SECOND EDITION
PSYCHOLOGY, THE HYBRID SCIENCE

FRANK B. McMAHON

Southern Illinois University at Edwardsville

PRENTICE-HALL, INC.,
Englewood Cliffs, New Jersey

SECOND EDITION

PSYCHOLOGY, THE HYBRID SCIENCE

Library of Congress Cataloging in Publication Data

McMAHON, FRANK B
    Psychology, the hybrid science.

    Bibliography: p.
    1. Psychology. I. Title. DNLM: [1. Psychology.
BF121 M167p 1974]
BF121.M295 1974   150   74-1468
ISBN 0-13-732909-1

SECOND EDITION
PSYCHOLOGY, THE HYBRID SCIENCE
FRANK B. McMAHON

Printed in the United States of America

10 9 8 7 6 5 4 3 2 1

Credit lines for selected illustrations appear on page xv

Prentice-Hall International, Inc., London
Prentice-Hall of Australia, Pty. Ltd., Sydney
Prentice-Hall of Canada, Ltd., Toronto
Prentice-Hall of India Private Limited, New Delhi
Prentice-Hall of Japan, Inc., Tokyo

TO JAN

CONTENTS

PREFACE xiii

ACKNOWLEDGMENTS xiv

CREDITS xv

CHAPTER ONE
THE BEGINNINGS OF PSYCHOLOGY 3

Philosophical Origins: The Greeks 6
Philosophical Origins: The Middle or Dark Ages 8
Philosophy Versus Observable Fact: The Renaissance 10   Summary 11

CHAPTER TWO
PSYCHOLOGY: THE EXPERIMENTAL SCIENCE 15

A Time of Unprecedented Discovery: The 1600s 16
Experimental Psychology and the Scientific Method 17
Reporting Experimental Findings 23   Summary 40

CHAPTER THREE
PSYCHOLOGY: PARTNER WITH BIOLOGY
AND PHYSIOLOGY 43

The Age of Darwin: Using Animals in Psychology 45
Evolutionary Patterns of Men and Animals 48
The Psychology of Behavior 59   Summary 78

CHAPTER FOUR
THE UNION OF PHYSIOLOGY
AND PSYCHOLOGICAL THEORY 81

The Age of Pavlov and Watson 82
Physiology and Behavior: Hunger and Thirst 93   Summary 101

CHAPTER FIVE
PSYCHOLOGY AND PHYSIOLOGY:
MOTIVATION AND EMOTION 103

The Physiology of Motivation 105   The Physiology of Emotion 110
Theories of Motivation and Emotion 113
Theories Restricted to Emotion 118
Theories Restricted to Motivation 121   Summary 126

PART TWO
PERCEIVING
AND
LEARNING

CHAPTER SIX
THE WORLDS OF PERCEPTION 131

Physiological Mechanisms 133   The Eye: Basic Physiology 141
The Reproduction of Images 144   Speed Reading 151
Perceptual Cues 152   Perception and Misperception 156   Summary 161

CHAPTER SEVEN
PERCEPTION AND PSYCHOLOGY 165

Psychological Perception 166   Probability, Chance, and Odds 171
The Era of Extrasensory Perception (ESP) 175   Summary 182

CHAPTER EIGHT
THE COMPUTER VERSUS THE PSYCHE 185

Physiological Mechanisms of Memory 188   Operant Conditioning 198
Summary 207

CHAPTER NINE
LEARNING 211

Attention 213   Transfer of Training 217
Techniques for Learning 223   Forgetting 226
Programmed Learning and Teaching Machines 233   Summary 236

CHAPTER TEN
THE EXOTICS OF PSYCHOLOGY 239

Hypnotism 240   Biofeedback 247   Sleep 249   Summary 259

PART THREE
THE
PERSON

CHAPTER ELEVEN
THE ERA OF THE UNCONSCIOUS:
SIGMUND FREUD 263

Summary 276

CHAPTER TWELVE
CONCEPTS OF PERSONALITY 279

Personality and Physique 281   Social-Psychological Theories 285
Learning Theories of Personality 289
Personality Theory of Self-Actualization 294
Cultural Theories of Personality 297
Influence of Society on Personality 301   The Self 303   Summary 304

CHAPTER THIRTEEN
MEASUREMENT OF PERSONALITY 307

Projective Techniques 309   Testing the Test 313
How Useful are Projective Tests? 316   Objective Personality Tests 318
Summary 324

CHAPTER FOURTEEN
ASSESSING INTELLIGENCE 327

The Binet Intelligence Test 331   Other Types of Intelligence Tests 337
Intelligence 340   Summary 356

CHAPTER FIFTEEN
RECOGNIZING TALENT AND CREATIVITY 359

Specific-Aptitude Tests 360   Achievement Tests 361
Tests of Creativity 363   Summary 370

PART FOUR
THE BECOMING PERSON

CHAPTER SIXTEEN
THE CHILD: SOCIAL DEVELOPMENT 373

Developmental Patterns of the Child 375
The Influence of Heredity and Environment 376
Patterns of Maturation 378
The Effect of Culture and Family on Children 384
Society and Sex-Role Development 387   Summary 396

CHAPTER SEVENTEEN
THE CHILD DEVELOPS
INTELLECT AND CHARACTER 399

Cognitive Growth 400   Piaget's Theory of Cognitive Development 404
Human Character Development 409
Psychological Factors in the Home 412
Physiological Factors in Character Development 417   Morality 419
Summary 424

CHAPTER EIGHTEEN
THE ADOLESCENT: REBEL WITH A CAUSE 427

Physiological Changes in Adolescence 429
Psychological Reactions to Growth Problems 433
Adolescent Defiance 434   Sexual Behavior in Adolescence 436
Homosexuality 443   Summary 450

CHAPTER NINETEEN
ADOLESCENTS: DELINQUENCY AND DRUGS 453

Juvenile Delinquency 454   Family Relationships of the Delinquent 457
Characteristics of Delinquent Personalities 458
The Psychological World of the Delinquent 458   Alcohol 461
Drugs 462   LSD 469   Summary 473

PART FIVE
PEOPLE

CHAPTER TWENTY
BEHAVIOR OF PEOPLE IN GROUPS 477

Social Structure 479   Social Grouping and Territoriality 481
Psychological Factors in Group Structure 484
Verbal Communication in Groups 490
The Function of Rules in Group Behavior 492   Summary 494

CHAPTER TWENTY-ONE
SYMBOLS, RITUALS, AND AGGRESSION 497

Symbolism in Group Behavior 498   Ritual in Group Behavior 500
Magic in Group Behavior 502   Violence in Groups 503
Techniques of Persuasion 510   Summary 521

PART SIX
TROUBLED
PEOPLE

CHAPTER TWENTY-TWO
NORMAL AND ABNORMAL BEHAVIOR 525

What Exactly is Mental Illness? 526   Issues in Mental Health 529
Mental Health Through the Years 534   Summary 541

CHAPTER TWENTY-THREE
WHAT CAUSES MENTAL ILLNESS? 543

Freudian Theory 544   Sullivan's Theory 545
Rogers, Maslow, and Existentialism 545   Learning Theory 546
Problems Creating Mental Illness 547
The System of Defense Mechanisms 549
Faulty Interpersonal Relationships 553   Kinds of Mental Illness 554
Kinds of Neurotic Reactions 556   Kinds of Psychotic Reactions 562
Summary 572

CHAPTER TWENTY-FOUR
TREATING MENTAL ILLNESS 575

Psychiatrists and Psychologists 576   Relieving Mental Illness 578
Styles of Psychotherapy 579   The Effectiveness of Psychotherapy 591
Summary 592

REFERENCES 595

A STUDENT SELECTION
OF FAVORITE PSYCHOLOGY BOOKS 636

GLOSSARY 637

INDEX 651

PREFACE

An author who tries to write a comprehensive psychology text, one that includes all the facts and controversies of psychology, dies long before he finishes the task. To me, this did not seem desirable.

I have tried, therefore, to provide a unified book by selecting major viewpoints in psychology as best I could determine them. I hope that some of the things I say will provoke you to disagree, because only in this way can a science move forward.

I hope you enjoy the book and learn something from it.

F. B. M.

ACKNOWLEDGMENTS

I would like to express my appreciation to the following cast, whose names appear in alphabetical order:

Jack Barrow	Edward Lugenbeel
Minor Chamblin	John Molino
Richard Glessner	Herbert Nolan
Jeanne Hoeting	John Peters
Margaret Horton	Hugh Peterson
Judi Katz	Wendell Rivers
Edna Kimball	Richard Schultz
Ken Kleinman	Neale Sweet
Natalie Krivanek	David Walker

and the hundreds of authors who provided me with copies of their articles for use in this book.

F. B. M.

CREDITS

Grateful acknowledgment is given for permission to use selected full-page illustrations for chapter openings from these sources (text pages follow source names):

Acme, 476; Robert J. Adragna, 184; The American Museum of Natural History, 130; Joe Baker, 2; The Bettmann Archive, 2, 306, 358, 398; Black Star, 426; Exxon Company, U.S.A., 210; Forsyth for Monkmeyer, 238, 278; FreeLance Photographers Guild, 2, 326; C. Greger for Monkmeyer, 262; Lambert Studios for Frederick Lewis, 164, 372, 496; Mahon for Monkmeyer, 452; Frank B. McMahon, 102, 524, 542, 574; The New York Public Library, 306; Harry Rose for Frederick Lewis, 80; Flip Schulke for Black Star, 42.

Grateful acknowledgment also for permission to use the following figure illustrations:

Figure 3-2. From H. F. Harlow, "Love in Infant Monkeys," *Psychobiology*, June 1959, p. 102. Copyright © 1959 by Scientific American, Inc. All rights reserved. Page 52.

Figure 3-3. From E. H. Hess, "Imprinting In Animals," *Psychobiology*, March 1958, p. 109. Copyright © 1958 by Scientific American, Inc. All rights reserved. Page 53.

40a-c. From *Physical Control of the Mind* by Jose M. R. Delgado, figure 24 (a set of 3 pictures) in Volume 41 of *World Perspectives*, planned and edited by Ruth Nanda Anshen. By permission of Harper & Row, 1969. Page 110.

SECOND EDITION
PSYCHOLOGY,
THE HYBRID SCIENCE

CHAPTER ONE
THE BEGINNINGS OF PSYCHOLOGY

The earth is a collection of atoms bound together into a ball of rock and metal eight thousand miles in diameter. It weighs 6 sextillion tons, and it is one of nine planets bound to the sun.

On this ball stands man, a miraculous combination of chemical compounds, mostly water.

The earth is $4\frac{1}{2}$ billion years old; man is 2 or 3 million years old. Man is the lesser understood [Jastrow, 1967].*

In 3000 B.C., the Sumerians, who gave us the wheel, the plow, and cuneiform writing, thought the moon, sun, and stars were all kept in place about the earth by a tin roof spread high overhead. The arrangement was controlled by the gods of creation. Man himself was wondered at, but in that vast and mysterious universe he seemed quite insignificant.

*In psychological articles, reference or index numbers are not used. The last name of the author and the year of publication appear instead. For the above citation look under "J" in the "References" section at the end of the book.

1-2   We understand man through the universe and the universe through man: Leonardo da Vinci's "Proportions of Man" (*Jeroboam*) and a photograph of earth from space (*NASA*)

3 Some victims of "dancing mania," by the elder Breughel (*Culver*)

Four thousand years ago, it was "logically" reasoned that if the sun's movement could produce floods (now known to come from melting snows) and the moon produce movements in large bodies of water (lunar tides), then man, his wars, and his fate must be influenced by planetary movements. These movements were carefully charted and predictions were made about man's behavior. This "science," astrology, was one of the earliest forms of psychology. It is still popular today, though scientists give it no credence.

From the time of ancient man to the last century, the vast majority of discoveries, findings, and applications have centered around understanding and controlling the environment in which we live. Only in the last hundred years have many serious attempts been made to understand man as he interacts with that environment. In the last half of the twentieth century, the moon has been landed upon, and its surface found to be a waterless and rocky wilderness pitted by collisions with meteorites. The temperature of Venus has been taken, a blistering 800 degrees Fahrenheit. The upper atmosphere of the earth has been loaded down with hundreds of orbiting, manmade "planets." But man himself is still wondered at; in this vast and mysterious universe, his constitution is much discussed but still little understood.

During this same time period, d-lysergic acid diethylamide (LSD) has been labeled a mind-expanding (and possibly mind-damaging) drug and has been found to produce symptoms of extreme disorganization. LSD is not modern. The same compound is found in nature as a fungus that may appear on infected rye grain.* Such contaminated grain is thought to explain the strange outbreak of "dancing mania" in 1374 [Brown, 1963]. LSD *is* new in an important sense, however, for it figures in one among many investi-

*LSD can be made from a fungus that is also found on wheat and rye grain and *may* wind up in bread.

5

gations conducted by a new generation of astrologers. Many of their maps are now chemical, but the goal is the same: understand man—somehow.

The phenomenon of electricity has been the subject of endless speculations and decades of experimentation, but only recently have we discovered that behavior can be controlled by electrical stimulation to the brain, so pick your point in time, then, to begin. Move up to the present day and the story will be the same; man is always seeking to understand himself through the universe, or the universe through himself. The basic question is: What am I?

PHILOSOPHICAL ORIGINS: THE GREEKS

The Greeks represent a mainstay in psychology: philosophical speculation about man's nature. This type of speculation is considered by many psychologists to be too unscientific for the twentieth century. However, it is a useful starting point in man's quest for understanding. And there are two important reasons for beginning our discussion with the Greeks. First, the completeness of Greek thought is somehow magical, amazing. Except for refinements made possible only by sophisticated measuring devices, the Greeks anticipated almost every psychological idea that exists today. This breadth can doubtless be attributed partly to the tremendous freedom allowed the Greek citizen by his society. His mind was free to think about the world as it desired, was even allowed to reject all traditional explanations. As one author has pointed out, when Athens was fighting for her life, the Greek playwright Aristophanes ridiculed the leaders, the cause of the battle, glorified peace—all to full houses [Hamilton, 1942].

Second, the flavor of Greek thought and speculation is responsible directly and indirectly for the changes that have taken place in psychology throughout the years. The word psychology itself comes from the Greek words that mean soul (*psyche*) and a discourse or discussion (*logos*). Through the years we cover in this text, although the label *soul* will change, the idea will remain essentially the same. The Greeks discussed it endlessly, and it still has a hold on man's beliefs that won't let go. Freud, for example, more than two thousand years later, denied the existence of a soul but said (1) that the unconscious is in us but it can never be seen or even heard from, except indirectly, and (2) that the unconscious has no sense of time—it is, was, and will be at the same instant without reference to a past, present, or future. Notice the similarity to the Christian soul, which always was, is, and will be without reference to time.

a look at man through Greek eyes

If you were to walk along an Athenian street on some winter's night in the fifth century B.C., you might run into a barefoot, ugly, paunchy man shuffling along in a tattered garment. You would be likely to shy away from him, as many people do from the twentieth-century societal dropout. If you remained and were fearless enough to stop and talk with him, you would very quickly be interrogated. *"To ti?"* he would ask, no matter what you were discussing [Wormser, 1962].

The man is Socrates, and his question—"What is it?"—is part of the very famous Socratic method. The Socratic method involves an armchair analysis of man, his mind, and his soul; "armchair" describes the process of sitting and analyzing without ever getting off one's duff. This kind of behavior is representative of Greek thought about man. It was very original and productive for intellectual stimulation. When psychology becomes a science, however, it will react to this speculative approach and go to the furthest extreme from it—if something can't be measured with an instrument, it just isn't. But that's the future.

What is man, then, to the Greek? Plato, Socrates' student, said that man was desire, emotion, and knowledge. Desire—sexuality—comes from the loins, emotion comes from the heart in the force and flow of blood, and knowledge comes from the head. Differences in personality stem from differences in the proportions of these three elements [Durant, 1933].

Maybe that wasn't the answer. So Plato tried a different explanation: "Is the blood the element with which we think, or the air or the fire? Or perhaps nothing of the kind—*but the brain may be the originating power of the perceptions of hearing and sight and smell and memory and opinion may come from them*" [Plato, 1952; italics added].

Such remarkable insight! Not until the late 1700s did objective evidence support his hypothesis about the brain.

One more example, this time regarding epilepsy and personality disorders. From the brain "the melting down takes place, most especially in the case of children in whom the head is heated either by the sun or by fire . . . and phlegm is excreted . . . and is the cause of his disease" [Hippocrates, 1952].

The man who wrote these words was Hippocrates, a famous Greek physician, the family doctor of 400 B.C. He is kept alive today by the Hippocratic oath taken by physicians when they graduate from medical school.

4   Evans's "Orukter Amphibolos" (*Transportation Museum, University of Michigan*)

The ideas that the brain melts or that the heart is the seat of emotion seem pretty far-fetched, but they were germs of ideas that were to stimulate thought all the way to the present day. Ideas, no matter how bizarre, have a form of permanency; and if they are good ones they have a profound effect on people's lives. For instance, you probably have been overwhelmed by the prospect of trying to find a parking place in the school lot. One of the men responsible for this was Oliver Evans who, because of an unusual occurrence, conceived the design of a motor car. A boyhood friend once told him about the explosion that could be made by filling a long tube with water, plugging the ends, and throwing it into a fire. Bang! Evans then had the idea of a propelling mechanism for a vehicle. In 1804 he came out with one of the first cars, improbably called the Orukter Amphibolos. It was thirty feet long and weighed fifteen tons, but look where it led us [Ketchum, 1959]. As you will note shortly, Greek ideas will also reappear in history with a bang.

A few important points about the Greeks ought to be kept in mind. Notice the flavor of the statements made: speculative, philosophical, not based on any laboratory investigation. This was the beginning of psychology; it was armchair psychology. Nonetheless, you will find as we progress that a large proportion of Greek thought was correct. More important, Greek thought was responsible for the rejuvenation of psychological and scientific thought after the Middle Ages, as we will discuss below. The philosophical method was a good one for its time, and today many of the ideas promulgated are still quite recognizable. For example, Plato spoke of "those desires which are awakened when the reasoning and taming and ruling power of the personality is asleep," a direct and obvious reference to the twentieth-century assumption that dreams can express desires which are normally held in check during the waking hours.

And there was Aristotle, who, as he walked through his large zoological garden, became convinced that the varieties of life species could be ordered and linked, one to the other, in a progression—facts upon which Charles Darwin later capitalized and which had a profound effect on the study of man as an animal in psychology [Durant, 1933].

PHILOSOPHICAL ORIGINS: THE MIDDLE OR DARK AGES

The ages called dark came about many centuries after the Greeks. The time was one of almost no science; "information" was received only from high church authority, and Greek speculation was temporarily missing.

An example of Dark Ages thought can be detected in Saint Thomas Aquinas, who wrote in the 1200s about the factors responsible for pleasure in man: "Operations (behaviors) are pleasant insofar as they are proportionate and connatural to the doer. Now, since human power is finite, operation is proportioned to it according to a certain measure."

This statement requires some translation, but it demonstrates the flavor of the Dark Ages (called dark in contrast to the supposed enlightenment of the Renaissance that was to follow). Aquinas was saying that certain behaviors are pleasant only in that God has seen fit to give man pleasure in the proper proportion; the pleasure available to man is of divine origin (directly from God) and of a certain amount. Likewise, pain in man is of divine origin and of a certain amount.

Whether one believes the divine-origin hypothesis is a matter of personal persuasion. Closer inspection of Aquinas' statement, however, reveals the relevance of his comments to the strange atmosphere of the Dark

5 *Garden of Earthly Delights*, by Hieronymus Bosch. Overdoing pleasure presumably would bring this eternal pain upon the participant (*Prado*)

6–7 In the left-hand picture the seventeenth-century witches seem rather light-hearted. But just like today the ones on the right had their problems: the picture shows a hold-up in a witch's laboratory (*Bettmann Archive*)

Ages. The concepts of pleasure and pain, their origin and significance, were no longer open to speculation as they had been with the Greeks; instead, information on all matters was dictated by God through the church. Scientifically speaking, this chain of authority presented a very basic problem: all writings were controlled and censored by the church; the church claimed absolute authority for the truths that it revealed to the public.

Unfortunately, the freedom of the Greeks was gone; reasoning was tightly bound to the authority of the church. One area where theology and science were interwined, for example, was in the attitude of religious bodies toward witchcraft [Wolf, 1959]. Witchcraft continued to be seen as quite genuine even by intelligent judges and church dignitaries. A brilliant man, Martin Luther, wrote, "Many devils are in the woods, water, wilderness, ready to hurt and prejudice people." Witchcraft manuals appeared; one contained methods for proper identification during a witch hunt—for instance, look for red spots on the skin that resemble the "devil's claw" [Coleman, 1964]. And for the mentally ill there was little help: those so disturbed were sometimes cured by the application of hot irons to their heads to "bring them to their senses."

Basically, the Dark Ages were dark in the sense that freedom of thought did not exist, and all problems were referred to divine origin—but history took an ironical twist. Searching for explanations of the official religious truths, very devout men began to explore the universe, which had been created for the benefit of man. In doing so they hit upon things that contradicted the church's teachings. One of these major discoveries, which we will pursue in reference to its effect on man, was that the earth is *not* the center of the universe. The men who discovered this fact at first couldn't believe it, but once they did, they were in for trouble from both the church and their own consciences [Wolf, 1959].

**PHILOSOPHY
VERSUS
OBSERVABLE FACT:
THE RENAISSANCE**

At this point Greek thought again emerges and lightens up the Dark Ages, showing itself in a period called the Renaissance. Greek thought again leads to freedom of speculation. And speculation, as you will see in Chapter 2, leads to scientific discovery.

The scientists were clearly in a dilemma. The 1500s saw the rediscovery of Greek thought, and scientists compared what they observed in their telescopes with what they had read in Greek literature. Keep in mind that at this time the earth was regarded as the center of the universe, with the sun revolving around it; man was thought to stand on a motionless planet. There were two reasons for believing this notion. First, man was a special creation of God, and the earth had been made for him; everything centered around him. Second, it *looks* and *feels* as if the earth is stationary, and everything does seem to be moving around it.

The scientific writers of this time had only the works of men who lived before the Dark Ages on which to rely for insight. Among the most important of these writings were those of the Greeks, and they suggested the possibility that the earth was not the center of the universe. Unfortunately, the Greeks emphasized the universal concept of the circle; they found it to be the ultimate in form. This emphasis created problems for Copernicus, one of the men who during the 1500s followed up on the idea that the earth was not the center of the universe. Copernicus, much as he benefited by Greek ideas, got hung up on the oneness of the circle. He spent a lot of time and calculation trying to fit the planetary system into a series of balls all of which were rotating one around the other in circles. His hypothesis—that the earth rotates on its axis and revolves around the sun as one of many planets—was startling and heretical. But, even though ridiculed, he was convinced he was correct [Wolf, 1959]. To his frustration, many of his mathematical calculations about planetary orbit wouldn't work out. The answers are simple in hindsight, but they were overwhelmingly difficult at the time.

The man who overcame Copernicus's difficulties was Johannes Kepler, a scientist who worked in the early 1600s. His solution was to try elliptical paths for the planets and see if the orbital calculations would work out. They did.

At this time another man of importance, Galileo Galilei, also supported the hypothesis that the earth was not the center of the universe. Publishing scientific ideas like this one was so dangerous that Galileo's book, *The Dialogue,* was written more or less like a modern stage play, with various characters sneaking in some of the author's own views on the nature of the universe. What else could he do? A large number of "authorities" refused even to look into his telescope to see his findings!

In the end, as you know, the facts triumphed; but in the meantime, an old, sick, and tired Galileo died prematurely as a result of continuous

8   Nicolas Copernicus, surrounded by the instruments of his science, astronomy; notice that he is holding a spherical model of the planetary system (*Yerkes Observatory*)

9 Anthony Quayle played Galileo in
this production of Bertolt Brecht's play,
Galileo Galilei. Compare the model in
this picture with the one Copernicus is
holding (*Martha Swope*)

imprisonment and trials because of his belief. The charges were briefly
summarized in a court transcript of April 1633: "Respecting the controversy
which has arisen on the aforesaid opinion that the Sun is stationary and
that the Earth moves, it was decided by the Holy Congregation of the Index
that such an opinion, considered as an established fact, contradicted Holy
Scripture and was only admissible as a conjecture" [de Santillana, 1955].*

SUMMARY   We have covered a great deal of history in a few pages. Each of the topics
is a book or two by itself. From the point of view of psychology, however,
you might look at it this way: psychology had its roots in philosophy,
especially the philosophy of the Greeks. Greek thought contains the finest
early thought known to man. Its highly speculative nature started psychology
out as a "nonscientific" science, meaning speculation without physical proof.
Even up to the present day, this speculative technique will weave its way
through psychology, on the grounds, many say, that only in this way can
we fully understand man. In any case, Greek thought led to great discoveries
about the nature of the universe and to an unprecedented age of mechanical
and scientific innovation.

   This change in the attitude of scientific investigation removed man
from the realm of the sacred, and he soon became something that could
be studied, explored, and taken apart. A reaction to these early and very
philosophical leanings will lead (as we'll find in the next chapter) to a
counterreaction: "Prove it"; "If I can see it, I'll believe it."

*Quoted in G. de Santillana, *The Crime of Galileo* (Chicago: University of Chicago
Press, 1955), p. 258; reprinted by permission.

11

Until we get there, let me quote a statement from a mid-twentieth-century scientist: "Life, therefore, is one with the movements of the stars and the planets, the heat of the sun, radiant energy, volcanic eruptions, and simple chemical reactions. . . . While this thought simplifies our concept of the universe, it only magnifies the mystery of it all" [Snodgrass, 1966].

PART ONE
THE HYBRID SCIENCE

CHAPTER TWO
PSYCHOLOGY:
THE EXPERIMENTAL SCIENCE

The study of man that utilized speculative and philosophical methods was hit hard by discoveries that the universe was less than magical and that man was rather like a machine which could be taken apart. Psychology, as you will see shortly, is going to try to imitate its brother, physical science.

A TIME OF UNPRECEDENTED DISCOVERY: THE 1600s

What is known of Isaac Newton suggests that he probably never had time to sit under a tree and be hit on the head by an apple. However, he did have time to recognize that if he threw an apple, or any other object, it would gradually begin to fall to earth. He also looked to the sky with a scientific eye: why didn't the moon fall to earth? He calculated its speed— about 2300 mph—and then the solution dawned on him. At this speed, the moon is moving so rapidly that it can't fall to earth like an apple. But if it's going so fast, why doesn't it fly off into space? For that too he had an answer. The moon was just the right distance away and its speed was just slow enough that force from the earth pulled it downward, causing it to turn and move in a continuous orbit rather than fly off into space.

Newton discovered this force, gravity, in the 1660s. His achievement is considered by many to be the greatest feat in the history of the physical sciences. Science was now working with something that had been considered beyond the realm of man's explorations. The impact of the new science is very graphically illustrated by the emergence at this time of a sect called the religion of Newton. The incredible statement upon which the religion was based was: "Universal gravity is the sole cause of all physical and moral phenomena" [Manuel, 1964]. Man as a philosophical or spiritual creature was in for a rough time.

In medical science until the Renaissance, information was gleaned from 125 volumes written by one man who had obtained his anatomical knowledge from examining slaughtered animals. These volumes contained such questionable tidbits as the statement that the human being has twenty-seven different kinds of pulse rate—including wormlike, wavelike, and antlike [Nourse, 1964].

The human body had been considered sacred, not to be cut into. With the coming of the new science, dissection became commonplace and

10   Isaac Newton analyzing a ray of light (*New York Public Library*)

16

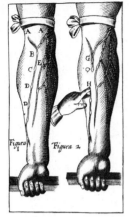

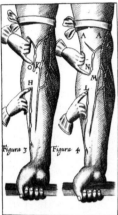

11 A drawing from Harvey's notebooks shows how he mapped the circulatory system (*New York Academy of Medicine*)

the internal workings of the body much less puzzling. For example, by 1750 a man named William Harvey had discovered the function of the valves in the heart for controlling the flow of blood, and he was very close to determining the exact nature of blood distribution by the heart. This finding didn't form a religion, but like Newton's it did add more fuel to the mechanistic atmosphere: circulation of the blood made man look even more like a machine [Matson, 1964]. The living organism was not very mysterious, it was thought, since it was a rather elaborate form of water pump; at least, if blood flow was mechanical, other such discoveries were not far off.

Most medical discoveries marked a milestone for psychology as well, because psychology concerns itself with the human being's physiological functioning as it relates to his psychological behavior. Man was becoming an operable machine, so to speak, subject to internal examination and exploration.

Science moved rapidly:

The body lost some of its mystery.

The telescope came into prominent use.

The weight of air was measured.

The microscope was invented.

The rush was on to conquer man and his world. The basic physical tools of science were now at hand. Rather than relying completely on rhetoric and persuasive speech—and particularly on the speculative style of the Greeks—the pendulum of scientific thought had swung to the importance of *demonstrating* to others the validity of scientific discoveries. Only by demonstration could the myths of speculation be dispelled [Conant, 1951].

Aristotle, for example, *thought* the brain was in the heart. This notion was something upon which the philosophers of his time could speculate endlessly. With the coming of the age of science, it was just a matter of years before actual physical stimulation of the brain (in the head, not the heart) was to produce visual images, thoughts, muscular movements, and the like. Speculation was being replaced by direct experimentation.

EXPERIMENTAL PSYCHOLOGY AND THE SCIENTIFIC METHOD

The wisdom of the ancients was certainly not always wisdom. Generations accepted the notion that if a spider was put in the middle of a circle made from the powder of a unicorn's horn, the spider just couldn't crawl out of the circle.* Nobody had ever tested this wisdom; it was "fact" and did not require testing. In England, a group of revolutionist-scientists formed a secret society called the Invisible College (it has been pointed out that the college

---

*The unicorn is mythical, but so-called unicorn dust did exist, whatever it was made of.

had to be invisible because there was large-scale persecution of heretical ideas). This secret society was composed not of malcontents but of serious scientists with serious objectives. (Robert Boyle, brilliant discoverer of many chemical laws, was a member.) An early report from this organization said: "A circle was made with the powder of unicorn's horn and a spider set in the middle of it, but immediately ran out" [de Kruif, 1926].

At first glance, the whole issue of unicorn dust and spider seems clearly a waste of time, but it isn't. Here was an actual scientific experiment and an important one in the sense that it captured the flavor of the times— demonstrate! demonstrate! First to be attacked was a common myth. A principle of the scientific method, then, is that a theory must be accompanied by some demonstrable evidence that what one is saying is highly probable. For example, only by repeated experimentation with satellites was it possible to plot the actual flight of spaceships to the moon. Just guessing at the path to take would have been disastrous.

Not only the vast universe, therefore, but even the world we cannot see began to come under scrutiny. Even this miniature world presented problems; for instance, where did it come from? Only the scientific method, as it is called, which involved careful experimentation, could give some of the answers.

"I've got a bug" is a complaint we often hear from friends who have the flu. Such a statement is so common that we rarely stop to think about it—but there was a time when the bug was completely unknown. No one dreamed that such things as microorganisms existed and could infect a person and cause sickness or death. Who found them? Certainly, you'd think, some white-coated, distinguished gentleman working long hours in a laboratory. Not quite. In the late 1600s Anton Leeuwenhoek (pronounced lay-ven-hook), a high-school dropout who worked first as a dry-goods salesman and next as a janitor at a city hall in Holland, developed a fixation

12   Rembrandt's painting reflects a critical breakthrough for science—dissection of the human body in order to study its systems

for grinding lenses and looking at things through these lenses. He examined everything he could find—ox eyes from the butcher, parts of a fly, bee stingers, the legs of a louse. One day, in his obsession for looking at everything through his lens, he turned his eye to looking at just plain, ordinary water and was the first man ever to find microorganisms; he called them his "beasties," which were "very prettily a moving" [de Kruif, 1926; Dubos and Pines, 1965].

Leeuwenhoek's experiment was quite a bit more complicated than the unicorn dust one and got a step closer to the method of psychological experiments of the twentieth century. The issue confronting this man was where the beasties came from. Taking the first step in any experiment, he formulated the following hypotheses:

1. The beasties were created out of nothing.
2. They crawled into the water from dirt.
3. They fell from the sky.

To test these conflicting hypotheses, he took some rainwater from the drainpipe at home and examined it under his microscopes (he had well over a hundred of them). There the beasties were. Was it certain that they fell from the sky, then?

No, there were other possibilities. One of them was that the microorganisms lived in the drainpipe and managed to get into the rainwater *after* it had fallen from the sky. Leeuwenhoek took a clean porcelain dish out into the rain, far away from anything else. He captured some rainwater and very carefully covered it up to take inside and put under his microscope. He found no microbes. They didn't fall from the sky. Modern-day psychological experiments are more sophisticated, but they contain the same ingredients as Leeuwenhoek's experiment.

A psychological experiment is identical to what Leeuwenhoek did; however, scientists have developed specific terminology for various aspects of the experiment. First of all, an experiment must have what are called *controls*. Put very simply, the experimenter must control his experiment in such a way that he can prevent extraneous, unwanted factors from influencing the results he obtains. In the microbe experiment, there were at least two possibilities. The microbes could have lived in some dirt or they could have come from heaven into the water. By his not standing under a tree, which would collect dirt, Leeuwenhoek *controlled* that problem—that is, he removed it as a factor. By doing so, and thus finding the pure rainwater to be without organisms, he focused attention on the drainpipe and its dirt as a contributing cause to the development of microbes.

Leeuwenhoek wanted to determine the conditions under which microbes existed. In psychological terminology, the existence of microbes would be called a *dependent variable*, meaning their presence is dependent upon certain conditions. In this case, he postulated that they were dependent upon dirt.

Being dependent has another side: a child who is dependent relies upon someone who is *independent*. In other words, the independent adult is responsible for what happens to the dependent child. In the experiment, the existence of microorganisms is dependent upon what? It must be dependent upon something, and psychologists call that something an *independent variable*. Leeuwenhoek tried varying the conditions of the experiment, first collecting water from the drainpipe, then collecting pure water. By alternating his method of collection, he was varying the independent variable, or the factor that is independent and can be manipulated by the experimenter. This manipulation or change should produce an effect on the dependent variable, as it did in Leeuwenhoek's experiment: in one case, microorganisms were present; in the other, they were not.

Having gone this far with the train of thought, we may find it worthwhile to do a twentieth-century experiment in psychology using once more independent variable, control, and dependent variable. The study will involve what psychologists call *set*—a tendency to see things continuously in the same way. Our experiment in set will demonstrate how it affects reasoning, and show how a psychological experiment operates.

the concept of set   The history of aircraft can shed some light on what psychologists call set. Basically, set means a tendency to solve new problems the way old ones were solved, or to continue to use objects in the environment the same way they have always been used. Only those who can break out of set are able to come up with great new inventions.

Man has always dreamed of flying. Ancient myths, legends, and works of art are filled with winged creatures having manlike bodies. For century after century, man observed the behavior of birds. Without fail a bird seemed to fly by flapping his wings, and man assumed, with some logic, that this was how *he* could fly. Early attempts at flight generated hundreds of dramatic but pathetic pictures of men with very elaborate wings attached to their arms. Many of them jumped off cliffs in the unfortunate hope that they would be able to fly before they hit the ground. This line of reasoning was doomed to failure. For one thing, birds have hollow bones that make

13 This man, strapped to a huge contraption, succeeded no better than others who tried to fly by "flapping their wings" (*Musée de l'Air*)

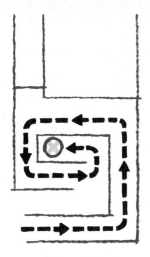

2–1 Left-handed maze

them very light. For another, the flapping of the wings is not primarily responsible for their ability to fly. Instead, the use of their wings in a manner that maximizes the flow of air over and under the wings' surface gives them continued uplift.

The lift provided by airflow was discovered by photographing the effects of wind on variously shaped objects in the first wind tunnel—in 1871. For millennia, man's progress had been retarded by a set: every time he saw something fly, he assumed it was flapping its wings in order to do so. No solution came in sight until someone broke set and came up with a novel idea: leave the wings immobile, since they give the lift; add a motor and propeller to get *forward* motion (not upward motion). The eventual outcome was that on December 17, 1903, a proud father received the following telegram from his son:

SUCCESS FOUR FLIGHTS THURSDAY MORNING ALL AGAINST TWENTY ONE MILE WIND STARTED FROM LEVEL WITH ENGINE POWER ALONE AVERAGE SPEED THROUGH AIR THIRTY ONE MILES LONGEST 57 SECONDS INFORM PRESS HOME CHRISTMAS

OREVELLE* WRIGHT [Josephy, 1962]

an experiment with set   How can psychologists demonstrate set in the laboratory? Notice that Figure 2–1 illustrates a paper and pencil maze of the type we all have worked at one time or another.

This particular maze is designed so that the goal can be reached only by making continuous left turns with the pencil. Suppose we take a group of people (called *subjects* in psychological experiments) and have them solve eight such mazes, all in a row, all with left-hand turns. At this point we give the subjects a traditional maze requiring both right-hand and left-hand turns. We find that they have difficulty with it. Could we conclude that we had induced a set for left-hand turns and that this set interfered with the subjects' being able to solve the regular maze? Well, possibly the logic has a major flaw here. Set is indeed a likely cause, but how do we demonstrate it? For instance, the regular maze may simply be more difficult to do than the left-handed maze.

A way out of this dilemma does present itself; here is how it works. We train a group of subjects on the left-handed maze. We take another group of subjects who essentially resemble the first group, but we give them no training. Finally, when the first group is through with its training, we give the regular mazes to both the groups and time them. If both groups contained essentially the same kinds of people to begin with, and we find that the "left-handed" group does less well on the regular maze, then the major difference between the groups was the set established by the first maze for making left-hand turns. The second group used in the experiment is called

*Sic.

a *control group*. Control group can be explained further by looking at another experiment. Suppose that a drugstore advertises a special cap to put on a baby that will make him learn to walk. You put the caps on a dozen babies and leave them on. By and by, the babies do indeed learn to walk. Can we conclude that the caps were effective? What's wrong with this experiment?

The solution is easy. Take a group of babies and don't let them wear the silly cap. They will walk just as soon. What have you done? You have *controlled* the experiment by eliminating the beany in one group. This control allowed the actual reason for the result (walking) to come into focus: normal maturation and development of muscular coordination. The point was demonstrated in the experiment by using a control group, a group that had had nothing done to it. If you had not had a group that matured without benefit of the beany, the evidence would not have been experimentally clear, even if common sense told you that the beany was irrelevant.

So, too, in the maze experiment, a control group is needed. We need to know whether the left-handed maze is influential in developing set. To learn this, we use a group of subjects who do not perform on the first maze, but only on the second (regular) one. We are controlling out the influence of the left-handed maze training, eliminating it as a factor for one of the groups.

Thus we have one group, the control group, that solves only the regular maze. Another group, the *experimental group*, is given both the left-handed maze and the regular maze. This group's behavior is thought to demonstrate the core of the experimenter's belief in the influence of set, and hence it is called the experimental group (the group on which the experiment is actually performed).

An independent variable (the factor that can be manipulated by the experimenter) results from giving one group both mazes and the other only one.

The dependent variable is the outcome of the experiment as affected by manipulation of the independent variable. In other words, the results are dependent on whether the subjects are given both mazes or only one. Putting the subjects through both mazes or just one is the variation of the independent variable—the part controlled by the experimenter.

So set does occur, but this fact was determined only by using an independent variable, a dependent variable, and a control group.

space-age psychology Not all experiments are carried out in the laboratory. Many of them cannot be. Some require the natural setting within which the person operates. A current and serious problem, for example, is the effect of the jet aircraft's speedy transportation on pilots and passengers. Each of us has a rhythmical pattern of temperature, respiration, and heart rate, and each of these increases and decreases throughout the day, with maximal and minimal points occurring about the same time each day. These rhythms are in turn regulated

14 Imagine how a person's normal rhythmical patterns must adjust to flight to the moon—or beyond (*NASA*)

by the number of hours of light and darkness that we experience [Rohles, 1967]. When a normal person reaches his individual low point for the day, coordination can be impaired to the same extent it would be after drinking 6 oz. of straight whiskey—in some states the legal intoxication level [Klein, 1971].

Jet air travel makes it possible for a person to change this light-darkness cycle by flying across an ocean and arriving at a place where night is beginning at what, for him, is one o'clock in the afternoon. This shift in light and darkness has been found to provoke extreme fatigue, some difficulty in making decisions, and an imbalance in the normal rhythmic cycle. The psychological and physiological effects are being studied with an eye to solving the problem.

To study the effects of disruption of the light-darkness cycle, the scientist uses the same experimental procedures followed inside the laboratory. Seeking to illustrate that the effects come not merely from the fatigue of flight itself, the experimenters use a control crew (control group) which flies an equal time and distance, but to South America, so that the light-darkness shift does not occur. The control group does not show the effects of light-darkness change that occur in the experimental group.

In other words, the independent variable comes from a process of maintaining or altering the usual light-darkness cycle; the dependent variable is the result of the alteration: fatigue, trouble in making decisions, and disturbance of the rhythmic cycle. The control group which does not undergo the critical part of the experiment contrasts with the experimental group.

In an interesting uncontrolled (completely uncontrolled) study which took place in the summer of 1972, a softball game was played between a group of "straights" and a group high on wine and marijuana. The straights won, 13–12, which was a pretty close game [Aldrich, 1972]. With this kind of information, what kind of conclusion can we draw about the effects of marijuana? None, because the "study" was not controlled. One of the most obvious things coming to mind is that there might be a notable age difference between groups, with the "highs" probably younger. If this were a real study, we would want to know how much drugging occurred in the experimental group; we would want to know whether the marijuana smokers were experienced smokers or not, which alters the effect of the drug; we would want to be sure that the control group, the "straights," hadn't stuck in a few professional players to prove their point.

REPORTING EXPERIMENTAL FINDINGS

graphic analysis

In some studies, the experimenter varies the instructions on a particular task so as to vary the amount of pressure put on the individual to solve a problem. As pressure to solve the problem increases, anxiety increases and efficiency decreases drastically. (Sometimes this process seems to be an integral part of our educational system.) A related study shows the effect of anxiety on test performance. A discussion of these studies will serve to show the

KEY

1	2	3	4	5
♂	X	T	<	Z

2	5	1	4	2	3
X	Z				

5	4	1	3	2	3

TEST-TAKER
WRITES IN SYMBOLS
USING KEY ABOVE

2–2 Digit-symbol task

operation of graphs and how they help to clarify the results of a psychological study.

One experimenter administered a questionnaire to a large group of students [Saronson, 1952]. From the information he obtained through the questionnaire about their feelings and responses to test situations, he was able to pick out two smaller groups. One group was what might be called high-anxious—in layman's terminology, high-strung, prone to nervousness, or quite jumpy in a tight situation. The other group was low on the anxiety rating, meaning calm, not nervous or jumpy under pressure. The two groups were given a test in which each subject worked individually on the task of changing geometrical figures into numbers. He used a key in which the subject looked at a series of figures that were already numbered (see Fig. 2–2). The test was too long to be completed in the time allotted, yet the subjects were given the instructions that they were "expected to finish."

Hypothesis:[*] There will be fewer correct responses the higher the subject's level of anxiety.

Independent variable: Assignment of two groups to the task; experimenter is varying the type of subjects taking the test, grouping them as high-anxious or low-anxious.

Dependent variable: The actual scores made, since they are dependent upon the anxiety level of the subjects.

Control: The experimenter eliminates those who did not score either high-anxious or low-anxious. In this way he emphasizes the two groups he wants to study, and he assumes that because they represent extremes on the scale, the chances that anxiety will be the important factor in the results will be greatly increased.

The subjects were given five chances to succeed at the task. In other words, they took the test five times in succession. In psychological terminology these five chances are called five *trials*.

Here is a report of the results: The scores varied from 27 through 43 for the five trials for each of the groups. The low-anxious group scored consistently higher (better) for each of the five trials, and in every case did better on the task than the high-anxious group. At the fifth trial, the low-anxious group continued to score better than the high-anxious group.

Although this verbal report is accurate, the results of the experiment are difficult to visualize, no matter how well the report is organized or written. This problem comes up frequently in the reporting of psychological experiments. *Graphs* are used to clarify and organize facts visually. A graph of the experiment above is shown in Figure 2–3.

[*]The results the experimenter expects to obtain.

The horizontal line at the base of Figure 2–3 is marked off to indicate the number of trials (1, 2, 3, 4, 5). The vertical line at the left indicates the scores obtained by the subjects. A legend, similar to one found on a road-map, shows the reader which line within the graph represents which group under study. The lines themselves connect a series of dots. Each dot represents a point on the horizontal axis (trial line) and a point on the vertical axis (score line).

The two arrows you see in Figure 2–3 do not appear in real graphs, but have been added here to explain how the position of the dots is determined. Assume that the experimental results show that on trial 2 the average score of all the subjects in the high-anxious group was 35. An arrow moves from 35 on the score axis (vertical) over to the right until it meets an arrow coming up from trial 2 on the trial axis (horizontal). The point at which they meet is the point where the dot is placed. Put another way, the dot represents trial 2, for which the average score of subjects equaled 35.

With that out of the way, notice how easy it is to see the results of the experiment just by looking at the graph. The dotted line (high-anxious) is consistently below the straight line (low-anxious); high anxiety, then, appears to inhibit maximal performance level through all five trials. If this explanation is not fully clear, go back to the paragraph on page 24 in which the results of the experiment were described, and compare the verbal description with the graph in Figure 2–3.

You will see hundreds of graphs in scientific reports. They all follow the *same* principle.

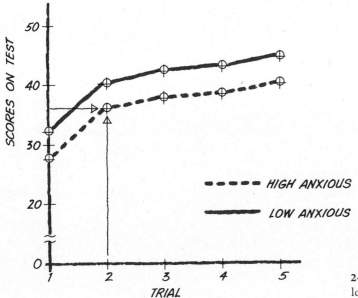

2–3 Performance of high- and low-anxious subjects

correlation Almost all psychological studies involve comparisons. The intelligence of a student is compared with his school grades; problems in the home are compared with delinquency rates; amount of narcotics taken is compared with amount of disorganized behavior; and so on. A statistical (mathematical) tool is used to make these comparisons; it is called *correlation*

We are probably justified in saying that a great many psychology students are frightened by numbers of any sort. Those familiar with history, however, can take refuge in the fact that a genius like Albert Einstein was not unusually precocious in mathematics (of all areas!). He failed his entrance examination to the Zurich polytechnic school, and when he finally made it through school he said that he did not want to think about scientific problems for a year because the examinations had so injured his mind [Snow, 1966]. Dr. Werner von Braun, the space scientist, once failed algebra. Take heart.

Nonetheless, to understand psychology you must understand results expressed as correlations. We will proceed step by step through the formulation of the concept of correlation and then show how it is used.

A famous psychologist, Francis Galton, worked in the late 1800s. First of all, Galton was aware of certain findings of his time, in the area of biology, that were labeled co-relations. Basically, the meaning of co-relations in biology is simple: the length of an arm, for example, is closely related to the length of the leg, so that if one has long arms, one will probably have long legs. Phrased differently, just as the length of the arm varies from person to person, so the length of the leg varies from person to person, the long going with the long and the short going with the short. The biologists called this the co-relation of structure. They assumed that some common cause in the structure of man produced organs that are co-related. If you take away the hyphen and add an *r*, you can say: long arms are correlated with long legs. If the ratio of arm length to leg length were always perfect to the exact centimeter, then we would have a perfect co-relation or correlation between the two: as one became longer, so would the other, to the exact centimeter. Such a perfect correlation obviously never happens, though it's theoretically possible [Dennis, 1948].

It was up to Galton to figure out a method for comparing things that were related to one another but not to the exact centimeter: this comparison required the use of mathematical and graphical analysis.

Galton was an inveterate improviser and inventor. He set up a room at the International Health Exhibition in London in 1884 where for the equivalent of three cents you could enter a room and have all your measurements taken—height, weight, breathing power, hearing, sight, strength of grip, and so on. This exhibit was profitable for Galton in a scientific and a nonscientific sense [Miller, 1962].

Galton collected a tremendous amount of information, and he was overwhelmed by stacks of numbers that he didn't quite know how to handle.

After attempting various other combinations, he finally put the heights of parents in one table and the heights of children in another.

Nothing could be more obvious than the fact that the heights of the children are correlated with the heights of the parents (see Table 2–1). Parents who are tall have children who are taller than the children of parents who are short [Garrett, 1951]. For example, the offspring in family C (69.5 in.) are taller than the offspring of family E (68.2 in.). And the parents in family E are smaller than those in family C. Therefore, a relationship must exist between height of parents and height of children.

Table 2–1   Average of heights of parents and offspring (in inches)

Family	Parents	Offspring
A	72.5	72.2
B	71.5	69.9
C	70.5	69.5
D	69.5	68.9
E	68.5	68.2
F	67.5	67.6
G	66.5	67.2
H	65.5	66.7
I	64.5	65.8

How does one go about expressing a relationship between two things? One common way to express relationships is to say one of the following:

The offspring's height is closely related to the parents' height.
The offspring's height is somewhat related to the parents' height.
The offspring's height is a little bit related to the parents' height.
The offspring's height is not related to the parents' height.

Each of these statements expresses a certain co-relation between size of parent and child, but the scientist coping with this problem is not being very accurate if he says that height of parents and children are closely related, somewhat related, a little bit related. These statements are subject to wide interpretation.

You can see by looking at Galton's table of heights that the two variables are related, but how can you express this relationship mathematically? With Galton's background work as an aid, mathematicians figured out that if one plots the points between height of parents and height of

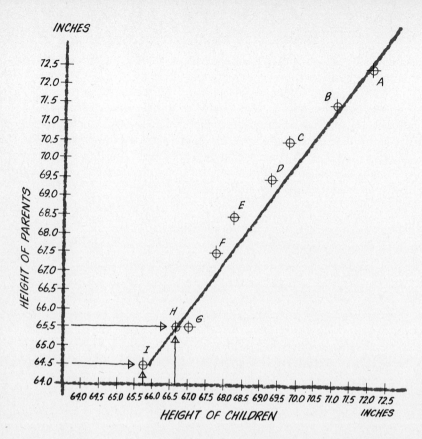

2-4 Correlation of average heights of parents and children as determined by Galton

children (Table 2-1) and then draws a diagonal* that comes as close as possible to all the points (Fig. 2-4) and still is a straight line, then the amount of distance *between the dots and the line* will indicate how close a relationship there is between the two different characteristics (height of parents and height of offspring).

For example, Figure 2-5 (hypothetical) shows a perfect relationship; there is no difference between the points and the straight line. Figure 2-6 (hypothetical) shows a weak relationship; there is a great difference between the points and the line of best fit. It is possible, with highly accurate graph paper, actually to measure the distances between points and the diagonal line and place them in a formula to determine the degree of relationship. Rather than do all this measuring, however, we can obtain the same results by dealing with the numbers *directly*, by means of a mathematical formula, which you will not need to know at present in order to understand the use of correlation [J. E. Freund, 1960].

---

*It is not critical at this time to understand why the line must be diagonal. The mathematical computation involved requires that it be so. The reader wishing to pursue the issue is referred to texts cited as references in this chapter.

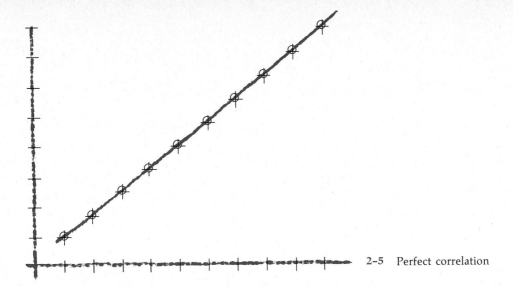

2-5   Perfect correlation

**how correlations
are read, interpreted,
and reported**

Correlation, then, is a measure of the apparent relationship between two different things. The preceding section presented correlation as a measure used to determine how closely the height of the children was related to that of their parents. Without mathematical correlation, scientists conceivably could use the words "lots," "some," "pretty much," "a little," "very little," but such statements are very inexact. The mathematical formula for correlation produces numbers that have basically the same meaning as words but possess a degree of refinement not possible with words alone. The numbers

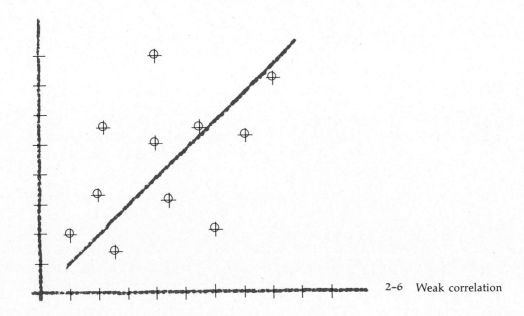

2-6   Weak correlation

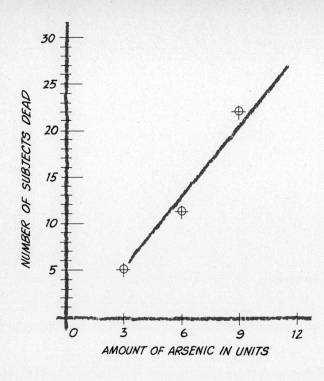

2-7 Correlations of amount of arsenic taken with incidence of death

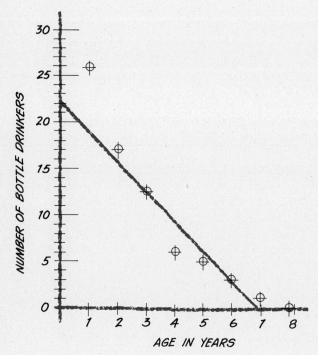

2-8 Correlation of bottle feeding with age

for correlation vary from 0 to 1. Zero means no relationship exists, while 1 means a perfect relationship exists.

One word of caution: it is a rare student who does not confuse correlation with percentages at the beginning. A correlation is not in any sense the same as a percentage. Correlational numbers *look like* percentages. They are *not*. Nonetheless, at least one similarity does exist—the higher the number, the more the two items seem to vary together.

Suppose the members of your class have the following test scores in history: 5, 24, 56, 60, 100. Suppose on an algebra test the same class members have the following scores respectively: 35, 100, 80, 50 and 75.

Obviously, subjects perform quite differently on one test, compared to another, but how do we state this difference without using words? What relationship is there between the scores on the history test and those on the algebra test? Correlation is used to get the answer because it compares two different sets of scores. The two sets should be only minimally related, and the correlation should be low. In fact, it is .23.

The size of the correlational number indicates the strength of the relationship; the higher the number, the stronger the relationship:

Typical correlations: .00   .15   .38   .59   .70   .89   .90   1.00
Relationship getting stronger - - - - ->- - -> - - - - - - - - - - - ->

The number .00 means no correlation exists; 1.00 means perfect correlation exists. All numbers between 0 and 1 are possible between these two points.

Visually inspecting, without computing, you might guess that in Figure 2–4 the correlation is roughly .85; in Figure 2–5 it is 1.00, and in Figure 2–6 it is about .30.

For example, suppose we want to correlate amount of arsenic intake with incidence of death. We take three groups containing 30 subjects each. To group 1 we give three units of arsenic, and 5 subjects die. To group 2 we give six units. and 11 die. To group 3 we give nine units, and 22 die. From the three groups of 30, we get death rates of 5, 11, and 22 respectively (see Fig. 2–7). Apparently the relationship is not perfect, or all the dots would coincide with the line. Some people must be sturdier than others. But notice that we get a *high positive* correlation between taking arsenic and dying, though not a perfect positive correlation.

Next, we could perform a hypothetical experiment relating bottle feeding to age. As age increases, bottle feeding will decrease. At age five there are a few hangers-on, and maybe one by age seven. Look at Figure 2–8, where this correlation is plotted. Something is different. For one thing, the straight line is running in a direction opposite from the ones seen previously. For another, even though the line fits pretty squarely between the dots, if you report something like this—"Correlation between age (through age 8), and bottle feeding is .90"—you are saying that as age *increases*, bottle feeding *increases*, which obviously is wrong. Yet we know there is a strong relationship between age and bottle feeding. To allow for this kind of a situation, the *correlation coefficients*, as they are called, operate in the negative (minus) direction as well as the positive (plus) direction; both mean the *same thing* in terms of *degree* of relationship. A negative .70 correlation (−.70) is just as strong as a positive .70 correlation (.70). The difference is that the negative correlation means that as one variable (age) goes one way (increases), the other variable (bottle feeding) goes the other way (decreases). The positive correlation means that as one variable goes one way the other variable goes the same way (as height of parents goes up, that of children goes up).

Correlations will appear with some frequency in this book. Before leaving the topic, you might try your brain on some obvious correlations to make certain you understand the principle. Their use will become clear when we deal with real problems later on.

1.   Correlation between getting frequent and severe beatings as a child and having a happy childhood; + or − ? High or low? Negligible?

2.   Correlation between the price of rice in China and the frequency of earaches in your family: + or − ? High or low? Negligible?

3.   Correlation between sincere kisses and happy marriages: + or − ? High or low? Negligible?

Answers:

1.   As beatings increase, happiness decreases, so a high negative correlation exists.

2.   The two variables are not related; negligible correlation exists.

3.   As kisses increase, happiness increases, so a high positive correlation exists.

The following *rough* guides can be used to interpret correlation coefficients:

From .00 to + or − .20 denotes indifferent or negligible relationship.

From + or − .20 to + or − .40 denotes low correlation; present but slight.

From + or − .40 to + or − .70 denotes substantial or marked correlation.

From + or − .70 to + or − 1.00 denotes high to perfect relationship [Garrett, 1958].

a word of caution   Correlation coefficients show the degree to which two things *vary together*. They do *not* necessarily show a cause-and-effect relationship. One might notice that as the number of fire engines going to a fire increases, the severity of the fire increases. If you were to apply a correlational analysis to the situation, you would find that the correlation between the number of fire engines and the fire's severity would be close to 1.00. The conclusion? The fire engines *cause* the fire to be greater.

The scientist's conclusion would not include the causal factor at all, but would merely point out that these two things co-vary together. While he would be bound to report these results, since they are objective findings, his logic and common sense would suggest the possibility of a relationship which is not cause-effect.

You *could* rearrange the situation and say that intensity of fire increases the number of engines and you could make a case for a possible causal relationship. However, your case does not revolve around the correlation. It revolves around how you interpret it. The correlation in both cases merely reports that two things vary together, not that one thing causes the other.

the normal curve: fitting people into groups

A striking human paradox confronts the pollster, the psychologist, and any other student of behavior. Whenever people are asked to rate themselves, they gravitate toward the middle of the road, possibly to make certain of having lots of company. No one knows just why this happens, but if a poll is taken of a large group of people, including equal numbers of the rich, the poor, and those in between, and they are asked to state which social class they are from—upper, middle, or lower—the interviewer will find well over 80 percent in the middle class, according to their own evaluations.

Here's a paradox, because little or no evidence exists that people consider themselves to be the same. To take an extreme, in some primitive societies where there is supposedly no competition, people assume a form of rank ordering in which the one who competes the least is the best. Their competition is based on *lack* of competition. So people constantly divide themselves up.

The desire of people to be divided up can be seen on the national level. Karl Marx's theory failed to completely take hold partly because it did not take enough account of differences between individuals. His theory of the perfect society of classless men is a rather drab one, and may have been a reflection of his own life. Physically miserable most of the time, he was often known to pawn his coat and shoes just to have enough money to stay alive. Worst of all, he suffered from serious and painful boils; he made the remark, after writing most of one afternoon, that he hoped the "bourgeoisie as long as they live will have cause to remember my carbuncles" [Heilbroner, 1961]. We do indeed.

Marx's theories had a tremendous impact on the development of today's Communist countries, even though Marxism is not the only theoretical background for any of these countries. Such great countries as the USSR have attempted to make people as equal as possible; yet this ideology is giving way to private ownership of television sets and the desire to have the

15-16 (*Sovfoto*)

commodities of capitalistic countries, and even to replacement of traditional uniform clothing with individual and colorful fashions. Thus, within the Soviet system innumerable concessions are made to the will of people to be individuals. One system used is a merit-badge rating. On his travels through Russia, one man found that the typical Russian male has earned a merit badge which he wears on his vest. A common one is the Master of Sport. A fellow with whom he spoke wore a badge designating him a Master of Motorcycle Racing [Van Der Post, 1967].

Separate groupings, then, are inherent in nations because nations are composed of people. And a clear characteristic of people is the desire for classification and organization, accompanied by the tendency to consider one thing better or worse than another, or perhaps merely to designate people as belonging in differentiated groups.

The scientist is even more fanatical about putting things and people into categories, and he uses diagrams to represent these categories. Take the case of the investigator who by the use of numbers must differentiate the wealth of various groups in the U.S. For example, how many families in the U.S. make under $2000 a year? How many make between $5000 and $10,000, and how many make between $17,000 and $20,000? Grossly approximating for purposes of illustration, we could say that 3 million families fall into the first category, 15 million into the second, and about 3 million into the third.

Suppose that you draw a line to equal, in length, the number of families in each category:

```
                               3 million
Under $2000        - - -↓          15 million
$5000-$10,000      - - - - - - - - - -↓
$17,000-$20,000    - - -
```

You have created a visual representation of income and families divided by category. If you wanted to include more data, you could draw

34

a line for each of a large number of income categories making wealth appear to be a little more equally distributed than it actually is; you would obtain something approximating this diagram:

Number of families

1.	Under $2000	- - - -
2.	xxxxxx	- - - - -
3.	xxxxxx	- - - - - -
4.	xxxxxx	- - - - - -
5.	$5000–$10,000	- - - - - - - -
6.	xxxxxx	- - - - - - -
7.	xxxxxx	- - - - - -
8.	xxxxxx	- - - - -
9.	$17,000–20,000	- - - -

(The larger the number of families, the longer the line.)

Now you can turn the diagram on its side, connect the points, and remove the lines:

The curve is called a bell-shaped or *normal* curve. It represents the distribution (in a rough fashion) of such a large number of things in the world that psychologists use it frequently to illustrate characteristics of certain groups or to categorize persons along a certain dimension. It is used to visually represent how large numbers of people are distributed.

You can see how it works if you take a hypothetical curve of cleanliness. Most people (the norm, or normal—that is, what is to be expected) are going to be in the middle in the more-or-less clean group. Assuming that the soap operas get their message across, there will be a large group of people right around the middle (see the 0 line in Fig. 2–9). Some groups of people are going to deviate from this norm, or normal position. At the far right of the curve in Figure 2–9 might be the superclean, the bathtub dwellers. As we move along the curve toward the superclean, the number of individuals becomes smaller and smaller. Sliding to the left, we

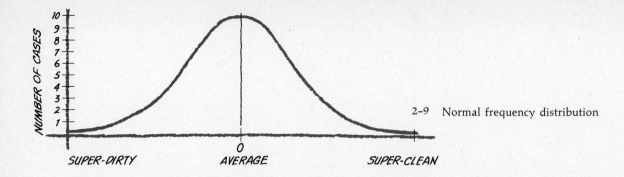

2-9 Normal frequency distribution

move away from the norm toward the superdirty, represented at the far left, and fortunately they also are in the minority. The technical name for this figure (2–9) is a *normal frequency distribution*. This means that after having counted (determined frequency), we have a distribution (arrangement) that fits the normal (quite frequently found) arrangement of things: few superdirty, few superclean, most in the middle (Fig. 2–10).

Height of individuals is a characteristic that will fit this curve. Another is intelligence-test results, which would include the very bright and the very dull, one at each end of the curve, and the average in the middle.

Figure 2–11 shows the percentage of subjects (persons, things, events, etc.) that would fall within a certain area of the curve if the curve were perfect. It is never perfect, but sometimes it comes close. The largest group of people fall into the middle (68 percent); 95 percent of the subjects are included within the second set of lines; and at 99 percent, the third set of lines, nearly everyone is accounted for. For example, 68 percent of a

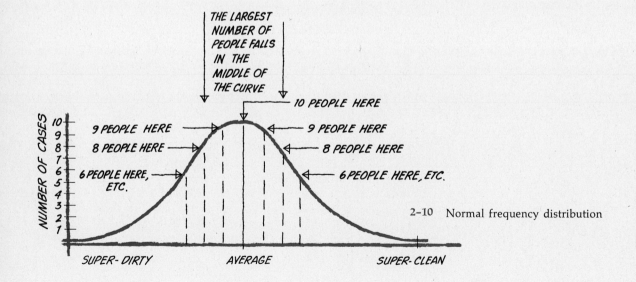

2-10 Normal frequency distribution

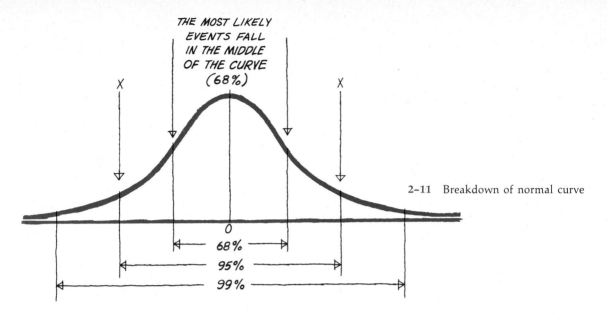

THE MOST LIKELY
EVENTS FALL
IN THE MIDDLE
OF THE CURVE
(68%)

X

X

O

68%

95%

99%

2-11   Breakdown of normal curve

typical group is average clean.* All people vary somewhat, but they can be classified according to these individual differences. Some are cleaner than others, some brighter than others.

The student new to psychology usually finds the concepts of statistics† somewhat difficult to grasp so early in his study. The purpose of this discussion has been to acquaint you in a general way with a distribution curve. The normal curve is a representation of the manner in which people are distributed in reference to certain characteristics, such as intelligence or height. The normal curve does not fit all situations, however. The normal curve is an idealized one, so of course the psychologist will run into other ones, some of them very oddly shaped. For example, if fifth-grade children were given a third-grade test, they would get most items right, and the curve would look something like Figure 2–12.

Reverse the procedure and give the fifth-grade test to the third-graders and the curve will look something like Figure 2–13.

The last two curves are not normal curves, and the percentages discussed earlier do not apply to them. They do, however, give a graphic representation of many numbers pertaining to grouped individuals, and they can quickly supply a general idea of performance, removing the need for tedious research into the numbers obtained for each subject. Since they are so frequently used, it is important that you grasp the general idea of what

*That is, if we had studied and placed 100 individuals in the curve, 68 of them would fall between the two lines indicated.

†Statistics include any numerical process used to group, assemble, organize, or analyze information received.

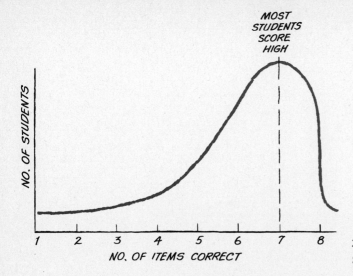

MOST
STUDENTS
SCORE
HIGH

NO. OF STUDENTS

NO. OF ITEMS CORRECT

2-12 Test results of fifth-grade children given third-grade test

these curves are, how they are constructed, and how to determine the number of people or times represented [J. E. Freund, 1960; Tyler, 1965].

mode, mean, and median: representative numbers

Three major mathematical measures are used in psychology to condense information into accessible form. If we had five scores of 25, 26, 24, 24, and 21, for example, we could get a number that would closely represent all these numbers by adding them together and dividing by the number of entries (5). The result, 24, is very close to representing all these numbers, and this number is called the arithmetical *mean*—what the layman usually calls the average.

These numbers present no problem, but if we took the scores 3, 5, 6, 7, and 30 and figured the mean, we'd obtain 10.2, which would not

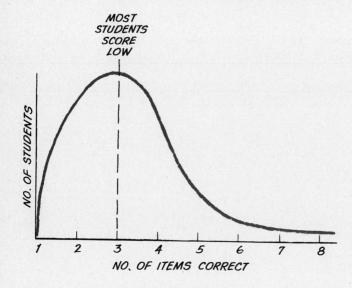

MOST
STUDENTS
SCORE
LOW

NO. OF STUDENTS

NO. OF ITEMS CORRECT

2-13 Test results of third-graders given fifth-grade test

be very representative of the many small scores we have (four out of five are below 10). The major problem with the mean, therefore, is that it can be inflated by a few deviate numbers. This problem is also an advantage, since the mean is sensitive to extreme scores and includes them in its calculation. As you will see, neither the median nor the mode takes extreme numbers into consideration. However, in our present case, to get a representative number as best we can, we have to use what is called the *median*, or halfway mark—the midpoint of a list of ordered numbers. Since we have an odd number of digits (5), the midpoint or median will be the middle number, 6; this number is much more representative of the scores than 10.2. If your list of numbers is even, merely take the middle two numbers in the list, add them together, divide by 2 and you have the median.*

The third representative numerical measure is the *mode*. It is very simply calculated: it is the most frequently appearing number. The mode is adequate if you have a set of scores such as 3, 7, 9, 9, 12, and 14 because the mode 9 occurs close to the middle of the series. On the other hand, it has the inherent problem that the most frequent might appear at a strange place: 3, 3, 3, 9, 9, 12, 14, and 17. Here the mode is 3 and certainly does not represent the group of numbers.

Of the three kinds of representative numbers we have discussed, the mean is probably the most frequently used. It is typically used with other statistics, but it can be used by itself. To try to bring together some of the material we have been covering, it might be worthwhile to go over an actual study which used the mean to draw conclusions about the effect of an independent variable.

One of the more serious problems with mental patients who have been incarcerated for extended periods of time is that they tend to lose some of their sense of self-identity and will go along with just about anything they are told to do. The psychologists conducting the study wanted to find out if the patients could be trained to be more assertive. The subjects, patients, were divided into two groups, one experimental and the other control. For the first part of the study the subjects were all asked to perform what was called an "unimportant project" and "busy work," which was to paste colored pieces of paper onto larger white sheets. They were told it was basically a meaningless task. There were fifteen pieces of paper to be glued. One point was scored for each piece of paper glued, so the higher the score, the less assertive the patient was.

In the next step of the study, the experimental subjects were trained in learning to assert themselves. The control subjects were not. After training was over for the one group, all the patients were called back for a second "interview" and again asked to paste pieces of paper as they had been before. Does assertion training have an effect? Take a look at Table 2–2. The left

*3, 5, 5, 6, 7, 30. Add: 5 + 6 = 11; divide by 2. Median = 5.5.

column shows the mean number of papers pasted up for both the experimental group and the control group before training. The right column shows the number of pieces pasted after the assertion training for both groups. [Bach et al., 1972].

Table 2–2 Results of assertiveness training with mental patients
[Bach, et al, 1972]

Group	Before Training	After Training
Experimental Mean	12.63	5.63
Control Mean	12.63	12.50

Before leaving this topic, a use of the normal curve and the mean together should be mentioned, so you can see some interrelationship between them. For example, if a psychologist assumes he has a normal distribution in the group he is examining, he is in luck because his results can be fit to the normal curve shown in Figure 2–11. Note the midpoint or zero shown in this curve. The psychologist makes the midpoint his *mean*, and he can then determine how far a particular person is from that mean by plotting that person's position on the fixed normal curve. For example, if a person is at either point labeled X in Figure 2–11, we know that at least 95 percent of other members of the group are between him and the other X, so he is pretty far out.

It takes quite a while, usually, to fully grasp the significance of the material in this chapter. The important thing is that you have a general idea of what is going on. As the book progresses, I have included statistics with the results of various studies, based on the assumption that you have a working knowledge of this chapter. Almost every study reported in the book is based on the use of some statistical measure discussed in this chapter, but it seemed best to wait a while before using them until you get a feel for the whole field of psychology.

SUMMARY

The 1600s were years of remarkable discoveries in the physical sciences, and these discoveries laid the groundwork for procedures used by modern psychologists. The discovery of microorganisms led to a fairly early experiment involving three critical experimental concepts: independent variable (that which is manipulated by the experimenter); dependent variable (that which changes as it is influenced by the independent variable); and controls (those factors not under study that might influence the results and so are removed or held constant by the experimenter).

A more modern psychological experiment using similar techniques studied the concept of set, the tendency people have to repeat previously learned methods of problem solving. Another such experiment demonstrated that high levels of anxiety reduce problem-solving efficiency.

Statistics are a way of grouping and consolidating information for clarity and simplicity of interpretation. Graphic analysis, for example, has the advantage of visually illustrating a large amount of information. Three methods of grouping information are mode (most frequently occurring score), median (middle score), and mean (arithmetical average). Correlation is a numerical representation of results and shows the degree to which two things vary together, but does not demonstrate cause and effect.

The normal curve is a bell-shaped curve that graphically represents the frequency of occurrence of many psychological and physical variables. Because of its regularity, it is a useful tool for standard interpretation of distance from the center or mean.

CHAPTER THREE
PSYCHOLOGY: PARTNER WITH BIOLOGY AND PHYSIOLOGY

What is psychology? Many would answer, "Well, it has something to do with the mind. That's what it is." Most people feel that we have not only a body that performs certain mechanical functions, but also—and more important—a vague *something else* about us that is the domain of psychology. This something else is usually called the mind.

Belief in the mystic nature of the mind probably has been around as long as man has been able to speak. Tracing back the word *psyche* ("mind" or "soul"), we find that it seems to have originated in Greek or Latin as a word meaning "breath" or part of the concept "breath of life."

The body has been studied mainly as an operating machine, and "mind" has retained a supernatural connotation. But body and what is normally called mind are intimately related, and psychology must study both. Scientists have been quick to learn that the body, which most of us take for granted, is a strange and powerful force in and of itself and has a direct effect upon the operation of what some call the psyche. Think of the person who has a fever that causes him to be "out of his mind." Functions that seem to be purely mechanical or physical are found to have great impact on the mind. Furthermore, the operations of organisms from the most simple to the most complex show a remarkable similarity, and physical behaviors are quite mystical in and of themselves.

A little world exists, for instance, that is stranger and more mysterious than that of astronomers, one whose creatures have an amazing sense of direction and abilities that no one to the present day fully understands. A relatively simple organism, the sponge, when alive and away from the kitchen, is basically a tubular structure into which water is drawn through many tiny pores, passed through various canals, and then dispersed through a vent back into the water in which the sponge lives. In a fairly large aquarium, you can take a living sponge and pull it apart with tweezers, then squeeze the bits of the sponge through a finely woven piece of cloth, and thousands of minute bits will fall through the water to the bottom. When these cells fall, they are suddenly free. What will they do? The bits of sponge will begin to swim in the water like tiny amoebae and will hunt around until two approach each other. They will fuse their little filaments and move along together until they find another stray. In a matter of days or even

44

hours a brand new sponge emerges with all the characteristics of the original one [Sinnott, 1955].*

This feat may seem incredible, even awe-inspiring, but the scientist must try to understand the mechanisms of such behavior.

Transfer your thoughts for a moment from the lowly sponge to man. Man has approximately 10 billion nerve cells. If you were given the choice of understanding either a sponge or man, which would you rather tackle? Only the most industrious would pick the human. So too with psychology. If the simple sponge has such an intricate pattern of behavior, isn't man's behavior surely a complex maze that will leave us bewildered?

If man is so intricate, how can he be studied? The answer to this question had been a long time in coming, but the door was finally opened in the middle of the last century by Charles Darwin.

THE AGE OF DARWIN: USING ANIMALS IN PSYCHOLOGY

Any psychology text will contain a proliferation of animal studies: studies about rats, geese, planaria, even cockroaches. One reason for these studies is simple: if man's complexity makes him difficult to understand, maybe he can be reached more easily through the close scrutiny of animals, which are in many respects simpler organisms. You might protest that man is not at all like an animal, but this is not correct. Physically, and to some extent psychologically, he shares much of his basic structure with animals.

Charles Darwin was one scientist responsible for a great deal of psychology's preoccupation with animal experiments. You will recall the discussion of how man's status in the universe was lowered and how the universe itself was brought under scrutiny. This change of status made man a little less untouchable and mystical and set the scene for the appearance of Darwin's very famous book of the middle 1800s, *The Origin of Species*, which proposed the theory of evolution. Darwin was not the first to suggest the idea that animals evolved, but he was the first great organizer of information about the long history of changing species that conceivably led up to mankind. The principal result of his studies was to make man more open to scientific investigation by suggesting that he was of animal origin.

As a young man, Darwin "enjoyed"† a luxury that many of us long for—a sea voyage around the world. He made the journey on a 242-ton brig, *H.M.S. Beagle*, and during the voyage spent much of his time collecting worms, rocks, and specimens from the sea. His major preoccupation was geology. He had close friends active in this field, and he considered his geology professor about the only one he could tolerate, understand, and stay awake around. Geology concentrates on a very slowly evolving earth

17   Robber crabs, from the notebooks Darwin kept during the *Beagle's* voyage (*New York Public Library*)

---

*Adapted from Edmund W. Sinnott, *The Biology of the Spirit* (New York: Viking Press, 1955), by permission of the publisher.
†He was constantly seasick.

whose land structure changes over periods of millions of years. Darwin's interest in geology has led some historians to believe that many of his ideas center around a subtle comparison between the geology of the world and the "geology" of man: if the world evolved, maybe man did, too [Adams, 1969].

Unfortunately, Darwin was sick most of his life. His active mind was always ahead of a faulty body that restricted activity. But he was fortunate in having a wife who considered it her mission in life to be his nurse, and as he lay on the couch feeling as if he had a permanent case of the flu, she spent many hours reading to him and caring for him. During this time, undoubtedly, many of his ideas came to fruition.

One such idea was the "survival of the fittest." By this Darwin meant that in each generation only those animals that possess characteristics which enable them to cope with their environment are likely to live on, and they will transmit these characteristics to their offspring. Thus, animals with the equipment most favorable to survival last longest and pass their advantageous equipment on to their young.

Many people ask if evolution stopped with the advent of man. In our present highly protected and mechanized world, where medicine and science allow even the weakest to keep going, the "new" survival of the fittest seems to be a *psychological* survival. We no longer need the equipment to eat raw food, cut our way through the forest, or fight off wild beasts. All we have to do is cope with the machine age, and those who do cope the best will remain [Irvine, 1955].

Turning back to the animal kingdom, we may consider an example of evolutionary change. It is thought the early horses had four-toed feet, a characteristic not advantageous for running. As slower horses died out over many generations, those with a middle toe remained and the side toes disappeared, leaving the horse with just a middle toe (its hoof) touching the ground, as shown in Figure 3–1. This hoof has helped the horse to achieve excellence as a runner. Adaptation, an evolution of adjustments, is

3–1 Evolution of the horse's hoof

18 A patent-medicine poster of 1873 makes satirical reference to Darwin's theory of evolution, first published in 1859 (*Library of Congress*)

manifest all around us. Such a miracle is the bird's hollow bones, which not only allow him to fly, but are "tubes" which act as part of the oxygen-intake system for sustained high-altitude flight which requires oxygen consumption beyond human capacity [Schmidt-Nielsen, 1972]. And tiny minnows of the stream protect themselves by changing their color so they blend into their background [Von Frisch, 1963]. The variations are endless.

Darwin was proposing that species evolve from more primitive organisms to those better adapted to their environment. It is important for psychology that man followed this pattern, for he developed from an apelike creature that in turn probably evolved from other species. This is not to say that the monkey who swings himself around on a rubber tire at the zoo or the gorilla who weighs 670 pounds is our direct ancestor, but that both man and ape have a common ancestor as branches of the tree have a common root. Misinterpretation of Darwin's intention regarding the relationship between man and ape brought about a world war of words, especially in the area of religion, because his views *seemed* to be at variance with the idea that man was created by God. Evolution has been hotly argued ever since Darwin first proposed his theory. In a public debate at that time, a high-ranking bishop sarcastically asked a friend of Darwin's whether he had evolved from an ape on his grandmother's or his grandfather's side. His reply was that it was better to be descended from an ape than a bishop.* Actually, most churches today admit the possibility of evolution, with the qualification that at some point during the lengthy process God gave man his special abilities.

Darwin himself was not irreligious; in fact, he believed in God during his early years and only later became an agnostic (not an atheist).† Perhaps one of his greatest sins, or at least the one made public, was that as a child he used his exceptional mind to figure out ingenious methods for stealing fruit from the family garden. He gave these delicacies to older boys in the neighborhood because he admired their "swift running ability" [Irvine, 1955].

As a scientist, Darwin was proposing indirectly that man, being but a more elaborate version of basic animal life, could be studied by observing in detail the less complex behavior of lesser animals. That is, if man is an animal, although a complex one, perhaps the study of less complex and more easily understood forms will reveal the mechanisms underlying *human* behavior.

Another reason for using animals in psychology is that they make it possible to use surgical techniques. To understand some operations of

* It was not until late 1969 that the Supreme Court finally settled the issue—that teaching evolution was legal.

† At one time Darwin actually studied to be a clergyman, as well as a physician. His father thought he was too stupid to be a good physician, but he had hopes for his son's bedside manner.

the human brain, for example, certain portions would have to be removed to see the effect on behavior. Two methods are available: wait until someone is unfortunate enough to have a brain injury, and then study the effects of this injury; or cut out part of the human brain and see what happens. The second procedure is frowned upon; the first is too accidental and random.

Animals, moreover, reproduce more rapidly and abundantly than humans. Many animal generations will be born and studied within one human generation. A scientist can study the effects of a drug on the behavior of a rat, on the behavior of its offspring, of its offspring's offspring, and so on, without dying of old age himself before the results are known.

A final point: very little breadth is allowed in experiments with human beings. Not so with animal babies. A number of extreme environmental variations and their effects can be demonstrated; the effects of total isolation, for example, or of frigid temperatures can be observed and analyzed.

Using animals involves certain disadvantages, many of which may already have occurred to you. The major one is that man is the most complex of animals, and analyzing one animal to understand the other corresponds to analyzing the electronic adding machine to comprehend the computer. Both have the same electronic components, but beyond that there are vast differences. To complicate the matter, man is equipped with hindsight and foresight, which means that he can bring into the present situation a tremendous amount of information and interpretation from his past, and even more important, he seems to be able to predict his future. This is not to say he can do so in a mystical way, like a fortune-teller, but he can forecast certain complex probabilities. Man, therefore, is much more intricate than the animal, who seems to base his behavior on only limited previous experience.

EVOLUTIONARY PATTERNS OF MEN AND ANIMALS

Nonetheless, we have frequently approached animals from a rather restricted human point of view. Valiant attempts to make chimpanzees speak have resulted in the chimps producing only a few incoherent sounds. Once the scientists broke set, however, they found that the chimps can indeed "talk," as long as you don't use human speech as your technique for judging. The chimps don't have the proper vocal apparatus, but they do use their hands constantly, so they can learn to speak precisely and coherently in proper sentence form up to a hundred words using sign language. And our hairy friends are quite good at using symbols. With a magnetic board on which are placed various symbols for words—nouns, verbs, concepts, and adjectives—a famous chimp, Sarah, can communicate in coherent sentences, using 130 words. She can even follow complex instructions if the experimenter puts the symbols on the magnetic board—for example, saying "Sarah insert apple [in the] pail [and the] banana [in the] dish" [Premack and Premack, 1972; Harlow et al., 1972].

Even though the study of animals can lead to some justifiable conclusions about the behavior of man, the two groups obviously differ in crucial ways—the major difference being in the intellectual area (which will be discussed later).

Although we recognize this difference, we find it very difficult to determine exactly where to draw the line between man and animal, for there are some remarkable parallels in the behavior of the two groups. Most of us tend, for instance, to think of lower animals and insects as creatures wandering around the earth, doing whatever is necessary for subsistence but doing it automatically, by instinct pure and simple. Evolution seems to have disappeared from their world and ours. But this assumption is not correct; even in insects we may look at examples of a continuing evolutionary process which is markedly similar to that of complex human patterns.

In human cultures, for example, a familiar custom is the presentation of a dowry to the bride's future husband, who in many cases may need some help in defraying the cost of supporting her. In our own society, however, the woman presents only herself in all her glory, but past customs still make themselves felt: the father of the bride foots the bill, and the bride's friends give her a shower so that she need not arrive completely empty-handed. Despite a gradual change, the core behavior remains.

A species of fly, the dance fly, follows a dowry system before mating, and that system has come about in a fashion very like the evolution of the human pattern. Four different kinds of fly seem to have evolved dowry behavior patterns. In the first kind, the male fly catches an insect. He then carries it to a swarm of flies, finds a suitable female, and presents her with the insect, performing a very intricate dance to make himself even more attractive. The female accepts the insect and the two of them go off into the shrubbery to mate. The female eats the insect during the mating process, apparently without offending the male's sensibilities. In the second type of the same group, the male wraps up the insect rather inefficiently. Sometimes the gift is lost, but even then, the mating takes place. The male of the third kind seemingly wearies of the chase and often substitutes something easier to get in place of a captured insect—for example, the petal of a flower. He still has a successful conquest if the petal is wrapped in a silken case. In the fourth type the male presents only an empty silken wrapping, and the ceremony of mating proceeds as planned [Van der Kloot, 1968].

In this example, the mating ritual develops from an initial arrangement that is more or less practical to a final stage that seems to be largely symbolic. Although many might disagree with our conclusion, we may use some imagination and draw a loose parallel between this case and the change from a full-fledged dowry to a symbolic one at the human level.

On an advanced human level it is possible to see an evolutionary process from the practical to the symbolic. Hunting provides a more complex example than the dowry. We can assume that Stone Age man hunted mainly to survive. As far as we know, these early, smaller-brained humans had

19 Cave drawings—
psychological comment on
conditions of early man
(*Monkmeyer*)

only stones, clubs, and sticks to use in getting food. Neanderthal man brought technological advancement by inventing the spear, which enabled him to hunt even the giant mammoth, an animal that resembled an elephant but was quite a bit larger—13 to 15 feet high [Ross,1961].

Sometime during the period following Neanderthal man came a time of severe deprivation and hunger caused by lack of game. Elaborate human symbolism evolved in the form of exaggerated plenty. Just as the Indian rain dance seems to have developed from a lack of water, so too did early man begin to symbolically portray grossly pregnant women and animals in cave drawings. Hunting and capture of the prey had entered a symbolic stage beyond the practical necessities of getting food to compensate for a physical lack. It is this symbolic evolution, on a high plane, that seems to distinguish man from animals.

Today we can see further symbolic exaggeration of the original hunting behavior. Many men have rifles and an arsenal of accessories that would be effective even against an overgrown mammoth—but these men do not need to hunt to live. Wealthier hunters go on safari, bringing back skins and stuffed heads as trophies, but they do not need to eat their prey. The ultimate step in this evolution of hunting is the rifle camera—a "rifle" that does nothing more than take a picture of the game through its sights.

To demonstrate that evolution is an ongoing process rather than a clearly delineated set of stages of the past, one can look at the Australian aborigines of today: a group of people who are so primitive in a technological sense that they have no written language and only the crudest implements and tools. This tribe still worships ritualistic rock paintings of animals as sacred relics. Thus various stages of evolution exist all at one time.

The worship of paintings or the behavior of the well-fed man with the rifle, somewhat like the dance fly presenting the empty wrapping, make little objective sense unless one understands the sequence of events that preceded such behavior.

Although, as we have seen, animal behavior and human behavior exhibit some striking similarities, they are by no means entirely the same—or even very much the same. But many examples of animal behavior do shed light on human behavior and, furthermore, suggest that we probably come into the world equipped with many of our basic behaviors upon which the environment elaborates.

**the imprinted animal
and child**

Evolution, then, involves changes in species through various generations and apparently is common to both animals and men. We seem to be born with certain basic behavior patterns already built in—a very unusual and intriguing phenomenon. Just as a flower will follow an orderly sequence and blossom at a preset time, so too animals and humans develop certain characteristics only at certain times in the growth process. The animal and the human being seem to unfold like the flower; there are certain sequences of events over which we have no control. For example, we will later discuss in detail the phenomenon of walking, which can't take place before the organism is ready, but will occur automatically as long as the animal is healthy. The point is that animals are like seeds in many respects; if you plant a seed at the wrong time of year, it will wait until the proper time to begin its growth.

This has been graphically illustrated in the case of ducks. At a certain time in their lives they are programmed to accept a mother, and if a mother is not around, some strange things happen.

One early naturalist* who explored this behavior was Dr. Konrad Lorenz. He had a whole house full of animals; in fact, at times so many animals were wandering freely about the house that his children, when left unattended, were kept in cages for their own protection. Part of his menagerie included some mallard ducklings. He found that shortly after hatching from their eggs, the ducklings would follow him, assuming that he was their mother, but only if he quacked like a mother mallard, which, incidentally, took quite a bit of practice. The ducks also required that he walk in the squatting position because his standing height was not sufficiently motherly; he was too large otherwise, and they lost sight of him. Dr. Lorenz was proud of how well his experiment was going when, one day, in his words:

> I suddenly looked up and saw the garden fence framed by a row of dead white faces: a group of tourists was standing at the fence and staring horrified in my direction. . . . For all they could see was a big man with a beard dragging himself, crouching, round the meadow, in figures of eight, glancing constantly over his shoulder and quacking—but the ducklings, the all-revealing and all-explaining ducklings, were hidden in the tall spring grass from the view of the astonished crowd [Lorenz, 1952].†

In his experiment, Lorenz was illustrating a point quickly picked up by psychologists: even among animals, the mother object does not necessarily have to be the actual mother—the animal was programmed only to recognize *someone* as its mother. In psychology, this programming is called *imprinting*. To put it loosely, the animal's brain—at a certain time—is embossed or imprinted with a mother image, or what it considers to be its mother. When the appropriate or inappropriate object of this need is presented to the duck at the *correct time* in its development, the object is labeled mother somewhere in the brain, and this label is frequently difficult to erase.

Psychologists took Dr. Lorenz's idea to the laboratory to study it further. They made a plastic, *male*-colored‡ mother-substitute for the

20   Konrad Lorenz and companions—in this case, geese (*Jeroboam*)

---

* A scientist who studies animal behavior as it occurs in nature. That is, he observes animal behavior without interfering with it.

† From Konrad Z. Lorenz, *King Solomon's Ring* (New York: Thomas Y. Crowell, 1952), p. 43; reprinted by permission.

‡ Male and female ducks have different coloring.

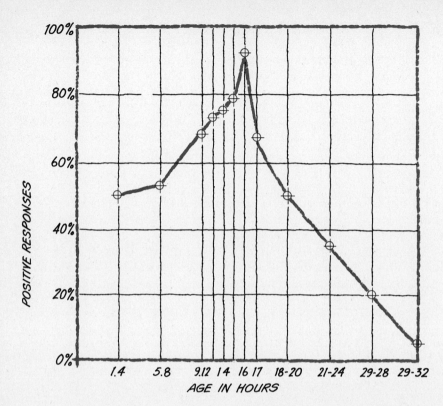

3–2 Ducks' response to imprinting

duckling. The duckling was then placed in a small pond where it was circled by the motor-operated plastic model and imprinted. After the imprinting experience the duckling was given a choice of following a male-colored or a female-colored model. Consistently it chose the male model, even though this choice would be inappropriate in nature.

The experimenters did not try to compete with Dr. Lorenz's imitation of the duck call, but instead used a tape recording during the imprinting [Hess, 1959]. Their experiment was not quite as colorful as Dr. Lorenz's, but some interesting facts emerged from it. First, ducks are clearly imprintable; second, ducks are imprintable only at a certain time in life. This second point can be seen in Figure 3–2. Note that there is a critical age* in hours (16) at which the duckling is most responsive to obtaining a mother.

In the laboratory, ducks have been imprinted to unusual items such as milk bottles and toilet floats, which may have made the ducks wonder what problem the experimenter had. In any case, laboratory imprinting is reversible,† whereas imprinting in nature is not. In nature, the mother becomes permanent. The difference between the two types of imprinting seems to lie in a continuous conversation between the mother and the

*Called *critical period*, which means that a certain event can occur only during a specific time period in the animal's growth.
†In other words, the animal can accept a different "mother."

52

duckling. This conversation begins before the egg has hatched; inside the egg the baby peeps and the mother clucks softly in response. These "discussions" go on before, during, and after the hatching, and since each mother duck has a slightly different manner of clucking, experimenters suspect that this is one of the methods for firmly imprinting a specific mother into the duckling's brain [Hess, 1972]. This difference between laboratory and natural settings may account for the success that Dr. Lorenz had in imprinting: his duck-to-duck conversation. In some new and really tantalizing studies, it has been discovered that both left and right handed human mothers reflexively hold their newborn with their left arm, pressing him against the heart. Some believe this well may be a primitive form of imprinting via heartbeat and rhythm [Salk, 1973].

Similar studies of imprinting and the critical period have been carried out with monkeys. These studies demonstrate that if a monkey has not received motherly stimulation before he is a certain number of weeks old, he will grow up to be cold, aloof, and unfriendly to his own offspring. Apparently physical stimulation in the form of love must occur at a certain time or the monkey does not develop normal "family" relationships. Although monkeys have a need for stimulation of some kind, they prefer a certain type. For example, baby monkeys were placed in a cage with two surrogate (substitute) mothers, one made of wire, the other made of soft terry cloth. A bottle of milk was hooked to one or the other mother. Both these "mothers" were available to the baby monkeys. The wire mother provided food for one group of monkeys; the cloth mother did the same for the other group. Figure 3–3 gives the results of this experiment.

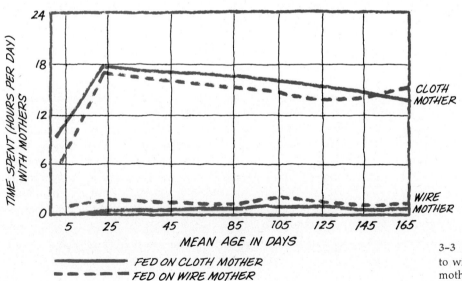

3–3 Monkeys' response to wire and cloth surrogate mothers

21-22 The baby monkey was willing to feed from the wire surrogate mother, but spent most of its time with the soft, touchable cloth mother
(*Harry Harlow*)

No matter how the monkey was fed, he spent a great deal of time with the cloth mother and little time with the wire mother. The explanation for this behavior was that the soft texture of the cloth mother provided comforting tactile stimulation for the monkey. Since the hunger drive is considered basic and its satisfaction of ultimate importance, one would expect the monkeys to prefer the feeding mother, even though she was made of wire, but this was not the case; the monkey's choice demonstrates a high-level need for the stimulation of touch. Of course, if the infants can have their cake and eat it too, they will: a cloth surrogate mother that feeds is preferred to one that does not [Harlow, 1970].

To a small child few things are more fascinating than a mechanical teddy bear, but to a monkey infant such a device is extremely frightening. The experimenter performed a fear test by placing a mechanical teddy bear in the cage with the monkey. No matter whether the monkey had been fed by a wire or a cloth mother, there was a strong tendency to run to the cloth mother for protection. This was true even if the wire mother had fed it. As time progressed, the cloth mother became more and more the "permanent mother," the source of comfort [Harlow, 1959]. Evidence that a critical-period phenomenon was involved was emphasized in one instance in which the experimenter was not prepared for the arrival of an infant monkey. He had to hastily fashion a surrogate cloth mother and used a round ball for the head. In the meantime he worked frantically to make a new head with a face for the surrogate. But he finished too late; when he put the new face on the surrogate mother, the monkeys had already decided that a faceless mother was theirs, so the monkeys turned the ball around to the side which had no features, and were then content [Harlow, 1970].

In experiments where monkeys were completely deprived of a mother object in any form, the results were unpleasant. When these monkeys grew up and had infants of their own they either ignored them or mistreated them so badly—for example, pushing the baby's face into the floor—that the infants had to be removed [Sackett, 1968].

The need among monkeys for a comforting mother, real or surrogate, during a critical period seems to have a parallel in human infancy, a time which also requires the comfort of physical contact. In some countries during World War II, for instance, it was nearly impossible to take care of the large number of homeless children placed in orphanages, other than to occasionally change diapers and prop up a bottle to feed them. In only a few orphanages were people available to hold the children during the feeding period and give them some physical attention during the day, even for short periods. A study that compared the death rate in the two types of institutions found the rate to be lower in the orphanages where the children were fondled more frequently. The mortality rate was so much lower that it could not be interpreted as just a coincidence. It is not the mere fact of institutionalization that is critical, but the interplay between the guardians and the children that is important. Recent studies show that some children who come from relatively grotesque backgrounds and have been institutionalized because of this have reached adolescence in good shape, both physically and psychologically, because they were provided with a close adult friend. It may sound trite, but love and affection do wonders [Wolins, 1970].

In general, animals have the most stable psychological development if as an infant they have soft bodily contact, rocking, and physically warm "mothers." It is no stretch of the imagination to assume these are very important in human infants* [Harlow et al., 1972].

Other studies have covered the critical period and imprinting in the lives of dogs. Apparently these animals have a six- to nine-week critical period for the formation of social attachments. After about twelve weeks, a dog that has been kept in isolation will tend to remain undomesticated, or at best shy and strange. Thus, as a general rule, a person would not want to purchase a puppy older than twelve weeks which has been isolated in a kennel, especially if the dog is a potentially dangerous and highly sensitive breed such as the German shepherd.

It is not unlikely that humans have similar critical periods. For instance, a comparison has been made between the wagging of the tail of a dog, which occurs at a specific time and produces a social response from others, and the smile of a baby, which appears about forty-five days after birth. Both the smile and the wagging tail are means of receiving love from others.

Learning a foreign language with a correct and natural accent is another example. This achievement is usually possible only with children less than twelve years old. Some change seems to occur beyond this age which prevents full development of foreign-language speech sounds. Here again we are probably dealing with some form of critical period [Scott, 1962; Scott, 1950; Fuller, 1967; Nash, 1970].

Considering how knowledge of animal-human parallels has grown in the last century, it is probably just as well that Darwin's publisher didn't get his way. When he first received the manuscript of *The Origin of Species*, his evaluation was preposterous and humorous—especially since Darwin's work has become one of the world's most famous books. The publisher suggested that Darwin change his manuscript to include only some information on pigeons, because, he said seriously, "most people are interested in pigeons" [Barzun, 1958].

Although it is true that humans are not identical to animals, much headway has been made in understanding people by studying animals, and this progress was prompted by Darwin's work. For instance, as one author

---

*One infant monkey contacted an ice-cold surrogate mother and "fled screaming in horror and never returned to the mother over a 30-day period" [Harlow et al., 1972].

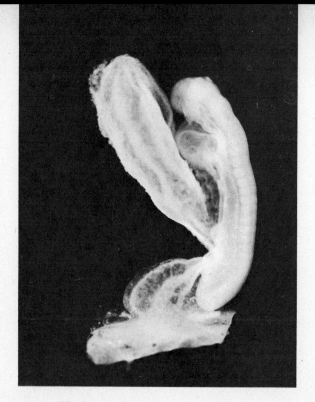
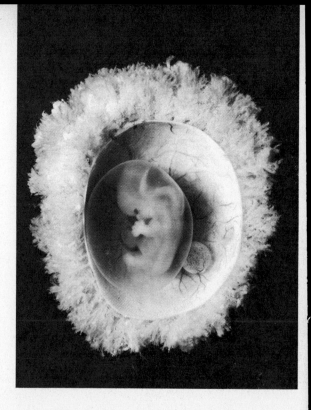

23a–d The human fetus at
four stages of growth—23
days, 40 days, 56 days, and
70 days (*Chester Reather*)

has pointed out, our generation is intent on blaming parents for whatever
happens to children, but some studies of imprinting and critical period in
the area of human childhood stimulation seem to indicate that *not* all children
are desirous of excessive cuddling and fondling. From the very beginning,
a small number of them seem rather cold and indifferent toward their
parents, although they still require *some* stimulation. While this behavior
obviously contradicts any hypothesis that proposes universal need for
physical stimulation at a critical period, the study nonetheless is an outgrowth of earlier animal studies and may lead to further understanding of
apparent innate differences in certain aspects of children's personalities
[Nash, 1970].

Along the same lines, and to be discussed more fully later, we now
know that the human being cannot survive loss of all stimulation from the
environment. We are just not equipped to handle such deprivation. Studies
of animals and the subsequent application to human beings should not,
therefore, be passed over lightly.

**preprogramming
in children**

Examples at the human level show that a child is, to some extent, preprogrammed for his ability to walk, a natural process that begins sometime
between nine and fifteen months. Waiting for this to happen, however, is
a long and trying process for the mother, especially at about nine months,
when the child is just able to stagger to the standing position, grab things
from a table, and smash them on the floor. To achieve this unenviable feat,
the child follows an orderly sequence of development: raise the head, roll

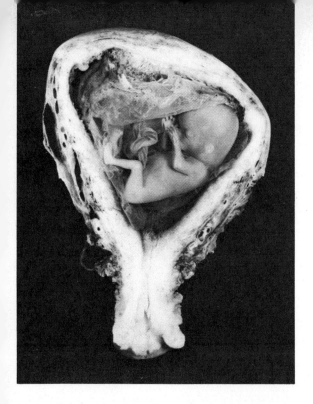 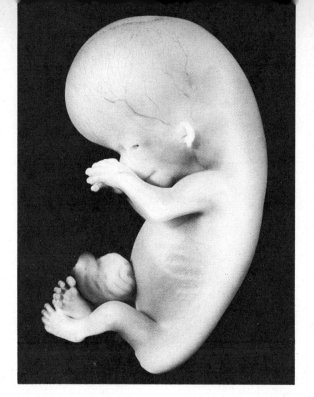

over, sit with support, sit alone, stand with help, and so forth [Mussen, 1963]. To the casual observer this process seems to be a learned one—but we may wonder whether the child would be able to walk without any previous training.

One method of answering this question would be to find a culture in which the child is not "trained" to walk. A striking example is the Hopi Indian tribe in which children are handled by methods entirely foreign to other American women. The culture is one of the few in the United States that has almost entirely resisted the encroachment of our so-called civilization. Its tribal ceremonies have not changed; the Hopi still catch live eagles and still perform a snake dance, and they won't disclose the secret method used to get the snake to cooperate. Their culture is so strong that one Hopi, White Bear, who left for the outside world and played with a big-name band for twenty years, finally returned to the pueblo, donned his costume, and once more became an active participant in the rain dances and other tribal ceremonies [Hawgood, 1967].

In some of these Indian cultures the husband retires to his bed when his wife is about to give birth; he may rest for a couple of weeks. In the meantime, his wife has the child, but she is not allowed to relax as her husband has been doing. Instead, she straps the child to her back so he can be transported while she performs her chores. The child remains bound to his mother's back for many months, and his movement is restricted so that he does not have the opportunity to "learn" to walk as other children do. Despite this restriction, when the child is let out of his carryall, he is able to move about, after a minimal amount of practice, with the same degree of efficiency as other children. Obviously, the child is preprogrammed, in a sense, to walk at a certain stage, and he will do so. Psychologists call this automatic process **maturation**, meaning that the body and the person are maturing at a fixed rate and will perform when ready, not before. There is a critical period ending just before eight weeks when a child shows reflexive "walking" movements just as many animals do. With special exercises during this period the child can be made to walk one month earlier than control children [Zelazo, 1972]. Whether it is worth the trouble is highly debatable. After the critical period, attempts have been made with twins to *train* one twin to perform bodily functions such as walking while the other is left untrained. The trained twin will not walk any more quickly than the untrained one. Nature must take its course [Gesell and Thompson, 1929].

The human baby is the most helpless of all creatures. Many feel this is so because the baby is in the process of developing a very elaborate brain the likes of which no other animal has. Even so, he follows an orderly sequence which gives the appearance of an evolutionary history: at one point the human embryo exhibits the beginnings of fish gills, then goes onward in its development. All evidence suggests we begin as animal and surpass this stage to reach humanness.

An intriguing study illustrates this sequence and suggests that man develops as a lower organism at the outset; but when the higher brain mechanisms via culture and learning take over, a considerable amount of so-called animal behavior is obscured. In the study, babies a few weeks old were placed face down in water for a short period. Each baby automatically held its breath and made swimming motions.* However, by four months of age the child was no longer able to do this; he got water in his mouth, flailed his arms, sank under, and struggled—all of which illustrates that he is destined for a nonaquatic life [McGraw, 1939].

instinctive behavior   Basic behaviors such as swimming ability seem to exist in humans, but they are likely to be covered up or to disappear completely because the organism is destined to be human. One must exercise caution in describing human behavior in terms of animal instincts, for individuals show almost endless variation, probably because some of their animal needs have been suppressed by social learning. Such a need is the sex drive, which celibate priests, Buddhist monks, and others have with difficulty overcome. Furthermore, people have been known to disregard even the instinct for survival —for example, the kamikaze pilot† in World War II, the Vietnamese Buddhist who immolates himself, and the soldier who gives up his own life

---

*The baby cannot swim at this age, so don't throw him into the water.
†Pilots who flew on suicide missions, carrying only enough fuel to get to the target and crash into it.

to save that of another. The point is that the term *instinct* must be used with care, for certainly human behavior is not explainable in these terms alone, even though parts of it are.

Psychology has never quite rid itself of a stigma from the early part of this century, when the fashion among psychologists was to label almost everything instinctive, including spitting, smiling, going to parties, and so forth. In fact, psychology got so much on its own political bandwagon that in the 1920s psychologists endowed man with 5,759 separate instincts, too many for any scientist to cope with [Bernard, 1970]. The claim that instincts are motivators in human beings has now been pushed aside by a large number of psychologists for this very reason. With rare exceptions, instinct as such has been abandoned as a working concept in psychology just because it became so easy to say, "Oh, that's an instinct."

The need for emotional and physical response from others, which we saw in the study of monkeys and human babies, is so universal that many feel this need is what might be called instinctive. But even here the human being probably is subject to his cultural environment, which later produces many variations, ramifications, and elaborations on the desire to be touched—for example, in the area of sex. If we look closely at the animal kingdom, including man, it seems obvious that regardless of later training and its strong effect, man and animal do come equipped with some basics—but to call them instincts, especially in humans, is too vague. Further, this label leads to a dreaded (for the scientist) circularity: a mother takes care of her baby; therefore, she has the maternal instinct; she has the maternal instinct; therefore, she takes care of her baby.

Hopefully, the scientist can avoid this circularity and sort out the so-called instincts from the learning, but the problems posed by this sorting process are extremely complex, because learning begins at the moment of birth, or perhaps even earlier.

THE PHYSIOLOGY OF BEHAVIOR

With this section, our discussion begins to focus on a great number of physiological centers of the body and their effects on psychological behavior. Beginning students usually enter the psychology classroom most preoccupied with finding out what is responsible for their friend's strange behavior, what kind of person will commit an ax murder, and, of course, a great deal about sex—so there is typically some resistance to the subject of physiology. But, interestingly enough, all these aspects of life have some connection with physiological mechanisms, so a discussion of them is generally fruitful.

If you feel this division between physiology and psychology, you are not alone. Chapter 1 referred to the philosophical origins of psychology, which were followed in time by an extremely rigid physiological emphasis on the part of many scientists; and for a long period psychology was split in half, with one division going the physical-measurement route and the other holding out for philosophy. The unfortunate dilemma is explained by Benjamin Franklin (always available with a quote), authority on lightning rods, kites, and beautiful women, not necessarily in that order. When the founding fathers were drafting the Constitution, ensuing battles between large and small states for adequate representation reminded Franklin of a "famous political quote" (which was his own). He said the representatives were like a thirsty snake with two heads, which came to a division on the road; one head wanted to go to the right and the other to the left, and the heads not being able to agree, the snake died of thirst [Van Doren, 1948]. Fortunately, the philosophy-physiology conflict is no longer quite as large an issue, but at times it has come close to the snake problem. Although psychologists work in many different areas of emphasis, more and more often these areas, both physiological and psychological, overlap and provide many answers that could not have been gleaned separately.

Unquestionably, physiological factors influence not only the supposedly more interesting things like psychopathology (abnormal behavior), sexual activity, and the mysterious phenomenon of hypnosis, but almost

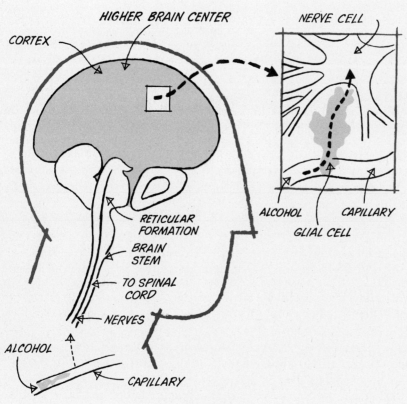

THE BRAIN   3-4   Outline of pathways of alcohol to the brain

all aspects of everyday activity as well. We need, therefore, a basic grasp of physiology in order to understand the total organism.

brain and nerves   Without becoming too involved in semantics, a distinction is often made between the mind and the brain. The mind is the layman's version of the *special* part of us that thinks, feels, desires, and the like, whereas the brain is the physical organ which psychologists feel is, in large measure, responsible for most of these more complex behaviors. A philosopher has pointed out this difference by analogy: the coat which you hang up on a nail will fall if the nail comes out. However, this does not demonstrate that the nail and coat are one unit, only that they interact. Thus, consciousness or mind depends on the brain, but the two need not be identical. Suppose you are physically fatigued. How this will affect your mind depends not on the fatigue but on the fashion in which you acquired the fatigue; if from swimming, the fatigue is usually pleasant; if from work, you probably feel irritation and little pleasure. For the time being, we will be dealing with the physical brain—but notice the interconnection between the psychological and the physiological that is constantly present [Durant, 1933].

Everyone is familiar, for example, with the changes that take place when people have had too much to drink. Some become placid, some maudlin, some hostile; some content themselves with wearing lampshades for hats, and some kill themselves or others. Obviously, one cannot say that just the "mind" is involved; something physical is also responsible for the behavior.

When a person is drunk, basically what has happened is that the highest and most civilized portion of his brain has been put to rest for a period of time. To accomplish this, the alcohol reaches the cells of the brain only by an indirect route. It first must arrive at the stomach, where it is gradually absorbed by the stomach walls and enters the bloodstream. During this slow process, most of the alcohol waiting its turn to be absorbed is passed into the intestine, where its progress is very swift (this speedy absorption accounts for frequent processions to the rest room) [Modell, 1967].

The alcohol passes from the bloodstream into the brain by seeping through capillary walls (very small blood vessels), through screening cells called glial cells* into the actual nerve cells of the brain. The resultant chemical action first works on the *reticular formation,* the alertness control of the body. This unit (Fig. 3-4) is very important in keeping active the *cerebral cortex,* which is the highest brain center of man. In the case of drunkenness, of course, the reticular formation helps the cortex to become less active.

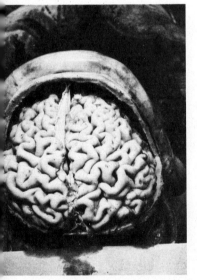

24   The human brain, viewed from above. Notice the wrinkled, wormlike convolutions of the cerebral cortex (*Gabriele Wunderlich*)

---

*Glial cells are small chemical units that exist in great abundance in the brain. They are thought to be chemical screens, and some investigators think of them as feeders or nourishers for the brain cells.

The cortex is a very thick sheet of gray-colored nerves that goes over and around the basic animal brain and is protected by the skull (Fig. 3–7). The tissue is wrinkled and folded like spaghetti or noodles lumped together; in this way nature utilizes all available space, which it could not do if the cortex were flat.* As one moves up the evolutionary scale, the amount of convoluting (wrinkling and folding) is of some importance; it seems to correspond *roughly* with the amount of intelligence† [Wooldridge, 1963].

Once the reticular sentry has been knocked out, the cortex begins to function with less and less organization. Ideas and images may flow more freely, but their sense often becomes harder to detect, especially to the sober listener. The action described above can be shown by noting the various divisions of the cerebral cortex that are shown in Figure 3–5. Looking at

---

*If you have a large ball of spaghetti, you have many more surfaces or greater surface area than if you had a comparably sized lump of dough, which has only a smooth outer surface.

†Intelligence is extremely difficult to define. What is intelligent for a dog versus a cat, for example? However, in gross comparisons—e.g., between dog-monkey-human—this principle holds true.

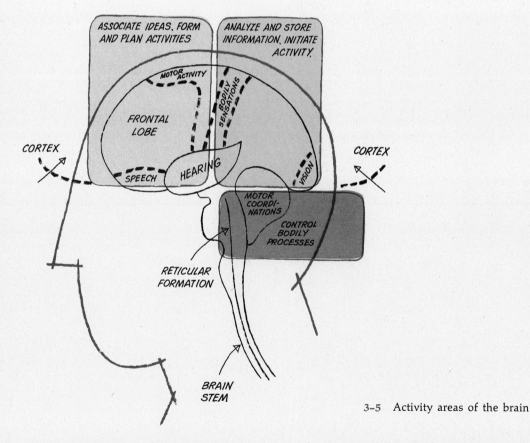

3–5   Activity areas of the brain

WOLCOTT'S INSTANT PAIN ANNIHILATOR.

Fig 1. Demon of Catarrh. Fig 2. Demon of Neuralgia. Fig 3. Demon of Headache. Fig 4. Demon of Weak Nerves. Fig 5.5 Demons of Toothache.

25   In this Civil War poster, headache is attributed to tiny devils carrying the Confederate flag (*Library of Congress*)

this figure makes it relatively easy to understand why the scientist points to the physical effect of alcohol on the cortex as the major contributing factor to the behavior of people who drink too much. One can almost trace the path of the alcohol through the brain, merely by observing the outward behavioral signs of the person. The brain is divided into sections, and each has a major task assigned to it. The most notable effects of alcohol, which most of us can detect in our friends, seem to be on the speech area, motor coordination, and vision. The frontal area has the major task of planning activities and associating ideas, two behaviors which are quite unreliable in those who have had too much to drink.

As this book progresses, we will devote considerable discussion to the brain. Before any of it begins, we should emphasize that the brain is not as simply divided as Figure 3–5 makes it appear to be. Hearing, for instance, can be interrupted by injury to any one of at least thirteen areas scattered all over the brain, even though the major hearing area *is* located where it is shown in Figure 3–5 [Luria, 1970].

background of nerve and brain discovery   From a historical viewpoint, perhaps the most striking facts about nerves and the brain is the length of time it took to discover them and the naive opinions that people often held about their nature. But then, as we carry out our day-to-day activities, we seldom think of any functioning part of our body—that is, until it starts to malfunction. A headache, for most of us, is a dramatic sign that we have a head; most of the time we take it for granted. Early scientists did not go so far as to take the entire body for granted, but the first problem they faced was the existence of many prohibitions against experimenting with the human body; the second was the lack of adequate tools with which to work.

Many ideas about the brain have not consistently proven helpful or favorable to the advancement of science. On the American frontier, for example, around 1800, a good cure for a headache was shaking the rattles of a rattlesnake (the reasoning was that if snakes could cause pain, they must be able to cure it, too). The cure for a head wound was a little more involved—the wound was dipped in cold cider vinegar and wrapped in a bandage of squirrel brains. Giving a sign that he was more advanced, the frontiersman in the northern wilderness used foresight and engaged in preventive medicine: all he needed to do to prevent headaches was to hook the right eye of a wolf inside his right sleeve [Dunlop, 1965].

In a way, it's a wonder that any progress was made. Nonetheless, all discoveries should be considered within the context of the general level of scientific progress; there is little question that great resistance to intellectual change or discovery exists, no matter how logical the scientist may be and how illogical general beliefs.

the nerve

The brain operates both chemically and electrically. Its operation is based on the functioning of the *neurons* (nerve cells) within it. Billions of these neurons exist in maximum concentration within the brain. These nerve cells are so small that some areas of the brain contain 100 million of them within a single cubic inch. At any single moment in time, any one of these neurons may be in communication with up to 270,000 of its neighboring neurons. The nerves,* aside from providing sensation and stimulating movement for the body, constitute the very elaborate *association areas*,† which exist throughout the cortex.

The existence of the nerve is common knowledge today, which puts us ahead of Descartes, the philosopher-scientist of the late 1500s, who was convinced that our behavior is a result of animal spirits that flow between the mind and the body. This theory may or may not have been a step ahead

26 Dr. Frankenstein's monster shows the positive effects of a blast of static electricity to his neural network (*Bettmann Archive*)

---

*Nerves, like most of the rest of us, are made up of cells. The individual nerve cell is called *neuron*. A group of neurons, which together transmit electrical information, is called a *nerve*. Nerve cells with their attachments are shown in Figure 3–6.

†Association areas are portions of the brain with highly complex interconnections between neurons. These areas are assumed to be locations for the unification of our many thoughts, actions, and feelings. A major association area (the frontal area) is shown in Figure 3–5. Others are shown in Figure 3–7. However, association areas are scattered throughout the brain.

of earlier thinkers who considered behavior the result of special fluids that flowed through the body and were characteristic of an individual. For example, if you had a rather draggy, dull personality, you were behaving under the influence of phlegm pulsing thickly through your tubes.

In the 1700s an anatomy professor by the name of Galvani set up a laboratory rather like that of the monster maker Dr. Frankenstein. One of his instruments was a static generator, the kind that produces large, colorful blasts of static electricity when cranked. One day, while Galvani was dissecting a frog, his laboratory assistant was standing over to the side and grinding away at the static machine. The frog's leg, which was sitting on the table, began to twitch, and continued to do so as long as the machine was on. Galvani concluded that the leg had "animal electricity" in it. This *was* a decided step forward in understanding nerve operation.

Following Galvani's discovery, further work was done by a man whose last name is in common use, Allessandro Volta, a professor of physics who explained Galvani's findings—electrical current flowed through the frog's leg. Once scientists discovered that the nerves operate on electrical current, it was only a short time before they noticed that the nerve was

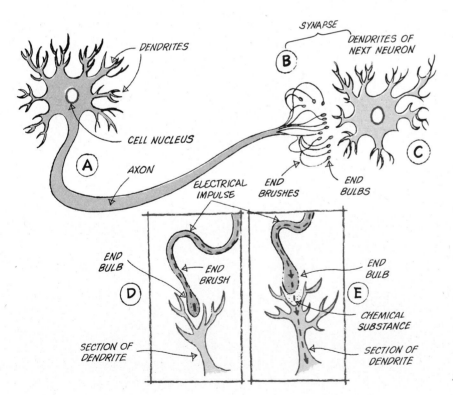

3-6   Nerve cells

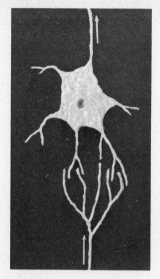

27   Clay model of synapse. The terminals intersect so that the nerve impulses pass from one nerve cell to the next in a chain reaction throughout the body (*Jeroboam*)

responsible for all of man's movements, his learning processes, and his thought patterns.

The nerve cell (Fig. 3–6) starts off its growth looking more or less like any other cell, and then the cell begins to spin out fibers that extend in specific directions to meet other nerve cells (Jacobson and Hunt, 1973). Eventually the cell looks like an octopus with branching tentacles. All but one of these tentacles bring stimuli *to* the cell body at the rate of 200 mph; they are called *dendrites*. The remaining tentacle is elongated and runs out from the cell body proper, its length depending on where the message is going and what pathway it will take. This long fiber is called an *axon* (Fig. 3–6A). The axon terminates in units that resemble a bulb if it is connecting to the dendrites of another neuron (Fig. 3–6B, C). Axons connect to muscle or gland cells, dendrites to sensory receptors. What the cell and axon look like will vary to some degree according to the function each is serving, but the general idea is conveyed in Figure 3–6. When two neurons interconnect, they do so indirectly, for there is a space between the end of one neuron (called an *end brush* because of its appearance) and the dendrite or receiver of the next neuron (Fig. 3–6D). The electrical signal that travels from one neuron to another does so by disturbing the chemical constitution of the bulb and releasing "chemical messengers," which disturb the next dendrite and activate it electrically (Fig. 3–6D, E) [Gardner, 1968; Morgan, 1965].

Oddly enough, LSD is a chemical remarkably similar to the fluid found at the junction of two neurons; this junction is called a *synapse* (Fig. 3–6B). Although they do not know for certain, many scientists conjecture that the ingestion of LSD causes the synapses to be connected in a more or less random order instead of by the normally desired pathways—hence the strange visions and sounds, the thoughts that collide, fuse, and come out in a very distorted form.

The nerve is the basic unit of behavior. Furthermore, it is basic to brain operation.

the brain   Early medical men were not as concerned with the head as physicians are today. Difficult as this is to imagine, the brain as we know it just did not exist for them. Medicine had other preoccupations. For example, a typical and long-lived practice in medicine was bloodletting, which was usually performed by applying leeches to the skin. This theory was not so preposterous—presumably injurious fluids were being removed from the body. It didn't work very well, but still it made some sense. Early medicine was busy with what could be seen, especially the discharge of various fluids from the body. In this area, a rather encouraging writing of the early physician, Hippocrates, has been lost to young people. He felt that acne was a good thing to have, since it represented a discharge from the brain of fluids that caused malady.

28   Robert Fludd, the physician who proposed that the brain contained three parts: intellect, imagination, and sensation (*Culver*)

29   Dr. Fludd's drawing shows man's soul in harmony with the universe (*Bettmann Archive*)

Dr. William Harvey came much closer. His major contributions were toward understanding blood flow, but he also tried to study the brain by use of logic. Observing that animals that did not possess a brain nearly as elaborate as man's still could perform movements and behavior patterns, he reasoned the brain itself could not be responsible for *all* of man's behavior. He granted that elaborate behaviors can come from the brain, but ordinary muscle movements and reflexes must not, since animals have them too. In his preoccupation with the heart, the area in which so many of his discoveries were made, he decided that the nonbrain, nonvoluntary behaviors were controlled by the heart. Today we know that much of what he said was correct. But the location of automatic control is not the heart but the spinal cord, the long bundle of nerve fibers running from the brain stem to the tailbone. The spinal cord handles most reflexive movements; usually automatic actions are short-circuited from the brain, which probably explains why we are more upset after a near-collision than at the time we are first involved in it. Initially our reflexes operate automatically to avoid the accident; afterward our higher brain centers are mulling over what could have happened to us. We would all be long dead if we had to stop and *think* every time such action was required. We will discuss the spinal cord later in this chapter [Harvey, 1952].

Even though the term *brain* was in use, and the brain had been located in the head, it was poorly understood. Its functioning was described in various ways, a few unique: a well-known physician of the 1600s assumed the universe was composed of three entities—God, man, and earth. He then described the brain as composed of three parts comparable to these three elements: intellect, imagination, and sensation. His drawing of the brain shows the inside of the head as three circles attached to one another by tubes [Wilson, 1964].

The first genuine breakthrough in understanding the brain came, in the early 1800s, in a bizarre fashion. A theory that today is considered completely false and inaccurate focused everyone's attention on the brain. It was interesting enough to bring out the rattlesnake-shaking people, who in turn brought down the wrath of the scientists upon it.

The man responsible for this revolution was an obscure medical student, Franz Gall. A vital ability of the medical student is memory, and in the early 1800s Franz Gall ran into difficulty because he was unable to remember as well as others. Rather than admit a failing on his part, he began to carefully scrutinize his fellow students and convinced himself that the best memorizers had protruding eyes (which he did not have). Thus, he directly connected certain physical factors with mental faculties; in this case, the protruding eyes indicated a facility for memory which he didn't have [Krech, 1962].

Gall did well enough to graduate and devote his life to studying anatomy. With the very limited knowledge of the brain available and with Gall's belief that the faculties we possess are reflected in our physical characteristics, he soon came out with his theory of *phrenology*, the study of bumps on the head as related to personality.

Feel your skull. Notice how uneven it is. You have a depression here, an enlargement there. Elaborating on the protruding-eye theory, Gall's phrenology stated that certain areas of the brain are enlarged if a person possesses a certain faculty in more abundance than his fellow beings. Thus, if you have an enlargement or bump about where your temples are, according to Gall, you have a personality that enjoys destruction; if you have a bump on the top of your head just to the left of the middle, you have a lot of faith; if you have one near your soft spot, you have a lot of self-love, and so forth. The list is almost endless.

In only a short while, some of the less scrupulous had set up shop, complete with the accouterments of fortune-tellers—colorful robes, capes, music, etc.—and they were analyzing people according to the bumps on their heads. The rattlesnake people flocked to the phrenologists and returned happy as rich old ladies who have just visited some mystic adviser.

Scientists were in an uproar over the unscientific procedure of phrenology. The biggest problem with this theory was one of proof, called *validity*, which refers to the accuracy of conclusions drawn. Put in other words, validity means: Do these bumps actually indicate what they are supposed to indicate? As you can see, it was impossible to verify any of the claims. How benevolent is one? Is one consistently so? How is this related to the bump in the "benevolent area"?

Of importance to our discussion is the fact that phrenology caught on with the public to a great extent, and its popularity brought violent objections from scientists. No matter what failings phrenology had, however, it focused the scientist's attention on the mind as *localized in the brain area*, something that had been largely ignored until that time.

A neurologist, Pierre Flourens, entered the scene and helped the scientist's cause. He began cutting away parts of the brains of pigeons, chickens, and rabbits, otherwise leaving the animals intact. He demonstrated by this procedure that if a certain part is cut away, the animal will lose locomotion, for example. If another part is cut away, the animal will lose what Flourens called "intelligence." Science breathed a loud sigh of relief after Flourens's work: here was scientifically demonstrable experimentation showing behavior control, not the broad assumptions and mysticism in which phrenology engaged. But the brain area had become important.

Scientists already had discovered that electrical impulses lie at the root of many of our acts. Not much later, in 1870, two men, Fritsch and Hitzig, came up with the novel idea of stimulating the brain with electrically activated wires. They found that when a certain area of the exposed brain

30   Dr. Gall interprets the skull of King Louis Phillippe of France; notice the very large bump, denoting faith, on the top of Louis's head (*Bettmann Archive*)

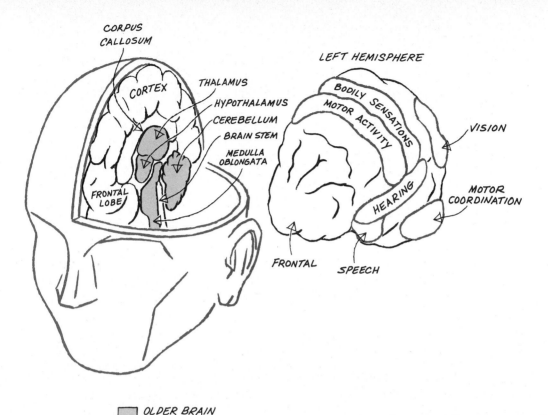

CORPUS CALLOSUM

CORTEX

THALAMUS

HYPOTHALAMUS

CEREBELLUM

BRAIN STEM

MEDULLA OBLONGATA

FRONTAL LOBE

LEFT HEMISPHERE

BODILY SENSATIONS

MOTOR ACTIVITY

VISION

HEARING

MOTOR COORDINATION

FRONTAL

SPEECH

OLDER BRAIN (SEE FIG. 3-11)

3-7   Structure and activity areas of the brain

was touched—for instance, the motor area shown in Figure 3–5—an involuntary motor response (a response of the motor system: arms, legs, trunk, etc.) occurred as a function of the particular area stimulated. This major discovery, of course, was impetus to much of what is now known about the brain. At last, in general form, the nature of the brain was known: it is electrochemical; it contains nerves; it is the major controller of complex behavior; it is divided up into sections, each of which is primarily responsible for specific behaviors.

basic structure of the brain If you look at Figure 3–7, you may notice an interesting characteristic of the brain: it has a major division into two parts, as if nature tried to provide an extra, as she did with eyes, ears, and so on.* When the brain is intact—that is, if you move the two halves in Figure 3–7 together—it appears to be one unit.† In the intact brain a depression, called the *fissure*, running along

---

*Of course, no one knows why we have two of anything.

†Figure 3–7 can be very helpful in obtaining a perspective on the brain. Notice that the part on the far right of the figure is identical to the view shown in Figure 3–5. The inner portion (middle of the figure) will be discussed as we progress.

the top from the back of the brain to the front, marks where the two halves are united. If you were to pull these two halves apart (as Fig. 3–7 shows), about midway down the middle of the brain you could see an area labeled *corpus callosum*. When the brain is together, this unit contains a number of nerve fibers that run from one half of the brain to the other, forming a communication network. The corpus callosum is also referred to as the transfer area because it transfers information received by one-half of the brain to the other half.

The division of the brain has been of considerable interest to experimenters, especially in terms of what is called *hemisphere dominance*. In the right-handed person, the *left hemisphere* dominates, which means that speech, deciphering of language, and fine finger movements (for the right hand) are controlled by the left half of the brain. For years it had been assumed that the opposite was always true for left-handers, but this is erroneous: the left hemisphere is dominant for speech and verbal activities in a number of left-handed people; for others it is not. Thus, the left hemisphere dominates for right-handed people, but the *right hemisphere* may or may not dominate for left-handed individuals.

In general, movements of the right side of the body are controlled by the left hemisphere, and vice versa, especially when we are dealing with fine motor control such as delicate maneuvering of the fingers, but again this need not always hold true. The corpus callosum under certain circumstances will act as an overload device and transfer information to the opposite hemisphere. For example, if a right-handed person is performing a physical task, he will be using his left hemisphere, but if we blindfold one of his eyes and deliberately overload the left hemisphere with all kinds of messages, the other hemisphere takes over the motor movements while the left one is working on the material coming in.

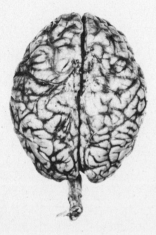

31   The two hemispheres of the brain, seen from above (*Gabriele Wunderlich*)

The old story that forcing a left-handed child to learn to write with his right hand causes *brain* confusion and results in insanity is misleading. Forcing a left-hander to try to write with his right hand is psychologically frustrating and like asking someone who is five-feet-ten-inches to play professional basketball. The brain doesn't explode electrically; the person is just not designed for that task. A change can be forced, but the psychological price is too high and the person's performance is never quite up to par [Geschwind, 1972; Brinkman and Kuypers, 1972; Dimond and Beaumont, 1972; Kinsbourne, 1972].

Basically, operation centers are located in many areas throughout the brain, and damage to one of these areas frequently results in its function being taken over by an area in the opposite hemisphere as the result of action by the corpus callosum. Should the right-handed adult receive minor damage to the left hemisphere, the lost abilities are often taken over by the right hemisphere, although the amount of restoration varies with the area damaged. Even in full restoration, which is rare, performance is somewhat primitive compared with what it was before the injury [Sperry, 1968]. In a few cases of injury and disease to the human infant, one half of the cortex has to be removed. When this has happened, the other half took over the functions and the brain developed into a fairly normal brain, if the patient was not too old. But with age, once a hemisphere becomes dominant, any major surgical undertaking results in only limited improvement.

Many studies of the corpus callosum have been performed on chimpanzees because they have essentially the same cortical arrangement as humans. The corpus callosum was severed in these animals, and one eye was left connected to one half of the brain, the other eye to the other half. A strange and intriguing situation developed: when the eyes were alternately blindfolded after this surgery, and the animal trained to do task A with one eye and task B with the other eye, the chimp learned two different tasks as if he had two brains: the eye that learned task A couldn't recognize task B, and vice versa. On the other hand, if the corpus callosum was left intact, the information learned in one hemisphere was transferred to the other, even if one eye was blindfolded.

In the few cases where surgery has been required on humans, cutting the fibers that connect one half of the brain with the other produced the same results; in addition, human beings were able to learn two different tasks simultaneously [Gazzaniga et al., 1965].

Even stranger in cases of hemisphere disconnection, some people apparently wind up with two consciousnesses; that is, they behave in some instances as if they have two different processes of thinking [Sperry, 1968].

A common phenomenon—a child's reversing letters of the alphabet when he is first learning to write—has raised a lot of speculation. One explanation which is fairly plausible is that hemisphere dominance has not yet been fully established and therefore some confusion arises when the child tries to reproduce the letter. Such confusion occurs because when information is transferred from one hemisphere to the other, it produces a "mirror image" in the opposite hemisphere. For example, the letter h in one hemisphere is recorded as ⅄ in the opposite hemisphere. Hemisphere disconnection in animals clearly indicates that this sort of reversal does take place, so by inference we can explain a baffling bit of human behavior [Corballis and Beale, 1971].

Of considerable interest to psychologists in reference to specific brain localization was an unusual case that occurred in 1848. A roadwork foreman by the name of Phineas P. Gage, while blasting away some rock to build a railroad right-of-way, was unfortunate enough to have the explosive go off prematurely. A pointed iron stick in the shape of a toothpick, about four feet long and about an inch in diameter was blown through his jaw, straight up just behind the nose, through what is called the frontal lobe (Figs. 3–5 and 3–7), and out the top of his head. Mr. Gage survived the incident—which is called by scientists the "American crowbar case"—but to Gage it was not just another incident in the annals of science. There was a marked change in his personality. He seemed to have lost control of much of what we call social decorum: he became like a child, having fits of temper when he didn't get his way; he made elaborate plans which he then canceled; he swore profusely at any time or place.

Mr. Gage's experience illustrates that to a large extent the frontal lobes are responsible for what we call social control and "personality." Even today, in some extreme cases, a surgeon will destroy portions of these frontal lobes in a mental patient who is uncontrollable; he drills through the forehead and then uses an instrument to permanently damage some cells and connections to the frontal lobe. The result, as with Gage, is usually an altered personality. The surgeon hopes that the person will become more manageable, and clear alterations in the personality do occur: the person usually becomes bland and colorless. The surgeon, however, always runs the risk of producing another Gage rather than a docile, harmless patient [Coleman, 1964].

We cannot assume that the personality is exclusively and centrally located in the frontal lobe. However, this portion of the brain is a major area of nerve fibers important to emotional response; hence, destruction of this area alters personality.

Throughout this book, discussion will focus on other portions of the brain as they become important to the topic at hand. For example, memory storage involves certain brain areas, thirst and hunger other portions, and the up-up-and-away growth of adolescence still others.

It would be unfortunate, however, to end this general discussion of the brain without mentioning the "ultimate" in experiments illustrative of this amazing unit. During an operation in the mid-twentieth century, a neurosurgeon discovered that by touching an electrode (an electrically active wire) to a specific portion of the cortex, the patient relived, as if in a movie-dream, a sequence of his life—for example, a birthday party, a trip taken, an incident in childhood.* As long as the electrode was held in place, the patient continued to live the incident, as if it had been stored on video-tape within the brain; when the electrode was removed, the "movie" stopped. If the neurosurgeon was able to hit the exact spot again with the electrode, the movie continued *from where it left off* [Penfield, 1959].

To avoid the possibility of fakery or vivid imagination by the patients describing their experiences, the physican capitalized on the fact that our brain cells do not feel pain or touch: he would ask the patient to report what he was seeing while the electrode was supposedly in place, although it was not. The patient was quick to reply, "nothing," until the

---

*The stimulated portion is the bottom area in Figure 3–5 of the section that looks like a finger and is marked "hearing."

electrode was again actually touching the brain—so the experience is quite genuine.

One might logically conclude that memory is located in this section of the cortex: this is true to some extent, but some patients lose some memory when injured in this spot; others do not. The safest bet is that memories are located in many spots throughout the cortex, including portions of the older brain (Fig. 3–11).

the spinal cord   Neither the human nor the animal brain is the *only* part of the body responsible for behavior. A frog, for example, has a cortex, and experimenters wondered how it would behave without one. They beheaded a frog in the laboratory, eliminating his brain. The question facing the scientists at this point was, is the frog dead? And in one sense it was not, for some of the internal organs continued to function for hours. For example, if the frog's foot was pinched, what was left of the frog would draw its leg up and away from the stimulation. One can be pretty certain that at this point the student watching the demonstration ran from the laboratory, terrified by what seemed an illustration of an eerie life after death. What had happened, in fact, was that the spinal cord had continued to function independently of the brain [Von Frisch, 1963].*

Now to the human. The human child who withdraws his hand from a fire is doing the same thing as the frog—performing a reflexive (or automatic) act. This simplest human reflex, shown in Figure 3–8, involves behavior such as the child withdrawing his hand. The first moments of withdrawal utilize the spinal cord, without calling on the higher brain centers. The impulse moves up the sensory nerve to the spinal cord and out the spinal cord via the motor nerve to the finger being withdrawn.

*Years ago in France scientists tried talking to freshly guillotined human heads to see if they could answer—they couldn't.

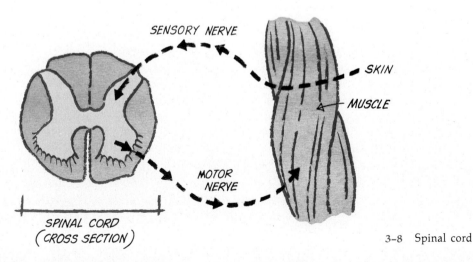

SENSORY NERVE

SKIN

MUSCLE

MOTOR NERVE

SPINAL CORD (CROSS SECTION)

3–8   Spinal cord

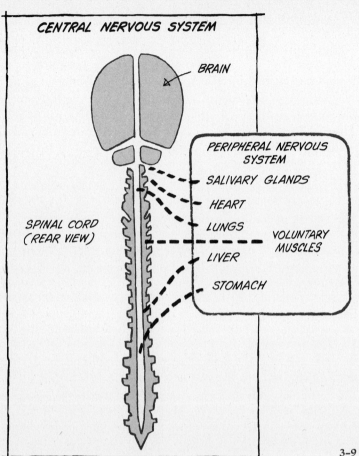

CENTRAL NERVOUS SYSTEM

BRAIN

PERIPHERAL NERVOUS SYSTEM

SALIVARY GLANDS

HEART

LUNGS

VOLUNTARY MUSCLES

LIVER

STOMACH

SPINAL CORD (REAR VIEW)

3-9   Central and peripheral nervous systems

The view of the spinal cord that you get in Figure 3–8 is called a cross section. If you had a friend cut you in half somewhere in the stomach area and then you took the bottom half of yourself and looked down on it, your spinal cord would look as it does in Figure 3–8. This drawing is an interior view of one of the bony knots you can feel if you reach behind and run your fingers along your back. Inside each of these knots (especially in the part that looks like a bat) is a complex array of neural connections which have nerves going to and from them to automatically control the stomach, kidneys, intestines, salivary glands, and so on, as well as motor functions. The back (or *dorsal*) side contains the incoming *sensory* fibers called *afferent sensory neurons*. The front (or *ventral*) side has the *motor fibers**** running from it, called *efferent motor neurons*.†

* For performing motor functions such as movement.
† It is not difficult to distinguish these two terms. *Affect* comes from the Latin for "acted upon" or "influenced" and *effect* to "work out" or "do." Therefore, the fire acts upon the afferent neuron and the effect or working out of the problem is accomplished by the efferent neuron.

74

The spinal cord and the brain together make up the *central nervous system*. Once the neurons have left the spinal cord or the brain, they become the *peripheral nervous system*, "peripheral" meaning on the outside of the central nervous system (Fig. 3–9).

Notice in Figure 3–10 that the simplest response, the *reflex arc*, would probably follow line *A* or line *B* and involve the receptor neurons, spinal cord, and motor neurons (motor refers to hands, arms, legs, etc.)

On the human level, any act more complex than the instantaneous hand withdrawal (reflex arc) would involve the higher brain centers and would most likely be referred to the cerebral cortex during the trip of the nerve impulse. At the cortex, orders would then be given for appropriate action. An example of this latter situation is diagrammed in parts *C* and *D* of Figure 3–10. A good example of this process would be the child who has burned his hand making a decision whether or not to tell his mother.

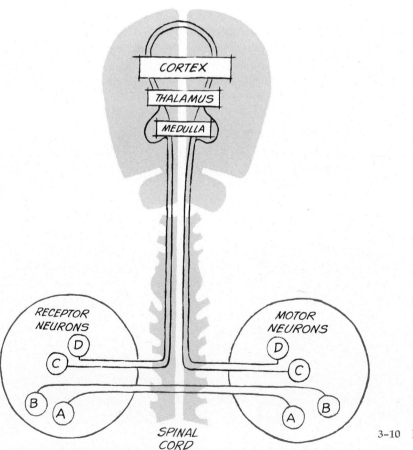

3–10   Reflex arc

32 Cross spider web
(*Jeroboam*)

The word *simple* has frequently been used in connection with reflexes. It is somewhat deceptive. A couple of authors have made the point that a reflexive act, even in lower animals, is no piddling thing. For example, the web shown in Figure 32 is from a cross spider. She builds this web with about 30 feet of silken thread for each 20-square-inch space. The web weighs about one–ten-thousandth of a gram, and the spider sits in the middle waiting for her prey, into whom she will inject a lethal poison. There is no evidence that a spider has reason, consciousness as we know it, or artistic creativity. Alive and in one piece, the spider has brain power rather like that of the poor decapitated frog. Significant for showing the amazing complexity of so-called simple reflexes is that the spider has only *one* set of muscles to perform a task that would require a considerable amount of learning on the part of a human. We should not sell short the simple reflexes when a reflexive system that has only one set of muscles far exceeds our capabilities in minute architectural design [Snodgrass, 1966; Henahan, 1966].

If you were given a choice of having either your cortex or the older brain surgically removed, which would you choose? Your initial reaction might be—take away the rest of me, but leave the cortex. However, if you look at Figure 3–11, you might change your mind. This drawing shows the major parts of the brain which we are thought to have inherited from animals, or at least which we have in common with most animals. These portions regulate the daily life processes of our body and together compose what is referred to as the *older brain*. This term arose because evolution

33 In 1506 Albertus Magnus, in his *Philosophia Naturalis*, interpreted the human brain as having three cavities (*Bettmann Archive*)

suggests that the cortex is a later development which "grew," so to speak, around and atop this older brain. You will notice, for example, if you look back at Figure 3–7, that part of the older brain, the medulla and cerebellum, is sticking out through the base of the cortex at the rear.

The brain is composed of a newer and older portion. If you study the older section and its various functions, you'll be able to pin down its various functions, in a general way (Fig. 3–11). The medulla is responsible for most automatic functions such as breathing and heart pumping. The thalamus is a central relay station for messages coming and going, and it

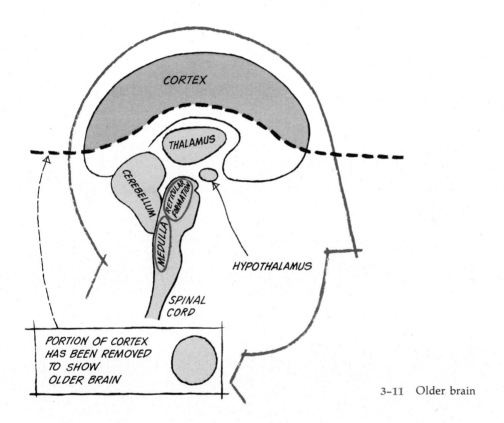

3–11   Older brain

also dispatches specific messages to appropriate centers of the brain. The cerebellum (Figs. 3–5, 3–7)*, which was shown earlier when we were discussing alcohol, is for balance and coordination. The hypothalamus regulates many of our needs—for example, our need for food and water. We cannot

*Labeled "motor coordination" in those figures.

survive without our cortex, but children born without one can live up to two months and can perform some physical movements such as moving their arms or sitting up [Delgado, 1969]. So, if it were not for the complex connections established between the older and newer brains, we could be a fairly complete organism without our cortex.

SUMMARY

Physiology and biology are integral parts of psychology because, from the lowest animals to the highest, there are physical properties that seem to drive organisms to the completion of certain acts. Charles Darwin's remarkable theory of evolution suggested that studying simple organisms was a method for understanding mechanisms found in man. The use of animals in the laboratory is somewhat inadequate because animals are not as complex as man, but it has the advantage that surgical operations, testing of new drugs, and the like can be performed on animals.

Many animals show obvious imprinting in which time is critical in the development of patterns of behavior. Studies with one of the highest nonhuman forms of life, the monkey, demonstrate what appears to be the imprinting of the need for physical stimulation. Other studies strongly suggest that humans have the same basic need.

Sequences of behavior in an orderly growth development, called maturation, are found in children. A certain amount of time is required, and during this time an automatic developmental process takes place—for example, learning to walk. Further indication of automatic behavior is the evidence of evolution occurring as the child moves from embryo to childhood in apparent sequence, at one point going through a stage in which swimming seems to be automatic.

The very high level of human intelligence comes from the cerebral cortex, a convoluted, folded mass of billions of neurons. The cortex is divided into areas that correspond to behaviors such as motor activities, sensation, vision, and hearing. Inside and underneath this cortex is the older brain, which contains the control centers for basic animal abilities—coordination, heartbeat, respiration, and the like. The brain is divided in half to form two hemispheres, one of which dominates the other. These halves are connected by the corpus callosum.

The operating units of the brain and nervous system are the neurons. They make up a nerve, which sends (motor) impulses and receives (sensory) impulses. The transmission of the nerve impulse is electrical in nature, but it is initiated by chemical activity in both the neuron itself and at the synapses, which are junctions to other neurons.

The spinal cord has two roles: (1) it is a relay station for incoming and outgoing impulses to and from the higher brain; (2) it is an independent operator which performs reflex actions. The brain and the spinal cord together make up the central nervous system. Nerves leave the spinal cord and connect with the heart, liver, intestines, motor control muscles, and so on. Once they leave the spinal cord they constitute what is called the peripheral nervous system.

CHAPTER FOUR
THE UNION OF PHYSIOLOGY AND PSYCHOLOGICAL THEORY

The chapter just completed should provide some evidence that a substantial link exists between the operation of parts of the body and what we often think of as the mind, or whatever term we choose to designate our nonphysical selves.

Caught up in the climate of trying to imitate such physical sciences as chemistry and physics, psychology was quick to detect the slightest evidence that man was subject to physical laws rather than to vague or philosophical mechanisms.

So, as we pick up the thread of development again, psychology begins to go overboard in its preoccupation with man as a machine. As you will notice below, discoveries with animals led to considerable experimentation and speculation about man's being nothing but a mechanism that could be manipulated, controlled, and repaired just like any other bit of physical material.

Elaborate psychological theories about man came to be based on experiments conducted with him as an organic machine—and here we have the meeting of physiology and psychological theory.

THE AGE OF PAVLOV AND WATSON

One of the best known and most biting of satirists, H. L. Mencken, wrote a book, *In Defense of Women,* which clearly is anything but a defense. He said the physique of a woman could be differentiated from that of a man because

. . . she looks like a dumbbell run over by an express train. Below the neck by the bow and below the waist astern there are two masses that simply refuse to fit into a balanced composition. Viewed from the side, she presents an exaggerated *S* bisected by an imperfect straight line, and so she inevitably suggests a drunken dollar mark. [Mencken, 1950].*

His comments are intriguing, because although males might laugh at his satire, few indeed are the men who would not turn their heads to view the bisected *S.* We decide physical beauty to some extent by reason, to some extent by societal influences, but most of all by constant association

*From H. L. Mencken, *In Defense of Women* (New York: Alfred A. Knopf, 1950), p. 31; reprinted by permission.

with what is labeled as beautiful through advertising, contests, and the comments of friends.

Our conception of a physically beautiful woman is the composite picture of Miss America:

Height: 5′ 7″
Weight: 127 lbs.
Bust: 35 inches
Waist: 24½ inches
Hips: 35 inches

On the other hand, among the Kafir and the Hottentot tribes, women cultivate, by binding, very long and pendant breasts, which become so large that "the usual way of giving suck, when the child is carried on the back, is by throwing the breast over the shoulder" [Frumkin, 1961]. Such is not a Miss America contest winner.

The most intriguing thing about this situation is that we have quite fixed ideas about such vague things as beauty, and considerable agreement exists within each culture about what beauty is. In other words, we have within each culture certain more or less rigid ideas about beauty that are constantly brought before us as ideals; the more they are brought before us, the more we seek them. And the more we seek them, the more they become entrenched within our lives.

Obviously, styles do change—but consider the difficulty any style innovator has with *older* people who are accustomed to years of repetitive association. They become used to having things a certain way. Traditional laws of etiquette, for example, are extremely resistant to change. When escorting a lady, a man had to walk on the outside because the streets were muddy and unpaved. The same procedure is followed today, even though one has to travel a long way to find an unpaved road. Furthermore, nowadays the man might be more chivalrous if he walked on the inside, in order to protect the lady from muggers.

Men are slowly changing and wearing perfume and high heels, buying false eyelashes,* and having their hair dyed. The alterations are usually handled surreptitiously, however, because they buck society's former conception of masculinity, and because older persons are used to the opposite: raw, unretouched men. It is doubtful, however, that our men will ever compete with the Boloki tribe. The men of that tribe, in order to show their masculinity and attractiveness, chisel the upper incisors† to V-shaped points.

The area of religion provides a striking example of how ingrained certain behaviors can become, and how we tend to rely on habit and tradi-

---

* Yes.
† Teeth.

tion. One author, discussing the attempts of the great philosophers to break away from traditional Christianity, points out the psychological anguish these men went through in making the break, even though they thought they were doing the correct thing. A notable number of them developed psychologically based illnesses from the strain: they suffered loss of appetite and pangs of guilt, and expressed the desire to have their terrible struggle over with [Gay, 1966]. All of us know at least one person who has had a certain religious faith all his life, has been thoroughly trained in that philosophy, and then has attempted to break away from it, suffering extreme pangs of guilt while doing so.

On a less dramatic level, since Bell Telephone has begun using male operators these men have been subjected to unbelievable abuse by callers—just because people are used to female operators.

Later in the book we will take up specific issues of social influence, but first notice here that both the brain and the behavioral system of the individual respond to the world—interpreting various facets of it as beautiful/nonbeautiful, desirable/nondesirable, or psychologically painful/nonpainful as a result of constant association and repetition of these factors from within the culture itself. These are, broadly speaking, examples of what psychologists call *conditioning*. Using this broad definition, a person becomes conditioned by a process of constant association.

Pavlov and classical conditioning

One of the most basic forms of conditioning was demonstrated in the early 1900s by a physiologist, Dr. Ivan Pavlov, a quite colorful man in his own right. He was the image of an absent-minded professor—his wife had to remind him to pick up his paychecks. He was a man of unusual temper when his work was interfered with—he once exploded at an assistant for being late to work even though the man had to walk through the streets during a Russian revolution in order to get there [Miller, 1962]. Pavlov captured the imagination of the whole world of psychology. He was involved in a series of experiments on the behavior of digestive glands,* trying to measure the effect of gastric juices and understand the mechanisms of

---

* Glands are parts of the body that trigger chemical changes in order to prepare the body for a certain task. For instance, salivary glands secrete saliva for the digestion of food.

34   An unsung hero of conditioning experiments poses with Pavlov (center) and his assistants (*Bettmann Archive*)

4–1 Pavlov's conditioning apparatus

digestion, work for which he received the Nobel Prize in medicine and physiology.

It really irritated Pavlov to be even indirectly associated with psychology; he was certain he was dealing only with physical mechanisms. In fact, any of his assistants who used a psychological term like *mind* while in the laboratory were docked some of their salary [Watson, 1968].

His experiments are actually quite simple, yet they had a profound impact on the whole history of psychology. He performed surgery on a dog so that the stomach and esophagus were separated from each other, an operation that meant two things: (1) food taken by mouth would never actually reach the stomach; (2) food could be put directly into the stomach without having to travel through the mouth and esophagus.

Pavlov was quick to note a strange occurrence: food put directly into the stomach did not cause a secretion of digestive juices sufficient for normal digestion. As if this was not odd enough, Pavlov then discovered that even when no food was placed in the mouth, stomach, or esophagus, digestive secretions could be elicited. He noticed that both the stomach and the salivary glands of the animal responded to just the sight of food. The strangest event of all, however, was the third one: the animal would salivate at the mere sight of the *experimenter* who previously had fed him, even if the experimenter did not have any food with him. Here was the issue of major importance to psychology. If an experimenter who had never fed the dog came into the room, the dog responded with a so-what attitude—but not so if the experimenter had previously given him meat; the sight of this man triggered the full digestive process (Fig. 4–1).

As we continue this discussion, we'll use diagrams to clarify our terminology, which is a little confusing without them. To start off, here is the basic situation of food in the mouth, eliciting salivation:

Food in mouth (*S*) ——————→ Salivates (*R*)

Notice that food is a stimulus (*S*) and that salivation is the response (*R*) to this stimulus.*

This is simple enough to understand. If someone puts a piece of steak in your mouth, you will salivate. First, Pavlov showed that the animal had associated the experimenter with the food:

Sight of experimenter ——→ Receives food ——→ Salivates

Seeing the experimenter and receiving the food become associated one with the other. The combined association led to this situation:

Sight of experimenter (*S*) ——————→ Salivates (*R*)

Since it was obvious to Pavlov that animals will only salivate to the experimenter under these special conditions, Pavlov referred to the response as a ***conditional response***—that is, it could be elicited only if certain conditions were present. Using this system, we can change the diagram slightly for greater accuracy, replacing the *R* with *CR* ("conditional response"):

Sight of experimenter (*S*) ——————→ Salivates (*CR*)

Returning to the original situation, in which putting food into the dog's mouth elicited salivation, Pavlov noticed that *no* special conditions were necessary for salivation to occur; just putting the food in the dog's mouth was sufficient for copious glandular secretions. Therefore, Pavlov called the meat an ***unconditional stimulus*** (*UCS*), and the salivation in this situation an ***unconditional response*** (*UCR*). In other words, it was a natural response:

Food in mouth (*UCS*) ——————→ Salivates (*UCR*)

Since an experimenter, no matter how tasty a morsel, will not *naturally* elicit salivation, special conditions are necessary for him to do so—namely, the association with food. Seeing the experimenter, then, becomes a *CS* or conditional stimulus to salivation. This conditional stimulus elicits salivation, but since the salivation is not "natural"—no meat is present—it must have a *conditional* response. Therefore, we have a *CS* eliciting a *CR*:

Food in mouth (*UCS*) ——————→ Salivates (*UCR*)
Sight of experimenter (*CS*) ——————→ Salivates (*CR*)

---

*The term *stimulus* comes from the Latin meaning "to goad" or "to push." In psychology *anything*, physical or psychological, which goads the organism into a reaction of any type is called a stimulus.

Notice that seeing the experimenter is now properly labeled as a conditional stimulus (*CS*) because the sight does not naturally elicit the salivation response. A few diagrams back, we labeled the sight stimulus (*S*) merely to help get the discussion started. Notice also that salivation can be either a *UCR* or *CR* depending on how it was elicited.

About now you may be wondering what this has to do with anything. Actually, the results are both profound and simple in their implications, but the fact that these certain specific terms exist sometimes confuses the issue. They merely represent a logical sequence. Simply put, by taking a nonnatural stimulus (experimenter) and pairing it with a natural stimulus (meat), it is possible to get the nonnatural stimulus (experimenter) to bring about a reaction similar to the one elicited by a natural stimulus (meat). For instance, think of a large, juicy dill pickle. Are you salivating copiously? What has happened? You are salivating just at a word or thought; there is no pickle present. You have associated the word *pickle* (*CS*) with the natural stimulus (*UCS*), pickle. Here's a diagram for your reaction:

Eats pickle (*UCS*) ───────────→ Salivates (*UCR*)

Hears word *pickle*

Hears word *pickle* (*CS*) ───────────→ Salivates (*CR*)

Returning to the comments at the opening section of this chapter, we might consider how it is possible to view male behavior toward women in exactly the same fashion:

Sex need (*UCS*)* ───────────→ Sexual arousal (*UCR*)

Repetitive advertisements about the ideal body shape

Specific types of
    body lines (*CS*) ───────────→ Sexual arousal (*CR*)

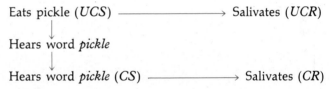 The type of learning Pavlov discovered even has international implications today, something he never could have foreseen. Everyone, for instance, is familiar with the overpopulation problem and the starvation of thousands of people that results. One solution to the crisis is to feed people protein powder made from ground-up fish; at present enough fish exist to feed a billion people for a year. However, most attempts at inducing people to eat the fish powder have failed. The conditioning of individuals within various cultures has been such that any new or unusual food is suspect, and thousands, without exaggeration, starve to death because they can't break away from their conditioning and eat strange foods [Henahan, 1966].

* The stimulus here is internal.

We have a situation which is basically the same as Pavlov's laboratory experiments.

At the natural level, a basic mechanism of unconditional behavior exists in which bad food elicits a natural response of sickness:

Eating bad food (*UCS*) ⟶ Vomiting (*UCR*)

(Foods to which we are unaccustomed are a matter of concern because they lack familiarity and may be sickening, e.g., eating ants.)

Being human, however, we operate with symbols and words:

Eating bad food (*UCS*) ⟶ Vomiting (*UCR*)

Unfamiliar food (*CS*) ⟶ Avoidance (*CR*)
(Symbolized: strange foods   (Symbolized:
  are dangerous)   cause sickness)

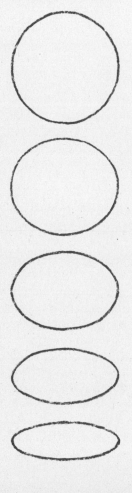

4-2 Pavlov's circle becoming an ellipse

Now that you have survived this far, I feel ready to point out that if you read any scientific article that deals with conditioning, you will not find the term *conditional*. Lest you throw your hands up in despair, let me quickly add that you will find terminology that comes close. An error in translation occurred when the word conditional in Russian was put into English, and it came out *conditioned* [Rosensweig, 1962]. Therefore, you will find that psychological literature uses the terms *conditioned stimulus* and *conditioned response*. These terms are identical to the ones we have used, but psychology has reconciled itself to living with the mistranslation.

A recapitulation might be worthwhile, and one of Pavlov's actual experiments wraps it up neatly. Pavlov had discovered that a neutral stimulus (for example, the experimenter) can become associated with a "natural" or unconditioned stimulus (for example, meat), with the result that soon the previously neutral stimulus (the experimenter) will elicit the same type of response as the natural stimulus (salivation). At this time the formerly neutral experimenter has become a conditioned stimulus and causes salivation, which has become a conditioned response. In other words, dogs do not normally salivate at the sight of an experimenter; certain conditions must be met for the salivation to occur.

One of Pavlov's experiments involved sounding a bell and then shocking the dog's paw, sounding a bell and shocking the dog's paw, etc. At *first* the dog withdrew his paw in an *unconditioned* or natural response, but after a few times of this pairing, the sound of the bell without the shock (conditioned stimulus) would induce the dog to lift his paw (conditioned response). This experiment showed that a primitive, automatic learning was possible in the animal when a basic physical behavior, reaction to pain, was paired with something neutral.

Another experiment was possible. In this case, once the dog was conditioned to lift his paw to the bell alone, the bell was paired with another stimulus (a light—the second unconditioned stimulus), and no shock was given. The dog would then lift his paw to the light even though this stimulus was well removed from the natural stimulus situation of the shock. That is about as far as such experiments can be carried without returning once more to the shock response, since shock is the basic drive.

These studies had far-reaching effects on psychology. Most of all, they suggested the possibility that we are a form of robot, responding more or less automatically to stimuli. One flaw in this thinking, though, is the fact that the dog and the human being cannot get far beyond the second conditioned stimulus (for example, adding other sounds and trying to connect them to the light) without the connection to the shock becoming too weak. Pavlovian conditioning by itself will not work to explain all human behavior. The type of conditioning he did is probably at the base of a large number of our behaviors, but some examples of human responses to beauty and food, while connected to some extent with Pavlovian conditioning, bear more elaborate explanation. We will go into other theories of learning that try to provide this elaboration.

In the meantime, it is safe to say that we are a pretty conditionable lot, and much of our behavior is the result of association and repetition of association.

conditioning and neurosis   Psychology perked up at Pavlov's work for another reason: he felt his experiments might offer an explanation for the milder form of mental illness called *neurosis*. As you will discover later, neurosis is not a simple problem. For the present, however, we might just define it as physical and mental upset resulting from an inability to resolve personal problems. Using this oversimplified definition, we can easily find a typical human situation for an example. Suppose a young woman hates her job, but her skills are not in enough demand that she can find another job. She has two options available to her, both bad: she can stay at a job she hates, or she can become unemployed. The stress that results from this situation is overwhelming.

Pavlov set up a laboratory experiment that resembled this difficult problem. He felt that conditioning created a similar "neurosis" in animals. Dogs were conditioned to salivate at the sight of a circle and not to salivate to an ellipse (Fig. 4–2; the circle became a *CS*). As the experiment progressed, Pavlov slowly made the ellipse more and more closely resemble a circle. Eventually the animals were unable to tell the difference between the circle and what had been the ellipse. Since they were given no reward for salivating to the ellipse they became more and more confused as to what their response should be. At this point the animals began to display erratic behavior from overactive physiological responses and soon were completely unable to function in the experimental situation, collapsing psychologically.

Pavlov thought of this animal neurosis in terms of conditioning; that is, it was a semimechanical occurrence without deep emotional involvement.

More recent studies tend to negate some of Pavlov's findings, at least in the sense that the mechanisms of neurotic conditioning are far more complicated than simple mechanical connections. In one study, for instance, sheep and goats were made neurotic by the use of shock. Even when the shock was discontinued, however, some of these animals continued to become more and more upset both physically and psychologically, almost as if they were falling apart because the shocking had been discontinued. Obviously such behavior requires a more elaborate explanation than a mechanical one.* No cure could be found for these animals—rest, change of scenery, and so on were all tried, but nothing short of surgery worked.

Even more interesting, perhaps, is the work with twin goats and sheep. The pairs were divided, and one twin received shock in a room with his mother; the other twin was left by himself when receiving the shock. Animal neurosis appeared only in the twin that was left alone [Liddell, 1954].

We should mention that from a historical perspective, Pavlov's work is essentially original and is today one of the oldest, most traditional systems. Hence, the system he used is referred to as *classical conditioning* to differentiate it from those of more modern vintage.

We now know that Pavlov developed a brilliant yet somewhat limited version of how we learn. At the time, his impact was profound, especially on the men who followed him.

John B. Watson and emotional conditioning

To many students psychology has the tone of an antireligious, antihumanistic science that has gutted man of "all that's in him." Although this view is largely erroneous, historically it has some justification. A man who independently adapted some of Pavlov's ideas, John B. Watson, was largely responsible for a period in the history of psychology in which man was indeed considered pure animal. He objected strongly to the belief, which many psychologists held, that man is a special creature with special attributes superior to those of animals, such as consciousness or soul. He maintained there is no way one could measure such things in a laboratory.

Watson was a sulky, argumentative student who felt most belligerent about philosophy, a subject he just couldn't understand. But in the early 1900s he did manage to get his Ph.D. and began experimental studies [Reisman, 1966]. One could make the inference that it was his distaste of philosophy which led him to proclaim loudly, clearly, and eloquently that man's behavior is nothing more nor less than a series of stimuli associated with a series of responses, like the performances of Pavlov's dog. Consciousness, while it might exist, is strictly the result of physiological components in operation. Thus, our feelings of love or hope are the results of some overactive muscle or gland system in the body. Pavlov had captured the imagination of psychologists interested in man as a machine subject to conditioning. Watson extended Pavlov's principles to include the idea that man in his entirety is nothing but automatic reflexes and movements triggered by stimuli and responses. Thus, as we will discuss shortly, man's

---

* Although any guess at the explanation would be presumptuous at the present state of the science.

"thinking" is, Watson argued, merely the response he has to the movement of his larynx and tongue. Watson's theory was called *behaviorism*, which, simply put, refers to the idea that our core consists only of our actions (behaviors). What we call by the exotic name of thinking is the movement (behavior) of vocal cords. Pavlov started off with the idea that at least part of man's behavior is automatic—Watson carried this idea all the way to include all of man's behavior.

Watson's theories were provocative; but more important, they were difficult to dismiss from a scientific viewpoint. For one thing, as we have mentioned, in the early 1900s the concept of "instinct" was getting out of control and Watson was quick to attack its vulnerability. Instead of instincts, he said, man inherits only a tendency to respond to certain objects—e.g., a mother figure—and conditioning takes over from there to form the complex creature we know so well.

35 a–c   An example of stimulus generalization, as Dr. Watson observed it. The baby's fear of a white rat is generalized to other furry objects (*Suzanne Szasz; Gabriele Wunderlich*)

A hospital was willing to allow Dr. Watson to experiment with babies, and from these experiments he concluded that we have three basic (physical) emotions to which can be conditioned any number of behaviors*: love, which comes from caresses given to children (the need for physical stimulation); rage, which children demonstrate, understandably, when they are physically restrained; and fear, which comes from the feeling of falling and from loud noises. Watson labeled these emotions as he did because *he thought* these were appropriate responses. Actually, later experiments have shown that emotions in a very young child are not that easy to label. It's difficult to tell one feeling from another if you see a child on film and do not know what emotion he should be experiencing in our adult terms [Sherman, 1927].

The experiment with a child's fear of loud noises led to one of the most famous cases in psychology. A child, Albert B., eleven months old, enjoyed furry animals, as most children do. A white rat was put into the room with Albert and he reached for it, showing no fear. Just as his hand grasped the rat, the experimenter struck a steel bar with a hammer, creating an awesome noise. This procedure was repeated until Albert soon had developed a genuine aversion to white rats. The experiment continued and it was discovered that Albert had developed a fear of *many* furry things he had not seen before—a fur coat, wool, cotton, even a Santa Claus mask, all objects having some similarity to the original feared object. The spread of response (e.g., fear) from a particular object (white rat) to similar objects (furry things) is called *stimulus generalization*, a term which suggests that the learner has moved from response to a specific object, to the same response to many objects. He has moved from the specific to the general. Notice what has happened here. The normally so-called complex motive of fear has been used as the unconditioned stimulus in a very mechanistic way, and the child has associated an avoidance response with many similar

*This view is no longer believed fully accurate.

things. What is normally thought of as complex higher learning has been reduced to simple conditioning principles.

Watson, then, even though he used the terms *love, rage,* and *fear,* thought of these behaviors as resulting from nothing more nor less than responding muscles and glands. His direct parallel between conditioning and what had been thought of as higher human processes was very unpopular among his colleagues, because no other theorist had expressed such an outspoken view on the matter. Also, social mores (standards of conduct) were not the same in the 1920s as they are today, and the excuse to quiet him that many had been waiting for was soon to come: Watson divorced his wife and very quickly thereafter married his laboratory partner. As a result of this scandal, he was dismissed from his position as professor at Johns Hopkins University and found other academic positions closed to him as well. So he moved into the field of advertising, where he was successful and had a continued outlet for his writings, especially those on child rearing. He was very influential with the public, who were always in search of some way to handle their little monsters [Reisman, 1966; Watson, 1968].

Watson's book on child rearing stressed conditioning of the emotions and behavior of the child. Some of his comments seem extreme by today's standards, but his views were popular, just as the child-rearing book of Dr. Benjamin Spock has been.* Watson suggested procedures that are remarkably similar to those currently in vogue for deconditioning an animal from constantly seeking your affection:

Treat [children] as though they were young adults. Let your behavior always be objective and kindly firm. *Never hug and kiss them, never let them sit on your lap.* If you must, kiss them once on the forehead when they say good-night. Shake hands with them in the morning. [Watson, 1928; italics added.]†

Scientists had some difficulty refuting Watson's theories. For one reason, some of them seemed to be borne out by experimentation. Watson startled the scientific world not so much by *claiming* that thinking is really the movement of our larynx muscles (voice box) and tongue, but by using primitive measuring devices to actually demonstrate that with many people who are deep in thought, subtle muscular movement is going on. His theory was that these movements are conditioned to the needs of the children when they learn to speak—that is, the need to express love, rage, or fear is basic; so-called thought is nothing more than a repetition of movements conditioned to seeking expression of these needs.

Since the advent of modern measuring techniques, it has become clear that we think with our whole body, not just with the larynx or even the brain. The body tenses up, for example, if we do nothing more than

* The comparison is somewhat limited: Dr. Spock's book is topped on the all-time best-seller list only by the Bible.
† From J. B. Watson, *Psychological Care of Infant and Child* (New York: Norton, 1928), p. 87; reprinted by permission.

think of lifting our arm. Recordings of the brain show appropriate electrical activity as if the arm were moving. Maximum tension develops in whatever area we normally use to perform the act we are thinking about. In addition, deep thought causes active movement of the muscles around the eye [Chaplin and Krawiec, 1968].

So Watson's work did not die. It was just accurate enough to have infiltrated, in greatly modified form, behavior and learning theory all the way to the present. You will detect Watson's handiwork in many discussions later in this book: For example, the burgeoning interest at present in body control, yoga, and states of meditation continues the argument of mind over matter or vice versa. Probably one of the most beneficial things we can learn to do in our present overwhelmingly rushed lives is to learn to sit down and meditate, just letting the mind wander freely. The result of this behavior is a form of superrest for the body. Meditation reduces breathing rate, blood pressure, and oxygen consumption equal to or greater than that found in the sleeping state [Wallace and Benson, 1972].

Watson's biggest theoretical flaw, ironically, is more or less philosophical: he assumed that muscle and gland behaviors cause thought, but there is no way to discount the opposite, that thinking results in muscle and gland behaviors, or the most popular view today, that thinking and behavioral response are operating one alongside the other.

Classical conditioning has continued, building on Watson's work, and has become classical in the true sense of the word. Although classical conditioning is a theory standing alone, it is significant in current psychology primarily as background material for more elaborate theories of learning. Nonetheless, some of our learning seems to come only from the classical arrangement that occurs when a basic drive, such as fear, hunger, or thirst, is paired with some other object.

Classical conditioning has not dropped by the wayside in the Soviet Union, however, where some rather startling results have been obtained with this technique. Soviet scientists have found that mechanisms earlier thought to be automatically controlled by the nervous system—breathing rate, constriction or expansion of the blood vessels, movements of the stomach, heart rate—can be controlled by laboratory manipulation. Using heat and pressure to change a person's internal environment can condition him to alter many of the behaviors formerly thought to be automatic. Soviet scientists have even been able to condition responses of the bladder, cardiovascular system, gastrointestinal system,* and the like to certain words [Razran, 1961]. Extensions of these studies will be covered more extensively in Chapter 10.

PHYSIOLOGY AND BEHAVIOR: HUNGER AND THIRST

One of the most pervasive trends in psychology, then, has been a proliferation of studies that involve the interaction of the body and the psyche. The

*Bladder, heart, and digestive systems respectively.

stress on man as a mechanism has continued in the tradition of Pavlov and Watson; but to the frustration of many psychologists, a gap always remains between physiological mechanisms and the individual person. Although we can find many physical mechanisms to account for behaviors, we have not found it possible to predict with great accuracy how the individual person will respond in a given situation.

Despite this problem, in this section our discussion focuses on attempts by scientists of all types to explain why man behaves as he does. The following discussion, for instance, is on hunger and thirst. If we could completely understand even these two phenomena, we would be well on our way to understanding why man acts as he does. Hunger and thirst are powerful motivators in human activity and physical mechanisms that strongly color our psychological behavior.

psychological mechanisms

He laid his mittens on his knees, unbuttoned his coat, untied the tapes of his face cloth, stiff with cold, folded it several times over, and put it away in his pants pocket. Then he reached for the hunk of bread, wrapped in a piece of clean cloth, and holding the cloth at chest level so that not a crumb should fall to the ground, began to nibble and chew at the bread. The bread, which he had carried under two garments, had been warmed by this body. [Solzhenitsyn, 1963]*

George and I couldn't afford to kill and eat the hens; we didn't want a feast. . . . So I traded the hen for a sweet potato a day for six weeks for George. They were better gardeners than we, had used human excrement from the first to fertilize with, at a time when we still shuddered at it; now they were harvesting sweet potatoes. . . . [On special days] George was given *two* potatoes! How he sang to himself those days, as he ate! [Keith, 1947]†

Two prisoners are speaking here, the first a man held for political reasons in a Soviet work camp in Siberia, the second a woman confined to a Japanese prison camp during World War II. Their comments say a great deal about the psychological nature of food—there is a religiousness about it, if you will, a respect and awe that seems to supersede just about everything else.

Psychologists have studied the effects of semistarvation in order to determine the changes that take place in the individual both physiologically and psychologically. The most famous of these experiments was conducted at the University of Minnesota during World War II. A group of conscientious objectors were used for the study. After a period of normal, well-balanced meals, the men were put on a twenty-four-week diet of semistarvation. The most notable physiological change was extreme weakness and inability to perform day-to-day tasks without difficulty, while psychologically the men's personalities altered drastically to include common traits

*From A. Solzhenitsyn, *One Day in the Life of Ivan Denisovich,* trans. R. Parker (New York: E. P. Dutton & Co., Inc., 1963); reprinted by permission.
†From A. N. Keith, *Three Came Home* (Boston: Little, Brown, 1947); reprinted by permission.

of nervousness, irritability, and lack of interest in other persons [Keys et al., 1950]. The average-sized healthy adult can last about seventy to eighty days without food; some die earlier, so it isn't a very enjoyable experiment to try. The brain is a very heavy user of glucose (sugar); in fact, at rest it consumes two-thirds of the blood's supply. With starvation this supply has to be reduced, which probably accounts for the symptoms mentioned above. When very young children are deprived of food their growth stops; if this condition lasts for a while, later feeding will not reverse the process and the child will never attain normal height. Worse, during the child's first year starvation results in permanent damage to the central nervous system, including a deficit in the number of brain cells [Young and Scrimshaw, 1971].

Other studies of starvation show that individuals in this conditiion tend to be completely dominated by a preoccupation with food. Their perception of the world alters to include food even where there is none. For example, if words that resemble *food* (e.g., *brood*) are very rapidly flashed on a screen, these people see the word *food.* Their descriptions of what they see in ink blots contain long lists of such items as knives, forks, spoons, and hunks of meat. To top it all off, in one starvation study, the men had pin-up pictures of food on the wall in place of traditional voluptuous creatures [Guetzkow and Bowman, 1946].

Food studies with animals produce similar effects. For example, rats who have been put on a semistarvation diet never recover from it; even when normal feeding is resumed they engage in *hoarding behavior*—that is, they continuously pile up food in the cage, far more than they will ever be able to eat. By inference, many psychologists feel that persons who have been through wars, famines, and depressions never fully recover: this explanation is often given for many mothers who sit their thirty-year-old "children" down at the table and won't let them up until they have completed the equivalent of two or three meals.

It is possible to say that when food is not available, the person focuses most of his energy and attention on it, but a close reading of the two books from which passages are quoted above shows that food did not become the be-all and end-all for the authors. Both writers who lived through the experience make clear that except for a minority, prisoners voluntarily share food with others who are dying or seriously ill.

36   In the Great Depression of the 1930s Okies in the Oklahoma dust bowl banded together in communities to obtain food and shelter. Some who lived through the Depression have never gotten over the hoarding habit, and put all their resources into a full refrigerator or a full bank account (*Library of Congress*)

37   Whereas the Okies organized in order to overcome deprivation, the passengers from the shipwrecked *Medusa* practiced cannibalism (*Louvre*)

Human complexity does not end there, however. It is appropriate at this point to just touch on a factor requiring considerable elaboration in Chapter 20—namely, the influence of group organization and structure on basic behavior, especially its disintegration. In the 1840s the Donner party, a group migrating westward in the United States, attempted to travel over California's Sierra Nevada in heavy snow after having crossed the formidable Nevada desert. Out of food, leaderless, and facing what seemed certain death, the members of the party engaged in cannibalism, eating the bodies of those who had died. The event is documented beyond question. Why it happened is a matter for speculation. One author feels that cannibalism was not uncommon in the jungle of America's early West. He quotes Kit Carson as having said that "in starving times no man should walk ahead of me" [DeVoto, 1943]. And he suggests that the Donner party turned into animals not only through bickering and fighting among themselves but also because the group may not have been the kindest to begin with, many of them previously having killed Indians "for fun." Another author points out that no evidence suggests that anyone was killed for the express purpose of eating him, and that were it not for the dead bodies, the children who did survive would not have made it through the ordeal [Hawgood, 1967]. The latter viewpoint is supported by the fact that only by cannibalism was it possible for 16 survivors of a mountain plane crash in 1972 to stay alive through more than 70 nights of freezing weather.

Nonetheless, it is always advantageous to take seriously groups deprived of basic animal necessities, a painful lesson being learned from the riots of the last decade.

social aspects   About a hundred years ago few people in the United States would eat tomatoes because they were thought to be poisonous. The Europeans fed corn to animals, but the Africans ate corn off the cob. It is obvious that food tastes are the product of both availability *and* the cultural habits of the society within which one lives. Some groups eat fried ants, but when they are served by an American party-giver, many people get sick—*if* they know what they have eaten [Kluckhohn, 1949].

We eat three meals a day, and yet we don't have to. No baby yet has come into the world demanding food only at 8 A.M., 12 noon, and 6 P.M. Furthermore, our drinking habits are dictated by social customs, even by as indirect a factor as the price of an item. In an experiment that illustrates the point, bottles of beer taken from the same batch were marked with different prices and labeled with letters suggesting three different brands, but the brand was not identified. Over a period of time the subjects in the experiment drank the beers and then were asked to decide which of the three they preferred by describing the beer with such terms as *rich-flavored, smooth, light, flat, biting, acid,* and the like. Even though all the beer was identical, the higher the price on it the better people liked it. This study is only one of many that demonstrates the premium our culture puts on price as an influential factor in our perception of what is tasty and what is not. Further, it illustrates that taste is not as simple as it would seem at first [McConnell, 1968].

Social pressure to drink is responsible for roughly $7 billion spent each year in this country on liquor, yet anyone who drinks can verify that the first few times they took one it was not a very pleasant experience; the taste was foreign and, to many, nauseating. The body adapts, nonetheless, and as the money spent for liquor attests, we soon come to actually desire specific drinks. Certain social stereotypes have become associated with various types of alcohol; the upper-class, high-strung executive is usually characterized as a martini drinker, and for years the beer drinker was pictured as a person who sits in his undershirt in front of the television set drinking quart upon quart and belching. Beer manufacturers spent millions of dollars to remove this image—successfully—at one point running a series of advertisements featuring what looked like a family gathering for Thanksgiving and emphasizing that beer is a family drink. The important thing is that drinking and eating have strong social tie-ins that color people's tastes and responses to various types and brands.

The mere fact that hunger is such a basic need lends impact to the dramatic activities of individuals such as Dick Gregory who have gone on hunger strikes for the improvement of unpleasant social conditions. People are shocked out of complacency (for a while, at least) when they discover that someone is capable of putting social need above physiological needs.

physiological mechanisms   The area of physiological hunger and thirst does not contain the amount of factual data one might desire because too many social and personality factors interfere. The lack of information has not resulted from an absence of enthusiasm on the part of experimenters. In the middle 1800s, for instance, a man was unfortunate enough to have part of his stomach left exposed after an accident, and he became a living guinea pig for experimenters. They noted changes in the exposed stomach resulting from emotion, eating, direct stomach feeding, and the like. The man eventually had had enough and fled to Canada, where he died. Not content, the experimenters wanted his stomach for the army medical museum. The physician trying to get the body for the museum received a classic telegram from the family: DON'T COME FOR AUTOPSY. WILL BE KILLED [Rosenzweig, 1962]. The family kept the body a long time so that it would decompose and no one would be able to perform the autopsy and get the stomach. Because of the stench, the body was kept outside the church during the funeral.

Nonetheless, from examinations of this man and from other experiments performed through the years, many things about the stomach are known. For example, the emotion of dejection reduces the amount of acid in the stomach and cuts down on the flow of saliva, both of which are necessary for adequate digestion. Anger, on the other hand, produces the opposite results: the stomach's mucous membranes become red and engorged with blood,* acid production more than doubles,† and the stomach begins vigorous contractions [R. F. Mason, 1961]. The moral is: Don't eat in the middle of a violent argument. Aside from the possibility of choking, you may get nauseated from the increased acid.

At first thought, then, hunger and thirst seem an obvious and perfectly logical state of affairs: My mouth is dry—I drink. I'm hungry, my stomach growls, I feel movement down there—I eat. Such is the common-sense approach and the place at which science began its study of the hunger and thirst mechanisms.

hunger One series of studies in the early 1900s involved subjects swallowing a balloon attached to an electrical recording device. When the balloon was inflated, stomach contractions were recorded in hungry subjects. The answer seemed to be that the stomach contracts when it is hungry and sends signals to a hunger center of the brain [Cannon, 1912]. Later experiments, however, found that the balloon itself was causing the contractions. That this was the case did not completely contradict the fact that the stomach, when empty, often does contract, and does have a subsequent effect on the sensation of hunger, but stomach contractions had to be discarded as being the only instigator of hunger feelings.

Further evidence that contractions alone were not responsible came when, for medical reasons, a man's stomach had to be completely removed. As people who have lost a leg report an itch "down there," patients without stomachs reported hunger pangs. Experimental studies with rats confirmed that the stomach by itself is not responsible for hunger feelings. Rats whose stomachs had been removed continued to eat in more or less normal fashion [Tsang, 1938].

Two other hypotheses for hunger feelings therefore came to the foreground: some center in the brain receives and sends out hunger signals; or the amount of sugar in the blood, ***blood-sugar level***, signals when it is getting low.

Experimenters, therefore, started examination of the hypothalamus (Fig. 4–3), which was already known to be a control center for many appetites of the body.

At least two sections of the hypothalamus were found to relate to the present discussion: a center that excites (instigates) certain behaviors and a center that inhibits (represses) certain responses. If the excitor center in animals was stimulated electrically, overeating occurred [Margules and Olds, 1962]. And when the inhibitory center was surgically removed, overeating occurred. These studies strongly suggest that messages of hunger or fullness are relayed to the appropriate portion of the hypothalamus, which in turn signals the organism to eat more or stop eating.

A low blood-sugar level is known to cause hunger, dizziness, fatigue,

4–3   Hypothalamus

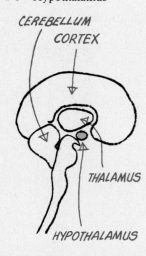

CEREBELLUM
CORTEX
THALAMUS
HYPOTHALAMUS

---

* Notice the redness in the face of someone who is angry.
† Thought to cause some ulcers of the stomach.

and irritability. These conditions become important in occupations where a person must be alert. Astronauts' wives, for example, take a course in meal preparation for their husbands in which high-protein foods are emphasized, since protein is converted more slowly and constantly into sugar (as opposed to rapid increase of blood sugar from eating a candy bar, *and* rapid depletion). This slow, even process will keep the blood-sugar level higher for a longer period of time. Hence, a low blood-sugar level and its resultant physiological effects, as well as stomach contractions, probably signal the hypothalamus that hunger is approaching [Bash, 1939].

Support for the blood-sugar hypothesis is found in studies in which hungry animals were transfused with the blood from satiated animals, with the result that stomach contractions ceased; thus we can assume that stomach contractions are at least partially related to hunger [Murray, 1964].

But what about the phenomenon we all experience of having an immediate decrease in desire for food after eating—a decrease that occurs before food has even had a chance to get to the stomach? We could just pass if off as the result of psychological factors—that is, the knowledge that we have eaten. While this awareness is obviously part of the explanation, there may be more to it. One theorist suggests we may have two sets of nerve fibers in the brain, one that signals hunger satisfaction for a short period of time and then dies out quickly, the other that records the many hunger stimuli and their satisfaction over a longer period of time so that the body is certain it is getting an adequate amount of food in the stomach and proper blood content [Deutsch and Deutsch, 1966]. We can speculate that the former type of fiber may be the one that signals immediate gratification of food desires even before the food reaches the stomach.*

One fact demonstrated clearly is that hunger can be reduced most effectively by placing food both in the mouth *and* in the stomach. Pavlov discovered this, and so have experimenters working with humans. Hunger, however, is reduced more rapidly by *mouth only* than by stomach only, probably the result of conditioning, but the two combined provide the most effective method of creating a feeling of satiation.

Thus, we do have some information on the basic mechanisms of hunger. All evidence points to natural, basic cravings, well regulated by the entire organism. Dogs, even mentally disturbed ones, rarely go around eating bushes or tree leaves. In fact, it is very unusual for undomesticated animals to suffer vitamin deficiencies; they seem to know automatically what to eat. Even captive animals such as cows and chickens, when given a choice of foods, pick the correct ones to balance their diets. For example, laboratory rats who lack vitamin B will choose foods containing this vitamin with a much greater frequency than other foods, although they do make errors of choice, as captive animals,† more than would be desired [Richter, 1937].

*In the same vein, notice later in Chapter 9, on learning, that we seem to have short-term and long-term memory systems.

†That is, not free in nature.

Human infants 48 to 90 hours old can tell the difference in taste between a dextrose (sugar) formula and plain milk, showing a decided preference for sucking milk [Dubignon and Campbell, 1969]. This type of study helps support the belief that we have a well-organized set of needs that has probably been distorted by our culture. In another study, a number of children less than four years old were given freedom to choose from a wide variety of foods placed before them at each meal. For a while the results looked disastrous; the children continued to choose one particular food over and over again. But then all of a sudden they switched to another food, so that by the end of the experiment they had achieved a balanced diet [Davis, 1928]. Humans, too, seem to have the ability to choose foods our systems require. For example, don't you every now and then crave a tomato or a carrot or a stalk of celery?

This experiment is dangerous to perform on your own offspring, because in our culture children are given all the spinach they want and little ice cream. Hence, at a young age we seem to develop a psychological craving for sweets that tends to overshadow our basic needs. One experiment the author has always wanted to try, but has never had the guts to, is to restrict the spinach and tell the child if he eats all his ice cream he can have a little spinach for dessert. Would the craving then reverse itself?

thirst   As we covered the material on hunger, we have also been covering most of the material on thirst, except that now we are dealing with dryness in the mouth and throat rather than stomach contractions in accounting for the need for a drink. Again the hypothalamus is the regulating unit. It is debatable whether the hypothalamus has two separate sections, one for food and one for drink. Some recent studies seem to show that electrical stimulation of this unit of the brain produces *mouth movements* for the purpose of either eating or drinking, and that the animal will eat or drink according to what is available; that is, he'll eat if food is at hand or drink if he has water [Valenstein, 1968].

If a quantity of water that would normally satisfy a dog's thirst is introduced directly into the dog's stomach, he will proceed to drink another quantity of water (by mouth) more or less equal to what he still thinks he needs [Adolph, 1941]. On the other hand, if a period of fifteen minutes is allowed to elapse before the dog is given a chance to drink by mouth, his body cells will have absorbed the water and he will not desire it. Thus, the amount of water contained in the body cells seems to be one signal for thirst. Most current explanations of this phenomenon indicate that signals occur in the hypothalamus as the water is absorbed and fed into the cells near that unit. Support for this explanation comes from studies in which the tissues of the mouth are bathed in sufficient quantities of water to suggest to the body that it has enough water. Even though the feeling of thirst may be satisfied for a short while, the animal soon seeks water again.

Like some animals, we do not have taste receptors that are sensitive to water, but our tongues do respond to temperature. Since our water needs are regulated by how hot it is, the body seems to control water intake according to the temperature of the water: less cold water would be needed if we are thirsty outside in the winter. In general, the cooler the water the more quickly animals similar to man stop drinking. It is possible, just by cooling the tongue, to temporarily reduce thirst, but this is because of conditioning—the body assumes that water will soon appear in the cells [Kapatos and Gold, 1972].

So again, we have a combination of more than one mechanism operating for a psychological need, this time dryness of the throat, temperature of the water, and balance of water in the body cells. That the hypothalamus is involved is pretty clear. If a salt solution is injected into an area near the hypothalamus, an animal will drink an excessive amount of water. If a comparable amount of nonsalt solution is injected into the same area, no such water "need" shows up.

SUMMARY

Repetition and association of certain behaviors in a given situation is called conditioning in psychology. Pavlov's classical conditioning, the earliest form to be thoroughly studied, involved pairing an unconditioned stimulus, such as meat, with a stimulus to be conditioned, such as a bell. The conditioned stimulus then elicited a conditioned response—for example, salivation to the sound of the bell.

Conditioning in animals that involves increasingly difficult discrimination leads to experimental neurosis in which the animal is unable to cope with the situation. Some human neuroses seem to resemble classical conditioning—for example, choosing between keeping a job you don't want and having no income.

John Watson used the philosophy of classical conditioning to some extent and tried to relate it to humans by suggesting that all human behavior, even thinking, is the result of some form of conditioning. Watson's work has been carried into the present day with refinements and elaborations on his basic theory.

Hunger and thirst are behavioral mechanisms with their central control panel thought to be located in the hypothalamus, a unit that receives messages indicating the need or lack of need for food or drink. The stomach does contract when one is hungry, although it contracts at other times also, but it apparently is partly responsible for the messages forwarded to the hypothalamus; blood-sugar level is felt to be another contributor to the feeling of hunger.

Water in the mouth temporarily reduces thirst, especially if it is cold, but water in the stomach is also necessary. Signals to the hypothalamus seem to come from the mouth and the stomach, the stomach sending messages indirectly through the body cells, which absorb water.

Factors which produce changes in the stomach include emotional responses, as well as general psychological factors such as cultural preferences, which dictate what is acceptable and not acceptable to eat or drink.

CHAPTER FIVE
PSYCHOLOGY AND PHYSIOLOGY:
MOTIVATION AND EMOTION

E motion and motivation blend together and are extremely difficult to separate, even though a differentiation is usually attempted to make it easier to study them. We will start out with physiological studies, but they are inadequate by themselves, and any discussion of physiology very quickly turns into fairly elaborate and complicated psychological theory. Why this should be so is not difficult to understand; some of our most intricate behaviors are based on poorly defined and vague motivations and our feelings are likewise subject to emotional responses that are more than a little difficult to pinpoint.

Possibly the novelist, poet, or dramatist has an advantage over the scientist. The beautiful writings of Antoine de Saint-Exupéry, a pioneer mail pilot, come to mind immediately. He speaks of his aircraft:

It was cold at the airport, and dark. The *Simoon* was wheeled out of her hangar. I walked 'round my ship stroking her wings with the back of my hand in a caress that I believe was love. Eight thousand miles I had flown in her and her engines had not skipped a beat [Saint-Exupéry, 1940]*.

38 Saint–Exupéry (right) and his partner Guillaumet standing beside the *Simoon* in 1928 (*French Embassy Press Division*)

This is the *emotion* of love, the same type of love a violinist has for his violin, probably the love a man has for a woman, and probably the devotion between a man and his dog. All of these things and more. But now, the problem: What is it? Where does it come from? Physiological explanations are going to be a bit of a letdown after the poetry of the written word, but the discoveries of science are nonetheless the end products of men equally involved in capturing our basic nature. The more elaborate theories taken up at the end of the section may seem too mundane for something as wonderful as love, but on the other hand they likely contain clues to the basic nature of emotion or motivation.

For all the praise of his wonderful flying machine, Saint-Exupéry, deep down, knew better. In the early mail planes, sometimes the engine did quite literally fall off at inopportune moments. In his chronicles, after the takeoff Saint-Exupéry doesn't have a chance to write many more pages before he crashes in the desert:

Our first day's nourishment had been a few grapes. In the next three days each of us ate half an orange and a bit of cake. If we had had anything left now,

* From Antoine de Saint-Exupéry, *Wind, Sand, and Stars* (New York: Harcourt Brace Jovanovich, 1940), reprinted by permission.

we wouldn't have eaten it because we had no saliva with which to masticate it. . . . Gullet hard. Tongue like plaster-of-Paris. A rasping in the throat. A horrible taste in the mouth [Saint-Exupéry, 1940].

And this man would be rescued, get back in another of those sometime-flying creatures, and be off again to the next crash. Here we have a clear-cut case of *motivation,* but again we are faced with the problems both of its origin and of its nature. Some of the more elaborate theories, like that of the famous Sigmund Freud, might attribute the motivation to fly as originating in a basic sexual drive, in the sense that a man needs to prove his masculinity; some might go (and have gone) so far as to equate the sensations of flying with those of sexual release itself. Or you might choose a different psychological theorist, who would have said that the flyer had a desire for power in a fashion similar to a mountain climber who takes up the challenge of the Matterhorn and tries to conquer it.

These theories are very broad, and we will cover some of them, but first we will try to approach hard-core fact as closely as possible in order to glimpse the physiology of emotion and motivation.

THE PHYSIOLOGY OF MOTIVATION

Motivation is thought to result from basic drives. An animal or a human being is hungry or thirsty, has a need for food or water, and is thus motivated to seek satisfaction of this need. Sexual desire is another need that leads to motivated behavior. A laboratory rat on a treadmill, for instance, will walk the equivalent of nine miles to reach his mate in heat. On the human level, with our current standard of laziness, it is questionable how many men would walk nine miles to get to a sexual partner, although they would be happy to drive.

sexual behavior

In order to understand sexual motivation, we have to grasp in a general way the operation of glands and hormones. Located throughout the body are various organs which secrete chemicals called *hormones* into the bloodstream. These organs are called *ductless glands* to differentiate them from "nonhormonal" glands that secrete through an opening; the salivary glands and the tear glands in the eyes are such nonhormonal (duct) glands. A duct is like a furnace duct in which the hot air is directed to a specific location; ductless glands merely dump their hormones into the bloodstream, and the blood takes over from there.

Certain hormones are thought to trigger the sex drive. In lower animals such as rats and chickens, sexual interest is removed when sex glands* are removed. Strangely enough, in the human, removal of these glands (testes in the male, ovaries in the female), which should end sexual desire, usually does not. In many cases sexual desire continues for an

* Called *gonads* (see Fig. 5–3).

indefinite period of time [Beach, 1956]. A number of studies help to explain the persistence of the sex drive, demonstrating that human sexual behavior is motivated by learning and association, and often is far removed from the original sexual objects themselves. For example, in extreme cases, sexual activity for some people centers around *fetishes*. A man may have a stocking fetish, a hair fetish, or a shoe fetish; the object of his fetish has previously been associated with women, and the object itself comes to provide *more* sexual interest than a woman does.

In a fairly large number of cases the sex drive is somewhat diminished in human females when ovaries are removed, an operation that results in loss of the female sex hormone, *estrogen*. These cases occur, however, in females who are psychologically not highly motivated toward sex [Bishop, 1953].

Possibly the traditional picture of the male as a wild, lustful creature is fairly accurate; women who have reached menopause and have experienced a decrease in sexual desire come to life again sexually if they receive the male sex hormone, *androgen*. Likewise, men whose desire is waning can be stirred to action again by the administration of additional androgen. In the early 1940s it was noted that the administration of female hormones to male rats induced homosexual behavior, and a flurry of activity in experimental circles sought to determine if intake of the *male* hormone by homosexuals could reverse their patterns of behavior and make them more interested in women. The experiment was essentially a failure, suggesting that homosexuality is not exclusively a hormonal problem. Nonetheless, hundreds of experiments continue to examine heredity, environment, chemical balance, and other factors in attempts to determine the causes of homosexuality.

Besides being intrinsically interesting, sex seems to provide an excellent model for the union of physiology and psychology. The basic drive is provided by hormonal output; but from that point on, culture, society, and the individual personality take over. For example, in those societies in which a woman wears a veil over her face, men go haywire just at the thought of seeing what is under the veil. The sex drive in this case has a foundation that intimately involves the physiological system, but refinements like the veil are not much more than conditioning. In fact, the whole body system becomes conditioned to certain stimuli. Thus, at the thought of seeing the face under the veil, the man's heart speeds up and his blood begins to pound. The state of excitement is associated with the mystery of the unseen, so we have participation of both the body and the psyche involved in sexual motivation.

pleasure and pain motivation

The attainment of pleasure and the avoidance of pain are frequently cited as primary motivators in human behavior. In lower animals, centers for both pleasure and pain have been found to be localized in regions close to our old friend, the hypothalamus.* Small wire electrodes can be implanted in the animal's brain, and he can learn that pushing a lever will send an electrical current to a part of his brain that will respond pleasurably to the current. Hungry rats, given the choice of pleasurable stimulation to the brain or food, will run faster to the electrical lever than to a lever that would give them something to eat. That intense pleasure is being derived from this stimulation is unquestionable: some rats self-stimulated themselves up to two-thousand times an hour for twenty-four hours straight [Olds, 1956].

To alleviate pain in humans, electrodes that produce a pleasurable sensation have been placed in portions of the older brain. Some degree of success has been reported with patients, who stimulate their "pleasure centers" when they feel the pain coming on. In a few cases, even patients with cancer who are under extremely heavy dosage of morphine—in fact, who are getting large quantities of the drug every two hours—have been provided with "pain boxes" for brain self-stimulation. By using this electric current, some patients have gone as long as three months without drugs [Murray, 1969]. Such success is the exception, but with improved techniques it may become the rule.

Pleasure receptors (receivers) on the outside of the body have been very difficult to locate, if indeed there are any. We do experience the pleasure of coolness in summer and warmth in winter, and the tactile (touch) stimulation of a loved one, through three types of receptors—warmth, cold, and pressure—located around the body.† The problem is whether this is pleasurable sensation in the same sense as, say, the pleasure of listening to music or watching cars being demolished in a destruction derby at the local racetrack, and to this no one as yet has the answer. It seems probable that what we receive as pleasurable skin sensations are heavily psychological and thus a matter of interpretation. Although body temperature is essentially the same all the time, a cold shower feels good in summer and not very good in winter. The caress of a woman is eagerly sought by most men, but the same caress from another man is usually not pleasurable.

Although pain, too, has a major psychological component, nonetheless we have clear-cut pain receptors called *free nerve endings* (see Fig. 5–1). Since most of them are located just below the skin, it has been suggested that rupture of these free nerve endings triggers impulses in the attached nerve fiber. These endings are classified as *mechanoreceptors* (mechanical receptors) because their actual mechanical movement, resulting from injury or pressure, leads to electrical-impulse activity.

Although pain is, of course, a physical phenomenon, we cannot avoid outside factors influencing everything we try to isolate. Amazingly

---

* Check Figures 3–7 and 4–3.

† Although there is considerable agreement on pain receptors, a lot of scientific argument has resulted over whether certain receptors can justifiably be labeled warmth, cold, and pressure. They are not necessarily that well defined.

FREE NERVE ENDINGS

EPIDERMIS
DERMIS
SWEAT GLAND
HAIR
FAT

5-1 Free nerve endings in the skin

enough, pain is to some extent learned. Fortunately, cases that demonstrate this fact are rare, but in the few instances in which children were reared in isolation (that is, with almost no love or stimulation), some of them showed little or no response to a cut or *minor* injury. This doesn't mean that no pain is felt but that reactions to moderate injuries are learned, probably within the social environment of attention from the parent [Freedman, and Brown, 1968]. How far the suggestion that pain is learned can be carried, since there have been few studies of children reared in complete isolation, is debatable. It makes one wonder, however, because when dogs are reared in complete isolation, they seem to have no concept of pain. They are quite willing to stick their noses into a candle flame—repeatedly—with very little response [Melzac and Scott, 1957]. There is some evidence of a critical period in developing brain receptors for certain types of stimuli, and the pain-response system for the isolated animal seems to have been bypassed [Fox, 1968].

In line with this finding, other studies have shown that tolerance for pain is largely in the person's mind (which is not to say he does not feel it). In the case of a child who wants to skip school for the day, the intensity of a stomachache begins to diminish as soon as he realizes that the schoolbell is ringing and he is still at home in his pajamas. Although in serious cases nothing will substitute for drugs as an aid in reducing pain, even in some surgical situations pain is largely psychological. One experimenter found that in 35 percent of the patients involved, pain was alleviated by the injection of a harmless solution which the subjects *thought* was morphine [Beecher, 1966]. Another study shows that if a patient enthusiastically expects a cure from experimental surgery (that is, surgery not critically connected to a specific ailment such as appendicitis), interesting results can occur. In this situation merely cutting the skin to simulate a "real" operation is often as effective as the surgery itself [Beecher, 1961].

The connection of neurons at the synapses provides innumerable alternate routes and way-stations for electrical transmission so that the impulses potentially can travel any one of several paths over routes similar to a complex highway cloverleaf. Thus it has been suggested that the pain impulse must travel through a number of stages; at each junction the impulse pauses briefly while the organism evaluates the intensity of the pain and decides whether to send the impulse on to higher levels of the brain. Each of us differs in our ability to tolerate pain, probably the result of both physiological and learned factors. For each there seems to be a certain level of intensity necessary and then the impulses flood over the dam [Melzack and Casey, 1970]. This idea may help explain why some studies point out that psychological factors such as memories, thoughts, and emotions modify pain by diverting the neural impulses away from higher brain areas. If these assumptions are correct, a person who has recently had an injection with a crooked needle by a jumpy nurse faces a new injection with the pain "floodwall" lowered in *anticipation* of feeling greater pain than would be experienced otherwise. Contributing to this subjective panic will be a highly overactive physiological system which has resulted from a cortical warning to the reticular formation (alertness control) of impending danger.

This overlapping, delaying, and rerouting of the nerve impulse is utilized by dentists, who have found in some cases that playing noise into earphones worn by the patient considerably reduces the experience of pain. An experiment with cats illustrates what happens to the pain impulses when other distracting impulses arrive at the same time. When an electrode is attached to a spinal neuron and a shock is administered, a "pain" wave is sent down the neuron. However, if a shock is administered at the same time a vibrator attached to an adjacent spot is activated, the pain signal is diverted and cut off in about half the time it would normally continue to conduct [Melzack, 1961]. In some humans suffering severe pain, a reduction is possible by electrical stimulation of the spinal cord [Melzack and Wall, 1965]. Apparently, the pain impulse never makes it to its intended destination.

Rerouting of pain impulses may partially explain the supposed effectiveness of acupuncture, an Oriental medical procedure now of considerable interest in the United States. In acupuncture, gold or silver needles are inserted in various areas of the body, and it is claimed that this treatment removes many symptoms of disease [Trent, 1972]. How much of this procedure is just the power of suggestion remains to be seen.*

One final point should be made regarding neural connections: not all pain fibers connect through multiple synapses. Apparently some fibers are short and provide a direct route to the spinal cord, a situation that

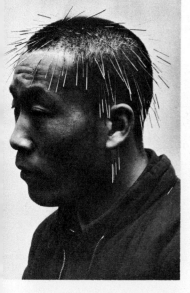

39 Acupuncture: the cure looks worse than the problem, but presumably it works in many cases (*Photo Researchers*)

---

* The first few pages of Chapter 24 cover the power of suggestion and healing—see also hypnosis.

accounts for the fact that we reflexively remove our hand from a hot object long before we "feel" the pain.

THE PHYSIOLOGY OF EMOTION

That overgrown pea-sized ball, the hypothalamus, is again called upon, this time to help explain our emotional reactions. For example, stimulation of the front portion of the hypothalamus produces symptoms similar to those found in persons who are reacting with either rage or fear. Pleasure centers are also located in the hypothalamus, something we already discussed, so it can readily be noted that scientists have found physical centers for emotional reactions. Stimulation in the thalamus also can result in anger, fear, or aggression, depending on the location of the electrical impulse [Bandler et al., 1972].

By cutting some of the nerve connections to the hypothalamus, physicians have been able to "tame" many uncontrollable mental patients, much the same as happens when tissue of the frontal lobes is destroyed* [Gardner, 1968]. Even though this emotional change may seem desirable, the results of cutting nerves in this area are unpredictable and may often make the patient worse off than before. Fortunately, the current trend is to handle most cases of mental disturbance with tranquilizing drugs and psychological treatment rather than with a knife.

Even study of the fear-rage portion of the brain has not been without its wilder moments. To prove his point, one experimenter connected a miniature radio receiver to this area of the brain of a bull and got into the ring with nothing more than a transmitter. When the bull charged, he pushed the transmitter button and the bull came to a screeching halt, presumably out of fright [Delgado, 1969]. It is likely that had the experimenter placed the electrode even one or two centimeters away from where he did put it, the experiment would have produced rage (or even pleasure), and we might have lost one of the few really intrepid innovators wandering around in the world of science.

40   True faith in science: Dr. Delgado trusts his welfare to an electrical impulse from a shortwave radio to the fear center of the bull's brain (*Delgado*)*

*See Figure 3–7 and the discussion of the "American crowbar incident," Chapter 3.

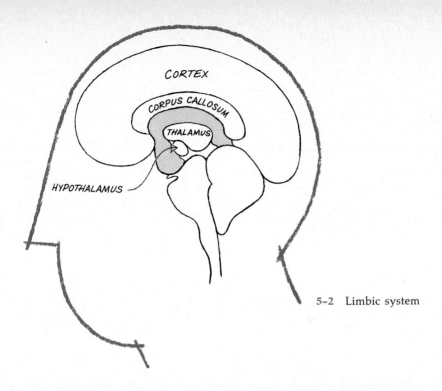

CORTEX

CORPUS CALLOSUM

THALAMUS

HYPOTHALAMUS

5–2 Limbic system

limbic system We have been discussing the hypothalamus and thalamus as if they were isolated units, but in the interest of accuracy we should briefly cover another area that has not yet been mentioned. Figure 5–2 shows a side view of the cortex with the thalamus and hypothalamus surrounded by a shaded portion. This darkened area is called the *limbic system*, and even has a miniature cortex of its own. The word *limbic* means "border" or "rim around," and as you can see in the figure it encircles the upper end of the brain stem.* Electrical stimulation in the shaded area can produce some unanticipated activities. As in the case of the bull, very small wire electrodes can be implanted in the *human* limbic system and activated by radio transmitter. Such implantations are usually a last resort for disturbed or seriously ill individuals, but they do occur. In one case, a patient with such an implant was sitting and playing a guitar when the experimenter introduced an electrical current to the limbic system; the patient jumped up and went into a rage, smashing the guitar [Delgado, 1969]. The same general area creates pleasure for the human [Brady, 1958*b*]. Individuals who are suffering extreme pain can have limbic-system implants for pleasurable self-stimulation, a fact mentioned a few pages back.

These techniques are not fully refined, but probably they bring images of thought control somewhat like that mentioned in the famous novel

---

*The hypothalamus, thalamus, and limbic system are all interconnected. In fact, some authors include parts of the thalamus and hypothalamus in the limbic system. This makes no real difference as long as you understand the three basic units.

1984. While it is true that a person can be punished or rewarded by remote control, the surgical techniques are extremely taxing, and the prospect of putting a receiver into everyone's brain is physically impossible. Furthermore, as you have already gathered, the location of the electrode is critical, and just a slight difference in placing it can change the response from pleasure to pain to rage to nothing. Considering the billions of neurons, perfection of this technique in the sense of "mass production" surgery is impossible in the forseeable future. Finally, humans do not show the same consistent effect of stimulation that animals do, probably because of the complexity of our brains [Deutsch, 1972]. Even though every event reported in the above paragraphs is accurate, we have passed over the numerous failures that occurred for the few successes. At least in our lifetime there is no evidence that we will ever be electrically controlled from an outside source, and it is improbable, although not impossible, for the future.

glandular system: emergency reaction

Important units in emotional reactions are the adrenal glands. There are two of them, located slightly above the navel, one on the right and one on the left (Fig. 5–3). The function of these glands is to secrete two hormones, adrenalin and noradrenalin. *Adrenalin* is most clearly associated with what are called *emergency reactions*—for example, fear. When dumped into the bloodstream, this hormone is partly responsible for the body's reaction to fight or to flee from a frightening experience: the heart begins to pump more rapidly to supply the organs with the necessary blood [Gardiner, 1937]. An increased need for oxygen is supplied from an accelerated breathing rate, and the liver releases a large quantity of sugar to provide the necessary energy for action [Funkenstein, 1955]. Muscle tension becomes extremely high in a fear state, possibly explaining why some people freeze solid if they hear a creaking on the stairs at midnight or feel the common phenomenon of induced paralysis when "glued to your seat" at a horror movie. One especially intriguing event that occurs in an emergency reaction illustrates the remarkable adaptability of our body: the blood's rate of clotting increases automatically. Despite any self-confidence you may have in a battle, the body's wisdom assumes you might not be a first-round winner.

The chemistry of anger reactions is not as clearly understood as is that of fear reactions. Anger seems to result from a mixture of adrenalin and noradrenalin.* Reactions that differ from responses to adrenalin alone include an increase in blood pressure and a decrease in heart rate. Muscle tension does not increase as much in anger as it does in fear [Ax, 1953]. In any case, in both anger and fear the body is prepared for an emergency.

---

*The exact role of noradrenalin is not fully understood as yet, although it clearly participates in these reactions, sometimes aiding adrenalin, sometimes helping to produce a different reaction.

THEORIES OF MOTIVATION AND EMOTION

Differentiating between motivation and emotion is extremely difficult. To pose a seemingly simple question about motivation and emotion is to become involved in a very complex answer. Does emotion motivate us? For example, do we seek a husband because we love, or do we love because we have found an acceptable man? One might say in this case that we are motivated to seek the emotion of love, but to make the problem more difficult, what about sexual behavior? Is sex an emotion or a motivation or both? If both, how much of each, and how do they interact? Generally, motivation is defined as that which moves an organism to behavior, but as you can see, it is not as simple as that.

This discussion is merely an introduction to the difficulties inherent in trying to differentiate between theories of emotion and theories of motivation and to forewarn you that they will blend together and sometimes become indistinguishable. Nonetheless, for some semblance of organization, motivation and emotion will be discussed under three headings: (1) theories that cover both motivation and emotion; (2) theories thought to be restricted to emotion; and (3) theories restricted to motivation.

learning theory

One prevalent and popular theory that covers both motivation and emotion is the *learning theory*. We will discuss learning theory in great detail later in the book, but for now it is enough to know that learning means the association or pairing together of events in a complex fashion to produce some type of behavior.

For example, in the area of *motivation*, a very poor child learns that money must be scrimped, saved, and hoarded just to survive. Later this fellow becomes a business tycoon who has a net worth of $5 million. He continues to pinch pennies, buys only one suit a year, and spends most of his weekends pasting trading stamps in a redemption book. We can say

41 Dickens's novel *A Christmas Carol* doesn't say whether Scrooge led a deprived childhood, but he must have learned somewhere to be a miser. Bringing in ghosts is not, however, the usual technique for curing stinginess (*Culver*)

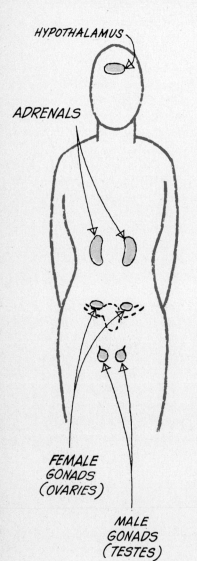

HYPOTHALAMUS

ADRENALS

FEMALE
GONADS
(OVARIES)

MALE
GONADS
(TESTES)

5–3 Significant Areas in
Emotion and Maturation

that in childhood he learned to be a miser and is motivated along the same lines for his lifetime.

The situation, of course, is not always so clear and simple. A person learns not only by association but also, to put it crudely, by what he gets out of it. For example, psychologist David McClelland feels that many people are driven by a desire to achieve, a desire to be recognized or successful [McClelland, 1953]. For instance, the millionaire who still spends his day trying to add another million doesn't need more money to satisfy his physical needs. Apparently he is obtaining satisfaction from trying to top his previous achievements by even greater achievements. If achievement is indeed a driving motive, each person learns techniques for satisfying this motive, and these techniques became habitual methods of behaving.

Motivations need not be so complex or all-pervading. I knew a man whose three brothers told him continually that the wing was the best portion of the chicken so that they could have the breast. To the present day this man is motivated to seek the wing whenever he eats chicken and is disappointed if someone else gets it.

In the area of learned *emotional* reactions, examples are around us by the hundreds. One that involves social training is that men do not cry as quickly as women. This difference undoubtedly comes from little boys' learning that "*Men* don't cry!" and "Be a *big* man. Don't cry!" Children do not naturally fear spiders, snakes, and rats, as you will recall from the experiment with little Albert and the white rat. But parents' comments of horror at a child carrying around a garden snake or a daddy-longlegs are obvious training factors in learning the emotion of fear.

Considerable experimentation has been aimed at sorting out which behaviors are basic to children at birth and which are learned, and the area of emotional behavior is a particularly difficult one. We will discuss sex differences at length later, but some recent studies are tantalizing in demonstrating differences in male and female children as young as forty-five hours old. Male children are considerably more active physically when they are asleep than females are; they twitch and jump and use their muscles more. Females are notably quieter in this respect, and, compared to males, they smile frequently during sleep periods [Korner, 1969]. From infancy male monkeys are wrestling, pushing, and shoving one another, while females are relatively quiet and shy, so there is little doubt that we are dealing *at the beginning* with some physiological difference [Bardwick, 1971]. The exact cause of these differences at this point in time is unknown, but the presumption is that the male and female sex hormones are responsible.

There is considerable variation in these characteristics during human infancy, but the most clear-cut difference between male and female children is in size and weight [Maccoby, 1972]. It doesn't take much imagination, then, to infer that parents respond differently to the male infant and female infant partly because of these behaviors. The father who feels his virility and masculinity is threatened if he does not produce a son arrives at the nursery already prepared for his new-born male offspring to show clear-cut evidence of baseball, fishing, and hunting potential. "Hello, Tiger!" seems a little inappropriate to be yelling through the nursery window, but it does occur, and the typical father will be looking for signs of "maleness" in his child.

Emotional responses of children, then, are probably learned primarily as a result of other people's reactions to them. Thus, the male is treated, even at this young age, as somewhat physical and aggressive ("male emotional behavior") and the female as quiet and sweet ("female emotional behavior"). To take but one example, the female is thought to be more sensitive than the male and more prone to emotional upset. These traits can actually be learned by the child from the parents' behavior. The point, I think you readily can see, is just how quickly learning can obscure any genuine physical differences that exist between male and female. Clearly, no scientific evidence indicates that females are more emotional than males, although most people believe they are, and believing apparently helps to make it so.

When you get to the chapter on learning (Chapter 9) you may want to return to this discussion and see how many other examples you can think of in which learning theory covers the way we develop our motivations and emotions.

homeostatic theory   Another theory, called *homeostasis*, deals with both emotion and motivation [Cannon, 1939]. The word *homeostasis* comes from the Greek and means "standing the same" or remaining in balance. Simply put, this theory is based on the assumption that we are motivated to behave *within certain limits*. Outside the psychological area, an easy example is that we are motivated to cut the lawn or shovel snow within the limits of physical fatigue and then we lose our motivation.

The homeostatic theory of motivation and emotion arose because bodily reactions are so well regulated in physiology. For example, the body sweats when hot and shivers when cold. These methods of cooling and heating are used to keep a body temperature of one degree above or below 98.6 degrees despite environmental temperatures ranging all the way from 20 below zero to 135 degrees above [Thompson, 1967]. Furthermore, the chemical ingredients of the blood are kept in very critical balance: oxygen level, salt level, and acidity must remain very close to a fixed point or we will die. In fact, an intriguing idea about these balances has been suggested: that we evolved from sea creatures and brought with us a tropical-temperature, salted blood-water—that is, the seawater equipment to bathe our organs continuously and thus remain in this homeostatic condition [Murray, 1964].

When moved to the field of psychology, homeostasis has been used to explain the fact that our body chemistry becomes imbalanced when we are hungry and thirsty and thus we are motivated to seek food and drink. Thus, we have motivation coming from an imbalance which needs to right itself.

The principle remains the same, but the situation becomes more complex when we move to broader human behaviors. It is believed that some alcoholics, for example, drink in order to escape certain realities they can't face. The thought of having accidentally killed his son is too much for Mr. X. If he thinks about it and faces the situation, then guilt, fear, and remorse (all *emotions*) become too great for him to handle. The homeostatic "psyche" prevents a breakdown by encouraging him to drink (*motivation*), an activity that in turn blots out the impending thoughts of what he has done and prevents an overload on the psychological system, just as a fuse will melt before the house current gets too high.

Again, for people who are afraid of speaking in public, a strong emotional component is involved. Before giving a speech, the person experiences an emergency reaction (mentioned in the previous section), apparently in preparation for the pending fearful situation. Homeostasis is thought to be operating in this case, trying to bring the body's level of activity up high enough to cope with the feared danger, so that the body and psyche are in balance.

The most complex level of homeostasis involves the operation of psychological mechanisms when decisions are made and actions carried out at the mental level rather than the physical level. This can often work to a person's disadvantage. Consider cigarette smoking. In one study every person filled out a questionnaire indicating how vulnerable he felt he was to cancer. These people were then divided into three groups. Within each group was a mixture of individuals who felt both high and low vulnerability to cancer. Next, each group was given a message. One group was given a low-fear message that involved a mild discussion of the possibility of getting cancer from smoking; the second group was given a moderate-fear message in which a film was shown depicting an actor in a doctor's office finding out that he had cancer. The third group was shown a high-fear message: a gory cancer operation.

The results seem to clearly indicate a form of psychological homeostasis. Those who felt themselves to be highly vulnerable to cancer showed *less* desire to give up smoking and have X-rays as the amount of fear in the message *increased*. Probably an intolerable level of fear was reached at some point and then the homeostatic mechanism, acting to prevent the person from being overwhelmed, reversed his thoughts and resulted in his deciding that he was not going to get cancer. In other words, the vulnerability previously felt was either masked or blotted out as the fear message became greater [Leventhal, 1967]. Without the same level of fear involved we can actually see the psychological homeostatic mechanism working. In a study on smoking and reading habits experimenters found that as subjects who

42 The overweight dormouse, just before hibernation begins (*Scientific American*)

smoked tended to have increased concern about their health they increasingly preferred reading material which supported the point of view that smoking was not injurious (correlation .50) [Canon and Mathews, 1972].

The homeostatic mechanism, then, does tend to maintain physical stability and probably operates on the psychological level in the same fashion. However, over the years pleasurable habits such as eating and making love can become a way of life that will sometimes cancel out the intellectual part of us, which might caution, for example, that we have a bad heart. One theory with some plausibility suggests that a limbic system accustomed to certain pleasurable experiences will override the logic of the cerebral cortex. The limbic system–cerebral cortex network has so many pleasurable connections for certain acts that a new idea—for example, a bad heart—doesn't carry much weight and overrides homeostasis [Young, 1967].

The theory of homeostasis is subject to other criticism. Some point out that at the animal level or the purely physical level the concept is workable, but when we move to the human psychological level the theory develops difficulties. How does one determine what the balance point is for a given person? Some people have a higher level of tolerance than others. Scientifically speaking, then, how could we ever establish what is the normal or average level at which the individual is in balance? Studying something is extremely difficult unless we know what is typical.* Is not the level of stress for the businessman higher (and still normal) in the winter than when he is on summer vacation? To further show how complicated this situation can become, a study using psychological tests on skydivers showed that fear of death decreased as the number of freefalls taken increased (correlation −.70) [Alexander and Lester, 1972]. Has fear of death really decreased, or is psychological homeostasis more effectively utilized by the more experienced jumpers?

These criticisms are legitimate, but they do not negate homeostasis. The critics of the critics, those who believe in homeostasis, counter with the argument that psychology is just not yet sophisticated enough to determine what is a normal level. They point out that even in nature there are different normal levels, and yet animals still operate on homeostatic principles. An intriguing example is the hibernating animal that begins to eat heavily in the fall to store up fat. A dormouse, for instance, who normally weighs four ounces, will double his weight for hibernation. At this point in time, the temperature-control portion of his hypothalamus swings into action: as winter arrives, each successive night his temperature gets lower, until it reaches a point just above freezing; then, to the rate of approximately one heartbeat each minute, he continues sleeping day and night until warm weather arrives [Mrosovsky, 1968]. Thus, it has been pointed out, the most

---

*If some people normally had temperatures of 105, some 94, some 98, how could you tell the degree of illness for each of them?

regulated portion of our world, the animal kingdom, has a *variable* level for homeostasis. Those favoring the homeostatic theory feel that eventually psychology will be able to predict what the base or normal level is for certain personality types, and using this base, better understand the psychological swings that are designed to protect the human organism.

THEORIES RESTRICTED TO EMOTION

the James-Lange theory

In the minds of laymen, probably one of the most famous psychologists after Freud is William James. In 1890 he wrote a book called *Principles of Psychology*, which is today considered a classic [James, 1890]. The major criticism from his colleagues—a most ludicrous one—was the accusation that his book couldn't be very scientific because the reader could understand it [Reisman, 1966].

The *James-Lange theory* of emotion was a unique one, and it still has not been discarded.* The theory is simple, yet often confusing because it is just the reverse of how we think our emotions operate. We think, for example, that we see an object that provokes emotion—a snake, say—and *then* we have an emotional response and we run. James reversed this: first we see a snake; next we respond internally (increased heartbeat, contracted stomach, etc.), and possibly run (increasing bodily response); finally, *because* our body is so keyed up, we feel the emotion of fear—reaction first, emotion second.

How did he arrive at such a seemingly upside-down conclusion? First, he says that the intellectual part of an emotion is dry and drab compared to what we *feel*. He follows this up with the idea that to think "snake" certainly does not create intense feeling. Therefore, first we react to the object physically (with tightened stomach, etc.) and then we *feel* the emotion as a result of the bodily response. The situation is somewhat similar to the difference between thinking about a girlfriend or boyfriend and actually touching her or him. The physical response comes first, and the emotion is a result that we feel from this physical response.

James's theory is a perfectly legitimate hypothesis, although it has been criticized, as you might expect. For one thing, under James's hypothesis, the injection of chemicals into the body should produce emotions because these chemicals alter the physiology, and once the physiology has been altered, the emotion should occur (for example, the injection of adrenalin should cause an emergency reaction). This does not happen. The so-called emotion that people feel after such an injection is reported as "not real," "false," "there's something wrong with the emotion."

---

* A Danish physiologist by the name of Lange appeared about the same time with a similar theory; hence its double name. This strange phenomenon—the same theory devised at the same time by two independent investigators—occurs over and over in the history of science. It should be noted that a contemporary of Darwin, Alfred Wallace, came up with essentially the same theory as Darwin at the same time.

Those who still insist that the James-Lange theory is correct counter with the argument that these injected chemicals are not produced by the body, and a falsely created emotion will of course seem false to the person experiencing it.

The major objection to James's theory takes the form of another theory, one that was implied in the earlier discussion of the physiology of emotion. It is called the Cannon-Bard theory of emotion.

the Cannon-Bard theory   This theory, named after its makers, centers around the discovery of the hypothalamus as a focal point of emotional response. Cannon and Bard propose that the object is seen and the hypothalamus is triggered to produce *at the same time* both the bodily reactions and the emotional response. Whereas James waited for the body to react first, this theory has both body and emotion reacting in unison. (The hypothalmic function was not understood in James's time, the early part of this century, and Cannon and Bard had more up-to-date information.) About the only major criticism of the *Cannon-Bard theory* is that in very extreme emergencies we *do* seem to respond first and then to react emotionally, as in a near-accident in an automobile.

the Soviet theory   No one as yet knows the answer to the problems of emotional theory. It is worth considering, however, some recent research in the field of physiological measurement and theory that stresses the cortex and limbic system as the two areas which are simultaneously operative in emotion. In the section on perception we will mention that the operation of the eye occurs by means of movement toward an object. This reflex is called the *orienting reflex,* meaning essentially that a portion of the body is oriented (for example, eyes to the object, ears to the right or left to locate sound, etc.) in order to assimilate that object.

Orientation is accomplished by the cortex, the higher brain center. We have already established that emotional responses are elicited by excita-

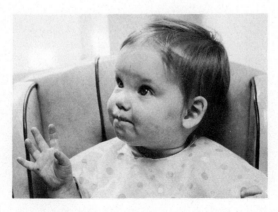

5-4   Orienting reflex

tion of the limbic system, especially the part called the primitive cortex, and by the hypothalamus.

Soviet scientists, combining these facts, have arrived at a most intriguing hypothesis to explain some of our emotional responses to objects in the environment. For example, why do we feel love or hate, respectively, when we *see* our mother or a stern school teacher? The experimenters propose that the original perception of the object (mother or school teacher) evokes an orienting reflex, which is recorded in the cerebral cortex, *and* a physiological response—internal physical changes from love or hate—which are recorded in the primitive cortex. The coincidental recording in the cerebral and limbic cortex creates a neurological* bond between the object and the emotion. Subsequently, when we see this object, the appropriate orienting reflex occurs in order to focus on it, and this reflex at once unites the higher brain center with the limbic area, resulting in an emotional response [Beritashvili, 1969]. This explanation might be considered a more elaborate Cannon-Bard, which in turn was probably a more up-to-date James-Lange theory, although you should remember these are separate theories in the eyes of quite a number of psychologists. They are not mutually exclusive in all respects, however.

the cognitive theory   The *cognitive theory* is easy to understand, but if it is claimed to be *the* theory of emotion, it is as difficult to support as other theories.† Stanley Schachter, the major proponent of this system, maintains that emotional responses involve an excitement of the physiological mechanism (e.g., heart rate, perspiration) but we only know (cognition) what emotion we feel by *labeling* it. Earlier we discussed the difficulty the experimenter has in distinguishing fear from anger in the individual. Dr. Schachter is not disturbed by this situation, because his theory proposes that we feel whatever we call it. In other words, if we are very muscular and a man attacks us, we call it anger; if we are weak, we call it fear. Essentially, then, we have a physiologically based theory, but the emphasis is on how we label the physiological changes we feel.

In support of his theory Dr. Schachter and his associates have performed experiments in which subjects were injected with adrenalin in the presence of other stooge subjects who were in on the experiment and supposedly had also been injected. The stooges acted either angry or unusually happy after their injection, and as the experimenter would have predicted under cognitive theory, the regular subjects tended to act in a fashion which resembled that of the stooges. In other words, they thought

---

* "Nerve network."
† *Cognition,* from the Latin meaning "to get to know," is used rather loosely in psychology to refer to almost any thinking behavior involving the higher brain centers of the human.

they were supposed to feel a certain emotion, and they behaved in that manner [Schachter, 1962].

One of the biggest flaws in this theory you already know: the injection of adrenalin tends to induce an unreal emotion. Therefore, you could argue immediately that if adrenalin was being manufactured internally, rather than being injected into the subject, the cognitive theory might not hold up. It is known, too, that different emotions result in the body's producing different hormones, although this may not directly affect the subjective feeling.

Even with these problems and a number of others which support the opposite point of view—that people can't readily identify their emotions—the theory should not be wholly disregarded, because at least it has called our attention to the importance of *suggestion* in influencing emotional responses [Shapiro, 1970]. For instance, an extremely competent commercial airline pilot boarding a jetliner and wearing old bluejeans and a World War II helmet with goggles might engender, just by suggestion and association, the emotion of fear, both physical and psychological, in the passengers.

Furthermore, cognition is intimately involved with verbal expression, and verbal expression in turn can create emotional responses. For example, in laboratory experiments in which the person is led to believe that he will experience pain, he becomes far more anxious than other subjects who are not led to believe they will be hurt. In fact, the person's actual "feeling" of pain increases in the former case [Hall, 1954]. This phenomenon is the reverse of Schachter's theory, in that emotions come from words rather than words from emotions, but the link between the two seems well supported.

Before leaving this theory, it is important to make the point that many emotions *as we know them* exist only through the use of language [Duncan, 1968]. A child has to learn the appropriate time for having feelings of guilt, remorse, shame, or envy. These will vary from one society to another; for instance, in some societies a funeral calls for sadness, in others joy.

The cognitive element, then, certainly plays some role in emotional response, but it doesn't answer all the questions which emotions pose.

THEORIES RESTRICTED TO MOTIVATION

hedonism

One of the oldest theories of motivation is called *hedonism*. It stresses that we seek pleasure for its own immediate gratification and avoid pain at all costs. This long-standing theory dates back before the Romans, who were known to induce throwing up during a meal so they could go on eating. Even Freud's theory stresses the drive of the organism to achieve pleasure as best it can during the waking state; if it doesn't succeed, then it will dream about pleasure. One way or another, pleasure is paramount.

There is little else to say about hedonism. Obviously, we all seek pleasurable experiences. Obviously, we try to avoid pain (most of us), so the theory notes only the obvious. As an all-encompassing framework, however, it is faulty and no longer held in esteem. One major difficulty becomes clear if we take a look at the psychological abnormality called *masochism,* in which a person actively seeks pain. A masochist is one who wants to be hurt, and such people do exist. By elaborate justification, it *is* possible to make a case for hedonism in this instance, but the bucket of information resembles a sieve because of all the stretching and bending over backward required to explain it. The explanation for masochism goes something like this: when a child, the person was spanked on his mother's or father's lap. This spanking, since it happened in connection with close physical contact, took on a tinge of sexuality (pleasure). The child came to associate the reception of pain with the pleasure of sexuality. Hence, the grown-up child seeks pain in order to derive pleasure. Both philosophically and psychologically, the flaw in this thinking is that hedonism states *flatly* that we seek pleasure and avoid pain. Such a theory either is or is not correct. One cannot, after the fact, twist the data to fit the theory by saying pain is sometimes pleasurable.

In any case, some intriguing discoveries may eventually do away with the hedonistic definition of pleasure that uses elaborate sexual explanations like the one above. What we call masochism may not be restricted to humans; in fact, a number of different animals seem to derive a perverse pleasure from electrically self-stimulating their fear and aggression centers. At present this behavior defies explanation; the fact remains that animals and men engage in this activity, which on the surface would seem to be unpleasurable, so pain and pleasure are mixed [Doty, 1969].

epicurianism   *Epicurianism* fits our problem a little better, and yet it has long been confused with hedonism. Epicurians desire a freedom from pain, but not specifically physical pain, and they do not stress direct avoidance of all pain. This philosophy allows for the fact that the long-term goal of pleasure is often fraught with unpleasantries that must be accepted for a greater good—a more "meaningful" pleasure. Primary emphasis is put on peace of mind through self-control [Gay, 1966].

For example, epicurianism can make some sense of a religious group called the Penitentes, who are still found in small numbers in areas between Santa Fe and Taos, New Mexico. During Lent, members of this group reenact Jesus' crucifixion literally, including the ritual of carrying the cross, wearing a crown of cactus, and often going through an actual crucifixion. Whether you agree with their behavior, some form of peace of mind does seem to be attained through such a painful process [Bach, 1961].

Epicurianism as a psychological theory is not used today, but half

43   Mahatma Gandhi based his life on the idea that great social change could be achieved through self-denial. He explicitly rejected the pleasure principle by fasting and practicing sexual abstinence (*UPI*)

a dozen current theories under different names are remarkably similar. Maslow's theory, covered in the last section of this chapter, is somewhat akin to epicurianism. We might well pause and look at the all-pervasive influence of the epicurian theory. Returning to the mail pilot, Saint-Exupéry, we see that he repeatedly comments on the psychological tranquility of the flyer who was completely in the hands of fate. Is this not the suffering of danger for a greater good? Saint-Exupéry describes this peacefulness:

. . . crossing peacefully the Cordillera of the Andes. A snow-bound stillness brooded on the ranges; the winter snow had brought its peace to all this vastness, as in dead castles the passing centuries spread peace. Two hundred miles without a man, a breath of life, a movement; only sheer peaks that, flying at twenty thousand feet, you almost graze, straight-falling cloaks of stone, an ominous tranquility. [Saint-Exupéry, 1942]*

These types of comments are almost universal in literature. Furthermore, philosophical explanations do not die just because they can't be verified by rigorous experimentation. The Roman Catholic church, for instance, explains that man must suffer in this life for a greater good. Protestant religions stress the need for sweat and toil to achieve good on earth and in heaven. Eastern religions advocate passive resistance and suffering for a greater good. In the 1970s one of the strongest philosophical movements is existentialism. Part of this philosophy suggests that the meaninglessness in our lives can be partly overcome by fighting the injustices rampant around us. In this way man obtains a "courage of despair" as he seeks right and truth despite the psychological pain [Tillich, 1962].

A teacher in a Tennessee high school sums up the courage of despair when she describes the plight of a determined black child:

I have looked at a Negro child in my classes, and I have wondered what it would be like to sit a whole year in a class and not have a living soul, except the teacher, speak to me. I have wondered what it would be like not to have anybody you could ask for a sheet of paper or a pencil. And what it would be like to have a new dress and not a single person say, "How pretty you look today." [Lewis, 1964]†

the hierarchical theory   Abraham H. Maslow's theory of motivation (Fig. 5–5) is based on a *hierarchy of needs*, a term which refers to the idea that basic needs must be reasonably well fulfilled before the next higher order of needs can be approached and met. Physiological needs like hunger and thirst must be satisfied before a person can progress to the level of safety needs. An example of safety needs is having a store of food for the future or a permanent dwelling to protect

*From Antoine de Saint-Exupéry, *Night Flight* (New York: Harcourt Brace Jovanovich, 1942); reprinted with permission.
†From A. Lewis, "Portrait of a Decade: The Second American Revolution," *New York Times Magazine,* November 2, 1958; reprinted by permission.

5-5 Maslow's hierarchy of needs

one from the weather. On the next higher level, the person seeks a sense of identity by, for example, belonging to a group. Once his identity is established and his belongingness-needs fulfilled, the person moves to attain self-esteem—for example, a position of importance in the group. The final need of self-actualization refers to the achievement of the person's purpose in life. If he wants to become a mathematician, he becomes one and thereby actualizes his self-potential. If talented musically, he is self-actualized by accomplishment in the field of music, and so on [Maslow, 1954]. Maslow found evidence supporting his hierarchy by studying self-accomplished people in such fields as politics, science, and art. These people do indeed seem to follow a hierarchy, as he suggests. Maslow's theory also fits quite well with the concept most of us have of ourselves. Basically he was saying that man has higher goals and motivations than animals, which he strives to achieve, but he can do this only by progressive steps upward.

A major problem, however, is that some people seem to skip over certain levels or ignore others. The trite but often accurate notion of the starving artist depicts a person who seems to be concerned mainly with self-actualization. He pays only fleeting attention to physiological needs and seems to ignore other needs.

Another example is the radical-activist who has seemingly run and jumped over physiological needs, and certainly has skipped around safety needs, and winds up somewhere near the top—perhaps attaining self-esteem by being a participant in a cause.

Maslow's theory is probably the most sophisticated motivational theory that does not emphasize basic needs like hunger, sex, thirst, and physical stimulation. These needs are more like stepping stones to higher things than ends in themselves. Maslow's ideas, therefore, are similar to the epicurian philosophy.

Maslow's theory sometimes brings the reaction, "So what?" because it is deceptively simple. A strict "correct" or "incorrect" is no more applicable to this theory than it is to others. It is important because it provides a rallying point for exploration of human motivation—a structure around which study can center. For example, he defines the healthy person not as one who spends his time *seeking* love but as one who already has it (belongingness). We can only develop a sense of self-identity if we are secure in the knowledge that someone else cares. Thus, as Maslow put it, a person fails to reach his full potential (self-actualization) because he is very busy trying to fill up the "hole which has to be filled, an emptiness into which love is poured" [Maslow, 1962, p. 39]. In a sense, motivation is misdirected and Maslow's schema helps provide an answer to the "why" of human behavior.

Maslow's system does not adequately explain all aspects of motivation, but it deals with slippery and complex concepts. For instance, Maslow feels, with considerable justification, that a person who has completely adjusted to our insane society has essentially rejected the true and meaningful depth of human nature. Few of us would disagree; his theory is beneficial because it provides a framework for understanding: the self-actualized person can disagree with society, but the insecure individual (who lacks belongingness) is preoccupied with seeking acceptance, and he goes along with the majority in trying to attain it.

other forms of motivation

Hunger, sex, and the like are what we might call negative needs—we seek to satisfy a lack within ourselves. Before leaving this topic, we should mention that today a considerable number of psychologists, in addition to Maslow, are working in the very difficult area of positive needs, those caused neither by obvious deprivation nor by the desire for special rewards other than possibly the reward of the act itself.

Harry Harlow, a pioneer in primate studies, has shown that monkeys will manipulate a complicated mechanical puzzle of hooks, latches, and sliding bolts just for the sake of doing it. These animals were not rewarded for their actions by petting, encouragement, food, or any other outside treat. Animals will also learn to perform certain acts just to see something different; for example, when a monkey discovers he can see a toy train on the other side of a door if he does what the experimenter wants, he will learn rapidly in order to see the train [Harlow et al., 1956].

We have just been discussing what are called the *manipulation motive* and the *curiosity motive* respectively. Psychologists have really struggled trying to understand the nature of these *nontissue needs.** The clearest findings to date indicate that animals from rats on up the scale will actively seek some type of variety or novelty in the world around them. The important factor seems to be change: even animals who are used to very complex surroundings—for example, living in a psychedelically decorated cage—will actively seek a new home with a simple pattern when given the choice. Presumably the animals are seeking the unexpected. Likewise the reverse: humans who have become accustomed to simple surroundings actively seek more complex ones [Munsinger and Kessen, 1964; Eisenberger, 1972]. The change in environment needs to be of a reasonable or moderate level or it will be viewed as unpleasant [Berlyne, 1969]. Thus, a group of rowdies who are tired of Sam and Mabel's Bar may seek variety by moving on to Harry and Sarah's Pub, but would feel quite uncomfortable confined by a coat and choked by a tie spending the evening at the Tenderloin Room of a swank hotel. Controlled experiments using water temperature as the independent variable indicate that once a person has adjusted to a certain temperature he will find the change of a couple degrees very pleasant, but respond to a major change negatively [Haber, 1958].

---

* That is, there is no specific tissue of the body that seems deprived, as occurs in hunger or thirst.

One intriguing study of animals shows that those exposed to continuous noise have little desire to seek more stimulation—they presumably have already been overstimulated [Berlyne et al., 1966]. Can we assume that this explains why television viewers are immobilized after a couple hours and have no desire to even seek the stimulation of standing up or walking around? Probably not—that's a dangerous and very speculative scientific jump—but some type of satiation (fullness) of the sensory networks must account for the dazed condition of the TV viewer.

Attempts have been made to explain the curiosity and manipulatory motives in terms of basic needs in the central nervous system [Eisenberger, 1972]. For example, the assumption has been made that the reticular formation* needs a certain minimal level of activation during our periods of wakefulness. If it gets too low, then we seek a change of activities to restore it to normal operating level [Fiske and Maddi, 1961]. Remember, however, that most of this is theoretical and there just isn't enough evidence yet to feel confident of the validity of these ideas.

The area of motivation is, then, both new and old. For many years it has been dominated by the negative theories of Freud, which are covered in Chapter 11. This is not to imply that Freud was either correct or incorrect, but merely to say that different and new viewpoints are always worthwhile, and that experiments with curiosity and manipulation motives are a refreshing change in that they examine positive rather than negative motivation.

SUMMARY

Although in many cases motivation and emotion are difficult to distinguish from one another, motivation is the driving force within the person which leads him to perform certain acts. These motives are called drives because they push the organism to action.

The sexual motivation of lower animals results from the operation of hormones, which are chemicals injected into the bloodstream from ductless glands.

Human sexual behavior is guided by hormones, especially the male hormone, androgen, but psychological factors easily obscure the actual effect of these chemical agents.

Two major driving forces are pleasure and pain. We have pleasure centers in the hypothalamic area—but specific pleasure receptors on the body are poorly understood. There is considerable agreement that free nerve endings are major contributors to our sensation of pain.

*The alertness control mentioned earlier in this chapter.

Both pain and pleasure are heavily subject to psychological forces in that we feel more or less pleasure or pain depending on what we have come to expect. The neural pathways of pain have been extensively studied, and these studies indicate that the nerve network is able to cut off or divert pain impulses.

Emotional responses also have specific brain centers, primarily the hypothalamus and limbic system for emotions such as rage or anger. Hormones play an important role in emotional behavior; especially notable is the effect of adrenalin, which stirs the body up to the point of an emergency reaction.

Numerous theories have been advanced to explain motivation and emotion. Some of these theories are workable attempts to explain both at the same time—for instance, learning theory, which proposes that we are driven toward certain satisfactions, but that the particular technique which we use to gratify these needs is learned. Learning theory further suggests that we learn emotional responses such as the fear of little crawly creatures.

Homeostatic behavior is most clearly noted on the physical level in the maintenance of equilibrium for bodily processes. Homeostasis is thought to regulate emotional behavior by preventing an individual from becoming psychologically unbalanced.

Among the theories of emotion is the James-Lange theory, which proposes that we react with an emotion physically first, and then we feel it psychologically—for example, we run, and because we are running we experience fear.

The Cannon-Bard theory stresses the operation of the hypothalamus in emotional responses and hence suggests that both the emotion and the physical response to it are mutually triggered—that is, they occur together.

The Soviet theory of emotion stresses physical response and emphasizes that an orienting reflex toward a potentially "emotional object" sets up an automatic cortical connection from previous learning, and we respond as we did in the past.

Labeling is the most important aspect of emotional behavior for the cognitive theorist. Differences in physical response are underplayed, and the theory focuses on what we *call* the reaction of the body, be it "fear" or "happiness."

Hedonism is the oldest and most obvious explanation for motivation: we seek what is pleasurable and avoid what produces pain. This theory does not take into account some actions that lead to temporary pain or discomfort for the greater good. Epicurianism, however, is based on this principle, which is carried to its ultimate conclusion in Maslow's hierarchical theory of motivation; this theory states that man is always seeking the highest level, self-actualization, but that he has to travel through other layers of behavior in order to reach that point.

Curiosity and manipulation motives are relatively new areas of study in psychology. Studies to date clearly indicate that these nontissue needs exist and that novelty is actively sought by all manner of animals as long as the change is not too drastic. The possibility that the reticular formation requires periodic stimulation has been offered as a tentative explanation for this behavior.

PART TWO
PERCEIVING AND LEARNING

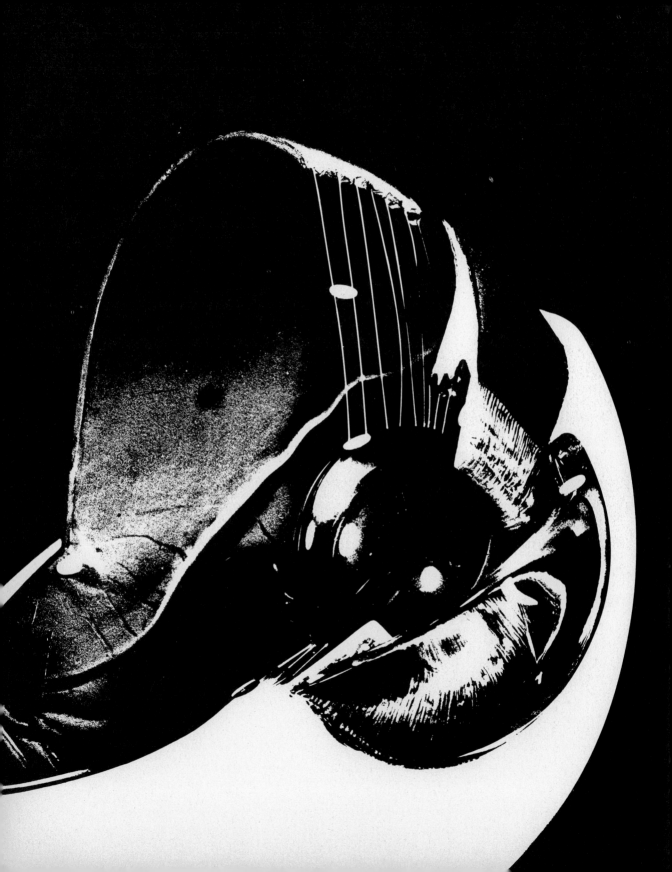

CHAPTER SIX
THE WORLDS OF PERCEPTION

The term *perception* refers to a person's ability to receive energy from around him and to interpret or understand the meaning of this energy. The most important sense for the human is vision, for our lives are dominated by what we see. Psychologists study all manner of perception—visual, auditory (hearing), tactile (touch), pain, and so forth. Because of the number of studies and the detail involved, just as a matter of practicality we will stress the most interesting and the most important of all—visual perception—in the present chapter and the one following.

Basically, perception is the extracting of information from the environment, but because we are so accustomed to having our perceptual ability, it is often necessary to call attention to the fact that we *do* perceive. An interesting analogy proposed by one author focuses on the dolphin, who sends out and receives clicks from his perceptual world. Using only this mechanism, it is able to determine the size, shape, and importance of the information received—that is, whether it has detected food, danger, or a place of refuge. The dolphin can even differentiate metal objects from other surface textures.

People do the same thing with their vision, although they are primarily concerned with receiving rather than sending out. The analogy still holds true, however, because the information received is processed by the brain, and in this sense the act is not passive. When a person is blindfolded, we get some clue to the process by which he perceives when he has his vision: he identifies objects by feeling curves, edges, and indentations in order to isolate *distinctive* features of the object. Take off the blindfold and his eyes do exactly the same things. Man's visual world would be complete confusion if the brain were not able to put objects into categories by concentrating on important and distinctive features like contour and shape [Gibson, 1970]. To illustrate, we don't "read" most words in an ordinary sense; instead, we are so used to them that we respond to their overall shape. In this example, the shape has been retained, even though the words have been run together:

TheDogThrewUp

Now, if we rearrange the shape, thus losing the normal contour of the words, we may have considerable difficulty in deciphering the material:

ThEdOgtHreWup

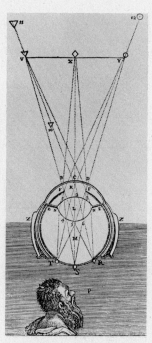

44 Descartes' diagram of the eye (see page 141 in this chapter) (*Jeroboam*)

Not only are we dealing with contour itself, but this contour becomes a symbol in the complex human brain. This can be readily noted once you find out that, if the shape is retained, even if the letters are backward we can read much more rapidly than we can in the sentence above, where the contour is disturbed. This is because the grouping of letters is important, not the individual letters [Kolers, 1972]. You should have only a little trouble reading this:

.ti tuoba yppah saw dna pu werht god ehT

Even in normal reading matter we can only process (that is, consciously recognize) about 3 or 4 letters per second—if we had to decipher each letter, this page would take about 20 minutes to read and this chapter about nine hours—a fate no one deserves. A final illustration that we treat letters as whole groups for a single symbol is dramatically demonstrated by experiments that show that when a person reads a word incorrectly, the word he substitutes usually has approximately the same length and contour and is usually the same part of speech as the word misread—that is, substitution of an incorrect noun for a noun, incorrect verb for a verb, and so forth [Kolers, 1972].

Visual perception, then, is based on contour and shape, on the grouping of letters, and on symbolic analysis of this information. The perceptual apparatus of the individual, however, is not simple; it involves memory, amount of attention the person is paying to the material, general intellectual level, presence or absence of physical impairments, and general health [Mann, 1970]. In other words, the perceptual apparatus involves a lot more than just aiming one's eyes in a certain direction.

PHYSIOLOGICAL MECHANISMS

light

If you stand on a sandy beach and gaze out to sea, soft and poetic thoughts may drift by, but if you wade into the ocean to any depth, you are suddenly aware of the strength and power of the energy in the form of waves. An ocean wave is a type of energy movement based on the same principle as snapping a whip; the energy starts at the snap of the wrist and is transmitted by a wave down to the end of the whip.

If you visualize either the ocean or the whip, you have a basic image of a representative form of energy transmission, the wave. Light, which moves in this fashion, has two basic components to its transmission: the frequency with which the waves are forming, and the distance between the top of one wave and the top of the next. Radio waves, for example, have an extremely high frequency of transmission; waves form at the rate of a million per second as the energy is moved through the air. Light waves move through the air at frequencies just below 1,000,000,000,000,000 (one quadrillion) cycles per second, if we concern ourselves with only the light we can see. In the case of the ocean, anyone can observe that as the frequency of the waves increases, the distance between the top of one wave and the

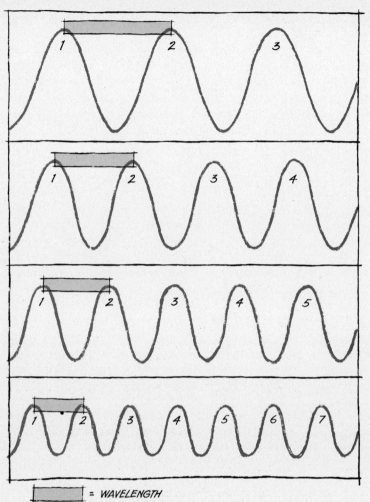

6-1 Wavelength and frequency

next (called wavelength) is going to decrease—as if there weren't time for them to form long wavelengths. This principle is illustrated in Figure 6-1.

The air is filled with energy transmissions that have a tremendous variety of wavelengths and frequencies. The radio has to lower the signals it receives to frequencies we can hear (20 to 20,000 cycles per second). Likewise the eye, even though it can respond to very high frequencies, is restricted in range to a very small portion of the light waves that exist in the atmosphere. As a result of the high frequency, light waves are going to be very short between crests—in fact, they are measured in millionths of a millimeter. Our range of vision in wavelengths is 380 mμ (millionths of a millimeter) to 780 mμ. Although at least 7 million different colors are potentially visible to the eye, the ability to see these lies in the response of the eye to this very restricted range of light waves. The three major colors are actually quite close together: yellow, 573 mμ, green 521 mμ, and blue 480 mμ.

Ultraviolet rays have an extremely high frequency and a very short wavelength. This gives them a penetrating power so great that people use ultraviolet lamps to get a suntan (burn), and must cover their eyes while doing so to avoid injury. The word *ultraviolet* means "beyond violet," as you can see in the bottom part of Plate I (opposite p. 144).

Rifles with special sniperscopes have been invented that are sensitive to another area we cannot see, the infrared ("below red"; see the top part of Plate II). These scopes pick up energy waves in the dark that fall beneath our eyes' ability to detect and transform them into visible energy [Neisser, 1968].

Ultraviolet and infrared are the two extremes at which the eyes cannot see—beyond violet and below red. Figure 6–2 shows the arrangement of energy waves in the air by frequency and wavelength.

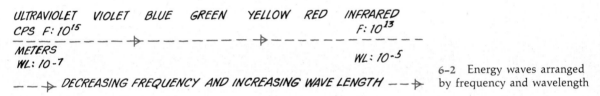

6–2   Energy waves arranged by frequency and wavelength

Color responses of the human visual network vary according to the transmission characteristics of the energy—that is, its frequency and wavelength. The light from the sun is called *white light*, which contains all the color wavelengths. When this white light hits various objects, the molecules of the objects vibrate at a certain frequency that breaks down the white light and sends to our eyes a resulting frequency that is absorbed by the elements in the eye and interpreted by the complete visual network. The interaction between the vibrating frequency of the white light and the molecules within the eye triggers the stimulus for the sensation of color. For example, the beautiful arrays of red and yellow we see at sunset result from two things: (1) the great distance the light is traveling at that time of evening (most of the high-frequency violet-blue waves have died out before reaching us); and (2) the diffusion or spreading out of the remaining light hitting air particles. One of the ironies of our big-city smog problem is that often the impurities of the air diffuse or spread the light of sunset into an elaborate pattern of varied colors, thus creating something beautiful from something ugly.

When white light vibrates at a high frequency, as it does in the atmosphere of the sky, we see blue. Snow, which has a crystallike structure, reflects white light without breaking it up; hence, we see white vibrations when we look at the snow [Hendricks, 1968].

Receptors within the eye are responsible for vision. These receptors absorb light rays from objects in the environment and turn them into electrical energy in order to operate the nerve networks from the eye to the occipital (visual) portion of the brain. These receptors are sensitive to and absorb most from certain wavelengths. Although the issue is so complicated that scientists cannot agree on exactly what method the eye uses to obtain all the different colors it does, they do agree generally that receptors within the eye receive a few major colors and combine, mix, or compare these basic colors in order to provide whatever color we are seeing.

We will discuss color vision in greater detail shortly; basically, the eye is receiving from different material the emission of different wavelengths of light.

receptors within the eye: rods and cones

Scientific discovery is often a matter of focusing on something we knew all the time but gave little attention to. This was true with visual reception units. The credit for a discovery goes to the one who calls our attention to a phenomenon, and a physiologist by the name of Purkinje was such a man. He noticed that as one stands and watches twilight approaching—that is, as it begins to get dark—objects that are red turn black quickly and objects on the blue-violet end of the spectrum (see Fig. 6–2) retain their brightness almost to the point of darkness. Using "logic," we tend to think of violet as a darker color than red, probably the result of our daytime experiences with "bright" reds and yellows. Why, then, would this *Purkinje phenomenon* occur? Shouldn't the blue-violet end become even darker?

The answer lies in the fact that within each eye we have receptors for two overlapping sets of wavelengths, giving us, in effect, two eyes for

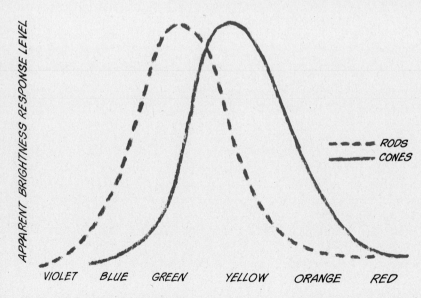

6–3　Response curves of rods and cones

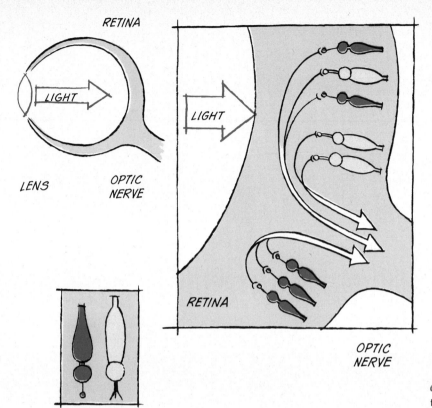

RETINA

LIGHT

LENS

OPTIC
NERVE

RETINA

OPTIC
NERVE

ROD CONE

6-4 Rods and cones
transmitting impulses
through the optic nerve

each one we have. One set of receptors is more responsive to the redder
end of the spectrum and is used for day vision. The other set is more
responsive to the violet end and is most effective for night vision (Fig. 6–3).
These receptors are called *rods* (more-purple end) and *cones* (redder end).
The names given these receptors are sensible if you look at Figure 6–4; there
is no reason other than their shapes. Each visual network for each eye has
a mixture of these units.

In the early part of World War II blue lights were used aboard navy
ships, based on the "logic" that this color is "darker" and therefore harder
to see at night. The results were disastrous [Ruch, 1967]. Look at Figure
6–3 and note how much more responsive the rods are in the blue area. A
change was very rapidly forthcoming and now ships in war zones have dim
red lights in all passageways leading to the outside. One reason for this
is that red is least detectable to the naked eye at night, if the light is kept
at low intensity; hence, there is less chance of being seen by the enemy.
Another use for these red-lighted areas is that sailors can stand in them
before going out on deck to take over the watch. As you know from entering
a movie theater, for at least the first few minutes you are bumping into
people and seats because of the time it takes for the eyes to begin a shift

from daylight cone vision to more sensitive rod vision. The sailor lets this shift take place before he goes out on deck, letting the rods take over with the least amount of interference—by using red light. This changeover is called *dark adaptation.** When complete dark adaptation has occurred (in about forty minutes), the eye has become at least a hundred thousand times more sensitive than during the day, although sharpness of vision, called *visual acuity*, is decreased because the cones are not operating.

Notice that Figure 6–3 shows the *relative* brightness of various wavelengths; it does not indicate that we cannot see certain colors. If you plead not guilty in traffic court for running a red light at night, saying that all you had was *scotopic* (rod) vision and not *photopic* (cone) vision, you will impress only a naive judge—or you may win because your argument is so unusual. It is true that the rods do not respond to red with the same efficiency as cones, but we see red lights at night so well because their intensity is high and the cones begin to operate. Driving down a well-lighted freeway, in fact, we are operating on photopic vision because the conditions are similar to daylight.

Remember, rods *do* respond to colored objects, but they do not "see" color. It is obvious that a bull responds to a matador's cape, but not because it's red. He will snort and attack no matter what color it is because the bull's retina contains almost all rods and he therefore cannot distinguish colors. Likewise, a cat has nothing but rods because he is a night creature. His vision is much better at night, but he can see during the day [Young, 1970].

color vision   One of the oldest theories of color vision has postulated three color receptors in the cone regions—red, green, and blue. The cones are responsible for color vision, and they have absorbing pigments for certain wavelengths—this much is known.† However, the red-green-blue theory is based partly on the fact that we can mix these colored *lights* to produce all the different colors we see. The eye probably does not operate in the same fashion as light mixture. In fact, mixing the pigments of red, blue, and green paints does not produce the same color combination as light mixture does. Some recent experiments have demonstrated that maximum color response is roughly in the blue, yellow, and green areas. Other experimenters have discovered that the ability to discriminate one color from another becomes clearest between green and red and between blue and yellow [Stone, 1971]. By now you should be thoroughly confused, though this is not my intention.

* The term *adaptation* comes up frequently in psychology. It refers to the organism's ability to change. The body can adapt, just as the eye does by increasing or decreasing sensitivity to external conditions. For example, in the last chapter, the hungry person increased his sensitivity to food (dark adaptation: increasing sensitivity of the eye to objects in dimness). The person who has eaten has adapted to a point of not needing food (light adaptation: decreasing sensitivity of the eye).

† The operating chemical substances of the cones are called *opsins;* those of the rods are called *rhodopsins*, but rods are for black-and-white and night vision.

Basically, color vision is not well understood. Most investigators seem to be content with the red, green, and blue cone theory—that is, we see colors as the result of a mixture of chemical and electrical responses from red cones, blue cones, and green cones [Young, 1970]. However, one reason for the rather considerable confusion is the individual variation in cone structure and basic equipment. We do not all "see" the same color, even though we may agree on a label for it, nor do we all have identical equipment for receiving color.

You might suppose that the solution would be simple: presumably, if color vision is a combination of three pigments, then individuals who have various defects in color vision should respond by cone absorption only for the colors available to them. Instead, however, some people require more red or more green light before they respond "normally" to these colors. Some experimenters feel that these people have a third, "mystery" pigment that does not absorb light in the normal fashion—that is, not specifically in the red, green, or blue range [Alpern, 1971]. And finally, to make matters worse, there is some indication that color defects are increasing in civilized groups, but tend, among primitive peoples, to remain low in frequency [Lindzey, 1971]. This finding is very difficult to explain.

A complete range of colors for the eye can be obtained by using only two "colors," one of them white light. By using filters it is possible to produce two different slides of the same picture. The first slide is shot in only one color; the second slide is colorless. When the two are super-imposed on a screen the picture comes out in full color. If a full range of colors is possible from only "two," one can speculate with considerable confidence that color perception is more than just a mixture of wavelengths. In this special situation experiments suggest that color sensations result from a complex arrangement in which some rods are responding to how light and dark the objects are and are mixing sensations received with the one-color cones. Thus, we have an instance of color being produced without the normally expected mixing of two different color cones [McCann, 1972]. In any case, this experiment emphatically points out the role of the retina, optic nerve, and occipital lobe* in processing the information received by the eye; that is, wavelength and certain absorbing pigments undoubtedly are important, but they do not contain within themselves all that is necessary to produce color. The remainder of the vision network must somehow operate to interpret what color we are seeing [Hurvich, 1969; Hendricks, 1968].

In line with the interpretation hypothesis, many years ago it was pointed out that color vision must be partly psychological in the sense that we see what we expect. For example, a white newspaper or book moved from outdoors in bright light to the indoors does not suddenly seem to dim,

---

*Back of the eye, nerve network from the eye, and the portion of the brain receiving visual information, respectively.

fade, or yellow, and coal is quite bright when in sunlight, but we still see it as black, certainly not as "light black."

Before leaving this topic it might be well to emphasize something discussed in the beginning chapters—all is not designed just for man. You may have wondered if this wide spectrum of light and color beyond the human range has any usefulness. Indeed it does. Just to pick two examples, bees are equipped with receptors for a favorite flower, the white bryony, which emits large amounts of ultraviolet, and the pit viper snake has infrared receptors for their own version of the sniper-scope [Manning, 1967; Johnsgard, 1967].

three worlds of vision An important principle, applicable to all human behavior, is illustrated by the "bright" coal and the newspaper discussed earlier. The human organism responds in reference to a combination of three dimensions: the external environment, or what is "out there"; the internal *psycho*logical world, which includes factors such as emotions or the concept of ***brightness and color constancy;*** and the internal *physio*logical world.

Recent experiments on the internal physiological world of vision are most intriguing. Even without the external environment, our visual apparatus is quite busy producing patterns, designs, and images of its own, called ***phosphenes***. If you want to create your own phosphenes, go into a completely dark room and relax, letting your eyes adapt to the darkness; soon you will begin to see pleasantly colorful designs resembling those of a kaleidoscope. If you do not like this sensation, you can be a part of what must have been a most exciting time in the early 1700s, the era of parlor games. Apparently for diversion from the ladies, Benjamin Franklin participated in this fun-time. Get the members of a group together, join hands, and have someone touch a static-electricity generator. Participants not only receive a shock but also see splotches of phosphene light, demonstrating that vision is partly electrical in nature.

Aside from such fun and games, the phosphene experiments suggest that the chemical-electrical network of the visual apparatus produces some of the mystical visions that people report; with intense concentration or with drug use, the light patterns become even more striking [Oster, 1970].

So, the internal world can operate by itself. However, most of the time the things we see around us are the result of all three mechanisms. A piece of coal looks black in the bright light because first, it has a certain texture and shape and certain specific characteristics for reflecting light (physical environment); second, we have the knowledge that it is a piece of coal (psychological factor); third, the neurons of the visual network, including the rods and cones, electrically *take an average* of the amount of light we are receiving (physiological factor)—thus, very light things are toned down, very dark lightened up.

Before moving on, the third factor mentioned above needs a little elaboration. If you are going to shoot one picture in the bright sunlight and another one at twilight the best pictures will result by changing the sensitivity of your film for each occasion and/or changing the settings of the camera. Basically what you are doing is taking an average of the amount of light and adjusting for it so the picture will not be washed out or black. The eye mechanism does the same thing, only it has to do it electrically within the visual nerve network. This is done very cleverly: if the brightness is very great, many of the neurons block or stop the firing of a large number of receivers within the eye; if it is dark, fewer neurons are blocked and your eye is more sensitive to light. We seem to be able to control this to some extent psychologically for objects we are familiar with [Werblin, 1973].

THE EYE: BASIC PHYSIOLOGY

The earliest theories of the eye are remarkably similar to the pervasive philosophizing discussed in Chapter 1. Basically, the operation of the brain was unknown; similarly, no one knew how the eye did its job. The eye was simply designed to see, and that was about it.

Descartes, the philosopher-semiscientist, was one person who was interested in doing more than talking about the eye. In the 1600s he removed the backs of human and animal eyeballs and noticed that objects were projected onto a piece of paper he held up to the open portion of the half-eyeball. He also scraped the covering from an intact ox eye and, looking through it from the back, noted that an image was formed there of whatever the ox eye was "looking" at.

Then, in the early 1700s Isaac Newton gave a remarkably accurate description of the eye in his book *Optics:*

Do not the rays of light in falling upon the bottom of the eye excite vibrations in the retina [the back of the eye]? Which vibrations, being propagated along the solid fibers of the optic nerves into the brain, cause the sense of seeing? [Newton, 1952]

The ideas of both Descartes and Newton are clearly important forerunners of the knowledge we have today about vision. Unfortunately, their views were to lead to an analogy between the eye and a camera, the idea being that the image on the film was the same as the image on the retina of the eye. This problem will be taken up shortly.

Even today, the eye is a source of endless mystery. You may have noted the subtitle of this book is *The Hybrid Science*, a phrase meant to suggest that work in many scientific fields will likely dovetail someday to help explain the origin and development of many of the fantastic organs we possess—assuming we don't destroy all living creatures before that is possible.

In any case, distinguished zoologists have recently performed careful experiments demonstrating that our world is populated with fantastic creatures—for example, lizards that carry around, atop the forehead, a third eye that is photosensitive* and regulates the light-darkness pattern of the animal, controlling the amount and extent of daily activity. This third eye may or may not have existed in the human—no evidence exists that it did—but one cannot avoid being intrigued by the speculation that we have within us a unit that has somehow evolved from this third eye and regulates our own dark-light cycles (as was discussed in Chapter 2). Reproductive and migratory patterns of many lower creatures are regulated by a light receptor in the brain. Birds don't fly south just to be home for Thanksgiving, but because they are responding to a change in the light-darkness cycle of the day as winter approaches. The receptors are not within the eye itself, because even blinded sparrows respond to light-dark cycles [Menaker, 1972]. The idea that humans have such receptors is without clear evidence, but the possibility is certainly intriguing.

Some of these studies have also shed light on the development of the eye itself. The eye is actually a portion of the brain, not a unit "attached to" the brain. One bit of evidence about this extended brain development is that at some stage of fetal development, tissue folds inward, forming a pocket similar to that in a baseball glove, and on the inward side of this pocket, toward the center of the brain, grow minute hairs called *cilia*. These hairs are essentially the same as those found in the nose; however, they bend and twist to form a structure that resembles discs stacked one atop the other, creating a conelike apparatus of photosensitive molecules. The stacking and curling process apparently is a later evolutionary development probably similar to our cone development. Thus, it would seem that scientists of all disciplines are zeroing in on some phenomenal discoveries relative to man's development [Eakin, 1970].

structure of the eye   Before progressing further, it might be well to examine the physical structure of the eye in order to avoid any confusion about terminology—for example, about the word *retina*.

Figure 6–5 shows a top-view cross section of the eye. The *cornea* is a clear outer covering behind which is a clear liquid. If you look at your eyes in the mirror and note its shiny covering, you are receiving a reflection from the cornea and the liquid behind it.

The "fingers" part of Figure 6–5 is the portion of the eye upon which lovers concentrate: "the color of your eyes," etc. . . . This part is called the *iris*. In a two-dimensional figure like this one, it is hard to visualize what the iris looks like. It is actually a circular muscle which opens onto the lens, and moves from larger to smaller and from smaller to larger circles so that it can control the amount of light entering the eye. To see it in operation, you have to work quickly, but you can catch it in the act. A bathroom mirror with an overhead or side light makes an excellent laboratory. Turn on the

* *Photosensitive* means having the ability to react to light, usually in a chemical fashion.

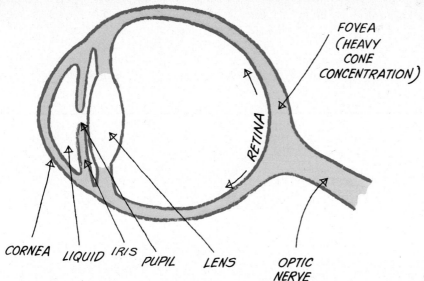

FOVEA (HEAVY CONE CONCENTRATION)

RETINA

CORNEA LIQUID IRIS PUPIL LENS OPTIC NERVE

6–5   Top view of the eye

light and cover one eye with your hand, standing so that this covered eye will be hit by the light when you remove your hand. Then quickly remove your hand and with your other eye watch how the iris closes from a large circle (dark-adapted, and open) to a smaller one.

What about the dark place in the middle of your eye? What is it? Nothing. The *pupil* is just an opening; it looks black because we can't see light reflected onto the *retina*, the back portion of the eyeball which lies behind the pupil.

Rods and cones, about 125 million of them, are located along the retina. Cones predominate in the center and are very heavily packed into the place marked *fovea*. In both directions from the fovea rods begin to predominate. Since we have only about a million nerve fibers running from the retina to the optic nerve, some doubling up of rods and cones is neces-sary, as Figure 6–4 shows. Thus, each rod and cone cannot have its own nerve fiber, although some cones do have their own fibers, which might help explain their ability to provide very sharp images. (Figure 6–4 is not a complete picture of all the actual interconnections, but should provide a general idea. Figure 6–9 is more detailed.)

The rods contain a chemical called rhodopsin which is sensitive to light and will change the shape of its molecular structure when hit by light. These changes are transformed into chemical and electrical energy that in turn produces responses in the optic nerve. Impulses move down the optic nerve to the vision center of the brain (occipital lobe*). All that light does is change the molecular arrangement; chemical reactions take over from there [Hubbard and Knopf, 1967]. The whole process takes about $\frac{2}{1000}$ second [Young, 1970].

* The occipital lobe is the vision center of the cortex. See Figures 3–5 and 6–9.

143

Basically, then, a chemical change results from light received by the rhodopsin in the rods. The rhodopsin "bleaches" out in response to the light waves and then restores itself when the light is removed. Driving a car at night, you can get a feel for this bleaching out when you are temporarily blinded by the headlights of an oncoming car. The bleaching is a chemical action that creates nerve impulses.

THE REPRODUCTION OF IMAGES

The camera became an analogue of how we see because of a strange property it possesses: it bends and deflects light waves so that what enters the top of the lens will be deflected downward and what enters the bottom will be deflected upward. The lens of the eye has a similar property; the image of an object projected through it onto the retina will be upside down. One reason the camera analogy is a poor one, however, is that we hold the camera as still as possible, click the shutter, and have an upside-down picture on the film. The problem is easily remedied by turning the photo right-side-up. If we had a stationary image upside down on the retina, we would be confused indeed. First, the world would seem upside down; and second, any projection that remains constant, in one spot, on the retina begins to fade from vision. Actually, the inverted image which we have on the retina

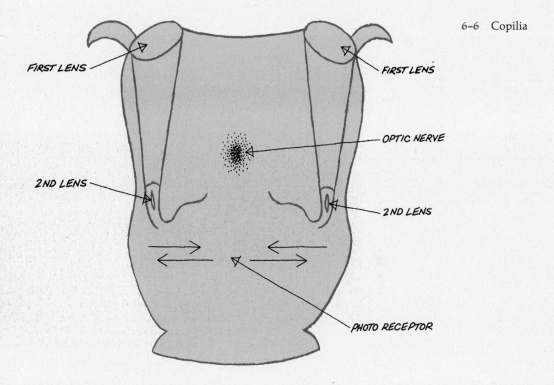

6-6   Copilia

FIRST LENS

FIRST LENS

OPTIC NERVE

2ND LENS

2ND LENS

PHOTO RECEPTOR

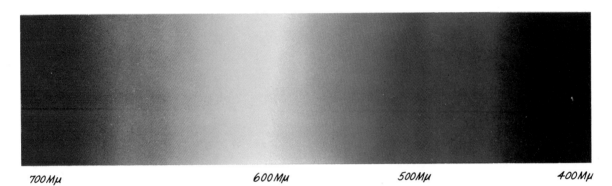

700Mμ   600Mμ   500Mμ   400Mμ

Plate I: The Visible Spectrum

Plate II: White Light Diffused Through a Prism

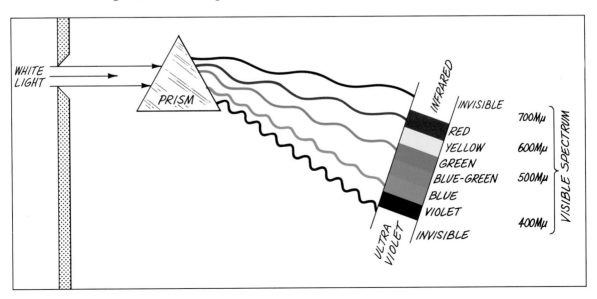

Plate III: Colors of a Sunset (Mark Jacobs)

Plate IV: Wavelength Sensitivity of Various Colors

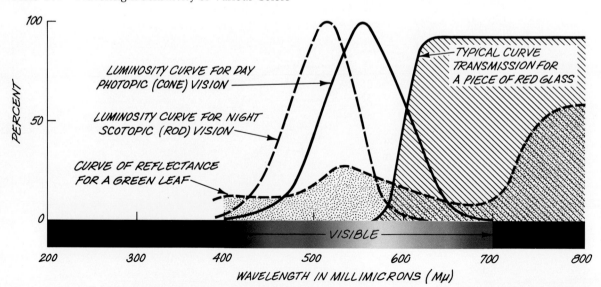

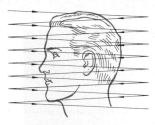

6-7 Television camera examines a figure sequentially

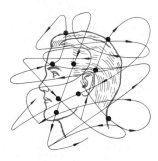

6-8 Human eye examines a figure in a complex pattern. Arrowed lines represent scan paths; dots, fixations.

makes no difference to the receptors of the eye because the eye does not process images as we see them in photographs; instead, it processes visual *information* from the environment, which will become clear in a moment.

A good analogy of eye operation can be found in one of the most unusual organisms on the earth, the *copilia*, a creature no larger than a pinhead (Fig. 6-6). As far as anyone knows, the copilia is not duplicated anywhere else in the world, except by coincidence in the television camera.* The creature has a photoreceptor and a second lens that move continuously, scanning the picture presented to the first lens (see Fig. 6-6) [Gregory, 1966]. This is basically how the television camera works, scanning along the picture in an orderly sequence so rapidly that we get a complete image of a man's head (Fig. 6-7), even though the camera picture is nothing more than a series of electron dots sent to photoreceptors and then reproduced at the television set.

Although we have only one lens per eye, we are in many respects similar to the copilia and to the television camera, although our eye movements are not as orderly as those of the camera (Fig. 6-7)—which, ironically, gives us a distinct advantage. Taking the head in Figure 6-7, our eye scans it in a fashion that can be represented by the drawing in Figure 6-8. Notice that the eye movements do *not* correspond to what we would consider a sequential examination of an object. How, then, do we see? We see because the eye is processing bits and pieces of visual information and fitting them together into a brain-centered *representation* of the object, taking special note, with each rapid eye *fixation*,† of changes, movements, alterations, and significant parts of the object which are sent to the brain in a neural code. Although Figure 6-8 suggests a random scanning of the object, recent studies strongly suggest that a *scan path*—a pattern of eye movements—varies according to the object being viewed. In storing objects for memory, the visual network may be recording some part of the object and connecting it with the eye movement needed to reach the *next* part of the scan path. Thus, just as we become conditioned to the pattern of right turns, left turns, etc., while driving home from school, the perceptual memory is becoming attached to certain sequences of eye movement. A physical movement sequence and a visual memory sequence become united [Noton, 1971]. But the exact position of the object, as you have seen, is not critical to development of scan paths or visual fixation. Therefore, we need not concern ourselves that the object is upside down on the retina. The whole image is not as important as specific features of the image. However, as you will read later in this section, if we deliberately turn the picture projected onto

*The coincidence makes one wonder. Might not the things we "invent" all be duplicated somewhere by some creature if we look long and hard enough to find it?

† Each darting and stopping movement of the eye is called a fixation. When we read a line of type, for example, the eye will make a few very rapid fixations to take in the entire line, grasping a group of words at a time.

the retina right side up, using a special lens, the perceiver is in trouble and has difficulty sorting out what is right, left, up, and down.

It should be added that we can scan scenes so quickly because we learn from experience where objects should be—and they generally are there. But our eye would stop for a long fixation if we saw a stuffed animal instead of a bowl of flowers as the centerpiece of a formal dinner setting [Biederman, 1972].

Some intriguing experiments have demonstrated that the eye and the brain have remarkable organizing abilities, and at the same time these studies have illustrated that we do not absolutely have to have the image in a certain position on the retina. The experiments underscore most of what we have been talking about here. First of all, in view of the fact that the image on our retina is inverted, what would happen if a grown man accustomed to years of seeing and responding to this inverted image were suddenly to find it placed right side up on the retina—in other words, inverted from its "normal" inverted position?

In the late 1800s a man named Stratton put an inverting lens over one of his eyes and kept the other blindfolded. Immediately after putting the lens in place, he tried to grasp an object that seemed to be on his right, but he reached to the left, and vice versa. Memory images of what things "should be" conflicted with what he saw through the inverted lens. However, after about the third day the environment began to look fairly normal to him, and by the fifth day he could operate with considerable accuracy. Objects appeared inverted to him only if he examined them carefully, but *if he was moving around,* everything seemed almost normal. You might notice how well this ties in with our previous discussion on the importance of eye movement in information processing.

As one experimenter points out, Stratton and experimenters who followed him seemed to agree that things *seem* normal unless very close attention is paid to them. There are many possible interpretations of these studies, but a workable one is that our eyes and brain are adaptable enough that they can process information even when the image on the retina is different from what it is normally. Nonetheless, years of adaptation to upside-down images on the retina have a more or less permanent effect on our handling of perceptions of the world [Gregory, 1966].

orientation reflexes   If you look back at Figure 6–5, you will note the fovea. This is the location in which cones are in maximum concentration for sharpest vision, and it is the spot used by the eye for brief fixations on various parts of an object. The importance of the fovea and its sharpness of vision is underscored by the fact that certain creatures—such as hawks, which must pursue and intercept their prey—have *two* foveae for each eye, one for side and one for forward vision. Presumably this aids in quick and accurate location of the victim and his path of movement [Charman, 1972]. These birds' sharpness of vision is also very critical; hence, the density of cones in the hawk fovea is 1 million per square millimeter, whereas in ours it is about 147,000 [Shlaer, 1972].

Outside the fovea, on both sides, are the *peripheral vision areas,* which are the locations of an increasing number of rods and diminishing visual acuity.

Peripheral areas are very important. Aside from the fact that they contain the heaviest concentration of rods and are most useful for night vision, it has been clearly demonstrated that vision moves inward from the outer side of the eye. That is, the peripheral region signals to the eye that a portion of an object deserves attention, and the foveal area then swings toward it. Once the object is centrally located, the peripheral area again signals the eyes to move their foveae to another area, and so forth [Mackworth, 1965]. Apparently these movements, triggered by the peripheral regions, are significant for survival in the sense that they are alert to any change. The eye will continue to follow anything blinking on either side; thus, highway signs that wink and beckon are extremely enticing and the eye is interested in these for a considerably longer time than is safe. This affinity of the eye for anything outside the foveal area might help explain a fact to be discussed shortly: the eye is interested in borders, edges, and outlines of objects, constantly returning to survey them. In fact, one author has mentioned that science has now verified what to some may have seemed merely a strange quirk—that is, the tendency of men to concentrate upon and follow the curves of women [Thomas, 1968]. Thus, as you can readily see, science is quite useful.

The movement of the fovea is called an *orientation reflex,* and this constant movement is the key to the reconstruction of objects found all around us. It has been pointed out that we can best clarify the position and shape of an object if it moves, or if our eyes move in relation to it. For instance, when you see a weather vane from a distance, you find it just about impossible to tell which direction it is pointing, especially when it stands at an odd angle—but let the wind move it slightly one way or the other, and you instantly can tell which direction it is facing [Neisser, 1968]. The orientation reflex was discussed earlier in reference to the Soviet theory of emotion in Chapter 5.

45 The tendency to see outlines before anything else has had an effect on Peter Max, among others (*Peter Max Enterprises, Inc.; all rights reserved*)

processing visual information

Experiments with live frogs have shed light on some of the intricacies of our own visual mechanisms. By attaching microelectrodes (electrical recording devices made of very thin wire) to the brain of the frog, it has been demonstrated that he responds electrically to various details of the object and takes action. For example, information is processed by at least two types of receptors found in the cat and the human eye, as well as in the frog's eye, namely, *moving-edge detectors* and *contrast detectors.* Contrast detectors provide an approximation of the shape of the object, and moving-edge detectors provide electrical responses for any movement in the field of vision. One intriguing component of frog vision not found in ours is a set of detectors that respond only to black, moving objects about an inch in diameter. The detector responds by immediately triggering the frog's tongue toward that object; the frog has an automatic bug catcher [Lettvin, 1959; Wooldridge, 1963].

The operation of these mechanisms can be understood a little more clearly by examining the visual apparatuses of the cat and monkey, which are considerably more complex than the frog's and similar to man's [Hubel and Wiesel, 1962]. This process is so fascinating that it is worth taking a little time to examine it. Use Figure 6–9 as we proceed. The first thing we respond to when looking around us is contrast—the relative brightness and dimness of various objects. Thousands upon thousands of light receptors in the retina process these light patterns. This is accomplished because certain cells when stimulated send an "off" signal from the retinal area (A in Fig. 6–9) to the ganglion cells (B in Fig. 6–9).* Others respond, when stimulated, with an "on" signal. By combining thousands of on and off signals the brain gets a rough estimate of the brightness, dimness, and general contrast of the objects being viewed. The thalamus (C in Fig. 6–9) has units in it that further refine the information going to the cortex. All these stages act as filters, so the cortex is receiving only the most important information—unusual contrasts or contours. At a more complex level, the occipital lobe is designed to receive slits, edges, and lines that are at specific angles, so if A is stimulated with one of these at a proper angle the information will be forwarded electrically to point D in Fig. 6–9. Part E of the cortex is designed to receive only more complex information, moving edges or lines, corners, and even parallel lines. The highest level, F, will integrate relationships between unusual lines, corners, slits, edges, etc., providing a representation of what we see in coded electrical form. Remember—only important parts or unusual parts of the scene are processed [Stent, 1972; Barlow et al., 1972]. What we have, then, is information of all kinds coming into the occipital cortex, where it is assembled into an understandable whole [Weisstein, 1969; Michael, 1969; Hubel and Wiesel, 1962].

Back a few pages we were talking about brightness constancy in the sense that coal does not seem bright black outside and white paper doesn't pale inside. Now you should be able to guess why (along with the guess of other experimenters). Presumably we "see" only the contours of these familiar objects and the brain is provided with only what seems an appropriate average amount of lightness for that object. In other words, the mechanisms we have been discussing distort the real-world object to fit the cortex's assumptions from past experience [Ratliff, 1972].

In summary, then, the visual apparatus contains many and varied processing centers and individualized response mechanisms. These specific cells, in combination, form a neural code to provide us with our visual information-processing machine.

---

* The term *ganglion* means a bundle or collection of nerves and synapses.

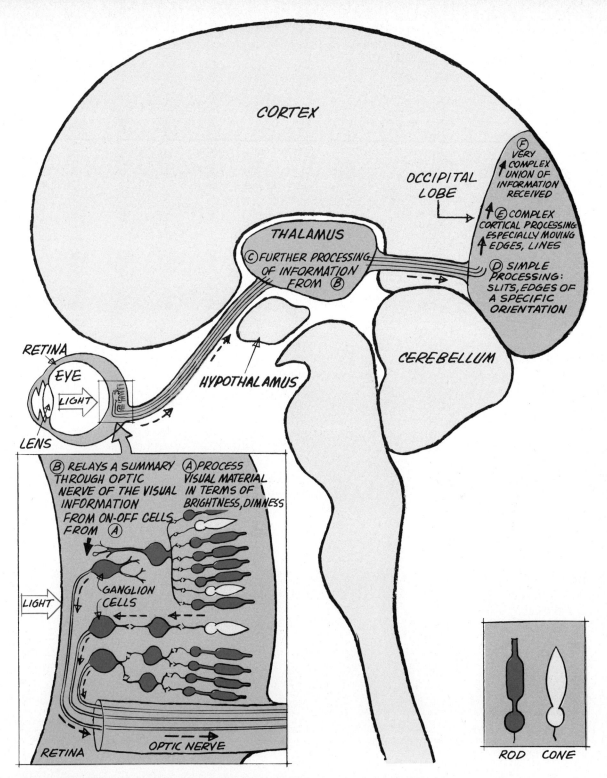

CORTEX

OCCIPITAL
LOBE

(F) VERY
COMPLEX
UNION OF
INFORMATION
RECEIVED

(E) COMPLEX
CORTICAL PROCESSING:
ESPECIALLY MOVING
EDGES, LINES

(D) SIMPLE
PROCESSING:
SLITS, EDGES OF
A SPECIFIC
ORIENTATION

THALAMUS

(C) FURTHER PROCESSING
OF INFORMATION
FROM (B)

CEREBELLUM

RETINA

EYE

LIGHT

HYPOTHALAMUS

LENS

(B) RELAYS A SUMMARY
THROUGH OPTIC
NERVE OF THE VISUAL
INFORMATION
FROM ON-OFF CELLS
FROM (A)

(A) PROCESS
VISUAL MATERIAL
IN TERMS OF
BRIGHTNESS, DIMNESS

GANGLION
CELLS

LIGHT

RETINA

OPTIC NERVE

ROD   CONE

6-9 Light energy is first processed at the back of the retina, A, impulses move
forward through the ganglion cells, B, through the optic nerve to the thalamus,
C, to the occipital lobe, D, E, F. See text, don't panic.

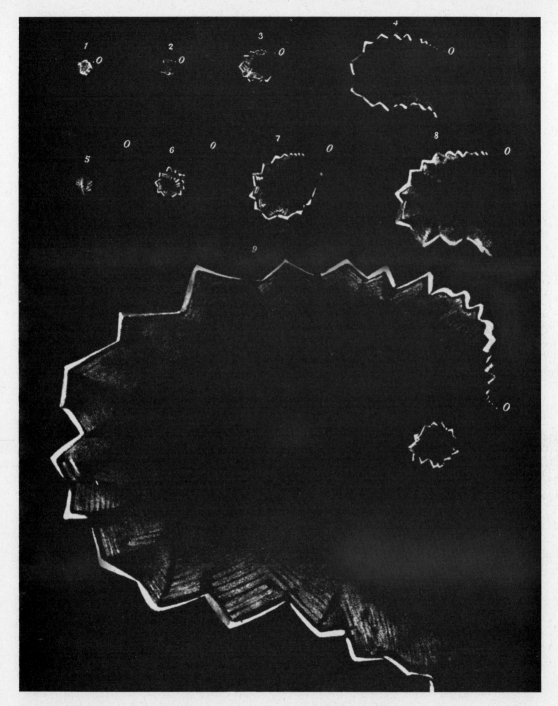

46　Persons with severe migraine headaches see the above designs, called "fortifications." Notice how these objects seem to reflect the actual operation of the visual network: they consist of lines, slits, and edges. One can almost see the eye in operation (*Scientific American*)

SPEED READING   If I were to tell you that one of the TV networks recently had a special on a high jumper who could jump 36 feet straight up, you might be charitable and think that I was led to believe this, that it certainly isn't possible. But what if I tell you—and here I speak the truth—that television specials and newspapers have given coverage to individuals who can read 50,000, 500,000, even a million words per minute, with the pages being turned so fast all you see is a blur. Now maybe you believe me—but *don't* believe what you saw or what you read because it can only be accomplished by some kind of trick. Only when the high jumper makes 36 feet will this reading speed be possible. Both are *physically* impossible. Each eye fixation can take in only 1 to 2.7 words, and each one takes about $\frac{1}{25}$ second. The *maximum* physically possible reading speed is 800 to a thousand words per minute [Taylor, 1965; Carver, 1971]. And we have an additional problem: for most people, if your reading speed is tripled, your comprehension of the material is cut to about one-third what it was to begin with [Maxwell, 1969a].

One thing people have trouble accepting is that the fixation process takes in so few words, something that we have been told can be overcome with training. Unfortunately, that is not true. One thing that leads us to believe that we are taking in more words than 2.7 per fixation is the *feeling* we get from the action of our peripheral vision [Taylor, 1965]. If you want to prove it to yourself, look at the meaningless passage below and you will get this feeling. Focus on the center "o."

yrfxidwgeasbonkutczhvpnjl

If you stared at the center "o" for a split second, you got the feeling you were seeing all the way out to the right and left [Kolers, 1972]. If you stared longer, you were cheating and your fovea began orientation reflexes toward the peripheral areas, movement that takes time. If you're skeptical, try it again; this time wait until you can actually *feel* the pull of your eyes to the right or left. As a matter of fact, one of the scientific criticisms of speed "reading" is that beyond 800 words per minute you become so conscious of your eye movements you pay more attention to them than to what you are reading [Carver, 1972].

The average acceptable *reading* rate for college students is 150 to 250 words per minute. The rate depends on the difficulty of the material; when the material becomes very difficult you actually begin to move your lips to say the words, and your reading rate has gone way down [Carver and Darby, 1971].

So, is there such a thing as speed reading, when reading means comprehension? No. Is there such a thing as speed *skimming*? Yes, and that is what so-called speed-reading courses actually teach—how to skim. The press gave considerable attention to President Kennedy because he was supposed to be able to read 1200 words per minute. We received no word from the press whether Presidents Johnson or Nixon could read, but we do know that President Kennedy had to be *skimming*, not reading.

You can skim at thousands of words per minute and pick out a few phrases to get the general idea here and there, but you cannot understand the material at these rates. Skimming is useful if you are trying to get a *very* general idea about what is contained in the material and you have to go through a considerable amount. Skimming will not work for college texts, however, unless you don't care whether you understand the content [Carver, 1971]. Skim only when you need to locate certain material or get a very general idea. If you want to learn to skim, there is probably a course at school; if not, try Maxwell (1969*b*) to learn how. For the ins and outs of skimming versus reading try looking in Carver (1971). Only as a last resort would you want to spend the 200 or so dollars involved in a speed-reading (skimming) course. Also, unless you really have a thing about gadgets, don't spend your money for so-called mechanical pacers. Experiments demonstrate that you can do as well or better using the palm of your hand as you move down the page [Berger, 1966].

The idea that speed of reading is positively correlated with comprehension or intelligence is very misleading. The reason some studies have shown this in the past is that when you have very slow readers in your group, they do have a problem understanding. Something is wrong with these particular people. Slow reading is the result, not the cause, of their difficulty [Carroll, 1964]. Some people have never learned to read properly, others have physical defects. If you are about average in your reading speed, exercise caution about speeding up your reading, because the faster you go the less you will remember [Davis, 1962]. If your reading speed is below 150 words per minute even on relatively easy material, then it probably would be worth a trip to the counseling office to see what can be provided in the way of reading assistance.

PERCEPTUAL CUES

size constancy

In the 1500s Spanish explorers found the Grand Canyon, the likes of which they had never seen before. Standing on the southern rim, they looked down more than a mile to the river flowing below; looking straight ahead, they could see the northern rim, in some places more than ten miles away. The Spanish judged the river to be about six feet across. The Indians living in the area knew better; they said it was actually about two miles wide [Hawgood, 1967].

How can we account for this discrepancy? Living a life that included few pictures, no movies or television, nothing in the way of mass media, and having migrated from areas where no Grand Canyon existed, the Spanish had few *perceptual cues* with which to make an accurate discrimination about something so complex as the width of a river that was quite

47 Perceptual cues in this photograph are interesting; turned upside down, the quonset huts become silos (*Wide World*)

distant. The Indians, on the other hand, were able to retain the concept "two miles wide" even from the top of the canyon because they had been down to the riverbed and knew that the apparent narrowness of the river was nothing more than the result of distance. The Indians' ability was related to the phenomenon called *size constancy*, a perceptual cue.

Size constancy means that with the aid of vision or of vision and touch, we estimate a fixed standard size for any given object and our brain retains this size. For example, we estimate a cigarette pack to be of a certain height and width. If we move the cigarette pack a hundred feet away from us, the pack looks a lot smaller, but we do not assume that it has shrunk. Instead, our brain decides that the pack is still about four inches high, but is farther away from us. We *can* be fooled, however, from lack of experience and false cues, as the Spanish were, or in a special case—for example, deliberate experimental manipulation. If we had a specially made cigarette pack about two inches high, and placed it a short distance from a subject in a laboratory, he would overestimate the pack's distance from him. The cigarette pack is smaller; hence, he would unconsciously reason, it must be further away. Some feel this experiment is tricking the eye-brain mechanism and that therefore these instruments are faulty. The reverse is probably true; if the brain didn't maintain perceptual constancy, our world would be a jumbled mess in which we could estimate neither size nor distance nor the position of one object relative to another. It is usually only when we deliberately trick the brain that errors are made.

depth perception   As we proceed, you might want to keep in mind that people develop certain abilities in terms of their experience, as was illustrated with the Spanish explorers. Hard as it may seem to believe, only in societies such as ours where there is a premium put on seeing pictures in depth do most people have this ability. Generally nonliterate people or those living in an entirely different culture do not see depth in drawings or photographs. For instance, the cube in Figure 6–15 is seen as flat [Deregowski, 1972].

Many early philosophers argued about the existence of an inborn ability to perceive depth (in the real world). Well, during a picnic at the Grand Canyon one day, an experimenter wondered whether her baby would crawl over the canyon, or if he already "knew better." Rather than use the real thing, she later designed what is called the *visual-cliff experiment* It utilizes a large table whose solid top is also covered with heavy glass, three sides of which have retaining walls of wood. The fourth side is left open, and the heavy glass extends many feet beyond the solid edge of the table so that it looks as if someone crawling beyond the edge will fall off (see Fig. 6–10). Babies from six to fourteen months old were placed on the table and enticed by rattles and goodies to leave the table and "fall" over the fake cliff of glass, but they would not leave it and go beyond the "edge" onto the glass [Gibson, 1960; Gregory, 1966]. Their refusal strongly suggests that, like many animals, the newborn baby has the rudimentary beginnings of depth perception, but the elaborate refinements necessary for fine discrimination come only with exposure and learning.

Depth perception is a perceptual cue; from it we get the feeling of both the distance and the solidity of objects. The 1950s were the heyday of depth perception; three-dimensional ("3–D") movies were introduced, in which the viewer wore special glasses, provided by the theater, which had different-colored plastic lens on each half of the spectacles. On the screen were projected two overlapping images, but separated slightly from each other, and differing in color. Because the glasses had colored filters, each eye received a slightly different image through the appropriately colored lens, giving the viewer a very lifelike depth effect of monsters creeping about in such exciting tales as *I Was a Teen-Age Werewolf*. The fad died out, partly because the glasses were a nuisance, but mostly because we can create a

6–10   Visual-cliff experiment

pretty effective three-dimensional depth effect with photographs just by using our other perceptual cues. And, of course, our ordinary vision is three-dimensional, so the movies were nothing new. In real life, each eye sees an object from a slightly different viewpoint, an effect called *retinal disparity.**

The bringing together of the images presented to each eye, to create the three-dimensional effect and a feeling of depth, is called *stereoscopic vision*

48–49   A stereopticon viewer and the two images used to create an illusion of three-dimensionality. Notice the lady's finger lines up at different points in the background (*Bettmann Archive*)

and provides for the sense of sight essentially the same effect that stereophonic sound does for hearing. The stereoscope, a forerunner of 3–D movies, was a device invented in 1833 to study this phenomenon. It presented two pictures separately to the two eyes, the pictures having been constructed by a pair of cameras separated a distance equal to that between our eyes. But man is sometimes a rather perverse creature. Dr. Richard L. Gregory, author of an excellent book, *Eye and the Brain,* points out:

> The stereoscope was a favourite Victorian toy, but unfortunately photographic subjects came to be chosen which, while ideally suited technically, met with such opposition that it was banned from the Victorian drawing room—a blow from which it has never recovered. [Gregory, 1966, p. 52]

accommodation   Another perceptual cue is called *accommodation*. The lens of our eye adjusts sharpness of focus for nearby and faraway objects by changing its shape from narrow and flat to elongated and wide (viewing the lens from the side).† As we follow an object in motion, for example, we have to alter accommodation to fit distance; it is assumed that as we do so, the visual center is informed of the shape of the lens, and this information provides a clue to its relative distance [Troelstra et al., 1964].

Furthermore, the eyes move inward toward the nose in order to see objects nearby, and they straighten out to see distant objects. This movement is called *convergence*, meaning that the eyes come together (converge) on a given point. The position of the eyes presumably transmits neural information to the brain, telling it how far away the object is.

---

* There is a disparity (difference) between the images seen.
† The lens is accommodating or fitting itself to the distance of the object for focus.

visual texture   *Visual texture* is a cue we don't often think about, but it plays an important part in estimating size and distance. The best example of visual texture is a gravel road. The part of the road nearest to us is seen as a conglomerate of separate pieces of gravel. As the road gets more distant, the gravel blends together more and more until we cannot tell if we are looking at a gravel or a paved road because the separate pieces are impossible to detect. Thus by the difference or change in texture as we see it, we determine distance and size.

other perceptual cues   A great many psychological factors are involved in perception, in the sense that we tend to see things in a certain way because we interpret how they *should* be seen. An example is the cue of *similarity*, in which we group like things together. In Figure 6–11a you will see three *squares*, one of "white" circles and two of "dark" circles. You won't see any squares consisting of two white and two dark circles (Fig. 6–11b) because you keep the circles separated on the basis of which are more alike. Moreover, you tend to see squares that are even more pronounced if four circles are added to one of the sets, as in Figure 6–12a.

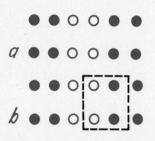

6-11   Similarity

You probably see Figure 6–12a as a square, even though it isn't. The eye has a tendency to fill in details, to form a whole and to see pictures that are made up of nothing but dots, as in newspaper photographs. Thus, the square in Figure 6–12a illustrates this integrating principle, called *closure*, which means we tend to close partial figures until they are complete. Figure 6–12b also illustrates closure.

One further comment on perceptual cues. Basic rules used by artists to get perceptual integration include having items in *close physical proximity*, the eye thinks they belong together [McKendry, 1963]. This rule is used in Figure 6–12a, but not in Figure 6–13.

PERCEPTION AND MISPERCEPTION

visual illusions   The author feels a tremendous kinship of bravery with Charles Lindbergh, who made the historic nonstop flight to Paris in a ship put together with sophisticated baling wire and lacking any glass installed in the open spaces at the sides. As Lindbergh reached the 3500 mile non-stop mark, having flown through a thousand miles of sleet and snow in his semiopen cockpit,

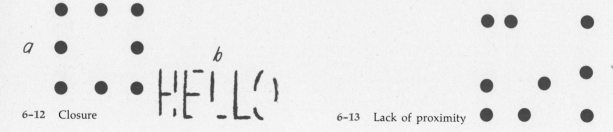

6-12   Closure

6-13   Lack of proximity

50 The "Leaning Tower" of Pisa provides (unintentionally) the sensation of being in a tilted room (*Bettmann Archive*)

he took his first bite of food in 30 hours. It was part of a sandwich, which he tried to get down by drinking water with it [Ross, 1968].

On a two-hour cross-country flying lesson, I almost choked on a hamburger after an hour of constant realization that I was 4,000 feet off the ground. My career was not quite as glorious as Lindbergh's. It terminated one day when the flight instructor told me to shut my eyes and guess what position the plane was in. I thought it was at a slight angle; actually, it was nearly upside down.

This type of misperception is common and occurs frequently when one flies through clouds without flight instruments because there is no visual reference point. Our most accurate perceptual mechanism, and the one that dominates the other senses, is vision, and when it gives false cues, or what are sometimes called illusions, we are in trouble.

Many carnivals and amusement parks have what they call rooms of mystery. Most of us have been in one at some time or another. When you walk through this room, you seem to be walking at about a twenty-degree angle, leaning backward. The guide attributes this peculiarity to some mysterious force of the universe resulting from magnetic pull in that particular area of the country. Actually, if you look at Figure 6–14 you will see the unique construction of the room and why we get the sensation we do. We are actually standing straight up and down, but the room is built on

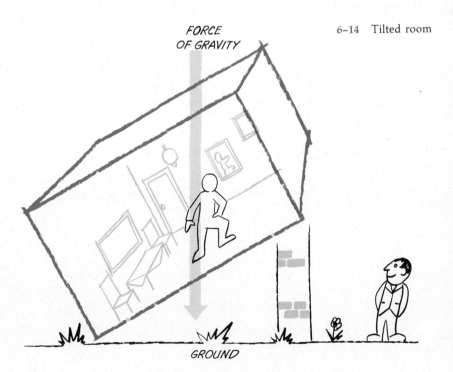

FORCE OF GRAVITY

6–14 Tilted room

GROUND

an angle, and our sense of *vision* notes that the room and its objects are at an angle to us. Therefore, since visually the room does not fit our erect position, our whole body feels that it is on an angle. The eye, deceived, sends messages to the brain that the body is in a normal room; if the room is normal, we must be standing at an angle, leaning backward [Leibowitz, 1965]. This, then, is an illusion, and an illusion is considered a misperception. You obviously *are* on an angle as you can see in Figure 6–14, but it is not necessary to be falling all over the place. When you walk up the ramp to get to the top of a sports stadium everyone is not stumbling around. The Six Flags Over Somewhere chain and some other amusement areas have these rooms. Try going through with a friend (you trust) and *keep your eyes closed.* Notice how simple it is to get through the room under these conditions.

Psychologists have long had an attraction for illusions, probably 80 percent for scientific reasons and 20 percent because it is enjoyable to fool people. One of the most famous illusions is called the *Necker cube* (see Fig. 6–15). As you watch the cube, it will continuously reverse its direction, appearing first one way and then the other. A traditional explanation for such reversals, and one that is still possible, is that the central nervous system, while responding to this figure, becomes fatigued with one position and alternates to another. The fatigue hypothesis has been used to explain why, given two alternatives, we vacillate between them [Orbach, 1963; Attneave, 1971]. One scientist suggests what might be a better interpretation of why we see this reversal: our eye is *in reality* given two perceptions at the same time, *either* one of which can be correct. Our visual mechanism, taking no chances, alternates between them. Some pretty convincing evidence supports this hypothesis: if a person is given an opportunity to touch a *physical* model of the Necker cube, visual reversals are reduced to a minimum, suggesting that the eye is thereby satisfied that what it is seeing is one way or the other [Shopland, 1964].

The evidence that we misperceive or misjudge physical phenomena when they are ambiguous can be illustrated clearly by a short discussion of a weight-lifting experiment. In this experiment, small colored weights (not barbells) are lifted between the thumb and forefinger, and comparisons are made with a standard weight. Subjects first must learn a color code for the weights: blue = light, red = heavy. Each weight is compared with the medium-weight standard and judged to be lighter or heavier. In the middle range, close to the actual weight of the standard, frequently blue weights were judged lighter and red weights heavier when no such difference existed. Hence, perceptual judgment is most subject to misperception and incorrect interpretation when an ambiguous stimulus is presented. In this case, the ambiguity lay in the fact that some of the weights were so close to the standard that it was difficult to discriminate, and color took over at that

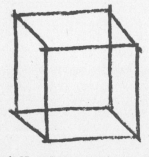

6–15   Necker cube

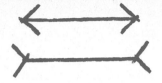

6-16   Müller-Lyer illusion

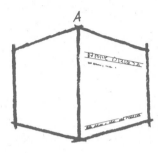

6-17   Another Müller-Lyer illusion

point. The situation is not dissimilar to the one in which touching a Necker cube helped to resolve ambiguity one way or the other, only in this case the ambiguity was resolved by calling on the "psychological" assumption that blue is light and red heavy [Bevan and Pritchard, 1964].

Another illusion is shown in Figure 6-16. This is called the ***Müller-Lyer illusion***. The two lines shown in the figure are the same length, yet the "arrowhead" line looks shorter. The traditional explanation for this misperception is that the arrowheads in one figure draw the individual's attention inward, and the arrow feathers in the other draw it outward, giving the illusion that one line is longer than the other. This makes some common sense, but seems to be an incorrect explanation; the idea that the arrowhead pulls the eye in and that this movement of the eye is responsible for the illusion has been fairly well discounted. One experiment along these lines shrunk the image so that it could be projected directly onto the foveal area, thus requiring no movement; another time, the speed of exposure to the eye was so rapid that it did not allow time for eye movement. In both cases, the illusion remained [Bolles, 1969].

Gregory views the illusion from a different viewpoint, and one that again makes considerable sense. Look at the drawing of the books in Figure 6-17. Notice that the Müller-Lyer illusion is present, but this time a commonly seen object is used. As Gregory notes, figure A in reality would have the corner of the book closer to us than figure B. Although both lines (A and B) are actually the same length, and the brain recognizes this fact, it doesn't "make sense" in terms of our everyday perception. For line B, which is farther away in Figure 6-17, as far as the brain is concerned, to be the same length as line A, it must in real life be longer. It isn't longer—but if the drawing were real, and the lines were to appear to be the same length in reality, one of the lines *would have to be longer*. The brain must make it so for the perception to make sense [Gregory, 1968]. Hence, the situation becomes not a misperception so much as an attempt by the brain to conform to and interpret appropriately what we commonly see.

Essentially the same thing occurs when we see a familiar object from a distance. A house seen from an airplane window looks like a miniature house; however, the eye compensates for the apparent change in size; rather than seeing a tiny house, we perceive it as a normal-sized house seen from a distance. You may notice that this mechanism is essentially the same one mentioned under the heading "size constancy."

useful illusions   Psychological factors and the central nervous system influence our perceptions, and this influence results in perceptual interpretation that can be useful in organizing our world. All illusions probably are helpful in *normal* life situations. Some are notably so, however. One such helpful illusion is the *Ponzo illusion* (Fig. 6-18); it assists us in depth perception. The uppermost

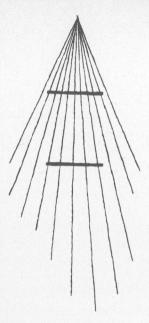

6-18 Ponzo illusion

6-19 Another Ponzo illusion

line looks longer than the lower line, doesn't it? Of course, you are wrong.*
They are the same length. Assume the converging lines represent a highway
or railroad bed, both of which normally get narrower as distance increases,
and we have placed two logs (rectangles) some distance apart (Fig. 6–19).
Since we know that the road is not actually getting smaller (size constancy)
in real life, then the uppermost log must actually be larger because it fills
up as much space in the picture of the road. Hence, our eye judges the
upper line as longer. Strictly speaking, our eye has interpreted correctly if
it were faced with the actual problem, although we have created an artificial
situation for it to cope with.

Another useful illusion, the illusion of movement, requires some
background material if we are to understand completely the issues at hand.
Few controversies have raged as vehemently as the one concerning whether
our perceptions are inherited or learned (we discuss this problem on and
off throughout the book). The issue is resolved today only by compromise:
most psychologists feel that perception is a combination of the two, learning
and inheritance. In any case, we might go back a few years to obtain some
perspective not only on perception, but also on the kinds of arguments and
trends that psychology followed in the development of these arguments.

When man came under scrutiny following Darwin's presentation
of the theory of evolution, psychology began to examine him in the laboratory, using the same techniques exploited by physicists and chemists who
in the late 1800s and early 1900s were making great progress in understanding the physical world. In chemistry most everything was thought to
be divided into combinations of various elements; for example, water is a
combination of hydrogen and oxygen. Psychologists in the laboratory gave
serious thought to the possibility that even that complex organism *man* was
so constructed; that is, man's perception, for example, is a combined series
of experiences which, added together, give a totality or a unity in the same
sense that hydrogen and oxygen give a totality of water. Each experience
is learned and then combined. Our perception of a house is a combination
of the learned perceptions of brick, shingle, wood, triangles, squares, and
so on.

The reverse was also true: if individuals were properly trained to
describe their experiences, it was thought, they could break them down into
elements. In this case, looking at a house objectively one might say that
it consisted of brick, shingle, wood, and so on. Early psychologists hypothesized that, knowing the core sensations and parts of perception, we could
eventually elaborate on this and predict man's feelings and behaviors just
as today the path, altitude, and speed of a spaceship can be plotted if we
know the thrust of launching, atmospheric conditions, and the like.

*This is an example of the triumph psychologists feel in using illusions to fool
people.

51a–c The neon sign on the Horse's Tail Tavern demonstrates the phi phenomenon (*Gabriele Wunderlich*)

Criticism was quick to arise from a group of psychologists in Germany who called themselves *Gestaltists*. They made the point that water is something more than hydrogen and oxygen; that is, once hydrogen and oxygen have combined, nature has produced a third substance, water, which is completely different from either hydrogen or oxygen. To use the house analogy, they said that a person does not see a collection of bricks with mortar and shingles, but instead he sees a *whole* unit, a house; and unless he is a building contractor, he never considers a house as a group of parts put together.

The word *Gestalt*, roughly translated from the German, means a "whole," something entire, something complete (as opposed to something in parts). In the area of perception the Gestaltists emphasized that we see whole things *already* unified, not a bunch of parts. We have already mentioned a Gestalt arrangement in the dots shown in Figure 6–11A. The three sets are seen as three complete units, not as separate dots. Maintaining that we come into the world *preprogrammed* to see things in units, the Gestaltists came up with some striking evidence for their theory, especially in terms of our illusion of movement. On the marquee of some old movie houses is a band of lights that gives the impression that the light starts at one end and moves along until it reaches the other end of the marquee. Another example can also be seen on the local drycleaner's storefront, where a band of lights forms an arrow, moves from the bottom of the sign up to the arrowhead, and then starts over.

The point that the Gestaltists stressed about this phenomenon is that we see an *inevitable* movement, and that we are born with this ability. We cannot break the movement down into separate lights going on and off; instead, we see a whole unit in movement. This is called the *phi* (Greek for "movement") *phenomenon*. Closely akin to it is the motion picture. As you know, a movie is nothing more than a series of still shots rapidly flashed on the screen at the proper rate so that we cannot avoid seeing movement.

One conclusion to be derived from this discussion is that the Gestaltists were correct in saying that many (but not all) of our perceptions and illusions are inevitable, that they seem to organize on their own without our help, and are useful for structuring our world. They especially emphasize the phi phenomenon and object, size and brightness constancies as proof of their point of view.

SUMMARY

Perception is a term that refers to the use of the sensory mechanisms for the purpose of interpreting and understanding our environment. The most important perceptual mechanism in human beings is vision, and the visual apparatus is used to select distinctive features from objects around us. These distinctive features are then integrated through the neural network, especially the retina, ganglion cells, and occipital lobe.

The eye receives its stimulation through light waves, which vary both in frequency and in wavelength. These variations, in combination with the molecular structure of various objects, provide the coloring we see. The receptors for light waves are rods and cones. Rods are used primarily for night vision and are responsive at the more-purple end of the spectrum of colors. Cones are for day vision and respond at the redder end of the color spectrum. In both cases, vision seems to come about from an electrical-chemical-molecular change in the visual network, especially in the rods and cones themselves. Apparently, most colors we see are a mixture of red, green, and blue, but the actual mechanism involved is poorly understood.

The eye itself operates as a scanning device, moving along and back and forth over the object and detecting important pieces of information about its makeup. The eye does not reproduce images in the same way a camera does, even though the objects seen are upside down on the retina.

Vision depends heavily on movement of the eye, or movement of the object in relation to the eye. The importance of this movement is basic to the orientation reflex, in which the eye receives signals from objects in the periphery of vision and swings the fovea toward that object. The fovea is the most heavily concentrated cone area and provides maximum sharpness of vision.

Information in the form of brightness-dimness, contour-contrast, lines, slits, edges, and so forth is processed by the higher centers of the occipital lobe into a coded representation of the environment. The processing starts at the photosensitive receptors of the retina, runs through the retinal ganglion cells, and then through the thalamus to various levels of the visual portion of the cortex.

The organization of our world relies heavily on perceptual cues, which are techniques the eye and brain have for judging the nature of the object seen. We judge distance and size by the mechanism of size constancy; we obtain a feeling of the solidity of objects, and to some extent their distance, by using our depth perception. Depth perception is aided by convergence of the eyes onto the object and by the accommodation of the lens for distance from us. Retinal disparity—each eye seeing a slightly disparate object—also provides depth and distance cues.

Illusions result from tricks played on the eye, although the eye is apparently following "logical" procedures that are beneficial in everyday life. Many misperceptions result from ambiguous objects like the Necker cube; other illusions are based on logical judgment by the eye and brain, but result from a form of trickery in the experiment or the drawing—for example, the Müller-Lyer illusion.

Considerable controversy has raged about whether we are natively endowed with certain perceptual mechanisms or whether we learn them. The visual-cliff experiment seems to demonstrate that at least some of our abilities are inborn. The Gestalt experiments, especially those demonstrating the organizing properties of the brain in producing inevitable movement, as in the case of the phi phenomenon, seem to bear out the fact that we are equipped with at least some basics of perception.

CHAPTER SEVEN
PERCEPTION AND PSYCHOLOGY

Most of the matters we discussed in Chapter 6 were closely related to the physical mechanisms of the eye itself. But the influence of what might be called *psychological perception* should not be discounted. Personality and environmental factors influence what is perceived almost as much as the visual network itself. Remember that what we "see" is partly in us, partly "out there." We guide our eyes to specific features of what we perceive and this guidance influences the end result (Gyr, 1972). The present, rather brief chapter is designed to fill in the gap between mechanical perception and very complex psychological behaviors.

PSYCHOLOGICAL PERCEPTION

To give an illustration of what we are talking about, a vast difference exists between perceiving a Necker cube and perceiving the sun as God. The latter event may or may not be more complex from the viewpoint of nerve cells operating, but it certainly contains factors not clearly detectable from examination of the eye and occipital lobe alone.

To a policeman's utter frustration, witnesses' descriptions of a holdup man vary from short and fat to tall and lean, with as many variations as witnesses. These descriptions probably differ as a function of the life patterns of each individual witness and are to some extent colored by certain types of characters we don't like. Our descriptions frequently fit a "bad guy" rather than the real person. Further, under extreme stress, perception is faulty, and witnesses are known to fill in the details "as they think they should be or as they want them to be" [Marshall, 1969]. An old saying points out that we see what we want to see; this is true, if one adds that we sometimes see what we are psychologically prepared for.

The Grand Canyon example was one type of misperception. A more complex one, psychologically, occurred in the 1500s when the explorer Coronado was led to the famous "Seven Cities of Gold" by an over-enthusiastic scout who had seen some mud puebloes glimmering in the distance during a sunset and thought he had discovered a city made entirely of gold [Hawgood, 1967]. He was obviously prepared to see wonders in this new world.

The implications here become quite profound and at times disastrous. I recently attended a trial in which a man was convicted of armed robbery. The defendant, who had no identifying characteristics such as scars or deformities, was "identified" twenty-four hours *after* the crime as he walked down the street in a blue coat "somewhat similar" to the one worn by the hold-up man. There was no physical evidence this was the man. It is likely the blue coat triggered a perceptual anticipation that the face that goes with the coat must be the same one as that of the robber. There is currently not enough information in this area of psychology, but it is an extremely important one. As attorney F. Lee Bailey points out, the greatest single cause of wrongful convictions is witness identification [Bailey, 1971]. In fact, with time and the decreasing ability to recall, we tend to reconstruct our memories in terms of our surroundings [Summers and Fleming, 1971]. This would suggest that by the time a trial comes up, witnesses are even more convinced of their identification because they are now seeing the defendant in the context of having been arrested, arraigned, and tried. Now it seems even more likely this is the guilty man.

We are usually not aware of subtle psychological effects upon our perceptions. One experimenter had individuals arrange sets of three numbers so that each number was spaced "an equal distance apart." For example, they were to arrange cards containing the numbers 1, 8, 9 and 1, 2, 9. Subjects unwittingly placed cards 1–2 and 8–9 closer together and cards 2–9 and 1–8 farther apart, apparently because 2, for instance, is numerically further away from 9 than it is from 1 [Teft, 1964]. This study is similar to the colored-weights experiment discussed earlier—only in the case of the numbers, a very subtle and unexpected psychological interpretation seems to be involved. Abstract distance is turned into physical distance.

psychological clues The abstract subtleties of perception are remarkable to say the least. Persons move from a very limited set of clues to arrive at very broad assumptions about others. Males inaccurately raise the hemline a couple inches in describing a particular girl wearing makeup and no glasses. In this controlled experiment the same girl with no makeup and wearing glasses is seen as having a hemline that is down two inches further than it actually is. If the girl is with makeup *and* glasses she is seen as serious and shy. Or, in another case, take off the glasses and she becomes "the sort of person with whom one would like to be seen but with whom one would hate to live." Put on glasses and leave on the makeup and the poor girl is now "antireligious." These broad, sweeping generalizations are even more remarkable when the subjects are interviewed after the experiment and you find out that they are not aware of the fact that the *only* thing being changed is makeup and/or glasses [Hamid, 1972]. Wearing apparel, in fact, is far more important than facial characteristics in judgments made about individuals [Hamid, 1968]. In a way, then, a case can be made for using school uniforms because unwarranted evaluations of others are reduced to a minimum since everyone looks approximately the same [Hamid, 1969].

Likewise, superficial characteristics make a difference in whether people will help you. In a study using "stranded motorists" (stooges), experimenters found that the more similar the motorist is in appearance to the person driving by, the more likely the latter is to stop and offer assistance. Sailors, for example, will stop more often for short-haired individuals than for long-haired ones. Long-hairs will stop more often for other long-haired persons than for short-haired ones* [Graf and Riddell, 1972].

Dramatic alterations of perception resulted from lack of food in the hunger studies reported in Chapter 4. Of the same type but of greater subtlety is a classic study in which subjects were to estimate the size of coins—pennies, nickles, dimes, and so on. The subjects were divided into two groups, the first containing people who were from poor homes and the second a group of rich children. The results are interesting. The poor children consistently overestimated the size of the coins, from which we might infer that money had much greater value (and hence size) for the poor children [Bruner and Goodman, 1947].

The reverse of this study is also intriguing—a case in which a person does *not* see something because for some reason he doesn't want to see it. Studies in this area use an apparatus called by one of those impressive and almost unpronounceable words, *tachistoscope*. A tachistoscope is a mechanical device, rather like a slide viewer, that is used for very brief and rapid exposure of words, pictures, or symbols. The timing can be set so that the picture is just visible for a split second and then gone, something many of us hope for when a neighbor invites us over to see the slides of his recent trip: John and Agnes in front of the Sphinx, John and Agnes hanging from the Eiffel Tower, etc. In any case, the tachistoscope has been used to expose subjects to so-called dirty words, of which no example can be given here except "----" and "------------." The outcome of these studies is interesting.† In some cases subjects saw and reported words that were similar in sound or spelling to the exposed word, but that were *socially acceptable*. In other studies some people did not even see the word, even though it was left visible for the same exposure time in which they could clearly see words that were acceptable [Carpenter et al., 1956]. We are dealing here with what is called *perceptual defense*, meaning that we often do not respond to what we don't want to see.

Probably this last sentence should be phrased differently. It is better to say that we are not *aware* of having seen a certain picture or word. Techniques of measuring electrical potentials (brain waves) have become sophisticated enough that the experimenter is able to determine when the brain is responding to certain objects presented to the eye by following the pattern and degree of cerebral electrical response. The tachistoscope, of course, can be used to flash something on the screen so rapidly that no one

---

*Unless you belong to the auto club, statistically you will fare better on your trip the shorter your hair.

†First, however, didn't you fill in the blanks mentally? Our perceptual apparatus desires completion (Gestalt psychology). Hence, censors merely call attention to what they are trying to get you to ignore.

can see anything at all—at least they don't think they saw it! These experiments have demonstrated that within the time span of sixteen hundredths of a second the brain can discriminate two different objects. Some experimenters have suggested this intriguing hypothesis: in the first step (which occurs so rapidly that we can hardly conceive of such a brief amount of time), the brain accepts or rejects certain objects; second, once this decision has been made, more complete eye fixation is sent either to the object, accepting it, or away from it, rejecting it. It was believed for years that we accepted all we saw and then filtered it out later if we didn't like it, but this assumption seems to be incorrect. The acceptance or rejection is instantaneous [Shevrin, 1969].

context In an earlier discussion on the eye and perception an illustration showed how dots or circles are seen together to form squares (Chapter 6). This process can occur in an even more elaborate fashion; in fact, it has led to such expressions as, "Tell me a man's friends, and I'll know him." Criminologists, for instance, have pointed out many times that policemen have a tendency to pick up long-haired men wearing black leather jackets with skull and crossbones or some such on the back just on "suspicion." Policemen share the common tendency to group *people* together as the result of *similar characteristics* whether or not the person's beliefs are actually similar to those of the "group" he resembles. In one of our many wars, this time with Japan, Japanese *Americans* residing in California were horribly mistreated and locked up in internment camps just because they looked like part of the group thought of as "enemy." The discussion of nazism later in this book well illustrates the lengths to which such supposed identification of like individuals can go.

Our perceptual mechanism assesses situations in *context*, too. In a string of items—*A, B, C, D, E,* for example—we would judge *C* by *A, B, D,* and *E* since the latter four surround or frame it. For instance, a bright red object is much more noticeable in a drab room than in a colorful room. Another example: we Americans, it is often said, are more preoccupied with our health than any other national group because we are surrounded by material goodies and we demand the same degree of improved technology for our bodies as for our possessions. Conversely, in countries less oriented to luxury, only a major illness is cause to see a physician.

Perception of the importance of a certain need, then, is taken in context. In a recent study, subjects were asked to judge the morality-immorality of certain actions. One group of subjects was given a list that contained items like "poisoning a neighbor's dog whose barking bothers you" and "habitually borrowing small sums of money from friends and failing to return them," mixed with mild actions like "playing poker on Sunday" and "fishing without a license." Another group was given the same set of items—for example, the poisoning and borrowing actions—only for this group these items were imbedded in a list of rather extreme actions: "putting your deformed child in the circus," "testifying falsely against someone for pay," and so forth. Context made a considerable difference. When the moderate items were mixed with the extreme items, the moderate set was judged considerably less immoral than when these same moderate items were mixed with mild items. In a subtle psychological fashion the subjects had contrasted the moderate items with the surrounding "atmosphere" and made judgments relative to them even though the subjects were instructed to judge each item on its own merit [Parducci, 1968]. Even though context has an effect on how we judge various items, it does not seem to notably affect how we judge a person's overall "morality." Subjects who are to judge the morality of an individual are unable to overlook one evil act even if it is embedded in a group with three good acts. Thus, judgments of a person who has supposedly prevented a suicide, rescued a family from a burning house, and donated a kidney has an overall morality rating that is low if he put razor blades in halloween apples. This situation follows the general laws of perception; can we *ever* avoid seeing the one unusual or unexpected thing? It would seem not at the present time [Birnbaum, 1972*a*, 1972*b*, 1972*c*]. The situation has broad social implications: can we never forgive the child molester no matter what else he has done? Are there certain crimes which are so psychologically overwhelming to us that we cannot forget them no matter what?

color Before moving on it might be worthwhile exploring briefly the world of art and perception. A number of artists are frustrated at the tremendous amount of current stress on color photography. Black-and-white photos or movies are generally better media for conveying a *message*. The reason for this is that black-and-white photos are not real in the sense that we do not see the world in this way—therefore, the black-and-white technique conveys a message to the receiver rather than just a faithful reproduction of a real-life color scene. Frequently when you use color in movies some of the symbolism disappears because there is so little "work" required on the part of the observer—he remains passive, he does not interpret [Gombrich, 1972].

This does not mean that color lacks psychological implications, since artists frequently use color for mood; their pictures, though, are typically abstract under these conditions. In our society there are clear-cut implications from the use of certain colors. Red is a highly stimulating color suggesting activity and assertiveness. Blue, on the other hand, is just the opposite, creating a mood of calm, tranquility, and inner peace [Gerard, 1972; Aaronson, 1972]. Other colors are a little more ambiguous in the type of response they create—but they do generate emotions. Yellow creates a strong emotional response—sometimes creating a mystical feeling or a feeling of explosion, even a subjective increase in the humidity and heat—all depending on who is viewing the color [Aaronson, 1972]. The implications are rather important: for example, red rooms or decoration in coronary units of a regular hospital or on the ward in a mental hospital containing agitated patients would be highly inappropriate.

PROBABILITY, CHANCE, AND ODDS

The topics of probability, chance, and odds may seem strange right in the middle of a discussion of perception. But since we are about to enter the exotic world of extrasensory perception (ESP), the subjects become quite appropriate. Actually, almost all the studies mentioned in this book are based on mathematical measures (statistics) that relate to probability and chance, but the topic is mentioned here for one major reason: many readers freeze up, as it were, at the minor complexities of these statistics, so I have chosen to discuss them when they will seem quite useful in reference to an interesting subject.

The basic issue in extrasensory perception is whether individuals even have such power. To take an example of how statistics might help, suppose that I were to predict that my next flip of the coin would be heads, and indeed it was. Would you then agree that I had special powers of prediction? Hardly—but why not? Simply because my prediction could have come true just by chance. In other words, my single prediction had a fifty-fifty chance of being right. I could have predicted tails and been correct; that is, I could have been correct just by chance.

No one knows what chance is; we do, however, assume that certain fixed laws operate in the universe and influence, for example, the roll of dice. In addition to these laws, there is chance itself, the unknown factors influencing the roll, which might be the tilt of the floor, the particles in the air, the angle of my hand, and so on. Even though the mechanical laws operate, unknown or chance factors constantly enter into any occurrence [Pierce, 1962]. So at any given time almost anything could occur just by chance maybe once, maybe even twice, or possibly a few more times. But suppose I could correctly predict the roll of dice 99 percent of the time for a thousand throws. I assume you would then give me the credit I deserve for my special abilities. Why? Because something other than chance must be operating.

The same is true with a subject like extrasensory perception, or even with the problem of finding that a person is a delinquent and comes from a broken home. I might be able to guess a card someone was holding just by chance alone. Or the delinquent may come from a broken home just by chance, and there might be no relationship between the home and his later behavior. We need a statistic that will determine just how farfetched it is to assume that chance is operating. If, for example, we were to apply a statistic to my 99-percent-correct predictions of dice rolls, we would find that the idea that chance alone is working *this often* is quite remote. In fact, you can be almost certain that something other than chance is operating, even if it is nothing more than my having loaded the dice. How far the results of a given study are removed from chance will be reported numerically in the same fashion as other statistics are. We will get to this in a moment, but first it might be worthwhile to start the discussion all over again with another example so that you are certain you follow what is going on, because almost all scientific studies are reported in terms of probability and chance.

One universal fact about human beings is that not everyone behaves in the same way. How, then, is it possible to make any statements regarding human behavior? We have already discussed correlation, but other statistical methods also give information about experimental findings. Suppose, for example, that we were to take the weights of a group of men found loitering on the corner somewhere and noted them to be 150, 165, 140, 160, and 325. Immediately we are struck by the highly deviant weight of 325, something expected very rarely. Also, we begin to speculate on how this man became so heavy. Maybe a glandular dysfunction, maybe overeating. No one, however, tries to speculate on how a man comes to weigh 140 or 160 pounds. There's nothing unusual about it.

Reverse the situation. An experimenter thinks he has found a drug that induces weight increase. He administers it to a group of four males and then examines them ten years later; he finds that their weights are 140, 150, 180, and 175. Assuming that their physiques correspond roughly to these weights, he has a very ineffective drug for increasing weight. Using another drug, he finds ten years later that his subjects weigh 325, 298, 310, and 170. These heavy weights are extremely rare. Because of this rarity, he can entertain the hypothesis that his drug induces weight gain. Just by chance he might get one unusual weight, but it is highly unlikely that just by chance he would obtain three out of four strikingly deviant weights. In other words, just by chance alone this event would be remote. The scientist is trying to demonstrate that the results he gets would be highly improbable if just chance was the only factor operating.

Psychological experiments, including social studies, ESP experiments, intelligence testing, predictions of group behavior, and so on, never produce 100 percent rare events, just as the last study above did not: 170 is not an unusual weight. On the other hand, the psychologist is looking for results that approach statistical rarity, and we will briefly cover this subject before proceeding in this chapter. The best place to start is with coin tossing.

In coin tossing, using a fairly new and untampered-with coin, the *probability* or odds that you will get either heads or tails is, in layman's terminology, 50:50 (in statistical language, $p = .50$).* In other words, *in theory* every 100 tosses of a coin should yield 50 heads and 50 tails. In actuality,

52   After providing basketball star Bill Russell with some "tips" on playing pool, Flip Wilson takes advantage of his friend's deviant height to sell elevator shoes to the unsuspecting (*National Broadcasting Company*)

---

*p stands for "probability."

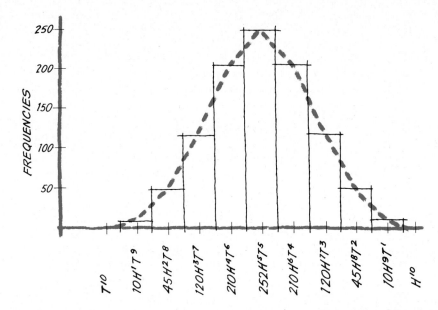

FREQUENCIES

250 —
200 —
150 —
100 —
50 —

$7H^{10}$ $10H^1T^9$ $45H^2T^8$ $120H^3T^7$ $210H^4T^6$ $252H^5T^5$ $210H^6T^4$ $120H^7T^3$ $45H^8T^2$ $10H^9T^1$ H^{10}

7-1 Normal frequency distribution in coin tossing†

for any given set of 100 coin tossings you might get 40 heads, 60 tails; 55 heads, 45 tails; etc. Chance (unknown or accidental) factors are operating to give slight variations in the number of heads or tails. The nature of these chance factors is unspecified, but they are assumed *not* to operate in a consistent fashion; in other words, they temporarily influence the appearance of heads a few more times or tails a few more times, eventually canceling one another out to result in figures close to 50:50.

If you have any money riding on the flips and they come up 20 tails and 80 heads, you would investigate the coin immediately on the grounds that something other than chance is operating—for example, a weighted coin. The discrepancy is too far removed from chance.

This is exactly what an experimenter does: he looks for results that are very remote from chance, just as it is very remote that 20 tails and 80 heads would occur merely from chance. (Note that it *is* physically possible for this to happen, but so rare as to be considered improbable.) It is more logical to search for a reason—a loaded coin—than to assume chance.

It is interesting to see what happens if you toss ten different coins 1,024 times.* First of all, even with so many coins the law of probability will still work. We could expect 5 heads and 5 tails from the ten coins more often than any other combination; next most probable would be 4 heads and 6 tails or 6 heads and 4 tails. Something to be expected *very* rarely would be 10 tails or 10 heads. Figure 7–1 shows a curve that quite closely

---

*You may wonder why the figure is 1,024 rather than 1,000. So do I.

†Henry E. Garrett, *Statistics In Psychology and Education*, 6th ed. (New York: David McKay Co., 1966). Reproduced by permission.

represents the results obtained from throwing a group of ten coins 1,024 times. You will note that a toss of 10 heads or 10 tails comes up only once in 1,024 tosses. The odds are 1,024 to 1 of getting either 10 heads or 10 tails.

Figure 7–1 looks suspiciously familiar. It is the normal curve you saw in Chapter 2. Again, as in Chapter 2, we can mark off the percentage of occurrences on the curve (Fig. 7–2). Take the combination of 10 heads. The point on the curve where it falls (arrow) is beyond the 99-percent level of the curve, actually a little beyond the 99.9-percent point, meaning that over 99.9 percent of all other combinations fall below this point on the curve. Looked at another way, 10 heads leaves only .1 percent (one-tenth of 1 percent) of the curve.

The whole curve, 100 percent, is going to equal 1.00 when the percentage is changed to a decimal (1.00). To find out how much of the curve representing 10 heads is left, we change 99.9 percent to .999 and subtract it from 1.00(0) and .001 is the remainder. This figure as a fraction is $\frac{1}{1000}$ and means that one time in one thousand (actually, in our case, $\frac{1}{1024}$) could this occur by chance alone. Thus it is *extremely* rare.

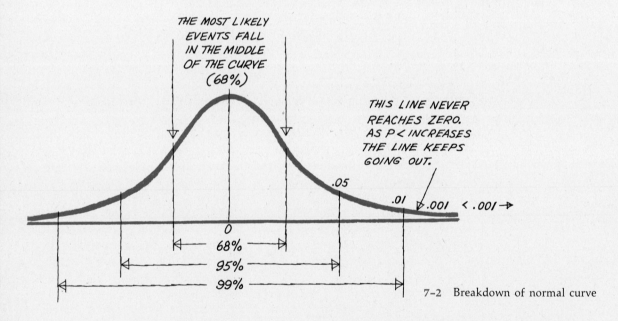

7–2   Breakdown of normal curve

In the sciences, even though we know that events *could* conceivably occur with a *p* (probability) of .001 and still be chance, such an event is so rare that the scientist assumes that the result is more likely caused by the independent variable he is using. Thus, if a scientist finds that statistics demonstrate that what he found in his study could occur only once in a thousand times just by chance alone, he assumes that chance is not the important factor, but that his independent variable is. For example, he might use a hypodermic needle treated with a special medication (independent variable) designed to kill pain. If sticking the treated needle into subjects prevents pain (dependent variable) in so many people that this painless reaction could occur *by chance* only once in a thousand times, he assumes that the medicine is working, not that he has witnessed a freak, chance event.

A final hypothetical experiment. By statistical methods, an experimenter determines the mean (average) heart rate expected for the population as a whole between the ages of twenty-five and thirty. The figure might be something like 75 beats per minute. This number could be set in the normal curve (Fig. 7–3). The experimenter then tries out a set of fear-producing sounds on fifty subjects. He assumes that a more rapid heart rate

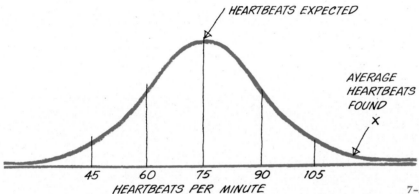

7–3   Effect of fear on heart rate

suggests fear. He averages all fifty scores together and finds for the group a mean (average) heart rate of 40 beats more than the average. This point appears at the letter *X* in Figure 7–3. He concludes that his sounds are responsible for this rare situation. The *X* appears at the 99-percent point in the curve; this is called the .01 ("point-oh-one") level, meaning that 1 out of 100 times such a finding could occur by chance. Put another way, only 1 heart rate in 100 would appear this high on the curve.

The .001, .01, and .05 levels are typically agreed upon by scientists as indicating significant (important) findings, and are reported in scientific studies as $p = .001$, $p = .01$, or $p = .05$, respectively. The experimenter decides before the experiment what significance he will accept.

THE ERA OF EXTRASENSORY PERCEPTION (ESP)

In some circles exotic phenomena such as ESP do not enjoy a very good scientific reputation. History provides a reason for this lack of regard. The United States was a wild and crazy place in the early 1900s, a mixture of supermoralism and an antithetical supermaterialism. Great technological progress was underway, and many felt that man was about to conquer all.

That age of optimism was marked by an atmosphere of tremendous material prosperity. Ironically, at about the same time a breakthrough of mysticism and the occult occurred, led by a profusion of spiritual mediums. Whether these ladies and gentlemen proliferated because people needed to experience *everything,* or because of an uneasy attempt at getting religion, is anybody's guess.

In any case, everyone was prepared to get rich, and prices were a little different from today: a turkey dinner cost twenty cents. One of the most famous and most poorly written series of books of all time—the Horatio Alger series—told the tale of rags-to-riches for every American. Alger wrote the same story 119 times with different titles and slightly different characters, and by the time the U.S. entered World War I (1917), 200 million copies had been sold and the books were still going strong. The common man aspired to become another George Eastman, of Kodak fame, who began as a three-dollar-a-week insurance clerk [Ketchum, 1959].

By late 1918, World War I was over, and enthusiasm spurted to even greater heights. In 1920 Prohibition began a futile attempt to dampen spirits, especially the alcoholic variety. Violations of Prohibition were staggering: in a single two-year period, the Justice Department had 3,500 civil cases on its docket and 65,000 criminal cases—with everyone drinking merrily on [Hicks, 1954]. Barnum and Bailey's circus marched right through the center of town in a mile-long parade followed by a herd of elephants trunk to tail. To add to the confusion, the sewing machine came into prominence at the same time that women were beginning to seek their freedom.

The public had also decided that everyone was going to retire to Florida. For 10 percent down people bought lots in Florida ranging in value from $8,000 to $75,000. But very few were buying the land to build on. They merely put down the 10 percent, waited a few days until the value had skyrocketed, and then sold, making a handsome profit. The next person who bought the land, with his 10 percent down, would wait a few days and sell at a profit. Values were not based on the land but on the assumption that values would rise. The situation continued like a chain letter until the realization dawned that hope, not land, was being traded. And there were no more buyers. The stock market, caught in the same fervor, crashed in 1929.

The scene before 1929, then, was ripe for a profusion of quacks, mindreaders, prophets, spirit mediums, and others. Telepathy (knowing through the communication of another) and clairvoyance (knowing on your own without a second party) were fashions of the day, come to prominence in this carnivallike atmosphere. Thus they were doomed to inevitable disgrace in scientific eyes. No one called more attention to the quackery (for his own publicity) than Ehrich Weiss, who took the stage name "Harry Houdini" by adding an "i" to the name of one of the world's great magicians, Robert Houdin. Houdini, in his own right, was probably the most colorful

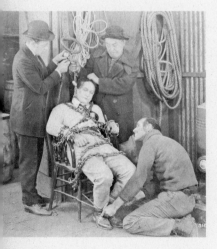

53   Harry Houdini in *Terror Island,* a Paramount movie (*Paramount*)

54 Zener cards (*Gabriele Wunderlich*)

con artist of all time. But at least he labeled himself an "escape artist," and the public knew he was a magician. He could get out of a straitjacket while hanging upside down in midair tied to a hook held up by a large crane. Or, thoroughly handcuffed and manacled, he could escape from a box nailed shut and lowered into the river.

Late in his life, Houdini began to expose mediums and mystics. The most famous case involved a Mrs. Mina Crandon. When male scientists were trying to determine if she was a fake, she had the rather distracting habit of wearing a kimona for her séances—and nothing else. Many professors certified her extrasensory powers—but they concluded that she was legitimate only after viewing her in her kimono. Houdini was determined to keep his eyes on her clandestine medium activities, and thus he was able to expose her as a fraud* [Gresham, 1959].

Harvard University was the center of legitimate ESP research in the 1920s, but some professors at the university became involved in the investigation of Mrs. Crandon; shortly thereafter Dr. Joseph Rhine, the biggest name in the history of legitimate psychic research (called *parapsychology*), arrived on the scene.

A most unfortunate thing happened to Rhine: he supported, in good faith, the telepathic abilities of a horse. Later, it turned out, as did many such animal experiments, that humans were unintentionally giving cues to the animals by slight nodding of the head, tensing of the body, and the like. By following these cues, the animals were able to add, subtract, multiply, divide, and even do square roots. So the legitimate science of parapsychology itself was off to a bad start, having been caught in the general mayhem of the time [Hansel, 1966].

Early experiments with humans involved the use of Zener cards, which are similar to oversized playing cards but have designs of stars, crosses, circles, squares, and wavy lines printed on them. In *telepathy* experiments, a "sender" looks at the figure on a card he draws from the deck and a "receiver," without looking, guesses what figure is on the card, supposedly receiving the message from the sender. In *clairvoyance* (knowledge without another person), the subject points to the back of a card on the table and says what he thinks the design will be when he turns it over. The Soviets have taken ESP quite seriously, especially in the last few years. They do not exercise the same rigorous controls found in the U.S. experiments which will be reported next, so we aren't too certain how valid their claims are. They maintain that they have demonstrated *psychokinesis*, the ability to move objects without touching them. One woman is supposed to be able to separate the yolk from the white of an egg, move a pitcher full of water across a table, and stop the heartbeat of a frog. Such feats

---

*In his report on the matter, Houdini was not one to pass up the priceless opportunity of indicating that he had *exposed* her.

have not been demonstrated under controlled conditions in the United States, so we have no evidence this can be done, even if you have a neighbor who claims she can do it [Krippner and Davidson, 1972].

Most experimenters are satisfied with odds against chance of 100 (10^2) to 1 or even 20 to 1.* A few ESP experiments have odds-against-chance levels between 10^{35} (1 followed by thirty-five zeroes) to 1 and 10^{70} to 1.† If an experimenter in any other area but ESP received such odds, he would be king of the mountain. But not so with ESP. One well-known psychologist has said that he will not accept ESP for a moment because it does not make sense. His remark is somewhat reminiscent of those who would not look into Galileo's telescope because what Galileo said they would see "didn't make sense."

In fairness, the history of ESP has been filled with fraudulent cases. In one it was found that the Zener cards were printed so heavily that they showed through the back side. Other subjects have been caught signaling to one another,‡ and many records of experiments have mysteriously disappeared after the results were published in journals.

On the other side, consistent evidence supports ESP, although the name "extrasensory perception" may itself be too mystical. For example, in one carefully controlled telepathy experiment, at the sound of a buzzer the subject was to open one of five boxes placed before her. She was screened from the experimenter and her task was to guess which box the experimenter would pick. On his side of the screen, he pushed a button for the box he chose. An automatic recorder recorded *only* when the subject opened a box *before* the experimenter made *his* choice of box. Out of 2,255 trials, the lady guessed correctly 539 times; the odds are 270,000 to 1 that chance alone was operating. Dr. Hans J. Eysenck discusses this kind of experiment in a very interesting book, *Sense and Nonsense in Psychology*. He concludes that ESP should be accepted unless one is willing to believe that some 30 universities and hundreds of highly respected scientists who believe in ESP are involved in a "gigantic conspiracy" [Eysenck, 1964].

Probably the biggest difficulty with the whole area of parapsychology is the mystic label "*extra*sensory perception" and the implication that some kind of magic is involved.

By analogy, a watchdog will be up and ready to attack long before we hear anything. To some observers this might be magic. To some it might

---

*$p = .01$ and $p = .05$ respectively.

† These p levels would run off the page in Fig. 7–2—they are that distant beyond the chance level.

‡ By facial tics, blinking eyes, mirrors, coughing, finger tapping, humming, and even the use of stooges who have raised and lowered windowshades or have used high-pitched whistles beyond the audible range of the aging investigators in cases where children were involved as subjects [Hansel, 1966].

55–55 A Stella May, one of many "spiritual advisers" who flourished in the 1920s (*Bettmann Archive*)

56–57 Tattered Tom's self-made rise to wealth and glory and prices in the corner grocery tell much about the attitudes of the twenties (*Culver*)

58 Drinking booze at the end of the twenties, when the Great Depression had set in (*Culver*)

be extrasensory perception, but not to us, because we have solved the problem. We know the dog has an excellent hearing range. Things that seem very special are not, once we know the secret.

Or take the following actual case involving human beings. Under very carefully controlled laboratory conditions, selected subjects were asked to determine the color of cards just by touching them. These individuals were completely masked; they had no opportunity to see the cards. Subjects did remarkably well, beyond* the .01 level in most cases, except when fatigue seemed to be setting in. For example, on blue-white discriminations of color, one subject obtained 68 percent success on 425 trials [Youtz, 1968].

Having read this far, you might conclude that *extra*sensory perception actually has occurred. So it has, if you stretch the use of the phrase—the situation involves an extension of our perceptual abilities at a level most of us would not have anticipated. If the colors are covered by filters that block the natural heat given off by colors, the subjects perform only a chance level. It seems pretty evident, then, that some individuals are hypersensitive (or *extra*sensitive) to heat, even the minute amounts reaching their fingertips from colored pieces of cardboard. Thus a very strange and mysterious phenomenon can be explained in natural terms. Phenomena such as telepathy are considerably more complicated than this, but conceivably some type of similar mechanism could be operating.

Ironically, this very sensitivity, possessed by many people, has led to criticism of ESP studies. Telepathy, if it is occurring, should be *mind* A communicating with *mind* B, but a large number of experiments are performed under conditions where even unintentional cues such as changes in breathing, eyeblinks, facial expressions, and the like, can operate to give the receiver the correct answer. Many also feel that the possible influence of so many cues other than ESP eliminates the statistic "chance" as a useful tool. The statistic might reflect high improbability that chance alone is operating, but then so does a loaded set of dice. Nonetheless, almost all psychological experiments compare results with chance, and few people level such criticism against them. In fact, the *Journal of Parapsychology* boasts two mathematicians per article to verify the statistics used; no other journals go to such admirable lengths.

One thought that immediately occurs to most of us is that some type of brain-wave transmission might be involved. Unfortunately, as far as can now be determined, although we do emit such energy it is in such minute quantities that its traveling any distance seems inconceivable. And it would seem that very elaborate and extraordinary devices would be required to detect such signals. Basically, this is one of the most pervasive

Beyond means even higher odds against chance than (1 in 100 in this case); it is sometimes abbreviated $p = >$ (not beyond) .01 or $p = <$ (beyond) .01.

criticisms of ESP and a major reason for skepticism: how could ESP work? Almost any problem in science has a number of fairly workable and logical hypotheses to explain the operation of a behavior. Light and sound, for instance, both operate on a wave-transmission hypothesis, but as one author has pointed out, very few plausible hypotheses suggest themselves as explanations of how ESP would work [Rothman, 1970].

Psychologist Gardner Murphy suggested that we mustn't ignore the area of ESP just because we don't understand it at present. Dr. Murphy's credentials as a professional include development of a complete theory of personality, presidency of the American Psychological Association, and director of research for the Menninger Foundation. We cannot pass him off lightly.* Dr. Murphy personally participated as a "sender" in telepathy experiments. The senders were in one room and the receivers in another room. The senders viewed, for example, slides and tapes that concerned former President Kennedy's assassination. The receivers, when interviewed, reported feelings of sadness, tragedy, and grief [Murphy, 1961; Moss, 1967].

Probably one of the most tantalizing cases I have run across really leaves one wondering. For background you should know that closing your eyes generates a specific type of brain wave, which can be recorded by an electronic device. Fifteen pairs of identical twins were studied in this experiment. In one part of the experiment, the two members of each pair were physically isolated from each other. In two of these separated pairs, it was found that when one twin closed his eyes, the brain wave pattern of the other showed a consistent and instantaneous change *as if he too had closed his eyes.* Even though this brain-wave change occurred in only two out of fifteen sets of twins, it certainly makes one a little doubtful about rejecting ESP [Duane and Behrendt, 1969].

Another similar study, done even more recently, also was controlled very carefully. From a group of picture postcards showing reproductions of famous paintings, a sender selected one. He remained in a room quite distant from the receiver, and tried to influence the receiver's dreams. The receiver was awakened each time he began to dream (another activity that can be identified by changes in brain waves). Of special interest is the type of material contained in the dreams the subject reported when he was awakened. For instance, one of the picture postcards showed Dali's famous painting *The Sacrament of the Last Supper.* Following are some key phrases I have selected from the subject's dreams: fishing boats; a dozen men; Christmas season; "the Physician." Notice that even though the receiver had no idea of what appeared on any of the postcards, his dream content had

---

*Obviously the mere participation of Dr. Murphy does not make ESP exist, but the point is that experiments are carefully done today and are far removed from the setting and atmosphere of the early 1900s; we can put more faith in the findings of current experimenters.

a constant theme of Christ while the sender was concentrating on the *Last Supper* picture (significance level $p = < .001$).

This type of result was common to all of this particular experimenter's studies [Ullmann and Krippner, 1970]. The study has been repeated a number of times by the same experimenter, each time with statistically significant findings when outside raters were given all the pictures and asked to match the dream material with the picture selected by the receiver in his dream material. A major center for the study of ESP has developed at the Maimonides Medical Center in Brooklyn, where the above experiments took place. The general trend of findings by these experimenters is that sleeping or hypnotized subjects perform quite well in ESP studies [Krippner, 1972; Honorton and Krippner, 1969]. One of their wildest experiments took place at a Grateful Dead* concert. Slides were flashed before the two thousand–plus members of the audience, and they were told to communicate the content to a subject sleeping at Maimonides, forty miles away. The experiment was successful and statistically significant [Krippner, 1972].

So there is strong evidence for strange (in the sense that we do not understand it) phenomena. What is ESP? How does it work? These questions future psychologists will answer and then look back on us and say, "How naive can you get?" At least experiments in this area are becoming more rigid and carefully controlled.

SUMMARY

Perception is strongly influenced by psychological factors, in the sense that we have a tendency to see what we want to see or what we expect to see. People misperceive the size of coins and the distance between numbers, and they often fail to see so-called dirty words. The mechanism involved apparently is some kind of protective device, called perceptual defense, and it is likely to be a homeostatic behavior.

What we see is also influenced by what is going on around us; if we expect someone to be a certain way, we may perceive him as actually being that way.

Probability is a statistical device which the scientist uses to determine whether his results are close to or far away from chance level. He hopes for results which are well removed from chance, at the p level of .001, .01, or .05, and at this point he infers that the results are turning out the way they are because his independent variable has entered the picture and removed the situation from just chance occurrence.

ESP has a bad name in psychology. This reputation seems to be the outgrowth of a number of unfortunate historical events and considerable

*Not an emotional condition, but a music group.

quackery in the field. Nonetheless, striking statistical and factual evidence supports the notion that some people do have abilities we do not understand. At the present time absolutely no evidence exists regarding how something such as telepathy occurs, but it is impossible to ignore the fact that dozens of careful studies indicate that it does.

002392 9240
002396 45

0023A4 6 1320
0023AA 4770 10
0023AE 9120   C
C023B2 47E0 1144
0023B6 9120 F00C
  3BA 47E0 1152
       9120 F00C
C02   118C
0023C6   00C
C023CA
0023CE 45
0023D2 CA02
0023D4 F4F1F1FCC1
0023DA 47E0 107A
0023DE CA02

CHAPTER EIGHT
THE COMPUTER VERSUS THE PSYCHE

There are two basic views of man, one of which deals with him at almost a molecular level and the other which sees man as operating on a very broad humanistic plane. Consider for a moment the following two passages:

It is absurd to think that if we could throw out technology, we should escape our human dilemmas. On the obvious level, technology is a set of tools, and the important question is, for what purpose are these tools used? On a less obvious level, it is true that technology does shape our image of ourselves in conditioning the kind of information we listen for. But the critical threat with respect to technology does not lie in those two: It is that we succumb to the temptation to use technology as a way of avoiding confronting our own anxiety, our alienation, and our loneliness. When a man is anxious about thermonuclear war, he can hope that with a few more missiles we shall be safe. When anxious about loneliness he can go to a psychoanalyst or learn some new operant conditioning technique,* or take some drug, so that, at so much an hour or a dose, he can be changed into the man who will love and be happy. But technology used as a way to evade anxiety makes man even more anxious, more isolated, alienated in the long run, for it progressively robs him of consciousness and his own experiencing of himself as a centered person with significance.

The ultimately self-destructive use of technology consists of employing it to fill the vacuum of our own diminished consciousness. And conversely, the ultimate challenge facing modern man is whether he can widen and deepen his own consciousness to fill the vacuum created by the fantastic increase of his technological power. It seems to me that, and not the outcome of a particular war, is the issue on which our survival hinges. [May, 1967]†

One of the most important and fascinating fields of modern science is genetics.‡ In the last several decades, geneticists have learned a great deal about how nature prepares the blueprint and detailed plans for construction of each of its creatures. This blueprint exists in the nucleus of every cell in the body of each animal. The design information is organized into tiny specks called chromosomes, visible under a high-power optical microscope. Every human cell contains 23 pairs of chromosomes. Each cell of the fruit fly contains 4 pairs, of the mouse 20 pairs, of garden peas 7 pairs. Under the much greater magnifying power of the electron

*Method of helping the "mentally disturbed"; discussed in Chapter 24.
†From Rollo May, *Psychology and the Human Dilemma* (New York: Van Nostrand Reinhold, 1967), © 1967 by Litton Educational Publishing, Inc.; reprinted by permission.
‡Study of the inheritance of characteristics from parents.

59–60   The 1970s, like the late sixties, promise to be a time in which people will look for human ways out of "the vacuum of their own diminished consciousness" (*Paul Fusco*)

61   Chromosomes—an electron microscope photograph (*Jeroboam*)

microscope, a structure is observed in each chromosome that is consistent with its division into a large number of still smaller parts. These smaller subdivisions of the chromosomes are called genes. The gene is the basic unit of heredity. It has been established that the principal working part of the gene is a gigantic molecule of deoxyribonucleic acid—DNA, for short. Each DNA molecule carries a coded message, written in a four-letter alphabet. Each of the four letters is represented by one of four different types of standard molecular fragments, or "nucleotides." These letters are arranged in a linear array along the "backbone" of the DNA molecule. The resulting message, conveyed by the several thousand genes that comprise the chromosomes of each cell, has a length of about ten billion letters—a few more for a man, a few less for a mosquito! This is the equivalent of 1,000 large volumes of ordinary printed material. The original copy of the set of manu-facturing instructions with which each animal starts its life comes to it in the fertilized egg—half from its mother, half from its father. As this original cell divides, and the resulting cells divide again and again to form the final adult organism, the one thousand–volume library of manufacturing instructions is faithfully duplicated at each cell division until, in a human, about one hundred million copies have been made. And it is this library of instructions, and this alone that determines whether the resulting animal is to be a flea, an earthworm, or a man. [Wooldridge, 1963]*

Careful reading of these two introductory comments may at first show little relationship between them; nonetheless, they cover two aspects of an important problem for a student of the sciences. On the one hand, you can't help becoming engrossed with the amazing and awe-inspiring aspects of the DNA molecules discussed by Dr. Wooldridge in the second

* From D. E. Wooldridge, *The Machinery of the Brain* (New York: McGraw-Hill, 1963), p. 87; reprinted by permission.

quotation. On the other hand, Dr. Rollo May, the first author, an outspoken psychologist, cautions us about the potential conflict in becoming completely enmeshed in the intricacies of science to the exclusion of man.

These quotations are appropriate for a second reason: as you read this chapter and the next one, you will notice a subtle (sometimes blatant) shift from minute details to broad theories that are based on only a few small bits of information regarding the operation of the details. At times man is treated as a whole unit; at times he becomes little pieces of machinery—albeit fascinating pieces. This constantly shifting emphasis is probably the result of the conflict mentioned at the beginning of this book, the discord between the broad "philosophical" examination of man and so-called scientific explanations.

Third, learning and memory theories are divided into two major approaches, one quite similar to the genetic model—that is, a chemical approach—and the other dealing with very broad aspects.

PHYSIOLOGICAL MECHANISMS OF MEMORY

When you read this section, you should return to earlier chapters, especially the illustrations there, if you find yourself getting lost at any point in the discussion. If we are to follow current research on the subject of memory, we must deal with some of the smaller physiological units of the organism, most of which have already been covered in a different context.

transmitting information

Memory and learning, of course, involve the transmission of information; we intend here to cover some recent hypotheses that attempt to explain how man learns and how he retains what he learns. One prominent theory involves the synapse, mentioned in Chapter 3. You will recall that the synapse is a junction between two neurons, or nerve networks. An electrical impulse travels down one neuron to the synaptic junction, or space, over which it must travel to arrive at the next neuron. This transfer is facilitated by a chemical substance between the two neurons: the electrical impulse or wave* can "jump the gap," so to speak. One theory of memory is that learning makes the chemical substances at the synapse more readily available for certain sequences of nerve impulses. Once this occurs, the nerve impulse can move over the synapse with greater ease; hence we have less difficulty in bringing back by replay that series of nerve impulses.

Evidence seems pretty clear that isolated groups of synapses respond to certain memory tasks. Suppose, for example, that you were learning a line of a poem. With each recitation of that line, the synapses connecting a certain group of neurons for that memory respond to repeated learning with more and more of the chemical substances at the synapse; eventually

---

* The electrical impulse is described as a wave because when it is measured it appears on the electronic device in the form of a wave.

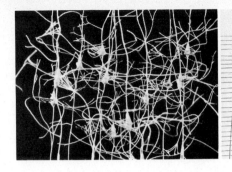 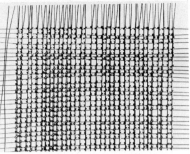

62–63 Two structures that do the same thing—synaptic junctions in the human brain, and the high-speed memory unit for an IBM 360 (*Will Burtin; IBM*)

it is a simple matter to "fire" the sequence and retrieve that memory. The neurons are "connecting" to make a path for that memory.

Chemicals that block synaptic transmission or increase its effectiveness have been injected into animals. If the drug is one that tends to prevent synaptic transmission, tasks that have been learned are apparently forgotten. And drugs that facilitate the transmission of impulses actually seem to increase memory beyond the degree to which the task was first learned [Deutsch, 1966, 1968]. The hypothesis of synaptic transmission proposes, then, that waveforms* from one neuron interact with waveforms from another neuron to produce a new pattern when learning takes place; when that learning—memory—is utilized, the proper waveform is searched for. For an analogy, this union of waveforms might be likened to what you get when your speedboat creates waves in the already existing waves of the lake. The result is a combination of the two wave patterns but different from either of them.† In the brain, waveforms alter the chemical structure (see protein structure in next section) at or near the synapse and probably store at least a portion of the memory somewhere in that area. The waveforms conceivably could be as individual as fingerprints [Pribram, 1969].

A slightly different version of the synaptic theory suggests that the chemical transmitter substance at the synaptic terminals acts as a switch which sometimes inhibits (blocks) activity in connecting neurons, sometimes facilitates a particular firing sequence. Thus, we form a so-called wiring diagram for certain learned or reflexive acts.

There is evidence that the chemical transmitter per se is changeable and can both block and facilitate neural behaviors. This was discovered by comparing the behavior of those synapses with chemical units with others lacking chemical transmitters. The *electrical* synapses do not alter their behavior—that is, do not sometimes inhibit, sometimes facilitate, thus suggesting that change comes from the chemical units themselves.‡ The

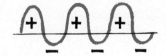

* *Waveform* refers to what is *seen* on an electronic device for measuring alterations in voltage. Electrical voltage changes from positive to negative as it moves along the nerve. The result on a measuring device might look like the figure at left.

† There is not an actual union of waveforms; waveforms are merely a representation of the union of electrical impulses.

‡ Most synapses are chemical; earlier discussion centered on this fact. However, a few are electrically operated.

189

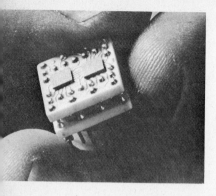

64 Another memory unit. This one "remembers" half a million bits of information (*IBM*)

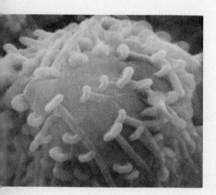

65 Synaptic junctions in the sea slug (*E. R. Lewis*)

synaptic theory helps explain basic behaviors and memory, but even if it is the answer to complex memory, probably many years will elapse before these behaviors and memory are understood [Kandel, 1970].

The exact location for storage of memories is unknown, but a large number of studies suggest that any given memory is not likely to be stored in only one location. You will recall the discussion in Chapter 3 of the "split brain" experiments. These studies at least suggested that a memory is stored in more than one place, because what was learned with one eye and stored in one-half of the brain was transferred to the other half of the brain. Experiments seem to indicate that, rather than storing memory X in spot X, the person's memory storage is spread throughout the brain, especially the brain stem (older portions of the brain) and the cerebral cortex (see Figs. 3–5, 3–7).

It is doubtful that a specific memory—such as that for a rose—is located in just one place. Instead, it is likely that different parts of the memory system combine to reproduce the concept "rose." For instance, if you want to bring back the memory of a rose, a number of different units could be activated by a pattern of neurons firing for each one:

Rose $\longrightarrow$ Flower $\longrightarrow$ Plant $\longrightarrow$ Kept in pot
$\downarrow$ $\downarrow$ $\downarrow$
Symbol   Fragrance   Location of pot
$\downarrow$
Love

Note that we have the possible combination of at least eight different memory sections, and you can figure out many more. When you think of a gardenia you activate some of the same circuits—flower, plant, fragrance, etc. Thus, if this theory is correct, nature has a very efficient method for storage which just brings together the appropriate elements necessary for a given memory [Frijda, 1972; John, 1972].

The exact mechanism of constructing memories, a new and highly complex area of study, is poorly understood. Bits of information seem to be located in various places and then brought together in *association areas* (see Fig. 8–1). These areas comprise a fantastically large number of neurons (and, of course, synapses), and they are assumed to serve the function of integrating bits of material until a completed memory is made. The principle is not dissimilar to the numbered-dot pictures, familiar to most of us in childhood, in which the task was to draw a line from dot number 1 to 2 to 3, etc., until suddenly before us was a picture of a duck—whereas before we had only numbered dots. We probably never come up with a *picture* of a duck in our minds, but we do come up with a coded representation that serves quite well.

One final hypothesis about association areas is that their primary purpose is to explore relatively unusual or complex objects or thoughts.

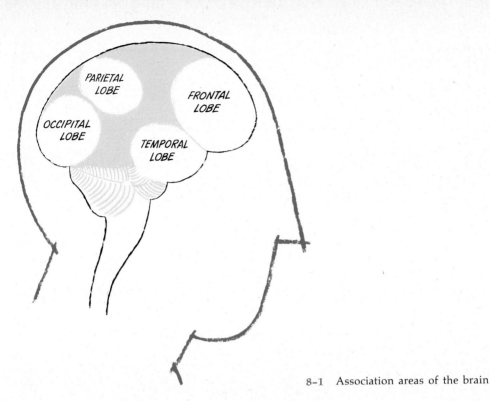

8–1   Association areas of the brain

Commonplace objects like a chair are probably stored in compact fashion so that little searching is necessary and minimal association is needed to put the information together [Pribram, 1969].

storing information   The question arises exactly how the units of memory are stored. Considerable experimentation has been done in this area. Basically, memory is thought to be stored in a ***protein molecule***. Protein molecules are responsible for the structure of the living cell and the occurrence of chemical reactions within the cell. These molecules are made up of highly complex building blocks which are put together into long, twisted chains of acids called *amino acids*. Viewing a diagram of the inner structure of the protein molecule is much like seeing a madman's dream of the world's most complicated Tinker Toy. You need not understand chemistry: the point is that amino acids have the ability to link together and form highly complex molecules of protein—and the structure of this protein is such that it can contain an overwhelming amount of chemical information. We assume that this chemical information can be "translated" into what we think of as memory information. Thus, since we do know that protein in various forms contains most of the information about the body and directs its operations, it is not illogical to speculate that protein might also contain memory information.

The actual development of proteins is fairly well understood. Return

191

for a moment to the very beginning of this chapter, to the quotation about DNA molecule. That discussion referred to the inheritance of characteristics—for example, decisions about what species we will become, where our noses will grow, the shape of our ears. DNA's function is to be the mastermind for all bodily processes, probably including memory.

To help in following the discussion, a few points should be outlined:

1.   DNA* constructs a chemical called RNA.† This RNA contains an exact duplicate of the information in the DNA. The DNA itself is in the inner core of the nucleus of the cell.
2.   RNA can send out "RNA messengers" (MRNA) to direct the amino acid chains to construct a certain type of protein.
3.   Electrical stimulation activates a chemical agent in the neuron; the neuron activates the DNA to activate the RNA, which behaves as in 1.

This is not as complicated as it seems at first. Diagrammed: Electrical stimulation ⟶ Activates neuron's chemical agent ⟶ Reacts with DNA ⟶ Sends out impulses to RNA ⟶ MRNA created ⟶ Directs specific protein buildup [John, 1967].

What has happened? Basically, electrical impulses arising from some sensation (for example, seeing a low-slung, powerful car called the Blue Zombie) have formed a memory molecule representing, in coded fashion, this wondrous machine. In order for the memory to be so formed, some have speculated, information from the general neural network—for example, concepts such as "blue," "low-slung," and "powerful"—has combined with protein structures which we already have for "automobile." Since we certainly have nothing to equal the Blue Zombie, information other than just "automobile" must be borrowed from other networks.

When we use our memory, then, our brain searches for those protein structures that will fire the neurons that adequately decode and provide a representation of the Blue Zombie.

Considerable evidence supports the idea that such a protein molecule for memory exists. Rats learned how to get to food placed at the end of a maze (a long, twisting series of pathways with many dead-end streets). Protein inhibitors were then injected into the animals, and a day or so after the maze-learning took place, the task seemed to have been forgotten [Flexner and Flexner, 1968].

long- and short-term memory   Even if current movies have become too sophisticated, you can sit up at night watching the old ones on television and be sure to run into a tried-and-true plot of a few years back. A man is struck on the head while

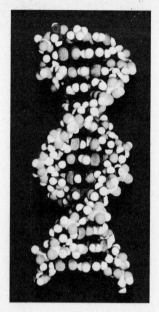

66   A model of the DNA molecule (*Abbott Laboratories*)

---

* *Deoxyribonucleic acid.*
† *Ribonucleic acid.*

watching a murder and forgets "everything." The murderer follows him around, not knowing the man has lost his memory, fearful of being exposed by him. The audience waits for the man's memory to return. Although the situation is corny, one of its real-life aspects is interesting. A good, solid blow on the head *can* produce *amnesia* (blocking of memory). Most intriguing, however, many people who have amnesia can recall events from the distant past but cannot remember anything recent; as memory returns, it starts with the events most distant in time and moves forward. This fact was one of the first clues we had to the existence of *long- and short-term memory*. The idea behind these clues is simple. The longer we have a memory, the stronger its mark on our brain and the more difficult it is to get rid of. Newer memories can be temporarily erased by blows on the head or electrical shocks. Brand-new memories—for example, incidents that occurred just before an accident—can often be permanently removed. Brand-new memories are supposedly short-term until they have been transferred to storage or long-term memory.

Laboratory evidence for the existence of short-term memory comes from experiments similar to the following one. The experimenter speaks three letters to the subject; these letters are called *nonsense syllables* because they do not resemble any known words—for instance, FAQ.* The experimenter then immediately reads off a three-digit number—for example, 574—and asks the subject to count backward from it, out loud, without stopping (573, 572, etc.). After a time, the subject is asked to recall the three letters. The point to the experiment is that a conscious task like counting backward interferes with holding the nonsense syllable in short-term memory, and therefore it is lost; only a few subjects are able to remember the three-letter combinations under these circumstances. If we assume that learning must first enter the short-term circuit and go around in there for a period before entering the long-term circuit, this experiment suggests not only the existence of a short-term circuit, but also that one can interfere with it [Peterson, 1966].

Physically, the two mechanisms seem to be at least partially independent. In rats, electrical stimulation of some parts of the brain disrupt short-term memory while the same electrical input to a different portion disturbs long-term memory. In the few cases of human brain injury that have been studied, injuries to one portion will affect short-term memory and those to another part the long-term. These studies are not conclusive, but certainly suggestive [Kesner and Conner, 1972].

Other studies of short- and long-term memory continue to demonstrate that we have these two mechanisms. For example, if a visual stimulus

67   *(Gabriele Wunderlich)*

* Nonsense syllables are used in experiments of this kind because familiar combinations of letters—for example, *pat, hat, rat*—are more easily remembered by some people than others. A man with a wife named Pat would probably have an edge over men with wives having other names.

is presented to the eye twice within 60 milliseconds,* the two presentations of this bit of information apparently join together in the short-term memory to increase the ability to retain this material; however, if a stimulus is presented once and the experimenter waits beyond 60 milliseconds to present it again, no "adding up" takes place. The short-term memory apparently processes its information during this time interval. Beyond that interval, it seems to treat the incoming visual material as brand-new and goes through the whole process of transferring it from short- to long-term memory from the very beginning [Jackson and Dick, 1969].

Motivation and distractions also affect short-term memory [Shiffrin, 1969]. On the positive side, the typical male college student could conceivably be given the telephone number of a beautiful female, (314-321-2522) and then asked to recite the alphabet sideways, upside down, and backward, and still retain the number. We are assuming that a *reasonable* amount of motivation exists in these studies, not an overwhelming amount. Distraction is an ever-present problem, especially if you are listening to some bore talk on and on: even the wallpaper becomes important, in your reveries, and everything slips through the short-term circuit and dissolves into oblivion.

One of the major current hypotheses about the structure of long-term memory relates to a process discussed before: once the information is "moved" from STM to LTM,† amino acid chains link together to form a protein molecule for that memory. To test this hypothesis, fish were trained in an aquarium that had been divided in half. A light glowed in one half just before a shock hit that side. The fish soon learned to swim to the other (safe) side as soon as the light came on, in order to avoid the shock. These fish showed striking evidence of having LTM; some of them could remember the task as long as a month later.

Next, a *protein inhibitor* was injected at various intervals to determine what effect this would have on memory. The results appear to support the LTM hypothesis:

1. Injection *before* training: a fish could learn the task (STM unaffected). However, immediately after training he forgot the task (no LTM).
2. Injection one hour *after* training: memory unaffected (LTM already operative) [Agranoff, 1967].

The exact amount of time needed for processing in long-term memory is unknown. However, if material is presented in one-second intervals, remembering this material is difficult compared to three-second intervals between presentations. In the latter case, the material has had time to be "absorbed" by the LTM. Of course, none of these figures can be added

* Thousandths of a second.
† Short-term memory and long-term memory, respectively.

or subtracted because we don't know what is going on inside the head. Nonetheless, it is highly probable that the one-second rate somehow interferes with LTM learning: that is, the LTM itself requires a specific period of time for its operation once the material has passed the STM, and one-second intervals just don't provide enough time for LTM to complete an effective storage process. Furthermore, as with STM, material that is most meaningful is most easily stored in the LTM [Raymond, 1969].

Thus evidence points to the existence of both short- and long-term memory. Short-term memory is a temporary process used, probably, to hold the material until we decide on its merit. From that point it is forwarded into a permanent state. Possibly STM is a continuous but temporary firing of synapses to hold the memory, and LTM is an actual protein change. A plausible current theory of how these mechanisms operate together goes something like this: The STM units are activated by a stimulus—for example, a car—and the LTM mechanism is activated for units that correspond to the image of a car from previous experience. When STM and LTM agree on the basics, this information can then be fed into permanent storage. When there are notable differences—for instance, with the Blue Zombie—the incoming STM will not correspond exactly with the existing LTM, so if the memory is going to be made permanent the LTM will have to activate additional circuits to take care of these differences [Atkinson and Shiffrin, 1971].

unusual memory   You probably have heard about strange cases of unusual memory, so they deserve a little attention. There is a report by reputable experimenters of a man who could repeat word for word two and a half pages of print after reading them once, although his comprehension was rather limited [Anastasi and Levee, 1959]. And there are indeed persons who can give you the day of the week a particular date fell on within the last eight years or can do the same thing up to the year 7000 with a very high level of accuracy. The strangest part about these cases is that most of the persons have a low IQ and show little ability to reason abstractly. Hence, they are termed *idiot savants*, a not too complimentary term meaning an idiot with great learning. A number of rather exotic interpretations have been advanced about these persons, but in recent years these have generally been discarded.

The most acceptable current theory is that the idiot savant is not particularly gifted by nature, and this is easily demonstrated by an examination of persons with normal IQs who have been in solitary confinement: the need for some type of inner stimulation is so overwhelming that these persons devise all manner of elaborate methods of mathematical calculations or rote memory. Since the idiot savant has a low IQ and difficulty in abstracting, he is generally subjected to a *social* solitary confinement. The calendar technique or feats of rote memory are sufficiently startling to most people that the individual attracts attention because he can perform these feats. The more attention he attracts, the more he will perfect them. Thus, if any of us wanted to devote almost all our time to perfecting one of these techniques we could do it with little difficulty, but we lack the social need of the idiot savant [Hoffman, 1971]. So, there are instances of unusual memory, but in most of them the person has to give up something in order to have this ability.

One of the strangest cases occurred in the 1930s. A man identified by the psychologist only as "S." had what you would call perfect memory, something that sounds really worthwhile, but isn't. The man could remember any amount of material given to him in the laboratory, and he could remember it for fifteen or sixteen years. As a matter of fact he went through his own private hell because he could not forget anything, even events from childhood.

S. mentally turned words into visual images, and if someone would talk too fast, the images would collide, get mixed up, and cause him considerable confusion. Even worse, he was unable to avoid attaching feelings, emotions, even sensations of taste to various words, at times creating a chaos of continuous images and sensations. On occasion the word-images that appeared to him as someone spoke would seem to be covered with smoke and fog, and the more people talked "the harder it gets," he commented, until he couldn't make sense of anything.

This case has received considerable attention recently because of the discoveries of STM and LTM. The best explanation at present is that he had a defect of the STM which did not allow the images to fade rapidly enough when moving into LTM. The man was not unusually bright in everyday terms: he had trouble thinking in abstract terms and in generalizing. Even though he had a memory beyond our comprehension, he had to pay a price [Luria, 1968; Bruner, 1968].

photographic memory and memory storage

A phenomenon that has intrigued students and researchers alike for years is photographic memory. In the early 1950s a famous television quiz show featured contestants "sealed" in soundproof booths. Millions were fascinated by one man who could quote without flaw a passage from "randomly" selected encyclopedia pages over which he had glanced just before air time. The show was taken off the air after a scandal revealed that in many cases the contestants were given answers beforehand. Regardless of the TV chicanery, such a thing as photographic memory does indeed exist; psychologists call it *eidetic imagery*.* Its workings are not so spectacular as the glamorous fraud of the quiz show contestant—but an image with complete detail does seem to remain in the person's view. A small percentage of the population has the ability to look at a picture of a chain and, when it is removed, count the links still seen in front of them. Most estimates suggest

*From the Greek for image, pronounced "eye-det-tick."

that 5 to 10 percent of children have this ability, but eidetic imagery is almost nonexistent among adults.

The procedure for examining eidetic imagery is simple. A child is shown a picture, the picture is taken away, and the child "sees" the picture on the table in front of him, usually for thirty seconds to a minute. If the picture includes a zebra, the child can count its stripes. However, if the child moves his eyes away from the table, the picture he sees "skips off the end of the table" and disappears. You will recall from earlier discussion that images on the retina are processed by nerve networks into slits or lines before they reach the occipital lobe of the brain. It would seem that the eidetic child has a rare ability to hold the incoming image back from the processing center. Possibly this image is a chemical bleaching similar to that in the case of rhodopsin, which remains for a period of time [Haber, 1969; Barber, 1959].

Most intriguing, however, is the discovery that if the children are asked to *name* what is seen, or give it a label, the eidetic image disappears. This little bit of information is fascinating to speculate about in light of the STM and LTM experiments. Naming an object seems to be the logical first step in storing material in the LTM, considering that man is highly verbal and uses symbols frequently. The very fact that the eidetic image disappears when naming takes place suggests that storing and holding such an image cannot occur simultaneously. The eidetic child cannot *store* the whole picture: the most he can do is retain it for a short period of time. Like the rest of us, he can store it by labeling the parts, but when he does, the eidetic image is gone. It would appear, then, that our learning is piecemeal, and that we learn each part in turn to form a coded version of the whole. And the reverse is possible: when we remember the material, we take the pieces and put them together into a whole.

the cognitive map

Putting things into a whole is called a *cognitive map* by some psychologists. You may recall that early behaviorists (Chapter 4) felt man to be a robot—a series of stimuli connected to responses. For example, when we drive home, we have formed a learning chain: right turn—left turn—left turn—right turn, etc. When it comes to driving home, however, most of us can see the obvious flaw in the assumption that we are nothing but stimuli and responses: if the road is blocked at a certain point, will we then be stuck, unable to find our way? Evidence suggests that rather than being *just* a connection of bits and pieces, then, the animal brain and the human brain have the ability to form an overall picture of the situation by uniting appropriate learned responses.

A psychologist, E. C. Tolman, demonstrated that a mechanistic stimulus-response chain is not necessarily true even in rats. Tolman's rats were placed in a complex maze with food at the end. Once they had learned the route to food, obstructions were placed in their way and new routes put in. Even when the maze became very complicated, the rats were able to re-sort and rearrange the different portions of it in their minds and quickly find the route to food. These experiments argue pretty strongly in favor of what Tolman called the *cognitive map*, the ability we (and the rats) have to reorder and reconstruct pieces to give a whole picture of the situation in which we find ourselves [Tolman, 1946].

We have been discussing learning and memory in minute detail. As mentioned earlier in the chapter, certain approaches to learning and memory take a very broad approach. These theories attempt to explain why memory occurs, only they do so in gross rather than molecular terms. The two approaches are not exclusive of one another, however. Both can exist side by side. The latter approach follows below.

OPERANT CONDITIONING

You probably recall the discussion of Pavlov and his dogs (Chapter 4). As you read there, an animal can be conditioned to behave in a certain fashion (for example, to salivate) at the ringing of a bell. This conditioning was accomplished by pairing or associating the bell with the normal salivation resulting from a natural event (for example, having meat on the tongue). It was discussed that some human learning results from this classical arrangement. By way of a refresher, consider an anecdote that illustrates the kind of thing psychologists tried to destroy years ago (animal anecdotes), during the proliferation of theories based on "instincts." (Having a captive audience, I find it difficult to resist.) I have a German shepherd who looks mean and growls menacingly at strangers, even invited guests. A veterinarian once, in the course of treatment, inflicted pain on the dog. Several weeks later, a visitor to the house was greeted not with the customary growls but with whimpering and cowering in the corner; it finally dawned on us that the visitor was wearing a light-colored trenchcoat that looked much like the vet's white lab coat. The association was still in the dog's mind between the doctor's white coat and the natural element of pain, which is to be avoided. By way of human analogy, in the 1950s, especially in California, seeing anyone with a black leather jacket and a motorcycle was enough to send townspeople scurrying home. This reaction was a simple conditioned response growing out of many real incidents in California towns where black-leather-jacketed gangs had literally taken over.

Despite these examples, considerable learning cannot be relegated to this procedure alone. Another type of learning covers a broader range of behavioral acts than does this kind of conditioning. You will recall that Pavlov's theory was called classical conditioning, a term that stressed its tradition and age. The second major learning theory is called *operant con-*

68   Author and assistant (*F. B. McMahon*)

ditioning. It is more elaborate than Pavlov's theory, and it can be understood best by comparing it to classical conditioning. In classical conditioning, learning takes place *inevitably*, so to speak; salivation is something that can't be controlled, is inevitable, when meat is presented. Operant conditioning, on the other hand, covers many situations that are not directly connected with such inevitable learning. The theory stresses that men and animals, given adequate motivation, learn as a result of movements (*operations*) which they perform. Operant conditioning still assumes motivation behind behavior, but this motivation need not be as explicit as that in classical conditioning, in which a reaction to meat is unavoidable. Hunger, of course, can be a motivation in operant conditioning, but other less obvious motivations appear—for example, the curiosity or manipulation motive.

B. F. Skinner   We left John Watson back in Chapter 4, but at the time I mentioned that his mechanical theory of behavior was not going to disappear, so here we are again. Burrhus Frederic Skinner is probably one of the best-known psychologists around today, at least to the lay public. Since it is more or less traditional to have fathers-of-things, Dr. Skinner is considered the father of operant conditioning theory. Like Watson, Skinner is not concerned with philosophy and speculation about why man does certain things; he regards man as an animal who responds to what is going on around him in a mechanical fashion. Skinner even made it a point during his college years to disrupt philosophical or ritualistic activities such as debates and commencement exercises—but this was before he joined the faculty. Before graduating he gave up disrupting things because of an overwhelmingly intense affection for physiology and psychology; he even passed up movies, plays, and dates for the cause [Skinner, 1967].

    Skinner believes that man is completely dominated by what happens in his environment. If the environment is rewarding, man produces and is happy; if not, then we have criminals, deviates, and unhappy creatures. His preoccupation with the proper environment led to a most unusual event in psychology: he reared his daughter in a specially designed "air crib" where the environment—air temperature, humidity, light, and so forth—was completely controlled. The child was not confined by either diapers or blankets. The "diaper" was a continuous roll of sheetlike material that was fed in one side of the air crib and exited the other side.*

    In the 1930s Skinner developed a box for studying animal learning. Unbeknownst to the animal, it contained a lever that, if pushed, would deliver food [Skinner, 1938]. The unit is known as a *Skinner box*. Animals usually begin by performing many operations—leaning against the side,

---

*The rumor got started that the child became insane, but she grew up more or less normal—like all the rest of us.

69 This pigeon, who resides in a Skinner box, has learned to get food by pecking at the hole in the cage (*B. F. Skinner*)

climbing on top of the box, touching parts of the cage. Sooner or later the animal pushes the bar and suddenly food arrives down a chute. Eventually he learns that the operation of pushing the bar produces food, so he repeats the act; thus, he has been subjected to operant conditioning.

A man learns that, with some women, patting them results in a slap in the face, and with others instant love. In either case the man is being operantly conditioned. His *actions* (operations) bring definitive results and learning. The distinction between classical and operant conditioning, then, is the relative degree of freedom of action which the creature enjoys. The operation of the bar is a relatively free action; it is not forced on him. Of course, once the animal has been conditioned operantly, Skinner would no longer consider him to have the same degree of freedom of action. In the human male the association between certain body lines and the sex drive may be classically conditioned, but the actions of a male toward a female are rewarding or not rewarding, and learning to use or avoid a technique will occur because of the results the action brings.

trial and error

Not everyone agrees, but it is probably fair to say that most psychologists consider the behavior of an animal in the Skinner box as *trial-and-error learning*. This kind of learning is exactly what the name implies—different actions are tried until one of them brings some kind of success. Trial-and-error learning assumes that some (unknown) motive is responsible for the animal's actions, bringing about his random movements, but the broader human motives fit here where they don't fit with classical conditioning. For example, people try to solve a Chinese puzzle, a device in which a number of wooden pieces are interlocked in an inscrutable Oriental fashion and must be disengaged. Solving such a puzzle obviously involves trial and error, and a preoccupation with these elements seems clearly to involve operant conditioning rather than classical conditioning [Thorndike, 1911]. Solution of the puzzle comes from a more obscure motive than a natural and basic one such as hunger satisfaction.

reinforcement and reward

An important ingredient of operant conditioning is *reinforcement*. This word suggests the same thing in learning as it does in carpentry or building: when something is reinforced, it is made stronger. Reinforcement in learning refers to the strengthening of a tendency to respond. For example, over a period of time, the likelihood increases that the animal in the Skinner box will begin to push the bar more frequently than he will perform other actions.

Reinforcement is traditionally assumed to work best as the result of *reward*.* Our rat in the Skinner box receives a reward of food for pressing

*In general most psychologists assume reinforcement occurs because of reward. Skinner prefers to use just the term *reinforcement* because he says you can't always tell what the reward is. Many psychologists use the two terms interchangeably.

the bar. This reward reinforces his tendency to push the bar again to receive more food. In a similar fashion, shock can serve to reinforce a response if the reward is escape from pain; that is, if pushing a lever results in turning off the current, the animal's tendency to push the lever is strengthened.

Psychologists have indulged in many discussions, some pleasant and some not so pleasant, about the nature of reward. The problem lies in the vagueness of the term itself and certainly in the difficulty in describing what makes a reward reinforcing. There are some clues around, but they will not answer the many hairy questions that occur to you.

At the basic level, we already have discussed the remarkable power of electrical stimulation on the "pleasure centers" of the brain; in fact, animals given the choice of food or stimulation prefer stimulation, as you may recall, so something about this stimulation must provide quite a kick. Rewarding the basic needs of animals—for instance, the need for food—clearly results in a form of internal electrical brain activity. Presumably the reward centers of the hypothalamus record these pleasurable experiences and hence reinforce this activity.

Reinforcement is not this simple, however. It may be intimately tied in with even more complex electrical activity: once an animal has received a reward, any circumstances that suggest he is about to get another one cause major electrical neural activity in the reticular formation. This activity is directly related to the degree of motivation and strongly suggests a high level of *anticipation,* which is probably quite rewarding. Once anticipation has been fulfilled, the animal will seek this satisfaction again [Olds, 1969].

You may have experienced the reward and reinforcement of anticipation yourself. Think how you anticipate your vacation each year. It's significant, however, that for millions of people, vacation is more gruesome than time spent at work—nagging spouses, picnics with sand in the food, long, hot drives, etc.—yet the following year anticipation rears it head again. Something about the anticipation itself must be rewarding and lead one to perform the act again.

shaping   Pigeons can be trained in very elaborate behavior by a technique called *shaping.* Shaping refers to a process in which a desired sequence of behavior is eventually obtained from the animal by rewarding each act in the sequence. Thus, pigeons could be trained to play table tennis or to dance in figure eights. Many movements have been shaped or molded into a whole. In the figure-eight example, for instance, each time the pigeon makes a proper circular move—even if it just occurs randomly—the creature is rewarded, so he will do it again. The shaping proceeds until a complete chain of movements is associated together to produce the figure-eight dance. Using these techniques Skinner tried to aid the war effort when he trained pigeons to guide a missile by pecking on various buttons. The idea was

70 Rare camera footage of a rare moment in history: pigeon vs. pigeon in ping pong (*B. F. Skinner*)

all right, but by the time the missile was loaded with the equipment necessary for the pigeons to perform, there was no room left for explosives.

Operant conditioning in the form of shaping has been quite effective in a number of cases involving severely disturbed mental patients. One patient, for example, had been a trial and tribulation to the staff for a number of years because she would urinate on the floor, feign heart attacks, and worst of all would choke herself. Everytime someone came to her aid or tried to stop her by traditional means, it seemed that her behavior got worse instead of better, so an operant conditioning procedure was instigated. Whenever she behaved in an inappropriate fashion everyone on the staff walked away from her and ignored her. When she stopped acting in unacceptable ways, the staff paid close attention to her, thereby providing her with a strong reward for "good" behavior. And each time she went two hours without choking herself, she received a reward that was very important to her, cigarettes. The patient did not return to her old ways during the whole course of treatment; she found that the attention she needed could be obtained in acceptable ways [Matefy, 1972].

The examples mentioned above all demonstrate what is called *continuous reinforcement,* which means that *each* time a desired behavior occurs it is reinforced by reward.

intermittent reinforcement

Skinner's techniques with his pigeons produced some interesting principles of learning. One of these is called *intermittent reinforcement.* In intermittent reinforcement the reward comes every so often (intermittently) rather than every time. Thus, a pigeon pecking at a disc for food might peck 5 times and receive food, then receive it again after 7 pecks, then after 3 pecks, and so forth. When an animal is reinforced in this manner, it has been possible to get him to a level of pecking 10,000 times before getting another reinforcement just because he can't tell when the next one will come [Skinner, 1957]. The same principle works quite well with slot machines. Since players don't know exactly when the reinforcement is going to come, they keep right on pulling; every now and then they get a few coins back, just to keep them going toward the big reinforcement, the jackpot.

The type of intermittent reinforcement we have just discussed is called *variable-ratio reinforcement.* Ratio in this context merely means number, so the animal is being rewarded for different (variable) numbers (ratio) of responses: five pecks, seven pecks, three pecks, and so forth.

What would happen if you kept the ratio the same, so that the creature is rewarded everytime he performs a certain number of acts? For example, what if the pigeon is rewarded every five pecks? This is called *fixed-ratio reinforcement,* and as you might expect, the pigeons will peck as rapidly as possible.* Ah! Maybe this is the solution to getting factory workers

*Note this is still a subtype of intermittent because reward is not continuous.

to put out more for the same amount of money. What happens, though, is that perverse human nature enters in. In Russia a few years ago this experiment was tried in a factory that made nuts and bolts. Since they were being rewarded for the number of units they turned out, the workers figured that they could get twice the number of units by reducing the size of the bolt one half. Of course, the next step is that if you reduce the size further you can get three times as many bolts. The result was millions of bolts that would fit nothing. And what happens if a large automobile manufacturer decides that the men on the production line can turn out more cars per hour? One suspects that, human nature being what it is, it doesn't take long for the men to find out that the only way to cope with this is to put screws half way in to save time or leave out certain parts. Even when fixed-ratio reinforcement is effective—for example when some worker decides to out-produce others, group pressure forces him to slow down.

Although there are more, for our purposes, it might be worthwhile mentioning just one additional type of schedule, called *fixed-interval rein-forcement*. If pigeons learn that they are going to be rewarded every five minutes no matter how fast they peck, they become very casual about the whole matter. They will walk over to the pecking disc, hit it once, saunter away for a while and then return, hitting it again. Their pecking will only increase toward the end of the five-minute period. If you look at Figure 8–2 you will quickly note that Congress operates just like the pigeons. There is no particular reason why the production of bills should not be more or less continuous, but with the reinforcement of anticipation of vacation time there is a sudden flurry of activity. Note how steep the curve becomes as the summer months approach and with them adjournment [Weisberg and Waldrop, 1972].

The basic importance of schedules* of reinforcement and shaping is that these seem to be general principles by which both animals and people learn. At least in theory, if we can control the techniques by which people learn or alter behavior, we can control the people themselves. This firm belief has led Skinner to suggest the possibility of a utopia in which we all live happily ever after with just the right amount of reinforcement. His contro-versial book *Beyond Freedom and Dignity* is based on these principles [Skinner, 1971]. Fortunately or unfortunately, depending on your point of view, there is little evidence that we understand the basics of human behav-ior sufficiently that this could come to pass at any forseeable time.

obscure motivation
and reward
Even though reward seems relatively straightforward, not all psychologists have been content to see it as a complete explanation of the motivation for

---

* Each of the arrangements mentioned—for example, fixed-interval, variable ratio— is called a schedule.

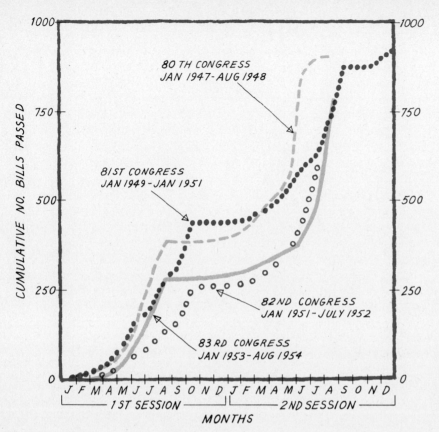

80TH CONGRESS
JAN 1947- AUG 1948

81ST CONGRESS
JAN 1949 - JAN 1951

82ND CONGRESS
JAN 1951 - JULY 1952

83RD CONGRESS
JAN 1953 - AUG 1954

CUMULATIVE NO. BILLS PASSED

J F M A M J J A S O N D   J F M A M J J A S O N D
├─── 1ST SESSION ───┤   ├──── 2ND SESSION ────┤

MONTHS

8-2 Cumulative number of bills passed during the legislative sessions of congress from January 1947 to August 1954

learning. Reward as a concept works fairly well when we are dealing with specific satisfactions—money, sex, food, and the like. What, however, are we to make of someone like the solver of crossword puzzles? Such a person spends considerable time learning to be better at this task, and the inveterate solver can immediately give you the four-letter word meaning "incidental or occasional" and beginning with the letter *o* (*orra*). Probably nobody else in the world except crossword puzzlers knows what this word means or what word will fit. In any case, here the reward leading to reinforcement is certainly obscure. It is not satisfying to assume that "he does it because he does it."

There *is* a possible answer, however, and it requires reference again to Gestalt psychology. One Gestalt principle is *closure*, a bit of human behavior that most of us seem to share, the desire for a completed whole. If we see an almost-completed circle, we tend, when reproducing it, to close the gap. In music, the technique of completion is frequently used; the melody is played all the way through, not stopped in the middle. One might speculate that the crossword puzzler's motive is similar: the completion of a task, rather than an inherent value in the task itself.

Closure is a perfectly legitimate hypothesis for explaining some behavior. Another suggestion is that animals and humans learn tasks for their own sake, not for any specific goal or purpose. For example, rats have been allowed to wander through a maze that held *no* food reward at the end, and hence there exists no apparent reason for the rats to learn the intricacies of the maze. Another group of rats was trained in the traditional fashion, with a reward of food at the end of the maze. The unrewarded group showed few signs that they were learning the maze, as we would expect. However, experimenters were in for a surprise: on the eleventh day of training, food was placed at the end of the maze for the group that previously had been unrewarded. After a few trials these rats were as good at running the maze as those that had been regularly reinforced [Tolman, 1930]. They had been learning the maze all along with no apparent reward. Only with reward did the learning that had been going on all along appear in their performance in the maze. The experiments showed that even animals must have some pretty complex and vague motives aside from just the basic drives. The learning in these experiments is called *latent learning.* Latent means something that goes on "beneath the surface" or is not obvious at the time. Latent-learning experiments were designed to emphasize the possibility of learning merely for its own sake.

Psychologists are not completely satisfied with explaining latent learning for its own sake; therefore, something like the curiosity motive is proposed to help explain the behavior. Thus, for the scientist *not* to search

71   In painting the *Card Players*, Cezanne relied on the principle of closure; he left some contours incomplete, knowing that the human visual apparatus would fill in the missing parts (*Louvre*)

for a cause is almost impossible, even if the cause does not clarify the matter to any great extent. It is maintained, for example, that *some* motive must underlie latent learning, some motive other than just the presence of the maze in the animal environment. Or do people and animals learn *just* by being exposed to or being around some material?

A rather clever experiment was devised to examine the question: can mere exposure to information provide learning? For the experiment, laboratory assistants were told that they were going to test some students' ability to memorize words. In order to test the students, the assistants would be *exposed* to the words the subjects had to learn, but they would have no known motivation to learn them. As the experiments turned out, the assistants did indeed learn some of the words just by administering the memory tests to the subjects, but the mere exposure was not as effective as motivated learning, even if the motivation was nothing more than alerting the person to the fact that he was supposed to be learning. This is one of the reasons psychologists attribute the curiosity motive to latent learning [Postman, 1955].

Motivation to learn can come in odd packages, however. Experiments that were similar in many respects to the one just reported demonstrate that learning can be facilitated in both observers and subjects just by the experimenters showing enthusiasm [Berger and Ellsburg, 1969]. Conceivably, this emotional contagion may explain why even students who are half-asleep in class seem to learn more from an instructor who has some emotional involvement in teaching.

There seems to be little question that learning is a positive emotional experience. As a child, a person may play for hours with a chemistry set; grown up, he may find chemistry *class* a deadly bore because all emotion has been stripped from it. I'm not zeroing in on chemistry; our whole educational system suffers from contagious boredom rather than excitement.

Even when motivation to learn has been established, the effectiveness of learning involves a personal emotional component: the *attitude* of the individual toward what he is learning. Individuals tend to learn material—or at least to reproduce more of it after learning—when that material is favorable to their viewpoint, so a student's attitude toward a topic affects the amount of material learned. This phenomenon is called *selective attention;* a subject selects that which agrees with his opinion and focuses attention on it. This does not mean that a person can't learn material with which he disagrees; it's just more difficult to learn. Given an opportunity, the person has little trouble bypassing his memory banks with disagreeable information [Malpass, 1969].

hedonic psychology   Just in case you were about to leave this chapter and dismiss it as a collection of strange schedules of reinforcement, it seemed that a little life might be brought to a sometimes dry subject matter by introducing the master creator of dissent and confusion, psychologist Timothy Leary. In case you don't place him right away, he is the drug-psychologist who created a furor in the 1960s by suggesting that everyone "Tune in; turn on; drop out." Since that time Leary has been in and out of various countries for a while avoiding prison on a twenty-year sentence for possession of an ounce of marijuana. It is hard to know whether to take him seriously; in the words of one biographer he is a "pleasant con man," but his rather deviant ideas seem to capture the imagination of many [Slack, 1973]. In any case, some of his thoughts are good for stirring the imagination.

Leary's current campaign is directly related to much of the material contained in the present chapter. Many psychologists have advocated the positive aspects of conditioning as a means of exercising social control and maintaining "correct" behavior in the individual. Leary takes the opposite point of view. He claims that psychologists have gone too far already in their use of conditioning because our reward system in the school and home is designed to produce individuals who can do little but conform to the dictates of society. By so doing, most of the rewards received are external to the individual.

He certainly is correct when he says that many have taken to heart the principles of conditioning as a solution to problems, but he takes an extreme opposite point of view: psychologists should do an about-face and should discourage working for external rewards that create conformity. Instead, he believes, psychologists should teach people to seek internal gratification, living only for internal pleasure, pleasures which the body can create on its own—in a word, we should become hedonists (see Chapter 5). The ultimate internal pleasure under his system is the ecstasy produced by electrical shock to the brain, or, as you might have suspected from the author of these ideas, being on an LSD trip [Leary, 1973].

Basically, he is saying that man should live without a society, should live within himself, and obtain whatever pleasures the body can provide. So, Leary is making a comeback, but the important point is, how do these ideas affect your thoughts and feelings about conditioning? Which world would you rather have, or must we choose between only these two approaches?

SUMMARY

The present chapter and the following one are based on material which moves back and forth continuously between two major viewpoints in psychology: the detailed, mechanical approach, and the broad-scope, semi-philosophical view of man. Illustrated by the two introductory quotations, these outlooks are still important in psychology. Both approaches are fascinating in their own right, and they do dovetail in many places. For the most part, however, you must unite them for yourself; most theorists take one side or the other, or at least emphasize one of them.

One current theory of memory storage rests on the assumption that when we learn material, it is moved from the STM to the LTM, and at the LTM the chemical substances of the synapses are altered to form preferred routes for electrical transmission, which actually triggers the memory. In some unknown fashion, these memories probably are stored in protein molecules, which in turn are responsbile for the electrical activity of the cells.

Memories are stored in various areas throughout the older brain and cortex of man. Given an appropriate opportunity, the complete memory seems to be reconstructed by drawing on bits of information stored in the protein molecules.

The construction of a memory molecule seems to result from electrical stimulation, which triggers a chemical agent. That agent reacts with the master chemical DNA, which in turn sends out RNA messengers to chemically organize the protein.

One of the foremost indicators that we have a short- and a long-term memory is the behavior of the person who has amnesia. In this case, most recent memories disappear first; hence, it is assumed that these memories have not solidified to the same extent as older memories have. Short-term memories are especially susceptible to interference from distractions that occur while the material is being learned. Long-term memory is most influenced by major structural changes, such as the introduction of protein inhibitors. Photographic memory, called eidetic imagery, is intriguing not only in its own right, but because it demonstrates something we will discuss in greater detail later on—that we seem to have two memory-storage systems, one of them for imagery and the other for symbols or labels; the eidetic person loses the visual image when he tries to label it.

While classical conditioning is based primarily on the unavoidable response of the organism to a natural stimulus, operant conditioning stresses that we learn by certain acts on our part. These acts, or operations, are associated with certain rewards, and the acts are thereby reinforced or made more likely to recur. Shaping of behavior involves reinforcement of parts of a complete act, rewarding the animal at various stages until he has the whole activity fixed in his repertoire of behavior. Basic techniques of operant conditioning involve continuous reinforcement, in which the animal is reinforced for each desired act and intermittent reinforcement, in which the animal is rewarded according to a schedule set up by the experimenter.

Most learning is thought to be of the operant type, although classical conditioning does play a major role. Furthermore, some types of learning are at present poorly understood—for example, learning because of a so-called curiosity motive. Psychology seems to be moving in the direction of more complete exploration of these more elusive motives, to supplement the myriad of studies on such basic drives as hunger and sex.

CHAPTER NINE
LEARNING

In its early days, psychology's interests were concentrated at the university level, first as a part of philosophy and then as a field of education, a discipline in which many psychological principles could be applied. Learning has been one of the largest areas of experimental study in psychology, and a good-sized library is available on this topic alone. In this chapter we will cover selections of some general principles of learning, since it would be impossible to cover all the issues, side issues, and discussions going on in the field.

To illustrate some of the principles of learning and some of the theories involved, we may well start with four statements. I beg the indulgence of the reader here: rather than asking questions now about this material, please read through it, and we will refer back to the passages as we progress.

72   (*Wells Fargo Bank*)

1. I pledge allegiance to the flag of the United States of America and to the Republic for which it stands. . . .

2. Raoult's law states that the depression of the freezing point and the elevation of the vapor pressures of liquids which are dissolved are in proportion to the number of molecules of substance so dissolved.

3. If you are attacked by a dog, hit his nose hard and fast. Put your forearm in front of you and jam it into his open mouth. Bring your other arm around behind the dog and press it against his neck. Force his head backward and over your arm snapping the neck.

4. In the late 1800s a Wells Fargo stage bandit named Black Bart was known throughout the West for the poetry he left behind after his getaway:

> I've labored long and hard for bread.
> For Honor and for Riches,
> But on my corns too long I've stood,
> You fine-haired Sons of Bitches.
>
> Black Bart, the Poet (Hawgood, 1967)*

*From J. A. Hawgood, *America's Western Frontiers* (New York: Alfred A. Knopf, 1967), p. 235; reprinted by permission.

212

ATTENTION   Now we are in a position to discuss a major principle of learning, *attention* Attention, of course, means exactly what it says: the key to the learning process seems to be a focusing on the material presented. Number 4 above is an attention grabber. It is quite direct and to the point—startling, in fact. There probably isn't a reader among you who can't recite the last line of Black Bart's poem right now without having to check back. If we were to graphically present the learning of the complete poem it would look something like Figure 9-1.

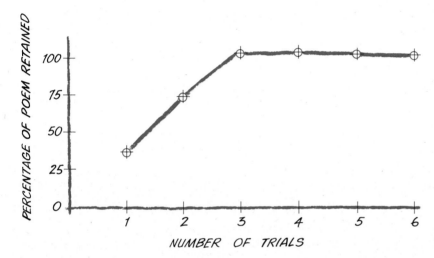

9-1 Learning curve for Black Bart's poem

In other words, Figure 9-1 shows that on the first few trials* we would probably make errors, but learning would take place rapidly until it reached 100 percent mastery. We could then go around reciting it, thereby becoming attention grabbers ourselves.

Compare Black Bart's poem with number 2, Raoult's law. Learning this material is going to be more conventional for the nonscientist because motivation is moderate, and so is attention. The learning process is more of a struggle. The definition itself can be learned, but after a short period a considerable amount has been lost. Over a period of time and trials, if this learning is averaged out, the curve will look like Figure 9-2. Note that the curve representing learning moves gradually upward with practice, but certainly the curve is not nearly so dramatic as the one in Figure 9-1. This gradual *learning curve* (Fig. 9-2) is *the* learning curve. That is, it is the curve most frequently found in experiments on learning, whether the task be a

* Trials are the same thing as practice sessions or, in a typical experiment, the number of times the subject performs a task.

(normal) poem, principles of mathematics, a passage from a book, or a speech to be presented. This gradual learning curve has for many years stood as the king of learning curves; other types appear much less frequently.

The difference in learning curves shown in Figures 9–1 and 9–2 suggests that through the clever use of color, design, and attention-focusing statements—that is, dramatic focus of attention—the student can more quickly reach an associational phase, the point at which material is integrated. As a matter of fact, some have been concerned that classroom surroundings which are too colorful, interesting, or lively could actually draw attention from what the teacher is saying and deter the learning process [Trabasso, 1968]. Therefore, the proper use of attention-getting devices in learning is critical. For example, did your eye move to the pictures on the opposite page? At the very least they should be distracting.

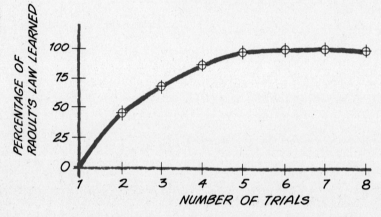

9-2 Normal learning curve

overlearning If you are like most people, when you read passage number 1—"I pledge allegiance to the flag . . ."—you didn't stop where the printed passage did, but continued on a few words beyond that point. You set into motion a process that is written indelibly somewhere in your brain, just like "Mary had a little lamb, its ——— — ——— – ——," etc. Yet when you first learned these lines, your attention was at best moderate, and you may have had little desire to learn the verse in the first place. Now it is thoroughly ingrained.

How do psychologists account for such permanent storage? By a process called *overlearning*. This term sounds strange at first, but when we are dealing with material that is only moderately interesting, overlearning often saves the day. To understand overlearning, we need first to focus on what is called the *forgetting curve* (descending line in Fig. 9–2; solid line in Fig. 9–3). A large amount of conventional material is forgotten very rapidly at the beginning, a short time after learning, but the "loss" begins to taper off to a point (*A*) at which retention will tend to remain (Fig. 9–3).

73-74-75 (*Suzanne Szasz,*
State of New Hampshire

The dotted lines in Figure 9–3 are the same as the solid upward line in Figure 9–2; both represent learning. In Figure 9–3, however, we learn the material to point *P*, meaning that we are able to recite it through *one time* perfectly. Right after this one recitation, the curve falls rapidly to point *X*, where it begins to taper off to point *A*. Point *A* represents the percentage of the original material which we tend to retain. So we start over with a second learning, and we go beyond one perfect recitation to three perfect recitations (3*P*); however, this time the curve falls to point *B*, somewhat higher than *A*. If we keep repeating this process, we can achieve perfect mastery of the material (point *D*), even after the curve falls over an amount of time with no recitation. Because we have learned the Pledge of Allegiance so many times, we don't forget it.*

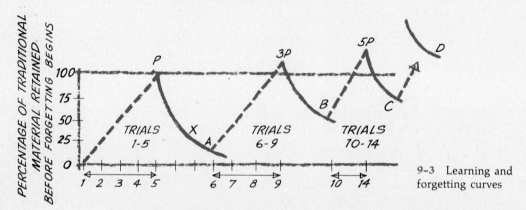

9–3   Learning and forgetting curves

Why is this situation called *overlearning?* If the curve of forgetting continues to fall each time you learn, in order to reach point *D after* the curve has fallen (which it always will), you require many additional rehearsals. Since you have learned beyond the original one perfect recitation, you have in essence overlearned the material. The term *overlearning* is somewhat deceptive. It really means learning over and above one perfect recitation. Notice in Figure 9–3 that you have reached the 100 percent retention point on trials 1 through 5. On trial 5 you have perfect (100 percent) retention only for one recitation, at which point error (or forgetting) begins to enter the picture. Therefore, you only held the 100 percent mark for a short time, so you must overlearn or learn well beyond one perfect recitation to hold the 100 percent mark indefinitely.

You may have wondered why, as an adult, you can still ride a bicycle. You do not retain that capacity because a motor skill—one that uses the muscles—is necessarily easier to remember than an intellectual skill. Rather, because you have ridden a bike—or tied your shoe—so many times,

*Figure 9–2 is a smoothed curve and doesn't show the dips *between* trials that you see in the detail of Fig. 9–3.

you have in theory overlearned the skill to such a degree that you don't have any trouble achieving 100 percent perfect every time. Your forgetting curve would not reach below the level necessary for continued perfect performance. (Notice again that the forgetting process begins right after that one perfect recitation; you don't have 100 percent permanent retention on the first perfect recitation.)

TRANSFER OF TRAINING

Another major learning process is *transfer of training*. The principle is relatively simple: training in task *A* will help learning or training in task *B*. For example, policemen are regularly given firing-range practice in which they shoot at human-shaped targets that dart, hide, and suddenly reappear. Since volunteers to act as targets are in short supply, these artificial targets are the best the police can do in most cases. The assumption is that this task (*A*) will transfer (carry over) to task *B*—actually firing at a moving human fugitive.

A more complicated transfer of training is found in the elaborate airline complex in Kansas City, Missouri. Exact replicas of aircraft cockpits are used to train pilots for genuine emergencies. These computer-controlled units simulate in precise fashion what would happen and what it would be like in a real aircraft during a particular kind of emergency. The pilot's responses to the situation are interpreted and transmitted by computer so that his fake aircraft will "behave" exactly as he tells it to. This simulation is a cheaper way to find out if the plane would crash than doing it "live." Pilots are also trained in real aircraft, of course, and they seem to transfer a considerable amount of learning from the simulator to the real plane. During an emergency in a real plane, the pilot may well behave as he did in the simulator—and the outcome will presumably be the same, for better or worse. Few learning situations are brand-new. We would be quite slow if we had to learn everything "new" from the beginning; instead we frequently transfer similar principles from one task to another.

Now to the more subtle aspects of transfer of training. Our second example, Raoult's law, would be much more comprehensible if we had previous training which somehow was related to the behavior of gases and molecules. In other words, a chemistry buff would have little difficulty understanding what that law is all about because he had learned similar aspects of other laws in the past. Principles of learning in the classroom are based on transfer of training. In the area of mathematics, for example, many of the later operations of calculus are based on similar modes of thought and actions found in algebra, which in turn are related to those of arithmetic. So learning is most effective when a number of components of a learned task are similar to those of previously learned tasks. For instance, many French, Italian, and Spanish words are similar, so that if we learn one, either of the other two becomes a little bit easier.

doctrine of
formal discipline

Education somehow has become synonymous with an unpleasant, unhappy experience. The thought that it might be fun is drummed out of us by about the third grade. And it never lets up. Generations of students have read books or had courses in "how to study." One of the cardinal principles has been: make yourself physically uncomfortable while you study. Sit in a hard-backed chair so that you don't feel relaxed. This rule was just taken for granted. Everyone knew intuitively that learning environments must be unpleasant—that is until it was studied experimentally. You will be happy to know that grade averages are about the same whether you study on the bed or in a straight-backed chair, and just as many honor students lie down as sit up while studying [Gifford and Sommer, 1968].

Education has also gotten a bit off the track in its fervor for the idea of transfer of training. First of all, considerable confusion existed about the exact role of the school in the 1800s, at the time when the public school system began. Originally, schools had been thought of as an extension of the home, and in this sense they played a major role in moral and religious training and character development. Unfortunately rules of conduct at school do not necessarily transfer to other situations. "Character development" showed itself not only in rules of conduct to be memorized but also in the philosophy that more difficult courses are "better" for the student. This view was probably partly based on the idea that "idle brains are the devil's workshop." A ray of hope for all belabored students showed itself when an educator's report published in 1859 (and mostly ignored) stressed the danger of insanity if intellectual training began too early* [Wishy, 1968]. This thought was clearly overridden in the next decade, when the *doctrine of formal discipline* became established. The doctrine of formal discipline stressed that certain courses, the very hard ones, were "mind-trainers"—Latin, mathematics, and logic. These courses were aimed at creating a form of generalized transfer, in the sense that the curriculum was designed to exercise the mind so that it would be capable of handling *any* difficult academic problem or life problem.

This theory of education suffered quite a blow in the 1920s, when a psychological experiment showed that those who had taken courses in cooking and sewing did essentially as well in reasoning tests as those who had specialized in the Latin-math type of course [Thorndike, 1924].

Further studies demonstrated that transfer takes place only when some similarity exists between the material originally learned and the new material. For example, Latin is helpful in learning Spanish, in the sense that learning about subjunctives and diagramming sentences can be used in one as well as the other. The student who has taken Latin would have an edge

76 Depiction of Victorian character development (*Culver*)

*This is a very appealing idea, but incorrect unless a parent or educator foists too much too violently on the child.

over the student who has not done so when they both enter a Spanish course since many Spanish words are similar to Latin words. However, there seems to be no such thing as mind exercise and training—despite the feeling of intolerable pain and exercise we get when we try to learn Raoult's law.

The important principle in transfer of training is similarity of the various aspects of the learned problem. For example, recall the problem with set in maze learning: once we had learned to turn one way consistently and then the direction was changed (Chapter 2). The general principle of problem solving was quite effective as long as we remained with the same type of problem, but when the procedure was switched, set had been established, and the wrong method of solving the problem was transferred, interfering with learning. In this case, what had happened was *negative transfer*, in which task *A* hinders rather than helps the learning of task *B*.

Negative transfer argues in favor of what might be called "flexible teaching," in which the student is trained to answer questions on his own rather than to perform rote memorization of factual material. Young children, for example, have some difficulty identifying people in photographs when the second or third photograph of the *same* person is taken from a different angle. Abstract concepts—e.g., "This is the same person from a different angle"—can be learned, however, and used for transfer, but only with flexible training. In one study, children were trained to identify several different people by being shown the *same* photograph of each person over and over again. Later on, these children did less well when the pose was changed than did children who had been trained using photographs taken of each person from different angles [Dukes and Bevan, 1967].

This example may seem pretty obvious to you—but the principle contains subtleties that are far-reaching. Rote memorization, a behavior somewhat similar to seeing the same picture over and over again, does not prepare the student for unexpected or unusual situations. Certain principles—for example, viewing things from different angles—can be transferred beneficially, but transfer of set is a hindrance in problem solving. As we will discuss later in connection with creativity, it is usually the person who can handle the unusual situation—or invent it—who is considered most creative.

generalization and transfer We have discussed stimulus generalization in reference to classical conditioning. In that situation, if stimulus *A* looked like or behaved like stimulus *B*, we generalized or extended our response to include stimulus *B* because it was like *A*. Notice that generalization, which can occur in operant conditioning as well as classical conditioning, is an integral part of transfer. For example, for a person who has previous training in chemistry, learning Raoult's law utilizes transfer because he immediately sees in the new principle similarities to those he already has learned. And if you were repairing a Honda, you would transfer what you knew about another make of motor-cycle; you could transfer your training from the repair of one to the repair of the other because of the two having so many similarities.

Transfer, which is based on generalization, can have widespread effects on social phenomena such as prejudice—an attitude that is learned from the attitudes, spoken and unspoken, of parents and friends. Minority groups, for instance, are set aside from others by a process of generalization. Blacks are among the most obvious victims of this process. In order for whites to justify the treatment of blacks in this country, it was necessary to create myths to counteract any pangs of guilt they might feel. Obviously, if one looks hard enough at any group, some of its members will turn out to be lazy, some not as intelligent as others. By locating these individuals, the whites tempered their unjustified behavior by saying to themselves and others, "Look there. Pete Jones is black. Pete Jones is lazy." At this point, generalization enters into the picture, accompanied by a large measure of faulty logic: If Pete Jones is black and if Pete Jones is lazy, then all blacks are lazy. Thus, a characteristic that belonged to a limited few is spread by the obvious color characteristic which makes the black identifiable and comes to encompass *all* blacks.

The situation is akin to that of the man who has an accident in his car. Both drivers are at fault, but the other driver is a woman. In order to eliminate any responsibility, the man starts off by assuming that the accident happened because this "woman driver" did not pay attention. The man is subsequently very quick to notice negative cartoons, surveys, or articles in the paper about women drivers. He is in the process of generalizing. Soon he will have accumulated enough articles favorable to his side that he can conclude that *all* women are poor drivers.

In both cases, generalization has occurred by the mechanism of transfer. We generalize or spread our reactions by transferring characteristics of black *A* or woman driver *A* to all members of the group. It is sometimes difficult to make the minor distinction between "transfer" and "generalization." This may help: we *generalize* because we see similarities; we move these similarities from object or person *A* to object or person *B* by a process of *transfer*.

discrimination   Pursuing prejudice further, we can get some interesting clues to the learning process in general. For example, we know people who hate *all* blacks *except* Joe Smith and Tom Jones, with whom they work and who are "okay guys." "But the *rest* of them . . . well. . . ." This situation is a case of ***discrimination learning.**** Basically this means that we learn by detecting differences, that is, discriminating between two or more things. The principle operates in

---

* Although the words are the same, the psychological term does not mean exactly the same as the popular term *discrimination*. In psychology the term *discrimination learning* refers to the ability to tell the difference between objects or stimuli.

this fashion. Suppose one is prejudiced against blacks. He establishes a set of standards for them: their noses are different; their hair is different. These standards might be called an *adaptation level* (see Chapter 6 for adaptation). In other words, just as our bodies have by now adapted to a point where we can tolerate a certain number of drinks or cigarettes a week, we have a fixed psychological adaptation level for what we expect in the behavior of a black. Four drinks a week might be the reference point. Blacks with lazy tendencies might be a reference point; they are expected and adapted to. New learning takes place when events are not in keeping with our adaptation level [Zeiler, 1963]. Twelve drinks can be as startling as the realization that Joe or Tom has human qualities—friendliness, honor, capacity for hard work, and so on. Our affection for their qualities has set these men apart (discriminated them) from the rest of the group that provides the adaptation level (reference point). In other words, learning takes place by discrimination of *A* from *B*, in this case discrimination of Tom and Joe from other blacks; and it takes place by altering our adaptation level.

We cannot neglect the role of attention here, either. We are attending to certain facets of the person that we never before knew were there. This is to some extent connected with the behavior mentioned earlier in the book regarding the orienting reflex (Chapter 6). Notice that we are picking out (orienting toward) cues to what a person is like rather than just using a generalized (and prejudicial) transfer process. We have reoriented our attention.

Many laboratory experiments narrower in scope than minority-majority relations have shown that accurate learning is a matter of attention to factors that are relevant to a situation as it really is—and hence is a matter of discriminating *A* from *B* [Hilgard, 1961]. Learning correct answers or responses in a classroom can be altered by correct orientation of attention to the type of material the teacher emphasizes. And the reverse can occur: surely by now you have been in a class where the teacher kept stressing (orienting attention toward) certain points and then you were asked test questions about everything he *didn't* stress!

clustering   In some respects, and despite its implications, the previous discussion of race was oversimplified, in that everything was placed into two categories, good and bad. The principle remains the same, however, when we move to the more complex learning arrangement called *clustering* or *categorizing*. Clustering at its *simple* level means organizing by "either/or" descriptions like "good/bad." In a more complex form of learning, we cluster by necessity because of the tremendous number of items we must group together. Nonetheless, these kinds of learning are again discrimination situations.

Notice, for example, that not all trees are the same: some have thick branches, some thin; some are evergreens, and resemble oaks only remotely; yet we categorize them all as *trees*. Also, we don't confuse a dog with a tree, even if the two are next to each other, as they frequently are. And we don't confuse a clump of bushes with a tree. What we are doing in this learning process is symbolically grouping similar aspects—for example, bark, leaves (we apparently consider an evergreen needle a form of leaf), trunk, and so forth—to form the concept "tree." How confused our world would be if we didn't cluster! Every single item in it would be different, and this proliferation would present insurmountable storage difficulties, even for our elaborate brains. Children who have been blind until about twelve years of age have not had the opportunity for visual storage and are extremely confused when they are able to see after an operation. For a period of time they can recognize a chair, for example, only by touching it. More to the present point, their world is chaos at first—a rooster and a horse are confused because they both have tails, and one boy whose sight was restored at eleven years thought a fish was a camel because its fins looked like a hump [Delgado, 1969].

Categorizing or clustering occurs on the physiological level by means of some mechanism of *coding* that is not yet fully understood but that will be discussed shortly. The terms *coding, categorizing,* and *clustering* are essentially the same for most purposes; the only major difference is that coding suggests that in storing material the brain uses some technique other than words, images, or thoughts as we normally recognize them.

Almost any characteristic common to all the items can be used for effective clustering. In memorizing lists of words, for example, those that rhyme or sound alike are grouped together by the memory storage system; apparently, we can even organize material on the basis of acoustic (sound) properties [Bousfield, 1969].

In learning experiments, lists of items are retained much better if some commonality exists among them [Bousfield and Wicklund, 1953]. More is recalled and items are remembered longer if lists have been categorized [Fisher, 1971]. Finding a unifying theme can be very helpful in learning school material. For example, the student of history must be able to recall many dates and events; usually, however, these data have a common element. We could, for example, group all the events that pertain to land expansion in the U.S. during the 19th century, making recall considerably easier. Using this commonality is similar to clustering.

Putting facts to be memorized into a meaningful framework facilitates memory considerably. In one study subjects in the control group were told to memorize a list of words, while subjects in the experimental group were instructed to devise a meaningful story woven around the words to be memorized. In the experimental group, median recall of the words was 93 percent; for the control group, it was 13 percent. Having to make up one's own sentences with the words in them is more effective [Bower and Clark, 1969; Bobrow and Bower, 1969]. These facts may help explain why Americans have so much trouble learning foreign languages in our school system. Typically, the student is given a list of words to memorize, the worst of all possible techniques. A little better, but still poor, and also very common, is the requirement of having to learn such preposterous sentences as *"La plume de ma tante est sur la table de mon oncle."* * Students in other countries must *speak* (i.e., construct sentences of their own) in the language they are learning. This "self-organizing" and integrating of words produces excellent memory.

TECHNIQUES FOR LEARNING

mnemonic devices

Sometimes clustering or organizing is not possible, and rote memorization is the only hope. Memorization can be aided by what are called *mnemonic devices,* unusual tricks or combinations that force us to remember—probably because they are attention grabbers. For example, when learning a new task—operating a keypunch machine, say—which requires a sequence of operations, we might remember the first two or three steps quite well but have difficulty with the fourth step but remember the fifth, sixth, and seventh. Sometimes, making up a ditty or a poem, or using an unusual word, can help you to recall that step. Since you know steps 1, 2, and 3 in the operation of your machine, you might say to yourself, "Step 1, then 2, then 3, MOTOR"—the latter meaning *Move Over The Orange Rachet*—"step 5, then 6, then 7." This technique may seem pretty involved, but psychologists have long known that the middle parts of lists of items to be learned are the most difficult, and sometimes we have to focus on them, accentuate them, in order to facilitate remembering.

Another typical mnemonic device is learning a ditty that will remind you of something that is difficult to learn. For example, one of my sons is supposedly learning to play the piano. In music there are things called notes placed on the treble staff (which I don't understand but some of you undoubtedly do). In any case, these notes are *E, G, B, D,* and *F,* so he has learned the ditty, *"Every Good Boy Deserves Fudge."* I don't know that this helps his piano playing, but at least he knows his treble staff.

Another mnemonic device frequently used by students is the descriptive-story technique, in which the words to be memorized are put into sentence form. Lists are always longer than this example, but to give you an idea of the technique, if you had to learn the words *sandal, blizzard,* and *rafter* in that order, you might make up a sentence like: "I lost my sandal while in a blizzard so I sat on a rafter to get my foot warm." The descriptive story probably works because it gives logical organization to the disorganized words. We discuss this further in the next section under principle learning. In any case, some studies indicate that the descriptive-story technique has at least a slight edge over other mnemonic devices in the long run. More

* "My aunt's pen is on my uncle's table." (All scientific books should have at least one sentence in a foreign language. You just had it.)

seems to be retained after eight weeks using this device than in using the other ones [Boltwood and Blick, 1970].

Rhymes are helpful also as a mnemonic device since they aid clustering. Apparently a rhyme is useful and easy to learn because it restricts the number of responses a person can give—that is, only so many words will rhyme, and this limitation makes memorization easier. The rhyming is not as important as the fact that it automatically limits the number of answers we have to search for in our memory. For example, a *poor* mnemonic ditty might include the word "hat," which rhymes with a lot of words—rat, cat, sat, pat, etc.—but there aren't many words that have so many rhymes [Bower, 1969].

Mnemonic devices seem to be effective only if they are used in the process of learning itself. In other words if someone has already learned some material and is then given a mnemonic device to try to retain it, the device is ineffective [Rust and Blick, 1972]. Presumably if the mnemonic method had been used at the beginning, the material would have been stored differently.

principle learning   A very useful aid to learning is called *principle learning,* or the use of principles in learning. Without returning to the quotations at the beginning of this section, see if you can give the essential facts about what to do when attacked by a dog—even though considerable material has been presented since then and you weren't asked to memorize it. Probably you can paraphrase it pretty well. Why? This method of defending yourself is based on a general principle we all learn early in life: pressure exerted on one point, with counter pressure on another point, will usually snap or bend whatever object we are working with. The same holds true with the dog's neck. However, even if you weren't able to recite the dog-protection plan offhand, principle learning will still work; now you have the principle, and one more reading and you will probably never forget it.

Here is another illustration of principle learning.

Memorize: 574   575   579   583   584   588   592   593

You can do this in about ten seconds. No? Well, once you understand the principle of the problem you can: start with the first number (the only one you really have to memorize). Here is the principle: add 1, add 4, add 4, then 1, then 4, then 4, then 1, etc. The principle is $+1$ $+4$ $+4$ $+1$ $+4$ $+4$ $+1$, etc. You can now recite 24 numbers, or more.

It is always best in any learning situation to try to apply a principle, or a "logic," to what you are learning [Katona, 1940]. For example, when reading about the mean or average in Chapter 2, notice how much easier it is to learn if you think of the mean as a number that combines all the numbers so it can represent them by just one number. Knowing the principle, you can figure out how any average is obtained. Contrast this method with rote memory: mean = sum of the individual numbers divided by the total number of individual numbers. This formula is without principle and therefore easy to forget, unless you overlearn it. Principles do not require the elaborate storage of detail that would be necessary if one had to learn, say, five different tasks separately. If the tasks have much in common, learning each is not very difficult.

consolidation theory

One of the most appealing theories of learning process is called *consolidation*. This theory seems to interest students because it involves resting—i.e., actually doing nothing. There is a slight catch, however. The student must study first, *then* rest. Theory has it that the memory storage system needs time for the material learned to consolidate or set. In other words, just as concrete solidifies with time, so will memories. Many studies have borne out this theory. An intriguing one showed that students who learned material and then immediately went to sleep were able to retain up to 20 percent more material than a control group that learned and stayed awake [McGaugh, 1967]. Direct application of this theory would indicate that an individual would be wise to take frequent (short!) breaks during study rather than trying to learn a considerable amount at one time. Experiments show that the rest period required for maximum efficiency in learning varies considerably with the type of thing being learned, but a good rule of thumb is to take a break whenever you feel your attention is drifting. Material learned just before going to sleep at night is very effectively consolidated by morning, but since you can't go to sleep every time you learn something, this technique is limited despite its merit.

Consolidation theory is obviously based on the principle of allowing the LTM enough time to bring together its "circuits" and alter the molecular structure to form the memory. Theoretically, then, the periods of rest prevent unwanted material from "firing" other circuits which would interfere with the original learning; that is, adding further material might interfere with that which is "setting."

One theory suggests that consolidation results from the solidification or making permanent of various protein changes within the LTM circuit. In an operant conditioning arrangement, the first rewarding set of circumstances—e.g., pressing the bar—starts an electrical network operating. A rest period follows; however, during this rest period any part of the original rewarding situation—for example, the corner of the Skinner box where the bar is—continues to remind the memory circuit of the total learning experience and its reward. During the rest period, this reminder triggers another firing of the whole memory sequence, thus strengthening it. The electrical firing during rest thereby continues consolidating the memory within the brain [Landaver, 1969].

In the last chapter we were struggling with memory facilitators and inhibitors. Chemical injections with animals have demonstrated that memory consolidation can be increased by chemical means [Alpern and Crabbe, 1972]. This holds intriguing possibilities for the future, one of which is the possibility of developing a drug which will increase consolidation in the human memory.

recitation theory

Saved for last is one of the least pleasant but most effective means of learning. This bit of behavior is one we have used since grade school—*recitation*—only here we are referring to silent recitation, which doesn't require you to stand up while performing the act. Recitation means repeating to yourself what you have just learned. To illustrate its remarkable effectiveness, subjects in one study spent almost 80 percent of their reading time stopping and reciting what they were learning. They recalled what they had learned *better*, in the long run, than a control group that kept on reading without taking frequent breaks for recitation [Gates, 1958]. Apparently, reading a paragraph or so and reciting in your own words what you have just read forces potentially wandering attention back to the material. This attention and recitation, in turn, probably facilitates movement from STM to LTM and theoretically provides a longer exposure for consolidation. As we will discuss later in greater detail, those subjects who continued to read, without stopping for silent recitation, probably brought in too much material, and it began to compete for a place in memory.

FORGETTING

Next we need to take up some of the factors responsible for the increase in errors (forgetting) that was evident in our discussion of the need for overlearning. However, first I should point out that psychologists divide memory into different kinds. Two kinds that are frequently differentiated are *recall* and *recognition*. Both are forms of memory, but recognition is "easier" than recall. Recall is a specialized memory that requires the bringing back of many *details* learned, as in an essay test. Recognition works in the familiar multiple-choice test. (Which one is correct: *A, B, C,* or *D? Recognize* the right answer.) Compare, for example, the relative ease of making an identification from a police lineup (recognition) to the formidable task of providing a full description of the culprit for the police artist (recall).

memory storage and referencing

Recognition is important because it demonstrates how little we actually forget under certain circumstances. For example, we can recognize a face we have seen, even if we can't give a name to it. All of us have been involved in the "double-take" routine; we see someone familiar, but his name is often elusive. The memory is intact, but we can't bring back the details. If these details come back later, then we have engaged in recall *and* recognition; if not, recognition alone. Our high level of recognition ability strongly suggests that we forget a small proportion of things that we have learned [Schwartz, 1969; Shepard, 1967].

Some rather startling recent studies may help to explain the difference between the two types of memory, recall and recognition. Apparently the brain has two different memory systems, one for visual memory and one for linguistic material that has been coded and stored. Subjects in one study had the capacity to recognize 85 to 90 percent of 2,560 slides they had viewed. Two of the subjects who scored in the 90 percent range saw 1,280 slides in one day. Apparently, memories in visual form are stored without coding and probably in "pictorial form" [Haber, 1970]. This visual storing may or may not explain the study, discussed previously, of eidetic children who lost the image when they tried to store the name of the object, but it certainly seems to fit the facts.*

In studies in this area there has been a consistently high level of recognition in which subjects could recognize many words and sentences, as well as pictures. For the time being one can only assume that this storage was visual. Entire words and sentences were stored intact, without coding, without moving them to the memory bank in the normal fashion, as we do when we have to memorize something for its *content*—that is, specific word storage. When we are memorizing for content and permanency, we code the material. Items in the recall bank apparently require coding and specific categorization. At present there seems to be a general consensus of opinion among psychologists that recognition memory involves very little, if any, searching through the memory banks, whereas recall in detail is a complex searching process [McCormack, 1972].

coding theories   How do we store this material? An experimenter in the learning field has devised an ingenious hypothesis: We code memories by category—i.e., in a fashion similar to the library system, by classes like history and philosophy, and maybe by sections such as friendly and unfriendly people, etc. [Shiffrin, 1969]. Since we know that recognition does not deteriorate over time to the same extent that recall seems to fade, we might want to assume that recall is difficult because we have a retrieval problem.

Retrieval means bringing back learned material. We might store some learning like this:

> **Philosophy** (main category)
> **Plato's book** *The Republic* (subcategory)
> **Thought 1 of Plato** (subcategory) (discussion of man)
> **Contents of thought 1,** items *A, B, C, D, E, F*
> (these contents all refer to specific items about man)

Now, in this storage scheme, retrieval by recognition requires a limited search by the memory process, compared to what is required for exact recall. All that is needed for recognition is agreement with the statement that a general type of discussion of man occurred. This could be determined without looking at the specific items *A, B, C,* etc. And the brain's

---

* Visual storage for recognition must not involve the traditional STM or it would disappear. The underlying process is presently unclear.

scanning process in recognition is extremely fast, approximately 25–30 symbols per second. So, if this system is correct, recognition could occur very rapidly [Sternberg, 1966]. In *recall*, however, we have to search in detail through all the different items *A, B, C, D, E,* and finally *F.* This task is much more complex. Furthermore, as time goes on we will add many more items under philosophy, and recall will become even more difficult. So-called forgetting, then, is probably related to the difficulty we have in bringing back the correct material, not to whether the material is in the memory.

Accuracy of retrieval might also be related to the amount of space, figuratively speaking, that we devote to a certain topic. File clerks tend to put a lot of material under "miscellaneous," which overloads that category; but the experienced secretary would not make this mistake. Specialists in specific areas will have many more main categories and higher subcategories and fewer miscellaneous groupings. For example, the mechanic would have more main categories for things related to automobiles than would the philosopher. This abundance of categories aids retrieval because fewer items fall into each category.*

The importance of this grouping cannot be overemphasized. Specialists in particular areas can avoid the Jack-of-all-trades-master-of-none problem because they are quick to place items in the proper category. The brain is always ready to group a new item separately if it detects a difference in the new material. Experimenters have demonstrated, for example, that the same series of numbers is treated as a different category when pauses are placed at different positions between the numbers. For example, the brain has difficulty recognizing 17 683 as 176 83 [Bower and Winzenz, 1969]. The specialist's brain presumably sees commonality rather than difference. Thus, we are all specialists in trees. We have learned that the evergreen (17 683) is "the same" as the oak (176 83).

Further, mnemonic devices are effective probably because they create a category all by themselves. In other words, having MOTOR stand for "Move over the orange rachet" is unusual enough so that the information will not be stored in a common category; hence, the learner will have less competition when he attempts to retrieve it.

Although forgetting seems to be a problem of retrieval, bear in mind that LTM is involved here; no assumption is made that we store in LTM every bit of material to which we are exposed. Obviously a considerable amount is lost in STM. As a matter of fact, some experimenters feel that information in the STM decays (disappears) within 30 seconds without active recitation.†

*It is important to say again that this is a logical, probable hypothesis, but not actually a "fact."

†Do not be confused about the many rates of learning or forgetting mentioned in this and the previous chapter. Different studies arrive at different conclusions, unfortunately. The 30-second rate is merely an easy, round, and approximate number and is probably accurate enough.

trace and decay theories

Trace and decay work together. The *trace theory* assumes that learning leaves a mark or "pathway" on the brain. An old theory, it preceded most experiments with synaptic transmission and was used to account for forgetting. According to this theory, the trace *decayed* over time, just as old buildings do. Once *decay* had occurred, the memory was gone.

The theory of trace and decay is simple enough in that it is easy to understand. However, it does not fit all the facts, especially with reference to LTM. In fact, the theory has been modified over the years, and now it is used primarily for STM only, whereas in the past it encompassed all memory. It is assumed that the very rapid (thirty-second) loss of material in the STM must be a form of decay in that the material "dies out" rather than moving to the LTM [Melton, 1963].

As I mentioned, the theory does not fit LTM. One example of its failure is that old people tend to live partly in the past, reviving some memories that are fifty years old or older. Obviously, little decay, if any, has occurred here. Many of these memories appear with frequency only later in life, so it is doubtful that overlearning was involved. Forgetting does result from the passage of time, so decay cannot be eliminated as an operative factor. It does indeed produce forgetting; but, according to most theorists, it is least potent in the LTM, where, for example, the aged person's childhood memory is stored.

interference theory

The forces we call interference are thought to be more potent than decay in producing forgetting. Very simply, *interference theory* suggests that we forget because of conflict between new and old material in the memory banks.

One interpretation of interference is that we forget because new material interferes with the *processing* of what is being learned. In other words, just the introduction of some types of new material can cause processing difficulties with material that has been learned and is being stored. For example, the mere passage of time (decay) does not produce as much forgetting as the introduction of new material when a subject is trying to remember a sound, such as a musical tone. Suppose you are in the process of storing tone A; well, the introduction of tone B shortly after A results in considerable interference, confusion, and difficulty in remembering A. The new tone, like the original one, requires processing, and is thus more likely to interfere with remembering tone A than would just a blank space of time with no learning [Massaro, 1970a; Massaro, 1970b].

Another theory of interference suggests that we forget because the new material is similar to the old. This theory does not stress processing as much as just plain conflict between the new learning and the old. Thus, interference is most pronounced when the material from the past learning and that from the present learning are somewhat similar but not identical. By analogy, if television channels 3 and 5 were assigned the same frequency

77 Jet-trail is not unlike the brain's "trace and decay" (*UPI*)

for operation, they would compete with and interfere with one another. We would get parts of each channel, and considerable confusion would ensue. Interference results in essentially the same manner; we get a mixture of learnings, as it were. One of the most common examples of interference is the person who has been driving a standard-shift car and then drives one with an automatic transmission. For some time the person will be frantically depressing an imaginary clutch in the automatic car. Early methods of handling a car have been transferred to the new car, only now these methods cause the person to make mistakes. The incorrect transfer results from the similarity of the situations. This mistake is not forgetting, as we usually think of it. It is interference with new learning, which causes the person to have difficulty learning, which is a form of forgetting [Ceraso, 1967].

specific types of interference: proactive and retroactive inhibition

Another example of interference of the same type is concerned more directly with learning as we normally think of it. Turn your mind back to that wonderful time in childhood when you had to learn, "Now I lay me down to sleep . . . ," etc. You had this line and the rest of the poem down pat, and a week later the teacher brought in a new poem that began, "How I rave so much of sheep . . . ," etc. When you tried to learn the sheep poem, you made mistakes because the similarity of the sleep poem interfered. Perhaps you came out with, "Now I rave so much of sleep." In scientific terminology, the lines of the first poem are inhibiting (or blocking) the learning of parts of the second poem. This blocking is called *proactive inhibition: pro*, "forward" (in time) plus *active* (in blocking or inhibiting). For example, look at Figure 9–4. Notice that as far as time is concerned, we learned the sleep poem first and the sheep one second.

Number 1 is "moving forward" from the past and inhibiting the learning of number 2. Hence the confusion when we try to recite the sheep poem.

There is another kind of inhibition. Suppose that we learn the sheep poem thoroughly and then try to recite the sleep poem. Problems again: the sheep poem is going to move backward in time and interfere with our recitation of the sleep poem, the reverse of Figure 9–4. This process is called *retroactive inhibition*. A tax is sometimes retroactive, meaning that we have to pay for some period in the past. Hence we are moving backward. In the automobile example, if we get thoroughly accustomed to driving an automatic shift and then return to a clutch car, we can expect at least one day of other drivers honking us off the road. We will stall at a lot of intersections because we forget to step on the clutch. What we learned recently (the automatic) is interfering with past learning which we are trying to relearn (the clutch drive). This is shown in Figure 9–5. Therefore, retroactive inhibition is taking place (inhibition coming from the present and causing difficulty with something learned in the past).

9–4   Proactive inhibition

1   2
SLEEP ———▷ SHEEP
(TIME ——▷)

9–5   Retroactive inhibition

1◁——————— 2
CLUTCH   AUTOMATIC
(◁——— TIME)

Basically, then, what we learn in the past interferes with what we are learning in the present and what we learn in the present tends to inhibit what we have learned in the past.

enforced forgetting:
extinction

Sometimes it is desirable to give someone a little assistance in forgetting. Take the case of the enterprising young child who learns that he can put his finger on the tip of a spoon filled with food, bend it backward, let go, and get a slingshot type of action. This behavior is one we'd like him to forget. One night at dinner, however, he does this trick and gets a startled laugh from his mother. The laugh will act as a reinforcer of his tendency to do this sort of thing. The parent is then faced with the need to discourage the child.

One technique of "unlearning" that has been employed by experimenters is called *extinction.* Extinction basically means ending or extinguishing a response. In the laboratory, extinction results from pairing behavioral acts with *no reward.* For example, a rat that has learned to press a bar to get food is put into a situation in which the bar pressing no longer gives food. After a while the rat pushes the bar less and less frequently, especially if he had been accustomed to receiving a reward *each* time he pressed it.*

Applying the principle of extinction to the food-flinging problem would suggest that the next few times the child does his trick, the parents should ignore him. The odds are good that when he gets no reward—that is, no one pays any attention to him—he will no longer feel an incentive to perform his act. Hence, it will extinguish [Johdai, 1955].

The statements just made—that the object is no longer rewarding, and that incentive is lost—seem straightforward and logical enough. However, they constitute only one theory of why extinction works. An alternative is that the organism, when not rewarded, goes on to learn a different behavior that will overshadow the original response. Thus, the child may replace operating the spoon-catapult with putting a finger in his milk. Although the spoon trick no longer elicits a reaction from his mother, he finds that finger-in-the-milk is very effective. The original behavior has not been completely forgotten, but it is extinguished by a competing behavior that is found to be more effective [Guthrie, 1952]. There is a moral to this, which we will discuss in greater detail later, but animal studies emphasize dramatically the fact that removing one behavior is maximally effective if a different preferred behavior is reinforced at the same time. Animal studies are easier to control in many respects, so they are quite useful in handling something as complex as this problem. Some studies with humans seem to bear out the finding that one behavior is replaced by another. Hence,

---

*That is, continuous reinforcement, when stopped, extinguishes behavior more quickly than variable-ratio reinforcement.

it seems logical to reward the child for eating properly before milk dipping replaces food throwing [Catania, 1969].

The most recent theory suggesting why extinction occurs is that frustration is conditioned to the response. In other words, since getting food is no longer the result of pressing a bar, the rat associates frustration with the bar, and extinction occurs. Therefore the rat avoids the frustration that it experiences when it responds to the stimulus of the bar but gets no subsequent reward [Wagner, 1966].

Behavior that is essentially identical has been noted in humans, so it is fairly safe to assume that frustration operates to extinguish a response in our case, too [Blixt and Ley, 1969]. Frustration actually causes the response—for example, bar pressing—to increase in intensity for a short while, but this is not unusual. Have you ever been very patient about a flooded carburetor, and finally, when it just wouldn't start, jammed down the accelerator with all your might, flooding the engine hopelessly? Frustration can lead to a temporary increase in activity, but as frustration builds up, the behavior usually dies out.

Studies support all three hypotheses: loss of incentive, replacement, and frustration. It is, in fact, possible that under certain circumstances any one or more of these explanations is valid. At present the hypothesis that is most thoroughly substantiated is the frustration theory [Berger and Ellsburg, 1969].

enforced forgetting: punishment

Another method for handling the food-flinging incident is clouting the child on the head. Punishment is one of the most popular methods for trying to induce forgetting. The fact that punishment or the threat of it is used so frequently is ironic, because the weight of evidence indicates that it rarely prevents unwanted behavior. For example, murder cases are about as frequent in states having capital punishment as in states that have no such penalty [Sellin, 1959]. No evidence supports the idea that jails and prisons prevent crime; in fact, there is evidence that they tend to foster crime. And animal studies of the effects of punishment suggest strongly that the negative approach causes such extreme frustration that the animal begins to respond in a maladaptive way—that is, continued punishment brings little improvement in the animal's behavior. Instead, it keeps responding in a fixed manner, even though it is punished. This maladaptation is often seen in children who are punished repeatedly; they seem to develop give-up-itis and make few attempts to correct their behavior [Ball, 1969].

Punishment also has unpredictable outcomes, even on the national level. Bombing a country is obviously a punitive measure, but the Vietnam War illustrated how the enemy, instead of changing its behavior patterns, tended to persevere. Individuals are frequently strengthened into a tight-knit group by having a common outside enemy.

Oddly enough, punished behavior does not disappear. Laboratory studies with animals have shown that punishment does tend to block or inhibit certain responses, but it does not change the behavior permanently. Instead, when the punishment wears off, so to speak, the behavior pops up again, just about as strong as it was originally [Skinner, 1938]. Thus, although punishment does extinguish a response in some animals, the response reappears when the punishment is halted. The return of men to criminal activities after serving a jail sentence (called *recidivism*) is so prevalent that it is impossible to ignore the parallel between animal and human behavior in this case. Thus, even though many return to crime because they have nothing else they can do and they have learned the trade of crime, punishment is not a deterrent.

About the only effective use of punishment comes when a positive alternative behavior is rewarded at the same time as an unwanted behavior is mildly punished. In this case, the rewarded response takes over and seems to replace the punished one [Estes, 1944]. On the practical level, be the organism rat, child, or prisoner, reward seems the most effective means of changing behavior. (The specifics of punishment relating to child behavior will be dealt with later.)

One final reminder: neither extinction nor punishment removes the *memory* of an act. They merely reduce the probability that the act will recur. "Forgetting" occurs in the literal sense very rarely, but it is a convenient term to use.

PROGRAMMED LEARNING AND TEACHING MACHINES

At least three major factors stand out in effective learning: attention to the material, repetition, and reward. To capitalize on these three, mechanical methods of teaching have been devised.

Any reader who has had even moderate exposure to school materials since the late 1950s will recognize that a major change is taking place in learning aids. This change is in the area of programmed learning. *Programmed learning* is presentation of school material in an organized sequence that follows an elaborate overall plan (a program). Hopefully, *any* learning device has some organization, but programmed learning is carefully structured into units that fit together to form a whole picture. Later units are designed to build on learning that has taken place in earlier units. Thus a program of mathematics might start out with the simplest units of addition, progress to multiplication, and eventually arrive at algebra.

Of course, this method can be seen as applying to all kinds of general classroom and textbook learning. The unique thing about programmed learning, which cannot be detected in its name, is that it is essentially *self-instructional*. A programmed text is a book in which questions are left unanswered on the line being studied, but answers appear beneath the blank space, to the left of it, or on a following page. For example, opening a programmed psychology text in the middle, it might read:

> Reinforcement is a process of strengthening.
> When a tendency to respond is strengthened, it is＿＿＿. (reinforced)
> Reinforcement is quite frequently based on some rewarding event. Therefore,
> A response given a reward is said to be＿＿＿. (reinforced)
> When a response is reinforced, it is＿＿＿. (strengthened)
> Without a reward, a response tends to die out, or extinguish. Therefore,
> Unreinforced responses are usually＿＿＿. (extinguished)

The student fills in the blanks as he progresses through the program, checking each answer as he goes along, and using the information he learned in that item to successfully complete the next item.

Programmed-learning techniques have been known since the 1920s, but not until 1954, when B. F. Skinner devised his teaching machine, a form of programmed learning, did the idea catch on. Skinner is the major proponent of operant conditioning, and, as you will see, teaching machines fit his theory very well. A teaching machine is like a programmed textbook except that it is an automatic device. A question appears in a slit, and with it a blank square in which the student writes his answer. He can then operate a lever to put the correct answer on display and compare it with the one he wrote.

This device fits Skinner's theory of operant conditioning in several ways. First, a response is emitted—i.e., written down; hence an operation (operant) is performed by the organism. Second, this operation results in reward and reinforcement when the correct answer is obtained [Skinner, 1954]. Skinner felt strongly that the organism had to have a reward, in the form of getting immediate knowledge of results for each question. Actually, writing down the response is not necessary. The same effect can be obtained by having the student choose one answer from a list of multiple-choice items; here, the choice is the operant [Schramm, 1964].

Further experimentation has indicted that learning takes place even if the correct answer is shown only occasionally. Obviously this technique entails the danger of learning wrong responses, so the occasional-reward system requires a program of superlative quality that leads to as few undetected errors as possible.

Despite disagreements about whether every trial must be rewarded and whether the answers should be written down or chosen from among several possibilities, the teaching machine provides a patient teacher that does not become exasperated. Further, it has the advantage of allowing the individual student to set his own pace. Students who have difficulties can

78 Skinner's original teaching machine was a plain metal box, but it started a revolution in personalized instruction that provided instant feedback and reinforcement (*B. F. Skinner*)

79   A little girl studies math with the help of a teaching machine (*IBM*)

go over and over the material and never feel ashamed. Fast learners can move ahead without being held back by those who need more time.

Programmed learning does work well. However, a question naturally comes up: How does it compare with direct instruction by a live teacher? Contradictory evidence touches on this issue. The teaching machine is clearly better than a poor teacher, and it is excellent for use in schools that are seriously understaffed. On the other hand, studies have compared the teaching ability of a program maker's program for a teaching machine with his live presentation of the material, and students generally do better with the live teacher than with his program. However, only the exceptional teacher seems able to compete effectively with the machines, and the machines are clearly here to stay [Annett, 1967]. Machines are probably better, at least at present, for more factual learning, while the teacher is better for discussion of abstract problems.

ADD ⟶ SUBTRACT ⟶ MULTIPLY (ERROR MADE)

MULTIPLY

MULTIPLY ⟶ DIVIDE

ADD ⟶ SUBTRACT ⟶ MULTIPLY ⟶ DIVIDE

9–6   Learning chain

Teaching machines nowadays are a far cry from Skinner's early machine. The teaching machines we use now are connected to computers, electronic typewriters, and cathode-ray tubes (like the tubes in TV sets). Students can "talk" to the computer by using its typewriter; the computer can select key words from the student's answer, analyze them, and present a correct answer on the TV screen together with a new question that follows from the answer given. If the student makes an error, the computer can redirect its questioning so as to provide more background information on the topic the student answered incorrectly [Atkinson, 1968].* With an excellent program design, the specific problem causing an error can usually be detected by the machine and the student led down a separate path until he understands that concept. Notice in Figure 9–6 that an error in the chain of learning multiplication would lead the student back to more multiplication until it was completely understood (top diagram). If the student did well in multiplication problems, then the computer would not deem further

* Work is now going on with talking computers. You talk to them over a telephone and they answer [Alpert and Bitzer, 1970].

instruction necessary and would continue on with division (bottom diagram) [Suppes, 1966].

As teaching machines become more and more sophisticated, student and computer will be able to hold more or less complete discussions, even in areas that are difficult to program like philosophy and English literature. Computers are already adequate; the difficulties lie in determining how best to program the material, and those solutions are not far off.

SUMMARY

The learning capabilities of the human mind are fantastic; however, we can pinpoint a few important factors that contribute to the learning process. One is attention, the process of focusing on material to be learned. In general, the greater amount of attention, the greater the amount of learning retained, although most learning of any kind will follow a gradual curve when the amount of material learned is plotted on a graph. This gradually increasing curve of retention falls rapidly when trials of learning are halted; hence, in order to learn material thoroughly, a process called overlearning must be employed.

Learning is facilitated by transfer of training. Simply put, we rarely learn in a vacuum; instead, we call on similar things we have learned to aid us in a present task. Thus transfer is based on the similarity of material.

No evidence indicates that the mind can be trained or exercised, so to speak. The doctrine of formal discipline, which has been widely used in the school system, apparently is a failure if it is used in attempts to increase *general* mental capabilities.

Even though formal discipline is not a workable concept, we do see instances in which training spreads out to include other material, a process called generalization. Generalization refers to the fact that we tend to group similar things together, and it helps to explain some unpleasant phenomena, like racial prejudice.

The other side of generalization is called discrimination learning, which means simply that we set things apart on the basis of what differences we can detect between dissimilar materials.

Memory is facilitated by clustering and mnemonic devices. Clustering involves bringing together separate types of objects or thoughts on the basis of some commonalities—for instance, the grouping together of evergreens and oaks into the category "tree." Mnemonic devices are techniques that emphasize certain aspects of a situation, usually in an odd or startling fashion so a person will have little difficulty bringing the material back.

Memory is aided by rest, under the consolidation theory, in that frequent breaks are recommended so the material will "set." Just the opposite is true with the principle of recitation from the viewpoint of the amount of work involved. This principle stresses continuous rehearsal of the material in order to fix it firmly in the mind.

Apparently two types of memory exist, short- and long-term memory (STM and LTM). The short-term material dies out quickly if it is not stored in the LTM. One explanation for this loss is the decay theory, which equates memory with traces in the brain that are lost by a fading process. All memory seems to be affected by interference. In interference theory, new material competes with older material for space in the brain. Two common types of interference are retroactive inhibition and proactive inhibition. Retroactive inhibition takes place when present learning interferes with what we have previously learned; proactive inhibition is interference with what we are trying to learn from previous material, moving forward in time to the present.

Extinction is a form of forgetting based on the assumption that without some type of reinforcement, particular learned materials tend to lose their value and disappear. Extinction is most effective if some alternative act is rewarded at the same time as the other is fading out.

Punishment is a highly ineffective method for erasing a learned behavior. Its outcome is unpredictable, and when the punishment is removed, the learned act reappears because it has been suppressed, but not removed.

Programmed learning is a technique that utilizes the method of presenting small amounts of information to the subject in an organized fashion, providing him with the correct answer at certain intervals, so that he not only profits by his mistakes but also is rewarded constantly for each correct response by the knowledge that he has given the correct answer.

CHAPTER TEN
THE EXOTICS OF PSYCHOLOGY

A touch of truth seems to cling to many older theories of man and the universe. Generations to come may find that some older ideas are correct, and perhaps even that some of our era's ideas are right. For example, nowadays we attribute the motion of planets largely to gravity. *Gravity* is a modern term, but it is not much clearer than some older theories of planetary motion although the older vocabulary *seems* more absurd.

HYPNOTISM

One such idea claimed that a universal magnetic field not only is distributed throughout the universe but also is contained in man himself, and that this field is controlled by the movement of the planets. In the late 1700s Anton Mesmer (from whom we got the word *mesmerism*, which means the act of using a magnetic personality) decided that he had special magnetic powers which he could align with forces from other persons, curing personal or physical problems by "rearranging" the magnetism of his patients. If you had nothing to do one afternoon, some money in your pocket, and of course some physical or psychological problem, you could take a trip to "Mesmer's." Once there, in a grandly decorated room you would find a huge wooden bathtub filled with iron filings, water, and ground glass (?). Protruding from the side of the tub was a series of iron rods, one for each patient to use to touch an afflicted portion of his body, or just to hold in his hand if the problem was not localized. These arrangements were all very nice, but they did not work until Dr. Mesmer appeared in the room and began to exert his magnetic influence on the bathtub and the people. Surprisingly, many people were cured by this routine. If by chance you were unable to attend, Mesmer sold his magnetic powers in bottled form.

Many historians feel that the application of hypnosis to groups began in this way. To differentiate it from individual hypnosis as best we can, Mesmer's bathtub procedure would be labeled *group suggestion*. As we will discuss later in the book, one should not underestimate either the restorative or the destructive powers of group suggestion. In a well-documented study in the 1960s, 40 women working at a clothing mill came down with a completely unexplained illness marked by nausea, rash, and dizziness. The press attributed the outbreak to the report, made by a few of the women, that they had been bitten by a "strange bug." The disease became epidemic, eventually spreading to roughly 200 employees. Most of the employees then

80 A lady enjoys the benefits of Mesmer's magnetic bathtub (*Culver*)

240

claimed to have been bitten by some small bug which eluded exterminators, microbiologists, public health officials, etc. Every available bit of evidence pointed to the conclusion that no such bug was on the premises, yet its "bite" spread symptoms and illness. The most logical explanation is that this epidemic was an instance of the power of suggestion. Similar "epidemics" occur, with some frequency, in which schoolchildren, office workers, and the like are stricken by a completely indefinable disease that leaves just about as spontaneously as it enters the picture. The element of panic seems more important than any actual infection or bug [Kerekhoff and Back, 1968].

Evidence to support the power of suggestion is even more abundant on the positive side. How, for example, could a man like Mesmer have "cured" people unless he did it by the power of suggestion? Certainly the passing of magnetic fluids is highly improbable.

The word *hypnosis* comes from the Greek word meaning "sleep." There is a superficial resemblance between sleep and what is called the hypnotic state, but the two are clearly not the same. *Hypnotism* is a technique of relaxation and suggestion in which the hypnotist reduces outside interference and convinces the individual to relax and put himself in the hypnotist's hands, so to speak. The person is not sleeping and does not lose consciousness; he does tend to act somewhat drowsily, but he is aware of what is going on about him and can be in control of the situation if he wants to be.

The method most frequently used to put a person "into a trance" is to require concentration on some object, perhaps a moving coin or a shiny watch. This method is often the easiest way to produce a trance, probably because it fits the expectations of the person being hypnotized. *Any* rhythmical behavior is conducive to creating a trance, however. A voice speaking in measured patterns will work; even listening to a recording of one's own breathing has been effective [Kubie and Margolin, 1944]. Many of us are at least partly hypnotized by monotony. A case in point is highway hypnosis, in which gazing steadily at the white line can lead to disaster. The phrase "You are getting sleepy" is well known to the layman as the hypnotist's tool, but one experimenter has been successful in inducing a trance state by looking individuals in the eye and saying, "Phoz"—a meaningless word [Moss, 1965].

The variety of techniques seems to indicate that hypnosis is not as special and mysterious a thing as the popular press plays it up to be. At least two basic factors are probably involved in being hypnotized: a relaxed state and a heightened degree of suggestibility. The power of suggestion is easy enough to demonstrate. Without ever seeing you, I can use the written word to bring your attention and *feeling* to a portion of your body of which you are not even aware at the present moment. Notice, once I have called this to your attention, just how inevitable and forceful are the feelings you experience, and yet you have not been hypnotized, merely had your attention directed and channeled. All the time you have been reading this paragraph, you were not aware of your right foot. Now, just by my suggestion, you can feel it. Assuming you are wearing shoes, I can further suggest that the shoe is slightly heavy, in fact confining, and maybe you should wiggle your toes. Even if you don't have shoes on, it might be a good idea to wiggle your toes, just to get some circulation in them.

This is not black magic, but merely a suggestion which points out that your powers and abilities can be controlled and focused. Notice how simple it would be to continue this suggestion and get you to feel hot, cold, faint, depressed, and so forth.

Hypnotists, especially of the stage variety, are noted for some of the unusual feats which their subjects perform—for example, displays of great strength. These feats, too, seem to be well within the realm of the average person—given the correct set of circumstances. It becomes a matter of concentrated effort and motivation. Many readers have seen a hypnotist suspend a person between two chairs, one chair bracing him under the neck and the other supporting the legs, and then proceed to stand on the person or break a concrete block resting on his stomach. These feats are possible, with a willing and trusting individual, even without hypnosis [Reyher, 1961]. The trick is based on physical characteristics of the body as an object. The chairs must be strategically placed, and the person must be trusting and relaxed; no harm comes to him because the "trick" is based on principles of weight distribution.

Insensitivity to minor pain has also been demonstrated in unhypnotized, but distracted, individuals [Barber, 1963]. In a moment of excitement, for example, we can cut ourselves and not even notice it.

None of these comments is intended to negate hypnotism as a useful and quite "real" tool. You should simply consider that although many people can operate in some particular fashion after they have been hypnotized, many can do the same thing without hypnosis.

uses of hypnosis   One effect of hypnosis that has intrigued people for generations is *age regression*. In age regression, the patient is taken back to an earlier period

81   The lady has been hypnotized so that she remains rigid between the two chairs
(*The Bettmann Archive*)

of his life and asked, while in a hypnotic trance, to relive that period. This aspect of hypnosis has been fascinating because it elicits childlike behavior that is generally appropriate to the particular age being relived. Indeed, it is often remarkable how close the person comes in mannerisms and speech. One notable flaw is that on psychological tests of problem solving the subjects frequently score better and solve problems differently from the way a child would have [Barber and Glass, 1962; Yates, 1961]. Some investigators therefore feel that unconsciously the person is removing himself from the present and acting *as if* he were that childhood age rather than actually becoming the age. Regardless, it has been found time and again that memories which have been forgotten, especially those thought to cause psychological difficulties, can be brought back and discussed, and that is what is important. Viewed from another angle, it might be said that a person can relive his past much more effectively while under what he thinks is hypnosis [Reiff, 1960].

Hypnotism has also been suggested as an effective method for coping with learning and study problems in school. Evidence suggests that the general relaxation during hypnosis increases the ability to learn for many people. The problem of occasional grogginess is usually offset by the fact that hypnosis seems to allow a person to pinpoint and focus on the subject matter at hand [Schulman, 1963; Amadeo, 1963]. The major benefits derived from hypnosis in education, then, seem to rest in its potential for improving concentration or relieving anxiety. Hypnosis itself may not be necessary to obtain these results, but for many it is a useful tool [Krippner, 1970]. As for creating "great brains" or geniuses from those with little potential, these effects are science fiction.

There has been considerable speculation about the possibility of forcing someone to perform "immoral" acts in the hypnotic trance. In some cases subjects have been enticed to throw (fake) acid into the experimenter's face, or even to walk into walls, or occasionally to pick up what they think to be a rattlesnake (a rope).* However, careful examination of these studies by a number of investigators has led to the general conclusion that the subject relied heavily on the hypnotist's integrity, on the belief that he would not tell the subject to do something harmful. In this regard, two things are important: first, if the experimenter tells the subject under hypnosis that the subject is on his own and must take responsibility for his own actions, probably the subject will not perform the antisocial act; second, people can often be encouraged to perform socially disapproved acts without benefit of hypnosis. Hypnosis can increase the tendency to commit such acts, but presumably the leanings were already there [Orne, 1962]. At the present state of knowledge regarding the matter, it seems that only those who have

---

*It is always possible that the subject is quite well aware that it is a rope. As one individual pointed out, you have to be pretty nearsighted to mistake the two.

a tendency to want to perform illegal acts can be persuaded to do so under hypnosis, but unscrupulous hypnotists *have* succeeded in getting people to cooperate in antisocial behavior. One physician had himself a 23-year-old (unpaid) secretary who was a former patient he had hypnotized. She caused him a little difficulty when she began talking in her sleep to her husband about the daily sexual encounters with the physician [Kline, 1972; Barber, 1961]. Since we are not certain of all our impulses, some caution in selecting a hypnotist is probably advisable.

the nature of hypnosis

Generations have argued about what hypnosis is, and the topic has developed a mystical quality not unlike the confusion generated by ESP. Hypnotism has taken to the stage, and with a flair and flourish fantastic things are done. Usually, the performer creates the effect of having just arrived from the Orient, and he is generally dressed in a manner to reinforce that effect. Through "hypnosis," either of himself or of others, he or the other person will walk across hot coals, "stop" the heart, or lie on nails. These acts are usually performed in the name of yoga, suggesting that they come from the mysterious East. Actually, the Indian yogi does not spend much time doing this sort of thing; his is a discipline that seeks union with the Supreme Reality and is a very serious life undertaking not concerned with nails, coals, or stopping the heart.

Hypnotism, by the way, is not required to perform any of these acts. Although I wouldn't want to prove it, time and again it has been shown that anyone can lie on a bed of nails if he is completely relaxed and the nails are spaced close enough together. And anyone can walk on hot coals; one intrepid chemist has demonstrated that anybody can enjoy this sport if he has the proper timing and confidence. The surface of the skin has enough natural moisture to prevent either blistering or burning of the feet *if you know how to do it* [Dalal and Barber, 1969].

"Stopping the heart" takes some practice. First, and quite obviously, *no one* can actually do this because blood would stop flowing to the head and the person would die. The brain receives 15 percent of the total blood supply of the body and 25 percent of the oxygen. If blood is stopped, the total supply of oxygen in the brain will be used up in about ten seconds [Thompson, 1967]. However, one can learn to control the muscles and manipulate the body in such a way that they hold back the venous blood from returning to the heart so that a stethoscope cannot pick up the sound of the heartbeat.

Theodore Barber, one of the most thorough investigators of hypnotic phenomena, has written more than a hundred essays and books on the topic. His work is refreshing and enlightening. All of it obviously can't be done justice here, but some of his insights should be noted [Chaves, 1968].

Dr. Barber points out that there is no such thing as a special

82   This lady may not have been hypnotized— but the audience has been (*The Bettmann Archive*)

83 Charcot demonstrates hypnosis to a group of doctors and medical students; see also page 264 in Chapter 11 (*Culver*)

"hypnotic trance"—that is, there is no way to determine if a person is in a so-called trance because he can get identical behavior without going through any hypnotic trance induction. Subjects told to close their eyes and "hypnotize themselves" get the same trancelike appearance, respond to suggestions in the same way, and otherwise behave just like people hypnotized by more formal methods [Barber and Calverley, 1969].

Important factors involved in performing hypnotic feats are the subject's attitudes, expectations, and motivations and, of course, the confidence of both experimenter and subject in what they are doing [Barber, 1965a]. Hypnosis is somewhat like attending a movie. If you are "with it" and involved, you can participate in and share the confidence of the hypnotist as you do the protagonist in the drama [Barber, 1970]. If the person is motivated to perform and is convinced that the task is not impossible, he can perform as well as one who has been formally hypnotized [Barber, 1965b]. It is not necessary to call the system hypnotism and then go through the suggestion process of "you are getting sleepy," and so forth [Barber and Calverly, 1965].

Hypnosis is now popular in connection with cases such as childbirth, so naturally the question arises whether this technique is effective in alleviating pain. From earlier discussions of pain, the reader should by now realize that pain can be consciously controlled and reduced. Hence, hypnotism is a very effective tool for *normal* childbirths, for example. It is not so useful, however, in dealing with more extreme pain. For years the story has been passed down from one psychological historian to another that completely painless surgery was performed in India in the early 1800s but that the discovery of ether about the same time led to the downgrading of the importance of hypnosis in surgery. The medical profession has borne the brunt of criticism for ignoring hypnosis and favoring anesthetic drugs, but this has been misplaced aggression because hypnosis never has been a very effective tool for surgery. Barber, in returning to the original reports of the Indian physician, finds that even he reported that such surgery was not painless, although better than nothing [Barber, 1969].

None of these studies is trying to downgrade hypnosis. The problem is one of unbalanced emphasis; credit belongs not to the magic of hypnosis but to the amazing powers each of us possess if we just use them. Some people need a hypnotist to help them, but all the hypnotist does is bring out the person's own abilities.

One prominent theory holds that hypnosis is the behavior of a person as he thinks he should behave under hypnosis. Hypnosis becomes a matter of the subject's confidence and motivation; he puts himself at the mercy of the hypnotist and acts out or lives the suggestions made to him. This theory suggests that if a person is told to forget something, he acts out the role of the forgetting person. Probably the role-playing occurs

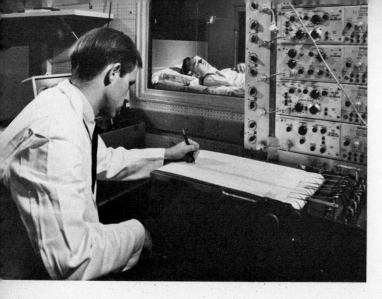

84 Sleep laboratory. Monitoring of REM, NREM, and dreams (*The New York Times*)

unconsciously; the person is not fully aware that he actually has this power on his own and that the hypnotist acts merely as a tool for activating it [Sarbin, 1950].

Earlier we discussed how a vibrator can relieve pain impulses (Chapter 5). The hypothesis was that neural impulses can be rerouted, so to speak, or sent away from an area of the brain that might register pain. In hypnosis, similarly, it is possible that once the power of suggestion has taken hold, many people exercise control and suppress impulses that might make them behave in a manner contrary to the desires of the hypnotist. At first this idea may seem preposterous—but recent experiments have shown that people can control their brain waves. We will cover brain waves in the next section, but it should be mentioned at this point that the brain gives off electrical impulses that can be measured by a recording unit called the electroencephalograph (EEG). When awake but relaxed, a person's brain frequently shows the *alpha rhythm,* a fairly slow change in electrical impulses; when drowsy, the person's brain exhibits many different rhythms, but generally they are even slower and resemble a gently rolling sea when recorded on paper.

Experiments in the laboratory have shown that a person can distinguish his alpha rhythms from his other rhythms, and, furthermore, that he can actually control having alpha rhythms or not having them. These subjects know little or nothing about brain waves or rhythms; they are controlling primarily by what they "feel" [Kamiya, 1968]. The relevance to hypnosis is that if we can control our brain waves (and some scientists have already shown that we can control our heart rate and the size of our blood vessels), we needn't stretch the imagination very far to say that we might also control neural impulses and the material that registers on the brain. In fact, Dr. Barber has demonstrated that both hypnotized and nonhypnotized subjects are able to create for themselves a "hypnotic blindness" that blocks off the brain-wave patterns which normally show up when visual stimulation is present.

hypnosis and sleep   All evidence points to error in the early assumption that hypnosis is a form of sleep. For example, brain waves under hypnosis do not resemble those during sleep, and reflexes are not the same: the knee-jerk reflex induced by the tap of a rubber hammer occurs in hypnosis, but not in sleep. Nonetheless, we find that during the early stages of sleep a person can be made to perform rather as he would under hypnosis. The person might be told, for example, "Whenever I say 'itch,' you scratch your nose." The subject will not remember having been told this; yet, up to five months later, and again in the early stages of sleep, he will respond to the cue word "itch" automatically by scratching his nose [Evans et al., 1969].

These similarities do not mean that sleep and hypnosis are identical; they are not. They may have much in common, however, and a case can be made for extreme relaxation when asleep. This brings us full circle—relaxation can lead to suggestibility or sleep, and suggestibility is probably the major component in hypnosis.

BIOFEEDBACK

In recent years a most exciting field of psychological study has gained considerable prominence, *biofeedback training.* For generations it had been assumed that certain bodily occurrences such as blood pressure, respiration, heart rate, stomach activity, and so forth were beyond man's voluntary control. Thus arose a term for specifying these various activities of the body, the *autonomic nervous system.* This term is still used, but it is misleading because translated it means "self-run" or "beyond voluntary control." We now know that we can control many of these functions even though in our day-to-day living they are autonomic.

Some studies of the behavior of the autonomic system are very simple, but have profound implications. For example, when subjects think of emotionally toned words such as *sex, rape, ——,** and *death,* their heart rate increases [Schwartz, 1971]. This may even seem obvious to you, but think for a moment about what the study shows: basically, thought process can actually control the behavior of a supposedly automatically functioning unit.

There is some misunderstanding about what biofeedback training actually is. It is *not* a system by which a person is hooked to a machine and the information from the machine is fed back to a certain organ of the body. It *is* a technique in which a machine monitors changes in the biological behavior and the subject sees or is told what the machine is indicating. Hence, biological functioning information is fed back to our conscious mind.

* Isn't this ridiculous?

At that point we take account of this information and try to achieve conscious control of the body. For example, the experimenter tells the subject at some point that his blood pressure and heart rate are synchronized. The subject determines what this feels like to him. Other times the experimenter tells the subject that he is out of synchronization and the subject determines what this feels like. Soon the subject is able somehow (we don't know how) to control the integration of his blood pressure and heart rate [Schwartz, 1972]. In other words, each time information is fed back to the person this person makes a conscious effort to readjust himself to obtain a desired result [Miller, 1971].*

alpha training   A current area of research is in the area of control of brain waves, a topic touched on briefly a few paragraphs back. The *alpha wave* of the brain is a relatively slow-moving wave occurring during relaxed wakefulness [Lindsley, 1960]. Early experimenters found that yoga meditation produced alpha waves and that the strength of these alpha waves increased as the state of meditation deepened. In fact, in deep meditation the alpha wave cannot be disturbed by external stimulation, which is remarkable because usually when something is going on around us we have a much more rapid wave [Anand et al., 1961; Krippner and Davidson, 1971; Davidson and Krippner, 1972]. This means that we can indeed withdraw from the world around us, once the technique is perfected. Using biofeedback the subject is told when he is generating alpha waves and when he is not. With training the person can learn to generate alpha waves on his own. Persons in the alpha state feel very relaxed, commenting that the "mind is very calm" and essentially all is well [Kamiya, 1969]. Skeptics thought that subjects were just saying this, and there was little or no relation to the brain-wave pattern, but when a control group was used in one study and incorrect information was fed back regarding their alpha waves, they were unable to attain a subjective state of well-being, so it isn't just hocus pocus [Paskewitz et al., 1971].

The possible uses of biofeedback are widespread. One author suggests that Maslow's last item in the hierarchy, self-actualization (Chapter 5), involves the ability to block out or resist external influences, and that one very useful tool for this is self-control of one's alpha state [Davidson and Krippner, 1972]. A number of alpha training courses have arisen in the last few years. While basic alpha training in relaxation may be useful, some of the commercial claims exceed this and one needs to exercise the same caution here as with choosing a hypnotist [Green, 1973; McKenzie, 1973].

The field of biofeedback is also quite promising for medical care. There is little reason to doubt that within another generation persons with

---

*Note that since the person is performing an action (internally) to get a desired result, this is operant conditioning, not classical conditioning.

heart problems or other malfunctions will check into a hospital and, as part of their treatment, learn biofeedback to help control malfunctioning organs.

SLEEP

Probably one of the most popular pastimes, judging from the amount of time people spend doing it, is sleeping. We spend about a third of our lives in this never-never land. An unexpected aspect of sleep, though, is that it is not the true unconsciousness many of us think it to be. In many respects we are like the cow who sleeps with her eyes open, or the clever, economical dolphin who sleeps with one eye closed for a couple of hours and then switches to the other eye. A sleeping man, supposedly out like a light, is potentially alert to unusual sounds. You may recall the reticular formation discussed earlier; this unit, of which we still have much to say, is ever ready to become alert, even in the sleep state. For example, strange phenomena occur in the case of a mother who has a small child: she can live near a subway track and sleep soundly through the racket and din of the trains, yet the slightest movement of her child will bring her out of bed and to her child's crib.

Sleep is related to the *circadian rhythm*.* Basically, the circadian rhythm is a cycle that people follow as they progress through each twenty-four hours. During this period, temperature, activity of the cerebral cortex, bodily activity, and muscular activity vary in degree of excitation or inhibition (deexcitation). Each person has his own rhythm. This individual rhythm can even be noted in each of a pair of Siamese twins (two children joined together at birth). Although Siamese twins share such common factors as a single blood circulation, each has its own separate rhythmic cycle [Alekseyeva, 1967]. "Night people" and "day people" also exist and can be distinguished partly by body temperature. Although body temperature does not *cause* one to be more or less active, it is one of many factors contributing to the activity level of a person at a given time.

Although we do inherit our circadian rhythm to some extent, as the case of Siamese twins shows, our rhythmic patterns can be influenced by learning. The typical day factory worker, for example, will reach his peak of body temperature (roughly 99°F) and of activity during the day; sometime during the night he will reach a low of roughly 97°F. If a worker is moved to the night shift, for the first few weeks he is usually irritable, restless, and prone to error or injury because bodily activity does not correspond to the old rhythmic cycle. Dramatic shifts in the sleep cycle—for example, two weeks of day sleep after an established pattern of night sleep—create a major disruption of dreaming, a necessity, and bring about persistent spontaneous awakening at times when this would not normally occur [Weitzman, 1970; Luce, 1971]. Even minor disruptions of one's normal

*From the Latin *circa,* "about," and *dies,* "day."

patterns alter the sleep cycle. It seems as if nature conspires against our having fun. Each time you go to bed at an unusual time, the normal sleep cycle is disrupted and there is a loss of time in deep sleep [Webb and Agnew, 1972]. After a week of fun and late hours you should feel really rotten and deserve it.

Some people find it next to impossible to make a complete shift to a new bodily schedule, but they are a minority. The astute observer will notice that a pet dog will often learn to stay awake a large part of the day and sleep during the night. He can do this, presumably, because, like the human, the dog has a cerebral cortex that can adjust and control rhythmic functions. In cases where a child is born without a cortex, or where a dog's cortex has been removed surgically, the organism spends most of its time sleeping, staying awake only long enough to eat. We assume, therefore, that a connection exists between the cortex and learned patterns of sleeping [N. Kleitman, 1949].

Aside from the major circadian cycle, the typical adult runs on a cycle of about ninety minutes throughout the twenty-four-hour day. In other words, every ninety minutes, more or less, the body goes into a rest cycle. Most of us have learned to control this tendency to rest, for the most part, except for a number of students I have had through the years. It is intriguing that every ninety minutes or so throughout the night, a period of dreaming occurs; the normal waxing and waning of the body seems to demonstrate itself more clearly at night when we are not in a position to control it. The shorter cycles are hard to detect in people—but cats clearly show the same type of cycles, only they are thirty minutes long. Undisturbed, your cat should have a dream about every thirty minutes [Hartmann, 1968a]. Studies with animals show that there is also an *annual* rhythm similar to that involved in hibernation (Chapter 5), but of more interest is the fact that annual rhythms are being located in humans—there are annual rhythms in weight change, urine chemical content, and episodes of mental disturbance which have been discovered so far [Pengelley and Asmundson, 1971].

Experimenters have been trying to figure out why many people are able to awaken themselves at a specified time without the aid of an alarm clock. One interesting possibility is that the brain keeps track of the number of ninety-minute cycles, and when the right number has passed, it sets off a physiological "alarm" [Zung and Wilson, 1971].

physiology of sleep   Sleep is a form of "idling" of the organism. The sleep state involves a notable decrease in temperature, heart rate, and respiration.* The first few hours of sleep are the deepest; blood pressure drops abruptly with the onset of sleep and remains low during this initial period. The body has gone into something like a short hibernation, and it shows decreased responsiveness to external stimulation. You can't "catch yourself" falling asleep because

---

* Except during dreams.

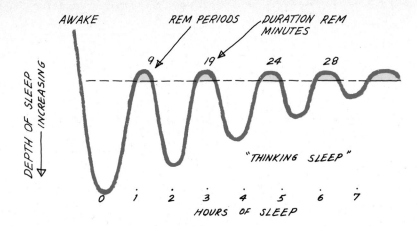

AWAKE REM PERIODS DURATION REM MINUTES

9 19 24 28

DEPTH OF SLEEP
← INCREASING

"THINKING SLEEP"

0 1 2 3 4 5 6 7

HOURS OF SLEEP

10–2 Representation of a typical night's sleep†

et al., 1971]. More about these people shortly. At the moment the Antarctic experiment probably would be interpreted as demonstrating nothing more than the fact that we carry our circadian rhythm with us wherever we go.

kinds of sleep   There are actually two kinds of sleep. To understand them, you need a little background. First, one of the stages of sleep is called *REM sleep*. REM stands for *rapid eye movement* and refers to a period in which our eyes are moving in all directions, rather like our eye movements when we are awake. The other kind of sleep is called *NREM;* as you might guess, this is *nonrapid-eye-movement* sleep.

Many intriguing hypotheses have been postulated to account for the rapid-eye-movement portion of sleep. For example, awakening a subject immediately after REM has shown that this period is usually the one in which dreaming occurs. Some have speculated that the eye movements correspond to actually "watching one's dream," as it were. This is possible, but newborn infants have a lot of REM sleep, and since they can't see very well in a coordinated fashion at this early age, one would be hard pressed to account for what they are watching [Dement and Kleitman, 1957]. Nonetheless, one might speculate that to dream or see an image in sleep triggers eye movements, just as perception triggers eye movements in the wakeful state. In general, then, rapid eye movements in sleep correspond to periods of dreaming, although the person does not necessarily dream during the whole period of REM, which can last from 5 to 40 minutes.* Note that people born blind do not have REM periods with visual imagery, which strongly suggests that REM and dreaming are intimately connected. The brain is never fully at rest, however, as you will note in Figure 10–2. Mental activity

* We don't know how long a dream lasts on the average, but there is no evidence that it is instantaneous. Presumably it fills in a substantial portion of the 5–40 minute interval.

†Notice that depth of sleep fluctuates throughout the night. REM periods usually occur during light sleep and their length increases as the night progresses. Dreams as we usually think of them occur during REM. "Thinking sleep" refers to images, thoughts, and brain activity without the distorted quality of dreaming. Reproduced from The New Psychology of Dreaming by Richard M. Jones (New York: Grune & Stratton, 1970, pp. 32, 37).

during the NREM period at times seems to resemble our daytime thoughts or daydreams ("thinking dreams" in Fig. 10–2). These events do not have the distorted, unreal quality of REM dreaming (Koulack, 1972; Jones, 1970). So, REM contains what most of us traditionally think of as dreams.

REM sleep is a necessity. If a person is awakened every time laboratory equipment indicates that he is about to go into REM dream sleep, he experiences extreme irritability. A control group awakened during NREM does not show this irritability. Another result of being deprived of REM sleep is a tremendous buildup, to the point where the person given the opportunity to sleep uninterrupted may have up to 30 REM periods in one night whereas about six would normally be expected.* Part of the REM sleep period can actually be quite a deep sleep. When discussing hypnosis, I mentioned that the knee-jerk reflex is missing in sleep; in many cases of REM sleep, actual paralysis occurs temporarily and for short periods. Such paralysis may well account for those extremely unpleasant nightmares we have in which we are trying to escape from some villain and can't move our legs to run. It appears that at this particular time we would not be able to do so.

So-called sleeping pills tend to block dream periods, and in this respect they are injurious. In a few studies where small numbers of subjects made continued use of some of these drugs, dream deprivation seemed to "wear off," and the person returned to more or less normal dreaming activity even though he still was taking the drug. Nonetheless, a few selected drugs do not interfere with REM. In general these would seem to be preferable, if the person's physician feels the other effects of the drug are appropriate [Hartmann, 1968b, 1969].

dreams   Some people claim they never dream. They are not liars; they are just wrong. We all must dream. The longer one sleeps, the more likely he is to *remember* a dream; this is because the later stages of sleep are lighter and contain occasional awakenings, so the person has more partially awake time to become aware of dreaming and is more likely to recall the dream [Taub, 1970].

Dreams resulting from factors outside the person have been the subject of considerable speculation. Grandmothers' tales inform us that eating heavily before going to bed will cause dreams, that catching one's toe on the sheet might cause the feeling that you can't escape, and so on. A handful of studies have examined occurrences during sleep and their

---

*Some studies are currently going on that are trying to relate the poor sleep of the mentally disturbed to some of the symptoms they have, which conceivably could result from lack of sufficient dream periods. Although the study of sleep and REM is new, as early as 1840 it was suggested that there might be some relation between loss of sleep and "insanity." In the middle 1800s, the *American Journal of Insanity* suggested that brushing teeth before going to bed was good because it put one in a restful mood and might help ward off insanity [Caplan, 1969].

influence on dream content. For example, early studies have shown that spraying water on a person during an REM period results in dreams that include "water material" in about 40 percent of the cases.*

A recent study using the best technical aids now available has shown the effect of external stimuli on dream content. Applying a mild electrical shock to the wrist of the sleeping subject and awakening him at various stages of REM and NREM, researchers have arrived at some interesting conclusions. First, when the person is in an NREM stage of sleeping—that is, not dreaming—stimulation does not trigger a dream. Second, stimulation at the beginning of the REM period does trigger a dream, or at least causes that electrical stimulus to be incorporated somewhere into the dream. Third, applying shock during alpha dreams,† which would cause momentary awakening during the early stages of REM, facilitates incorporating the shock into the dream directly or indirectly; that is, either there is a dream about a shock or a dream about some portion of the wrist.

Our dreams seem to be triggered by the limbic system or by other internal mechanisms, and for the most part we do not respond to external stimulation during REM, so this period apparently is restricted to some type of internal stimulation of the brain [Berger et al., 1971]. If an external stimulus of sufficient strength is introduced into the room or onto the person, if it will "fit the story," and if REM is in its early stages, the stimulus will probably be incorporated into the dream [Dement, 1957; Koulack, 1969]. When a wife has been out of town and she overhears her husband report that he had some really great dreams, the odds are that the dreams were conjured up by the brain itself, rather than an especially strong *external* stimulus—or at least he can use this argument as a defense.

Freud felt that the dream state is necessary as a means of ridding ourselves of less desirable impulses in the safety of a fantasy world. No evidence supports this idea, but it cannot be discounted completely, since current data‡ indicate that we *must* dream. Current theories of dreams do not stress the Freudian hypotheses. Today most theorists believe we dream for one of the following reasons: (1) dreams are a necessary discharge of energy built up in the electrical network of the brain; (2) dreams clear the nervous system of leftover thoughts or emotions from the day; (3) dreams reorganize the central nervous system's electrical firing, which has become disorganized by lack of stimulation from the environment; or (4) dreams keep the brain stimulated during a time when it is receiving relatively little from the environment [Jones, 1970]. These theories make some sense if we

---

*And many uncontrolled studies where dorm mates put a sleeping person's hand into a pan of water to see what would happen.

†Dreams during which the stimulus creates an alpha (awake) brain wave for a few moments.

‡A broad term referring to the pieces of information obtained from an experimental study.

assume that infant and adult REM sleep is similar; but, it is difficult to visualize complex Freudian impulses in very young children and it is also difficult to explain discharge of thoughts and emotions (no. 2) in rats, donkeys, mice, and elephants, who also have REM periods of dreaming [Jones, 1970].

The NREM state seems to be related to physical fatigue more than to any other specialized physiological need. This relation to fatigue is implied by the fact that very young children seem to require a long NREM sleep before entering REM sleep. Some authors have hypothesized that children need a lot of NREM sleep because their central nervous systems tire more easily. As people grow older, however, the REM stage begins more quickly, often within 50 minutes or so after the beginning of NREM, possibly because the central nervous system has matured and grows tired less easily.

The nondream sleep period, which seems to be related to physical needs, remains about the same when long sleepers are compared with short sleepers. Interesting studies are now being performed with both groups; long sleepers seem to need more dream (REM) sleep. Some experimenters suggest that somehow the additional REM sleep is useful to people who are relatively anxious or depressed. This is just speculation. Nonetheless, long sleepers have twice as much REM sleep as short sleepers [Hartmann et al., 1971].

In and of itself, the existence of dream REM from birth tends to support the hypothesis that a primitive cortex found also in animals of a higher order is receiving impulses from the brain stem, no matter what has gone on in the outside world before sleep began. Later in infancy, when a connection is made with thought patterns of the cortex, this likely produces more complex dreams [Roffwarg, 1966]. People who have been insulated from stimulation by wearing earmuffs and gloves, or by being suspended in water so they can feel little or nothing, within a short time begin to have hallucinations; later, if allowed to sleep, they have considerable REM. Thus, it would seem, the body generates its own stimulation if none is supplied from the outside world.

In recent years, *sleep learning* has become a popular topic. In sleep learning, the theory goes, a tape recording being played in the room while the person is sleeping supposedly embosses the material on the brain, with no effort at all from the learner. This idea is so simple and wonderful that there must be a catch in it somewhere. There is. When we are in a deep sleep, no material is being learned by this method; it isn't even being recorded by the brain. Throughout the night the depth of our sleep fluctuates. The more we come out of the sleep state, the better the tape recorder works, and when we are almost awake, it works quite well. The obvious problem in this situation is that we learn only in proportion to the degree of wakefulness [Oswald, 1962]. When is our maximum learning, then? When we are awake. Actually, sleep learning has a disadvantage beyond that of not being very effective: the tape recorder keeps us from getting a good night's sleep and awakening refreshed, at which point we could do our best learning.

dream content   Dreams are such a source of interest that it is not difficult to find people who carry around pocket-sized books about dream analysis so that during a coffee break they can review the parade of the previous night. Apparently people have always considered dreams to have mystical qualities. Many guide their lives by dream content; and presidents and statesmen, according to endless bits of lore, have failed or succeeded by following or ignoring their dreams. Much of this lore can be accounted for by the uniqueness of some dreams, by their bizarre content, and by their seeming so far removed from everyday life. We all remember the wild and gory ones and, of course, those that seem to have prophesied some important event in our lives.

Sad it is to note, however, that most people's dreams, most of the time, are commonplace. The settings are common—home or office—and the content involves normal people doing *relatively* normal things. All people dream, and they frequently populate dreams with everyday concerns, only occasionally going off on a fling [Hall, 1953]. The assumption that dreams are bizarre has probably resulted from the stress on those of disturbed individuals who do indeed have bizarre dreams. Well-adjusted persons seem to have notably distorted dreams only when going through a period of turmoil [Carrington, 1972]. The factor that calls attention to normal dreams is that even though the setting and characters are relatively commonplace, the combinations are often quite odd. Aunt Harriet, who has had one date in her life, is observed kissing someone atop Mount Everest. One explanation is that the brain, if it is firing more or less randomly, is mixing things together, rather as if you were randomly splicing bits of old home movies together. Another possibility is that the brain is reenacting the activities of the day for the purpose of removing material which is unwanted or unnecessary. The latter theory assumes that some material is highly active in the brain—for example, some concern we want be be rid of. The earliest dreams of the night seem to be directly related to actions or emotions of the day which we have not completed or resolved [Jones, 1970; Berger et al., 1971]. Such speculation leads us back to Freud's hypothesis and again is quite difficult to demonstrate. One recent intriguing idea is that sleep is necessary primarily to provide REM periods. It has been pointed out that, physiologically, sitting quietly can conceivably provide an amount of rest equal to that of NREM; following this line of reasoning, sleep is for the purpose of discharging the brain via REM periods. This theory contradicts the idea that the purpose of sleep is to alleviate fatigue, but both hypotheses are workable.

In support of the discharge hypothesis, it has been shown that if subjects see a film that contains aggressive behavior (e.g., fighting) before going to sleep, less aggression will show up in the dream content. Possibly it has already been "discharged" [Foulkes et al., 1967; Foulkes, 1967]. In the same vein, a number of dreams are found to compensate or balance out what went on during the day. For example, subjects who pedal a bicycle during the day may dream of lying on a hammock, or subjects who have been socially isolated may dream about people and having some kind of social relationships with them [Berger et al., 1971].

Some things seem well established: every 90 minutes or so we have an REM period and a dream. A dream appears to be a reenactment of a sequence of events in which various parts are connected, only more randomly than when we engage in "normal" perception. In both dream and waking states, perceiving involves sensory relays and receptors to the brain stem as well as the cortex, and the same brain areas seem to be used in both states. And the "in-between" state, the period of NREM, involves body rest and occasional so-called thinking dreams which resemble daytime thought or daydreams (see Fig. 10–2).

Dreams have another intriguing aspect—color. At this time, the reason for having dreams in color or in black and white is completely unknown. Dr. Calvin Hall, a leader in dream research, has been unable to detect any important differences between the content or the activities within dreams that could account for their being in color rather than in black and white (or vice versa). But just for the record, it is interesting that about 29 percent of our dreams are in color, with women dreaming more in color than men [Hall, 1951]. Unfortunately, I know of no adequate hypothesis for the difference in color or the difference by sexes. So dream up whatever hypothesis you can.

nightmares   Before leaving the topic of dreams, a few words should be said about nightmares. There certainly has been a great deal written about the subject, but very little actual experimentation until recently. Although we don't know very much about them, there are some general findings that might be of interest. First of all, regular nightmares occur during REM periods—as you would expect—and typically involve thoughts about death, injury, or being trapped in unpleasant surroundings. Nightmares are infrequent: only about 5 percent of normal subjects, and about 7 percent of those considered psychologically disturbed (mental patients), have them as frequently as once a week. To date the evidence is just too vague to say that people who have nightmares also have clear-cut psychological problems, so for the time being we have to view these events as extensions of occasional unpleasantness in our everyday environment.

There is another kind of nightmare which you may have been lucky enough to avoid. In adults it is called an *incubus attack*, which comes from the Latin meaning to have a devil lying upon you; in children it is called the *night terror*. Again there is no clear evidence that these result from psychological disorder although, like nightmares, they do appear in persons who have physical problems such as difficulty in sleeping or restlessness, which may or may not be psychologically caused [Hersen, 1972].

Of particular interest in light of earlier discussions is that the night terror or incubus attack occurs during the deepest sleep stage of NREM.

The trigger for these overwhelming nightmares seems to be a startling noise or other rather strong stimulus during the tail end of the deepest NREM. The reaction in these attacks does not seem to fall into a category of a dream as much as an extreme overload of the reticular formation when it is least expecting it. In other words, whereas the body gradually prepares itself for approaching REM periods by a continued increase in physiological activity, it is caught completely unprepared for a startling stimulus during NREM deep-sleep relaxation. It would seem that the physical overload may either trigger the terror or occur about the same time as the terror; respiration increases dramatically, the person feels like he is being choked, and heart rate zooms upward unbelievably fast—probably about as fast as it can get, from around 60 to 170 beats per minute—in just a matter of seconds. These reactions may create the feeling of impending death and overwhelming panic [Kahn et al., 1972; Hersen, 1972; Fisher et al., 1973]. One final note: you may recall that during REM periods the images going through the brain have an unreal quality whereas the NREM resembles reality considerably more; this may explain why the death or injury fear in incubus attacks, which resemble reality so closely, causes sheer terror in the individual. It is very close to an overwhelmingly terrifying event when awake.

SUMMARY

The exact nature of hypnosis has intrigued man for generations; however, even today the phenomenon remains a mystery. Experiments in the last few years have demonstrated that a "hypnotic trance" can be brought about in a person just by telling him to go hypnotize himself. In other cases, suggesting that a person is able to perform certain feats has led to behavior remarkably similar to hypnotic trances.

Not everyone, however, can be hypnotized or made suggestible. And in general the formal behavior of swinging some object in front of the subject's eyes seems to be just a technique, not a requirement.

Hypnotism—or, more correctly, the power of suggestion—has been quite useful in creating behavior such as age regression and minor-pain reduction. Some students have also benefited from hypnosis in their studies. Little evidence supports the notion that a person can be made to perform acts "against his will," and the technique is not very helpful in cases of severe pain. In other words, even though we don't understand its exact nature, hypnosis or the acts connected with it seem to be a part of almost every man's capabilities, whether or not he has been put in a trance.

Hypnosis and sleep probably have some common basis in the reaction of the reticular formation, but each state is a separate behavior, and reactions of the sleeping person are not the same as those of the hypnotized person.

Sleep is basically related to the circadian rhythm of the body, a cycle of activity which in our culture is most pronounced in the contrast between nocturnal and daytime behavior. The state of sleep induces an "idling" of the body, with most of the basic operations slowing down markedly, until such time as the reticular formation is activated to bring about a state of alertness.

The two types of sleep are REM and NREM. REM sleep is characterized by rapid eye movements and dreaming; NREM sleep lacks these phenomena and seems to have alleviation of fatigue as its main purpose. Dreams can be induced in a person, but only if an external stimulus is presented sometime in the early stages of REM. Most dreams are internally triggered, and their content is basically simple and of an everyday nature; bizarre dreams probably stick in our minds because they are unusual, but they are the exception, not the rule. Dreams are clearly a necessity, and their content probably is the result of some type of random firing of the neurons in the cortex rather than the reflection of unconscious impulses.

Nightmares are relatively infrequent during REM and even less frequent during deep-sleep NREM. The latter nightmares are called incubus attacks in adults and night terrors in children, and they seem to be triggered by some stimulus which startles the person during his deep sleep. The body is unprepared for a nightmare during deep NREM and overreacts, creating the terrifying feeling of overwhelming disaster. At present experimental evidence is unclear about whether nightmares or incubus attacks (night terrors) are correlated positively with personality disorders.

PART THREE
THE
PERSON

CHAPTER ELEVEN
THE ERA OF THE UNCONSCIOUS: SIGMUND FREUD

Below is the beginning of a speech given by the Austrian psychiatrist Sigmund Freud in 1909 at Clark University in the United States.

Ladies and Gentlemen: It is a new and somewhat embarrassing experience for me to appear as lecturer before students of the New World. I assume that I owe this honor to the association of my name with the theme of psychoanalysis.

The tone is one of humility from a man who was not very humble. However, the speech marked the beginning of positive reception in the United States of a theory that was to have monumental impact on psychology—causing vibrations that echo down to the present day. So possibly on this occasion he did feel humble—or at least tentative—in trying to find acceptance for his ideas.

Dr. Freud was to reach the pinnacle most men only dream about: to be read, quoted, and studied on an international scale by devotees whose intensity approached religious fervor. At the time he made the address at Clark University, he was by no means acclaimed as a great authority. He had attained limited recognition for research on methods of preparing specimens for examination under the microscope, but he had only gained infamy in the eyes of his colleagues by what they saw as an overenthusiastic use of the newly discovered medical tool, cocaine [Reisman, 1966]. Now he was proposing an idea that seemed preposterous: *Human behavior is determined by unconscious processes.* Further, he suggested to openly puritanical audiences that sex was our guiding light in life, the energy source and wellspring of activity. So the odds were against him.

86 Sigmund Freud in 1932 (*Culver*)

But the odds always had been. Being a Jew at that time meant that medicine was one of the few fields open to him, and a physician is what he reluctantly became. That career was to be short-lived because of Freud's terrible aversion to the sight of blood. He also tended to become more preoccupied with what the patient was saying than with his physical complaint. Except for an excellent bedside manner, he was ill equipped for the profession of medicine as it existed at that time [Rieff, 1959].

In the late 1800s, Freud got to know a famous neurologist* named Charcot who was active in the field of hypnosis, which was gaining consid-

* A physician-specialist who is expert in the area of nerve operation and function.

erable attention from the medical profession (see Chapter 10). One evening, discussing a patient who was the wife of an impotent man, Charcot made the point that her psychological problems originated in the sexual area. Some biographers feel this statement had a permanent impact on Freud: his theory is famous (or infamous) for its sexual base [Freud, 1938].

Of greater importance, patients who had been hypnotized were found to talk more freely and to relive experiences they had seemingly forgotten. Freud mentions the case of a woman who was unable to drink water and stayed alive by eating fruit and melons. Under hypnosis this woman one day recounted that as a child she had found the dog of a hated servant drinking out of one of the family's glasses. After mentioning this experience under hypnosis, the woman's abhorrence of water disappeared— and Freud became quite intrigued with hypnotism as a psychological tool.

In the 1880s another friend of Freud, Dr. Joseph Breuer, was treating a woman for symptoms of dizziness, fainting, and coughing spells. Breuer became so interested in the case that he was analyzing the woman the greater portion of the day and sometimes into the night, a schedule to which his wife objected violently because the woman was so attractive. Probably, at this point, he contemplated turning the woman over to Freud for treatment. No matter—one day he just vanished from the patient's life, but not before the grand finale in which the woman, learning that the relationship with Breuer was to end, had what is called a hysterical childbirth. This very unusual bit of behavior involves all the symptoms, pains, and activities of actual childbirth, but there is no baby available when it is over. Breuer hypnotized the woman once more, removed this problem by suggestion, and then disappeared [Schultz, 1969].

As far as Freud is concerned, what matters is that Breuer discussed the case at length with him and mentioned how many of her symptoms and problems disappeared even without hypnosis, just from the process of talking.

And Freud had tried hypnosis for a time, but felt that it didn't get to the root of the patients' problems. Probably because of Breuer's comments, Freud became intrigued with the importance of the patient and the doctor *talking* about the problems, and he gave up hypnosis.

At this point you likely can fit the pieces together yourself. Freud felt that events from our individual pasts—especially those that are upsetting to us—are removed from conscious memory but are still "in us." These events can be reached by the relaxation of hypnosis, but an even better technique is discussing one's life in an atmosphere of freedom and privacy.* If basic problems are *not* released into consciousness, the result is needless

---

* This technique, Freud's method for curing mental illness, is called *psychoanaylsis* and is discussed in Chapter 24.

87 Freud's couch, where it all began (*Edmund Engelman*)

anxiety, frustration, and conflict. These upsetting events are stored in what Freud termed the unconscious.

Why the sexual emphasis in the theory? It was not only the comment of Charcot which brought it about, but also the fact that Freud's patients consistently talked about childhood sexual experiences and desires once he had gained their confidence. Freud felt that these conflicts were responsible for most of their difficulties. He was later to find out that most of the events were imaginary, but not before he had formulated his theory of sex as a basic drive. Even after discovering how much the patients had exaggerated, he neatly fit into his theory the importance of sexual symbolism and imagery, especially in dreams. Although patients had sexual *fantasies*, he reasoned, they still were having difficulties because of them.

By then Freud had formulated the theory that early sexual desires and needs, which are forbidden, cause guilt. These guilt-producing desires are therefore **repressed** (pushed down) into the unconscious, only to appear later in adult life as conflicts and anxiety.

The sexual hypothesis was elaborated, apparently following Darwin's evolutionary principle in the sense that it was biological and it fit into a developmental sequence. That is, our earliest sensual experience—broadly defined, our first sexual activity—involves the mouth: we are fed by our mothers. (This stage is called the *oral stage* of development.) This phase is followed by toilet training and an emphasis on the supposedly pleasurable experience of elimination, the *anal stage*, during the second year; next comes a period of preoccupation with sex itself as a sensual experience, the *phallic stage*, generally thought to appear between three and five years of age. And if the individual is lucky, he finally makes it to heterosexual interests, the *genital stage*. Freud thus focused on the various openings of the body, put them into a developmental sequence, and labeled them erogenous* zones, meaning areas of sexual pleasure. At each of these stages much of our energy and preoccupation is devoted to that particular portion of the body.

These stages of development might be likened to an assembly line in which a machine is being manufactured and assembled. A defect can arise anywhere along the way, but the end product will still operate fairly well until it is put under stress later on, at which time the weakest or most defective part will be the first to go. So also with the Freudian system: if during the oral stage we felt deprived of enough sucking at the mother's breast, the stress of later life may cause us to revert to that oral stage and behave in a way that seeks to make up for the previous loss. (This behavior is called *regression*—"moving back to.") For instance, alcoholics are thought to be preoccupied with use of the mouth, and hence are considered, in Freud's theory, to be overdependent—just as the one-year-old child is; they

* From *eros*, sexual love (the other kind is *agape*, spiritual or divine love).

are attempting to compensate for early oral deprivation. Or the child in the anal stage, if his situation was unusually traumatic, may have developed a preoccupation with retention of bowel movements; his later personality might reveal this problem through miserly behavior in which the person retains or hoards money, stamps, or other material things.

One of Freud's most provocative ideas is the Oedipus complex, a somewhat misleading label borrowed from a Greek play in which a king's son named Oedipus, who is taken from his home without ever knowing his parents, returns later, kills his father in an argument, and marries his mother. The Oedipus complex, which develops during the phallic stage, is a slightly different version of the same story. The male child of a family desires the mother sexually and seeks to destroy the father's affection for the mother.* No one knows for certain where Freud got this idea, but he considered resolution of the Oedipal phase to be crucial to a child's proper development. That is, those who couldn't resolve the jealousy toward the father and the desire for the mother would have later psychological problems.† Of course, anyone knows that jealousy occurs in every family, so few people would dispute this aspect of his theory, but the specifics, especially sexual desire for the mother, have come under criticism time and again, and we will cover these in detail in a moment.

Freud spent many years in exhaustive self-analysis and examined in detail his every dream, thought, and reverie, in connection with both his past and his present. In his own childhood he had a loving but very stern father and a mother who gave him continuous love and attention [Ford, 1963]. Quite possibly he framed the Oedipus complex after his own life as he saw it in retrospect, and he also may have been influenced by the sexual fantasies of his patients. Furthermore, the Victorian era within which he was reared provided a stern father and a loving mother for almost every child, and Freud's friends probably made a number of comments about this family situation which later reinforced his ideas about threatening fathers and permissive mothers.

The Oedipus complex has been one of Freud's most difficult theories to examine carefully because it is obviously not very easy to measure childhood sexuality. Nevertheless, it *is* possible to look at a few current studies about parent-child relationships and make some inferences regarding Freud's hypotheses.

---

* Freud did not spend much time discussing the problems of the female in this regard. Although he did cover the female child, the situation is far too complex and lengthy to become involved in at this point. In general terms, the female child is sexually attracted to the father (the Electra complex). Most of the references used in this section explain the system fully for those who desire to pursue it.

† In Sophocles' play, Oedipus learns of his errors, and his guilt is so great that he puts out his own eyes and spends the rest of his life wandering the earth, doing penance for his behavior.

That fathers are a major influence in the development of "femininity" in girls seems to be fairly well established. Fathers treat their daughters in an entirely different fashion from their sons. (This is not the case with mothers' behavior toward their male and female children.) For example, fathers punish their sons physically, but rarely their daughters. This situation suggests that sexuality, at least from the viewpoint of the daughter, is not as much an issue as the fact that she is learning to be cared for, to be dependent and supposedly "feminine."

Daughters who are close to their fathers tend to become involved in long-term romantic relationships with men which lead to marriage, whereas those who are not close to their fathers frequently engage in antisocial acts and have excessive sexual interest. There are two ways of interpreting this: the Freudians would point out that the romance, with an underlying sexual basis, is merely transferred from the father to the marriage partner. Freud emphasized that what happened early in life determined what would happen later.

A second, non-Freudian interpretation would be that frustration caused by lack of intimacy leads the girl who is not close to her father to seek excessive sexual outlets [Biller, 1970]. The non-Freudian interpretation would suggest that the basis for the father-daughter relationship involves the traditional male-female roles in which the father is the protector of the daughter and she finds safety in his love; this role is then transferred to her future husband by means of a long, safe courtship. The frustrated daughter may be seeking sexual activity later in life as a means of obtaining some form of love—of any sort—and she finds that the sexual method is a workable technique. Either interpretation is possible, but a study to be taken up shortly tends to cast doubt on the early sexual interest of the child.*

On the one hand, Freud apparently is correct about the importance of the early years in the formation of certain personality characteristics. Absence of the father before the male child is four or five years old seems to reduce what is called "masculine orientation"—the tendency of the boy to think of himself as masculine. This probably comes about because most children develop a preference for being male or female sometime prior to the five-year mark [Ward, 1969]. On the other hand, this would strongly suggest that Freud was incorrect in assuming that masculinity, supposedly biological in origin, operates automatically; instead, masculinity would seem to be learned by imitation of the father.

Males who do not have a father, but who have contact with other adult males, do not seem to suffer from loss of masculinity. Again, we seem

---

* *Sexual* in its specific sense. A child is interested in sensual pleasure as opposed to sexual feelings.

to have a case of social learning rather than basic male sexuality. Certainly one cannot say that resolving sexual desire for the mother by overthrowing the father can possibly be involved in this case, for the boys are not even faced with the problem and do not show any unusual masculinity difficulties.

Boys without fathers show considerably more fear about the unknown of sexual activity than those who have a father available [Biller, 1970]. This seems to point out that the child needs to learn how to be sexual. In Freud's hypothesis of the Oedipal conflict, the child whose father is *present* should be more afraid of sex because he is competing directly with the fearful father figure for his mother.

For his work Freud is considered a pioneer in child psychology, in the sense that he called attention to the "sexuality" of children. By the age of six, the odds are overwhelming that a child has masturbated. The big question here, however, is whether this is sexual activity or more a matter of sensual gratification. Masturbation in the teenage period is usually accompanied by sexual fantasies, so there is little question that by then the activity is sexual in nature. In any case, Freud felt that guilt and anxiety were connected with sex at a very early age.

It is ironic that before the 1850s children were treated harshly and forced into strict moral training. By 1860, child-rearing books had come out which stressed that it was "not necessary to frighten the child" and that psychological and permissive methods were best used [Wishy, 1968]. Then Freud came along and upset the applecart again, pointing out how animalistic children can be. And this approach has been followed by a wave of permissiveness in which many people fear that repressing a child sexually is bad for him—but this view takes considerable adjustment on the part of the parents and never has been very successful.

Although Freud eventually tempered his sexual emphasis to encompass a more sensual outlook than sex as such, he always held that sexual energy (called *libido** or *libidinal energy*) is the wellspring of all behavior. The sex drive is biological in nature, and the theory seems to have been borrowed from the heavily biological, nonphilosophical orientation of scientists of the time† [Watson, 1968]. In any case, these libidinal desires seek expression and in doing so create tension in the individual; this tension needs release. If release cannot be found in actual life, the desires appear as a dream or as fantasy modes of expression which are not as threatening to the individual. Release of desires can also appear as a psychological disturbance; for example, a man's fear of women might result from his having had incestuous wishes about his own mother, which he repressed because they

---

* From the Latin word for "lust."

† To the reader objecting at this point: yes, Freud's system is obviously quite theoretical and philosophical, but he claimed that it was based on biological behavior and his theory assumes that biological drives are at the root of all behavior.

were "wrong." The part of the unconscious that contains these basic impulses is called the *id;* the id contains our untempered animal drives.

Like most men, Freud was unable to avoid the time in which he lived. He borrowed many of his ideas from the physics of his era. For example, his time was quite preoccupied with mass and force and energy transfer. The internal combustion engine, as well as hydraulics, was in the forefront of scientific interest. Basically, the id and the engine operate on the same principle. For example, in Figure 11–1 if cylinder *A* contains water and a force is exerted on it (arrow), the water will flow through the tube into cylinder *B*. Likewise, the most direct route for an id impulse (arrow) would be actual expression of the desire by letting it come out through cylinder *B*—that is, doing whatever we want. However, if cylinder *B* is blocked by repressive forces of parents or society, the pressure might cause the tube to burst unless these unacceptable thoughts can pop out at relief valve *C*—in dreams or fantasies. This principle of equilibrium, you will notice, is also very similar to homeostasis.

The id is opposed by society, in the guise of parents; we do not

11-1   Id, ego, and superego

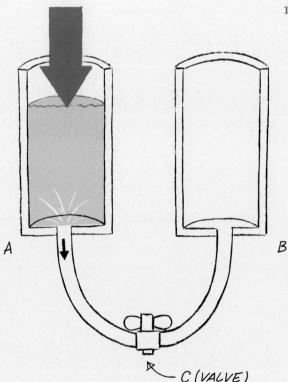

A   B

C (VALVE)

just act out any desire or whim of the moment. This opposing force Freud called the *superego,* which is approximately a synonym for conscience.

Although such a thing would rarely happen, the superego and the id could be in balance; if you look again at Figure 11-1 and assume that the id is *A* and the superego is *B,* and an equal amount of pressure is coming from both, the person is in control of the situation psychologically because the forces are in balance.

Freud referred to a third portion of the individual, the *ego.* The ego is little different from what most of us term our *self.* The ego is conversant with the world around us and tries to mediate between the desires of the id and the repressive forces of the superego. It acts as a control panel in attempting to regulate the psyche in order to maintain balance. The ego can use the relief valve *C* in Figure 11-1 to discharge id energy by dreams or fantasies.

Readers sometimes think that Freud was suggesting that we have all three—ego, superego, and id—from the beginning. Actually, he was proposing that the biological id is the major driving force and that the superego evolves from the same energy source because the rules of society more or less force it into this position. Without these rules the id would be the sole driving force. Present-day psychoanalysts stress the *ego* as a central driving force and maintain that the ego develops as the result of social pressures, especially from the mother or father. The concept of ego is emphasized because in a way Freud put his own theory in a bind by suggesting that rational, controlling behavior (superego) somehow evolved from a completely irrational unit (id) [Langer, 1969].

The major thrust of Freud's system is that in essence man is an animal covered over by a thin veneer of society's accepted behavior. This view represents a logical extension of Darwin's work on man as animal and the work of later psychologists who followed Darwin. Some evidence in archaeological records supports Freud's thinking, but his appraisal of man would probably have been most appropriate 3 or 4 million years ago. Man was then a predatory animal. Later, when he developed tools for tilling the fields and engaging in general agriculture, his domination over nature allowed people to settle down into units of society [McNeill, 1963]. Since that time the validity of Freud's view of man as primarily id-animal becomes more remote with each era. For example, in the twentieth century, studies have shown that modern man is far less excited by the nude body than by one which is partly covered [Hirning, 1961]. This response in no way resembles animal behavior. Nothing turns people off quite as much as everyone walking around nude, but it doesn't seem to interfere at all with animals' sexual interest.

The ritualistic behavior of sex in a refined culture is so elaborate that it is often difficult to find the id, if such there be. In fact, some

88   September Morn,
nowadays not a very
shocking picture
(*Metropolitan
Museum of Art*)

later followers of Freud, who emphasize the ego and are called neo-Freudians (new Freudians), have modified his theories considerably and focus on
the social and cultural aspects of behavior. They stress, for example, that
toilet training is a process of interaction between the child and the mother
that seeks to resolve where, when, and how the child goes to the bathroom,
rather than putting the emphasis on going to the bathroom itself as a sensual
experience molding later behavior. The overall pattern of behavior between
the mother and the child will determine how the child turns out—that is,
whether he has certain messy habits, is abnormally clean, or is relatively
normal when he grows up.

Far from being "animal behavior," the complex interplay of sexual
forces within society can be demonstrated by the following real story,
reported by one of the first "publicity men"; the picture he refers to, *September Morn*, was an infamous one.

I applied for work at a small art shop that had printed a lithograph of
a nude girl. The picture sold at ten cents apiece, but nobody would buy it. I could
earn my month's rent if I had an idea for disposing of the 2,000 copies in stock.
It occurred to me to introduce the immodest young maiden to . . . the head of the
Anti-Vice Society. . . . I telephoned him several times protesting against a large
display of the picture which I myself had installed in the window of the art shop. . . .
When he arrived in front of the store window, a group of youngsters I had hired
especially for this performance at fifty cents apiece, stood pointing at the picture,
uttering expressions of unholy glee. . . . "Remove that picture!" he fumed. . . . The
Anti-Vice Society appealed to the courts. . . . Overnight the picture became a vital
national issue . . . and seven million men and women bought copies at a dollar
apiece [Reichenbach, 1931].*

Similarly, the American carnival appeared on the scene in 1893, but
interest and attendance were very poor. The promoters talked a prominent
clergyman into denouncing the carnival because it had a very indecent dance.
That did it. Attendance soared, and carnivals became a resounding success
for decades [Truzzi and Easto, 1972].

Freud, perhaps influenced by seeing the disaster of World War I,
added aggression to the drives that make up the basic human instincts.
Under his final system, the id contained both sex and aggression as the prime
motivating forces. Aggression has not changed considerably with civilization,
but with Freud it seemed to be almost an afterthought.

Assessing the value of Freud's work is extremely difficult. We have
devoted considerable space to him and we'll continue to do so, because he
has had an irradicable effect on the history of psychology. Innumerable

*From H. Reichenbach, *Phantom Fame* (New York: Simon & Schuster, 1931),
reprinted by permission.

articles, books, and discussions of our own day can be traced back to Freud's work, in the sense that they either incorporate some of his ideas or that they *react* against them. Some feel that Freud's greatest contribution to psychology was not his "discovery"* of the unconscious, but his focus of attention on man as encompassing two processes of thinking: first, a seemingly rational progression of thoughts controlled and organized by society; second, the irrational, impulse-driven process of thinking that surfaces in the ramblings, incoherencies, and profanities of the seriously mentally ill [Peters, 1965].

Freud emphasized two events as "proof" that the unconscious exists. First, he claimed that dreams are prevalent and that they are quite bizarre† and frequently disconnected. Dreams are id products. During sleep, when the ego is not as alert and has its defenses down, the id can operate virtually unhampered. Second, he emphasized "slips of the tongue," or the frequently inexplicable behavior of saying things we don't mean. For example, assume that in our unconscious we are holding an extreme dislike for our father. Sometime, in calling out to him, we might say, "Oh, bother!" Freud felt that the unconscious, seeking discharge, substituted the *bo* for the *fa* and in this way was discharging some of the energy connected with this unacceptable dislike. All of us have made such a slip and then wondered why in the world we ever did.

The strictest behaviorists of the present day, those who demand scientific evidence for an unconscious, cannot get it. They argue with some legitimacy that the existence of the unconscious cannot be proved or disproved because it is not located anywhere in the body; at best we are getting only an indirect manifestation of it—which means we can *interpret* dreams as being highly symbolic, even if they are not. "But why go to the trouble?" they ask. A dream can quite clearly be a random association process of various events of the previous day: since the brain is continuously firing, even when we are asleep, might not it be a matter of just connecting various thoughts together?

As for repression, couldn't this be explained just as well by saying that it is forgetting? Many valiant attempts have been made to pin down Freud's hypotheses and examine them carefully in the laboratory. The Freudian hypothesis runs something like this: if an individual's self or ego is threatened, he will repress the threat and push it down into the unconscious. One way to test this is to have individuals take an examination in

---

*It would be simple enough to go back to the Greeks and show that all the components of Freudian theory were available to them. It was Freud's structuring of the theory and emphasis on it that made him great.

†More recent studies, as you recall, show that most people's dreams involve very commonplace events (see Chapter 10). Remember, however, that Freud's patients were not "normal."

which, for example, they must choose certain words which they think describe a series of inkblots. After this task, the subjects are divided into groups; one group is told that the results indicated they were psychologically disturbed; the other group—the control group—is told nothing. Now we can test the subjects to see how many words they recall. If repression is working, the experimental group should have pushed the words from consciousness because the words are threatening: they supposedly indicate that the subjects are psychologically disturbed. Does this happen? Well, the experimental group recalls many fewer words. At first glance, then, it would seem that repression works. But one experimenter has cleverly added another group of subjects. Instead of being threatened, however, this group sees the inkblots, decides on the words they want, and then sees a movie about which they "will be asked a number of questions." Interestingly enough, this group does as poorly in the recall of the inkblot words as the threatened group, and in response to essentially the same types of words! What have we got, then? We have an alternative explanation to repression and pushing into the unconscious—namely, competing material in the brain causes forgetting. When the threatened subjects were interviewed later, they were found to be so preoccupied with the bad personality reports that they were thinking about them rather than the words. Thus, memory interference is clearly a plausible explanation, in lieu of repression into the unconscious, a possibility supported by the fact that for the movie group, just straight non-emotion-laden interference produced the same amount of "forgetting" [Holmes and Schallow, 1969].

Considerable space has been devoted to this study to illustrate three important things:

1.   Freud's work, though brilliant, should not be taken at face value.

2.   Experiments are difficult and complicated, but attempts are being made to determine if Freud was right.

3.   It is equally plausible to agree with the "non-Freudians": repression is not mystical; it is just forgetting.

Some of the major attacks on Freud have come as a result of his feeling that the theories as he presented them are *universal*—that is, can and will be found in any culture. In the sexual area, for example, the male is dominant and the female submissive. The male child eventually imitates his father, who is the male model, and takes on his characteristics. However, the fixed concept of male-female patterns of behavior is patently false. Dr. Margaret Mead has made this quite clear in her studies of other cultures, in some of which the female is the sexually aggressive partner [Mead, 1935]. Customs change very rapidly and are related to pressures often far removed from the id. In the 1970s the role of women is changing drastically, a change that we will cover at length later in the book. Even in our own society it should be obvious that *any* universal is shaky.

In the 1940s boys who wore pink, or boys who wore green on Thursdays (?), were considered effeminate and were subjected to looks, hoots, and catcalls. Such color schemes, like the other modes of behavior we have been discussing, have a sexual connotation that is quite variable. Thirty years later, most men wear very bright colors. The color blue for baby boys comes from an old superstition that evil spirits threatened boys in the nursery and that blue, borrowed from the "heavenly blue" of the sky, would ward them off. Later legend suggested that baby boys were found under blue cabbages (a color often found in Europe) and that girls were born inside a pink rose [Brasch, 1967]. All this suggests that Freud's theory may have been correct in his own time, in his own home town; but the ways of mankind are so variable that anyone who says he has found a universal is out as far as he can get on the weakest limb of a tree.

Important current research reflects the complexities of sexual behavior patterns. First, however, you have to grasp a fine but very important distinction between sexuality and *sex-role behavior*. Sexuality is the innate drive for sexual satisfaction. Sex-role behavior can be completely removed from this drive, especially in early years. It is a learned behavior that differentiates boys from girls in a social context. Examples of sex-role behaviors in childhood are a little girl playing with her doll and her brother making war with his toy soldiers. These learned behaviors are expanded throughout the developmental years. Learned behavior can be observed in early adolescence in the young girl dressing and acting seductively, although she would be frightened to death by an overt sexual response from a man. In a study of lesbians (female homosexuals), researchers found that early sexual behavior of the subjects was almost identical to that of "ordinary" women. That is, start of genital play, masturbation, feelings of sexual deprivation, and so on, from childhood to the onset of adolescence, were not different for an "ordinary" versus a lesbian group. This similarity strongly suggests that *sexuality* as such may not be present in early years. If we were dealing with sex itself, the development of a lesbian would be different from an early age; she would be gravitating toward women in her desires and behavior. Instead, the lesbian acts "sexually" as heterosexually (male-female) inclined women do. On the other hand, if sex is not a basic desire from the beginning (that is, if the child is not sexual but merely interested in the genitals for pleasure's sake through the early years), the child has to *learn* first what sex really is and, more important, how one is to behave in the sexual situation. This process is called sex-role development and means that we are trained gradually in the ways of behavior as a male or female. Put another way, we learn how to be a man or a woman sexually and adopt that role—as if we were in a play—until that role becomes second nature. To oversimplify, the female child, according to this theory, who learns to respond to and be interested in other females does so not because of sexuality but because of observation and learning of social roles at home and in school. The sex-role behavior becomes lesbianism only when the girl is old enough to engage in sexual activity for its own sake. This tends to cast a shadow over Freud's hypothesis that the child is sexual by nature and driven by sexual desire from an early age [Simon and Gagnon, 1969].

It might be added that aggression is not a universal either. Although we may find it hard to believe that others don't have wars and go around shooting each other, this fact is indicated clearly by studies of other cultures.

Why, then, has Freud survived so long? One possibility is that he was correct, but unfortunately there is no clear evidence for this one way or the other, and of course the followers of Freud have watered down his theory considerably so that it no longer is what it started out to be. Other possibilities include the fact that Freud organized a system of personality that fit just about every contingency or behavior pattern and was extremely easy to follow, use, and understand; no one has quite matched him for this feat. And it should not be forgotten that Freud dealt in two areas of undying interest to man: sex and the intriguing symbolism and magic of a dream world we don't fully understand.

SUMMARY

No one in the history of psychology has had such a profound effect on its course as Sigmund Freud. While experimenting with hypnosis as a tool, Freud developed his "talking cure" and along with it the basic assumption that inner man is composed of an id, superego, and ego. Under Freud's framework, the id is the basic driving force of behavior, and it constantly seeks expression for desires that are animal-like needs. The talking cure supposedly can assist the analyst in reaching some of this buried material, at least indirectly, and in liberating some of the energy built up in the id.

Freud's theory was quite mechanical and biological; he divided the individual's history into stages of development, each one of which is based on one of the pleasurable openings of the body. If biological development is "normal," then man is able to reach a final stage—a fully functioning sexual life. Sex itself, in its broadest sense, is the mainspring of human behavior, but full attainment of its desires in a mature fashion is difficult for anyone to achieve. Most people get hung up somewhere along the way and have the energy of the id fixated at one of the stages. Later behavior is then focused on activities such as preoccupation with the mouth (oral), or hoarding (anal), or inability to have normal heterosexual relationships (phallic).

At the core of Freud's theory is the Oedipus conflict, a term referring to the incestuous wishes of the male child for his mother. Resolution of this complex is paramount to adjustment.

Freudian theory is losing its foothold in current-day psychology. A major reason for this loss of influence is the difficulty experimenters have in demonstrating the accuracy of some of Freud's claims.

CHAPTER TWELVE
CONCEPTS OF PERSONALITY

The discussion of Freud's ideas in Chapter 11 was somewhat misleading, in the sense that the structure of Freud's scheme strongly suggests that we can categorize individuals into certain types, based on what has happened to them during the years of development. Of course, this apparent simplicity has been and is the magic of the Freudian system. The "oral" person exhibits certain behavioral patterns. He is preoccupied with the use of his mouth; and because the baby at this stage is very dependent, so too is the "oral" adult. This theory is all well and good—at first glance it seems that people can be put into categories with some ease. The major problem is that personality is not that easily defined or simple. Since Freud, scientists have made innumerable attempts to explain how people got the way they are, and some of their theories will be covered in this chapter. People obviously are not so easily categorized as these theorists might have us believe, but in any case, each of them probably has something to contribute in explaining some of our behavior patterns.

Puzzling people move all around us. You are one and I am one. Evidence that each of us has a single, clear-cut personality is meager; in fact, a large number of studies indicate that each of us alters our personality and behaves differently, depending upon circumstances. Earlier, we discussed how our perceptual and memory systems are able, remarkably, to bring together quite disparate elements into one—the pine and oak, for instance, are both trees. Apparently the same ability holds true regarding ourselves. We do all manner of quite bizarre things that don't fit together objectively—like the good Christian tax evader—but these contradictions don't make us come apart or feel we are two different people—instead, I am just *me*, all one person. We see all parts of ourselves as fitting together; usually it is the psychologically disturbed person, ironically, who detects the discrepancies, and they are quite worrisome to him.

Personality theorists fall prey to the desire for unity for its own sake all the time. As one author has pointed out, for example, if a woman is sometimes fiercely independent and sometimes rather docile, the psychologist tends to lump these two behaviors together, concluding, for example, that she is actually quite independent and dominating, but to satisfy this need for domination, sometimes she must "pretend" to be docile [Mischel, 1969]. This is pretty tricky reasoning. The point is that personality theorists tend to oversimplify; at least be aware of this as we discuss personality.

Nonetheless, science cannot advance without some organization, and personality theories provide this structure—that is, something psychologists can at least "grab hold of" so they have some framework for discussion and experimentation.

Personality is difficult to define for at least two reasons. For one, personality is differently defined by different theorists. Freud, for example, would have said that personality is made up of behavior patterns resulting from the handling of sexual and aggressive impulses during childhood. Others see the origins of behavior differently. The second difficulty is that personality is the ultimate in complexity and variability. How do we explain Mr. Jones, who is the following: a tax evader, a shifty business operator during the week, a faithful and apparently sincere churchgoer on Sunday, a dynamo at work, and very meek at home? How do we explain the behavior of Colonel George S. Patton III, who sent out Christmas cards inscribed "Peace on Earth" and decorated with color photos of dismembered Vietcong corpses [O'Neill, 1971]?

What is personality? Any definition could give rise to legitimate complaints. But, in order to give the discussion some structure, a definition is needed: *personality* consists of relatively enduring behavior patterns that result in fairly consistent reactions to a number of different situations.

Personality theory attempts to pinpoint specific *types* of people, determine what is responsible for producing each of these types of person, and make predictions about their behavior that will hold true most of the time.

PERSONALITY AND PHYSIQUE

One of the easiest theories to understand, because it closely resembles "common sense," is the body-type theory, called *constitutional psychology*.* The most elaborate constitutional theory of our time started in the 1930s and came from the experimental work of Dr. William Sheldon. Sheldon's work was spurred not only by similar theories of the past but also the persistence of folklore that has tainted everyone's perception. If, for example, you ask someone to characterize a fat man's personality, chances are good that he will say, "Fat? Oh, a jolly, good-natured person."

Or a woman who is skinny and nearsighted: "A brain—a bookworm."

Or a man who is muscular and sturdy: "An athlete—spends most of his time walking up and down the sands of Muscle Beach and exercising."

Sheldon had a more elaborate system than these simple comments indicate—but basically he did divide people into three types: *ectomorphs*

---

*That is, based on physical structure or constitution.

endomorphs, and *mesomorphs.* These terms come from the combination of various root stems:

ecto = without; **morph** = shape   a thin person
meso = intermediate; **morph**   an athletic person
endo = within; **morph**   a fat person

Once he had established these basic types, Sheldon went about classifying hundreds of people, using his system called *somatotyping,* or typing of body shapes. He and his coworkers then attempted to correlate personality characteristics with body types. For example:

Ectomorph
love of privacy
mental overintensity
hypersensitivity to pain

Mesomorph
love of physical adventure
need and enjoyment of exercise
love of risk and chance

Endomorph
love of physical comfort
love of eating
oriented toward people

Surprisingly enough, Sheldon found correlations in the .80s and .90s between body type and personality characteristics. This was a startling finding, and one that suggested that personality characteristics do indeed correspond to physical attributes [Sheldon, 1936].

A

B

C

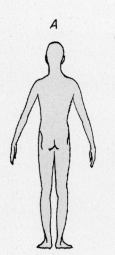 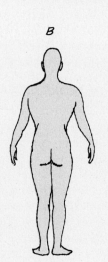 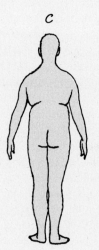

12-1   Three somatotypes among the thousands identified by Dr. William Sheldon

The matter was not allowed to rest with such an impressive set of statistics, however, and upon closer scrutiny the issue quickly became clouded. Other experimenters could not obtain such high correlations between body type and personality; in fact, they were generally low, frequently in the .10–.20 range [Tyler, 1965]. In addition, when ratings obtained from written personality tests—rather than from personal interviews, in which the experimenter could conceivably be influenced by *seeing* the person—were compared with the individual's physique, they yielded negligible correlations [Hood, 1963].

You might conclude that Dr. Sheldon himself was suspect, but your conclusion would be unwarranted. The problem resided in the fact that Sheldon and his experimenters did the ratings of *both* the physiques of the subjects *and* their personality characteristics. An experimenter who believes in his system cannot help being influenced by it. For example, when you see a fat man, it is human nature to search for and see traits such as love of eating and love of physical comfort and, often, to discount traits that might indicate another personality type, such as sensitivity to pain or love of physical adventure. So, in general, the relationship is minimal between body type and personality characteristics which are clearly defined and specific.

Because of the possible influence of one's theories or other such factors on results, the very elaborate systems of control mentioned earlier have evolved. Sheldon's work apparently fell prey to the pitfalls of distortion because the experiments were not carefully set up.

Common beliefs, folklore, call them what you will, thus present particular hazards for the experimenter, because sometimes they do hold a grain of truth. The experimenter has the task of sifting fact from magical fiction, and he constantly faces the problem that from childhood on he too has been influenced by "common sense" and folklore.

One belief that has persisted through the ages is that the ectomorph is an extremely brainy person. In the 1920s it was almost accepted as "fact" that the frail person who wore glasses was more often than not a "genius." This notion led to one of the most extensive studies ever performed. Dr. L. M. Terman examined a thousand gifted children, and his results showed that instead of being a weakling and sickly, the "typical" genius was healthy, socially active, popular, and well adjusted psychologically [Terman, 1959]. The issue is still active, though. A recent experiment clearly indicated that nearsighted people do much better scholastically than those who don't need glasses. The author of the study points out, among other things, that nearsightedness probably reduced participation in sports for the people in question and led to greater concentration on reading [Douglas et al., 1969]. More recent studies, however, suggest that the highly gifted student may have more personality problems than Terman found [Chambers and Dusseault, 1972]. There is considerable evidence that the very bright today are a far cry from those in the 1920s. There has been a gradual decline in the level of stress among students on achievement in reading, writing, and arithmetic and an increasing interest in social issues and the need for some practicality in what they are learning. Thus, the gifted of today may not be as aloof from world problems and may suffer personally for it [Epstein, 1972; Hawes, 1972]. However, there is no evidence that very bright individuals are crazy and there is minimal correlation between the ectomorph, brightness, and severe mental disturbance.

In the 1950s a husband-and-wife team, the Drs. Glueck, who have spent their lives studying delinquents, found that mesomorphs engaged in delinquent acts more often than individuals of other body types. Here we have an interesting scientific problem: Which is the horse, and which the cart? It stands to reason, at least after the fact, that sturdier people are going to go in for activities that are physically more aggressive. Since all mesomorphs are not delinquent, however, it seems somewhat remote that body type is directly involved in the sense that it causes delinquent behavior.

Some recent research on body types has taken a fresh approach to the issue of physique and personality. These studies, with most results sharing significance beyond the .05 level, have focused on the effect of one's body on one's own self-image—how a person sees himself, rather than how others see him. Male mesomorphs clearly like their bodies better than other males like theirs. And, in what one experimenter terms a throwback to frontier ideals of manliness, mesomorphic hulks of flesh are clearly viewed as most masculine *by males*. Females tend to view men of the less muscle-bound variety as more masculine [Darden, 1972]. This would suggest that the self-image of the nonmesomorphic male would suffer most in the early, formative years when boys are most concerned with the opinion of other males and have not yet taken note of what females have to offer.

Contrary to Freud's hypothesis that women envy men's bodies, women value their bodies more highly than men do. Both men and women are well aware of their physiques and focus considerable attention on them. Those who are chronically ill tend to view their bodies poorly, as opposed to a normal control group. Some of these results may seem obvious, but so did Sheldon's work, at first. The major difference between the two types of studies is that physique seems to affect one's perception of oneself rather than to reflect specific personality "types." The influence of one's body, then, can be quite potent. In a culture oriented toward the female body, for example, a woman with a poor self-image of her body can obviously have strong feelings of inadequacy [Kurtz, 1969; Kurtz and Hirt, 1970]. The importance of a woman's body in influencing judgments about her personality unfortunately begins at a very young age, and can make life very difficult for the girl who happens to be an endomorph. In one study, female subjects seven to eleven years old were asked to supply adjectives to fit pictures of silhouettes of the endomorph, the shapely mesomorph, and the

89   Carl Jung

ectomorph—there were no facial features, just silhouette outline drawings. The endomorph was seen as a cheater, mean, dirty, stupid, and so forth. The shapely mesomorph was characterized as neat, happy, helpful to others, et cetera. The ectomorph did not do as badly as the endomorph but was generally seen as weak and quiet [Staffieri, 1972].

Some conclusions can be gleaned from these studies. First, the body shape *does* elicit some emotional response from other people, but its major effect seems to be on the person's feelings about himself. In other words, personality may be nothing like the body type, but if others believe it is, this can cause considerable heartache. Second, body type appears to have *some* effect on personality. However, although many skinny people are intellectuals, not all intellectuals are necessarily weak or skinny. Not all athletically built men are automatically delinquents, nor are all delinquents athletic; not all fat persons are jolly like Santa Claus, and as you may recall if you ever went downtown at Christmastime when you were a child, not all Santa Clauses are fat.

I want to emphasize the second point, the effect of the body type on personality, because it puts the whole situation into perspective. In the late 1960s long hair became the rage among a significant proportion of male adolescents, including war protesters, draft protesters, and society protesters. The reaction of conservative adults ran to such opinions as "Jail all those kids with long hair" or "People with long hair are dangerous." An unwary experimenter *could have found* a high correlation between long hair and protest or even anarchic activity. Obviously, long hair is not a characteristic that determines personality or behavior, because all young people can grow long hair—but a correlation nonetheless is there. It *is* possible to say that among those causing trouble, many had long hair. It is not possible to say either (*a*) that long hair lends itself to illegal behavior, or (*b*) that long-haired people have personality characteristics which lead them to commit antisocial acts, or (*c*) long hair causes protesting.

SOCIAL-PSYCHOLOGICAL THEORIES

All of us have grown up in an era marked by preoccupation with the influence of parents on children, and considerable confusion exists, among professionals and laymen alike, regarding Freud's theory. In the last chapter, even though I tried to emphasize the biological aspects of Freud's theoretical framework, you needed to be especially careful not to fall gradually into the assumption that Freud was saying our parents influence us during the oral, anal—what have you—stage of development. He was not saying anything so simple. Freud based his theory on sequences of biological development patterned after Darwin's idea of the survival of the fittest. In the developing human organism, some people did not develop properly during a particular stage; something went wrong *biologically*, and they became fixated at that stage. Freud was, at best, only minimally concerned with what went on between mother and child. Only those who were physically programmed to survive the various stages made it in one piece. So Freud paid only lip service to the direct interaction between mother and child in a social sense.

Obviously this heavily biological orientation was not going to last long, because the influence of social factors was too strong for theorists to ignore. Freud's successors still cling to some of his ideas, but they have modified his theory in rather drastic fashion to include social factors. For example, we might look quickly at a current-day journal article written by a psychoanalyst. The author discusses the causes of obesity. From Freud's viewpoint, now, this overeating problem results from a malfunction of the organism that occurred during the oral stage. The person becomes preoccupied with oral activities such as eating because of this malfunction during the oral stage of development. However, the modern author stresses that the infant undergoes some *upsetting experience* during the oral stage of development—perhaps a rejecting mother—and that this poor *social* situation makes the grown person unable to read his body's signals regarding hunger and fullness. That is, inadequate loving during infant feeding (a *social* experience) leads to some biological disorganization, which is intimately tied to hunger signals from the body. It is now a known fact, for instance, that in general, normal-sized people can read such bodily cues as stomach contractions that indicate hunger, but obese subjects do not detect the contractions when they occur—in fact, they frequently indicate that they do not want to eat, but something drives them to it* [Bruch, 1969].

The important point here is that Freud's followers, the neo-Freudians, have altered his concepts to include important factors of social interaction, to a large extent deemphasizing Freud's biological-deterministic approach.

A contemporary of Sheldon was Dr. Harry Stack Sullivan, a psychiatrist and probably one of the most colorful writers in the personality area. Sullivan, a neo-Freudian, died in 1949, but fortunately not before he had worked out an extensive system of personality. Sullivan's system probably characterizes the neo-Freudians most clearly, so he will be discussed as representative of the group. You will readily notice in a moment his heavy emphasis on social factors.

To set the stage for this great man and his keen insight, a passage is quoted below from one of his books. Sullivan is explaining how people set up patterns of behavior to avoid social relationships that they find

---

*It is important to know that overweight is *not always* a problem of self-control or of psychological difficulties. Considerable recent research demonstrates that obesity is in some cases the result of purely physiological or inherited factors—e.g., an overabundance of fat cells, as compared to normal people. Exercise does help, but *these* fat people are coping with a physiological problem, not just emotional hangups or lack of "will power" [Mayer, 1968].

threatening because of earlier experiences. He says what many of us have thought:

> A certain small section of Manhattan society rise from bed in the later forenoon, dress rather carefully, gather up their husbands or wives—their concessions to social necessity, as it were—and proceed to the bridge club. There they engage in an intensely concentrated performance, almost without speech or with only very highly formalized speech. After a considerable number of hours at this, they go out and retrieve their social remnant—by which I mean their mate—get something to eat, and go through a practically meaningless routine of life until the next meeting of the group. . . . [They] live a life which is all bridge; the rest is a matter so obviously of boring and tedious routine that it is very impressive. [Sullivan, 1954]*

Why set up situations involving only minimal contact with people on a meaningful level? For the answer we need to look more closely at Sullivan's personality theory.

Sullivan was like Freud in stressing the importance of energy in personality development. To Sullivan, however, this energy appears more often as tension which a person develops, an excess of energy he feels when faced with a choice between two alternatives neither of which is very agreeable. Notice, for example, the phenomenon of pacing the floor to get rid of this energy when you are trying to solve a problem.

The child's first contacts are with his mother. The child directs his energy toward a "social" relationship with the mother, and she in turn either does or does not reciprocate with an adequate amount of love. In actuality, Sullivan seemed to be saying that personality exists *only* in terms of how others react to us and how we react to them. In other words, what we call personality is a matter of how we see ourselves and how others see us. In a somewhat symbolic fashion representing the mother, the baby develops a concept of the breast and nipple as an energy force that is either "good" or "bad." Thus, the mother is either friendly, loving, and satisfying or hostile, unforgiving, and rejecting. If the mother is not satisfying, then the situation is both psychologically and physically upsetting to the child.

Aside from feeding, mother-child interaction takes place in play, in bathing, in dressing, and in general care. Thus, the child is accepted or rejected and begins to form a concept, in Sullivan's words, of the "good-me" or the "bad-me." The child carries this concept around until he is able to formulate it into words (symbolic thought). A bad-me brings low self-esteem and, of course, a great deal of anxiety—both resulting from *social interaction with the mother*.

Sullivan's theory of infancy is presented here as an example of his ideas about social interaction. He does not suppose that important events

*From H. S. Sullivan, *The Psychiatric Interview* (New York: Norton, 1954), p. 153; reprinted by permission.

90 Charlie Brown seems to have a "bad-me" self-concept
(© 1971 United Feature Syndicate Inc.)

in human development end with the infancy stage. The juvenile stage follows, and the child begins to form social relationships with other children; after this juvenile stage comes the preadolescent period, which will be discussed in a moment. Of maximum importance throughout the developmental sequence is social interaction with others and its influence on the kind of human being the person is becoming. How he turns out is greatly influenced, of course, by the early concepts he has formed of himself. He will be able (or unable) to relate to others along the way depending upon the anxiety such relationships bring. If a person feels himself to be a bad-me, relationships with others will create a lot of anxiety because people are likely to reject him, just as his mother seemed to do. A person sets up methods for defending himself from full realization of this bad-me. In a sense, his defense is a fantasy world that counteracts the bad-me conceptions, a world that is unreal but protective. In grossly exaggerated form, such fantasy conceptions are often part of the thinking of the highly disturbed person who believes that everyone around him is wrong and he is right, or that everyone behaves strangely toward him because they realize his greatness and are envious. He is discharging anxious energy.

Sullivan's system allows that these misrepresentations may be corrected along the path of life. (Freud felt that the personality became fixed by the age of three or four.) Sullivan concentrated especially on the early adolescent period as a critical time for corrections. During this period the boy or girl forms very close attachments to members of his or her own sex. During this "buddy stage" the person is able to test out some of his distorted thinking and note the reaction of the peer toward him; if the friend is accepting, his reaction is very beneficial in helping the person to reorient or correct some of his misconceptions.

Sullivan felt that the rules of society are extremely restrictive and that these rules, enforced by parents, often lead to personality difficulties. During the buddy stage, the early adolescent often lives in a world that belongs just to adolescents; in that world, it is possible for him to find personal worth and self-esteem under a different set of rules, not closely bound up in the strange laws of parents or society.

288

Once the heterosexual stage begins, society reasserts itself, and very strongly, in rules about dating, sexual behavior, and the like. Thus, although salvation is *possible* after early adolescence, adolescence itself is a critical time. But the buddy stage has its hazards, too; if the person cannot find sufficient self-worth during this period, at least enough to give him the strength to wander into that frightening world of boy-girl relationships, then he is likely to become a homosexual, because to him that seems to be a safer relationship than one with the opposite sex [Sullivan, 1953].

LEARNING THEORIES OF PERSONALITY

Learning theory also emphasizes relationships with others, but from a slightly expanded point of view: we learn from the total environment and form our personalities by obtaining rewards from this total environment.

The following quotation, which will help illustrate the point, is from the autobiography of the famous black gospel and blues singer, Miss Ethel Waters. This passage about a world most of us know little about demonstrates the influence of early learning on later attitudes. Miss Waters's deep respect for prostitutes probably goes back to her favorable childhood experiences, reflecting an attitude or personality tendency begun at a very young age.

In any case, ignore me just for a moment and read the words of a great lady:

Along with a few other Clifton Street youngsters I acted as a semi-official lookout girl for the sporting houses. Though prostitution was a legalized business, there were occasional police raids. These came when church groups bore down heavily on the authorities or after one body too many, stabbed, shot, or cut up very untidily, had been found in some dark alley.

Any of us slum children could smell out a cop even though he was a John, a plain-clothes man. These brilliant sleuths never suspicioned that we were tipsters for the whole whoring industry. Usually we'd be playing some singing game on the street when we spotted a cop, a game like Here Comes Two Dudes A-Riding or the one that begins:

King William was King James's son,
Upon his breast he wore a star,
And that was called . . .

On smelling out the common enemy, we boys and girls in the know would start to shout the songs, accenting certain phrases. If we happened to be playing a singing game we'd whistle the agreed-on tune. The other kids, even those who weren't lookouts, would innocently imitate us, and in no time at all the whole neighborhood would be alerted. . . .

I've always had great respect for whores. The many I've known were kind and generous. Some of them supported whole families and kept at their trade for years to send their trick babies through college. I never knew a prostitute who did harm to anyone but herself. I except, of course, the whores who are real criminals and use knockout drops and bring men to their rooms to be robbed, beaten, and blackmailed. [Walters, 1951]*

Learning theory relies heavily on very early experiences which, often repeated, tend to become a style of life for most of us. Almost everyone can remember childhood acquaintances or relatives with whom he had many good or bad experiences. Today we probably still respond to people either positively or negatively according to their resemblance to people from the past—for example, you may meet someone and dislike him intensely before he even says anything to you. If you think back carefully, chances are very good that the person reminds you of someone you detested.

I have mentioned the influence of events from early life, as both Freud and Sullivan saw them. Learning theories also stress the past and assume that our present behavior results from previous situations. A major difference between learning theorists and Freudians is that the first group deemphasizes the unconscious. In learning-theory terms, the unconscious is often equated with forgetting or an inability to recall past events easily and immediately. If you are reminded of John Watson, you have good reason, for he was the forerunner of later behaviorist theory. According to behaviorist theory, the organism is subject to mechanical principles rather than to more exotic phenomena like the unconscious or the libido.†

The neo-Freudians discuss the varying strength of the superego and the id; Sullivan covers the importance of having a strong self-concept. The strength of these various mechanisms, however, depends on how the person learned to respond to his mother or to others in the environment and how they responded to him.

The panorama of personality theory, therefore, contains an important gap. The deficiency centers around the issue of exactly *how* the childhood ties, felt so strongly in later life, are formed. Both Freud and the neo-Freudians, including Sullivan, concerned themselves with the effects of early events on later behavior but not the specific mechanisms by which the early events find their way into our personality.

For the *how*, we turn to two prominent theorists of learning and personality, Dollard and Miller, who took many basic components of Freudian and neo-Freudian theory, added flavor of their own, and tied the whole framework to a system of learning and development. They stressed psychoanalytic principles, but you may find their outline useful in trying to explain how human beings develop, no matter which personality theory is used.

---

*From Ethel Waters and Charles Samuels, *His Eye Is on the Sparrow* (New York: Doubleday, 1951); © 1950, 1951 by Ethel Waters and Charles Samuels; reprinted by permission.
†The term *behaviorist* implies here, as it did with Watson, that we are little more than a series of learned behaviors tied mechanically together.

the pleasure principle   A working assumption of the Dollard-Miller theory is the *pleasure principle.* You have come across this principle before, in hedonism and in Freud's concept of the id gratifying its basic desires.* Dollard and Miller add to Freud's core—sex drive—such phenomena as hunger and thirst. The validity of adding these drives to sex drive is based primarily on studies of lower organisms. For instance, rats can be trained to push a lever, or pigeons trained to peck at a certain place, in order to obtain a pellet of food or a drink of water. Receiving food or water satisfies the basic need, resulting in a reduction in the animal's desire.

Similarly, using the Dollard-Miller system, the mother's nipple in Sullivan's theory can satisfy hunger, so that the human child derives pleasure from it. Obviously the child does not come to feel loved just from the nipple itself. Think back to Watson's experiment in which little Albert was afraid first of the white rat and then of white things and furry things; the effect of the initial connection spread outward to include things closely related to the original object. (The term used for this process is *generalization.*) Using the same principle, the child who has pleasurable feeding experiences can generalize them to the mother as a whole person, and eventually to people as a whole. Admittedly, this generalization is not going to come just from feeding alone, but from feeding combined with pleasant experiences of bathing, dressing, and handling. Thus the child develops a positive concept of parents and others from generalization based on the pleasure principle.

We might speculate here on the case of the prostitutes mentioned by Miss Waters. We can assume, not illogically, that all children have considerable anxiety and a great need for love; that is, experience provides many threats to one's basic sense of well-being that need to be pacified. Under the learning-theory system, this anxiety could have been reduced by the friendship of the prostitutes. Since anxiety is unpleasant, its reduction is a rewarding experience and will be sought over and over again.

An unknown boundary defines the point at which we have learned that we are loved or unloved; too little love tends to make a person feel unwanted and too much makes him overdependent. In the latter case, the child has learned that each time a problem of any sort arises the mother, in her excessive concern, will solve it for him.

If you learned at an early age to stop spitting food because your mother disapproved, you would in turn be rewarded by a smile or a loving pat on the head. Each act bringing this type of reward tended to strengthen the learning, ensured a continued good reaction from others, and helped form a good self-concept: "If everyone is loving toward me because of these acts, I must be someone very worthwhile" [Dollard and Miller, 1950].

On the negative side, a young child can learn a number of unen-

---

* In those instances, you may recall, we get carried away seeking our own pleasure and avoiding any pain or displeasure.

viable personality characteristics. For instance, although he may learn that when things go wrong, attacking his mother doesn't bring rewards (is unpleasurable), he may also learn that blaming his brother makes him feel better. If he consistently behaves this way, a child could develop a personality characteristic in which blame is never accepted, but always placed on someone else [Miller, 1952].

avoidance behavior   Or suppose that a little girl comes to fear her father, having learned that she doesn't make the correct responses often enough. According to learning theory, this fear of the father could develop into an *avoidance response*, in which the child tries to avoid the troublesome object or person, in this case the father. Conceivably this child could generalize the avoidance response to the father, building up a set of avoidance responses toward men in general.

Studies with animals reflect an interesting characteristic of learned avoidance responses: once begun, they become self-perpetuating. A dog was enclosed in a large pen with a hurdle in the middle; each half of the floor was separately electrified. On the side of the hurdle on which the dog was first placed, the electricity was turned on, causing him to jump the hurdle to the other side. After a few seconds, the electricity was turned on on the other side, and the dog jumped back again. A few seconds more, and the electricity was turned on again on the original side. Before long the dog began to jump over the hurdle a short time *before* the shock was administered. When he got to the other side, he waited until just before the shock came and then jumped. At that point the experimenter could turn off the shock entirely and keep the dog jumping until he became exhausted. The most important point is that the dog did not wait to see if the shock was still there [Solomon, 1964].

The parallel with human behavior should be obvious. A person who has a number of upsetting experiences with other people can quickly learn to avoid them. By doing so, he keeps from running the risk of being hurt; worse, however, he will never find out if another person will accept him. By avoiding people, he is constantly jumping before the shock, so to speak.

Before leaving the topic of the electrified compartments, I want to bring up another group of studies that *suggest* learned behavioral responses that might apply to humans. Again using dogs, the experimenter arranged a harness so that the animals couldn't escape repeated shocks no matter what they did. These dogs, when finally given an opportunity to jump over a hurdle, did not do so; instead, they remained on the electrified portion until the shock was over. They had learned that *no* appropriate response was available, that conditions were beyond their control, and they had given up. Repeated inability of the human child to succeed may induce such passive, give-up behavior.

It is possible—sometimes—to retrain people who have been subjected to continued failure—for example, by forcing them into situations in which they can only succeed [Seligman, 1968].

secondary drives   Learning theorists make allowance for the complexities of human behavior, notably by means of *secondary drives.* Basically, humans do not operate just at jungle level, relying only on primary drives (hunger, thirst, and sex); instead, they attach words, symbols, and meanings to the primary drives and behave in accordance with them. The concepts embodied in these words, symbols, and meanings are called secondary drives because although they mimic primary drives or basic needs, they have been altered by the association of symbols to them, which are themselves not basic or primary.

Suppose, on the human level, that we start off with a basic drive such as hunger. Hunger is a primary drive, meaning that it is of first importance to survival. But from childhood on we are trained (so that our parents can sleep) to eat only during the day, and even more specifically at 7 A.M., 12 noon, and 6 P.M. The human body does not need this regulation, nor does it need exactly three meals a day. Hence, our desire to eat at these specific times is the result of learning. Our "hunger" at 11:30 A.M. is not critical in the sense that a primary drive is critical; instead, it is a recommended behavior pattern of society. Hence, it is a secondary or learned drive. These secondary drives are often triggered by what are called *verbal cues* or *environmental cues* that have been attached to the secondary drive. A clock may be an environmental cue, for example. Often we are not certain how hungry we are until we see what time it is—an hour late for lunch. And purely verbal cues are everywhere: As you drive along the highway, you see a big red EAT sign. The word EAT triggers a secondary drive which results in your stopping to have a hamburger [Dollard and Miller, 1950].

Only if you have gone without food for a long time does the primary drive begin to operate again. However, the secondary drive is still with you. The secondary drive probably triggers mirages of hot-dog stands to a man wandering through the desert without food or water. "Hot-dog stand" is a secondary symbolic image associated with the basic drive of hunger.

91   An environmental cue, if you happen to like that kind of food (*Gabriele Wunderlich*)

Another example, one that is more directly related to personality, may help to clarify this point. At first a child needs physical love and reward. That is a primary drive or need. Notice, however, that after he has spent a short time in kindergarten, the child works frantically to see how many gold stars he can get the teacher to paste on his forehead. He is operating under a symbolic secondary drive that began as a primary drive, the one we might call a need for acceptance and love. A cue that triggers the seeking of stars could be anything from seeing others with many stars on their foreheads to hearing a word of praise from his mother when he arrives home looking like a highly decorated spaceman.

Word cues also operate on the negative side. Suppose that a child is burned a number of times on a gas stove. The pain initiates a basic, animal-like avoidance response, a primary drive, but the words *dangerous, stay away,* and the like, are verbal cues. They set up a secondary drive, so that the child learns symbolically, by the meaning of these words, to avoid fire and later will avoid things labeled "dangerous."

In diagrammatic form:

Child sees fire→Word cue "dangerous"→Secondary drive of avoidance→ Child refrains from putting hand into fire.

These, then, are some aspects of learning theory. You should have detected the basics—that is, learned associations by classical or operant conditioning. These combine so that we form the core of behavior patterns which in turn form our so-called personalities. At least one major problem in the learning theory of personality is reflected in the objections of Dr. Carl Rogers. The learning theory is too mechanical for some. Rogers represents a school of psychologists that believe that behavior is not based primarily on physiological needs, drives, or avoidance behavior, but instead on a "higher" driving force within the human which impels him toward complex personality patterns. That is, the person seeks a form of spiritual reward, not in a religious sense but in a self-fulfilling sense. As you may recall, we have approached this controversy before in the discussion of hedonism as opposed to Maslow's hierarchy of needs.

PERSONALITY THEORY OF SELF-ACTUALIZATION

Carl Rogers stands in contrast to Freud, Sullivan, Dollard, and Miller. His theory stresses the individual, who "determines his own fate"; hence, he has been popular in the United States, a country impressed by individual achievement. Although Rogers does not disclaim the unconscious, it is not a part of his system, as it was with Freud. Rogers differs from Dollard and Miller by treating the individual as a whole unit rather than as the sum of a number of stimuli and responses. And, compared with Sullivan, he deemphasizes the stages of development and the overriding importance of social influences.

His theory does resemble others we have studied, however—notably one that seems closely related in basic concepts, Maslow's theory. Although Maslow has not been discussed in this section on personality theory, he had a considerable amount to say about it. For example, Maslow's "hierarchy of needs" focuses on the whole person as that person works toward a unified goal. But Maslow was concerned, as you may recall, with goals that satisfy specific needs, a distinction about which Rogers says little.

self-actualization   Rogers assumes that from the beginning each of us has a potential for *self-actualization.* Maslow used this term frequently, but you will see some important shades of difference. For Rogers, self-actualization might be, metaphorically, a set of guiding principles the potential of which is present in us from childhood, like seeds always present but in need of water.* We strive constantly to fulfill these principles in order to become whole and

* Rogers called the self-actualized person "fully-functioning," but I have taken the liberty of using the same term as Maslow did for clarity, since the two are almost identical.

unified persons. Rogers emphasized the present rather than the past; that is, within reasonable limits, what happened to us in the past is correctable in the present if the person is allowed to utilize the forces within himself. In other words, the basic potential for development is already there, but the person must become aware of it [Rogers, 1942, 1951].

Throughout his life a person develops *self-regard* (or fails to develop it); this term basically means he finds himself intrinsically worthwhile. Self-regard—a positive concept of oneself—is not to be confused with being "stuck-up" or self-centered. And of course everyone has days when he feels worthless; but a person who has basic self-regard values himself and his role in life. He is not depressed by the very thought of his existence.

Such a person must have regard for others' worth, as well, in order to be fully rounded out; he is able to accept those around him. And if a person has high regard for himself and for others, he can achieve self-actualization. The basic personality—shy, aggressive, happy, sad, etc.—results from how well the person handles his self-concept, that is, how he views himself.

You may still see this process as identical to Maslow's theory, so some distinctions should be mentioned. First, Rogers feels that a person has the potential for self-actualization from the beginning of life and is working toward it (see Maslow's diagram, Fig. 5–5). Under Maslow's system, self-actualization is possible only *after* more basic needs have been met. Second, in Maslow's theory the fulfilled person is usually one who has reached the apex of achievement in a selected area of life. For example, the woman who wants to become a physician and does become one is satisfied with her life situation and therefore stands at the top of Maslow's hierarchy. Under Rogers's theory, the same young woman can attain a feeling of her own worth even if she doesn't achieve exactly what she desires. This woman may enter any occupation, even if she does so just through economic necessity, but she can still be self-actualized if she feels she is doing her best, is producing satisfactory results in life, and has high regard for herself and for others. Ideally, of course, the highest level of self-regard is achieved through full realization of one's life goals.

Self-actualization is based on a feeling of one's own worth. But it is difficult to see how this feeling can be achieved without having at least one person who cares for you as a person rather than for what you can give him. In other words, a friend can provide you with the self-confidence you need in order to regard yourself in a favorable light and to use this confidence as a springboard to doing worthwhile things.

Thus, Rogers has a system of counseling people with problems that rests on the listener's accepting the person and caring about the integrity of the person rather than about his actions. (This system will be discussed in detail later.) The counselor's concern and acceptance constitute what is called *unconditional positive regard* for the patient. This kind of regard can be understood best by using an example from the area of criminology. Suppose the counselor is working with a person who has stolen something; the counselor's task is to demonstrate by his actions toward the patient that he feels that, "Yes, you have committed a crime, but the *crime* is not *you.* You as a person are basically worthwhile. The crime is an action that does not reflect the basic you. The basic you is good and working toward self-actualization. I accept unconditionally this basic you, even though your crime may leave something to be desired."

basic development   As I have mentioned, development under Rogers's system is not based on a fixed set of stages—Oedipal, phallic, nipple, buddy, etc. The important fact of development is how the person sees himself and evaluates his worth or value at any particular time. In other words, during Freud's "phallic stage," the person meets up with a set of "laws" to which all humans are subject; this stage is a time of preoccupation with sexual self-gratification. This is not necessarily the case under Rogers's system, for even though the child may be preoccupied with sex, he may also participate actively in a youth group or in some other project that he finds fulfilling. Thus, personality development is an individual matter and proceeds in an individual fashion; it is not bound by any fixed "laws" of developmental sequence.

During development, Rogers emphasizes, each of us is subjected to different experiences. We incorporate these experiences into our frame of reference if they are appropriate to us. In doing so, we form a self—maybe a self who is outgoing or private, friendly or unfriendly, excitable or un-ruffled, and so on, but we form our own concept of what we are like. Once we have established this framework, we allow into our consciousness external things that fit our world and block out those that do not. Rogers calls this process *symbolization,* meaning that we recognize certain things as appropriate to us and make them into symbols for ourselves. For example, if you believe stealing is wrong and you see someone caught for doing it, you might symbolize this scene (put it into your own framework) as verification of what you believe. If, on the other hand, you see someone getting away with stealing, the incident will not be fully integrated or symbolized, at least to the extent that you would integrate an event that reinforces your viewpoint. In other words, by the process of symbolization one continues to build his basic personality tendencies in a certain direction, selectively "verifying" his beliefs each step of the way.

Symbolization may be easier to understand if we call on another prominent social scientist, Dr. Leon Festinger. Festinger points out that we integrate events around us by a "balancing technique." For example, I am a man, and I love Barbara. I hear someone say Barbara looks like a witch and has bad breath. This remark will not integrate or fit with my feelings or thoughts about her appeal. So, in order to rebalance my perception of her, I am likely to convince myself that whoever said that about her is just envious. Or it *is* possible that I could agree with him although it's not likely. If I do agree, then I must stop loving Barbara or say to myself that I never did. Otherwise my thought patterns and my feelings do not agree. Festinger's proposal, which is a *theory of cognitive dissonance,** states that we must maintain a balance within our thought or feeling processes. The system is somewhat similar to physical homeostasis because we keep dissonance in balance or reduced.

Rogers is saying roughly the same thing: I will reject the other person's statements about Barbara (that is, I will not make them into symbols for myself); or, if I accept them, then I didn't have a genuine love symbolization of her to begin with.

Rogers elaborates his symbolization process by saying that a person seeking self-actualization is accepting and rejecting, sifting through the environment as it were, to get the pieces to fit together into a workable whole. People who have personality problems have not learned to symbolize adequately in the direction that would lead them toward self-actualization.

For Rogers, then, development is an individual thing. Each of us is basically motivated to seek our self-actualization, and we do so by the technique of symbolization. Rigid or fixed developmental stages are under-played in his system.

CULTURAL THEORIES OF PERSONALITY

Dr. Carl Jung (pronounced "young") was one of the most brilliant and interesting men in the chronicles of personality theory. For a time Jung was a follower of Freud, but the two men disagreed on many things, especially the importance of sexuality and Freud's emphasis on the mechanical aspects of human behavior.†

For a long time Jung's theory has been considered as lying outside the mainstream of psychological thought. Recent years, however, have seen a resurgence of interest, generated partly by the mysticism inherent in his system. He cannot be ignored, and his influence on current theory is un-doubtedly there, although it is subtle. Jung's quasi–religious theory of personality stresses a driving force in the individual; this force is rather similar to the one that impels the self, in Rogers's theory, only it is much more elaborate, as you will soon see [Spinks, 1967].

Jung's influence was most notable in the 1920s, when he represented a counterforce to Freud's theory. His popularity waned over the next four decades, during which time psychology continued to fight any mystical or

---

Cognitive refers to thought processes; *dissonance* is lack of agreement. A person tries to reduce cognitive dissonance and to align two dissonant cognitions (that is, two contradictory thought processes or feelings). Dissonance sets up tension and the individual changes his perception in order to reduce this tension.

† The battle was rather bitter. Jung called Freud neurotic and Freud said Jung was crazy [Brome, 1967].

magical theory and remained preoccupied with those aspects of human behavior that are subject to experimental analysis—or at least those that can be measured. Jung's ideas again appeared on the scene in full force during the late 1960s and early 1970s. One might speculate that once again psychology is struggling with the problem that a human being will not sit still indefinitely with the label "machine" tattooed on his chest. This unwillingness to accept the status quo seems to be what makes psychology the hybrid science; it has trouble settling down into one specific area. Man is constantly interrupting the scientists, saying, "I am something more than Freud or Watson claimed!"

Jung made specific criticisms of the mechanistic viewpoint. Who do we all think we are, he wanted to know, to ascribe the power of love, or the magnificent intellect of such great philosophers as Immanuel Kant, to the "all-powerful matter" of the brain cells? In a way he was claiming that this is a bluff; in fact, we are taking the traditional attributes of God and just moving them over under a different name—"the brain cell" [Jung, 1933].

Jung objected to psychology that constantly ignores what is obvious: the human being continually sets up goals, purposes, and needs that are religious in nature. Man is endlessly trying, by ritualistic acts, to unite himself with a greater good or a more powerful being. For example, in a nonreligious analysis of the Roman Catholic Mass, Jung points out that the human consciousness of the priest and the congregation becomes part of a "divine happening" * by a symbolic union with God. Man is always striving for union with a greater good [Jung, 1958].

How does all of this occur? One of Jung's basic concepts is that man's personality is a part of ancient myths and traditions passed on from one generation to another, much as one receives certain hair or eye color; the major difference is that abstract thoughts and symbols are being inherited. By careful analysis of old records, prehistoric paintings, and relics, Jung was able to demonstrate that man, in each succeeding generation, seems to follow a pattern in what he worships, what he believes, and how he behaves. These patterns are so similar that he suggests the basic pattern is inherited. Man's attitude toward the sun provides a prime example of such consistent behavior. All known primitive peoples recognized the sun as *the* powerful force in the universe. At times the sun has been worshiped as a god; even in our modern civilization, people focus considerable attention on it, trying to capture its energy and understand its nature [Jung, 1925]. In other words, each generation of human beings inherits the general idea of the sun as a great force.

Likewise, each generation inherits a concept of "mother"—one who cares for us and has maternal feelings—no matter what word is used for

92   A mandala, Jung's symbol for the oneness of human experience, made concrete in universal myths and archetypes

---

*Jung used the word *happening* in 1955. Today it has a more than familiar ring.

93 An earth-mother from prehistoric culture; modern men have named her the *Venus of Willendorf,* assuming that she represented a standard of beauty to Paleolithic man (*Museum of Natural History, Vienna*)

this person. This concept may have originated in the basic idea of earth-mother—the earth as a mother that provides us with food, shelter, and care. The expression "Mother Earth" is certainly an old one. Our greedy non-Indian friends of early America ran into this problem head-on when they tried to buy land from Indian groups that felt deeply about the earth as a mother. As one author has pointed out, this attempt to buy pieces of earth was tantamount to asking them to sell their mother [Josephy, 1968].

If Mother Earth is a universal—that is, the concept of protectiveness is available to all men—it is so, Jung maintains, because each new generation inherits the concept. Somewhere in man's long history, he says, an *archetype* of motherly behavior developed. An archetype is an original; in many respects it is like the master recording that is used to press records which are later sold to the public. Generations of mothers resemble this inherited archetype without being aware of it.

Jung suggested that in the process of copying the archetypes, many a person tends to obscure what would be his or her actual personality. He called this fake personality a *persona,* derived from a Latin word for the mask worn by actors in Greek and Roman stage plays. According to his theory, many of us adopt masks that conform to what we are supposed to be, rather than letting ourselves be what we actually are. We make up mask-personalities. Many women who assume the role of mother, for example, do so to the exclusion of other aspects of their personalities. They become preoccupied with diapers, soapsuds, and baby foods, and this personality can become so complete that even on the rare night when their husbands take them out, somehow the subject gets around to soapsuds, baby food, and possibly even diapers.

Personality, then, is a combination of inherited universal tendencies and social roles.

social learning   You may be ahead of the discussion already, having anticipated one of the reasons Jung lost favor with scientific psychology: Today most psychologists interpret what Jung called role behavior* as learned social imitation rather than actions resulting from an inherited archetype, although basically they have adopted Jung's theory without the inheritance aspect.

The outcome for human beings, whether interpreted as social learning or inheritance, is the important fact: We often become what society tells us to become; we behave as we are expected to behave. For instance, a judge who appears at the bench wearing nothing on top but an undershirt is immediately suspect because we expect certain characteristics in a judge, and one of them is a dignified appearance.

A notable example of personality characteristics that are socially induced appears in a fascinating novel about coal miners in England. The author mentions that the miners' life style calls for them to have extremely

*Taking a role, as an actor does; adopting a persona.

aggressive personalities over the weekends. The miners usually report faithfully on Friday night for a forty-eight-hour drinking and fighting spree. And then, in a rapid turnabout of personality, during the work week:

> Now everybody is back at work, and this pocket in this heading in this seam resounds to the thud of metallic fracturing explosions of picks sunk into coal, of shovels ramming into piles of loose coal, of five teams of men moving wordlessly in damp semi-darkness, of picks and shovels clanking and plunging. Ten men in pit boots and leather belt and pit helmet and naked to the gods of the interior earth.
>
> There is something about their nakedness. When I first crawled into this seam politeness required that my eyes take no special note of what was, in a stranger's eyes, a jarring sight: the simple nudity of men who, if they had the choice to make, would have their clothes on. Down here, these men reserve a special respect, almost a gentleness toward each other's nakedness. There is no horse-play, no punching around, and I do not think it is only because their energy must be conserved for the job. It is as though, in shucking off his clothes to stand revealed, and therefore in a large sense defenseless, the collier derives from the very nakedness of his coal-smeared flesh a unique self-respect, an unfleshly dignity which is both elemental and deep driven. The fraternity of the naked worker need not be fierce. [Sigal, 1960]*

Social conditions and the society within which these men live are obviously producing personality characteristics—for example, aggressiveness—which differ in degrees and kind from other social groups.

Talking about individual personality persona, and how it is influenced by society's expectations, an extremely frustrating situation plagued the late Walt Disney. He had created an image that is world-renowned, and he was invested by one and all with a specific artistic talent gained from the fame of his cartoon characters; yet he was unable to effectively draw Mickey Mouse, Donald Duck, or Pluto. Disney sometimes dropped hints to his artists that he wanted to learn how to make a quick sketch of Mickey for autograph seekers. Obviously overall he was a tremendous success, but as you can see, his fictionalized persona had an irritating little piece missing, and he was trying to correct the fault so he could live up to social expectations regarding his personality [Schickel, 1968].

Or to take another example, when Dwight Eisenhower was president, he had a popular image of being a homely, friendly, guy-next-door type of man who read western novels in his spare time. To protect this (erroneous) social role he had his speechwriters deliberately write terrible speeches. If by chance they came up with a good phrase, he would delete it [O'Neill, 1971].†

---

*From C. Sigal, *Weekend in Dinlock* (Boston: Houghton Mifflin, 1960); reprinted by permission.

†Nixon was heavily criticized for rarely talking to the press. Eisenhower had a different technique—he deliberately made as little sense as possible in his press conferences. When faced with a sticky question, he assured his press secretary, he had a sure-fire method for handling it: "I'll just confuse them" [O'Neill, 1971].

**INFLUENCE OF
SOCIETY
ON PERSONALITY**

A discussion of personality would not be complete, then, without mention of this cultural (social learning) view of development. We may each possess individualized modes of behaving and we may or may not develop according to the other systems mentioned here, but there can be little question that our personalities are shaped by our culture and by the attitudes and rules of behavior found in a given society. Later, it will become important to notice that even "mental illness" is often little more than a label reflecting the fact that a society expects certain things from people and that people are labeled "mentally ill" because they do not fit these expectations.

The influence of society on the individual personality is as remarkable as it is universal. As with Sheldon's body types, a given society seems to maintain a tenacious and unyielding stereotype of personality for most occupational groups. The stereotype is influenced in turn by the behavior of individuals—for example, people who reach high positions in business become involved in administrative problems of seniority, salary increases, board meetings, and the like. These behaviors by their very nature tend to increase an interest in business, and the person often acts the part of a business executive because of this interest. The more these acts become a part of his life, the more he encourages the behavior and participates in it, and the circle goes round and round. The point can be made just by asking a few questions. For example, the driver of a Caterpillar tractor often takes home a salary equal to that of the vice-president of a small business. Now, compare the two for a moment. Which one follows the stock market? Which one plays golf? Which one plays pinball machines in the local tavern? Which one is more likely to deal with a loan company than a bank?

I am not suggesting that everybody always conforms to the settled expectations of society, or that these expectations always produce personality characteristics that are clearly distinguishable. But societal expectations *can* and do influence behavior, and one cannot ignore the high degree of such conformity in the formation of a persona. And one might ask, is there a point at which the individual actually begins to believe he is a certain type of person just from playing the role? Probably so.

Deviants from society are often considered a personality type, in the sense that they have certain characteristics which set them apart from others. An intriguing hypothesis has been offered about the formation of deviants.* It suggests that in any human community, deviants are used to define the boundaries for the behavior of that society's members, and hence are a necessity. In other words, just as a child learns the amount and severity of punishments as part of his rule-learning behavior, so society uses news broadcasts and newspapers—both of which are preoccupied with the prosecution of criminal behavior—to tell us what is permissible and what is not. Most people unconsciously watch the penalties carefully to determine what

---

* A *deviant* is one who violates the rules of society, usually to such an extent that he is deemed punishable. A society's most obvious deviants are usually kept in institutions.

behavior is acceptable and how far one can go. Such rules are constantly changing, and the deviants help to keep the rest of us informed.

Futhermore, much evidence suggests that one of society's traditional arrangements is designed to perpetuate deviant behavior, and even to train new deviants. Prisons are a standard environment in which deviants are thrown together in such a way that they exchange trade secrets. This training is enhanced because in a sense prisoners are members of an exclusive group, set aside from society itself in the same way as people who join a country club. They even undergo an elaborate ceremony—their trial—complete with incantations, wearing of special robes by the judge, formal seating procedures, and the like, all designed, in a way, to provide a formal initiation into the deviant role. And society never actually removes the stigma when the prisoner has served his sentence, almost as if society wants to keep its deviants and thereby designate acceptable role behavior for others and specify certain behavior patterns for the criminals [Erikson, 1964].

The topic of society and personality is enormous. A few other related issues might be mentioned briefly: What about sex roles? Many men, for example, insist on remaining the "head" of the household. What impact does society's reaction, officially negative, have on the homosexual's personality? On effeminate males? On tomboyish girls?

What about "normal" behavior that seems rather bizarre to us? Consider the Dobu tribe of New Guinea. For the Dobu, normal behavior consists of being violent, dangerous, highly competitive, and, interestingly enough, cheating whenever possible [Benedict, 1934].

Many men require that sex be illegal, immoral, and "dirty" if they are to enjoy it. American society aids them considerably in attaining these goals. At the same time this society helps mold the personalities of prostitutes, many of whom have been pushed around so much that they are hard, cynical, male-hating people. In the case of prostitution, we could expect that women with certain personality needs would gravitate toward this kind of life—but notice how society accommodates the male by providing the forbidden fruit and expecting the woman to develop a purely commercial attitude toward what could be a warm human relationship.

How about the prostitute's enemies? The same set of circumstances that forms the prostitute provides rules of conduct, modes of behavior, and likely types of personality among members of the vice squad and citizen's organizations that want to "clean up the town."

role conflict Role theory takes many of its concepts from stage drama. A role is a part; everyone plays parts in his lifetime and we all have many roles. Our behavior is usually appropriate to the role we are playing. In the role of student, for example, some people take notes, some ask questions, and some fall asleep. The role of mother or daughter demands certain actions and behavioral characteristics.

Sometimes a situation occurs in which one role makes demands that are incompatible with those of another role being played simultaneously. The daughter role requires adherence to parental rules like being home by midnight, but the role of member of a social group may oblige one to attend an all-night party. Adhering to either role means violating the expectations of the other role. Such a situation is called role conflict.

Various aspects of one's "social personality" can come into conflict. Some men, as mentioned earlier, are avid churchgoers and Boy Scout leaders on the weekend and cutthroat pirates in their weekday business enterprises. A scandal breaks when a policeman is arrested for burglary and when the Mother of the Year is later jailed for beating up her children. Important role conflicts frequently involve a person who is caught between gratifying his base desires and living according to acceptable standards. Again, these roles seem to be a mask or persona, and it is difficult, to say the least, to determine what kind of a person Mr. Jones really is. This situation sometimes involves what might be called subcultures. A gangster behaves in accordance with the rules of his group when "at work," and by the rules of family, church, and fatherhood when not at work. He belongs to at least two subcultures.

A rare but much publicized phenomenon is multiple personality, in which conflicting roles come out into the open quite blatantly. Conflicts and guilt associated with double roles become so intense, psychologists assume, that the personality "splits" into two persons; each lives an independent existence, not recognizing that the other is "part" of him. The Eve Black–Eve White case of the 1950s is a famous incidence of split personality. Eve, who was really one person, had different personalities that switched back and forth. Eve Black was bratty and seductive, and Eve White was overly sweet. Eve Black spoke about Eve White as though she were another person, not recognizing "herself." During psychological treatment, a third Eve emerged, and she seemed mature and stable compared to the other two. After extended treatment, a fourth Eve, a more socially adjusted woman, appeared on the scene; she was the final, integrated person who made a healthy adjustment to life [Thigpen, 1957].

One theme has been stressed pretty much, but is worth repeating: We function as a whole unit—body, brain, emotions, and psyche. In a very elaborate study of a more recent case of four personalities in one, the authors found that brain-wave patterns differed for each personality; responses to emotion-creating words differed; and if one personality learned something in the laboratory, the other frequently did not remember it [Ludwig et al., 1972]. Each personality had a unity of its own.

THE SELF

A common thread tying together all the personality theories we have discussed is that each of us has a self. Some psychologists have put special emphasis on the self: Freud, who called the self the "ego"; Sullivan, who saw the self-concept as good-me and bad-me; and Rogers, who saw the self-concept as related to self-actualization.

The theory of self, however, presents some problems when faced with the facts of role conflict and multiple personality, because in these cases the self seems to be more than one. And emphasis on the self has been especially strong in the United States, where it may fit well with Americans' supposed concern for individuality. Segments of societies in other parts of the world have equated the self with society: A person is what his society causes him to be. A good example is contained in some Eastern philosophies that have taken completely to heart the belief that man is a part of society. Under these systems, the individual self is composed of a series of social roles which we juggle around as we play the game of life. The self is not independent [Watts, 1961].

Many Soviet psychologists reject the self completely, claiming that it and individuality are capitalistic concepts. One's frame of reference, then, becomes the focus for understanding any theory. To be as objective and honest as possible, one can only say that no evidence makes it necessary to reject the hypothesis of "self." I feel most comfortable with the theory that we are each a self, but that the self is influenced by individual needs, social learning, and social pressure.

SUMMARY

Personality theorists attempt to categorize behavior patterns fairly rigidly so that it is possible to examine them scientifically. It seems impossible, however, to use these labels on particular people, because each seems to be so many persons all at the same time.

The earliest attempts at classification came from Sheldon's constitutional psychology, which tried to classify individuals according to the shapes of their bodies. For a while it appeared that personality characteristics could indeed be classified by body type; however, other investigators were to demonstrate that the theory is rather weak. Nowadays experiments focus on the effect of a person's body type on his *own* perception of himself rather than how others view him.

Freud emphasized biological mechanisms as determinants of personality development, but to some extent his theories took a back seat to the more obvious one—that we are influenced by social factors. In other words, interactions between child and mother, or between child and friends, are critical in forming personality characteristics. One major proponent of this system was Harry Stack Sullivan, a neo-Freudian who claimed that a person forms his conception of himself by noting how others react to him.

Another system that stresses early experiences is the learning theory of personality development. This theory emphasizes that our personalities evolve as they do because we seek the pleasurable and avoid the painful.

If our hunger, thirst, and sex needs are gratified, we learn that we are loved and cared for; if these needs are frustrated, we are frustrated. A person tends to generalize these experiences; in other words, if his mother gratifies his needs, then he will tend to see others and the world as performing the same function. A person also engages in avoidance behavior, staying away from objects or people that he finds painful. Sometimes a person's personality is negatively formed in the sense that he learns to avoid others because he fears being rejected, as he has been in the past. Much human behavior is based on secondary drives; often people guide their lives in quest of something that makes little sense on the surface. A child, for example, can be quite acquiescent and agreeable to adult demands in order to obtain a reward that may seem trivial to us.

The learning theory is too mechanical for Rogers. He feels, rather like Maslow, that people are basically motivated in life to fulfill themselves by a process of self-actualization. In other words, a person can become self-fulfilling and happy if he develops a positive feeling toward himself and others (self-regard). Somewhat like Sullivan's position, a person forms a basic concept of himself, and then he symbolizes (allows within him) that which fits this self-concept and rejects that which doesn't fit.

Jung differs from other social theorists in emphasizing inheritance of certain personality characteristics which tend to fit stereotypes. He emphasizes the mother role, but the same principle applies to any other occupational or behavioral category within which a person finds himself. Jung's ideas have considerable appeal to the present generation because he emphasizes the religious, mystical aspects of human behavior and tends to shy away from the mechanical approach. His theory is called "cultural" because it leans heavily toward the person's becoming what a given society or culture wants him to become.

An extension of Jung's theory is role behavior, a form of social learning in which a person adopts a persona that conforms to other people's expectations of him. Cases of multiple personality illustrate how social role development may become so ingrained that the person literally evolves into each of the roles he has been using in the past.

CHAPTER THIRTEEN
MEASUREMENT OF PERSONALITY

It would be hard to find one of you who has not been subjected to psychological testing sometime in your life. Testing seems ever present, no matter what you want to do: get a job, join the army, go to school, whatever else you try to accomplish. You don't have to take a test to get into prison, but even there you will have taken one before you have worn out your welcome.

What *is* a psychological test? In general, it is an instrument that attempts to evaluate individuals by comparing them with other people who have taken the same test. In other words, when person X takes the test, the results are compared with the scores obtained by large groups of other people in order to determine if this person differs from the others, and how much he differs.

In theory, the test enables the researcher to perform his task in a more orderly fashion, from one person to another, than would be the case if the subjects were interviewed by individual psychologists. And, of course, it is much less expensive to administer tests than to conduct lengthy individual interviews. Each subject responds to the same test items, in the same order, and under the same time limitations, as every other subject—and, at least theoretically, his responses are subject to the same evaluation as everyone else's. Under these conditions, the variations in a person's responses should reveal something about his personality.

These theoretical assumptions will have to be qualified, or course, but they are the foundations upon which psychological testing is built.

Psychology did not enter the area of personality testing immediately after Freudian theory caught on. Instead, it waited until World War I, which created a great need for basic intelligence measurement designed to identify "untrainable" recruits. Intelligence testing came into prominence before personality testing. For our discussion, however, a few years here or there are not critical. By the 1920s, after intelligence testing had obviously become a success, personality testing was well on its way.

Our first topic will be measurement of the unconscious—at least, of thoughts, feelings, and desires which the subject presumably is unaware of or cannot express. Then we'll take up personality tests designed to measure general attitudes and conscious feelings and behaviors. (Intelligence testing is covered in the next chapter.)

PROJECTIVE TECHNIQUES

Freud emphasized the enormous influence of id impulses, which, he believed, were buried in the unconscious. A basic assumption of his theory is that a person is unaware of many of his needs and desires. Freud felt that these needs would come to the surface if the person were allowed to ruminate at will about his past. This idea is logical if it is further assumed that the id is actively seeking expression.

The idea that free expression can unlock a person's innermost thoughts is not unique to Freud. Galton, that inveterate improvisor who made money measuring people at the state fair, had the idea that one could use word-association tests to reach deeply into the mind. He would give himself a word as a starting stimulus, and then associate as many other words as he could with that word, always allowing complete freedom of association. For example, one version (obviously condensed) of the process might run thus:

House (stimulus word) ——→ Home ——→ Room ——→
My room ——→ Me ——→ In my room alone ——→ I am
lonely ——→ I was lonely as a child.

Galton did not extend the word-association technique as far as other experimenters have, but his ideas did help to shape the development of projective techniques. The projective technique, as you will see in a moment, provides a vague stimulus to which the test taker associates.

the Rorschach test

A man who did go further than Galton was psychiatrist Hermann Rorschach, who developed the famous "inkblot" test. Incredible as it may seem, this man's nickname in school was Klex, meaning "inkblot." Another translation of *Klex* is "painter," more likely the meaning intended, since Rorschach's father was a painter. Even so, the coincidence is rather startling, considering the fame of the Rorschach inkblot test.

Rorschach picked up the idea of using inkblots to measure a person's fantasy world when he read a student's dissertation* on the use of blots to study the fantasy life of individuals [Reisman, 1966]. Rorschach used real inkblots in the creation of his test. Dropping some ink in the middle of a piece of paper and folding it in half will create symmetrical designs like the one shown in illustration 94; this is exactly how Rorschach made his inkblot test. After considerable experimentation, Rorschach finally settled on ten blots that are now used universally to administer the test. Few paid any attention to the test until after his death, however.

The *Rorschach test* is used as a tool to ferret out aspects of a person's unconscious and to estimate his overall thought processes and self-image. It is based on the assumption that the psychologist examining the subject's responses to the blots can detect facts about the person that he himself cannot see.

94 An inkblot like those used in the Rorschach test (*Gabriele Wunderlich*)

* A dissertation is a long research paper, usually a hundred pages or more, written as part of the requirements for a master's or doctor's degree.

13-1 Unidentified stimulus

Suppose for a moment that Figure 13-1 is shown to three people. The first person says he sees a cactus, the second a flower, the third a fork. Such answers are normally not the responses of the unconscious, nor do they have deep meaning, but they are probably influenced by the person's past life. For example, a gardener might see a flower quite readily, a Nevada desert prospector a cactus, and a waiter a fork. The stimulus is, in fact, no more like one of these objects than the other two. Some correlation is assumed to exist between the subject's past experiences and his perception of the stimulus. Now consider a stimulus that is even less precise, the inkblot. The inkblot can properly be said to be nothing more or less than a blot of ink. What the person sees is his own production, a product of the imagination.

Rarely does the test taker give just one response—for example, cactus. He is encouraged to give many. The more responses he gives, the more difficult it will be for him to think of things to say, and he will have to reach deeper and deeper into his fantasy world. The more he reaches into the fantasy world, the more likely it is (in theory) that his responses will get close to the unconscious.

In interpreting the meaning of responses to the inkblots, the psychologist attaches importance not just to the objects seen but also to the way in which the person describes the objects. For example, seeing a bloody ax *could* have some significance, but meaning is also attributed to the person's seeing a bloody ax falling downward—that is, to an action of the object seen.* Movement is remote from the blot itself; nothing is actually moving there. If you say that you see two animals escaping from one another, it is felt that in order for you to attribute so much to the blot you must have an emotional investment in what you are saying. I'll pick an oversimplified interpretation to illustrate the point. The psychologist might say that you are trying to escape from something or someone, and that this behavior appears—disguised—in your claim that the animals are acting this way [Beck, 1951]. Or, to take some extreme examples, if you see eyes peering at you from all the blots, you might feel deep down that others are out to do you in. If you see every blot as a dark, gloomy, swirling mass of heavy clouds, one might suspect you of being depressed.

We can be more concrete and tie the Rorschach to Freudian theory. One typical study compared the number of food items and (food) digestive organs seen in the Rorschach by alcoholic Ss (subjects, always abbreviated Ss) and by a control group. The number of food items mentioned by alcoholic Ss was nine; members of the control group mentioned three; $p < .05$.† Digestive organs mentioned by alcoholic Ss numbered eight; control group, two; again, $p < .05$. This finding *could* support the idea, discussed in connection with Freud, that alcoholics tend to be orally dependent

---

* Seeing action in an inkblot is called an M response which stands for (M)ovement.
† The formulation $P < .05$ means that the level of significance was .05 or greater. See Chapter 7.

—and that is exactly what the study attempted to show [Bertrand, 1969].

The experiment illustrates an attempt to verify theory, but it does not "prove" the Freudian hypothesis. It is just as likely that constant "thirst" for liquor makes a person preoccupied with his mouth; this preoccupation may not be related to early feeding experiences or dependency, as Freud proposed. Nonetheless, it should give you some idea of how the Rorschach operates.

Projective test theory suggests, then, that a person's unconscious, given the opportunity provided by a vague, ambiguous stimulus, will attribute to that stimulus some of its energy, feelings, or desires. The person *projects* this inner feeling onto the stimulus, just as a movie projector projects its image onto a screen. The screen in this case is the inkblot, and the film is the person's emotion or feeling. The alcoholic, for example, projects his oral dependency onto the blot and sees food items and digestive organs.

the TAT   The Rorschach is the most famous and the most often used of projective techniques, but a close runner-up is a test called the TAT or *Thematic Apperception Test.* This test was devised by two psychologists, Dr. Henry Murray and Dr. C. D. Morgan, and its theory and operation are a little easier to understand than the Rorschach. The TAT contains twenty photographs or drawings (see Fig. 13–2). Each picture contains a *potential* theme, which the test taker is to develop in his own words. Notice, in Figure 13–2, that two women are placed in a position that suggests they are talking to each other. The picture provides primarily this one stimulus, and the person has to make up a story about what he *thinks* is going on. Obviously he has considerable leeway. Are the women whispering? Are they talking about him? Who are they? Sometimes patients see the two women as the same person; one figure is the conscience, or the devil encouraging the other half of the person. The possibilities are endless, and the choice of stories is thought to be individualistic behavior especially tailored to the test taker, then projected onto the stimulus [Morgan, 1935].

Apperception is simply a special form of perception of an object or situation that includes attitudes, feelings, and emotions. The word *theme*, unfortunately, is familiar to every reader. In this context it means to tell a story. The Thematic Apperception Test, then, is a test designed to bring out themes or stories that are related to a person's perception of what is happening in his private world.

13–2   TAT-type picture

Murray and Morgan assumed that just as it is often possible to get some idea of an author's values, beliefs, and problems by reading his books, so in this case the test taker becomes an author and reveals some of his hidden problems, which may have gone unrecognized.

Suppose someone says of Figure 13–2:

This is my grandmother talking to my mother. I was caught stealing something from the cookie jar, and they are trying to decide what kind of punishment I should get.

In theory, this "story" could shed considerable light on the test taker's background, some of his early problems, some of his present problems as they relate to the past, and, frequently, the important matter of how he views himself in relation to others. But a caution is always necessary: in a semi-humorous vein, John Steinbeck warns that authors sometimes write about things that *don't* happen to them—in the hope that they never will [Steinbeck, 1969].

The underlying assumption is that projection is operating here much as it does in the Rorschach test. The TAT, however, provides a firmer structure within which both the subject and the psychologist can function. In other words, a person taking the TAT can develop stories from the material provided in the picture; the Rorschach rarely lends itself to complete stories. If deeper meanings are being tapped and the psychologist is skillful enough to ferret them out, the TAT seems to provide a clearer picture of problem areas and conflicts than does the Rorschach. But comparing the tests is very difficult, if not impossible. The Rorschach is said to measure the operation of the unconscious self; the TAT takes the unconscious and ties it to social relationships and a person's view of himself and others.*

Some psychologists prefer the TAT to the Rorschach, and vice versa. Many use both tests. Many feel that neither is necessary; all that is required is a fairly direct interview with the patient, assuming he is able and willing to give information of a deep and personal nature. Many feel that the projective test provides this information more quickly than an interview, and still others feel that projective tests are too tricky, both to administer and to interpret, to be of much use [McMahon, 1969].

If the usefulness of the projective test is in question, then a logical query is: Why bother to use it at all? Aside from the need to obtain important personal information about the patient, one problem is ever present, especially with mental patients: trying to determine an exact diagnosis; that is, what is the patient's problem and how serious is it? The diagnosis becomes important, especially in court cases, where it may be critical to determine whether or not the patient is legally sane.† Diagnosis is most important for the patient's own welfare—for example, is he dangerous to others? To himself? Simply explained, a *paranoid* person believes that others are trying to do him harm. Believing this, he is potentially dangerous because he may "strike back" at his imagined "persecutors." A *depressed* person—again, the definition is oversimplified—is one who has little hope for the future and is liable to end it all. He may harm himself if he is not

---

*Probably it is safest to use "unconscious" in its broadest sense—that is, things of which we are only partially aware at most.

†*Insanity* is a *legal* term, not a medical one. Many people who are seriously mentally ill are not "insane" in the eyes of the law. The legal issue usually revolves around whether a person knew right from wrong at the time he committed the crime. Nonetheless, many psychologists feel that the projective tests can give an accurate enough picture of personality to aid in determining the legal estimation of insanity.

correctly diagnosed (and, of course, treated). Presumably the projective test can assist in such diagnoses.

There is a serious question whether the traditional diagnosis, made in a hospital by the psychiatric staff and based on intuition and case history (a record of the patient's past life), is very accurate. In one study, for example, thirty-two professional staff members of a hospital, including psychiatrists, neurologists, social workers, and psychiatric nurses, diagnosed the *same* patient and came up with fourteen *different* diagnoses [Nathan, 1969].

Many psychologists, therefore, feel that the test instrument can improve diagnosis. Those who believe in and use the projective test feel that human beings are extremely complex, and that the tests enable them to find the subtleties of behavior that are keys to personality. Unfortunately, statistical studies do not always bear out the claims made for the tests. With some legitimacy, users of projective tests blame this failure on the inability of experimenters to arrange an experiment in such a way that it can be determined just how accurate the tests are. For example, if a psychologist says that a patient's projective test indicates a tendency toward suicide, who wants to prove the point by using an experiment that waits to see if the patient commits suicide? Instead, the patient needs to be carefully watched and protected so as to prevent him (hopefully) from carrying out his suicidal tendencies—but at the same time this prevents accurate determination of the test's ability to predict.

Many psychologists support the use of projective tests for a simple reason: These tests usually are administered on a one-to-one basis—one patient, one psychologist—and the administration process itself provides an opportunity to observe the person "in action," in an unusual setting, to see how he behaves.

TESTING THE TEST

Even though statistics don't always confirm the claims made for projective tests, they have proved helpful in analyzing the tests themselves.

How does the psychologist know if a particular test is any good? As we discussed earlier, certain statistics are a great help in evaluation. These statistics are basically correlations; if you understood them, the following material should present few problems.

First, a test must perform two tasks: (1) it must measure what it claims to measure; and (2) it must measure in a consistent fashion.

validity   If I devise a test that is supposed to be a "Test of Accounting Ability," for example, it must give some indication of how good an accountant the test taker is. This accuracy of the test is called its *validity.* A ticket for a plane trip is only valid if it will get you on the plane; if it doesn't, it has no validity, and its claim to being a useful ticket is incorrect. A test of accounting is valid only if it does what it is supposed to—that is, if it measures some of the skills required to be an accountant.

A test that consisted of spelling words used as an accounting test would probably not be valid. The same test used to predict success in English composition might well have high validity.

Any personality test, then, is valid only if it can tell the test administrator something definite about the personality; if it can't, then it isn't valid.

reliability   The second important aspect of a test is whether it is consistent. This factor is called *reliability*. By analogy, a reliable person is one on whom you can count to do something regularly; for example, a worker who shows up for the job only now and then is not reliable. If we had someone take our accounting test four times, once on each of four successive days, and his scores were 15 percent, 95 percent, 80 percent, and 20 percent—all on the same test—then this test is not reliable. It cannot be counted on to yield a consistent score, and the test administrator will have no idea which of the many different scores is the correct one, or the one that best represents the person's performance. The test will not produce consistently.

Reliability is an especially difficult problem in the area of projective testing. With the Rorschach, the problem is acute because a person frequently does not see the same thing in the blot on Wednesday as he does on Monday. Thus it becomes very difficult to compare "scores" to see if they are remaining about the same.

If we go through the two measures step by step, they are not difficult. Suppose, for an analogy, we have three eccentric oil wells owned by an eccentric millionaire. First, we establish two ground rules: (1) a valid well is one that does what it claims to do, deliver oil; (2) a reliable well is one that delivers consistently.

Eccentric well number 1 delivers oil in spurts, and does so consistently. This well is both valid and reliable. It delivers oil, and the delivery can be relied upon.

Oil well number 2 delivers water, and does so consistently. This well is reliable in that it consistently gives water, but not valid, because it doesn't do what it is supposed to—deliver oil.

Oil well number 3 delivers oil, but just whenever it is in the mood to do so. It may deliver oil at completely unpredictable times. It is valid to some extent but not reliable.

Again, then, validity is whether the proper thing is delivered, and reliability is whether it is consistently delivered. A good psychological test should have both aspects.

measuring validity   How valid and reliable are the projective tests?

In order to measure the validity of a projective test, we have to correlate whatever the test says about a person with what we actually find out about him; thus we find out if the test is measuring what it is supposed to. This is no easy task. Assume that in a TAT, a patient sees a little boy sitting and crying because he has been locked in a closet by his mother. This response can be interpreted as meaning that having been locked in a closet as a boy by his mother is the cause of the adult patient's fear of elevators. How do you verify the correctness of this interpretation? Suppose you ask him. If he says yes, you might as well not have bothered to give the test because you could have found out anyway. If he says no, you have two alternatives: He has repressed the idea, in which case he couldn't say yes anyway; or the conclusion you drew from the test is incorrect.

Because of this difficulty in verifying such hypotheses, the majority of validity studies for the Rorschach and TAT have studied bits and pieces of hypotheses. For example, with the Rorschach, the limited hypothesis of oral interests among alcoholics is a typical subject for a validity study. In an admirable attempt to validate the Rorschach on a broad scale, an experimenter correlated college success with Rorschach indicators of maladjustment and came up with a moderately good − .49. Other testings with different groups have failed to reach this level of correlation [Munroe, 1945]. Perhaps maladjustment as indicated by the Rorschach is not relevant to college success except in extreme cases.

Most validity studies made on parts of the Rorschach have yielded correlations of .30 to .40 [Cronbach, 1960]. A typical study examined the S response in the Rorschach. When a person sees the "empty" spaces in the inkblot, and refers to them, his response is called an S response (space response) and is thought to be connected with a negative attitude.* Logically, a validity study of the S response would have raters (friends, fellow workers, psychologists, and others) fill out a check sheet or rating form indicating the negativity of subjects. This information would then be correlated with the number of S responses given by various subjects. In just such a study, the correlation was .35, showing a fair but not exciting relationship [Bandura, 1954].

Validity studies of the TAT have not been much better. Correlations between TAT stories having aggressive themes—i.e., stories that clearly include aggression—and actual aggression by the patient have been very low [Anastasi, 1968].

What can be concluded about the validity of projective tests? Unfortunately, very little. Although a few studies have produced correlations at the .60 or .70 level, many of them have been flawed [Cronbach, 1960]. Most of the studies leave a big question mark in the experimenter's mind. The correlations are high enough to be interesting, but not high enough to really strengthen the case for the projective testers.

assessing reliability   To assess the reliability of projective tests, the experimenter compares the content of the same person's responses in two or more testings of either the Rorschach or the TAT. We have already discussed that M(ovement) and S(pace) responses are considered important. Theoretically, if the same person takes the test more than once, the number of such M and S responses given the second time should be about the same as the number given in the first testing.

---

* I don't understand the logic of this, but it is a fact of test interpretation nonetheless.

Reliability, then, is measured by correlating the number of responses the first time with the number of responses the second time for the various categories such as space or movement.* Likewise, with the TAT, the themes developed in the second testing should resemble those brought out in the first testing.

Two major problems present themselves when we consider reliability studies of projective tests. First, slight alterations of the person's mood conceivably could alter the pattern of responses in the Rorschach. Second, since the TAT consists of pictures, themes seen in the movies or on television possibly could alter the content. A person who was much impressed by a murder mystery seen the night before testing, for example, could give responses that he might not duplicate in the second testing, a week later.

In any case, the reliability studies look very much like the validity studies. For major categories of perception (space, movement, animals, blood, etc.) in the Rorschach, reliabilities range from about .45 to .70. These correlation coefficients are only fair, because reliability scores are generally higher than validity scores.† When very small and unusual detail is emphasized (picking out and describing a very small portion of the blot) in the first testing with Rorschach, it is rarely found on a second testing, and the reliability coefficients range from .40 to zero. For major themes in the TAT, reliabilities ranged from .60 to .90 in a large number of different studies [Lindzey, 1955]. For many others, the reliability has ranged from − .07, which is obviously poor, to .34, which is fair at best [Child et al., 1956]. These studies contradict one another; to date, the reason for this contradiction has not been determined. One easy answer to the problem is that some people are more consistent than others, but this is a weak way out of the dilemma.

The reliability studies are really little better than the validity studies. Again, however, you are cautioned that there are two points of view about this data. To the statistician and "purist," the results conclusively rule against the effectiveness of these tests at the present time. To the user of projective tests, the results are discouraging, but they do not reduce his firm belief in the practical usefulness of the instruments, no matter what statistics show. The matter is primarily one of faith, but not necessarily naïve faith; some few excellent psychologists can provide impressive predictions of future behavior by using projective techniques.

HOW USEFUL ARE PROJECTIVE TESTS?

In the last few years a number of experimenters have been exploring different facets of the projective test. They have demonstrated problems only hinted at in the past, problems that will have to be corrected before the tests can become maximally effective.

---

*There are other methods of calculating reliability, but this one is common and illustrates the principle.

† Scores on tests other than projective tests are usually in the .80s and .90s for good, solid reliability [Eichler, 1951].

First, in projective tests, as in other kinds of tests, no one has figured out how to avoid the problem of the influence of daily activities and external events on the internal personality [Holt, 1970]. In other words, assuming the test is completely accurate in measuring how we feel *inside*, how can it sort out external events? If a number of things have been going wrong for the person during the week before he takes the test, he may be feeling depressed—but this temporary state of mind may not be an accurate reflection of that vague thing, the "real" personality.

Second, the most serious difficulties seem to lie not so much in the ability of the test to bring out important information about the test taker as in the integration or bringing together of these facts. Raters can agree, for example, that a person has a problem with stuttering, or nightmares, or fear of water, but their agreement tends to disintegrate when they try to explain the facts in a unified fashion. For instance, although most raters might agree that these three problems exist, they might not agree about how to interpret them—for example, "inner stress caused fear of darkness, water . . . ," or "stuttering caused by insecurity." These statements may be a combination of the personality of the rater—that is, possibly some of his own problems—plus his ability to bring the facts together; in other words, the rater becomes more an author than a psychologist with the source of his material of unknown origin [Dana and Handzlik, 1970].

Projective tests, probably because they are so vague, have a built-in problem: the interpreter of test results carries his own biases into the interpretation. The rater tends to project his own personality into the situation. For instance, in one study raters were found to be describing the personalities of others by using adjectives which fit themselves [Dana and Handzlik, 1970]. In another study, two teams of expert raters were asked to analyze a single set of responses to a Rorschach test—except that one team was told that the test taker's father was a bus driver and the other told that the father was a lawyer. The raters interpreting the responses of the "bus driver's" son tended to see more abnormality and less chance for recovery than those interpreting the responses of the "lawyer's" son—even though the responses were exactly the same [Levy and Kahn, 1970].

The problem is striking: The psychologist, being usually middle-class, has a bias against working-class people. Possibly one difficulty here is that the life style of working-class people is typically different from that of the psychologist. In general, the working-class person is more physical than intellectual, and not as verbal as a middle-class person. *Verbal* means interested in using words and bandying ideas about. In many ways this lack of interest in language is not appealing to the verbally educated psychologist. Finally, the working-class person is generally at a disadvantage when confronted with the middle-class ritual of testing that goes on until the victim is exhausted. He is thus bound to feel a little less at ease than the middle- or upper-class person [Levy, 1970].

OBJECTIVE PERSONALITY TESTS

Attempts to measure personality have, with a few exceptions, been slanted toward the negative. That is, efforts have been made to determine what is wrong with the person rather than what is right with him. Objective testing is no exception. There is a reason for this emphasis: One researcher has estimated that during World War I soldiers who were emotionally disturbed cost the military an average of $75,000 each in care before discharge. Even the U.S. government balks at such payments when the number of patients is in the hundreds of thousands. As a result, during the war, psychologist R. S. Woodworth was commissioned to develop a personality test that would screen out disturbed men in as little as twenty minutes, compared with the ninety minutes to two hours it usually took to administer and score the typical projective test. Dr. Woodworth is thought to have developed the first extensive written personality test; it consisted of two hundred items to which the person answered "yes" or "no." Examples of items typically found on this kind of test are:

I wet my bed frequently.	*Yes*	*No*
I often have nightmares.	*Yes*	*No*
I had an unhappy childhood.	*Yes*	*No*
I get along well with most people.	*Yes*	*No*

This test was to have been administered to inductees so that those who scored poorly could be released from service before they cost too much money. As luck would have it, the war ended before the test was used [Eysenck, 1964]. Nonetheless, the test became a model for hundreds of objective personality tests that followed.

Before discussing the development and interpretation of such tests, I might explain the use of the word *objective*. A test is called *objective* only in comparison to the *projective* test. The projective test presents the test taker with items (blots, pictures) which are, in themselves, not specific and are thought to have little or no built-in meaning. The objective test item, however, has a specific meaning, and hence is thought to be objective; that is, the item does not rely completely on the fantasy life of the test taker. To respond to an inkblot by saying, "I see someone who has an unhappy homelife," is obviously projection since the inkblot itself supplies no evidence of this. On the other hand, the test item, "I have an unhappy home life," is structured so that either a "yes" or a "no" answer will relate to home life. Hence, the item is objective or *factual* in content and scoring.

Objective personality testing, then, began toward the end of World War I and has continued to develop up to the present time. These tests did not result directly from personality theories but seemed to evolve along with them and were colored by the theory in vogue at any particular time. You will notice that as we moved from the theory of Freud and projective testing into other personality theories, emphasis shifted from the unconscious and deeply rooted personal problems and centered on the person as he develops into a *social* being. This change of focus is evident in objective-test items, which are concerned primarily with social adjustment—that is, how well the person has adjusted to his environment. These tests ask questions that center on a person's reactions to others, how well he gets along in life, what social behaviors he has learned or failed to learn, and what concepts of himself he has formed.

Theoretically, this information can be obtained from a projective test, especially the TAT, but the objective test is more direct, in the sense that it is concerned with specific problems [Jones and Jones, 1970]. The purpose of objective testing is to develop a picture of an individual's personality—how he feels most of the time, how he behaves characteristically. Again in theory, the test items are designed to provide a sampling of the person's home life, sex life, social life, and, to some extent, his fantasy world.* From this sampling the psychologist attempts to obtain an overall measure that will predict how the person is apt to behave in particular situations. As you will see, however, the tests rarely approach anything near this degree of accuracy.

content validity   Mention was made earlier of validity, the ability of a test to measure what it is supposed to measure. The items on many objective personality tests have a special kind of validity that is called *content validity.* Content validity refers to the assumption that the items are valid *in and of themselves,* just because of the type of question they are asking. In other words, the test is measuring what it is asking about, and what the test is asking about is supposed to be what it is measuring.† Since we supposedly are dealing with tests designed to locate people who have personality problems, the content of such questions as, "I wet my bed frequently," "I often have nightmares," and "I had an unhappy childhood," by their very nature should locate personality problems. Hence they have a kind of automatic validity.

Psychologists have learned, however, that content validity can be a very dangerous thing. For one thing, this kind of validity cannot be reported in terms of correlations because no comparison is necessary between test items and real-life adjustment; instead, the items themselves are *automatically* valid. Another danger can be seen by looking at the item, "I had an unhappy childhood." A person could answer "yes" and still be fairly well adjusted. Many of us had unhappy pasts that are compensated for by a good life in the present.

Again, many of us have nightmares once or twice a week. Is this frequent or is it not? The problem is that each of us could interpret the word *frequent* differently, some feeling that once a week is "frequent" and some feeling that nothing less than twelve times a week would be "frequent." The point is that items which look pretty obvious on the surface are not

---

*By direct question such as, "I daydream a lot."

†Content validity is present in objective tests other than those used by psychologists. A history exam made up of true-false and other objective questions, for instance, is measuring what it is asking about (your knowledge of history), and what it is asking about is supposed to be what it is measuring.

that easy to interpret. As you will find later on, these tests can pick out disturbed people, but they also tend strongly toward labeling as "disturbed" a large number of people who are fairly well adjusted.

Finally, the items themselves present problems. Ask just about anyone if bedwetting is a symptom of mental maladjustment, and he will say it is. However, both bedwetting and thumbsucking are behaviors about whose significance there is very little agreement, and very little proof. Some youngsters wet their beds and seem quite "normal." In older people, this symptom would be significant, but as many times as not the problem is physiological rather than psychological. One needs to be wary, then, of test items that look scientific, sound deeply psychological, and yet may mean nothing.

establishing norms   An objective personality test usually has established *norms*. A *norm*, which has the same root as the word *normal*, is the result of a process in which a test is administered to a large group of people in order to establish the "normal" or expected number of specific kinds of responses obtained. For example, 200 objective-personality-test items might be administered to a group of nonhospitalized, seemingly well-adjusted people in order to establish the number of items which this group will answer unfavorably. (The word "unfavorable" has a connection with content validity. For example, answering "yes" to "I often have nightmares" would be considered unfavorable and an indicator of maladjustment.)* We might very well find that out of 200 items, a so-called normal, well-adjusted population answered an average of 25 items in an unfavorable fashion. A score of 25 or below would be established as indicating that the subject is adjusted; 26 or above would indicate a maladjusted person. To refine the test even more, one might administer it to a group of hospitalized patients on the assumption that they are mentally disturbed. If their average score was 50 and their lowest score 35, we have refined our norm so that we know that scores between 25 and 35 (highest normal and lowest abnormal) are in a gray area and are subject to errors of interpretation.

Most objective personality tests are administered to many different kinds of groups, and the norms for these groups are published in a manual accompanying the test. Thus the test administrator can compare the results he obtains for a particular person with the many different groups of individuals that have been used as standards.

faking   Understandably enough, very few of us are willing to expose some of our inner feelings in public, and of course the personality test has the potential for such exposure. A common test item runs something like:

I have adjusted satisfactorily in my sex life.   *True   False*

---

*Earlier we discussed nightmares and the fact that there is little evidence that they indicate maladjustment. Nonetheless, they are typically considered such on objective tests.

Under many conditions a person is just not willing to give out this information, and as a result the objective test suffers greatly from the problem of faking. Since faking the answer in order to increase one's social desirability is a simple matter, psychologists were plagued with this problem from the first objective personality test on. Faking is most pronounced when the personality test is given as part of a job interview, a common practice today. Many feel such a use of the tests is an invasion of privacy, and it is difficult to quarrel with their point of view. Hence underground presses have gone into the business of providing the "correct" answers or suggesting techniques for doing well on personality tests, and these guides are available at a price to prospective employees.

Psychologists have not been remiss in trying to correct the problem of faking. Two kinds of tests beyond those discussed so far have been devised to combat this problem. In fairness to the authors of the tests, I should mention that their main purpose in developing them was to rid the test results of *unconscious faking* rather than to trick prospective employees; most personality tests have been devised to help mental health workers and the patient himself, not prospective employers. Unconscious faking under these circumstances results from the inability of many people to see flaws in their own personalities. If we sit down and try really hard, most of us find very little of consequence wrong with us, whereas others seem able to spot our flaws accurately. In this sense, then, the test is trying to help the test taker.

One attempt to reduce faking is called the *forced-choice technique.* In the forced-choice method the test is constructed so that the person can't come out smelling like a rose. Often he must choose between two equally undesirable (or desirable) items, deciding which is more applicable to him. For example, choose one: "I am frequently lonely./I am sometimes depressed." This technique can be highly irritating to the test taker. The situation may be likened to the question: "Have you stopped beating your wife?" You lose either way. In general the forced-choice method has shown some promise, but studies have indicated that "faking good" can still be done by the more astute individual.

A second kind of objective personality test designed to reduce faking and to avoid the issue of social desirability is the *empirically keyed test. Empirical,* a word used by scientists, means no-nonsense, factual information. To "key" a test is simply to score it.* Empirically keyed tests, then, contain test items that are scored in a completely objective fashion—that is, there is no "nonsense" of *interpreting* a test item's meaning; it is simply scored.

---

* The word *key* is a holdover from early scoring techniques in which a template (key) with holes in it was placed over an answer sheet and the number of responses showing through the holes was counted. Although this scoring system is still used, large-scale testing is processed by machine and requires special pencils that put down a heavy coat of magnetized lead on the answer sheet. This coating is picked up electrically.

How empirical keying works will become clear in a moment. First of all, the test consists of a very large number of items (200–500) many of which have no *obvious* meaning as far as personality is concerned. For example:

I like to go to the movies.   *True*   *False*

I like to play checkers.   *True*   *False*

I read a lot.   *True*   *False*

This large number of items is administered to a test group—say, of psychiatric patients—and to a control group of "normals" not receiving psychiatric treatment. The responses of one group and the responses of the other are tabulated. *The content of the items is not interpreted.* The important factor is how the people in each group answered each item. For example, perhaps the majority of psychiatric patients checked "True" in response to the statement about liking to go to movies; perhaps the "normals" check "False." In the empirically keyed test, preferring movie going to checker playing or reading becomes one small indicator of maladjustment—simply because a majority of psychiatric patients, who are thought more likely to be disturbed, had that preference, and a majority of "normals" did not. Later the test can be administered to an individual and if he checks "True," he scores one point toward disturbance.

This kind of test also contains items in which the content appears to be important but isn't. You will frequently find items like:

I had an unhappy childhood.   *Yes*   *No*

However, with empirical keying, if the majority of psychiatric patients check "No," this item would *not* be counted toward mental disturbance when checked "Yes" by a person taking the test later on. To some extent this kind of test eliminates social-desirability problems, but the results still fall far short of great predictive value, although they often prove useful. Even though this type of test may seem rather strange when you first think about it, it seems to work fairly well simply because it has so many items and various types of individuals frequently fall into similar patterns of behavior.

reliability and validity   Little that is definitive can be said about the results of objective personality test results, a situation that you may find frustrating. Experimental studies show that sometimes the tests perform their function well and sometimes they work poorly. Important factors that influence the results are the cooperative outlook and self-knowledge of the test taker. Reliability is generally low, around .50. Occasionally the reliability of a test given to a specific group will reach the .90 area. As you will recall, reliability refers to how consistent the test is from one administration to another, and .50 shows that the test answers tend to remain relatively inconsistent. This means, in turn, that the accuracy of the instrument is frequently quite weak because it is hard to keep the person's *"test"* personality the same from one administration to the next [Anastasi, 1968].

When we discussed the Rorschach and TAT, we were concerned with validity. The validity at issue then was called *predictive validity*—that is, how well does the test measure what it is supposed to measure, or how well does it predict the illness of an individual? In evaluating predictive validity, the test results are compared with some other measure. For example, test scores might be compared with the degree to which mental health workers later discover that a person is disturbed. The predictive validity of objective tests—that is, the agreement between behavior and test results—is as uncertain as the reliability scores, but again it tends to be on the weak side. Some validities go as low as .15, but most are .35 to perhaps .50 [Cronbach, 1960]. Do not be confused; earlier it was mentioned that many objective personality tests have content validity. This does not mean you cannot also check your validity, and when you do check it, as we did with the Rorschach, you are using predictive validity—how well the test predicts behavior.

general problems An example may illustrate the major problem of the objective personality test. The difficulty lies not so much in finding disturbed people as in finding *too many* disturbed people—that is, labeling normal people as disturbed. In military use, the tests save a considerable amount of money. A test was used to examine 2081 Seabees, and the results correctly picked 281 sailors later found to be emotionally disturbed (predictive validity). It missed sixteen disturbed men. However, the test also labeled 244 sailors as mentally ill who later proved to be well adjusted. These 244 men lucked out as far as military service was concerned, and the Navy saved probably five hundred hours of face-to-face interviewing by psychiatrists and psychologists [Harris, 1960]. Nonetheless, notice the danger in this situation: labeling 244 persons "disturbed" when they are not is just plain bad news.

I hope that you will not leave this section with the feeling that personality tests are "no good." Many serious flaws have been mentioned; these problems hopefully will be corrected in the future, with the use of insight and imagination. Moreover, without some personality tests, things would be worse; for example, you may feel that interviews and personal evaluations of people would have a better track record. As a matter of fact, from what little is known of this area, ratings of people by their supervisors are less accurate than personality tests (a fact that fits in nicely with our theory about how a person puts his persona to effective use). Few studies have compared ratings by different supervisory groups in any detail. One quite extensive study compared pre-employment ratings of teachers with their ratings after a full year of employment in the school system, using all the teachers in a whole county. The study examined 508 teachers' records as rated at the end of the year's employment and compared them with ratings from other sources at the beginning of the employment year. Even after two years of intimate contact with supervisors, the end-of-year ratings on such factors as relationships with children, community relationships, and

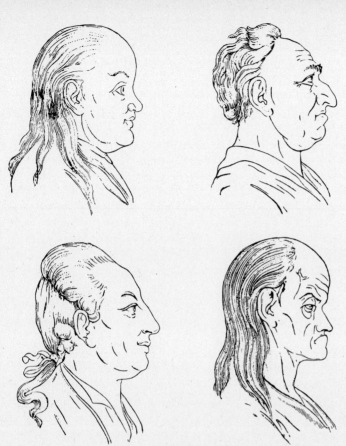

95 In the middle ages, before personality testing became scientific, a person's facial characteristics were thought to reveal his personality traits. See top left, phlegmatic; top right, choleric; lower left, sanguinic; lower right, melancholic (*Bettmann Archive*)

personal qualities agreed with previous ratings .08, .06, and .06, respectively. For these 508 persons, 2221 ratings were available, which is a considerable number, so the likelihood of this inaccuracy being a chance finding is remote. Very few psychological tests have this poor a record. Why there was almost no agreement is unknown, but that an individual's personality frequently eludes classification by others is pretty clear [Browning, 1968].

SUMMARY

Psychological tests of all kinds, both those discussed in the present chapter and those in the following chapter, got their primary impetus from the tremendous need for screening soldiers during World War I.

Personality tests are broken down into two basic types, projective and objective. The projective test is designed to ferret out impulses, desires, and needs of which we are only partially aware. The basic principle of this kind of test is that the test taker is given a stimulus which is vague or ambiguous and asked to tell the examiner what he sees in this stimulus. Because the stimulus is not clear-cut, projective-test theory assumes that the person takes some of his own inner thoughts and projects (throws) them onto the stimulus, thereby disclosing some aspects of himself that he might otherwise not be able to let out.

The Rorschach inkblot test is probably the most renowned of projective measures. It consists simply of inkblots to which the patient responds. Interpretation of the meaning of his responses is based on an elaborate theory of the significance of seeing color, movement, space, etc. in the blot. In general, the validity and the reliability of the Rorschach have been poor. Experimentally oriented psychologists feel this record indicates that the test is of little use. Others feel that the problem is to find some way of constructing an experiment that will fairly tap the potential of the projective test.

The TAT is more highly structured than the Rorschach, in that it provides picture-stimuli to which the test taker responds. This test is also more useful in eliciting stories rather than isolated impressions, so the test is assumed by many to provide a more complete picture of the patient. However, validity and reliability studies have not been much better for the TAT than for the Rorschach.

Establishing validity is basically a matter of comparing test results with some outside measure of what the test is supposed to be testing. In other words, the test results are correlated with something that resembles what the test is designed to predict. Reliability is a correlational measure which compares the test with itself over more than one administration to determine if the test is fairly consistent in the types of predictions that it provides.

Objective personality tests provide fixed statements and a number of alternative answers that can be given to these statements. The primary emphasis in these tests is a measurement of the degree of social adjustment which the person has made, although a number of test items always pertain to a person's private life.

Any objective test can have what is called content validity. Simply put, content validity refers to the assumption that test items are measuring what they are supposed to be measuring. No numerical data are possible. This type of validity merely relies on the ability of professionals to determine what a test should contain.

Because an objective personality test has fixed statements and fixed answers, comparing the answers given by different groups of people is a relatively simple matter. Therefore, norms are established for all objective tests. That is, an expected, "normal" set of scores is obtained, and each test taker's score is compared to the norms to determine how much that person deviates from the norm. Even with these norms, the validity of a particular objective test can be poor, because this type of test has a tendency to overestimate the degree of personality difficulty. Nonetheless, reliability is a little better, and at least it is measurable, as compared to the projective test.

In general, most psychologists agree that administering personality tests is better than doing nothing at all, but so far the great promise these tests hold has not been realized.

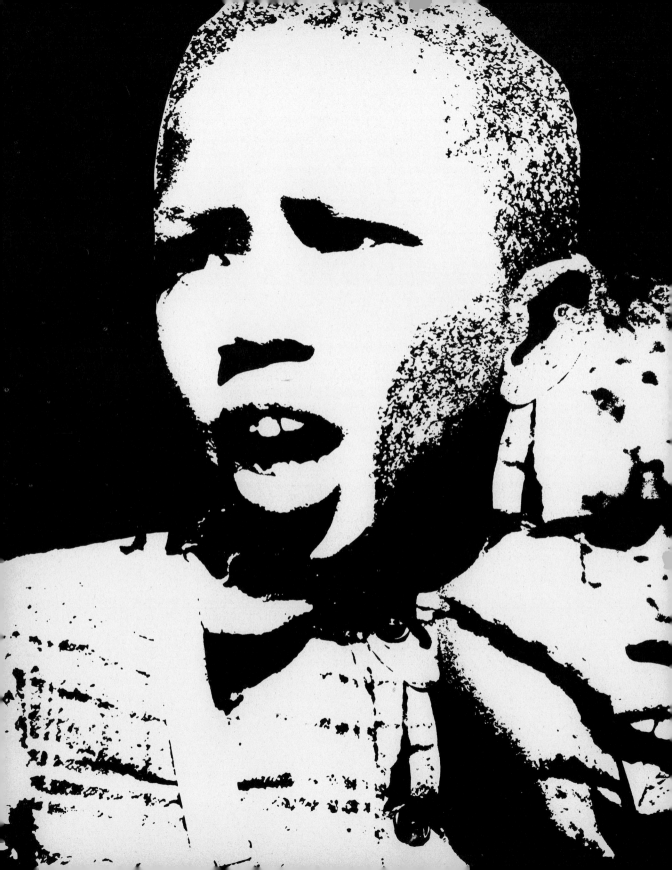

CHAPTER FOURTEEN
ASSESSING INTELLIGENCE

Of all the words used by professionals in psychology—and by the layman, for that matter—no one word seems so clear when we hear it, and yet is so nearly impossible to define, as *intelligence*.

Historically, considerable confusion has prevailed in scientific circles about just what this thing is. One view of intelligence focuses on a vague neural-network hypothesis—that is, the physical structure of the nerves in the brain differ from one person to another, are more complex, and so forth. These theories of physical difference were aided by Gall and Spurheim's phrenology, which emphasized the big-bump-for-intelligence hypothesis. Darwin's "survival of the fittest" also suggested, or at least implied, physical differences within any particular species—so here we have a case of intelligence varying as the result of differences in physical structure.

Another view emphasizes that biological differences are not as important as the technique the brain has for categorizing, organizing, and

96 Before the development of intelligence tests, various methods were used to determine intellectual capacity (*Bettmann Archive*)

relating what it *has* learned with what it *is* learning by a transfer process [Mancuso, 1969]. Conclusions are a long way off, but some new studies in the area of learning and memorizing ability seem to indicate that the difference between people of high and low intelligence lies partially in the *technique* they employ in the process of learning. In other words, the brighter subjects have a greater ability to symbolize, or at least to use symbols [Jacobson et al., 1969; Jacobson, Milham and Berger, 1970].

The use of symbols obviously could be based on certain inherited physical structures of the brain. On the other hand, it might be that symbolization is a matter of early training, at least in part; and this idea could eventually revolutionize education.

Intelligence per se, whatever it is, is not easily defined either as physical or as the result of education. As you will note in the following pages, intelligence is apparently a combination of physical factors and education, but it is poorly understood, not because the scientists haven't tried, but because even in its simplest form intelligence is extremely complex.

The following discussion traces the development of the concept of intelligence from a historical perspective. Only in this way may the reader grasp why the subject presents so many difficulties.

We may well start with a quotation from the late 1800s:

The determination of any fixed point or quantity in pleasure or pain is a matter of great interest . . . and I should be glad to include some such test in the present series. To determine the pressure causing pain, I use an instrument . . . which measures the pressure applied by a tip of hard rubber 5mm. in radius. I am now determining the pressure causing pain in different parts of the body; for the present series I recommend the center of the forehead. . . . [Cattell, 1890]

You may wonder what this quotation has to do with intelligence testing. Strange as it may seem, the "pressure-causing-pain" device was part of an early intelligence test. (Lest you shy away from psychologists and some of their unique devices, remember that nowadays intelligence tests don't employ apparatus that cause physical pain as part of the testing procedure.)

Nonetheless, the rubber tip was one of a group of test items used in early intelligence testing. Today this device seems ridiculous, but at the time, 1890, it made a great deal of sense because psychology was trying desperately to become a science in every sense, especially in its desire to measure as accurately as possible, modeling itself after sciences such as physics.

You may also recall that early philosophers stressed that mind and body are inseparable. Now comes some tricky logic. *If* mind and body are inseparable, and *if* psychology is to be an exact science, then measurements of the body should reflect powers of the mind. Put another way, the abilities of our mind can be measured in the behavior of our body, or so it was assumed. So early psychologists came out with mental tests that sought

97 A "pressure-causing-pain" device (*Bettmann Archive*)

primarily to establish physical measurements which would reflect mental abilities. Among the items in the test mentioned above was a measure of dynamometer pressure, or the squeezing device found at penny arcades and carnivals, whereby a man tries to impress his girl with a strong grip. Outside the laboratory, this unit usually has a dial which reads from "Superweakling" to "WOW! Superman!" Another technique used in early intelligence tests was a measure of how fast a person could move his right hand from the resting position through 50 centimeters of space.

The better you did on these tests—that is, the faster and stronger you were—the more "intelligent" you were.* In other words, in theory the *body* was reflecting the *mental* speed and strength you had.

Like any other new idea in science, this one could not be condemned just because it didn't seem to make sense. However, as you might suspect, considerable experimenting failed to establish any usable correlation between these abilities and school achievement, teacher competency, job performance, and the like [Wissler, 1901].

The idea behind the physical measurement test should not be ignored, however, since it started psychologists in the direction of devising tests that would measure intellectual abilities in a factual, scientific way. A renowned test maker, Dr. Alfred Binet, pointed out that diagnoses of mental ability had traditionally been performed by physicians "looking at"

*Regarding pressure-causing pain, it is difficult to determine if the author of this test considered *resistance* to pain or *sensitivity* to pain as an indication of "higher intelligence." He did not make this clear. It doesn't make any difference now, however, since it doesn't work.

the person and guessing how bright he was. This technique was not (and is not) a very accurate measure of intellectual prowess or lack of it. So at least the early intelligence tester had the right idea about *objective* measurement—that is, using standards by which one person could be compared with another.

Although some studies have indeed shown that examiners can estimate IQs fairly accurately in certain cases, the consistency of their estimates in general cannot match the consistency of data accumulated by administering the same items to hundreds of people every day [Wessler, 1970].

Even though physical measurement does not correlate adequately enough with intellectual behavior to be useful, the historical seeds were planted for the development of a test that would combine objective measurement with some measure of so-called mental ability.

THE BINET INTELLIGENCE TEST

In the early 1900s the French minister of public instruction faced a dilemma known to many school administrators of the time: He needed to know which students required special instruction and which should go to a regular school. Guessing a person's intelligence had proven of negligible value, and accurate determination is critical in making such an important decision. In 1904 he set up a commission to determine methods for distinguishing between bright and duller children. Dr. Alfred Binet was appointed to the committee. Binet had been active in trying to solve the riddle of intellectual measurement for a number of years. He was trained in law and was a playwright, but fortunately for psychology he became interested in intellectual growth, went on to get a doctor's degree, and headed the first psychology laboratory at the Sorbonne (University of Paris). He was also blessed with two daughters who acted as guinea pigs for his early experiments in intelligence testing [Varon, 1935].

Binet's thorough and frantic attempts at finding a method for determining intelligence included handwriting analysis and palm reading. Needless to say, these techniques were not very successful, but in any case he was testing as many factors as he could that might somehow reflect intellectual level. Those that didn't work were eliminated.

Binet and a coworker, Dr. Theodore Simon, began work in the late 1800s on their intelligence test. Binet never stated definitively what an intelligence test was to measure, but his writings suggest that he thought of intelligence as comprising at least four factors: direction, or the ability to set up a goal and work toward it; adaptation, or the ability to adapt oneself to the problem and use appropriate means to solve it; comprehension, the ability to understand the problem; and self-evaluation, the ability of the person to evaluate his performance and determine if he is approaching a problem properly. At the simplest level, some typical test items included naming the parts of the body or handing specified objects to the examiner when asked to do so. Older children were required to indicate which number was not in its correct position: 12, 9, 6, 3, 15. Even harder: "Repeat these seven digits after I am through giving them to you" (seven digits are then given orally). In later editions of the test a typical item for 12-year-olds is: "Bill Jones's feet are so big that he has to pull his trousers on over his head. What is foolish about that?"

Binet's basic operating principle was simple: Find test items which, for most ages, could be solved by many children but not by all.

The first Simon-Binet intelligence test came out in 1905. Each test item had been administered to a large group of children of varying ages before the test was published. The items were then put in order of increasing difficulty. If, for example, all five-year-old children could pass a given item, it was found to be too easy and moved down to the four-year level, or to a level at which some youngsters still had difficulty with it. If an item was too hard for almost all five-year-olds, it was moved to the six-year level. Of course, some fairly hard items were left to distinguish bright from dull. After doing this exhaustive work, the men had a test that consisted of items for each age level from 3 to 15 years.

mental age
We would expect that the average five-year-old would be able to pass many of the test items at the five-year level, for that is how the test was designed. At this point Binet used what is called the concept of *mental age*. The child who is chronologically five years old would be said to have a mental age of five years if his performance was average for his age. Binet accomplished this alignment of the two ages by assigning to each test item a certain number of months' credit of mental age. For example, if there were six test items used at the five-year-old age level, each test item would count as two months' credit of mental age, for a total of one whole year at age five if every one of the six is answered correctly. Notice at this point that if the average five-year-old youngster starts the test at the five-year level and passes all the five-year tests he probably could pass those for four and three years, so he is automatically given credit for these.

Each year contains 12 months' credit toward mental age, and the youngster is automatically given credit for two years (the age at which the test begins). If he then earns 12 months' credit at three years, 12 months' credit at four years, and 12 months' credit at five years, he has accumulated a total credit of five years of mental age. If his actual physical chronological age—the age at which he measures his birthday—is also five years, then he is perfectly average. Rarely would a five-year-old answer all the questions up to the last of the five-year items and then miss every one following that point, but for clarity we'll assume that this can happen. *If* a chronological five-year-old has been tested and found to be a mental five-year-old, we can use mathematical manipulation to get that child's *intelligence quotient*

(IQ). A quotient, of course, is merely a number obtained by dividing one number by another. For ease of handling, a nice round number, 100, was used as the center point of the test. So 100 became the ideal average in mathematical computation of mental and chronological age.

Notice how we get this IQ of 100. Take the mental age (MA), divide it by chronological age (CA), and then multiply the result by 100. (We multiply by 100 to get rid of the decimal which will appear if the numerator and denominator are not the same.) Thus, we get the following for our ideal average five-year-old:

$$\frac{5}{5} \times 100 = 100 \text{ IQ}$$

When we say someone has an average IQ, we imply that his mental age and his chronological age are the same. Not every "average" person, however, fits the 100 mark exactly; in fact, the range for average IQ is generally between 90 and 109.

Consider the case of a dull person; we suspect from the outset that his mental age is not as high as his chronological age. If this is so, the IQ formula will reflect it. Suppose a boy has a physical (chronological) age of five years, but when we add up his months of mental "credit," we find that his intellectual age is four years. Putting this into a formula, we get the following:

$$\frac{\text{MA}}{\text{CA}} \times 100 = \text{IQ}$$

$$\frac{4}{5} \times 100 = 80$$

The child's IQ is 80, which is dull. On the other hand, the five-year-old who has a mental age of six has an IQ of 120:

$$\frac{6}{5} \times 100 = 120$$

This IQ is considered to be in the bright normal range because the child's mental age is significantly higher than his chronological age.

the normal curve and IQ

It might be well to review the section on the normal curve (Chapter 2), since intelligence scores, as measured by the early Binet-type tests, fit the normal curve fairly well. The reason is that most people do not have exceptionally high or low intelligence, and as you move along the curve toward these extremes there are fewer and fewer persons, just as there are fewer and fewer superclean and superdirty people. It just so happens that many attributes and abilities in life fall into the normal curve: most people gravitate toward the middle, and a minority are at the "abnormal" ends. Notice how closely Figure 14–1 fits the ideal normal curve. This figure is called a bar

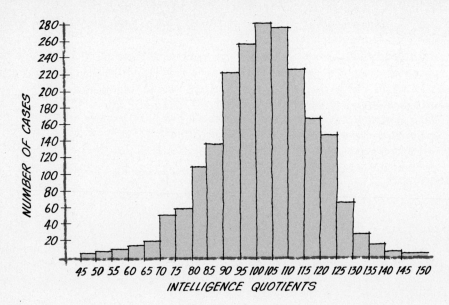

14-1 Histogram showing the curve of IQ

graph, or *histogram*. A rough approximation of the typical curve, which is smooth-looking, can be obtained by drawing a line from the middle points of the top of each bar, from the left, up one side and down the other in Figure 14-1. If you do this you will see how closely the intelligence curve fits the normal curve. Even without drawing the line, the general outline is fairly obvious. Interpreting the histogram is about the same as interpreting the regular curve. For example, Figure 14-1 shows that approximately fifty subjects tested had an IQ between 70 and 75, 280 had scores between 100 and 105, and close to sixty subjects had IQs between 125 and 130.

Later intelligence tests,* capitalizing on this tendency to fit the normal curve, were designed so as to fit the *ideal* normal curve. In this way, statistical computations can be made, and IQ arrived at without worrying about the slight fluctuations of an *approximately* normal curve. Dividing mental age by chronological age has also disappeared over the years with the use of this ideal normal curve, but the principle behind the measurement has remained the same. In other words, statistical manipulation no longer requires use of mental age and chronological age in order to determine an IQ. The IQ is arrived at by locating a position on the ideal normal curve (see Fig. 14-2).

In any case, the numerical IQ provides approximations for the degree of intelligence of a person.† From these numbers, judgments are made regarding a student's potential. For example, 148 or above is very superior, 64-76 is borderline mentally retarded if you use Figure 14-2 [Merrill, 1938].

---

* Including later editions of the Binet.
† We have not yet even begun to struggle with what intelligence *is*. For the moment, assume that we know.

validity of the IQ test   Experiments have been conducted comparing the results of IQ tests with students' later achievement in schoolwork. Representative correlations show that achievement in history and IQ scores correlate about .59; reading comprehension and IQ scores correlate .73; biology and IQ, .54 [Bond, 1960]. Thus intelligence tests do predict future scholastic ability fairly well. The astute observer will immediately counter that the correlations are not in the .95–1.00 range, so some errors must have been made in prediction. In this he would be quite correct. The IQ test is a useful tool for obtaining a fairly accurate picture of the scholastic potential of a large number of students, but test results must always be viewed with caution, especially if the school performance does not seem to reflect the IQ score. It is important to remember that the primary usefulness of the IQ test is to predict school ability—the goal Binet originally had. Sometimes the tests can be grossly misused. For example, to become a policeman in Boston one has to take an "IQ test" which requires defining words like "pyromaniac" and "lexicon"—hardly appropriate for becoming a policeman [McClelland, 1973].

Test conditions often can influence accuracy of an IQ score. I recall that when blessed with the happiness of being in Navy boot camp, I was subjected to the standard tests for recruits that made it possible to assign us to jobs suited to our abilities. It seemed to me that the men who scored highest were given cleanup and KP duty, while those who scored lowest got the highly technical and complex intellectual tasks, but possibly that was my imagination. In any case, we were awakened at four o'clock one cold winter morning, taken to a dark, damp building before having breakfast, and given four hours of intelligence tests. Testing conditions were not exactly conducive to maximal effort or interest, and undoubtedly they had considerable effect on the scores obtained.

Later we will discuss another problem, the effect of *social environment* on intelligence testing, but I should mention at this point that individuals from poor homes, poor schools, and poor sections of the country do not perform as well on intelligence tests as do other, more fortunate students. The conclusion cannot be drawn that these people are basically less bright. The environment itself seems to have a profound effect on everyone.

Physical health also has an effect on test taking. It is difficult to get excited about test taking when you are half-dead with the flu.

The difficulties that beset test taking are almost endless, but you should be aware of them; in too many cases, a single IQ score has been obtained for a student and has stayed with him throughout his school years. For this there is no excuse.

reliability of the IQ   The IQ test is far from perfect, but it is far superior to guesswork. The IQ scores obtained from a large group of people tend to remain close when the same group is tested years later. That is, correlating early scores with later scores for the same people will yield fairly substantial reliabilities.

Using the Stanford-Binet as a representative test, studies show that the test is consistent and especially reliable the older people are when they first take it. That is, if a group takes the IQ test at four years of age and then at 12, the two sets of tests will correlate (i.e., have a reliability) in the low .60s. If the first test is taken at age six and the second at 12, the reliability is in the .70s; scores at age eight correlate with scores at 12, for the same group, in the .80s [Honzik et al., 1948].

Although we could hope for perfection, we may safely say that despite some notable fluctuations, by and large the IQ test is a reliable measure.

standardization   The intelligence test does, however, make errors, sometimes as much as 30 points [Sontag, 1958]. However, errors are not typically this large. You may wonder, considering that we know of these errors, why the intelligence test is used so often. The reason is that the test is the most accurate measure we now have of what we call mental ability. Talking with a person can be misleading, as can evaluations based on attitude, dress, mannerisms, or speech patterns.

The intelligence test has a major advantage over guesswork in what is called *standardization*. Standardization is a process of making a test uniform from one administration to the next; in other words, it is made

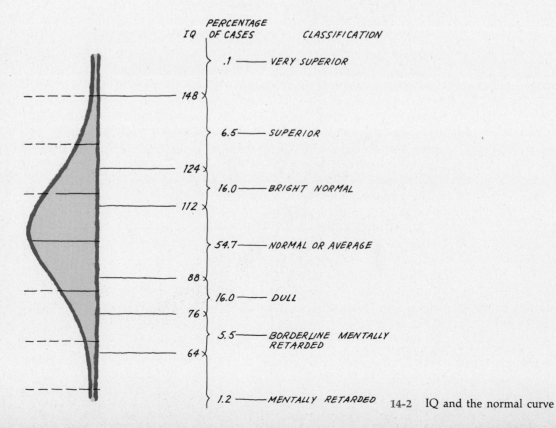

14-2   IQ and the normal curve

standard. This point is quite important: the *same* set of questions is used for each individual of a given age group being tested; if different questions were asked, person *A* could not be compared with person *B* because one set of questions might be easier or harder than another set.

Standardization requires that the test administrator read to the test taker the *exact* question to be answered. Each question is read in exactly the same way every time the test is administered; this uniformity prevents coaching, aiding, or rewording of the question that might give one child an advantage over another. Standardization also requires that results be uniformly compared; for example, person *A* and person *B*, both 14 years old, are compared with the same group of 14-year-olds used to construct the test.

OTHER TYPES OF INTELLIGENCE TESTS

We have been discussing the Simon-Binet intelligence test, which came out in 1905. Over the years this test has been revised; poor items have been removed, items have been updated, and so on. The current edition of the test came out in 1960; it was constructed at Stanford University and is called the Stanford-Binet intelligence test. This test can be used for ages three through about 18 years, and it is sometimes used for adults, but it is considered a poor measure for this older population.

The Binet is the most widely used intelligence test in history, but it has a major flaw in that it is highly *verbal*. "Verbal" refers to the kinds of questions asked on the test. A substantial proportion ask for definitions of *words*, for solutions to *word* problems involving reasoning, and for *verbal* abstractions such as (for age seven), "Brother is a boy; sister is a _____."

The results of a highly verbal test will be biased in favor of the well-educated upper-middle-class and upper-class white population. These groups have emphasized achievement in school, and school achievement in turn is mostly a process of defining words, doing a lot of reading and writing, and solving verbal and arithmetical problems.

In fairness to the Binet-type test, remember that our society places great emphasis on verbal skills for management positions in business, advanced degrees, literary endeavors, and the like. These positions go principally to people who have verbal skills. Nevertheless, the Binet test does skip over many people whose basic abilities have not been developed or whose intellects haven't grown along verbal lines. The function of the intelligence test is to *predict* future success and achievement, but since it relies heavily on *past* achievement, the Binet tends not to identify many people who have had inadequate training in verbal skills but who still may possess *potential* for learning and accomplishment in intellectual endeavor. This problem faced Dr. David Wechsler in the 1930s, and the problem was acute.

the Wechsler Adult Intelligence Scale

Wechsler, a psychologist at New York's Bellevue Hospital, had the difficult task of evaluating a large number of local derelicts. Many of these men were semiliterate, had not attended school beyond the early grades, if at all, and were social outcasts, even though some undoubtedly had intellectual potential. The Binet test clearly would be inappropriate for such a population because it is highly verbal. Dr. Wechsler hit upon the idea of a two-part intelligence test. The first part contained *verbal* items similar to those of the Binet, but the second part was a series of tasks that comprise what is referred to as a *performance test*.

A performance-test item relies minimally on verbal skills but nonetheless requires reasoning ability. It involves problem solving without extensive vocabulary. This test was right in line with Wechsler's evaluation of intellectual ability; he believed intelligence to be the purposeful and rational ability to deal with the environment (problems which are around us) [Wechsler, 1958]. Ability to solve problems without putting the stress on words—on verbal solutions—could be indicative of intelligence, then, and for this reason he created the performance scale.

Some performance-scale items are:

Picture completion.   The test taker is shown a series of pictures from which some important part is missing—e.g., at the simplest level, a pig with his tail missing. The subject is asked to indicate what part is missing.

Object assembly.   The test taker is given a picture of a familiar object—e.g., the outline of a person—cut up like a jigsaw puzzle and asked first to recognize the object and then to put it together (testing the ability to symbolically move parts together into a whole).

You will notice that these tasks involve reasoning ability, awareness of the environment, and ability to integrate the environment—all tasks assumed to have something to do with intelligence; yet there is no stress on words.

The items of the performance scale are graded like those of the

98–99   The picture-arrangement subtest from the WAIS; block design test (*Psychological Corporation*)

Binet—according to difficulty—and arranged according to the age groups passing them. Again, an IQ is derived based on the underlying principle of mental age, but the Wechsler IQ is obtained by statistically computed tables; and no direct calculation of months or years is used, as in the early Binet. Since Wechsler also devised a verbal IQ scale, it is possible with his test to obtain both a *performance IQ* and a *verbal IQ* and to compute a combined score for the two of them. The advantage of the double-IQ system is obvious: If a person scores very high on the performance test and very low on the verbal test, the tester probably ought to take a close look at the education and background of the test taker. He may be very bright, but lacking in training. Very high verbal scores and very low performance scores are rare, but such a combination could conceivably indicate problems with motor coordination or with the motor area of the cortex.

Wechsler's first test was designed primarily for adults. It is presently called the *Wechsler Adult Intelligence Scale* (WAIS for short). The WAIS has statistical averages (norms) for comparing an individual's score with those obtained from thousands of persons in the age range 16 through 74. Since it is specifically for adults, the WAIS is more accurate for older people than the Binet, which was designed primarily for children.*

individual and group intelligence tests

Both the Wechsler and the Binet tests are administered individually. A psychologist sits at a table with the student or patient and asks the questions or demonstrates the problems contained in the test. These two *individual tests* take a little over an hour each to administer in this fashion. Some feel that the lengthy administration allows the examiner to grasp finer shades of meaning in the person's answers than do other intelligence tests. He also can allow partial credit for partially correct answers.

The biggest disadvantage of the individual test is the very high cost. At the bare minimum, the price is about ten dollars per student. Some other intelligence tests cost five to seven cents per test, and naturally these are given more frequently. These *group intelligence tests*, as the name implies, are administered to large groups of people at one time. This is possible because the test is entirely written—that is, the test taker has only to make the correct answer on a piece of paper. The items found in group tests are naturally limited to those that can be answered by a pencil mark; nonetheless, they include questions similar to those in the individual test—e.g., defining words—but in the group test alternatives are offered; for example:

A hat is (*a*) to smell; (*b*) to look through; (*c*) to wear; (*d*) to smoke.
What number is missing? 1-3-5-___   (*a*) 6; (*b*) 7; (*c*) 8; (*d*) 9.
Ear is to *hear* as *eye* is to: (*a*) *tear;* (*b*) *see;* (*c*) *spectacles;* (*d*) *eyelash.*

Considering the amount of time and effort it takes to administer the individual test, you would expect that validities would be considerably

*There is a *Wechsler Intelligence Scale for Children* (WISC).

higher than with the group test. This is true in selected cases because a number of poor group tests are on the market; however, the better group tests show some impressive correlations. For example, one group test correlates with school achievement tests (how well a person has learned the subject matter) between .70 and .84, depending upon the group tested [Allen, 1944].

The stability or reliability of the group test is also impressively high, especially when it is used with young people just past the early teenage period. Some tests correlate between .84 and .90 when the scores during the teenage period are compared with scores of the same individuals at thirty-three years of age* [Anderson, 1960].

INTELLIGENCE

At first you may be puzzled by the heading of this section; surely we have been discussing intelligence for a number of pages, haven't we? We have not; we have been discussing intelligence testing—and as you will see in a moment, that is a slightly different issue. Most of us know people who have tremendous skill in problem solving in everyday life; we know students who do extremely well in school and businessmen who are very successful; yet many of these people do not obtain unusually high scores on intelligence tests. And we all know "brains" who seem pretty stupid to us.

The reason for this discrepancy is that psychologists do not know what intelligence actually is. The definitions of intelligence presented by men like Binet and Wechsler seem workable and appropriate, but they are not able to fully encompass that unknown quality which *is* intelligence. Thus, although the items in available tests reflect and involve intellectual processes, they do not include everything which goes to make up intelligence. The reliance of tests on problem-solving tasks is the best that anyone has been able to come up with.† The important point is that the intelligence test undoubtedly measures factors involved in intelligence, but it does not measure *all* that constitutes intelligence [Guilford, 1967].

This topic brings up an important issue in psychological-test construction, one that we avoided when validity was mentioned earlier. We skirted the issue because at the time it might have been confusing. Now, however, if you understand the issues of intelligence just mentioned, you should have no difficulty with the present topic—construct validity. The intelligence test is based on construct validity.

construct validity   First, as a refresher, validity has been defined as the ability of a test to measure what it is supposed to measure. Correlations between test results

---

*Possibly this results from some form of "solidification" of abilities with age?

†You may recall the effect of Oliver Evans's discovery of "jet propulsion" (see Chapter 1). The current generation of psychologists or students may suddenly see the light, as Evans did, and then we will have one of the most important discoveries yet in psychology—how to measure intelligence of all kinds with a high degree of accuracy.

and actual behavior help to establish validity. If behavior agrees with test scores, then the test is doing a good job of sorting out people; its scores are highly correlated with behavior, and it has high predictive validity.

This sort of validity is not too difficult to understand. Another way to determine if a test is measuring what it is supposed to measure is merely to get experts to agree that the test is performing as it should. The expert mind determines what a test should contain if it is to measure a certain behavior. If no one verifies the *actual* validity of an engineering test, for example, but instead just assembles a group of engineers and has them make up test items which they feel measure engineering ability, these experts have *constructed* a test, and the test has **construct validity**. In theory, the test is designed to measure what the experts claim.

This idea is often confusing, so it might be beneficial to recapitulate. No one knows specifically what factors go together to constitute intelligence. Wechsler and Binet hypothesized what they, as experts, felt went into intelligent behavior. Their tests had construct validity. Earlier in the chapter we discussed how accurately the tests predicted how a person would do in school or on the job. That was predictive validity. Even if we had not run the predictive-validity tests and ignored that issue completely, the test could still have been administered on the grounds that it had construct validity.*

One final set of questions may have come to your mind. Does a test with construct validity *necessarily* measure what it is supposed to? No. It merely assumes the experts are correct. Does a test with predictive validity measure what it is supposed to? Yes, if the correlations are high.

Wechsler, for instance, *constructed* a definition of intelligence: He called it the purposeful and rational ability to deal with the environment. As long as there was some agreement among other experts that this definition was reasonable and workable, Wechsler could then proceed to devise items that seemed to fit the construct. For example, his construct implies that we can deal with our environment most effectively if we are able to detect certain problems in it; therefore, a person who notices that the pig's tail is missing in the picture-completion test is better able to deal with the environment than one who cannot see this lack. Wechsler's item, then, had construct validity—the item fits into his construct of what constitutes intelligence.

No correlations are possible in construct validity, as they are in some other kinds of validity I have mentioned. There is nothing to correlate with anything. This type of validity refers simply to a method for developing ways of measuring whatever hypothesis an experimenter has. Since intelligence tests are developed on the basis of constructs, it is important to keep

---

*Note that construct validity refers to a broad hypothesis made by the experimenter. Content validity (chapter 13) refers only to specific types of material used in a test.

in mind that an intelligence test measures *what we think is intelligence*, not actual intelligence. No one knows for certain what actual intelligence consists of. Remember, the construct definition leads to this: People differ in their ability to answer IQ-test items, and because they differ they have different IQs. We are not talking about *real* intelligence because we don't know what that is [Cantela, 1958].

is intelligence inherited? Francis Galton actually started psychology off in the direction of exploring intelligence as an inherited factor. Since intelligence tests had not been invented yet, Galton had to figure out on his own which people were most intelligent. He decided to find individuals who had reputations for being original, being leaders of opinion, being world renowned. These were his intelligent men. He then calculated that such men existed at a ratio of one for every four thousand persons in the general population.

He interviewed as many of these men as he could locate and read biographies and published accounts of scientists, poets, musicians, and military men; he even included a few wrestlers and oarsmen, so that brawn as well as brain was a part of his study. From these people, he picked a thousand persons whom he could label "eminent"—that is, those who were original, world-famous leaders of opinion. He discovered that these one thousand came from only three hundred families. Galton therefore concluded that inheritance was the critical factor. Using these "facts," he published his book *Hereditary Genius* in 1869; it made a strong case for intelligence being a hereditary characteristic.

To add further support to Galton's work in reverse, two infamous families appeared in the literature of psychology. In 1877, a member of the Prison Association of New York took a tour of county jails, and in one jail he found six members of the same family! He called the family by a pseudonym, "Jukes." The lineage of this Jukes family was later traced out by another investigator, and he found, first, that over a 130-year period the family had increased from five sisters to 2094 people. And one-half of this unusual group was feeble-minded. Furthermore, he estimated that over a seventy-five-year period the Jukes family alone had cost in excess of one million dollars for relief and institutional care [McClearn, 1962]. Even in today's inflation-prone economy this figure would be staggering. The important point, of course, is that this study seemed to indicate that lack of intelligence is inherited.

The second infamous family was the Kallikaks. During the Revolutionary War "Martin Kallikak" (a pseudonym) had an affair with a feeble-minded girl he met in a tavern, and this liaison resulted in the birth of a feeble-minded child. After the war Kallikak became respectable, married into a respectable family, and produced normal children by his wife. When the genealogy was traced, the tavern girl's descendants turned out very much like the Jukeses, and Kallikak's respectable family turned out more or less normal.

These studies seemed to be pretty convincing demonstrations for inheritance of intelligence. However, it is important not to forget that the environments, the living conditions, the incomes and opportunities of the two families were entirely different and could have had quite an effect on their respective "mental abilities," although Galton wasn't much concerned with this possibility.

Typical studies today, which tend to show the importance of environment, may be represented by one study that found a correlation of .48 between children's IQ and an estimate of the cultural level of the family (amount of books in the home, number of years of school, etc.). Another study also supported the environmental hypothesis:

IQ of child correlated with culture measures: .51

IQ of child correlated with economic factors: .52

IQ of child correlated with father's occupation: .45 [McClearn, 1962]

So there are arguments for both heredity and environment.

However, that is jumping ahead slightly. It is interesting to note that because of his studies Galton started a "science," *eugenics*, which occasionally crops up today. Eugenics advocates selective breeding of the human species, as breeders control animals so that only the best stock is bred with the best stock. As you will see, more recent evidence of inherited intelligence is not as clear-cut as Galton felt it to be, but even if his case was clearly made, our world would be strange indeed if it contained nothing but "intellectuals." For one thing, we would run the risk of never getting anything done while everyone sat around talking about it.

The dilemma remained, though. The problem was to determine if environment or heredity was responsible for the similarity between parents' intelligence and thus children's intelligence. The solution seemed imminent when it was discovered that like-sexed twins (two boys *or* two girls) often come from the same egg of the mother, whereas differently sexed twins (boy and girl) always come from different eggs. Basically, the implication of this discovery is that if twins come from the same egg, their intrauterine environment (within the mother) will be the same, and so will their inherited characteristics. With twins from *different* eggs, their environment is probably the same before birth, but their heredity is unquestionably different. For the first twelve months, in fact, motor coordination, eye-movement control, general alertness, and so forth correlate in the .80s for identical twins (same egg). For nonidentical twins the correlations are in the .60s and .70s, the difference between the two sets of twins $p = <.05$. So we definitely seem to be dealing with inherited differences, but only part of this is inherited "intelligence." A considerable amount of these early correlations are probably related to physical similarities, because as age increases the IQs tend to correlate with factors such as cultural level of the parents, economic conditions, and father's occupation, as mentioned earlier [Wilson, 1972; Calloway, 1972].

After birth another factor becomes important: Are the twins reared together, or are they separated? If they are separated, living in different homes, then their environments are going to be different. Most of the studies performed to date can be summarized with a fair degree of accuracy by Table 14-1.

Table 14-1   Correlations between "intelligence" of twins and nontwins reared together and apart [Burt, 1958]

Identical twins,* reared together	.92
Identical twins, reared apart	.77
Nonidentical twins, reared together	.55
Siblings (brother and sister, brother and brother, or sister and sister, but not twins) reared together	.53
Siblings, reared apart	.51
Unrelated children, reared together	.26

* From same egg; hence, same heredity.

A 15-point correlational difference exists between identical twins reared apart and those reared together. We can assume that the *environment* of twins reared together is much more similar. This environment, in turn, produces the differences in correlations between identical twins reared together and those reared apart.

The difference between nonidentical twins reared together and identical twins reared apart is a striking 22 points of correlation. This spread suggests that a hereditary base is involved, since entirely separate environments do not alter intelligence as much as the different heredity of nonidentical twins. Siblings reared apart correlate about the same as nonidentical twins reared together. This would again suggest a hereditary component, because siblings would have certain characteristics in common. The situation becomes more striking when unrelated children are compared with the siblings; unrelated children living together correlate only .26 as compared with correlations in the .50s for siblings.

The results obtained in observations of unrelated children reared together would suggest—with caution—that the .26 correlation could be largely attributed to environment.

Many studies have been made in this area other than the ones just summarized. The findings show a consistency that cannot be denied. There-fore, certain conclusions can be drawn with some degree of safety:

1.   No study has clearly demonstrated that heredity is not a factor in intelligence. In fact, the larger proportion of them show basic intellectual potential to be something inherited from parents.

2.   Environment is a critical factor in the enrichment of this intelli-gence, and a meager environment can reduce the potential of a particular person.

You might very well draw conclusions other than mine. This does not mean that either of us is right or wrong; instead, it demonstrates that a variety of interpretations can develop from the same set of figures. This is especially true at the human level when someone tries to make a division between two extremely complex variables such as heredity and environment.

race, culture, environment, and intelligence   The discussion of construct validity should help you to understand some controversial issues centering on race and intelligence. If intelligence tests are artificial devices, not pure measures of intelligence, then test results are going to be strongly influenced by outside sources such as culture and environment. Remember that the intelligence test was constructed *by* mid-dle-class white Americans, and it works best *for* them; hence, highest scores will generally be obtained from this group.

A striking example of cultural influence is the poor showing many Indians (i.e., from India) make on the intelligence test. Looking at numerical values of test results alone, you might assume—erroneously—that Indians as a group are not very bright. Digging a little deeper, however, brings some interesting facts to light. Most intelligence tests put a premium on time; in other words, a set time period is allowed for solving the various items.* But many Indian groups just do not put a premium on time limits, as white middle-class Americans seem to do. A well-known historian has suggested that one of many possible environmental influences contributed to this "timelessness": Since very early in their history, Indian people have been located primarily in an area of monsoons (heavy rain periods), and they experienced no pressing need to attempt exact prediction of the seasons. Growing periods were announced loud and clear by the onset of rain. Other civilizations, not having the monsoon cycle, had no accurate warning of seasons and therefore they developed calendars and time-keeping devices that relied on the moon, sun, and stars. Thus, these peoples tend to be more conscious of time [McNeill, 1963]. No one is saying this factor alone is responsible for different reactions to time; but clearly many subtle environ-

---

* This limitation is for standardization purposes. The problem-solving period is kept the same from one person to another so that no one individual has the advantage of extra time.

mental influences on behavior, when absorbed by the culture, may influence test results. These factors would influence intelligence-test results but probably have nothing to do with basic intelligence, so any statements about differences in intelligence as reflected by such tests must be interpreted with caution.

Even Binet's construct of intelligence as a directed, rational, and purposeful act by the individual can suffer when one moves from one culture to another. Some African societies that demonstrate all the general qualities of intelligent human behavior—for instance, the ability to symbolize—hold cultural beliefs that contradict Binet's conception. For instance, in one culture presently existing, a person is not believed to be in full and direct control of himself or his personal environment; instead, he is subject to the influence of objects that guide his fortunes. One rule of this society is that a person should not admire a tree or its fruit because it can influence him in such a way that he will have a poor marriage. No matter what you think of this belief, it makes the important point that culture can directly influence constructs about intelligence. We have no reason to assume that even more subtle beliefs are not operating in all societies, and within specific groups these will alter their "intelligent behavior" as defined by a test [Irvine, 1970].

Other studies have indicated that ethnic origin can make a difference, especially in verbal skills. Evidence points to an understandable handicap for Spanish-American children because they are in a home environment of more than one language with an emphasis on their parents' native tongue. To some extent this makes acquisition of English-language verbal skills more difficult [Christiansen and Livermore, 1970].

Little is understood about racial differences, though we have more than enough myths—for example, that the dark skin of the black is an advantage in regions of intense heat and sunlight. Actually, the "white" (lightly pigmented) person fares much better in such climates. We are unable to clearly interpret racial differences at the present time. What appear to be notable alterations in physiological construction apparently are just variations on the same theme; their evolutionary significance, if any, is unknown [Montagu, 1962].

Clearly, inherited differences do exist between groups of people. For example, if a person from the Arctic region dips his arm in cold water, the blood vessels enlarge; with people from the temperate zones, they contract. Blood groupings, skin pigmentation, and specific diseases are also subject to inheritance by certain groups of people. No one really questions that distinctive racial characteristics do show up.

The issue is different, however, when we reach areas such as intelligence. Geneticists, experts in inheritance, point out that there is no reason to suppose that the genes of one group—whites, for example—combine to produce superior intelligence. There is no reason for high-IQ genes, if there is such a thing, to accumulate in one race as opposed to another [Bodmer and Cavalli-Sforza, 1970]. As one author points out, the abilities to make tools, engage in symbolic language behavior, and understand abstract relationships are universal human characteristics [Wolff, 1970]. Despite individual differences between people, these characteristics are so necessary to human survival that differences are very unlikely to amount to much more than variations typically found in ear size, nose size, or eye color. In all three variations, size and color have no relation to the ability of that organ to function. Assuming that such a relation did exist would produce some strange results! The Chinese throughout history have been world renowned in mathematics. Can we assume that this excellence results from certain skin pigmentation, ear size, eye shape, or what have you?

Intelligence testing of black children ordered ceased by California court

The U. S. Federal court for the Northern District of California has upheld a class-action suit temporarily enjoining the state school system from administering intelligence tests to black children.

Robert F. Peckham, presiding judge of the U. S. District Court in San Francisco, ruled that IQ tests taken by the city's black school children are culturally biased and ordered them ceased.

The plaintiffs in the case were the parents of seven children who were labeled mentally retarded and placed in remedial classrooms. The court decreed that separation from normal education on the basis of questionable IQ scores was in violation of the civil rights of the children.

While 9.5 percent of the school age children in California are black, 27.5 percent of the children in the state's mentally retarded classes are black.

The decision ordered the California State Department of Education to refrain from placing black students in classes for the educatable mentally retarded "on the basis of criteria which places primary reliance on the result of IQ tests."

100 (*American Psychological Corporation*)

And there is that classic argument about brain size. Following the evolutionary scale, we know that the most intelligent being, no matter how one defines intelligence, is man. A very high correlation exists between the brain size of different animal species and the ability of those species to solve problems; the largest brain is man's.* The average brain capacity of man is about 1350 cubic centimeters. For comparison, the chimpanzee has a capacity of approximately 400 cc. The range of brain capacity between white and black is negligible. The brain on the average seems to be slightly smaller among blacks, but the difference is meaningless, for many very intelligent people have brain capacities as low as 1000 cc, well below the average person of whatever skin color [Montagu, 1962, 1964]. As long as man's brain size remains above 800 cc, brain size has little or no relationship to intelligence. Differences in intelligence show up among individual people, not between races. Furthermore, there is no such thing as a pure race.

You might think that all this is perfectly obvious, but recently courts have had to rule that in many cases IQ tests can be unconstitutional when

---

*There are a couple rather *big* exceptions. Some elephants have brains that weigh 13 lb; whales, 19 lb. However, the principle still holds true: the elephant's brain is small *compared to his size*, being $\frac{1}{1000}$ its weight; the ratio for the whale is 1/10,000. Man's brain-to-size ratio is $\frac{1}{60}$ [Asimov, 1965].

comparing blacks and whites [Fleishman and Bartlett, 1969]. Being relatively new to the field of IQ testing, you may wonder what all the commotion is about. It boils down to the very simple fact that *on the average* the tested IQ of blacks is five to ten points lower than that of whites. At the highest end of the IQ scale are both blacks and whites, but *statistically* there is an overall difference between them [Cartwright and Burtis, 1968]. This difference in IQ has enjoyed fairly wide publicity in the name of prejudice, so many social scientists have leaped into the fray to point out that intelligence is just like a muscle that needs exercising; if the black child isn't given this opportunity for exercise, obviously a difference in IQ can be expected [Tyler, 1965].

Jensenism   It is sometimes remarkable how emotional issues can cause even renowned scientists to throw out what they have learned. By the time you have reached this page in the book, you are well aware of the need for control in experiments and would strongly question experiments faulty in this respect. But when emotion enters the picture things get very confused. In 1969 psychologist Arthur Jensen came out with a "scientific" study which claimed that blacks are intellectually inferior because there is some defect in their heredity [Jensen, 1969]. The study was pretty much like this hypothetical one: I take a trip to New York and find myself a corner on some street—for example, Wall Street. The next step is to stop the first fifty whites I see to use as my white subjects. I have to do a little hunting, but eventually I find fifty blacks who are in the general area for my black subjects. Then I administer a test to both groups on stocks, bonds, corporate mergers, mutual funds, selling long and selling short, and so forth. At the end of the study I find something remarkable: Blacks are incapable of learning about stocks and bonds. The difference is obvious in the test results I got. (Never mind the fact that there are very few black stockbrokers.) And the press picks this up and gives it front-page treatment. So much for the basics of what happened with Arthur Jensen.

Both studies lack adequate control, but what matters is that Jensen's study was real and he concluded that blacks have inferior heredity and are incapable of learning to the same extent as whites. Amazingly, he came to this conclusion admitting that the environment has been known to change IQs in some cases as much as 70 points [Brace and Livingstone, 1971]. No matter; the press had a field day with the results of his study.

Nor has controversy over the Jensen study subsided. One anthropologist comments that he thought the pure-race theory had died with the demise of Nazi Germany, yet every time you turn around "Jensenism" pops back up [Brace, 1971].

What, then, is the basic issue? It is relatively simple. Jensen compared blacks and whites on their ability to answer IQ-test items and found that blacks did less well. So, we already know this, but he concluded that environment is not responsible for the difference and that heredity is. The conclusion was unwarranted, for the social environments in the two groups were not the same; therefore, differences between intelligence could just as easily be attributed to environmental differences and have nothing to do with heredity. Even Binet warned just after the turn of the century that his test should only be used with persons who have the same basic environment [Brace, 1971]. The Society for the Psychological Study of Social Issues in 1969 condemned the Jensen findings because the study was not experimentally sound.

Then the situation became worse because a Nobel Prize winner agreed with Jensen. Thus, Jensen picked up a supporter—which is all right, except that the supporter was given the Nobel Prize for inventing the transistor radio, not much in the way of qualifications for supporting the study [Brace, 1971]. Experts in heredity just do not agree with the conclusions of Jensen. In the words of one well-known geneticist, there is no way to discount the influence of environment on a test which is partly designed to measure the influence of environment [Attland, 1971].

The issue is not whether intelligence is inherited. We already know that this is true to a large extent; but we also know that environment is quite influential, especially when we have a white middle-class test as our measuring instrument: specifically, the test is construct-validated for whites [Dawes, 1972].

The criticisms of Jensen's study and of the use of the white IQ test for blacks and other minorities are overwhelming. In semioutline form, here are a few of them: (1) Chicanos (Mexican Americans) score very low on white IQ tests. Isn't it stretching credulity to add them to the list of people with "poor heredity"? Shouldn't we be looking at the test instead [Mercer, 1972]? (2) Persons from different ethnic groups have entirely different ways of organizing their world. Questions like "What do you think of capital punishment?" have different meanings for the deprived and for the advantaged [Cole and Bruner, 1972]. Doesn't almost any question elicit different responses depending on where you live and how you were brought up? (3) Questions asked in a specific dialect and in a nontesting environment bring about very-high-level answers from the so-called socially deprived [Cole and Bruner, 1972]. (4) Whites seem to be trained from childhood to develop school-oriented verbal ability. Is there a similar premium on words in the black communities, and even if there is, how does one get the black child excited about his prospects for success in the white world [Garcia, 1972; R. Watson, 1972]? (5) To make matters more complex, motivation enters into intelligence-test performance. Studies have produced some strange results in this area. Black students who were tested by a white examiner could solve a difficult problem when the task was labeled as a measure of hand-eye coordination; but call the same task a measure of intelligence, and they performed poorly. The authors suggested that in the second case the students were so highly motivated to "do well" that the white examiner by his very presence was "freezing them up." He represented too much of a threat with his intelligence test [Katz, 1964; R. Watson, 1972].

Now for the acid test (white middle-class Anglos only, please). Look at some of the sample items from Dr. Robert Williams's "BITCH" test in Figure 14–3, a test designed to sample the black environment and provide

14–3 Dr. Robert Williams's "BITCH" test items

DIRECTIONS: *Below are some words, terms, and expressions taken from the Black experience. Select the correct answers and put a check (✓) mark in the space provided on the right of the test sheet. Remember, we want the correct definition as Black People use the words and expressions. There is no time limit. Twenty to thirty minutes should be sufficient time to complete the test. (Answers at bottom of page.)**
GO AHEAD.

		A	B	C	D
Alley Apple (a) Brick (b) Piece of fruit	(c) Dog (d) Horse	1.			
Black Draught (a) Winter's coldwind (b) Laxative	(c) Black soldier (d) Dark beer	2.			
Blood (a) A vampire (b) A dependent individual	(c) An Injured person (d) A brother of color	3.			
Boogie Jugie (a) tired (b) worthless	(c) old (d) well put together	4.			
Boot refers to a: (a) Cotton farmer (b) Black	(c) Indian (d) Vietnamese citizen	5.			

* Answers to the "BITCH" test: 1—*a*; 2—*b*; 3—*d*; 4—*b*; 5—*b*. Items from the BITCH (Black Intelligence Test of Cultural Homogeneity). © 1972 by Robert L. Williams, Ph.D. Reproduced with permission.

1. *Vocabulary:* choose the word which has the same meaning, or most nearly the same meaning, as the word in dark type at the beginning of the line.

   javelin   **A.** bleach   **B.** coffee   **C.** jacket   **D.** rifle   **E.** spear

2. *Sentence Completion:* choose the word that will make the best, the truest, and the most sensible sentence.

   There's no book so ——•—— but something good may be found in it.

   A. good   **B.** true   **C.** beautiful   **D.** bad   **E.** excellent

3. *Arithmetic Reasoning*

   A man has to take a 300-mile trip by car. If he goes 40 miles each hour, how many miles does he still have to travel after driving $5\frac{1}{2}$ hours?

   A. 180 mi.   **B.** 100 mi.   **C.** 60 mi.   **D.** 2 mi.   **E.** none of these

4. *Verbal Classification:* think in what way the words in dark type go together. Then find the word on the line below that belongs with them.

   cotton   **wool**   **silk**

   A. dress   **B.** sew   **C.** fibre   **D.** linen   **E.** cloth

5. *Verbal Analogies:* look at the first two words and figure out how they are related to each other. Then, from the five words on the line below, choose the word that is related to the third word in the same way.

   then ⟶ now : yesterday ⟶

   A. tomorrow   **B.** time   **C.** today   **D.** here   **E.** past

14–4   Lorge Thorndike "IQ" test items

some measure of the ability of the black child. Can you answer them as well as the items from the typical IQ test in Figure 14–4?[*]

suggestive studies on IQ changes

Although the IQ for most persons tends to remain relatively stable, there is rather convincing evidence that outside influence can change it. The stimulation a favorable environment can provide apparently raises the IQ. Black children who were moved from the South to a northern city gradually increased in IQ as they remained longer in the North. We have no reason to expect that heredity alone (inherited intellectual ability) was responsible for the change [Lee, 1951].

In another study, an experimenter tracked down 25 children who had been in an orphanage together 21 years before the time of his study. At that earlier time one group, thought to be fairly bright, was kept at the orphanage, where its members received adequate but rather impersonal care.

[*]I won't tell you how I did on the BITCH test, but I do have to say that before going to press I had to verify every test-item answer with the author, Dr. Williams.

101 Some environments make it tragically clear why those who live there don't do well on intelligence tests (*Bruce Davidson, Magnum*)

A second group, thought to be mentally retarded, was separated from the original group of 25 and moved to a school for the mentally subnormal. These "retarded" children were later adopted by parents who provided them with individual care, love, and a family. Under these circumstances the supposedly retarded children made an average gain of 29 IQ points. The group remaining in the orphanage lost an average of 26 points. The changes seemed to result from such external factors as maternal care and affection [Skeels, 1966; Hunt, 1969].

A third, related study found that the IQ of retarded children decreased more rapidly if the children came from *better* environments before being placed in an institution, as compared with children who came from unpleasant environments to begin with. The authors suggest, with considerable logic, that the move to the institution generated a kind of hopelessness, in the sense that things were worse for the children and their motivation decreased along with IQ. Since these cases did not involve brain deterioration, we have no logical basis for assuming that intelligence decreased—only IQ, as reflected in motivation [Butterfield and Zigler, 1970].

In another study, specific interest in a student, at least in the sense of expecting him or her to do well, seems to have had an effect on IQ scores. Professional interest in the fluctuations of IQ reached a peak in 1968, with the publication of an amazing and controversial study of the effects of a teacher's expectations on the outcome of a pupil's IQ tests. In other words, the experiment asked, is it possible that if the teacher expects the pupil to do well in class work—that is, expects him to be brighter—the child actually will perform to that expectation even on an IQ test? Among the previous studies that were instrumental in the design of this study, one is amazing enough in its own right: Animals, including rats and even worms, were found to perform more "intelligently" in laboratory studies if the lab assistants were led to believe that a certain group of rats or worms was brighter than another group, even though there was no actual basis for this belief.*

The basic study was designed in the following manner: Grade-school pupils were given a test that supposedly could pick out students who were "very likely" to suddenly blossom into excellent pupils.† A group of students with no unusual attributes, either positive or negative, was selected for this treatment, and the teachers were allowed to find out that these pupils were about to go into their (supposed) "blossoming period." This group was the experimental group. The other students in the school were the control group, and nothing at all was said to the teachers about them. Thus, on IQ scores, the experimenter could compare the effects of the teachers' expectations for a group that was supposed to blossom with regular students' scores. The results are shown in Figure 14–5.

Notice in this figure that the first- and second-graders made remarkable gains in IQ points, apparently as a result of teachers' higher expectations. For example, 21 percent of the students in the experimental group increased 30 IQ points. If this is not amazing enough, three first-graders in the experimental group increased 69, 45, and 40 points respectively (not shown in Fig. 14–5) [Rosenthal, 1968].

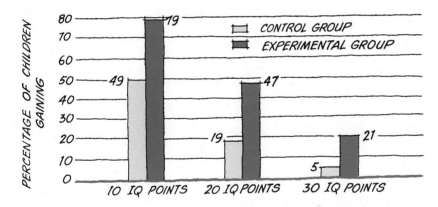

14–5   Teacher's expectations and increase in IQ for first and second graders

The same dramatic increases did not hold for grades beyond the first and second. Apparently, in the earliest, most pliable years, the expectations of an authority figure can have a pronounced effect on a child's performance, even in the area of IQ-test taking. Carrying this argument a step further and relating it to an earlier discussion, we may easily speculate

* One possibility, which has not been thoroughly explored but has been proposed by thoroughly reputable scientists, is that the breathing rate and body temperature of the experimenter change according to what he expects, and the worms or rats might be responding to this [Ratner, 1968].
† There actually is no test that can predict this phenomenon with a high degree of accuracy.

that IQ scores of black children may be *depressed* if teachers expect that these youngsters will not perform as well as white children.

When a group of women subjects were told that they were in competition with men and it was suggested that the examiner expected them to outperform the men, their WAIS IQs were significantly higher ($p < .05$) than those of a control group who were told that the tests were simply being administered to get a sample from the school [Dirkstein and Keplart, 1972]. These studies suggest pretty strongly that when dealing with subjects who sometimes are expected to have depressed scores, expectations in the positive direction can alter the results.

A word of caution is in order, however, regarding the dramatic increases of IQ shown in Figure 14–5. This study hit the psychological and educational worlds like a bomb, and it has endured heavy criticism since it was published. One major objection has been about the experimenter's statistical analysis; his figures indicate that the effect in question is more widespread than it actually is [Barber and Silver, 1968]. A second study performed by a different experimenter tried to duplicate* the study and failed to get the same results, although in this case the subjects were not quite as impoverished intellectually, which may have made a difference [Clairborn, 1969]. A third study has shown that if the subjects *know* they are doing well or poorly on a task—that is, have a form of self-knowledge—the effects of an experimenter's (and probably a teacher's) expectations are reduced [Wessler, 1968]. A fourth study demonstrates the possibility that if the experimenter (and teacher) is very objective, the subject is not much influenced, because the experimenter holds his attitudes or feelings in check [Wessler, 1969].

Despite all these difficulties, the data in Figure 14–5 are quite real; these changes did occur. Most objections focus on how widespread such results are. From our viewpoint, the important thing is that in some cases, especially with very young children, most scientists would agree that IQ can be changed by outside influences which have little or nothing to do with intelligence as such.

This study became so famous that a number of years had to pass before it could be done again because the teachers were on their guard, so to speak. However, the author of the study took a stab at it again in 1973 and was again successful in demonstrating the expectancy effect.

In the meantime, the educational and IQ world is busy trying to cope with another severe jolt. One of the most traditional and basic defenses of the usefulness of the IQ has been that when you get into the lower ranges (IQs of 30, 40, and 50) the evidence is pretty clear that much in the way of verbal training is hopeless. Not so, however. Psychologist Renée Fuller

---

* Called *replication* in science.

has figured out a way to teach children with IQs as low as 30 to read, a task formerly thought next to impossible. Dr. Fuller's system is very clever. Her training method involves four senses. These children learn the alphabet by building each letter out of blocks (lines, circles, and angles are all that is required). The child is thus using his tactile (touch) sense, his kinesthetic (muscle) sense, his visual sense, and, when he hears the letter, his auditory sense. This method has resulted in vocabulary building, IQ improvement, and acquisition of the ability to read. Besides calling to task Jensen's assumption that IQ is not related to environment, the success of Fuller's results may open up wide horizons for changes in techniques of teaching [Schmell, 1972; Shuman, 1972; Fuller, 1972].

The final study relating to "intelligence" changes is most intriguing, although next to impossible to perform on humans: it may be that mental work actually changes the animal brain. Rats who were raised in a stimulating and enriched environment, for example, with plenty of activities to perform, actually develop a thicker cortex and a heavier brain than rats in a poorer environment. One notable change is that the synaptic junctions of rats reared in an enriched environment are about 50 percent larger than those of a control group [Bennett et al., 1964; Rosenzweig et al., 1972]. Memory and learning tasks also increase the diameter of some of the neural cells and the amount of branching in the dendrites of the neurons [Rosenzweig, 1968]. Could this happen with humans, too? Right now, we have no reason to think it couldn't.

I have the somewhat sinking feeling about this time that you might have formed the impression that the IQ is worthless, and it would be very disturbing to leave you with this impression. In general, if you are dealing with a middle-class white, the IQ is a useful tool for predicting academic success. Also, despite the very important studies by Fuller with very-low-IQ individuals, the intelligence test can be beneficial in locating persons who clearly have deficits in learning ability and who require special attention.

The IQ is under heavy attack, and it deserves this fate because for years it has been a god that supposedly could see through us all and it has been used by the schools in this fashion. The test is clearly invalid for predicting intelligence for Chicanos and blacks, although it will provide a "white IQ" for these individuals. The work of Williams with his "BITCH" test fills a temporary need for some kind of measure of how much a minority group has absorbed from the environment; it is not, however, the final answer, because we need a single test that can measure individuals from any group. The IQ test has been king so long that psychology is suffering from a terrible case of set—and this set needs to be broken.

Intelligence, then, is an extremely complicated topic. We may hope that more solutions are on the way. Or you may take the casual approach of Alexander Hamilton toward intelligence. Attacks were leveled at Supreme Court justices during his time, as they are now, and one such criticism was that intellectual ability declines with age and some justices are very old indeed, and getting older. Hamilton, in *The Federalist*, very neatly side-stepped the issue by pointing out that all the judges couldn't be senile or incompetent at the same time and that this afforded protection to the public.

SUMMARY

Every manner of device, technique, and question has been used to measure the ability labeled intelligence. The most successful measures of intellectual ability, to date, have been the verbally oriented tests, since they tend to correlate highly with one's degree of success within our revered system of education.

Two of the best-known individual tests of intelligence are the Stanford-Binet and the Wechsler Adult Intelligence Scale (WAIS).

The Binet test is a highly verbal test originally designed to provide a mental age that could be compared with a chronological age to give an IQ. Although the same principle exists in present-day intelligence tests, the normal curve is used, and the IQ is statistically computed without direct reference to mental age.

The Stanford-Binet test items are designed to measure a sense of direction in problem solving, the ability to adapt, comprehension, and a self-evaluation of how one is approaching the problems. These constructs were originated by Binet in the development of his test.

The IQ test has high validities and reliabilities as compared with the personality tests discussed in the previous chapter, although the tests are subject to notable error on occasion.

All IQ tests are standardized, which means that the administration of the test is uniform—that is, the same for each test taker.

Wechsler defines intelligence as the purposeful and rational ability to deal with problems around us. Although this definition is similar to Binet's, it does reflect an orientation that stresses many types of problem solving, including physical-motor and nonverbal problems like those found in the performance scale of the WAIS and WISC.

Group intelligence tests are similar to objective personality tests in that they are administered using paper and pencil, and the choice of answers is usually limited. They are considerably cheaper, therefore, and a good test can yield high validities and reliabilities.

Although obvious differences exist in the inherited characteristics of individuals, including intelligence, little or no evidence supports the idea that racial differences include a difference in basic intelligence. In any case, intelligence as measured in most IQ tests is a construct primarily applicable to white middle-class Americans, so in many instances the issue is a straw man. Black children can "raise" their IQ by living in more intellectually stimulating neighborhoods and attending better schools. IQ also changes with love and with special attention, apparently even from the positive expectations of a teacher.

It appears correct to say that intelligence is inherited to *some* extent, regardless of race, but environment can have a notable effect.

CHAPTER FIFTEEN
RECOGNIZING TALENT AND CREATIVITY

In this day of "test first, talk to the person later," few of you can say that you have not taken an intelligence test. However, it *is* possible that you have never taken one. In any case, we need to discuss a number of tests that often resemble IQ tests but are not intelligence tests.

An intelligence test is designed to predict in a *general* way how well a person will do in the future. For example, you could probably bet on the success of a person whose IQ is 130, whereas you would be on shaky ground with someone whose IQ is 30. The IQ test, then, is actually trying to estimate potential intellectual ability.

Another type of test resembles the IQ, but tests something different. It is called an aptitude test. The word *aptitude* is part of our everyday vocabulary; we say that so-and-so has an aptitude for medicine, or for law, or for engineering, or for auto mechanics. We mean that the person has a specific potential for a certain type of endeavor.

In many respects the aptitude test resembles the IQ test, but intellectual ability as measured by the intelligence test is designed to predict general academic success, not specific potential.

SPECIFIC-APTITUDE TESTS

The differences may become clear when we ask about the measurement of specific skills—potential abilities (aptitudes) for office worker, secretary, mechanic, or bookkeeper, to name a few. These abilities are not covered by IQ tests, so *aptitude tests* have been devised for these specific areas. Many of the same problems plague aptitude tests as intelligence tests. Nonetheless, specific-aptitude tests are worthwhile attempts to predict the future for an individual in a given area. With a few exceptions, most of these tests are taken with paper and pencil.

Here are some typical tests:

Mechanical comprehension: Attempts to predict in fields such as refrigerator repair, auto mechanics, and general repairmen in the mechanical field.

Typical item: If gear X is moving in the direction of the arrow, will gear Y move (*a*) clockwise, or (*b*) counterclockwise?

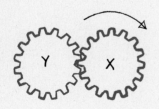

This item and many far more complex ones are used to measure one's ability to understand mechanical devices. Each person's score is compared with

360

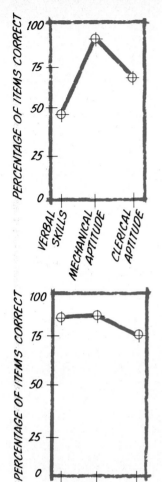

the scores of people who are already successful in the area of mechanical skills.

Spelling: Attempts to predict potential in fields such as secretarial or office work. (Other such tests include typing, correcting sentences, and the like.)

Typical item: Which word is spelled incorrectly? (*a*) horse; (*b*) house; (*c*) humit; (*d*) hanger.

Clerical speed and accuracy: Attempts to measure some of the skills necessary in clerical, filing, and other office jobs. A timed speed test.*

Typical item: Find the underlined test item and mark it on your answer sheet.

Test Item	*Answer Sheet*
MS MQ <u>MP</u> MF	A. MF MQ MP MX
A7 <u>B2</u> AB C3	B. C3 B3 B2 A7

This sampling should give you a general idea of how specific-aptitude tests work. There are, of course, many others. None is accurate enough to predict like an oracle the success of a person in a given field. However, counselors, especially job counselors, are often faced with the problem of guiding a person in the right direction, and here the tests are helpful. They give fairly reliable clues to areas of potential success.

Figures 15–1 and 15–2 present what is called a *profile*—that is, a graphic representation or "picture" of a person's skills. The item marked "verbal skills" on the profile is a test of verbal reasoning ability, and it is used because it correlates well enough with overall intellectual ability to provide a rough guide to general intellectual functioning.

We can make a superficial analysis of these profiles to show how they could be interpreted. Notice in Figure 15–1 that the person is below average (50%) on verbal reasoning but high on mechanical aptitude. Contrasting this with Figure 15–2, we might say that the individual in the second figure looks as if he might be suited for mechanical engineering, whereas the first person might be better in an occupation involving mechanical repair work. Of course, further and more elaborate testing would be necessary.

15-1/15-2   Samples of aptitude profiles

ACHIEVEMENT TESTS

Another type of test is given in grade and high school to measure the student's progress. In many ways it resembles examinations given in history, English, or psychology. In these tests, the questions are used to gather information on present ability, not to predict how well a person will do in the future. The scores indicate how well he has done in the past—that is, what he has

---

* The more items completed correctly in a fixed length of time, the higher the score.

learned or how much he has achieved in a course. Thus, the tests are called *achievement tests*.

By analogy, then, an aptitude test tries to measure how deep the well is, and the achievement test how far the well is already filled up.*

At this point, problems of test construction enter. If a person has some potential, he will have learned something in the past; or, put in technical terminology, if he has aptitude, it will be reflected in his achievement.

The problem can be illustrated with a hypothetical test question:

Columbus discovered America in (*a*) 1492; (*b*) 1700; (*c*) 1859; (*d*) 1950.

This test item could be considered appropriate for fifth-grade students. Almost any fifth-grader would know the answer because he has absorbed the information from his environment just by being around and by paying attention to what he hears or reads.

One more bit of logic in test development needs to be added: *If* a person has absorbed from his environment in the past, as the fifth-grader has done, we may assume that he will absorb and learn in the future. The duller students will have forgotten the answer by the fifth grade. Hence, the question *could* be used as a measure of aptitude for history because those who know answers now will know other answers in the future. Therefore, the question is one likely to appear on an aptitude test.

Suppose, however, that we move this same item down to the second-grade level as part of a year-end test. It then becomes an *achievement*-test item, attempting to measure how much specific material in a course one has learned, since that is usually the time at which you have to memorize such dates.

By this time you are objecting, and legitimately so—we've got the same question doing both tasks. But notice that it is this specific problem that the makers of aptitude tests face. Can a person be intelligent and not have a background of school-achievement–type material? And, furthermore, how can the test maker avoid developing test items that measure school learning? School learning, then, does interfere with aptitude and intelligence scores. The test maker faces a monumental task in thinking up items that will not give the school learner an advantage over the dropout when the two may have equal potential.

Despite these problems, every attempt is made to *minimize* the influence of school learning. Wechsler's goal in using the pig without a tail as one of his test items was to find something *everyone* was exposed to, regardless of schooling. Again, the assumption is that if everyone looks at the pig, the brightest will see that the tail is missing, whereas the dullest may not. Sad to say, even in this case the story does not end happily: It has recently been discovered, to the horror of many, that quite a number

---

*The intelligence test tries to measure how deep the well can go, in a *general* way.

102 a, b, c Some objects that may be unfamiliar to people living in different parts of the U.S.: sheep; a lottery ticket; subway token (*USDA; N.Y. State Dept. of Taxation; Gabriele Wunderlich*)

of children living in concrete New York City have *never* seen a pig, a horse, or a cow. A psychologist who had never been out of New York City before startled a group of grade-schoolers in West Virginia when he commented on the big cows that were wandering through the schoolyard. He had a hard time believing they were pigs (which they were) because he thought pigs were much smaller [Horton, 1972].

Once again in theory: If when taking a test you must solve a number of mechanical problems without formal training, then you probably have taken a mechanical-aptitude test. If you are a mechanic and take a test on mechanical problems, you have just taken an achievement test. In a sense, the use made of the item is more critical than the item itself in determining what kind of test we are dealing with.

TESTS OF CREATIVITY

Suppose that two subjects are presented with a picture of a man sitting in an airplane and they write down the following responses to this picture stimulus:

> 1. Mr. Smith is on his way home from a successful business trip. He is very happy and he is thinking about his wonderful family and how glad he will be to see them again. He can picture it, about an hour from now—his plane landing at the airport and Mrs. Smith and their three children all there welcoming him home again.
>
> 2. This man is flying back from Reno where he has just won a divorce from his wife. He couldn't stand to live with her anymore, he told the judge, because she wore so much cold cream on her face at night that her head would skid across the pillow and hit him in the head. He is now contemplating a new skid-proof face cream. [Getzels and Jackson, 1962]*

There is a striking difference between these two stories. The first is a standard, to-be-expected tale. The second is unexpected, novel, and humorous, showing a talent or flair for the unusual. This section will be concerned with tests that attempt to measure this factor, creativity.

*From J. W. Getzels and P. W. Jackson, *Creativity and Intelligence* (New York: John Wiley, 1962); reprinted by permission.

First, however, what do psychologists know about the two "types" of people who produce these stories and why they seem to differ?

Invention is probably the product of unusual thinking. For example, people often say, when the solution to a problem is obvious, "Why didn't I think of that?" The answer was right before our eyes, but we didn't see it. Instead, we kept on solving problems the same old way. We were conventional, not unusual. We had a set.

Invention (and, we infer, creativity) is an ever-present necessity. Take the movie scene in a Wild West saloon where a man breaks off the end of a whiskey bottle and pours himself a drink. In real life, this procedure often was more a necessity than a dramatic gesture: Sometimes a cork can be wedged so tightly into a bottletop that 300 pounds of pressure are needed to remove it. The problem persisted until someone took a piece of metal, twisted it like a spiral staircase, put a sharp point on it, added a handle to push down at the top, and invented the corkscrew.

There is creativity in all of us. Before the age of fliptop beer cans,* every picnic or party required what was then called a "churchkey" (?), sometimes known as a beer-can opener. When and if it was lost, breaking set was amazing—rocks, nails, fingernail clippers, hairpins (a failure), tire jacks, and the like were used for the emergency.

In many ways it is strange that psychologists took so long to get around to performing studies on creativity with any frequency, but as you will see in a moment, the subject is a tricky one to examine. However, it is intriguing enough to have become a major area of interest.

First, it is necessary to come up with a workable definition of creativity before you can study it. To do this we must return to a previous topic, construct validity. Psychologists most often define the construct "creativity" as the ability to break set. This definition is fairly workable; scientific and literary inventions, whether in mathematics, in nuclear physics, or in poetry, inevitably involve uniqueness.

Such a definition unquestionably has some flaws. For example, disoriented mental patients in hospitals have drawn up very elaborate electronic diagrams for "world bombs." Breaking set in this case is the result of *disordered* thought, and since the bombs won't work, the thinking is not productive. And, of course, an architect can break set with innovative design, a creative process—but if he breaks set by violating laws of stress and builds a beautiful bridge that immediately falls down, his thinking is not creative.

These problems aside, if one had to pick the most prominent characteristic of inventors, it would be their ability to diverge or move away from the normal or expected. Also, one would normally anticipate that the end product of divergence would be useful or workable. The psychological studies of the creative discussed below deal primarily with schools and verbal material. Keep in the back of your mind, however, that creativity abounds in many situations and that real-life creativity is much harder to

*They said it would never work.

try to measure. One anthropologist discusses a very clever Eskimo man, Okluk. Desirous of attending a party many miles away and not having enough driftwood to construct himself a sled, Okluk had to figure out some way to get there. Hence, he soaked strips of walrus hide in water, rolled them up with salmon inside, and put these bundles outside to freeze. By lashing these solid pieces together he had a sled to make the journey. Incidentally, when he made it to the party, he "gave himself over to the joys of reunion with old friends, fed the walrus hide to his dogs, and stuffed himself on the salmon that was inside" [Weyer, 1961]. Such is real-life creativity, I suppose.

locating
the creative person

Almost all psychological studies of creativity involve making comparisons between creative individuals and the so-called noncreative in order to determine what characteristics divide one group from the other. In general terms, the creative people are located by two methods. The first is to call on members of a professional society to vote on who among them is most creative. This method has a built-in flaw: How does each voting member go about determining who is creative, and why? To this method's advantage, however, is the logic that the leaders of a professional group—for example, architects—should be able to pick which architects are making outstanding contributions. The second method for locating the creative people is heavily involved with the *construct definition* of creativity as "the ability to break set." Tests are administered to groups in order to locate those who break set, and these subjects are then labeled "creative" for purposes of the study.

Examining a typical test used to locate set breakers may make this idea clearer. The test is called the Uses for Things Test [Getzels and Jackson, 1962]. The test taker is given a series of words—for example, *brick, paper clip, sheet of paper*—and told to list as many uses for each object as he can think of. Using part of this test, see if you can locate the more creative person:

> **Subject A: Brick.** Uses: Barbeque pit, to build a patio, a house, decorate a garden, make a fireplace.
> **Subject B: Brick.** Uses: Hit someone with, use as a doorstep, use as a paperweight, grind up and give to an enemy in a red-pepper jar.

Another typical item in this kind of test is the essay you read at the beginning of this section about the man sitting in an airplane.

These two methods, then, are the major ways of locating creative persons—the test and the expert witness. Remember, creativity is a construct because we define the creative person as one who diverges from the expected, so we don't have a pure measure of creativity any more than we have one for intelligence [Nicholls, 1972; Anastasi and Schaefer, 1971].

studies of creativity
in schools

Creative students are wild, silly, unpredictable [Torrance, 1962]. You can well imagine how their behavior goes over with teachers in school. These students just don't fit the model "intellectual"; instead, they tend to be disruptive and frequently contradict the teacher. Their personal traits and values correlate with those that students feel the teacher expects to the extent of $-.25$. If you remember correlation, you will see that from the viewpoint of the creative youngster, what the teacher values, the student doesn't, and vice versa. In fact, most teachers don't consider the creative student particularly desirable, which is understandable to some extent [Getzels and Jackson, 1962]. Not all studies show teacher opposition to the creative student to this degree, but in general those who score high on the creativity tests are rated low by the teacher. Part of the problem is that teacher ratings reflect the educational system as a whole, and this system is geared toward straight academic achievement and conformity rather than innovative approaches to problems [Merz and Rutherford, 1972].

An intriguing study was performed with a group of middle-class Chicago adolescents [Getzels and Jackson, 1962]. Tests were used to locate the highly creative and less creative students within a school. Again, these tests differentiated students by sorting out those who did and didn't give unusual or unexpected responses. Some individuals were set aside as creative. This process left a group of "uncreatives," at least as far as test results were concerned. From the uncreatives, twenty-eight students were picked, each of whom had a very high IQ, the average for the group being 150. The highly creative students, twenty-four of them, had an average IQ of 127, which is fairly high but not as remarkable as the high-IQ, "uncreative" group. In tabular form, the two groups looked like Figure 15–3. This table

Fig. 15–3	*High IQ* ($N = 28$)	*Highly Creative* ($N = 24$)
IQ $\bar{X}$	150	127

shows that we have two groups, one called "high IQ" and the other "highly creative," labels determined by the tests. The symbol $\bar{X}$ refers to the mean or average; it is a shorthand method for expressing this term in figures and tables.* The letter N in the table you will see often in scientific reports; it is easy enough to remember: It means *N*umber.† So Figure 15–3 shows that we have $N = 28$ high-IQ subjects with a mean ($\bar{X}$) IQ of 150, and $N = 24$ highly creative Ss (subjects) with a mean ($\bar{X}$) IQ of 127.

To complete the table, we need to mention achievement tests, which were covered a short while back. In that section we referred to achievement tests as measures of how much had been learned, up to a given point in time, in areas such as reading comprehension, basic language skills, spelling, and what have you. Next, achievement tests were administered to both groups, the high-IQ Ss and the highly creative Ss. We could guess the outcome of the tests, considering the 23-point average difference in IQ between the two groups—but we would be wrong! (See Fig. 15–4.) Amazingly enough, the highly creative Ss did as well as those with high IQs on

---

*Some authors use M or $\bar{x}$ for mean: these symbols are the same as $\bar{X}$.
† Some authors use n for number.

the achievement tests, despite the great difference in IQ scores. Thus the implication is very strong that creativity makes up for lower IQ. In other words, creativity seems to be a potent factor in (real) intelligence which is not tapped by the construct-validated traditional intelligence test. We can

Fig. 15-4	*High IQ* (N = 28)	*Highly Creative* (N = 24)
IQ $\bar{X}$	150	127
School achievement test scores ($\bar{X}$)	55	56

draw this conclusion because the kind of study reported in Figure 15-4 has been replicated (done over)* with different groups and by different experimenters at least eight times—and six of these replications produced similar results to those in the original study [Torrance, 1960]. Indeed, it seems that psychologists have isolated a new dimension of mental ability. In any case, the correlations between creativity scores and IQ scores are consistently very low (usually in the .10–.30 range), so we known that the tests are measuring different factors† [Dellas and Gaier, 1970; Anastasi and Schaefer, 1971].

The purpose of the experiment we've just discussed was to locate creativity and pin down its characteristics and effects. I should mention, however, that students who scored high on both IQ and creativity tests were not used in the study. Since the experimenter was trying to isolate the characteristics of the two constructs, "creativity" and "intelligence," including this group in the study would have made sorting out the characteristics impossible. A person can, of course, be both highly creative and highly intelligent, as measured by these tests [Maier and Janzen, 1969]. Also, even though creativity tests and intelligence tests do not measure the same thing, a person needs a basic level of intelligence to be creative; in other words, he needs a core with which to work, and this core IQ is estimated to be about 120.

The ability of the creativity tests to predict future achievement in art, drama, literature, and music is good. Tests administered to students in the seventh grade were kept for five years, after which time the experimenters checked up on the students to see how active they were in artistic endeavors outside school, whether they had received any awards, had things published, and so forth. The correlation between creativity scores in the seventh grade and creative production five years later was in the .50s

---

*Replication, or redoing a study, with an entirely different group of subjects, is an important aspect of scientific studies. It is sometimes possible that your study produced unusual results because by accident you had an unusual group. For example, you surveyed fifty persons and found that 80 percent of those interviewed agreed that narcotics should be legalized. It is always possible that 80 percent of the group you interviewed were dope addicts. Although this possibility is remote, replication would soon clarify how widespread such an opinion was, and your results would probably change drastically.

† To demonstrate how tricky this problem can be, in view of the general attitude of creative people it is always possible that they do not take the intelligence test seriously and hence obtain a lower score in this test than in the more challenging test of creativity.

[Cropley, 1972].* The accuracy of these creativity tests is far greater for the "arts" than for the "sciences" [Nicholls, 1972]. The probable reason for this is that when you are dealing with physics, chemistry, and so forth you are bound by more rigid rules and guidelines. There is much more leeway in changing paints, notes, clay, or words than there is in altering chemical reactions or the laws of physics. Thus in the arts there is a little more room for producing the unusual.

personality characteristics of the creative

Some evidence supports the idea that subjects who are high in creativity have characteristics that differ from those who just have high IQs. A study was performed in which creative adolescents were located within a larger group of students by using both tests and ratings from teachers. All students selected for the study were high in IQ, but they were divided into a highly creative group and a less creative group on the basis of the test results and the ratings. Both groups were then given what is called an *adjective checklist* [Gough, 1952]. The adjective checklist contains a few hundred adjectives such as *interesting, thoughtful, sexy, absent-minded,* etc. The test taker is asked to check those words that he thinks apply to himself. Although the choices may not give a fully objective picture of what a person is "really" like, they do a good job of giving a self-evaluation of the individual.

The creative students, compared to those not considered creative, saw themselves as—among other things—original, spontaneous, rebellious, complicated, and somewhat withdrawn from most people [Schaefer, 1969]. Many other studies support this finding.

For example, an examination of creative women mathematicians found them to be on the whole self-centered, individualistic, and original. And creative writers tend to be independent and highly productive, to have wide-ranging interests, and to put great value on self-worth [Barron, 1965].

The thread running through most all of these studies is that the highly creative are dominant, forceful, attached to themselves, and innovative in thought and action. These individuals are very much wrapped up in their work and are strongly motivated from within themselves—that is, external rewards don't seem to have much meaning for them [Nicholls, 1972].

are creative people "out of it"?

Somewhere along the line van Gogh cut off his ear and continued to paint masterpieces. Edgar Allen Poe was an early version of the current-day trip taker and frequently wrote under the influence of narcotics. His are creepy but beautiful works of literature. And if you wander through the corridors of an art school on any campus, you'll find people whose dress and behavior are pretty weird.

Without question, a fair amount of creativity has come from the "mentally disturbed," as some would call them. Most likely only a few creative people are seriously disturbed, the remainder being merely eccentric, as some art students seem to be. The equation which suggests that

---

* In other words, the predictive validity of the test is in the .50s. If you don't know what I'm talking about you were speed-reading Chapter 13.

creativity is always accompanied by bizarreness is farfetched and has been shown to be unreliable.

Highly creative people tend not to conform to society, so this may account for their apparent deviancy. Thus, studies do show that the highly creative lean *toward* the abnormal on personality tests, but then this tendency is to be expected because sensitive people are the very ones who can create. Sensitivity will naturally breed an intense awareness of the problems and concerns of people and the world, and this awareness will push a person toward depression, anxiety, heightened awareness of the body and its malfunctions, and the like. The appearance of abnormality frequently goes along with the tendency to be different from others, and this seeming abnormality can develop an atmosphere in which a person rebels against society or the establishment—but such behavior is not necessarily a sign of mental disturbance.

How, then, does one tell the creative person from the truly disturbed? Most studies, as noted, indicate that the creative person has a strong sense of self-identity and strength—a firm conviction of worth. One author has said that the highly creative are both the sanest and the craziest people you will ever meet. The missing ingredient for those who are called "mentally disturbed," rather than "creative," seems to be that they lack this strong feeling of importance, self-identity, and "worthwhileness" [Barron, 1963; Mackinnon, 1962]. It seems that most creative people can tinker with the world of the bizarre—and, in fact, enjoy doing so—and still maintain their grasp on reality. Some lose their grip, unfortunately, even though their products remain exceptionally good, but this phenomenon is more the exception than the rule.

training for creativity

103   The Wright Brothers thought creatively; they were able to break conventional thought-patterns and understand how flying really could be done (*Culver*)

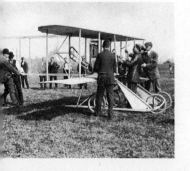

The paradox of our educational system is that the largest proportion of available dollars has gone into dissemination of factual information. The area of creativity has been ignored almost completely. Yet creativity appears to be basically quite a simple thing to teach. Not that everyone can become a creative genius—but it is possible that most people can be led into patterns of thinking that are potentially creative.*

One technique for creativity training that has caught on in industry is *brainstorming* [Osborn, 1963]. Faced with a problem, the president of a company may call in the members of his staff for a brainstorming session. The group sits around the table, and after being presented with the problem, everyone gives free flight to his imagination and flings out *any* idea that occurs to him, no matter how absurd it may seem. This technique has proven useful in generating many a good solution that at first seemed absurd but later proved to be remarkably appropriate. The larger the brainstorming group, however, the more effort is wasted and the more ideas are duplicated with many dead ends [Bouchard and Hare, 1970].

* If mass creativity is desirable. In the words of a couple of experimenters, too much emphasis on so-called creativity may defeat the whole purpose of creativity because it could deter "mental discipline and mastery of subject matter" [Dellas and Gaier, 1970].

104   Icarus and Daedalus, according to this woodcut made in 1493, took a conventional approach to flying; they tried to mimic birds' flight—Icarus failing, falling into the sea (*Bettmann Archive*)

Students in the classroom can be aided in improvisation. They are instructed to examine objects or events we all know and then to change them in their imaginations. Thus, a common object is named, and they must deliberately change its physical shape, size, color, texture, and the like, to "see what happens." In the case of a described event, they must change what led up to it and suggest what would then follow.

One method for teaching creative thinking is creative in itself. Students or employes are encouraged to think about problems from the viewpoint of another organism; that is, they are to pretend to be some creature from the animal world and try to figure out that organism's solution to the problem. One interesting result grew out of this procedure. The space program was faced with the problem of devising a way of sealing space suits. (The zipper we know is not airtight.) During a creative brainstorming session, someone suggested having insects run up and down the zipper area manipulating little latches—and this idea led to an actual, workable, airtight latch-zipper [Gordon, 1961].

It is thought-provoking to carry creativity training to its ultimate extreme, as at least one author has done. He suggests that if we want to truly induce completely creative thinking, we should teach children to question the Ten Commandments, patriotism, the two-party system, monogamy,* and the laws against incest† [Henry, 1963].

SUMMARY

Aptitude tests attempt to measure specific intellectual potential for specific tasks—for example, mechanical ability or clerical ability. Achievement tests, however, are measures of how well one has done in a specific area—for example, history or English.

"Creativity" is a construct based primarily on testing. Tests that measure a person's ability to diverge from the expected are frequently used to locate people who can be labeled "creative." The tests of creativity do indeed seem to measure something other than traditional "intelligence," and some studies strongly suggest that this ability is part of the broader, real-life intelligence which the IQ test cannot get at.

Persons labeled "creative" are frequently a problem in school; they do well on achievement tests, but they tend to be rebellious and unruly in the classroom. Although they are learning, they have difficulty sticking to the prescribed curricula. Nonstudent creative people are remarkably similar. In general they are independent, think very highly of themselves, tend to dominate, and are highly productive.

One need not be crazy to be creative. Although creative people deviate from society, they generally have full control of their faculties—they just don't like to follow along with the crowd, a preference that fits with their ability to break set.

* Each man having one wife, and vice versa.
† Sexual relations between family members.

PART FOUR
THE
BECOMING
PERSON

CHAPTER SIXTEEN
THE CHILD: SOCIAL DEVELOPMENT

Two stanzas by Lawrence Durrell deserve careful reading. He has captured in a few lines all of childhood—its anarchy, its joy, its games, and its painful, deadly seriousness.

All summer watch the children in the public garden
The tribe of children wishing you were like them—
These gruesome little artists of the impulse
For whom the perfect anarchy sustains
A brilliant apprehension of the present,
In games of joy, of love or even murder
On this green springing grass will empty soon
A duller opiate, Loving, to the drains.

•   •   •

What can they tell the watcher at the window,
Writing letters, smoking up there alone,
Trapped in the same limitation of his growth
And yet not envying them their childhood
Since he endured his own?*

105 Young girls working at a thread-winding machine (*Lewis W. Hine*)

Children have always been an enigma and a problem. They have been thought of as miniature adults and as the opposite, complete blobs. They have been deemed unmanageable, fully trainable, monsters, and angels.

They have been mistreated: Even as late as 1876, the highest court in Massachusetts, in supposed benevolence, held constitutional an act that limited the employment of children to *60* hours a week [Wormser, 1962]. Children have been brainwashed: Books have been published of such heavy moral tone that the youngest of today's readers would wince. In a book typical of the 1830s, *The Parent's Present,* the plot went something like this: guests urged a child to eat something his father had forbidden, since the parents weren't home. "Very true," (that my parents aren't here) the child said, "but God and my conscience are."† [Wishy, 1968].

And the confusion hasn't stopped: Today we are embroiled in a

*From the book *Collected Poems* by Lawrence Durrell; © 1956, 1960 by Lawrence Durrell. Used by permission of E. P. Dutton & Co., Inc., New York.

†Sometime when you are in the library, page through this amazing book, which covers all the wacky things children went through in order to survive in the grown-up world. The book is titled *The Child and the Republic.* See reference section at end of book.

374

106   Learning morality at his mother's knee (*Bettmann Archive*)

controversy about our children becoming too mature too quickly. A typical argument, for instance, is over what age, if any, a schoolchild should be allowed to see plastic models of genitalia.

Meanwhile, psychologists have been on the scene contributing their confusion to the situation; some advocate breast-feeding in all situations; some, strict discipline; some, permissiveness; some stress innate depravity on the part of children; and so forth. This confusion points to one difficulty in understanding a child's thought processes and development: children can't tell you about it for quite a long time, and then when they do speak, what they say is often alien to grownups.

One psychological study of the thirties does stand out. A man-and-wife team of psychologists adopted a chimpanzee, a lovable little seven-month-old female, which they decided to rear exactly like a human child to see what would happen. The chimp grew up with a human brother, and the two were treated identically. Indeed, the parents may have felt some panic for a while, when it seemed that the chimp was learning faster than their son—for example, his eating and drinking habits and obedience behavior were much more developed. Somewhat less than a year later their human son had overtaken and surpassed the chimpanzee in every respect except in physical strength and in the amount of hair he had [Kellogg and Kellogg, 1933].

The studies continue, but nowadays they are usually a little more sedate.

DEVELOPMENTAL PATTERNS OF THE CHILD

Certainly the chimpanzee experiment was not the first child study, but it was a very dramatic one, illustrating a point that is still central to child psychology: Development within species is orderly and specific; it has its own timetable and pattern. The growth rate of the chimp is much more rapid and reaches an apex more quickly. The child, on the other hand, is progressing at *his* own rate and cannot be "taught" until he is ready—that is, until he has reached a level of maturation at which the body and mind are ready to go along with the training.

Indeed, it is speculated with considerable logic that the sequencing and timing of a given species' development are most important factors in how complex the final organism becomes. The child living with the chimp was much slower at first, but later surpassed him because the child developed high-level symbolic ability. It seems that the chimp progressed rapidly, compared to the human, because quick development would have survival value for him in his natural habitat, the jungle. The human child labors under a major disadvantage throughout his younger years: He is not strong or well coordinated; usually he can't walk until he is more than a year old, and his crawling ability will not enable him to flee an enemy. The human child is more helpless than any other creature for a longer period of time.

Skeletal remains and archaeological discoveries suggest that man probably developed in the equatorial climate of Africa where he could survive in his seminakedness and with his helpless children. This region provided vegetables, meat, warm climate, and plenty of trees to hide in at night [McNeill, 1963].

The long developmental stage of the human seems to have at least two advantages. First, it has forced man, who did not have unusual physical skills, to develop his intellectual capacity to provide himself with tools and weapons. Second, it probably has been responsible for the high degree of cultural refinement and elaborate social structure humans have; societies were formed of closely knit males, females, and children for the purpose of protecting and caring for the helpless young ones.

THE INFLUENCE OF HEREDITY AND ENVIRONMENT

You may recall that the Indian child is bound tightly to his mother all the time children of other cultures are "learning to walk"; yet he is able to catch up and walk just as skillfully as an unfettered child. This ability illustrates the phenomenon of *maturation,* which in its formal sense refers to an orderly and sequential process of physical development. The importance of this process may be seen in the case of trying to "teach" a child to talk. It just can't be done until the physiological mechanisms of the body are ready for it. Of course, some stimulation from the environment is necessary—the parents have to do some talking so that the child will be able to learn sounds and words, but any formal training before the body is ready is fruitless [Strayer, 1930].

So-called intelligence training is another good example. Many devices on the commercial market claim to improve a child's intelligence. This isn't about to happen until the brain is ready; there is no such thing as getting a head start on the other kiddies. All the nerve cells of the body and brain are present at birth, but they must grow, develop, and branch out, and the best and only way to help this process is to feed the child. Once the child is ready, however, all manner of environmental factors play a role in development: health habits, diet, books in the home, "Sesame Street," and possibly devices for "training intelligence." In fact, recent studies have indicated that during the first two years many children will show evidence of being slow intellectually and then will suddenly catch up [Kagan, 1973]. The best that can be done is that the child be provided with a good environment. He will use it when ready.

107   It has been claimed that the "wild child," a boy who grew up alone in the woods, with no human contacts until a French doctor found him, had become a wild animal (*film by Truffaut, THE WILD CHILD, United Artists*)

The *basic* potential for development in any area is inherited from one's parents. They provide the equipment with which the child is to work. Early physical behavior patterns are remarkably regular. To demonstrate this point, we can call on Dr. Arnold Gesell, a man whose fame in child development equals that of Dr. Spock. His institute has carried on what is probably the most elaborate and lengthy series of child studies ever done.

He comments on an unusual case which he ran into among the thousands he studied, an incident which reflects the strong drive and control that inherited behavioral characteristics exercise on the body. The study involved identical twins; identical twins share the same inherited structure because they are formed from only one egg in the mother, whereas fraternal twins come from two eggs. Therefore, the identical twins inherit identical characteristics. At 28 weeks, two youngsters, identical twins, were put in the sitting position. Even with their legs spread apart, *both* of them would "rebound backward in an automatic manner resembling a sharp spring-like action of a knifeblade snapping into position." Among all his cases, Dr. Gesell had never seen such a reaction. That it was happening twice, right before his eyes, at the same time, *and* that within a week both youngsters simultaneously stopped having the reaction, is a remarkable demonstration of the degree to which the intricacies of bodily behavior can be exactly arranged, in sequence, by inheritance [Gesell, 1929]. The importance of inherited characteristics and physical development cannot be underrated in their effect on maturation.

The subtleties of inheritance often pop up in strange places. Tolerance for alcohol among adults has been found to be an inherited characteristic; one adult can drink an ounce of alcohol and become as tipsy as another who drinks three ounces [Jersild, 1968]. Of importance, however, is that we can alter this basic trait by gradually increasing our tolerance for certain behaviors. Such a modification was mentioned earlier in regard to homeostasis. For example, some groups have contests to see who can drink whom "under the table." The pros in this field have obviously altered their basic physiological tolerance for alcohol; for the uninitiated, similarly large amounts of alcohol would be fatal. An alteration is possible, however, only after the body has established itself, so to speak. Thus, through maturation we become able to run, but given the proper characteristics, through continued practice we could become track stars.

We discussed imprinting earlier in the book. At a certain time of life the duckling was ready to receive "mother" in whatever shape she might appear, including that of Dr. Lorenz waddling along in a squatting position. It seems rather obvious that the potential for imprinting is inherited, but once it is present, the environment can enter in: Some mother has to be provided for the process to be successful.

The degree to which an animal responds to the environment also seems to be inherited. Some few ducklings are minimally preprogrammed for a mother imprint. If you mate two of this type of duckling, their offspring also show little imprinting behavior. Here we have a case of heredity controlling the amount of the environment which the organism can let in [Hess, 1959].

Although physical maturation is required for the emergence of behavior, then, the environment can alter the specifics of a given behavior.

And, of course, the development of the body itself can clearly be influenced by environmental factors. A great deal of nervousness or fear in a child, for example, can produce sleepless nights, loss of appetite, and stomach troubles, to mention but a few physical changes obtained from environmental factors. Malnutrition can result in severe vitamin deficiencies and altered body chemistry. Proper food is especially critical in early years because without it cell division and growth of the brain may be retarded [Dayton, 1969]. Overeating can put a strain on the heart. The list is endless—you can add to it. The point to all this discussion is that both heredity and environment interact in complex ways to produce what we are and what we will become.

PATTERNS OF MATURATION

Patterns of maturation are essentially the same for all children. However, the *timing* of development can vary. The pattern of learning to walk, for example, is an orderly sequence—crawling, holding on to a chair or table, and walking—but the exact time at which any of these events will occur for a particular child is variable. The child will walk at about fifteen months, but new mothers often engage in a continuous contest to compare their children with others in the neighborhood. If Johnny walked at fourteen months and Tommy at sixteen months, then Johnny's mother may hold her son's supposed brightness over the other mother's head. These battles are based on a fallacy: Only a negligible correlation exists between motor development (physical skills) and later intelligence [Jones, 1949]. Of course, one must take this statement within the bounds of reason and logic. A child who is *very* slow to walk probably has lower intelligence, but the matter is quite complex. Slowness in learning to walk usually means something physiological is wrong with the child, which in itself is likely to influence intelligence. Very bright children can be moderately slow in walking if they lack the motivation to walk or even if they are overweight [Dennis, 1943].

Each child, then, unless something drastic seems wrong with him, should be allowed to develop on his own, according to his individual rhythm. Providing the opportunities to learn is important, but forcing the child will do far more harm than good because he will just become frustrated at his lack of ability.

growth cycles

Not all parts of the human being develop at the same rate. Growth follows a *cycle* so that some areas develop more rapidly, some more slowly, some spurt or increase dramatically, all in a short period of time. For example, at age eight, 95 percent of the child's brain development is complete, whereas the body as a whole has reached only 45 percent of its potential, and the reproductive system, which will cause some concern during adolescence, is only 10 percent developed [Harris et al., 1930].

social development

Most present theories of a child's social development are built on a rather negative foundation. An early theorist, who is out of vogue now, proposed

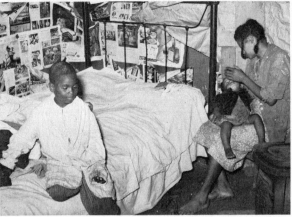

108-109-110 The effects of diet and environment on these children's ability to learn can easily be imagined (*Culver; Dorothea Lange; UPI*)

that the source of just about all troubles for mankind is the trauma of birth itself.* Dr. Otto Rank, who wrote during Freud's era, pointed out that the child lives in a warm and secure place, the womb, during the nine months of the mother's pregnancy. Then suddenly this child is thrust out into a cold, unfriendly environment. From this birth trauma, he theorized, none of us fully recovers; instead we carry around a degree of insecurity, and for some people the insecurity is so overwhelming that they collapse psychologically and are unable to operate in a productive manner [Rank, 1929]. You may have heard it said that someone wants to go "back to the womb." This little saying comes from Rank's theory.

Even though Rank's theory is no longer popular—probably because it is oversimplified and vague—it does lay the groundwork for understanding many theories that *are* currently in favor. Basically, many contemporary theories stress that the child becomes a social creature by bowing to the will of the parents because the child, finding himself in a frightening and insecure world, knows that only his parents are there to protect him.

More specifically, at this point, remind yourself of Harry Stack Sullivan's theory, which is typical of social development theory. You may recall that he stressed relationships between people as critical for the formation of an adjusted and balanced personality. In his eyes, no relationship could be more crucial to the child than the one with his mother. Sullivan said that a mother possessed either a "good nipple" or a "bad nipple." Basically, he used these rather graphic expressions to illustrate that when mother and child are not in harmony, the child sees the mother as dangerous and threatening, even though she should provide the security he needs after being flung out of the womb into the world. Naturally, a poor relationship between mother and child will be fraught with fear and anxiety. The child, therefore, will conform to the mother's desires in order to win or keep her favor; this need for security requires the learning of social amenities, such

* Trauma is an overwhelmingly upsetting experience.

379

as not going to the bathroom under the kitchen table, and other customs of society.

Some fairly recent theorists—for example, Dr. Karen Horney*—have combined the ideas of Rank and Sullivan, to some extent, in emphasizing that to the child the world is a threatening place, by its very nature, because he is helpless and needs the mother to temper his anxiety. This theory goes a long way toward explaining those people—we all know some—who tend to be very dependent and demanding as grownups. According to Horney, this sort of person is still seeking to reduce the anxiety he felt as a child, and he does this by demanding constant reassurance, even as an adult [Horney, 1950].

fears and anxieties   These theories would not be of much interest except for evidence which indicates that the child does indeed suffer from some of the problems mentioned.

First, an inherited component again seems to be at work, especially in the early years, for identical twins show fears that appear and disappear at about the same time [Freedman and Fraser, 1966]. A young child's fears seem to be quite specific—the most prominent, until the age of two, being fears of pain, falling, strange people, and most of all, noise.

Next comes the issue of anxiety. No term in the world seems harder to define. Experimenters who design a study in which they use anxiety as one of the factors measured (for example, the study in Chapter 2) have more than their share of troubles because they have to figure out some method for *objectively* defining what anxiety is. Often they are forced into a corner and have to rely on a person's report that he feels anxious. In any case, personality theorists have trouble defining anxiety, so we can probably get by with a definition of anxiety in children as a vague but pervasive feeling of being afraid. In fact, the major distinction between fear and anxiety is that fear is specific: You are afraid of a bear standing two feet in front of you; you are afraid of losing your job because you just lost the company $50,000 in sales. Anxiety, on the other hand, is a general feeling of nervousness in which you find it hard to pinpoint exactly what is upsetting you. Anxiety is characterized by sweating hands, feet, and armpits and sometimes by rapid heartbeat and difficulty in swallowing. Anxiety has no specific object of fear clearly in focus: You may feel anxious when walking down an alleyway in a rundown area of town, even though no one is around; you may be anxious about the possibility of losing your job, *but you don't know why;* it is just a feeling.

Child development theorists hypothesize that the youngster suffers from anxiety as the result of having been thrown into an alien world; he is afraid, but he does not know why. The ability of the mother to relieve the anxiety then builds a bond between them, and he must rely on her.

* Pronounced "Horn-eye."

All this makes logical sense to the adult, but with the young child we have no way of determining whether such anxiety is present. The barrier to this knowledge obviously is communication. However, if we define anxiety as fears of the unknown, then these fears do appear, and with greatest intensity some time during the third and fourth years. Comedian Bill Cosby does a routine in which a child smears Jello all over the kitchen floor so the monsters will slip and fall when they come to get him. We probably laugh at this bit because we can remember quite vividly some of our own experiences, which, though perhaps not as silly, were certainly just as frightening. In any case, by the age of four, anxieties have definitely set in; typical fears of the four-year-old are of the dark and of being alone [Jersild and Holmes, 1935]. Animal, bug, and monster fears, which are also prevalent at this time, are probably learned from the parents since very young children give no sign of shying away from such delicacies as cockroaches, snakes, frogs, what have you. By *inference*, however, the fear of being alone at least suggests anxiety, since no specific object of fright is present. Thus, those who support the anxiety theory maintain that it can exist before the age of four but not be evident because the child does not express it clearly. There really is no way of knowing for certain.

the role of the mother   Although we can't prove that a child has anxieties in his very young years, it is still a possibility. We *can* establish, however, that the child has fears, and at least in this area there is support for theories which state that a child needs his mother as a source of comfort.

It may be worthwhile to examine some of the evidence that a mother has influence over her child, even though the point seems obvious.* Some evidence comes from the study, mentioned earlier, of the need monkeys have for contact comfort when they are frightened; the monkeys chose the terrycloth mother in preference to the wire-mesh mother when frightened, even though feeding had taken place at the wire-mesh mother. We can assume, without stretching the point beyond credibility, that the child likewise benefits from being touched and loved. The fact that children who were left in understaffed orphanages tended to die reinforces the suggestion that there is a need for contact comfort. Fairly recent studies with human children indicate that they need social stimulation, or what we might call "being around people," as well as being touched by them. When deprived of social contact, children actively seek out someone to come into the room with them [Rosenhan, 1967].

Further evidence of a social stimulation process comes from studies of the act of smiling, which is a most unusual behavior seemingly reserved

111   Motherless monkeys huddle together for "contact comfort"—just as humans do (*Harry Harlow*)

---

*At first, taking the trouble to demonstrate "the obvious" may seem ridiculous, but a science should never take anything for granted. It was taken for granted that the earth is the center of the universe. It was taken for granted that a spider can't walk out of a circle of unicorn dust.

for human use. Smiling occurs long before it is clearly a social act—that is, some internal stimulus creates the smiling: Babies in the first month will smile when there is no one around. By the second month smiling occurs more often in response to some stimulus such as a pleasant sound or a caress, but it does not seem to be a matter of learning by imitation at the beginning because blind children will smile to the same type of stimulus [Jersild, 1968]. Later, however, the smile occurs in response to certain kinds of social stimulation such as being picked up or being smiled at, so a natural response becomes conditioned to certain events [Fitzgerald and Porges, 1971]. At about 6 to 8 months the baby begins to smile only for his mother, father, or other familiar person, becoming wary of strangers. By the tenth month the child begins to show strong attachment to his mother, and he demonstrates considerable distress at her absence [Coates et al., 1972]. The significance of the mother and the child's psychological dependence on her seems clearly established.

An issue with which psychologists have been struggling for many years is the one about breast-feeding an infant. Breast-feeding could be of critical importance in the child's social development, since it touches so directly on whether he feels loved. Many dire tales have circulated about the effects of lack of breast-feeding, but these stories have not been substantiated. The most recent evidence seems to indicate that no *necessary* correlation exists between breast-feeding as such and psychological maladjustment [Heinstein, 1968]. I use the word *necessary* here because the motivation behind the mother's decision not to breast-feed her child becomes important. If she refuses to breast-feed the child because she doesn't want him, then the issue of the child's adjustment is not going to hinge on breast-feeding in any case; instead, the mother's whole outlook toward him will probably tend to be negative. Much has been made about the lack of proper feeding and things like thumb-sucking, which some have claimed is a bad thing. But, the deeper we go, the less obvious such claims become because from birth on the female has a greater mouth-sensitivity than the male and is a much more persistent thumb-sucker. This *may* account for the fact that more women than men are obese or have trouble giving up smoking, but note that we are dealing here with an inherited difference, not necessarily a psychological problem [Korner, 1973].

In any case, mothers who don't want to breast-feed are often unable to do so. The desire not to breast-feed, although a psychological factor, in itself results in a physiological change in which the supply of milk the mother can provide decreases the more she wants not to breast-feed her child [Newton, 1968]. To try something in the way of compulsory breast-feeding would, in the long run, be a failure, producing frustration and negative feelings in the mother toward the child.

In many cases, mothers who do not want to breast-feed tend to associate breast-feeding with sexual activity and to feel a certain repugnance toward it for that reason. On the other hand, other women quite often find some sexual gratification in breast-feeding [Sears, 1957]. In this case, assuming that this pleasure does not make them feel inhibited or guilty, a mutual sensual bond (in the positive sense) can develop between mother and child. The contact of breast-feeding aids in normal, healthy development only if it is voluntary; the mother-child relationship seems to provide plenty of other opportunities for mothers who do not breast-feed to give similar love-service as they handle and care for their children.

Breast-feeding continues to be infrequent in the United States, with social pressure against it in public. It is a sad commentary on our rather weird society that the breast can be suggestively exposed in order to sell cars, but it is taboo to expose it to feed one's child.

learning social behavior

Just about any learning theory discussed in this book can be applied to some aspect of the child-socialization process. Skinner's operant conditioning is certainly appropriate. In some cases, Pavlov's classical conditioning fits, and, of course, Dollard and Miller's learning theory, with its Freudian approach, can be used. An interesting union of the Freudian, Dollard-and-Millerian, and Skinnerian approaches has been developed by a psychologist, Dr. Robert Sears [Maier, 1965]. His theory provides a rather detailed explanation of how a child might actually learn some of the social behavior his parents require of him.

112   A letter to Ann Landers (*Ann Landers*)

Q. I'll be brief and to the point. We live in a highclass neighborhood. Trashy people can't afford to buy homes in this section. Six months ago a certain young couple bought the house next door. They have two children—an infant girl and a little boy, about two and a half years old. The mother allows the boy to run around the yard nude. I find this very embarrasing and my husband doesn't like it either. Is there a law against it? We don't want to call the police but if our neighbors are violating an ordinance perhaps we should.

I had some ladies in for bridge yesterday and that naked kid next door was standing right in front of our house. He is cheapening our property. Please tell us what to do.

A. The sight of a two-and-a-half-year-old boy with no clothes on does not offend me in a house or a yard, but in our society people who appear in public are expected to wear some covering, and this means people of all ages. This is not a matter for the police, but do suggest to the mother that she put some clothing on the boy for protection against injury, if for no other reason.

According to Sears, the child comes into the world helpless and dependent, although he is too young to fully realize his dependence, as we adults may do. However, by *repetition* of the mother's behavior as she cares for him and fulfills his needs, the child *learns* the role of dependency [Sears, 1965]. In other words, he learns that crying will get attention; he learns that cooing and salivating sweetly gets a smile or a tickle; he learns that even throwing up on the rug gets attention, although not always the desired kind. In other words, he learns the role of being dependent on the mother for attention. Each time the child acts in a dependent way, his mother assists him, thus reinforcing the connection between *mother* and *satisfaction;* during this process, he reduces the anxiety which he feels because he is helpless in the world. At the same time this process is going on, the child is learning the procedure which his mother follows in gratifying his needs—for example, feeding him and cleaning him [Sears, 1957].

Then suddenly comes that unpleasant time called *weaning* when a child is removed from the bottle; just as bad, he is toilet-trained. All manner of unpleasant things, from his point of view, begin to occur. The dependency the child has learned will no longer elicit help; instead, his mother becomes uncooperative. Since the child has already learned what his mother does, he takes care of his own dependency exactly as she did—for example, feeding and cleaning himself. Now, once the child does these things, he is reinforced by his mother for the imitation—"Why, you did it yourself! Good boy!" *Imitation* has thus become rewarding, and the long socialization process of continuing to imitate her and continuing to be reinforced for it has begun. He will be trained by imitation in manners, social behavior, boy-girl behavior, and so forth.

THE EFFECT OF CULTURE AND FAMILY ON CHILDREN

We have been concerned indirectly with the effects of child-rearing practices on the later development of children and, by inference, with whether the child will turn out to be "normal." I will have a good bit to say on this topic later in this chapter and later in the book, but it might be worthwhile at this point to mention that child-rearing patterns are far from universal, even though we tend to think of the close mother-child relationships prevalent in the United States as being the norm. Even cultural subgroups in the United States are not uniform in their child-rearing practices. Chinese-Americans are reared in a very strict, but friendly, environment in which the children are directly responsible for their behavior, which reflects on the honor of the family. In contrast, Jewish and Protestant middle-class groups are notably permissive in their child-rearing techniques [Kriger and Kroes, 1972]. Thus, treatment of children is a direct reflection of cultural standards, but no evidence supports the notion that one way is the best—or the worst—or that one child-rearing practice consistently turns out "better" children than another.

deviancy   If we assume that child rearing affects adult life, a number of interesting studies have shown that deviants from the normal, in the *non*creative sense (the mentally disturbed), are typical in *all* societies regardless of child-rearing practices. In the United States we are prone to hospitalize people who demonstrate eccentricities; in most other countries, where neither money nor facilities are available, most such individuals are tolerated rather than institutionalized. The exact nature of the deviance that appears varies from country to country, and from group to group, but no evidence suggests that any society is doing such a good job of producing supernormals in its population that it needs to be proud. Even extremely sheltered and protective societies, in which people live "close to nature" and have all the necessities of life, don't have an enviable record. Some have better records than others—for example, a group called the Hutterites—but even they have their problems.

The Hutterites are a religious group living under a form of community rule in which everyone has the same living standard as everyone else. They do not suffer from lack of life's necessities because they are self-supporting and highly agricultural. Competition is minimal. Children are very much loved and carefully cared for; as they grow older, they mature within the framework of a solid community. Investigators have studied the Hutterites because rumor had it that they suffered from no mental illness. The fact is that while the Hutterites do not have, in proportion, the major mental illnesses found in the United States as a whole, they do suffer in reasonably large numbers from *depression,* a severe reaction in which a person feels he has little to live for. This depression could, in fact, result from the strict way of life they lead [Eaton and Weil, 1955].

None of this is to suggest that within a given group certain practices by parents do or don't lead to problems for the children. The specific issue at hand is whether any universally good child-rearing practices can be identified—and the answer probably is no. Sometimes we hear the complaint that Americans today are too permissive. The author of one study about the effects of family structure on children demonstrates that modern Greek culture is one of the few remaining in which the father has sole and total authority. Complete submissiveness is demanded of the children, although they are loved deeply. From the viewpoint of mental health, the presence of an authoritarian father has made little difference; Greek children are not all falling apart. In fact, their delinquency and dope addiction rates are almost negligible.

If the author's hypothesis is correct, this type of child rearing reduces the drive for achievement and has had only technological effects, in the sense that Greece is not considered very progressive in industrial development and innovation.* Still, some problems exist. These children,

_____
* This may be a blessing. Have you tried breathing lately?

when they grow up, do not seem to have the drive for productivity of their American counterparts [Triandis, 1969]. This hypothesis is interesting to pursue along another line. You may recall that creative children are those who have a habit of wandering off on their own and cultivating individualistic ideas. An authoritarian atmosphere tends to stifle this kind of creative development.

communal living: Child-rearing practices in the past decade have come under tremendous
the kibbutz   scrutiny, both in the popular press and in scientific journals, to some extent because of the Israeli kibbutz, in which is practiced a large-scale and unique method of child rearing. The word *kibbutz* comes from Hebrew for "group" and suggests what the society is: a group of people living an isolated, communal sort of existence together [Neubauer, 1965]. The kibbutz communities were formed because Israel needed a full work force in agricultural production and because many people apparently wanted to live a freer life [Bettelheim, 1969].

One unusual aspect of the kibbutz is that all children live together, separated from their parents, although they see them regularly, usually in the evening before going to bed. The rest of the day they are cared for by a selected group of people whose job it is to be substitute parents. Strange as it may first seem, kibbutz society is strongly child-oriented; the children come first whenever they are in need, often to the exclusion of many comforts which the parents might desire. This intense affection for the children may, of course, develop because the parents don't have to cope with the day-in and day-out drudgery of caring for them, or because they suffer guilt from not doing so.

The kibbutz differs from the typical orphanage in at least one important aspect: The children are not living in groups because no one cares about them, nor have they been abandoned or orphaned. Their living arrangement is a chosen way of life, and this makes quite a difference. Further, the groups encompass all children, not just those who are poorly adjusted in some way. Ample opportunity exists, therefore, for any child to find companionship with others who are compatible. In fact, the closeness the children feel with each other seems to be a vital part of the kibbutz child's normal development, as compared with some children in homes for the wayward, orphanages, and the like, where inmates are society's outcasts. The closeness breeds a sense of unity among the children that is often difficult to achieve in our society except in unusual families; in the kibbutz, people of the child's own age are always around who understand his unique world and share it with him.

The development among kibbutz children of a sense of intense loyalty to the group seems to stabilize their personalities, for no signs of major mental disturbance have shown up. Educational achievement equals or exceeds that of comparable American youth, which could result from the feeling of unified purpose which the group tends to foster (although Jews in general are known for high educational achievement) [Rabin, 1958].

About the only notable effect on personality is one similar to that among Greeks: As a whole the youngsters do not have the sense of individuality which is typically found in American youth [Bettelheim, 1969].

Elaborately planned day-care centers for infants are available in the United States. A few of these centers are designed to provide excellent care and stimulating experiences for the youngsters while the mothers are working during the day. Care is exercised that the children are provided with love and affection at this young age, when it is so necessary. Careful experimental studies not available with the kibbutz children have been performed, and the findings are approximately the same as those reported earlier. When compared with a control group of children who lived at home 24 hours a day, youngsters receiving day care in centers were found to differ unnoticeably in the child-mother attachment, to have more peer-group attachment, and to manifest no significant difference in social or emotional development. Of course it is important to remember that day-care centers carefully organized to provide love and stimulation do not make up the majority [Caldwell et al., 1970].

Even with group child-rearing practices, then—barring unusually cruel or bizarre social situations—the behavior of one society or another does not produce greater or fewer misfits, just different types.

SOCIETY AND SEX-ROLE DEVELOPMENT

Lists of numbers are often misleading (and often boring), but the following list, taken from FBI arrest records, is worth examining for a few moments. In a typical recent year a pattern of criminal activity, excluding traffic offenses, developed something like this:

> **Total male arrests:** 4,829,918
> **Total female arrests:** 688,503
> **Arrests for male drunkenness:** 1,408,594
> **Arrests for female drunkenness:** 109,215
> **Arrests for forgery and counterfeiting, male:** 26,515
> **Arrests for forgery and counterfeiting, female:** 6,947

You can infer some intriguing things about male-female roles, or *sex roles*, from these data. Sex role refers to behavior patterns and actions that seem to fit one sex rather than another.

Looking at the statistics, the most striking thing is that males are arrested so much more often than females. At first one may object that this situation is not very strange—but then we are used to the fact that males commit more crimes than females. Barring rape and some types of assault, there is no *basic* reason why this has to be. In a small number of other cultures, female aggressiveness is even greater than male aggressiveness.

Females are fully capable of committing crimes in close proportion to that of men. Take, for example, the crimes of forgery and counterfeiting: neither requires unusual strength or masculine skills, yet the men do most of the work in this area. Why should this be? The answer seems simple enough: There is man's work and there is woman's work, and strangely enough this notion carries over even into crime. The point is that training within a culture is so forceful and so pervasive that even the deviants tend to follow the pattern.

The statistics on drunkenness make the situation even clearer: Some well-versed members of Alcoholic Anonymous have estimated that the ratio of female to male alcoholics is about 1 to 5. Females are more adept at hiding their drinking problem, so arrest records show a ratio of something like 1 to 12 in favor of males. Many different factors may explain this, but they all fit into the sex-role theory. One factor which could account for the difference in arrests is that the woman's place to get drunk is at home, and man's is at the local bar. Furthermore, female drunks are usually escorted by men when they go out, so someone other than a policeman is available to take them home. Even so, a policeman is much more likely to take a woman to her home and a man to jail. Because a general social taboo* works against unusual aggressiveness in women, drunk women don't usually get into fights or disturb the peace with quite the same noise level or frequency as men.

Taking off from this example, we want to try to find out how some of these behavioral differences develop between male and female, and whether they are inherited or primarily the product of a culture.

Freud and the sex role   Sex-role development involves the child's incorporation (taking into himself) of methods of behavior that he learns from his parents. Freud did not explain such learning in the specific terms of Skinner, Sears, or Dollard and Miller. Instead, he referred to the learning process much as a layman would: We learn because we see and imitate; we learn to avoid fear and to seek love because we see and imitate; we learn to avoid fear and to seek love because when they are presented to us we choose one over the other. In other words Freud did not emphasize elaborate learning procedures; learning just occurred.

With that out of the way, according to Freud the first component of sex-role learning is a process of identification. *Identification* is a technique for fighting off the anxiety one feels as a very small child. We identify by modeling our behavior after various behavior patterns of another. For example, the child notices that the parent is able to cope with the environment better than he is, so the child incorporates into himself various characteristics of the parent based on the principle that they are useful.†

---

* A societal restriction against something.
† Strictly speaking, one incorporates by a process of identification.

This process may be a little clearer if we say that identification involves modeling ourselves after others for the purpose of gratifying our needs. For example, how many times have you or your friends said at a basketball game, "We've got to win"—even though you, like most of us, are probably not able to hit the backboard, much less get the ball through the hoop? The term *we* is used in the process of identification; the basketball team becomes a part of us and we become a part of it, and this gratifies our sense of identity with a group, or a school, or a city. And how many times do you wiggle, squirm, and tense your muscles during an exciting movie because you have identified with the hero who is in a predicament? In these cases we probably identify in order to gratify our need for excitement. In just this way, according to Freudian theory, the youngster becomes similar to the parent by identification, only identification is designed to reduce anxiety.

During the early years, the child, male or female, relies most heavily on the mother to take care of him, but identification, in Freudian terms, results from the child's physical characteristics—that is, the boy identifies with the father because the two of them have the same sexual organs, and the girl does the same with the mother. Freud elaborated on this quite a bit more than this brief outline can do, but at least we can use the idea of identification as a starting point when we look at sex-role development [Hutchins, 1952].

biological sex differences   Freud pointed out that each of us has a little male and a little female in us, regardless of our physical appearance, but in most cases the identification was completed with the parents of the same sex. Interestingly enough, chemical analysis has borne Freud out.* The male sex hormone, androgen, and the female sex hormone, estrogen, are both found in members of each sex, but one dominates the other. The dominance apparently produces some of the male and female physical characteristics. But we already know that this is true mostly in the case of animals below the human level; quite a few human males who have been castrated and lost their supply of sex hormones continue to be interested in and participate in sexual intercourse, and the same is true of women. Our discussion of biological factors in male-female behavior patterns would be simple if we were going to deal with mice, but since we are not, it is complicated.

Hormones that instigate actual sexual behavior probably do not

---

*The story of Freud's theory that we are all bisexual is an interesting bit of historical chaos. Freud apparently took the theory from a Dr. Fliess, a nose-and-throat specialist. Fliess based his theory on the idea that we all (supposedly) follow a cycle using the magical numbers of 28 and 23, based on menstrual cycles and the interval between them. Even though most men do not have menstrual cycles, the magic in the numbers seemed to intrigue Fliess. Freud did not go along with the numbers, but he did borrow the idea of bisexuality. Fliess felt that Freud stole it. A nose man got into this area, apparently, because the mucous membrane of the nose swells during sexual excitement [Brome, 1967].

DIANE

113–114 Sex roles and occupational roles are usually learned primarily from a child's parent of the same sex. The mother of Diana the Huntress may not have provided a very strong role-model as wife, mother, and housekeeper! (*Culver*)

operate in young children. These hormones usually become effective during the adolescent period, at which time sex hits the youngster like a sledge-hammer. So we need to turn to other physical factors that relate to sex differences in children. The most obvious is that the boy is heavier and bulkier than the girl all the way up to the age of ten.* There is no question but that during this period the male has superior strength and that this physical superiority will naturally turn him to certain activities in which many girls do not perform. You may recall that earlier it was mentioned that even as infants, males show a higher level of activity than females. These differences, then, are biologically determined, but the culture will super-impose its own standards on these differences [Mead, 1949]. Who, for example, would carry the female's lack of strength to the extreme of saying that she can't even open a door for herself? This bizarre notion could occur only in a society that is making into a norm of behavior a custom that probably originated in a moderate difference in physical constitution.

A disturbing truth has recently been discussed by a *female* psychol-ogist. *Males* have dominated the scene in expostulating ad nauseum† on the psychological and biological nature of women. These discussions have been based in part on two characteristics supposedly found in most animal communities lower than man: The females are submissive (by inference a biological factor), and the sex hormones of males and females *do* differ. However, a few recent studies, for example ones with stumptail monkeys, are calling into question the assumed sexual submissiveness of the female animal as a fixed biological behavior. Female monkeys in this species initiate sexual contact, engage in varied sexual techniques, have orgasms, and in general behave as male animals in the sexual area [Chevalier-Skolnikoff, 1972]. This type of study is important because it casts doubt on the idea that women have a specific biological inheritance making them automatically submissive creatures by nature. It should also be mentioned that animals are not able to change their social structures because they are not bright enough. So even if one could conclude that animals' sex-role differences are to a major extent biologically inherited, you cannot assume the same for women for a very simple reason: Hormonal behavior can be overridden by psychological factors, as in the case of inability to respond in sexual activity (frigidity in women, impotence in men), which occurs even without a physical hormonal imbalance or disturbance [Weisstein, 1969b].

Through the years, in a substantial number of instances, the sex of an individual has been ambiguous. The general term applied to these people is *hermaphrodites*. The external organs may not indicate what sex the person is; he or she may have a combination of sexual apparatus, or the

---

* At the age of ten this changes for a short period of time. See Chapter 18.
† To a sickening degree.

internal structure may reflect one sex and the external another. In general, with some psychologically painful exceptions, such a child has been capable of developing sex-role behavior in line with how he has been reared—that is, as male or female—which demonstrates the power of psychological forces over physiological constitution. Admittedly, the biological forces have some effect, and many (biological) girls who are reared as boys, and vice versa, have something "gnawing at them"; they do not feel that everything is in proper perspective as far as their sex roles are concerned. However, for our purposes the point is that social influence can be strong enough to do a fairly good job of overriding basic biological sex [Harrison, 1970]. This fact also suggests strongly that so-called female behavior versus male behavior may not exist except within the framework of society [Money, 1961b].

It is important to emphasize that psychologists don't really know very much about the *true* nature of women—or too much about men, for that matter. We will be discussing social sex-role development in the next section—but remember, we are talking about how people are trained, not what they are.

psychological sex differences

Early sex-role identification is forced on the child in blatant as well as subtle ways. Toys for boys are in stark contrast with those for girls. There is no inherent reason a boy would not want to play with miniature doll furniture while continuing to be enthusiastic about playing with miniature tanks or soldiers. In families where children are sent to a nontraditional nursery which reflects the parents' belief that sex roles are not fixed, the children do not show the usual tools-for-boys and spoons-for-girls interest. A control group of traditional children in a traditional school does show distinctive sex differences in toy preference [Selcer and Hilton, 1972]. More subtly, at very young ages girls are expected to be dressed properly and neatly whereas boys can look like they have been playing with sows all day. Girls are usually required to be around when the mother has a family visitor like grandmother; girls are more often expected to attend family functions, run errands, and even attend weddings and funerals of relatives and friends. Boys are more or less allowed to disappear for many of these occasions, setting up for them an early pattern of emancipation which shows up later when the husband disappears for long periods of time, supposedly to play golf or bowl. The girls, then, are being prepared for a domestic role that involves working around the house and being the mainstay of the family [Komarovsky, 1950].

In case you are wondering, societies do indeed thrive in which the men do the cooking and sewing while women go out for the day's hunt. The women, of course, bear the children, but they are then deposited with daddy [Honigmann, 1959].

As would be expected, the effect of the father and mother is critical for any child's sex-role development. For many years, following the Freudian tradition, it was assumed that boys identified with the father and girls with the mother. Now we know that the matter is a little more complicated. Fathers who are very warm and affectionate toward their daughters tend to masculinize them, producing a mild and harmless tomboyishness [Sears, 1966]. On the other hand, extreme strictness, *severe* control of aggressive impulses, or unusual physical punishment tend to feminize both the male and the female child. This result probably can be explained by the fact that the child becomes docile, at least externally, and appears to play a more submissive role.

Children also have some identification with brothers and sisters. Boys who have brothers and girls who have sisters tend to fit traditional male and female sex roles better than children of families where brothers and sisters are mixed. When mixed, the effect of siblings on sex-role development one way or the other is negligible [Sutton-Smith and Rosenberg, 1965]. In families where either the father or the mother is unusually dominant, compared with the other parent, the children tend to identify with the dominant parent, even across sex lines [Heatherington, 1965].

Boys whose fathers were not present during preschool years—that is, up to age five—tend to be less masculine in the sense that they are less aggressive and not quite as active in masculine sports, if these traits are important [Biller, 1970]. Many psychologists seem to assume that men should be football players and women powder puffs for "normality," but this notion is absurd. Certainly men who are not especially athletic experience some discomfort in our male culture, as do women who are not domestic, but even in extreme cases where biological sex (male-female) is ambiguous the rate of major mental disturbance is very low. In this respect mothers without husbands—for example, widows and divorcees—panic unnecessarily. When strikingly feminine behavior does occur in a boy it is not unusual for it to arise in a family where the father is present [Lebovitz, 1972].

The effects of father absence per se do not seem to disrupt children's conceptions of what the male role consists of, nor does it seem to interfere with a child developing a positive feeling toward the father or males in general. A study of lower-class families in the United States in which the father is missing and lower-class families in Japan in roughly the same situation indicates that children develop what appear to be normal, healthy attitudes toward males and the roles males play in a family. This does not negate the importance of the father, though, because in Japan a grandfather is usually present and the children develop more positive attitudes toward him than toward the absent father [Aldous and Kamiko, 1972]. The moral of these studies seems to be twofold: Children undoubtedly benefit from having both a mother and father, but disaster does not strike because a father is missing. These statements are made, however, on the assumption that the child is allowed to make friends with or be exposed to some adult male figures. Daughters of widows, for example, develop a fear of men unless some model is provided [Hetherington, 1973].

The Freudian hypothesis appears correct that identification of some sort does take place. This is especially true, for example, when the father is dominant; the son will be quite masculine. Otherwise, this identification is not simple and does not follow father-son and mother-daughter lines. A complex interplay goes on between the dominance of the parent and the identification. Some daughters identify with fathers; some sons identify with mothers; some identify with both; and the brothers and sisters have their effect [Stevenson, 1967].

the future of sex roles in America

Trying to guess the future is a difficult business, and one that has no place in a psychology book. However, certain trends do stand out, and we should touch on them, because children born this year and the next and the one after that are going to be affected by what is going on now.

Striking evidence indicates that in the present generation young females are moving rapidly toward effecting an integration of the sexes. Employment and education are two areas of profound change: No longer, at least on the books, is discrimination allowed in hiring practices or school enrollment procedures.

Experiments have shown that women are actually a little brighter than men until high school, at which time they begin—as a group—to falter in their intellectual prowess [MacCoby, 1966]. Unless we take the preposterous position that female intelligence suddenly begins to decline exactly at high school age, we have to admit that this slowdown is the result of a purely social process in which men have been fairly adept in convincing women that they are supposed to be pretty stupid. The attention being given to such social phenomena as the supposed decline in female intelligence will gradually change the intellectual role of women in the future.

Behavior such as that found in the high school girl's decline in intelligence apparently has its origin in childhood conceptions of the female role. In this regard, one author maintains that there is no such thing as sex role unless it is tied to marriage and the family [Sprey, 1972]. If you think about this for a minute, you'll realize that it is really very hard to conceive of there being an issue of the male role and the female role if it weren't for family arrangements in a society. In any case, when the mother in a family is relatively satisfied with her role as a housekeeper, the daughter grows up with approximately the same feelings. When the father is dominant in the marriage, again the daughter leans toward the more traditional housewife role. The woman who desires freedom from the role of housewife most often comes from a family where neither parent is dominant or where the mother is very dissatisfied with her role [Lipman-Blumen, 1972].

Notable changes have taken place in the way women handle their menstrual periods. In the 1940s and 1950s, women were expected to disintegrate during this time of the month; they "couldn't" swim, play games, or, in some cases, show up for work, and it was considered dangerous to take a bath. In other words, women were encouraged to be inactive.* As late as the middle 1960s we find numerous experimental studies still trying to dispel these myths. As you would expect, they show that neither exercise nor a bath—not even swimming—is injurious to health or well-being during the menstrual period [Siegel, 1960].

Attempts are being made to solve the problem of personality changes in the woman just prior to menstruation. These changes are predictable and seem directly related to a chemical alteration. For example, one study examined the level of anxiety in normal females just before and after menstruation began. The difference showed anxiety very high before and low after (significant $< .0005$ level). Other typical symptoms are irritability, depression, and a fear of death [Bardwick, 1971]. Recent studies with males indicate that they also follow a monthly rhythm with changes in mood, usually with a low point of apathy or indifference occurring at least once [Luce, 1971]. Presumably the future holds a chemical treatment for these unpleasant reactions.

Studies in the late 1960s comparing the sexual freedom of women at that time with their freedom during the 1940s seem to demonstrate that while sexual relations do not begin any earlier, the women who do engage in intercourse feel less guilt, more conviction that such behavior is appropriate, and most of all, a belief that women have a right to such freedom [Gebhard et al., 1967; Gebhard, 1969].

A comparison of *college students* in another study shows notable changes in sexual behavior between 1958 and 1968. The authors hypothesize that adult hypocrisy and consequent student skepticism about adult rules may be causative factors in the change. Premarital intercourse by women in the dating category rose from 10 percent in 1958 to 23 percent in 1968; in the going-steady category, from 15 percent to 28 percent; and among the engaged, from 31 percent to 39 percent. This study, like the one mentioned in the previous paragraph, indicates that "guilt feelings" have decreased notably during the same period [Bell and Chaskes, 1970]. The rather dramatic changes that have taken place in female attitudes toward sexuality

* Sometimes this came in handy. In the Old Testament, Rachel was involved in the thievery of some pictures. When the house was about to be searched, she stuffed them into the "camel's furniture" and lay down on top of it. The place was completely searched, except for the area where she was lying, because, as she pointed out to the searcher, she could not move: "the custom of women is upon me" (Genesis 31:35).

are found in a more recent study than the one reported above. Comparing 1965 females with 1970 females, the experimenter found that 70 percent thought premarital sex immoral in 1965 and only 34 percent in 1970, a change of 36 percentage points. Asked if a woman who had sex with a great number of men was immoral, 91 percent thought so in 1965 but only 54 percent felt this was true in 1970 [Robinson et al., 1972]. A new standard of sexual freedom for women does seem to be arriving.

Courts are beginning to recognize the right of a woman to sue in injury cases in which the husband is disabled from an accident in such a way that he cannot engage in sexual relations; formerly, this prerogative belonged only to the man if his wife was so injured. Nonetheless, the struggle continues with the belief found in the 1800s that women who claim sexual feelings are engaging in "vile aspersions."* Textbooks for medical doctors are really incredible in their ability to perpetuate clearly erroneous myths about females. Some books claim that women are not able to derive pleasure from sexual activity, that a woman's sex desire is based on a need to be inferior, that a woman cannot dominate in a sexual relationship, and that women desire procreation rather than pleasure from sex. These types of things appear in textbooks as late as 1971 [Scully and Bart, 1972; Brown, 1966].

115   *(UPI)*

In fact, as more studies emerge, the image of the male as a strong, rational, and aggressive individual is becoming rather muddled—at least in the sexual area. In what certainly is an unusual series of events, women in Greece have moved ahead of the men in their sexual liberation. That's not the strange part, though. Since the males want to marry virgins, the woman will have premarital intercourse with her fiancé until time for the marriage, at which point she will have an operation which gives her the anatomical appearance of a virgin [Safilios-Rothschild, 1972]. Meanwhile, back in the United States, mental health workers are reporting a dramatic increase in the number of males who feel the woman is being excessive in her demands for sex, which the men can't keep up with. According to the men, women have become too aggressive, and since many males are unable to handle this they seek professional help to restore their sexual ability [Crist, 1971; Grotjohn, 1971]. Obviously we are dealing here with a threat to the male ego. In a dead-giveaway statement one male patient exclaimed, "Who calls the shots [in sex], anyway?" [Ginsberg, 1972].

And finally, women's interest patterns—that is, goals, purposes, and activities—are shifting into alignment with those of men and, as would be expected, at the same time women demonstrate considerably less docility and acquiescence in their attitudes and outlook, especially the younger ones [Eagly, 1969]. At Stanford University, for example, only 4 percent of the

*Disgusting falsehoods.

female graduates in 1972 expected to be housewives. In 1965 for every six men planning to enter a profession only one woman also planned to do so. By 1972 this had changed to approximately four women for every six men [*The Stanford Woman*, 1972].

SUMMARY

All animals, including the highest, man, follow a specific sequence and timing in their development. Man is the weakest of creatures and takes the longest to develop, but the end product is the most complex level of intelligence known at the present time. The developmental pattern is called maturation and is influential in both physical and mental development. Although the *sequence* is fixed, the exact rate of maturation is an individual thing—for example, some children walk earlier than others, although this fact has no deep and important significance.

One of the earliest theories of development stressed that the child, upon arriving in the world, is faced with "birth trauma" after the peacefulness of the womb. Even though this specific theory is no longer very popular, it points out a common denominator found in the greater proportion of theories of child development. The child is a helpless creature, at the mercy of adult figures, and in order to survive in this world he must learn to conform to the demands of adults. The basic theory is that the child feels anxious in the world and relies on his parents to reduce this anxiety. This reduction comes about through imitation of the mother's actions and through the constant rewards he receives for conforming to her behavior.

No ideal method of child rearing exists. Some of the stricter societies reduce many social ills like delinquency and drug addiction, but they do so at the expense of full development of individual psychological freedom in the child.

The American family unit is not necessarily the perfect arrangement. Kibbutz children and children from very large families seem to survive quite well. Although the mother-child intimacy always held up as the ideal is pleasant enough, studies indicate that well-run day-care centers for working mothers are more than adequate and do not necessarily turn out a distorted child.

Culture exercises one of its strongest influences on sex-role development, which basically means that males and females are trained differently. In our culture the male generally is trained to be aggressive and the female passive. Traditionally, this process has been considered the result of the child's identification with the same-sexed parent, although many variations on this theme have appeared, and the situation is not simple.

If one is honest, he cannot say seriously that any *basic* differences exist between human males and females. Although they are biologically constructed somewhat differently, our society provides little that both sexes cannot do, if they are permitted by society to do it. Boys whose fathers are around at least until they are five years old seem to develop more within the stereotyped male role, but then this pattern may be nothing more than learning. The upheaval in sex roles is a major theme in America today, and we have no reason to anticipate that sex roles will remain as notably different in the future as they have in the past.

CHAPTER SEVENTEEN
THE CHILD DEVELOPS
INTELLECT AND CHARACTER

Aconversation between an experimenter and a four-year-old:

"Do you have a brother?"
"Yes."
"What's his name?"
"Jim."
"Does Jim have a brother?"
"No." [Phillips, 1969]

Is there something wrong with this child? Is his mental development retarded? That little discussion makes one wonder. Yet the answers are simple: not in the least, on either count. We spoke at the beginning of Chapter 16 about children being strange and sometimes incomprehensible creatures; and this exchange is just a sample of the thought processes of a four-year-old.

Until the age of two, roughly, intelligence tests give us few clues to intellectual development. Infant-intelligence tests contain items designed to measure mental development indirectly—items like ability to move the head at an appropriate time, ability to smile or make noise, or, much later, ability to turn the pages of a book. However, as you may have determined from the earlier discussion of the correlation between the age of walking and intelligence, these motor tests are generally of minimal value in determining mental ability as measured later by more sophisticated intelligence tests. Studies suggest that the early phases of development measured by the infant tests are different from the type of development that occurs later. The early tests measure the child's ability to operate on the environment in a physical way, whereas later tests are aimed primarily at mental development [McCall et al., 1972]. Occasionally the infant test and later intelligence tests actually correlate negatively, so we do have problems.

Despite these problems, a great many studies have attempted to understand the mental development of the child. Two leading scientists working in the field of children's cognitive* processes are Dr. Jean Piaget, a Swiss psychologist who has devoted his life to studying this area, and Dr. Jerome Bruner, an American educator. These two men have made remarkably complex, detailed, and thorough studies of thought-process

---

Cognitive in this sense refers to thought processes; the word comes from *cognition*, which, broadly defined, is perception or awareness.

400

development. Each theory takes more than one book to elaborate, and, of course, many other experimenters have done considerable work on cognitive development in children. All this is by way of introduction to the fact that, for better or worse, I have tried in this chapter to integrate their material into a coherent whole, and, for the sake of clarity, I have attempted to avoid as many of the controversies as possible. You can get more detailed and possibly different interpretations by consulting any of the reference sources as we progress.

**the child
at the beginning**

It seems almost impossible to determine what a child is able to see and how accurate his visual mechanisms are in the first 20 weeks—yet these determinations have been made in an ingenious set of experiments. You may recall the "visual cliff experiments" (Chapter 6) and the discussion about whether the child had to learn most of his visual "clues" or whether he had them innately, that is, came into the world with them. The experiments we will discuss demonstrate experimental techniques with very young children which strongly suggest that they come into the world already in possession of an amazing amount of visual integrative ability.

One part of the experiments involved using cubes of various sizes. Babies love games like "peek-a-boo," and by using this game it was possible to condition an infant to turn his head and look *only* at a cube of a certain size (30 centimeters—about 1 foot); someone played "peek-a-boo" only when the child turned his head and looked at the 30-centimeter cube. Once this conditioning had been accomplished, the experiment was ready to progress.

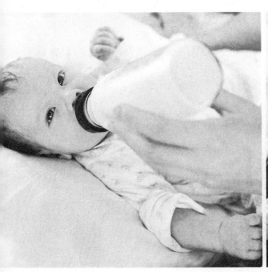

116 Vision dominates in the human child even though he likes to taste everything

First, the experimenters wanted to learn whether a baby a few weeks old is able to determine *actual* distance or is just responding to the size of the retinal object. He has been trained to respond only to a 30-cm cube placed one meter away from him; what will happen if we take this same 30-cm cube and move it *three* meters away? The size of the object on the retina is going to be much smaller than it was when the cube was only one meter away. Yet children generally will respond to this cube as they have been conditioned to, even though the retinal image has become so small. They still recognize it as the 30-cm cube. Hence, the child does possess the ability to determine actual distance, even though he has had no opportunity at this young age to learn it. This ability seems to be basic equipment.

Using cubes again, is it still possible to fool the child, in this case in regard to size constancy and interpretation of distance? You may recall that size constancy refers to our ability to perceive that an object is the same size no matter where it is moved. For example, a cigarette pack moved far away doesn't, in our minds, become smaller; it merely is farther away, but the same size. Or—and this is important—the *reverse* is true: If we see a cigarette pack which is far away but seems to be the same size as a cigarette pack that is close up, then we know that something is wrong with that cigarette pack. It has got to be larger if it is going to look the same that far away. In order to perform such complex interpretations, we need the ability both to perceive size constancy (the cigarette package or the cube remains the same size) and to interpret distance.

Depth perception can be fooled: the corners have been cut from the 9 and the 8 card. In physical reality the 9 is in front, the 8 behind it, and the 10 in the rear (*Felix Cooper*)

So, can you fool the child in these early weeks of life? Does he have both of these abilities? Take a *90-cm* cube and move it three meters away. Now the object the child sees will be the same size *on the retina* (it will appear to be 30 cm square) as the conditioned 30-cm cube. It seems logical that we can fool the child, yet in most cases we can't. Children do not respond with great frequency to the 90-cm cube placed three meters away. They seem almost to be saying, "You've got a 90-cm cube way out there." Although children are not that sophisticated, their visual mechanisms seem to be.

In another area of visual abilities we have been underestimating the infant: in his ability to perceive the solidity of objects. If a child is lying down and you move an object toward him, he shows little reaction. It had been assumed that he had to learn the solidity of objects by a combination of touch and vision. However, it has been discovered that an infant on his back is rarely fully awake. If you sit the two-week-old upright and move an object toward him, he perceives it as solid and tries to ward off the moving object by putting his hand between it and his face.

A child does, of course, have to *learn* many things about his world (and I will mention some of them as we progress), but as you can see, his basic equipment, which seems to include ability to judge size constancy, distance, and solidity, can't be sold short [Bower, 1966, 1971].

You may wonder whether a very young child is much different from other animals in the basic equipment he has which facilitates his special learning ability. In other words, is the human child different from animals? One method for finding out is stimulating certain receptors of the body and then measuring the electrical discharge rate of portions of the cortex. Most of us know, for example, that a dog's life seems to be centered mostly on his nose. This notion can be tested by stimulating various portions of the dog's body—for example, the eye by light, the ear by noise, or the nose by smell. Smell stimulation produces much more diffuse* electrical responses in the cortex than does any other kind of stimulation, thus verifying the importance of this sensory unit. And pig lovers will be pleased to know that nothing turns on the electricity for a pig like fooling around with his snout.

Finally, there is man. He comes into the world well prepared for his specific role; he is maximally specialized for *visual* stimulation, which will dominate all his responses. When given a choice between trusting his vision and trusting some other sense, human beings will use vision†. Visual skills predominate in the learning process as the child moves toward adulthood; especially important is the later development of an ability to read and use word symbols.

At this point we should refer again to the orienting reflex, discussed previously (Chapter 6) in reference to our ability to interpret the world around us by turning our attention to certain objects and events. It is important here to note that sight and sound are most likely to cause an orienting reflex in man, even in the earliest years, so man's abilities are specialized and well integrated. The child is well equipped from the beginning and his visual apparatus is especially useful.

Hopefully you remember something about the visual processing networks discussed in Chapter 6, so it might be interesting to discuss a few recent studies about the development of the child's perceptual networks. First of all you should be aware that most of the neural networks of the brain fully mature *after* the child is born, thus providing an opportunity for environmental influence in this development.‡ For example, monkeys reared from birth in darkness do not have environmental stimulation, and they do not show the ability to gauge various dangers in the environment, nor to follow moving objects when they are freed from their darkened surroundings [Riesen, 1965].

Likewise, the human infant relies on the environment, but the extent

---

*Spread out in many places (in the brain).

†Second in importance for people is hearing, which is critical to speech development [Adrian, 1947].

‡We are dealing now with more abstract visual ideas. This does not contradict the fact that the child has size constancy and depth perception very early. We assume the latter are required in nature for survival.

of learning is regulated by the maturation of the neural networks. A two-week-old infant is most interested in objects with sharp contours or strong light-dark contrast, something you may recall is one of the early stages of the adult human's visual processing network. Presumably this basic response is formed very early and stays with us through life; it is strongest, however, during the first two months. By that time the neural networks have begun to mature and the child has been exposed to objects in the environment. It is at this point in time that he begins to pay particular attention to specific details of objects. For example, if he is shown masks that differ slightly, he will spend considerable time looking them over. We assume that he is trying to group these different faces into a single category; that is, in adult terms, mask A is a "face," mask B is another "face," mask C is another "face," and so forth. Although we are not sure this is what he is doing, it is a good explanation, because by the age of three months he has lost interest in the masks and they bore him. With further maturation, when the child is about a year old, the same masks again become of interest to him and he will examine them at length. The explanation for this behavior, we think, is that by this time he has learned that *differences* in the environment are important. Thus, he has matured enough so that he is trying to organize the meaning of differences and what impact they might have on him, especially whether there is any danger involved for him. Evidence for this assumption is that just about this time—a little over a year—the child begins to fear foreign objects, strangers, and separation from his mother [Kagan, 1972].

What seems to be happening, in sequence, is that the child is moving from basic analysis of the contours of an object, to the grouping of objects, to the relatively sophisticated level where objects are differentiated one from the other and emotional responses are attached to these differences.

PIAGET'S THEORY OF COGNITIVE DEVELOPMENT

Jean Piaget is probably *the* authority on *cognitive development* in children. Piaget divides the development of the child into a few major categories and many subcategories, but the major categories are enough for our purposes.*

Piaget focuses on three categories or stages of cognitive development: the sensorimotor (that is, sensory-motor) stage, the concrete-operations stage, and the formal-operations stage, each of which will be explained in turn. Piaget implies that this developmental sequence is invariable—that is, the three stages develop out of and into each other in order, and the first must precede the second, which must precede the third. In general, his assumption seems to be borne out by the evidence [Zern, 1969]. It cannot

*Except as noted, the core of Piaget's ideas is contained both in his works of 1929 and of 1952.

be taken as dogma, however, because some studies show that the stages do sometimes overlap and that not all children follow this exact pattern [Kofsky, 1966]. But Piaget is close enough to correct that few difficulties can arise when we assume his system to be valid.

the sensorimotor stage

The stage, called *sensorimotor*, occurs during the first two years of the child's development. The child spends his time on two activities, *sensation* and movement (*motor* responses). The first learning experiences, or associations, result from motor operations; for example, the baby looks at, sees, and finally grasps a bottle, thereby receiving pleasurable sensation. These acts are indeed primitive, but motor behaviors are the cornerstone upon which learning experiences of a more complex nature will be built. Another example: for a period the child will kick off his covers; later this movement can become associated with the *feeling* of coldness, and then much later even the word *coldness* can become associated with both the action and the feeling. So, fundamental to the learning process are motor behavior (movement) and its connection with sensation, which is later tied in with symbolism.

At the beginning, actions are part of the object itself; that is, the child does not clearly distinguish between the act of reaching, the bottle itself, and the pulling of the bottle toward his mouth. A little later the action of reaching becomes separate from the bottle because the child reaches and retrieves other objects, too. Thus the bottle becomes but one of many things he can grab.

Once the object has been separated from the action, the child can use a symbol (word) in place of the action and obtain what he needs just by speaking—for example, by saying, "Bottle," to his mother. So the core of language development is tied to this separation of action and object [Neverovich, 1969].

The neural networks of the cortex are assumed to be quite undifferentiated at this early stage; in other words, the nerves have developed no particular pattern that will bring thoughts together into a coherent framework. However, it has been speculated with considerable logic that continued motor responses and sensations begin to develop certain fixed pathways of neural impulses and synaptic connections in the cortex as the child progresses through these actions and stages. An analogy for this change would be the continued overflowing of a river which eventually gouges out "favorite" pathways for the water to flow; the water will then have a tendency to keep flowing through these channels. Using this analogy, the neural "channels" eventually become organized thought processes [Hebb, 1969].

This sensorimotor stage includes an unusual phenomenon, which usually occurs at three to five months of age, and which illustrates the difference between the child's mind and the adult's. If the experimenter arranges the situation so that a toy, a ball, or some similar object, which the child has seen or played with, suddenly disappears (through a trapdoor, for example), the child shows little concern about finding it or even that it is missing. "Out of sight, out of mind" seems to apply perfectly. At first this phenomenon is perplexing to the observer, because children do love their toys. How could the toy disappear and the child seem not to care about its whereabouts? Probably this is best explained by the fact that in the early years objects have no continuity; each object is taken to be part of the environment if it is there and not part of the environment if it isn't. It seems to be that simple. On the other hand, we adults have *learned* that certain objects tend to remain and that certain persons, when they leave, will return.

You may recall that our visual systems are programmed to perceive movement. Well, up to about five months of age the child focuses on movement all by itself and pays little attention to what it is that is moving. For example, if a small white manikin crosses his field of vision, passes behind a screen, and emerges on the other side as a red lion, he continues to follow it as if nothing unusual had happened. Children older than five months typically look on the other side of the screen to see what happened to the manikin. A very basic response to movement itself, then, has gradually changed to a concern about the movement of specific objects—another bit of evidence of maturation and learning [Bower, 1971].

In the adult world overwhelming confusion ensues when objects disappear. "Candid Camera," a television series of a few years ago, once showed a sequence in which a man dining in a restaurant was called to the phone in the middle of his meal. While he was gone, his table and all identifying objects were removed and a palm tree put where he was sitting. When the man returned, his confusion and panic were obvious. Not so for the very young child: The world is what it is for any particular moment.

The experimenter can detect this so-called learning of *object permanency* * in operation by performing a different sort of experiment. If the object is *slowly* obscured from a child's vision by gradually moving a screen in front of it or by slowly dimming the lights around it until it is "gone," the child behaves differently: he looks for the object and seems to expect its return [Bower, 1967]. This kind of study shows the child actually going through the rudimentary stages of learning object permanency. In "real life," the learning process is similar: for example, the mother disappears from the room gradually, rarely falling through a trapdoor, and the child learns to expect her return, especially after she has repeatedly left and come back. In this fashion, objects finally become permanent and expected by the time the child is about a year old.

Interestingly, it may be the attachment of the child for his mother

---

* Objects become a permanent part of one's world in the sense that they are missed when gone.

that starts off or assists in the development of object permanency. One of the first signs of serious concern over missing objects shows up at about ten months—when the mother leaves, the child becomes very distressed and looks for her [Coates et al., 1972]. One might easily speculate that this primitive form of object permanency develops because it is related to a very important need of the child.

concrete-operations stage

Another stage* of the Piaget system is that of *concrete operations*. As you will notice, the child has been leading up to this stage by creating permanent objects in his world. Concrete operations occur in a period during which the child begins to manipulate the environment in a fixed, objective fashion. In other words, the world is fixed and genuine, with separate objects like our own reality (that is, concrete), and the child is ready to operate within and on it.

The child is able to name a picture in a book at 18 months, and by two years he has uttered his first sentence, though not many people can understand what it was he said [Shirley, 1933]. Thus, the formation of language is assisting the process during this concrete-operational stage. What had previously been actions—for example, grabbing and sucking on an object—are now translated into words like *milk* and *bottle* and exist in a "real world." This process of changing action into word is critical to the development of complete symbolic thought process.

Thus, before this stage begins, the child has learned that a hand reaching for an object can obtain it; but as his symbolism becomes more complex, he can substitute in his mind *before acting* the many possible different, and more or less effective, methods of action. For example, suppose a desired object is behind bars that are too close together for the child to get his hand through, but a thin stick is available beside him. He will eventually be able to figure out, by using mental symbols based on earlier arm and hand movements, that the stick can substitute for the reaching of his arm toward the object. He has engaged in symbolic substitution [Bruner et al., 1966]. Early patterns of activity have thus been dominated and regulated by word symbols.†

The pattern for cognitive growth has been set, but the child faces many stumbling blocks ahead during this concrete-operations stage. He must, after all, somehow develop our elaborate reasoning processes. For one thing, his world is still pretty self-centered—for example, he uses himself as the reference point in everything. The quotation at the beginning of this chapter makes this focus evident: The child is unable to "get out of himself."

---

*Roughly covering the years from two to twelve.

†Note how completely symbolic a sophisticated human society becomes. For example, in the area of finance, money is pure symbolism; all we are handing back and forth are pieces of paper, which we cannot even require the government to redeem for gold.

118 a, b, c   At a certain stage of development, the young child is able to understand that the same amount of clay was used to make all three of these forms. In other words, he grasps the concept of conservation. (*Gabriele Wunderlich*)

He knows *he* has a brother, but it is not entirely clear that his brother has him. He could not assume his brother's point of reference.

Conservation.   Even after the child has become fully involved in manipulating objects in his environment, he still has a big stumbling block ahead of him: these objects sometimes both remain the same and change—at the same time. At first this idea may seem confusing to you, because you are so used to it. However, we take some fantastic subtleties entirely for granted. Suppose you put a glass of Kool-Aid in front of a five-year-old. Next to this glass you place another glass, but an empty one that is taller and thinner than the glass with the Kool-Aid in it. Now, take the glass filled with the drink and pour the contents into the tall, thin glass. Ask the child which glass holds more. Even though he watched you do the pouring, he will say that the tall, thin glass has more in it simply because it looks higher. The child lacks understanding of a concept called *conservation*. Conservation simply refers to the fact that if we take an object, liquid or solid, and distort its shape, the object still will contain the same amount of material that it did in the beginning. In other words, the amount of material is conserved (saved) regardless of how we shape it, but this principle is obvious only when the child's world has become more abstract and less concrete.

One reason the child has problems understanding conservation, it is assumed, is that he focuses on just one aspect of the situation. Thus, he pays attention to one thing that he has learned in the past *generally* holds true: the taller the glass of Kool-Aid, the more soft drink in it. He fails to focus on both width and height. Understanding conservation requires him to integrate more than one dimension. Young children, for example, may be shown a long, thin pencil and a short, thick pencil and asked to differentiate between them. This is how they do it:

"This pencil is long, this one is short; this one is thin, this one is fat."

Once children have learned about conservation, however, they are able to integrate the two dimensions:

"This pencil is longer and thinner than the other one." [Inhelder and Sinclair, 1969]

Notice that this is actually a developmental stage which is part of concrete operations because the objects are becoming a part of the real environment which can be manipulated, handled, and altered with an understanding that the object essentially remains concrete and permanent.

One might think that *training* in conservation would help to speed up comprehension. This is not the case, however; continued demonstration of the principle of conservation, in visual form, helps a little, but for the most part the process of understanding proceeds at its own pace, apparently supplying us with another example of the regulated pace of maturation

[Beilin et al., 1966]. For instance, the six-year-old can be made to understand that the two glasses contain the same amount of Kool-Aid, but he will begin to doubt it if the experimenter questions his judgment: "But look, this glass is taller than the other. Are you *sure* that they contain the same amount?"

So the conservation principle is understood, but not fully entrenched. By about seven years—just one more year—the child ceases to become confused and understands "thinner and taller," and you can't talk him out of believing that the two glasses contain the same amount, even though one is taller than another.

The process of full comprehension probably moves slowly because of a cortical mechanism called "internal conversation." Basically this is the process we all use of talking to ourselves mentally. This internalized conversation goes on continuously, probably in the associative areas of the cortex, and because it is internal, it is not subject to constant correction by parent or teacher [Mead, 1934]. Hence the child can go a long time reinforcing and emphasizing to himself such early ideas as the notion that "tall" equals "more." In his own mind he does not confront much evidence to the contrary. Each new problem or tentative solution has to compete with these memories (conversations with himself) until compromise solutions are finally reached [Bailey, 1962].

formal-operations stage

From 11 or 12 into the adolescent and adult years, the person becomes more and more adept at the third stage of development, *formal operations*. Although this stage involves a rather elaborate theory in its own right, for our purposes we may simply point out that formal operations involve the complex and highly abstract reasoning of which most adults are capable. Formal operations involve the highly symbolic modes of behavior found in mathematics or logic; they even involve the complexities of moral decisions and the hypothesis making of psychologists. In any case, the formal-operations stage brings the child to the highest level, and that was our goal.

Thus, Piaget demonstrates that a maturational process occurs in the intellectual realm. Again, as in intelligence, you can't train a child beforehand, but schools and parents can emphasize various training at appropriate times in the development to enhance understanding during that period. For example, schools should emphasize conservation principles at appropriate ages.

HUMAN CHARACTER DEVELOPMENT

Moral development in its broadest sense varies, of course, from one society to another and from group to group within a society. Most parents attempt in one fashion or another to help their children develop into "useful" human beings for the particular society in which they live.

Training and obedience seem critical to a child's proper development. A large number of studies which we will discuss, however, are not

119   James McCord, Watergate defendant, is sworn in by Senator Sam Erwin (*Wide World*)

confined to young children, because it is necessary to find out what happens to adults who have experienced certain types of childhood.

Unquestioning obedience to training can be a dangerous thing. This is a theme we will develop later, in terms of the pressure of companions and society on the individual to do some grotesque things—for example, the atrocities of the Nazi movement. It may be worthwhile, though, to summarize a laboratory experiment in "obedience" that provides a concrete example of the extremes to which people will go and the undesirability of unthinking obedience. In an experiment that is now famous, a laboratory setting was prepared in which each of the subjects (young adults, not children) was told that he was to be part of a "learning experiment." His task was simple. On the other side of a screen from him sat a person who was "in training"; when this person (a stooge, though the subject didn't know it) made an error, the subject's task was to administer a shock as punishment. Each time an error was made, the subject was to increase the shock by manipulating a dial marked off in voltages. The dial was marked from "mild shock" through "danger" all the way to an unlabeled setting marked in red like a poison label, suggesting that this final point on the dial might trigger a fatal charge of electricity. Even though the stooges cried out "in pain" (although they were not really receiving shocks), the subjects obediently continued to give the erring "trainees" voltages of electricity that were supposedly large enough to kill them. More than 60 percent of the subjects obeyed instructions to give extremely severe shocks as a penalty for failure to answer questions properly. Since the "lethal" dose was not clearly marked, it is probably stretching credulity to assume that the subjects thought they were killing the people; everything indicates, however, that they thought they were injuring the trainees [Milgram, 1965].

Many readers might be skeptical about these results, thinking that the subjects had somehow caught on to the experiment and would not really be willing to do this in real life. Not so, however. In an identical experiment with puppies right in view, Ss shocked them just as they did in the other experiment. The shocks were sufficient in strength to cause the puppy to howl, squirm, bark, and jump around. The only element that the Ss had no way of knowing about was that the shocks were not intense enough to cause the pain that they thought they were causing. The dials on the machinery again suggested increasingly severe jolts of electricity were being administered [Sheridan and King, 1972].

The effects of unquestioning obedience came crashing in on the head of the average American who viewed the 1973 Senate hearings on the Watergate incident. Most of the testimony of those who were involved in the criminal activity centered around "I was only following orders."

We know, then, what some human beings are capable of doing, and unreasoning obedience is not behavior to be encouraged. The issue confronting parents, however, is how to minimize or correct things that society frowns upon without creating children who conform too much to orders and rules.

the roles of society and the parent

The difference between male and female crime rates has already been noted. It can hardly be attributed to biological differences alone. Parents handle male and female children differently, and this contributes to the difference, but probably the greatest responsibility for sex-role differences in moral behavior lies in the pressures exerted and the opportunities granted by our society. One experimenter, for example, had kept rather extensive personality records on a group of boys and girls from their preteen years and decided to call these people back to find out what kind of adults they were—that is, what changes had taken place in each one's personality and behavior over the years. He found striking evidence that outwardly the male and female roles tended to remain the same in at least two critical areas. Comparing the behavior of the grown women with their behavior as children, he found that the dependency and submissiveness they had shown as children tended to remain high into adulthood. Openly expressed sexuality and aggression tended to remain low for women and high for men [Kagan and Moss, 1962]. This seems to be a pretty clear indication that a large part of early sex-role development remains with the child for his life. Of course, exceptions do occur, but of all the training that takes place, sex-role training seems most tenacious.*

The enduring quality of sex-role behavior probably results from the sheer amount of reinforcement it receives. A boy, for example, is trained by his parents to "be a man," and at the same time he is taught to "be good"—that is, not to be openly aggressive or sexual. This training is ambiguous from the beginning, for the male child is sometimes encouraged to play war games and yet not to injure a neighborhood child. Physical aggression usually is reinforced. And later on society will encourage the man, in subtle fashion, to be sexually aggressive, especially during the early teens, an aggressiveness that is especially noticeable in teenagers' unsubstantiated bragging about their "conquests." The extent of this training becomes especially obvious when we consider the strong feelings evoked by the word *sissy*.

Young males receive training in aggression, somewhat tempered by "morality training." On the other hand, young females get rather consistent parental discipline in being feminine and dependent, so that women's impulses are constantly held in check. Society as a whole frowns on women's promiscuity, bar hopping, and fist fighting.†

It is important, then, to keep in mind that discipline and training,

---

*This is why it matters that young women are becoming less submissive and dependent, as mentioned earlier. Generations to come will feel the impact of this change.

†During World War II, I recall some notable exceptions among women who worked in munitions factories.

and the "morality" they instill, are clearly related to the child's sex role *as the culture or society interprets it.* The female traditionally has been required to be far more "moral." Psychologists of late have been expressing alarm about this double standard, especially in the sense that females are restricted from childhood in opportunities to develop a sense of achievement, independence, or self-assertion [Block, 1973].

PSYCHOLOGICAL FACTORS IN THE HOME

This discussion will focus on the many methods commonly used to make the child "moral." First, however, one psychological concept should be made clear before some of the experiments can be understood. The goal of the parent is to make the child's moral behavior permanent, in the sense that he will carry it with him through life. This process of instilling permanent moral principles is called *internalization*; the word refers to the process whereby external persuasion is used by an authority—for example, the parents—to get the child to incorporate *into* himself (internalize) the values of that authority, so we are dealing essentially with conformity. When these values have become part of the child, they have been internalized. If a child is forbidden by external authority to steal, for example, and the prohibition is reinforced by punishment if he does steal, the goal is generally to get the child to adopt this standard for himself. If he does come to believe that stealing is "wrong," he has internalized the standard; it has become a part of him.

Internalization is measured most often in psychological experiments by the technique of forbidding or punishing the child for handling or playing with certain attractive toys. The experimenter then leaves the room, and the child assumes that he is alone. The experimenter watches through a one-way mirror to see the effect of the prohibition or punishment on the behavior of the child, who thinks he is not being watched. Many of the experimental results to be discussed in the following section have been obtained by using this technique.

physical punishment

Punishment has been discussed before, but a few additional words pertaining directly to the child are necessary. Extreme physical punishment can lead to effects opposite from those desired, because this sort of punishment forms a very strong dependency relationship between parent and child. In other words, the child's behavior ceases to be self-directed; he always waits for the parent to tell him how to behave, rather than risk punishment. This overdependency exists even though, as studies have shown, such punishment also builds up resentment and hostility toward a parent [Zipf, 1960]. Extreme punishments such as locking the child in a room seem to produce the same effect: overdependency, and anger and hostility toward the parent. On the opposite side of the coin, when children are given a little leeway to act on their own, they show more independence, more initiative, and a personality reflecting more individuality [Watson, 1957].

One strange thing that sometimes occurs with animals, you may recall, is that they tend to persist in incorrect behavior even when punished consistently and severely (Chapter 9). This happens with children, too. Why would someone persist in doing something for which he is always punished? In some cases, it has been suggested, human beings find the punishment worth seeking rather than avoiding, in order to satisfy their own needs [Festinger, 1961]. I present the explanation for this behavior only for speculative purposes: no studies have clearly demonstrated the accuracy of this hypothesis, although it does provide logic for an illogical situation. The punishment "makes up for" the bad behavior which the child has just perpetrated. He feels absolved of guilt; the books have been balanced, so to speak, and a form of homeostasis or equilibrium has been reestablished. The child is likely to get caught in the forbidden act again and to be punished again. The punishment begins to be a part of his way of life, and he experiences a lingering guilt that is especially strong if he is punished severely. The child keeps working at establishing a balance between guilt and retribution, therefore, by setting up situations in which he will be punished.

This hypothesis certainly does not fit all situations, for we know that most children tend to avoid punishment—but one feels a need to explain so unusual a phenomenon.

Probably the most important aspect of studies on the persistence of punished behaviors is found where an act is *both* punished and rewarded —for example, when a subject receives both money and a shock for something he does. The person is being told, in essence, that he has been both good and bad. Thus, many people persist in a certain "bad" behavior because the "morality" or "immorality" of the act is just not clear. And the exact degree of reward, or punishment, or both, as *interpreted* by the individual, may not be clear. That is, he may find the reward in the act worth the punishment [Racinskas, 1969; Vogel-Sprott, 1969]. This kind of study illustrates why child-rearing experts emphasize that discipline must be consistent. Mothers frequently get so tired of the same old crime that they give up for a while and lock themselves in the bathroom. Since the child is not being punished, he gets the reward portion of the behavior until she recovers sufficiently to get him again. Thus, a forbidden behavior tends to persist.

We are all human, and it is obviously next to impossible to avoid smacking a child every now and then. In fact, to expect us to behave otherwise would be most unrealistic—and such superior conduct on the part of a parent will actually produce a rather distorted and unrealistic child. All is not sweetness in our world. The issue of punishment involves a matter of degree.

Reasonable punishment has been studied in some detail in laboratory settings. For example, children were put through a learning experience in which they were trained to handle certain toys and not to handle others.

As punishment for handling the forbidden toys, the subjects received a disturbing but harmless noise* through a set of earphones. This arrangement was used to form a high-intensity-punishment group. Another and less disturbing noise was used to form a moderate-intensity-punishment group. Some of the youngsters were punished 100 percent of the time for incorrect behavior, and others 50 percent of the time. Essentially, four groups were formed: high-intensity–100 percent; high-intensity–50 percent; moderate-intensity–100 percent; moderate-intensity–50 percent. In this way both amount and intensity of punishment could be studied as influences on internalization.

Internalization of learning was measured when the experimenter left the room and then noted the tendency the children had to touch and handle forbidden objects while he was gone. Girls internalized more from the high-intensity punishment than boys did;† one may speculate either that girls were not as accustomed to harsh treatment as boys or—the reverse— that boys "took it like men." These two possibilities aside, the most important conclusion of the study for our purposes is that intermittent punishment (not 100 percent) works quite well [Leff, 1969]. Continuous punishment seems to be unnecessary and, more important, ineffective as a training device. Apparently, we can punish the child but give him a chance to recover and learn rather than just stay put and get more of the same treatment.‡

punishment by withdrawal of love

Not too much can be said about this method; the data bear out whatever negative reactions you may have had when you read the heading. However, parents often do let children know, directly or indirectly, that "if you continue to act this way, I just won't love you anymore." To a small child, extreme anger or hatred can convey the same message.

Withdrawal of love for the person is different from disapproval of the act itself and what it represents. We can still approve of the child as a human being. Withdrawal of love probably reduces internalization of "morals" because the child gets to be more concerned with the loss of love than with the training issue in question. On the other hand, disapproval of the particular act seems to enhance internalization [Hoffman and Saltz-stein, 1967].

rewarding good behavior

Time and again it has been shown that reward is necessary in establishing internalization—that is, self-regulated moral behavior. The reward system is so common that it needs little explanation. It is what we all seek—for

---

*The children were allowed to hear the sounds before the experiment and were not subjected to a frightening experience.

† At least in this study. In general, the degree of punishment is not significant; in fact, the harsher it is, the less effective it tends to be.

‡ Notice that at first glance this study seems to contradict the ones on behavior that persists in the face of punishment and reward. Remember, however, that persistent misbehavior is relatively rare, so the second study applies in most cases. Discipline should be consistent in terms of disapproval but need not involve continuous punishment.

example, good food or candy, a movie, money, and so on. Reward seems to be as effective with children as it is with adults, or with rats who receive food pellets for pushing a bar. One method of using reward to enhance internalization is to offer the child something he wants if he completes a certain task, and then leave him alone. Once the adult is gone, the child models himself after the adult and in the process internalizes adult norms of behavior [Bandura and Perloff, 1967].

You may recall an earlier discussion in which it was mentioned that secondary reinforcements are important in learning. For example, the kindergarten child will work hard for a gold star that he can paste on his forehead. The star represents (and is *secondary* to) the most important reinforcer, praise from the teacher, but it is still very effective.* The point is that the internalization process begins with concrete rewards from others and progresses to a stage where the child monitors and regulates his own behavior. This self-monitoring leads to the reward, so the self-monitoring *itself* becomes associated with reward and acts as a secondary reinforcer. The child says to himself, "My, I am doing this and I am *so* good you wouldn't believe it!" He is rewarding himself with the gold star of self-praise.

Strangely enough, excessive or overdone praising of the child can create self-criticism in him. As one study has demonstrated, it would seem that as the praise becomes more unrealistic, the higher the standard the parent is actually setting for the child and he realizes he can never be quite that good [Davis and Brock, 1972]. This study, like many others, suggests the common-sense approach to children: act naturally with them and treat them realistically.

A number of people express concern about the use of rewards with children in the sense that they consider it bribery, but as one author has pointed out, they don't apply this same rule to a Christmas bonus or a raise in salary for themselves. In any case, studies to date indicate that rewards are a very beneficial method for changing behavior or encouraging a child to continue to do something. It is certainly desirable to have a person want to do something just for its own sake rather than because he will get a reward, but there aren't a lot of things in life that fit this description. Rewarding a child for reading is a good example, because at first reading is a chore; eventually however, it can become something worthwhile on its own, and external rewards will then no longer be necessary.

To keep greed at a minimum, most psychologists feel that natural rewards are the best kinds to provide—such things as special privileges, extra time off, and so forth. About the only real matter of concern in terms of rewards is the danger of rewarding someone after he has done something undesirable. For example, if a child has just torn up the living room, giving

---

*If you are a "purist," praise itself is a secondary reinforcer—that is, secondary to the primary reinforcer of actual mother love.

him a candy treat "to not do that any more" results in a basic form of conditioning in which the child is actually being rewarded for creating havoc [O'Leary et al., 1972].

It is important to remember that children must sometimes let off steam. In an unusual study using a form of reward with nursery-school children, an amazing thing happened: virtually perfect control of the children was reported by the examiners. The experiment went this way: *if* the children sat quietly and watched the blackboard, they were rewarded at unknown and random intervals with the sound of a bell, at which time they were instructed to "RUN AND SCREAM," a behavior they were more than happy to perform. This technique was developed to such an art that the children would sit still and pay attention so they could earn credits for good behavior. The credits could be "cashed in" for many rewards, one of their favorites being the opportunity to push the experimenter around the room on his movable swivel chair [Homme et al., 1963].

A study of ten- to twelve-year-old boys is interesting for the light it throws on effective control of behavior. This study divided the boys into two groups, those who had a high degree of self-esteem and those who had fairly low self-esteem. Having high self-esteem might be defined as regarding oneself as a worthwhile person, one who feels fairly competent in social situations and is not afraid to express his own opinion. Those who had high self-esteem didn't necessarily have "good character," but under our broad definition we can infer that they were reared properly by some appropriate techniques which at least produce well-adjusted individuals. Well-adjusted people, in turn, could logically be expected to fit societal patterns within reasonable limits.

In any case, this study shows some of the factors that seem to be involved in having a good *self-concept.** The self-esteem of these young men was correlated with a home life marked by strict and consistent discipline that involved neither the withholding of love nor physical punishment, but instead emphasized the parents' genuine concern for the child and interest in him [Coppersmith, 1968].

Apparently, then, childhood training is most effective when it emphasizes the reward system, minimal physical punishment, and disapproval of the child's acts rather than of the child himself.

One additional word about punishment: the stress on minimal physical punishment doesn't mean that a child should never be spanked, shaken, or otherwise handled by an adult when he can't stand it any longer. A well-adjusted child can develop even in the face of physical punishment. It is all a matter of the parents' attitude and the degree of punishment.

---

* *Self-concept* merely refers to how one views oneself; one may have a good or a bad self-concept.

PHYSIOLOGICAL FACTORS IN CHARACTER DEVELOPMENT

Until recently the social sciences probably have overemphasized the psychological factors involved in behavior and character development. By this I mean that social scientists have turned toward parents, neighborhood environment, kinds of discipline, lack of love, and so forth to provide complete explanations for the development of character defects in children who get into trouble with society. In some states parents are arrested for the crimes of their children.

In general, it is legitimate to assume that these factors play a large role, but at times distorted logic has somehow slipped into attempts to explain away some unusual facts. For example, not atypically, in a particular family two out of three children, say, may turn out normally and have no difficulty with school, parents, or the law. But how about the "other one"— the bad one? How can we explain what happened to him? Why did he turn out as he did? The tendency has been to explain his problems in terms of *differential treatment*—meaning that this particular child was not as well cared for, not as much loved, or perhaps disciplined more strictly than other children in the family.

Other studies have tried to explain these cases in terms of the order of birth of children in a family—that is, whether the "problem" child was the first, in the middle, second of four, last, etc. The idea is that earlier children usually get more personalized care; the third, fifth, or tenth child has to fend for himself. But correlations between birth order and personality development have been only moderate. The early-born tend to be a little more dependent and to speak a little earlier, but these studies have not explained the gnawing problem of why, within one family, some children turn out "bad" and others don't.

Psychologists undoubtedly have been correct in assigning great importance and influence to the psychological environment of the home, but these factors are not the whole explanation.

Is it possible that certain *physical* characteristics of "bad" children also make them prone to getting into difficulty? Indeed, the study we will cover in a moment suggests in a remarkably persuasive way that a relationship may exist between physiological problems and such psychological difficulties.

Many studies in the United States have examined inheritance and physiological characteristics as they relate to personality difficulties. But in our country we suffer from a serious problem in attempting to study individual families and their children in great depth and detail: our society is constructed on a rather impersonal basis, compared to, say, some English communities which we will discuss. Because our social arrangements are impersonal, social workers and psychologists often meet suspicion among those they hope to study, because these researchers are not an integral part of the community or of the family that is having trouble. Thus, in fairness, we can say that we probably don't get information in the quantity or depth that is available to workers in other countries.

The particular study at issue took place in a town in Great Britain that has a unique makeup, probably because it is so small and because it is characterized by long-standing integration between welfare workers and families. The workers know each of the town's children well—their family situations, school problems, teachers, and so on. Thus, the experimenter was able to gather detailed information on family history and development. The closeness of professionals and families made it unlikely, for example, that a highly unstable family would go unnoticed.

The experimenter divided the families to be studied into three psychological categories: stable families; families that had more than their share of troubles;* and families that appeared to be very disturbed.† Using these three divisions, the study explored the possibility that *physiological* factors could be contributing to youngsters' being referred to authorities as problem children. The stable families contained a total of 31 brothers and sisters. Within this group, 5 children from 5 different families had been referred for delinquent acts like shoplifting and getting into trouble at school. None of the siblings‡ of these 5 children were found to be delinquent or disturbed. Here is the crucial finding: all 5 delinquent children showed histories of physiological problems, either before their birth (while the mother was pregnant) or afterward. In one case, for example, the pregnant mother had a serious lung infection; in another, delivery was delayed artificially to give a student nurse time to arrive. The delinquent children themselves showed various defects: epilepsy, speech impediment, respiratory infections, and so on.

In the second group—families that were slightly unbalanced—13 disturbed children from 13 families were referred to the authorities; these children had 55 siblings, of whom 44 were psychologically stable. Again, 12 of the 13 referrals§ had physiological defects—asthma, imperfect speech, tuberculosis, headaches, and chronic sickness, to mention but a few.

And in the third group, families that were psychologically very disturbed—15 disturbed children from 15 families were referred to the authorities; these children had 55 siblings, of whom 39 were stable. Among the 15 referrals, 14 had abnormal physical symptoms, and these symptoms were more pronounced and occurred more frequently than in the other cases,

---

* These families were slightly unbalanced; they were marked by overreaction and inability to cope with stress, some tendency toward moderate threats against children, and a fair proportion of angry confrontations.

† These families showed extreme hostility, confusion, psychological upset, and maladjustment.

‡ Brother(s) and/or sister(s) within the same family; in this case, brothers and sisters of delinquent children.

§ In psychological terminology, a referral is an individual referred to a mental health worker for assistance.

although essentially they were of the same type: epilepsy, speech defects, nose-bleeders, pigeon-toes, skin troubles, and so on.

Within all families, no matter what the level of disturbance, the greater proportion of children were *not* problem children and did not give evidence of serious maladjustment. Of 33 delinquent cases, 28 children (more than 80 percent) had somatic (bodily) or neural impairment, or the mother had a physiological problem before the child's birth. We simply cannot ignore the strong possibility that physiological factors are connected in some way with the children's maladjustment [Stott, 1966].

This does not mean that psychological influences can be discounted. We find, for example, that as we move from the most stable to the most unstable families, the number of *siblings of referrals* showing disturbance increased in the following order: 0 percent, 20 percent, and 29 percent. Environment and the psychological family situation *do* appear to be factors in abnormal development.

The author of this excellent study points out that in a large number of cases, children may inherit a potential for instability, just as they inherit dispositions toward certain diseases. With proper care, however, just as in the case of physical disease, these problems can be controlled or even reversed. Strikingly, in the "worst" families the physical problems seem to have been aggravated by the psychological atmosphere.

I have spent a good deal of time talking about this study because it illustrates how, with some ingenuity, factors which at first look difficult can be measured—for example, the possibility that physical factors influence maladjustment. Remember, however, as with smoking and cancer, that a *correlational* relationship can be demonstrated, but is not a "proof" of a cause-effect relationship. For example, it is conceivable that an unpleasant birth or physical defect in a child could cause the parents to treat him or her differently.

MORALITY

Human beings have concerned themselves with teaching morality to others since the first moment when there were enough people around to make cheating, stealing, and murder worthwhile. If you find yourself disappointed with this section on "morality" because it lacks definition and conclusion, you will be no more frustrated than experimenters who have struggled with the problem through the years. There is no point in trying to resolve what morality *is;* naturally, it is different things to different people—but most societies do typically hold that murder, stealing, and cheating are taboo, so the definition can rest on these behaviors.

We might as well start with the worst to give you some idea of the difficulties the experimenter faces. Whether or not you are religious, you probably will agree that in general the standards of most religions in the United States are in accord with most principles of morality as one typically views them. Using a recent and very elaborate review of studies on the relationship between religion and behavior, the difficulties we face can be illustrated clearly. One study compared delinquent girls with non-delinquent girls, and found the delinquents to be more in favor of Sunday church observance and the teachings of the Bible. Among delinquent and nondelinquent boys, no differences in religious attitudes were observed. Another study failed to establish any clear correlation, positive or negative, between antisocial behavior and religious attitudes. And a majority of inmates at a state reformatory said they had been regular churchgoers, and one-half of them felt churches were effective forces for good [Sanna, 1969].

These data don't attempt to downgrade religion but merely to point out that no area of study is more unpredictable than that which tries to pin down the effect of moral training and moral beliefs on moral *behavior*. Even belonging to the Boy Scouts and going to Sunday school fail to correlate highly with behaving morally [Hartshorne and May, 1928–1930].

A In *Adam's* Fall
   We Sinned all.

B Thy Life to Mend
   This *Book* Attend.

C The *Cat* doth play
   And after slay.

D A *Dog* will bite
   A Thief at night.

E An *Eagles* flight
   Is out of fight.

F The Idle *Fool*
   Is whipt at School.

120 The McGuffey reader, widely used in the U.S. during the 17th and 18th centuries, provided instruction in practical morality (*Bettmann Archive*)

The most famous study of morality was made in the 1920s. It showed a correlation of only about .30 between lying, cheating, and stealing by "normal" children in one situation and their tendency to do the same in another situation. The authors point out that antisocial behavior seems to be related to a specific situation for a specific child; in other words, Harry might cheat in one situation but not in another. Honesty is not something you either have or don't have. In fact, the experimenters found that our famous normal curve holds for honesty: very few children were completely honest, nor were many completely corrupt. These investigators, Dr. Hartshorne and Dr. May, also found that those children who cheated in a given situation expressed as much disapproval of the act as those who didn't.

Clearly, then, there is a difference between moral knowledge and moral behavior. People acquire moral knowledge in a sequence much like that of cognitive processes, but their moral behavior seems to be much more random as far as the results of studies are concerned. Some specific technique for producing moral children may very well exist; we just don't have any clear-cut experimental evidence—only clues—about what might produce moral behavior or what might inhibit it.

One recent study at least heads in the right direction. Pronounced cheating behavior occurs in subjects who have a very high feeling of self-satisfaction and a need for approval. These people seem to present such a high level of excellence, to themselves and to others, that they have to be certain of doing well on tests even if they have to cheat. This finding may become clearer when we add that the worst offenders are women college students who exhibit very great need for approval and self-satisfaction [Jacobson, Berger, and Milham, 1970]. Given a double threat—one to self-esteem and another to their roles as intelligent women in a man's world—these women apparently have been forced into cheating. Basically, the more that is at stake, the more likely the person is to cheat in order to get it.

moral knowledge Two leading students of children's moral development are Piaget and Dr. Lawrence Kohlberg. What follows emphasizes Kohlberg's system, while it draws on both his and Piaget's ideas.

The first period in a child's moral development has been called *moral realism* [Piaget, 1948]. Before the age of seven or eight, the child has little concern for the *reason* that specific behaviors are allowed or forbidden; he is a self-centered creature, and his mind does not seem flexible enough to fully comprehend the violation of rules as an interference with others (which, theoretically, provides the basis for morality). Another label for the early moral realism period is the *rules stage*, a term that suggests unreasoning adherence to authority.

The beginning of the child's move toward moral development has been called the *reward stage*. At this point, a conditioning process involves not only the blind punishment of the first stage, moral realism, but also some attempt by parents to teach the child by rewarding correct behavior. The child is beginning to focus on certain acts as good or bad—or at least as rewarded or punished. His moral development here is analogous to his development of the ability to discriminate an object as something separate from himself, a principle we discussed earlier in reference to Piaget's theory of cognitive growth. In other words, if the child has developed the ability to view objects in the world from an abstract perspective, as he does when he learns conservation, he is then able to relate to people in an abstract moral sense [Hardeman, 1972]. Between the ages of six and twelve, for instance, the child tends increasingly to regard lying as wrong because it brings unpleasant consequences rather than because it is forbidden [Medinnus, 1962].

The third stage might be labeled *disapproval by others*. Now such disapproval for misdeeds has been going on for quite a while, but at some time after the age of six the child begins to develop a broader form of social consciousness, and the disapproval of others creates anxiety and probably guilt.

The guilt and anxiety, it has been hypothesized, lead to the fourth stage, *disapproval of self*, or the ability to see why some of our own characteristics are not beneficial to others—for example, stealing to get what we want. This disapproval of self, if one subscribes to the homeostasis concept, will reduce both guilt and anxiety, since it is a form of self-punishment that helps to equalize the crime. Such disapproval, of course, requires both symbolic and verbal understanding of the issues at hand [Aronfreed, 1965]. Since the child is no longer so self-centered, and since he now symbolizes, he can follow the reasoning of "do to others what you would have them do to you."

The final stage is the *sharing stage*, which involves sharing of objects, goals, and rights with others. The basis for full development of this characteristic seems to be the striking need for acceptance by peers during the adolescent stage. The development of a flexibility in moral judgments—that is, being less morally rigid—frees the adolescent from the rigidity of parental rules and opens up for him the opportunity to be accepted by and to accept more of his peers [Birnbaum, 1972]. This ability obviously requires complex understanding, and it is thought to be quite fully developed by the age of sixteen [Kohlberg, 1963; Turiel, 1969].

**notes on
moral behavior**
One persistent problem with moral behavior is that it is difficult to sketch out any unifying theme which separates those who are moral from those who are immoral. The best approach may be to mention some of the data that have accumulated on morality, even though they are sometimes less precise than one would desire.

Social pressure   A person's morality is frequently subject to the behavior of those around him. On the negative side lynchings and mass murders have been with us for centuries; people who would never dream of committing by themselves so hideous a crime are swept away with the tide. On the positive side people are more prone to help others if an example is set for them by others. For instance, a fake situation was designed in which a supposed lady in distress was having the tire on her car changed, apparently by a passing motorist. This scene was arranged so as to be noticed by another motorist just before he came across another stooge—a lone woman standing beside her car, which had a flat tire. This experiment produced far more assistance for the lady with the flat than a comparable setup (the control situation) in which no passing motorist changing a flat tire provided the subject with an example before he got his opportunity to help [Bryan and Test, 1969].

Social class   Statistics indicate that the moral behavior of impoverished groups is poorer than that of the middle class.* Aggression and competition are greater in the lower classes than in the middle and upper classes—but remember that when you have most of the necessities of life, you have little need for this type of behavior [McKee, 1955]. More than likely, the higher incidence of aggression and competition in the lower classes is related to the fact that the lower class's behavior is more noticeable, more physical, and more likely to result in police action. The middle and upper classes probably harbor just as much aggression and competition, but it is more verbal, more "sophisticated," and more "acceptable."

Moral training   Here the concept of internalization of learning applies. Three studies will be discussed that pertain particularly to the internalization of moral behavior.

First, once a child has reached the symbolic stage, training in moral behavior seems to be instilled most effectively by rational explanation of rules, after punishment has been meted out and while the parent encourages the child and reduces the anxiety he has experienced from the punishment† [Aronfreed, 1965].

Second, internalization is not reinforced by the use of power—that is, threats of violence. The internalization of norms is interrupted by a definite negative reaction that works against the trainer's goals. Again, as in other studies, explanation fosters moral behavior more than anything else.

Third, children who are models of good behavior in school are not necessarily so at home, and vice versa [Walsh, 1969]. Children seem to need

---

*Obviously, this is a middle-class interpretation of what is moral.

†This strategy is somewhat similar to the optimal arrangement of providing a rewarding alternative to a punished act.

a safety valve, probably for the same reason that the Mardi Gras is held in New Orleans each year before Lent. The supposed privations of Lent are offset beforehand by a period of "letting go."

SUMMARY

Mental development follows a sequence. Since intelligence as we know it in adults is extremely difficult to measure in children, our ideas of this developmental sequence are based on inference and theory.

We do know that vision and hearing are the two most important senses of human development, and a number of studies have focused on the growth of these faculties. Some visual behavior apparently is inherited, as the experiment using 30-cm cubes demonstrates.

Piaget divides cognitive development into stages—for example, the sensorimotor, which starts out as crude motor behavior of grasping objects but soon turns into concrete operations in which the world of the child is populated with fixed objects that have a permanent reality and usefulness. Once the objects are permanent, the child engages in symbolic substitution in which these objects and the acts connected with them can be handled on a purely cognitive level. Conservation appears during this stage and involves learning the principle that the shape of objects can be changed without altering the actual amount of that object. By this time the world has become a genuine entity which can be manipulated, altered, and understood. The third stage mentioned, the formal-operations stage, is merely an elaborate refinement of earlier stages, but by this time the individual can engage in highly symbolic reasoning and solve complex problems and issues.

Morality is impossible to define to everyone's satisfaction, so in this chapter an arbitrary definition was used which suggested that murder, cheating, and stealing are generally not acceptable in most societies. Caution should always be exercised in trying to obtain blind obedience, however, since experiments indicate that subjects will do some rather grotesque things when they are not judging and thinking for themselves.

Learning the rules of conduct is based on a principle referred to as internalization whereby the child takes the externally imposed rules of behavior and makes them a part of himself. Training which involves physical punishment is generally poor, the more so the harsher the punishment, because resentment is building up at the same time as dependency, making an undesirable combination. It does not seem to be necessary to punish the child continuously or severely for internalization to work. Maximum effectiveness is gained by providing reward for acceptable behavior and mild punishment for unacceptable behavior.

One study was covered at length which strongly suggests that many problem children have physiological difficulties. This in combination with a rugged psychological environment correlates highly with delinquent behavior.

It has been theorized that moral development proceeds in stages also. The earliest stage consists of a self-centered child who must follow rules blindly. The next stage focuses on rewards, at which time the child begins to respond somewhat toward others, which leads to a stage when he feels some concern about those around him. This is followed by a stage of disapproval from those around him. The next stage is one of disapproval of the self for certain wrong actions, and, if all goes right, the person reaches the sharing stage, which is mature interaction between individuals with mutual concern for one another.

CHAPTER EIGHTEEN
THE ADOLESCENT: REBEL WITH A CAUSE

With the following passage, written by someone who seems to feel the age for what it can be, we arrive at that infamous period, adolescence.

Adolescents are funny people.

They do strange things for strange reasons, or no reason at all. One day they'll cut you down because you've got acne and the next day put in four hours' work for underprivileged children. Intelligent, incredibly stupid, rank, pure idealist, perceptive, blind, funky, noble, all kinds of things and nothing really. Superman and a big fat zero. Their insides are hanging out all over, just asking to get bruised. A weird world they inhabit, where a man-child's strength is measured by the way he can hunch over a steering wheel and jam his accelerator to the floor. They drive around endlessly and sit on their cars and the boys spit and the girls giggle and they feel each other up and they don't quite know what to do with it. Even when they do something with it, it's so damned frantic. And they are all so confused, but they know what they're doing. They know better than anyone else. Nobody knows better than they do, 'cause no one else has ever been there before, not *really*. So they drive around some more and throw beer cans out the window and smoke and shove each other and yell their favorite obscenities and it's all a kick.

Sometimes it's such a pain, such a real ache that they shut it all out and just quit. They don't talk, they don't eat, they just sit in their room and wait. When it goes away, until the next time, they're just a little bit closer to being "adults" and somehow you hope they'll never make it, not quite. [Wantland, 1970]

During this stage, adults are prone to say, "I just don't know what is the matter with them!" As you will discover, very little is the matter with them; teenagers are merely trying to sift through the garbage adults have been handing out for years.

121 a, b, c Adolescent behavior varies greatly in style-and isn't nearly as sinister as some adults believe. Almost no young people actually behave like the protagonist of *I was a Teenage Werewolf,* though lots of adults like to think they do (*Ken Regan, Camera 5; Lucia Woods; American International Pictures*)

PHYSIOLOGICAL CHANGES IN ADOLESCENCE

Unquestionably, the adolescent is different from both the adult and the child, and the purpose of this chapter is to explore some of the reasons for the differences.

Between childhood and adulthood, the most startling developments are physical. Sudden changes take place in sexual ability and physical growth. Boys shoot upward in height. Girls shoot upward and outward, and not always in the right places; girls during this period are subject to dramatic increases in weight which are not always reflected just in the Great American Fetish,* the breasts. These changes in physiology, together with the complete integration of cognitive processes mentioned in Chapter 17 and attainment of the adult or "sharing" stage of moral development, provide the American youth with all the equipment of adulthood, but he has little opportunity to utilize these abilities.

So we find that the adolescent period is characterized by cliquishness. Adults have long since passed their adolescent problems, and have probably repressed them. Children think adolescents are too old, and adolescents think children are too young. Essentially, adolescents are by themselves in the world. Their new-found, higher level of moral integration does not fit that of adults, who have become hardened by the "realities" of life. The result is the isolated grouping and superidealism of the adolescent. The fact that adults won't let adolescents into their world, then, forces the young to band together—sometimes in a rather bizarre but quite earnest fashion. How else can one explain such peculiar phenomena as the "gang" wandering around New York streets on a 105-degree summer day attired in black boots and leather jackets? This must be their way of telling the world: We belong together, we are different, see us, listen to us. These acts also provide the enjoyment of shock value, for nothing gets the adult more upset than simple little devices like wearing hair shaggy-dog fashion or shaven off; deliberately scuffing up your shoes; actually buying the product of a clever capitalist, sweatshirts properly shredded and torn by machine; going in for miniskirts, maxiskirts, old military uniforms, green neckties without a shirt, bare feet, and so on.

What is the meaning of all this? These behaviors are simply methods of bonding adolescents together because they feel different from their parents, alone to some extent, and rebellious toward "old ways." Conformity to such patterns reaches its maximum during the ages eleven to fourteen and begins a rapid decline at about eighteen years [Landsbaum and Willis, 1971].

Adolescence isn't necessarily either a painful time of life or an enjoyable one for any particular boy or girl. It can be one or the other, or both, but in any case the signals will be there, telling us that something is going on, and it is these signals we want to examine.

---

* A *fetish* is a psychological preoccupation with certain portions of the body or with wearing apparel; the preoccupation is sexual in nature.

hormonal changes We discussed the hypothalamus and its role as a mechanism controlling hunger and thirst, but the hypothalamus has other functions during the adolescent period, and again they are regulatory. The hypothalamus's communication network contains a unit that is of critical importance during adolescence: underneath it, hanging down like a slightly oversized pea and attached by a thick string of nerve fibers and blood vessels, is the pituitary gland (see Fig. 18–1 for detail and orientation). The pituitary gland is the master gland of the body. In childhood its primary function is to regulate growth, but during adolescence it has a major additional role.

The pituitary receives its orders from the hypothalamus, and it then issues its own orders to other glands that manufacture hormones, the chemical regulators of various cells in the body.* In this elaborate chain of events, a signal system is set up so that the pituitary will trigger these other glands, register their amount of activity, and then increase or decrease the hormonal flow from them as appropriate.

The hormones are directly related to major physiological changes during this period. You may recall that before adolescence begins, sexual

**Hormone comes from a Greek word meaning "to excite" or "to activate."

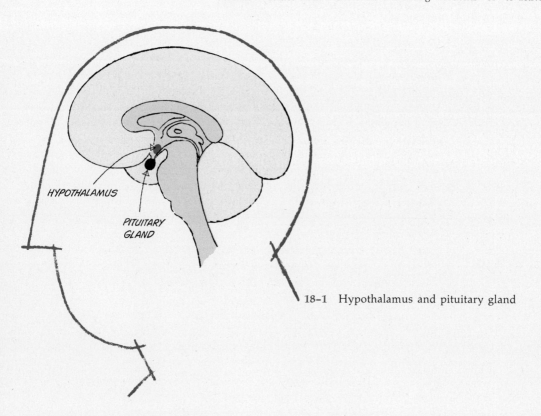

HYPOTHALAMUS

PITUITARY
GLAND

18–1 Hypothalamus and pituitary gland

maturity reaches only 10–20 percent of its maximal development. In other words, between the onset of adolescence and the age of twenty, roughly eight years, 80 to 90 percent of the development of sexual apparatus takes place. In a very dramatic fashion, therefore, the youngster is suddenly going to be confronted with burgeoning sex drives set in motion by hormonal activity. Moreover, this same hormonal triggering is responsible for other major changes—for example, a rapid *growth spurt.*

During the adolescent period, the pituitary stimulates two major glands, the adrenal glands and the gonads (sex glands). The adrenal glands you already know about (Chapter 5). The gonads are stimulated by hormones that haven't really come into use before, but which develop suddenly during this period.

Both the adrenal glands and the testes bring about a very rapid growth rate in boys between eleven and fifteen years of age. Some boys grow as much as four inches a year during their maximal spurt.

Both the adrenal glands and the ovaries trigger growth in females. The girls' spurt of growth usually occurs between nine and twelve years of age.* At maximal rate, some girls average three-and-one-fourth inches of growth a year [A. S. Mason, 1961; Beach, 1948].

Adolescence of itself need not be an unusually trying period for parents or youngsters.† Probably more often than not, it is something of a problem, especially in the United States. Comparisons with other cultures are not always fair, but frequently they help to shed light on some of our problems. For instance, Dr. Margaret Mead, the grand lady of the social science world, has extensively explored many other cultural groups. She finds that in societies marked by considerable sexual freedom and few rules of conduct for the adolescent, the transitional period to manhood or womanhood is relatively carefree. Many in our society will debate the wisdom or the morality of allowing such conduct for adolescents; nonetheless, the transitional period to manhood or womanhood is relatively painless in societies where strictures on behavior are few [Mead, 1928]. For better or worse, our rather restrictive society does present the adolescent with difficulties.

Restrictions as such, however, are not what cause the problems. The structure of the society seems to determine how adolescents will fare. In the kibbutz, for example, adolescent revolt is minimal—but the children have lived all their lives in groups in which their *peers*‡ provide a great deal of

---

* The age at which these spurts occur varies widely and can be determined only on an individual basis.

† Physically, the changes of adolescence are not too difficult to specify, but psychologically, as you will notice later, some changes that begin in the early teens drag out to the early twenties for many youngsters.

‡ *Peers,* as used here, means *age-peers:* people of one's own age group, usually those with something in common—for example, school grade, neighborhood, or extracurricular organization—although age group alone can be the common denominator.

personal security [Bettelheim, 1969]. They have little need to seek out or form "gangs" for the purpose of revolt. In the United States, on the other hand, the personal insecurity many adolescents feel seems to turn them toward others for the first time in a genuine common cause, and the result is often dramatic.

adulthood   Nonetheless, we must take our society as it stands for the moment and examine some of the problems it presents for adolescents. One major difficulty is how a male adolescent goes about entering manhood in our society. How, for example, does he know when he has become a man? At age twenty-one? When he gets a driver's license? When he gets married? Or starts to shave? Just looking at these items, you will notice immediately that no criteria govern the point in time at which a young person becomes a man and ceases to be an adolescent.

Adults tend to keep youngsters highly dependent on them for too long. In some fairly primitive tribes the transition is handled nicely, if you happen to be able to tolerate pain. When the young man is ready to enter adulthood, he is taken away from the community by the elder males, beaten with clubs, made to sleep in the cold without covering, and forced to eat food deliberately made disgusting by pouring half-digested antelope grass over it. The male is also circumcised in a rather bloody fashion, after which his penis is covered with leaves while he recovers. In principle, these initiation rites are like many of those for joining a teen club or college fraternity.

This procedure seems pretty gruesome to most of us, and maybe even to the participants—but when the boy returns to the community, he is a man, and *no one questions it.* He has no need for rebellion or for proving himself further [Whiting, 1958]. In contrast, our society fails to provide any ritual that clearly serves as a landmark for adulthood.

The adolescent rebellion of young women in the United States is quite complicated. First of all, the female is never really supposed to become independent. Although, like the male, she shows many signs of independence, these stirrings seem to be repressed by extreme pressure from society and by that sneaky little thing called "love," which puts her right back in the dependent role. As we have seen, the female role is changing, but it is still in a transitional stage and presents serious problems.

Moreover, for most youngsters in our society, education goes on and on and on. Even though the boy or girl is ready for marriage and a job, he or she is under constant pressure to stay in school and thus hold off fulfilling these roles, a situation that results in considerable frustration and creates a limbo state from approximately twelve years until the early twenties, in some cases going on through to twenty-eight or twenty-nine years [Ralston and Thomas, 1972].

Finally, it should be noted that *adults* have decided that voting, parenthood, army service, bar mitzvah, and even attaining one's legal majority aren't enough to ensure adulthood.

**PSYCHOLOGICAL
REACTIONS TO
GROWTH PROBLEMS**

Adolescents who have just survived their growth spurt look pretty awkward, usually tall and gangly. Over the years this phenomenon has led to considerable research on the *actual* coordination of adolescents. Many studies have measured the adolescent's ability to manipulate levers and follow targets; tests have been made of reaction time and strength. The results consistently show that the adolescent is in peak condition and has excellent coordination [Simons, 1944].

Psychologically, however, the situation is different. The adolescent's arms and legs *are* longer. He *is* taller, and he hasn't quite adjusted to his body, which seems to have run away from him. The resulting awkwardness of movement is quite noticeable, especially in social situations. Adolescents frequently lack the polish and self-confidence that most of us attain when our bodies have stabilized. On a concentrated, specific task, adolescents seem to be able to adjust their coordination fairly well, but when faced with a novel situation involving movement, they come off looking pretty awkward.

This set of events is not helped by the enormous production of hormones, especially those produced by the adrenal glands, which brings with it the embarrassing problem of skin eruptions like acne—and, even worse, the probability of sweating heavily and being thought socially offensive in our superclean society.*

Obesity is frequently a problem in adolescence. Its exact origin is unknown; depending on the individual, overweight can result from disorders of metabolism or hormones, or from psychological problems, or from a combination of these factors. To compensate for physical changes—for example, becoming very tall and skinny—the teenager can fall prey to overeating. The same pitfall seems to lie in wait for the adolescent who is lonely and unhappy. It has been consistently noted that food provides some relief from loneliness. For some people overeating becomes a habit rather like that of taking drugs: One immediate effect of heavy eating is a state of sluggishness and drowsiness which relieves tension. This "drug" effect is underscored by the fact that obese patients frequently eat even when they are not hungry [Swanson, 1970].

Although the origin of overweight may be physical, corrective measures should be taken, because extremely obese people face both physical difficulties and psychological discomfort, and the fat adolescent tends to become a fat adult. Only rarely will an adolescent "grow out of it," as mothers and fathers are likely to say. Far too often a fat person's feeling of self-worth is damaged considerably before action is taken [Stanley, 1970]. Admittedly, many overweight people are well adjusted. That is not the point. Especially in adolescence, overweight causes unnecessary heartache and loneliness even if the person survives psychologically.

Of special importance, from a psychological point of view, is that

---

* There is no certainty about a direct relationship between glandular production and acne, although this is one of those medical probabilities awaiting more definitive data.

girls have their growth spurt earlier than boys, a situation that can be embarrassing for both sexes. If a boy and a girl are about the same age and go out together, the taller girl feels like an Amazon, and the boy fears that if they dance, his nose is going to get stuck in her navel. These worries probably account for the tendency of girls to date older boys during this period. Girls generally take the initiative in dating patterns, as we'll discuss below, even though the boys are given the credit, or at least think they deserve it. In any case, far too many girls at this age fail to realize just how awkward and shy the boys really feel, despite their constant spitting and big talk. Whether to kiss on the first date is just as overwhelming an issue for most boys as it is for girls.

The dating pattern for females seems to be a learned social role that is forced on girls and one that few of them favor. Studies have shown that in the early stages of courtship, women are assertive. As they move into the going-steady stage, their behavior shows a combination of assertiveness and receptivity—that is, they act more dependent on the male. Finally, when they become engaged, women are outwardly receptive, although inwardly they are not entirely happy with this last role [McDaniel, 1969]. By the time the engagement takes place, the girls have tended to move from the habits and preferences of their peers back toward those of their parents, substantiating to some degree an idea mentioned earlier—at present most women do not seem likely to become fully independent, although there are strong leanings in that direction.

ADOLESCENT DEFIANCE

The adolescent has been said to live in an "intense present." He cannot seem to conceptualize death or even the distant future. He sees himself at the starting gate of life [Kastenbaum, 1959]. This point quickly becomes apparent to anyone who has gone through junior high school. On the day of graduation the future is all yours; nothing but the wonders of the world lie ahead. By and large, younger adolescents are most concerned with the immediate past and the present. Interestingly enough, many older adolescents shift to an orientation that includes the near future and the distant past. This switch would seem to fit well with the idea that the adolescent is in transition, on the one hand moving forward, on the other trying to hold to the security of the past. The late adolescent seems to be able to integrate past, present, and especially future, or at least to shift his relative interest in them [Cottle et al., 1969].

The adolescent wants to be on his own, to live his experience to the fullest. Parents are in the way, always worrying about driving habits, clothing, hair length, and social rules. More often than not, adolescent and parent clash head-on during this period. But the rebellion, as one might expect, is not much more than skin-deep.

Close scrutiny of the value system of adolescents shows that they

122 Sometimes adolescent idealism and adolescent rebellion merge to create a powerful movement for social change (*Wide World*)

have not forgotten their socialization through the years; it has been thoroughly entrenched in them. Although they are justified in attempting to make the American way of life more moral, more sane, and more humane—improvements that are badly needed—they are basically at one with their parents' *ideals*, and the separation of goals seems more deeply rooted than it really is.* Nonetheless, the adolescent boy or girl is trying to find out who he is—that is, obtain a self-identity that is independent of and yet a part of the parents' identity.

An elaborate study of 273 youngsters going to different schools, both public and religious, in different sections of the country, demonstrates remarkable agreement by these youngsters regarding the happy and successful life—and their view coincides with that of most parents. They see friendship, achievement, the ability to love and be loved, and the ability to persevere as paramount virtues; they shy away from domination, aggression, and overdependency [Thompson, 1969]. Probably the major difference between adults and youngsters is that the parents pay more lip service to ideals as the years go by, whereas the adolescents want to do something about them. Except in the areas of drug and sex laws, where the parental group remains very conservative and the younger group wants change in the direction of liberality, the major difference in the so-called generation gap is in the matter of degree. That is, adolescents take a more extreme point of view in their fervor for causes such as an antiwar movement or in their opposition to racial discrimination [Weinstock and Lerner, 1972].

Psychology texts commonly indicate that adolescents need parental guidance even though they are in the process of rebelling. This is probably more true in the United States than in some other countries. Our child-rearing methods tend to foster dependence, as a comparative study of fifteen- and sixteen-year-olds (median age) in Denmark and the United States has demonstrated. Danish society provides considerably more equality and democracy for the adolescent than does American society. Analysis of the adolescent in Denmark shows that he acts and feels more independent than his American counterpart.† Apparently, in the Danish child's early years self-direction and internalization develop as the result of stricter upbringing, so that the adolescent is as prepared as he ever will be to go out on his own. In the United States, on the other hand, child rearing tends to encourage dependence during the early years, and *specific rules* remain necessary during adolescence—for example, rules about television, dating, friends, and the like.

Strangely enough, in both Danish and American adolescents, parents' standards are more often obeyed than violated, but an interesting difference does show up between the two groups. In Denmark, desired

* It is the *parents'* ideals and behavior which do not coincide.
† With the difference between the two at the .001 level of significance.

behavior usually occurs when *no* specific rules govern behavior. In the United States, just the reverse takes place: Specific rules appear to foster proper behavior. Apparently, in our country internalization is still continuing during adolescence, whereas in Denmark it is complete by this time [Kandel and Lesser, 1969].

In any case, youngsters in *both* countries tend to respect their parents and to consult them, especially mothers. Other studies, aimed primarily at the United States, support this finding: When major decisions come up—things not involving clothing, hair, or length of skirt—the majority of adolescents indirectly turn to their parents and follow the norms their parents have set up [Brittain, 1967].

Authors consistently report that the typical American high school adolescent does not participate in demonstrations, use drugs regularly, act in a delinquent fashion, or engage in open rebellion. Typically, battles with parents are over trivial matters. Although early adolescents are preoccupied with sex, actual sexual relations take place infrequently, and nothing takes place that even borders on the widespread promiscuity usually claimed by a few sensationalistic news sources [Offer, 1970]. Just as a for-instance, two studies in 1972 encompassing 25,000 high school students indicated that over 70 percent of the students had never used drugs (Husni-Palacios and Scheur, 1972; *Who's Who*, 1972). At the college level, roughly 50 percent have not used drugs [Cross and Davis, 1972].

The typical adolescent in the United States does not find his self-identity until about the age of 20, a time usually considered beyond adolescence. Even in this period, he often experiences some loneliness at leaving home to attend college [Offer, 1969].

Major changes in attitude do take place in college, however, possibly more of them today than in previous generations. In a study covering a thirty-seven-year-period (1930–1967), notable changes have taken place in the value structure of the college student. Over this time period, the church system has come under major attack. Students have not changed much in their belief in a deity—instead, they are attacking what they consider organized religion's outmoded social structure [J. Jones, 1970]. Even so, most students, about 80 percent in one study, express an intention to stay in their religion—at least in name—and rear their children in it [Jacks, 1972].

SEXUAL BEHAVIOR IN ADOLESCENCE

No country in the world is quite like ours when it comes to sexuality. None could possibly exceed our record for hypocrisy. A bizarre case in point is a recent commercial regularly aired on nationwide TV in which a young woman is shown modeling a bra—worn *over* a sweater. Yet on these same stations viewers can watch innumerable war movies vividly depicting hideous scenes of violence. Movie rating systems require parental approval if a breast is shown, but no such approval if a man's hand is cut off in sadistic anger—as, for example, in the John Wayne movie *True Grit*. One cannot expect the American adolescent to develop a relatively healthy outlook on sex when we are constantly dangling sex in front of him with a smug "Look what we've got—but you can't have it." Admittedly, the issue of sex outside marriage is open to many arguments, both for and against; it doesn't make any difference what side of the fence you are on—the problem lies in our snickering attitude toward sexual behavior.

Only in the last few years has human sexual activity been explored in any depth. Before then, the major exception was Dr. Alfred Kinsey, of the famous "Kinsey Report," who in the 1950s made a significant breakthrough in the study of sexual habits and patterns. For showing the way, his institute was subjected to a considerable barrage of verbiage, usually accusation, when in fact his studies were characterized by high moral integrity and scientific quality. His studies on male sexuality had received considerable financial support, and things were going along relatively smoothly until Kinsey came out with his finding that females are sexual creatures as much as are men; this supposed attack on womanhood caused such an uproar that he lost his financial backing from research-funding foundations [Pomeroy, 1972].

It is important to remember that sexuality is physical, personal, and symbolic. Attaining an adequate sex life involves considerably more than perfecting a technique for producing pleasure. Sexuality is also a *symbol* of maturity or attainment that is connected only indirectly with sex itself. And sex activity must be considered within the framework of a society. For some people, sexuality means the attainment of a secure life; for some it is a ritual that causes anguish and guilt; and for some groups it even seems to be part of a religious ritual in which sexual acts are performed on rooftops so that the participants can get closer to the power of the sun god [Bach, 1961].

psychological and sociological factors in sexuality

Literate and civilized societies generally make little or no provision for sexual behavior outside marriage [Murdock, 1949]. One possible explanation is that as societies become more and more "sophisticated," they tend to impose more and more prohibitions and rules in any given area.

The adolescent faces two major problems in handling his sex drive. First, sexual maturation, or the ability to procreate, occurs earlier and earlier with each generation. Generally, sexual maturation is measured in women by the first menstrual period and in men by the growth spurt and by changes such as the full growth of pubic hair. Nowadays, puberty* is reached two-and-one-half to three-and-one-half years earlier than it was a century

* The period of getting pubic hair and hence, by inference, the beginning of maturity. From the Latin for "downy" or "hair."

ago. This is not the result of climate or of being more sex-conscious; it is the outgrowth of better nutrition. For instance, in areas marked by extremes of poverty and wealth—for example, Hong Kong—the rich mature nine months earlier than the poor [Tanner, 1968]. In the United States, the adolescent generally is prepared for sexual activity and/or marriage at an earlier and earlier age. Yet, as you know, teenage marriages are frowned upon, and so is teenage sexual activity.

The adolescent faces problems at the other end of the scale, also: the human life span is getting longer and longer. This means that youngsters who give in to an early marriage, especially women, are frequently asking for trouble. A woman married before 20 will see her children leave home by the time she is 45 or so, leaving her with 30 years of leisure for which she is ill prepared. And the man who marries early is tied down from a very young age. Margaret Mead has proposed the solution of creating two kinds of legal-marriage arrangements, one for those without and one for those with children. Licenses for the couple desiring a marriage-with-children would be harder to obtain. This solution would allow for companionship and freedom for both woman and man without imposing heavy responsibility—but obviously it is clashing head-on with issues of morality [Browning, 1969]. Nonetheless, the problem of the traditional marriage is there. What is the solution?

Sexual mores change. After all, the waltz was originally greeted with storms of protest because it was considered too sensuous. The exact direction of the change in this country is problematical, but some change must take place.

psychological and physiological factors in sexuality

Heterosexual relationships,* even outside marriage, are delayed for most adolescents for several years beyond the appearance of the hormonal sex drive. Adolescents flounder just as much, if not more, over their sexuality than they do over other social behaviors. To almost everyone's mind, the male is more sexually oriented than the female, but such an assumption is very difficult to evaluate. Kinsey's 1953 study is the only major attempt so far to examine the sexual habits of large groups of people. At that time he found that roughly 20 percent of girls had masturbated by the latter part of high school. However, this statistic does not take into account the sexual satisfaction girls receive from petting, kissing, and the like. To illustrate the possible distortion here, it might be well to point out that Kinsey also found that among women deprived of normal physical sexual outlets—for example, those who wind up in prison—68 percent have had sex dreams that end in orgasm† [Kinsey et al., 1953].

* Sexual relationships between male and female.
† Compared to approximately 30 percent of the whole female population, who occasionally have such dreams.

A small but recent study of female reaction to erotic literature has shown that, contrary to popular belief, women do respond sexually to such material, even when it is read in the presence of a woman experimenter. The author makes the point that Kinsey's finding that 40 percent of the female population reported they were *not* stimulated by such material possibly was too high a figure, simply because some women had probably never read erotic literature [Mosher, 1969]. Thus, women could have been predicted to be just as "sexual" as men. And now, additional studies clearly indicate that this is not only a possibility, but a probability. One study comparing the sexual arousal of males and females in response to films and pictures of heterosexual activity indicates that the two are not as far apart as had been thought. Sexual arousal occurred with males 86 percent of the time, and with females 65 percent [Schmidt, 1970]. Another study has shown only minimal difference between male and female reactions to photographic and literary erotic material. In fact women in the study were a little ahead of men in response to literary-type stimulation [Byre and Lamberth, 1970]. So the new sexual freedom of women seems to have brought to the foreground a decided interest in and reaction to sexual material, factors probably buried by cultural taboos in the past.

Data on men are pretty clear. Even in Kinsey's time, over 90 percent of men had masturbated by age twenty [Kinsey et al., 1948]. One probable reason for the difference between men and women in this area is that the male is more easily aroused because his sexual organs are not recessed, as women's are. Even male babies frequently have erections. One author has postulated that childhood erections may eventually turn into an association with sexual arousal [Korner, 1969].

In its early stages, a boy's sexual behavior is primarily physical. That is, the eleven-year-old is not usually involved in heterosexual relationships; instead, he engages in masturbation. Although his fantasies concern women as sexual objects, little in the way of romance inheres in these fantasies. On the other hand, the girl's major sexual outlet comes at least indirectly from social behavior in dating and thus, for her, sex carries a more romantic connotation. This may help explain why, later on, men are characterized as being more physical about sex than "love-oriented" women. Actual participation in heterosexual relations seems to be retarded in early male adolescence because the boy is preoccupied with women as objects of fantasy and as stimuli for physical release [Simon and Gagnon, 1969].

In its early stages, sex for the adolescent male is quite possibly used mainly to establish maleness for his own self-satisfaction. Without any intention of being funny, one might say that boys masturbate as practice in developing the male sex *role*, not actual sex behavior. The fantasies a boy has during masturbation are usually very aggressive and animallike, and only rarely does he actually behave this way in later relationships with women [Simon, 1969]. In other words, the boy's fantasy life is out of tune with reality; he seems to be using it to establish a supermaleness for a time, which is later toned down by actual heterosexual contact. He is becoming a male first and a sexual being second.

Why this concern over "maleness" looms so large may become even clearer if we explore another area of great importance to the young man, the size of his penis. Although this subject evokes considerable laughter in the locker room, thousands of male adolescents (and adults for that matter) don't find it very funny. A boy who has a small penis is literally frightened that he is not much of a man and will not be able to properly perform his male sex role as society seems to have set it down for him. For many more men than most people realize, the psychological implications are disastrous. To make the situation even sadder, our society has been incredibly repressive about circulating sex information. Only through perseverance and guts, in the mold of Kinsey, have two experimenters, Dr. William Masters and Mrs. Virginia Johnson, formed a scientific institute to study the organs and processes involved in human sexual intercourse.* From their studies we now know some very important things—for example, the flaccid (limp) size of the male penis only minimally reflects the size of the erect organ, and it certainly has nothing to do with adequate sexual performance† [Masters and Johnson, 1966]. For years, then, a man whose penis was small has been subjected to ribbing that was sometimes psychologically disastrous—and that ribbing was based on complete myth. Romain Gary, the French author, discusses this issue in terms of the novelists F. Scott Fitzgerald and Ernest Hemingway:

> It seems that Fitzgerald was tortured by the idea that he was "small." Hemingway conducted an experiment and assured his insecure friend that he was perfectly all right. To prove this beyond any doubt, he dragged Fitzgerald to the Louvre to show him the phallic dimensions of the Greek statues. How could two adults, two of the most famous writers of their time, arrive at such nonsense? What deep anguish does this American phallic fallacy hide? I have never come across this "dimensional obsession" in any other country. [Gary, 1970] ‡

Along the same line, the Kinsey Institute's later book on sexual deviance presents evidence that possession and use of pornography by males

*Masters and Johnson's book was published in 1966 (see references). The reader will find it pretty tough going, however, because of its extremely scientific nature. A paperback is available that clearly examines their findings, and an interested layman should have no difficulty with it [Brecher and Brecher, 1966].
†Essentially the same was found regarding the size of the vagina. Barring physical malformation, its size is not critical to sexual adjustment.
‡From *White Dog*. © 1970 by Romain Gary. Reproduced by permission of The New American Library, New York.

for masturbation fantasies is just as common among normal males as among those who are labeled "perverts" [Gebhard et al., 1965]. Without getting into the issue of morality, possession of pornography is quite common among men and can be considered a normal rather than an abnormal manifestation. Or, to be absolutely on the safe side, possession of pornography by its very nature does not make one perverted or, necessarily, leaning toward perversion. One thing is certain: Pornography seems to make many people lose their perspective. The forefather group of the CIA, called the OSS during World War II, came up with a typically brilliant plot. They decided to drop pornography over Hitler's headquarters, so that when he took a walk in his garden he would find all these obscene pictures and would go insane [Smith, 1972].

Despite all manner of protestations to the contrary, the federal government's 1970 *Report of the Commission on Obscenity and Pornography* was compiled from studies carried out in the finest scientific tradition. Had this report been a positive one supporting faith, hope, and charity, there would have been little disagreement. As it was, however, the report received a "moral" and political reaction rather than a scientific one when it was published. Basically, these studies undertaken for the Commission were unable to find a significant correlation between the use of pornography and sexual offenses, character disruption, delinquency, or crime. Exposure to pornography does not suddenly turn someone into a raving sex maniac. In fact, sex offenders and deviants in some cases have had less exposure to pornography during their adolescent years than have "normal" males [*Report. . .*, 1970]. Other studies seem to indicate that those persons who read erotic material (*Playboy, Penthouse*) are less disturbed, confused, and guilty about sex than those who avoid the material [Schill and Chapin, 1972].

Before leaving the topic, the comments of one psychiatrist certainly should be mentioned because they are so provocative. He points out that most of the antipornography drives are male-oriented. It is quite possible that women have been reading (their own brand of) pornography for years. As the author says, "You cannot sell pictures of nude men to women for erotic purposes; but that does not mean women do not have their own pornography. They do, but most men have not recognized it as pornographic because it would not excite a man: for instance, stories of romance, where what is emphasized is affection, closeness, courtliness, and a little lovely masochism that disguises gentle triumph over a manly man, but not sweating anatomy" [Stoller, 1970].

physiology of sexual activity Male and female sexual responses are related to remarkably similar mechanisms—for example, engorgement of the vagina or the penis with blood—and both the clitoris and the penis are responsive to psychological and physical stimuli.

Sexual enjoyment seems to be the result of a heightened response of the whole body—sweating, flushed skin, increased blood pressure, speeded-up pulse rate. Truman Capote, author of *In Cold Blood*, has likened sex to a sneeze, and the French call it a "little death"; both comments suggest the convulsive release that is involved. The overwhelming physiological reaction during sexual activity probably gives it the impact it has. The orgasm itself involves unmistakable muscular spasms in both male and female.

Sexual release is the same physiologically regardless of how it is attained; that is, climaxes achieved by masturbation, intercourse, or what have you are identical physiologically [Masters and Johnson, 1962]. The major differences in sexual response are psychological. In other words, reactions to sexual activity are functions of motivation, habit, and probably upbringing, rather than of physiology [Wittenborn, 1957].

Masturbation and sexual intercourse—within reason—do not harm or deplete one's life force*; nor do they cause insanity—or add years to one's life.

sexual activity and hormones

Higher primates, including man, apparently have to learn patterns of sexual behavior. Monkeys, for example, do not naturally copulate in a proper fashion unless they are able to observe the behavior [Harlow, 1969]. Other studies with higher animals show that the cortex exercises considerable control over sexual activity [Beach, 1967]. Considering the rich fantasy lives of humans, this finding seems borne out at the human level.

What role do hormones play, then? It was reported earlier that sexuality continues in men who have had their testes removed; however, the continuation does not seem indefinite, and loss of the male sex hormone eventually lessens sex drive. The human being probably operates for a time on psychological forces, and only eventually does the hormone loss have its effect.†

Females are known to experience an *increase* in sexual desire when the ovaries are removed, probably as the result of a psychological factor: The surgery prevents them from having more children and makes them more relaxed about sex. But this doesn't explain physiologically how an increase in drive can result when the ovaries are removed. The answer seems to lie in the fact that the male sex hormone, which the woman also manufactures, is responsible for female sexual activity to some extent even with the female hormone removed. In fact, injection of androgen (male sex hormone) into females does increase sexual interest [Money, 1961].

* Whatever that is, but you will hear about it quite frequently.

† This statement is an educated guess from the data available at present. The role of hormones in human sexual behavior—once it has become a habit—is unclear.

HOMOSEXUALITY

Homosexuality, a term applied to sexual relationships between two men or between two women,* is not a phenomenon restricted to adolescence, but this particular time period certainly encompasses the beginnings of external manifestations of homosexual interest. Hence, we take it up at this point.

Homosexuality is not an "all or nothing" phenomenon. Some people have isolated homosexual experiences and never return to this activity. Others have isolated heterosexual experiences. A moderate number of people are bisexual and engage in both types of activity [Kinsey et al., 1948]. The incidence of homosexuality, counting isolated events that occur as seldom as once in a person's lifetime, is about 50 percent for males and 24 percent for women [Kinsey et al., 1953]. Though these figures were determined using reliable survey techniques, in an area like homosexuality they should be taken only as approximations.

Two major psychological orientations bear on this kind of behavior. First is the assumption that homosexuality grows out of normal adolescent sex drives that originally are directed toward members of the same sex and that do not graduate to an interest in the other sex. Second is the "long-term" explanation in which the seeds of homosexuality are sown long before adolescence. This theory searches for causes in early childhood and family experiences that begin to show up in puberty.

psychological explanations

Harry S. Sullivan makes a great deal of the period of puberty as a factor in homosexual development. As the young man or woman grows into puberty, he or she is faced with a number of crises of an intimate, personal nature, but the youngster finds it difficult to discuss many of them in depth with parents or, especially, with members of the opposite sex. Sullivan calls this period the "buddy stage" because at this point the adolescent turns to members of his own sex with his intimate problems [Sullivan, 1953]. Relationships with same-sexed friends are now quite intense and emotional, and they involve physical contact.† At the same time, hormonal and psychological sex desires are rearing their heads, and these same-sex relationships increase in intimacy, at least on an emotional level. They do not necessarily involve sexual activity, although occasionally sexual encounters occur.

Further along in time, the adolescent should theoretically gravitate toward the opposite sex, and most do. But *heterosexual* relationships can be loaded with danger for some of these youngsters: either the relationship itself can be wholly unsatisfactory and frightening, or it can just fail to measure up to the same-sex relationship previously established. If this

---

*Homosexual females are also called lesbians.
†The type of intimate physical contact seen between football players: hugging and rear-end patting.

happens, the boy or girl may return to his or her homosexual ways [Sagir, 1969]. Actually, a fair number of later homosexuals have heterosexual relationships at some time during this adolescent period, and another substantial number have them after earlier homosexual experiences. The determining factor is the relative satisfaction of one relationship over another. Sullivan, then, concentrates on the adolescent period as the critical time of sex-partner development.

The Freudians (adherents of old, new, and modified versions of Freudian theories), on the other hand, stress early developmental patterns. Innumerable experiences and combinations of experiences exist in early development that *might* explain later homosexual behavior: fear of the opposite-sexed parent, which turns the youngster toward a member of his own sex; overidentification with (becoming too similar to) the same-sexed parent, either through fear of the other parent or through preference for the same-sexed one. You are already familiar with the possibility of a mother or father getting a baby of the "wrong" sex and rearing the child as if he or she were the desired gender. It has been postulated, too, that heterosexual relationships could be frightening because the child witnessed the *primal scene** and interpreted it as a fight or, lacking understanding, thought that the heterosexual act involved injury because it appeared to be violent.† Thus the child would avoid heterosexuality—and "violence"—by turning to a member of his own sex. Support for the primal-scene hypothesis is pretty weak, or at least hazy. In a study comparing homosexual sex-offenders in prison with a "normal" control group, 10 percent of the prisoners were found to remember witnessing the primal scene, as compared to 4 percent of the control group [Gebhard et al., 1965]. So, even if the primal scene is a factor, the difference is a minor one between the two groups and could not account for homosexuality in general.

A final postulation comes from Freud, and has already been touched on: Freud felt that everybody was at least a little bit bisexual.

By this time you may have begun to feel that Freud was obsessed with sex. Even if he was, it is always unfair to dismiss a theory on such grounds. Because of his sexual theories, Freud suffered verbal abuse from passing strangers as he walked down the streets of Vienna. He was called "dirty" and "filthy." He was even attacked at a meeting of neurologists and psychiatrists, where one professor said that his theory was a matter for the police [Brome, 1967].

All we can do is take each of Freud's ideas as it arises and examine the evidence that supports or challenges it. Basically, careful studies of

123   Some homosexuals are trying to alter society's attitudes in order to offset the negative effects on their own lives. Here, two men apply for a marriage license in Minneapolis, Minnesota. Marriage is one of society's most powerful forces for stability and social acceptance-and in Minnesota, marriage between two men is not illegal (*UPI*)

*That is, saw his parents engaging in sexual intercourse.
†If this view were accurate, the majority of males living in extreme-poverty areas where the whole family sleeps in one room would probably be homosexual—and such is not the case.

normal males show no evidence for this theory that everyone is somewhat bisexual in desires. Normal males are stimulated by pictures of nude female adults, adolescents, and children, in that order. They demonstrate an erotic aversion to adult male nudes, and slightly less aversion to adolescent male nudes. Freud was dealing with the abnormal—but still the normal males should show some interest if Freud's bisexual theory is correct. No such evidence exists, that I can find, in studies of normal males* [Freund, 1970].

In the case of female homosexuals, it has been hypothesized that an affectionate father causes overidentification with males and hence a tendency to be more masculine; by inference, the girl then leans toward homosexuality. A very careful study has shown this theory to be incorrect; in this study of adolescent lesbians, the fathers were overbearing and obnoxious, or not even present in the home, rather than overaffectionate [Kremer and Rifkin, 1969]. You may recall, too, that normal development of the female child is facilitated by affectionate fathers. Finally, female homosexuals are not necessarily masculine in outlook or behavior.

Learning of social roles by means of operant conditioning should not be forgotten; this kind of conditioning could apply to any of the childhood or adolescent influences we've been considering. Using this theory, the behaviors that are most rewarded, or those that bring most satisfaction, assist in developing a social role that fits this most rewarded behavior. If male-male or female-female relationships are most rewarding, they become the style of life.

Without wanting to take the easy way out, we may suggest that, as more data appear, any of these interpretations, or a combination of them, could well apply to a particular person; homosexuality probably is not a behavior that always results from a single set of circumstances.

physiological factors in homosexuality

Investigators have worked thousands of hours trying to find some physiological basis for homosexuality. Identical-twin studies have come into play again, with experimenters trying to determine if people with identical heredity would follow an identical route toward homosexuality. Indeed, studies have shown that a large number of identical twins do engage in homosexual behavior [Kallman, 1952]. However, as in the case of the intelligence studies, it is very simple to point out that similar environments could just as easily have led to sets of twins engaging in similar behavior.

Even more damaging to the case for heredity are many studies which have shown male homosexuals to be much more numerous than lesbians,

---

*There is always the Freudian "out" that the aversion of men for men is a way of covering up desire, but when you get into this kind of reasoning you are lost scientifically. Note that the paragraph above does *not* contradict the fact that we are bisexual in the sense that each of us has both male and female hormones.

and which have indicated that being in prison increases homosexuality. These studies demonstrate social and environmental influences as well as do the cases (mentioned earlier) of hermaphrodites who seem to develop sexual interests and leanings depending on *how they have been reared*—that is, as boys or as girls [Money, 1961, 1965]. The issue takes on special significance because some hermaphrodites may look like men but have the internal apparatus of women, and vice versa, but they play the role they have learned. A final argument against heredity, and an intriguing one, is suggested by the fact that very few homosexuals have children. Just by the laws of inheritance and survival of species, homosexuals should be a "dying race," but they are not [Cory, 1965].

Hormones have not been forgotten. To date, the evidence about hormones has been clear. Injection of a male hormone into male homosexuals and of female hormones into lesbians has no effect on sexual leanings; the hormones do not turn homosexuals toward the opposite sex. Imbalance of *estrogen** or *androgen†* does not seem related to heterosexual or homosexual activity [Ullman, 1969].

One finding, which should be viewed with caution, is nonetheless thought-provoking. A large proportion of male homosexuals, compared with a control group, experienced the onset of puberty very early; the average age was about thirteen [Gebhard et al., 1965]. This finding, even when viewed with the necessary caution, certainly lends support to one possibility: For a male who enters puberty very early, other boys are fairly accessible for sexual activity, while few girls are available to boys at this age. Obviously, not all boys who enter puberty so early turn out to be homosexual, but such a finding, when combined with some of the psychological factors mentioned, could be a clue to homosexual development.

the myths of homosexuality The greater proportion of homosexuals seem to feel that interest in members of their own sex is the result of hormonal imbalance, some inherited characteristic, or some physiological problem. None of these factors, as you have noticed, seems to be influential, at least according to present knowledge of the subject [Buss, 1966]. Many psychologists feel that homosexuals believe in these factors because doing so helps to justify the statement, "I can't help it." Other social scientists, as you will see in a moment, cannot see any particular need for homosexuals to justify their actions.

The heterosexual world has its own myths about the homosexual world. As a general rule, however, you cannot expect to identify a homosexual by his physical appearance or his mannerisms. Only a minority dress and act "funny," as "straights" might term it [Hooker, 1962]. Many men

*Female sex hormone.
†Male sex hormone.

125 Transvestites (males in female clothing) at a beauty contest. Sometimes sexual deviance takes bizarre forms (*Frank Teti, Camera 5*)

124 Socrates rescuing his lover Alcibiades from attackers. The great philosopher was a married man—and a homosexual (*Culver*)

who have the deepest of voices and the most masculine of mannerisms are homosexual, and many of the most feminine women are, too.

Except for occasional combinations that happen to fit the personalities of those involved, little or no evidence supports the widespread belief that one member of each pair takes the male role and the other the female role in living arrangements and/or sexual behavior.

Finally, among young-adult and adult homosexuals, the use of force—that is, homosexual rape, enticement, or even kidnapping—is extremely rare* [Hoffman, 1968]. Partners seem to be chosen in a traditional fashion, as they are in the heterosexual world.

is homosexuality normal?

Many readers may prefer that this section be deleted, but to do so would be to ignore a critical and controversial issue in psychology. Any such discussion is going to bring forth the wrath of certain people anyway. Did you know, for example, that in some states a person may be convicted of certain homosexual acts, such as sodomy, and receive a prison sentence of sixty years to life? That in one state the minimal punishment is life imprisonment at hard labor? It makes one wonder who is more bizarre, homosexuals or the people who support such legislation. One almost gets the impression that sex of any type, even between husband and wife, is illegal† [Sherwin, 1961].

Belief in the psychopathology‡ of homosexual activity is not universal. As most of you know, the ancient Greeks considered this behavior a normal activity as long as the person had heterosexual contacts on occasion. In fact, homosexuality is not uncommon among animals free in nature; many animals seem to have the capacity for both male and female sexual interests [Chevalier-Skolnikoff, 1971]. Many countries today have legalized homosexuality—which doesn't make it "normal" or "moral," but does help to

---

*This is not true in the case of adult homosexual offenders against minors. These individuals seem to be of a different mold.

†As a matter of fact, it nearly is, in most states. Laws are on the books prohibiting anything but "regular" intercourse between married people. Sex play of other kinds is illegal.

‡Abnormal behavior resulting from psychological disturbance.

447

ensure that it won't be considered a terrible crime against nature as it is in most of the United States.

One source of controversy in the United States is *The Gay World*, a book which despite its popularity is the result of careful, scientific investigation. The author, Dr. Martin Hoffman, has spent years investigating homosexuals in the United States who have regular jobs, do not violate other laws, and apparently lead relatively normal lives. Hoffman blames society for the ills of the homosexual underground; society, he maintains, by its prohibitions and laws *makes* homosexual behavior abnormal. In other words, he is saying, it is not so much the act of homosexuality that causes grief, but instead the laws that prohibit it and the society that finds it repugnant [Hoffman, 1968]. The core of his argument, as I understand it, is that millions of homosexuals don't want to be "cured." The immediate counterargument, of course, is that lots of mental patients either see nothing wrong with themselves or say they don't want to be "cured." So, this argument can be used against Hoffman, at least part way. If the mental patient is bringing misery on himself or others, as a large number are, there is some justification in trying to cure him. But there is another side to the coin: What if the mental patient, or the homosexual, is relatively happy and functioning well? Do we still "cure" him?

There are a few studies which bear on what are called normal homosexuals. A *normal homosexual* is defined as one who has not been in a mental hospital and to all ostensible purposes is leading a fairly productive life. Studies of 89 male and 57 female normal homosexuals suggest strongly that homosexuality as a way of life is already developed by the time of adolescence. Even before adult contacts occurred, most of the homosexuals reported that they had an orientation or leaning toward members of their own sex, and, as mentioned before, heterosexual contacts did not seem to alter these basic desires. Male and female homosexuals seem to follow social-role development in a fashion similar to that of other subgroups within a society. For example, male homosexuals are aggressive and comparatively unemotional in their contacts; they are also quite fickle. Female homosexuals are less conspicuous and more emotional, and they form longer attachments, at least half of them lasting four years or longer [Sagir, 1969; Hoffman, 1968]. In other words, the homosexual world seems to be a traditional subgroup of society which exhibits relatively traditional behavior patterns, except in the matter of sex preference.

Psychological tests and interviews of normal homosexuals have been unable to distinguish between heterosexuals and homosexuals; that is, homosexuals who have not sought treatment do not appear abnormal [Hooker, 1957]. Dr. Albert Ellis, probably the leading psychologist-sexologist of our day, immediately counters this finding with the criticism that since psychological tests are of such low validity, how could these findings be supported anyway [Ellis, 1965]? Ellis feels that the tests are in error and that the homosexual is not normal. You might want to refer back to our discussion of test validity where you will find the results depressingly low in many cases—but complete and summary rejection of all test results by such a respected person shows what a volatile issue homosexuality is. He feels that so-called normal homosexuals are "sex-shy." They may be, but you should view statements in these provocative areas with caution.

Other investigators point out that the "bizarre" ways of homosexuals get them into trouble with the law. By inference, then, they are abnormal because they are on the other side of society. This concept becomes quite confusing when closely examined: Many state laws forbid premarital heterosexual relations; are people who violate these laws also bizarre or abnormal?

Some psychological problems do seem to be connected with homosexuality. For example, the degree of emotional involvement between partners, especially males, is relatively low. Social-sexual contacts between homosexuals do not seem to involve the same amount of give-and-take found in heterosexual relationships. In other words, by this criteria, homosexuals are less able to form adult contacts that can be deemed mature. Male homosexual involvement seems to take the form of relationships that are quite shallow and somewhat reminiscent of the early pubescent male and his self-preoccupied sex life.* The male relationships, more often than not, are similar to a form of sexual release rather than the development of social ties on a one-to-one basis, although a moderate number of long-lasting, "monogamous" homosexual relationships do exist.

A typical study of female adolescent homosexuals, a small one involving 25 subjects, showed that these girls, although not under treatment, have trouble in school and at home and did not seem, to the experimenter, to be well-adjusted [Kremer and Rifkin, 1969]. This type of study always presents a problem: If the examiner were given 25 girls *labeled* homosexual (but actually not), would he find the same amount of psychological disturbance? Also, assuming that signs of pathology did show up, were these adolescent girls pathological to begin with, or did society's prohibitions make them that way?

Suppose you are the doctor. A patient comes to you with a number of problems. After a few meetings with him, you find out that he is homosexual. When you ask, he says that this area is one in which he doesn't

---

*Even the most impersonal sex relationship, however, is not completely devoid of emotion. In fact, one sociologist has noted an unusual situation in which the building where activities took place became an object of strong attachment. In one instance in which a public restroom used for homosexual activities was torn down, one of the frequenters took a black wreath to that spot at Christmas. Some emotion must be involved, although it comes out in unusual ways [Humphreys, 1970].

have problems, and he doesn't want to be "cured." How would you handle it?

SUMMARY

Adolescence is frequently a very trying time for the young man or woman, especially because major physiological changes occur during this period. Hormones are activated that have been quiet up to this point, and these hormones trigger dramatic increases in height, development of intense interest in sexual activity, and a number of minor changes such as voice changes, skin difficulties, and social awkwardness.

Changes of this nature are confined to the adolescent period, so it is to be expected that adolescents will band together with others who are experiencing the same difficulties.

Psychologically, the adolescent is reaching manhood or womanhood, which brings with it both the desire to be free and the somewhat feared independence of adulthood. Unlike other societies, the United States makes little or no provision for a transition from childhood to adulthood, a factor that leads to uneasiness and lack of direction for the adolescent.

Despite all these difficulties, adolescent rebellion is not a major problem except in the eyes of an older generation. Most adolescents do not get in trouble and tend to remain fairly close to the ideals expressed by their parents, but they seem threatening just because they dress and act differently from middle-aged people.

Sexually, the adolescent is ready for marriage, yet every other societal force works against such a move, and the youth has no direct sexual outlet. Increasing evidence points to the possibility that an interest in sex is just as prominent in females as males. Sexuality is intimately tied up with social roles, so it is difficult to determine the genuine desires and feelings of young people. For example, how much of the sexual bravado of male teenagers is playing the game, and how much is actual desire, is elusive. We do know that masturbation is frequent in males and moderate among females, and that girls find a sexual outlet in kissing and petting.

Homosexuality may have seeds early in life; in fact, most psychologists believe it does. During the adolescent period, however, manifestations of this behavior come into full bloom. One persuasive theory about homosexuality is that of Sullivan, who maintained that in early adolescence intimacy is commonly with members of the same sex and that if relationships with members of the opposite sex present difficulties, the youngsters tend to remain with same-sexed partners.

In any case, no evidence supports the idea that heredity or physiology are factors responsible for the activities of homosexuals. Almost all evidence points to its being a learned behavior. A very strong current trend is to argue that by no means is all homosexuality psychopathological;

instead, homosexuals can be classified as those who are normal and those who are abnormal, largely ignoring the homosexual behavior itself and focusing on the person's mental health, regardless of his sexual persuasion.

At present, however, this latter view is the voice of the minority; most psychologists still feel that homosexual behavior is abnormal.

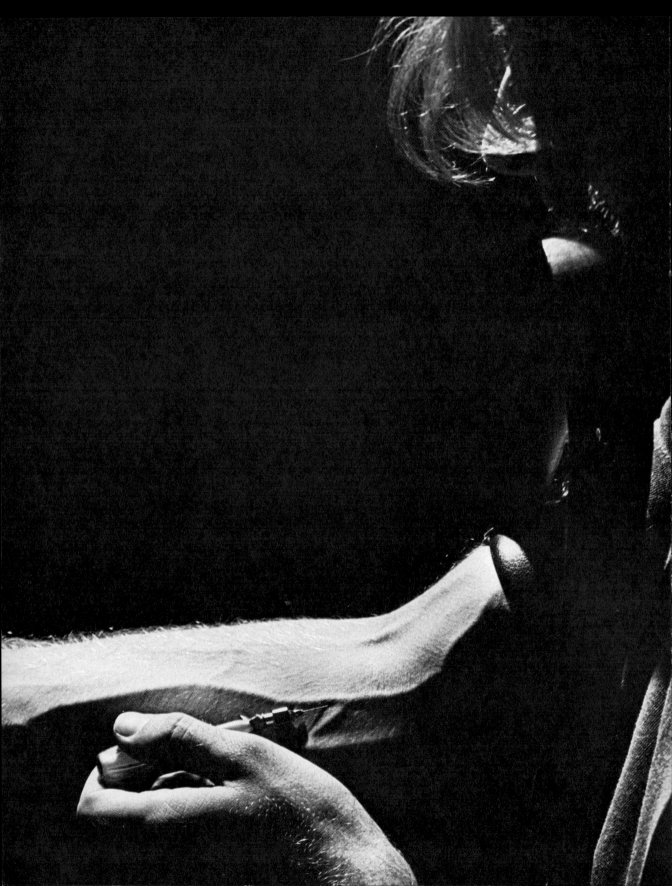

CHAPTER NINETEEN
ADOLESCENTS: DELINQUENCY AND DRUGS

**JUVENILE
DELINQUENCY**

An article in the *Ladies' Home Journal* lamented loss of interest in the Bible and religion, saying, "The younger man now reads with indifference of a score of murders every morning while puffing his cigarette . . ." [Wishy, 1968]. The popular press seems quick to call our attention to signs of pending moral decay. But this comment appeared in 1900. Such a remark has appeared at least once a year in every paper or magazine since Ben Franklin helped to decrease the amount of labor required to turn out printed material.

Part of the problem with juvenile delinquency is that it becomes as sensational as wearing a topless swim suit, long hair, or beads, or not taking a bath. No doubt delinquency is a problem, but it always has been. Delinquency rates do tend to increase and multiply each year.

A fair proportion of this increase, however, is the result of more sophisticated crime-reporting techniques. There was a time when the police had a talk with the boy or girl, and that was it; now there is little talk (except between authorities and the upper-class delinquent), quick frisking, detention, and a record of arrest.

We used to push over outhouses on Halloween; if any were left today, a youngster would pretty likely be arrested for this act rather than swatted with a stick by an irate farmer. And it is a rare child, rich or poor, who has not taken a pencil or a paperclip or something else from a store just to see if he could do it—but these acts are now officially "delinquent."

No one is making light of delinquency or of the fact that it *is* increasing, even if population growth and reporting techniques are taken into account, but no evidence proves that panic is in order. The majority of young people are about as good or bad as they ever were. Our focus will be on the problems of a minority. Within a given year, about 2 million young people between 15 and 19 are arrested for delinquent acts.

**delinquency
and social class**

Delinquency can be defined in various ways. Basically it involves theft, vandalism, or malicious behavior by underage boys and girls. *Social class* is an even vaguer term than delinquency. By scientific custom, society is broken down into three major classes: the lower class, comprising semi-skilled and unskilled people; the middle class, or white- and blue-collar workers; and the upper class, professional and semiprofessional people.

454

126–127 Delinquency and social class are not always easy to relate. Looking at these two groups of adolescents, you cannot readily tell which may be "delinquents" and which law-abiding and harmless (*Maude Dorr; Lucia Woods*)

Admittedly, this classification is hazy and overlapping and presents problems of definition, but you can get the gist of it and detect some differences between the groups that are probably justified.

For forty years an accepted fact has been that delinquency rates are much higher in certain areas of cities—namely, lower-class slums [Shaw, 1929]. Even today studies bear out this fact [Gordon, 1967]. It would be nice to leave it at that and say that slum areas breed delinquency, but the story is not so simple.

methods of reporting delinquency

First, a distinction has to be made between two methods used to record delinquent acts, the official report and the self-report. *Official records* reflect *only* the number of people arrested for delinquency; obviously, undetected delinquent acts don't appear in these records, but many conclusions are drawn from them, nonetheless, and are therefore questionable. One such conclusion is frequently reached—that lower-class people are more prone to delinquency, compared, for instance, with middle-class people. This finding is distorted: Police are more likely to let the middle-class person go with a reprimand and to arrest the lower-class offender.

Delinquency is relative. In fact, it varies enormously from one culture or subculture to another. Some countries define as a delinquent act collecting cigarette butts, climbing trees (!), and girls talking to strangers even though these same girls may be sexually promiscuous and not be considered delinquent [Gibbens and Ahrenfeldt, 1966].

The second method of studying delinquency, the *self-report*, is similar to a questionnaire. Social scientists use it with people from all classes, usually anonymously, in order to obtain information about their activities. To make this clearer, some typical items found on a questionnaire used in an elaborate study of 4,077 high school students are as follows:

Have you ever taken little things (worth less than $2) . . . ?
Have you ever taken things of some value . . . ?
Have you ever taken a car for a ride without the owner's permission . . . ? [Hirschi, 1969]

455

The self-report clearly has advantages over official statistics in locating behavior patterns that have escaped police detection. For instance, one of many recent studies involving the self-report technique shows that social class does not seem to be involved in delinquency. Class had appeared to be a factor because a large number of delinquents come from families that are on welfare or where the father is unemployed. If just these particular families are removed from the category "lower class," a large number of lower-class individuals remain who are *not* on welfare. When only these nonwelfare families are considered, self-report studies show that delinquent acts occur just about as frequently in the middle class as in the lower class [Hirschi, 1969].

One major factor in creating delinquency seems to be the destruction of family unity which results from being on the welfare role—not social class as such. For example, a child has trouble admiring an unemployed father; the child can't understand why his father is different from other fathers. And family friction over the man's job problems may add to the child's lack of respect for his father.

Self-report studies also show that upper-middle-class youth commit about as many offenses as lower-class youth, even though these adolescents are a little more "refined." Even so, authorities tend to punish these same offenses more severely when they occur in the lower classes—for example, offenses involving the use of alcohol [Pine, 1965]. In other words, official statistics aside, delinquency of one sort or another seems to pervade all classes of adolescents, but enforcement is not consistent.

An unexpected amount of delinquency occurs among even affluent teenagers. One often thinks of delinquency as a way of life among youngsters who are deprived. Yet interviews with upper-class delinquents indicate that they have all the material goods they need; some claim not even to want some of the things they steal. In some respects their behavior is probably not dissimilar in origin to that of the lower class—that is, upper-class delinquents maintain that they are egged on by their friends and have "a desire for kicks . . . excitement."

One major difference between classes, however, is the type of crime committed. The upper-class delinquent engages in typical, normal horseplay—for example, "mooning," or exposing a bare rear end through a car window, or the "mobile party," cruising the neighborhood while having a party in the back of a rented truck. But some of the behavior is rather vicious—for example, shooting at houses, painting cars, chopping down trees, killing pets. The poor delinquent engages in more "serious" crimes such as robbery, aggravated assault, and burglary [Tobias, 1970]. The main difference between the two groups apparently is that upper-class delinquents do not need material possessions, whereas lower-class delinquents act in ways designed to obtain objects or money.

**FAMILY
RELATIONSHIPS
OF THE DELINQUENT**

Delinquency shows a clear family pattern. For instance, a study in one state showed that *80 percent* of recorded delinquents came from families with previous criminal histories, a staggering figure. This percentage does not suggest, however, that heredity is deeply involved, except possibly among the few youngsters who had very low intelligence and didn't seem to comprehend the law. Actually, the case against heredity is fairly strong: For the majority, delinquency is a temporary thing and recedes as adolescence draws to a close.

Chromosomes, you may recall, are the basic material of inheritance. The popular press has given considerable attention to one study's claim that some prison inmates who showed violent and dangerous tendencies possessed an extra chromosome. The suggestion was strong that criminality was sometimes inherited. As happens frequently, careful studies replicating the original study have not been reported by the press. An educated guess at present, relying on followup studies, is that the chromosomal difference in the one study was a fluke. These later studies indicate no tendency toward violence among individuals with the extra chromosome. In fact their behavior was similar to that of people with a different chromosomal disorder, one that is typically considered to produce mild-mannered, unaggressive people. So this study seems to be a dead end as far as inheritance of criminal tendencies via chromosomes is concerned—and it certainly points out the importance of replication [Clark et al., 1970]. Taking dozens of recent studies into account, experimenters come to the conclusion that there is presently very little evidence of such a thing as a "criminal chromosome" [Owen, 1972; Hook, 1973].

Instead of crediting the heredity factor in delinquency, most authorities suggest that the family with a criminal background is pretty well splintered and a child growing up in that environment has the odds against him. Of course, it has been suggested that some imitation of the parents by the youngster is involved, which is probably true, but the core of the problem seems to be the confused and unpleasant family situation.

The family that lacks a father is more likely to produce a delinquent. Most investigators feel that the delinquency can be attributed not to the absence of the father as such, but to the chaotic family life that preceded his departure from the home [Siegman, 1966]. For instance, delinquents have a notorious family history of cold and rejecting fathers even when the fathers happen to be at home [Bandura and Walters, 1959]. Further, many youngsters are probably happy to see the father go, because he is typically brutal and alcoholic [Ainsworth, 1962]. Delinquents' parents, in general, suffer a higher proportion of physical ailments, emotional disturbance, and mental retardation [Glueck and Glueck, 1970].

A further ingredient that can be added to this unsavory mess is lack of communication between parent and child [Martin, 1961]. Communication, pure and simple, is not the real issue; many families indulge in considerable talking and shouting. Instead, the variable that differentiates the delinquent from the nondelinquent is the amount of *intimate* communication, the degree to which family members share goals and activities. For example, parents' genuine interest in where the youngster goes when he leaves the house is negatively correlated with delinquency. This correlation is found even if the parent might care but doesn't know for certain where he has gone: The critical issue here seems to be simply a personal concern about where he might be. The importance of this factor holds for all social classes [Hirschi, 1969]. These findings can be related to earlier discussions of internalization of parental attitudes. Apparently, the nondelinquent internalizes his parents' concern for his whereabouts; no matter where he goes, he feels that they are interested in what he is doing.

CHARACTERISTICS OF DELINQUENT PERSONALITIES

Delinquents, as we have seen, do not show a consistent desire for material goods, so material wants do not seem to provide the only reason for their actions [Reiss, 1963]. Instead, as you can piece together from my comments, the delinquent just doesn't know whether he is coming or going in life because no one *else* seems to care or will give him any assistance in finding out. Thus it may well be that many of his delinquent acts are perpetrated in order to get some attention, just as children frequently violate rules simply so that someone will pay attention, even if the attention takes the form of punishment.

The delinquent, then, seems to lack personality aspects that are associated with a deep, close family life. His sense of identity is missing: One study shows a *major* discrepancy between delinquents' evaluation of "me as I would like to be" and "me as I really am." Some discrepancy appears in all adolescents, but with delinquents it is notable [Deitz, 1969].

Other studies are clear in emphasizing "incompleteness." Even though this feeling in general is typical of adolescence, the delinquent is *quite* immature and fails to recognize his emotions or take them into account. Handling emotions of all kinds is usually learned in a reasonably peaceful family setting—but delinquent youngsters deny that they "feel anything," and they seem to lack a sense of personal worth or self-esteem, even though they may display a lot of bravado [Didato, 1969; Baker and Spielberg, 1970].

THE PSYCHOLOGICAL WORLD OF THE DELINQUENT

The delinquent is floundering, psychologically adrift; he is seeking and desperately needs attention. Traditional behavior—"being a good member of society"—hasn't worked, so he must turn to other people, those who share his dilemma, members of the delinquent gang [Coleman, 1961]. He joins the gang because he can't seem to find home plate or a sense of identity through family or home.

the school   Many recent studies point out that this problem is aggravated because the delinquent does not fit in at school either; in fact, many authorities feel that the school could be at least the final backstop in helping to avert delinquent behavior. Unfortunately, this is not the case. As a matter of fact, school is for many normal people the worst thing that has happened to them. In a survey of the most negative experiences in one's life, teachers caused more psychological upset and conflict than any other single group—including parents, friends, lovers, or siblings [Branan, 1972]. Anyway, the delinquent may possibly do poorly in school *because* he is delinquent, but as the studies we cover will demonstrate, this explanation seems remote. Apparently, the reverse is true: The youngster does poorly in school, and this failure helps to push him down the path of antisocial behavior. For instance, verbal achievement tests have a high negative correlation with delinquency; the world of the middle-class, verbally oriented school is beyond the abilities (or interests) of the delinquent, more often than not of a lower-class orientation.*

Cheating in school can result from difficulty in a student's **attention span**, or his ability to orient himself to the task. The typical recorded delinquent is a youngster who cannot orient and attend to verbal material and hence is much more prone to cheating behavior [Grim, 1968]. Thus, although school may be difficult or boring for the ordinary student, for the potential delinquent it is fatal. The potential delinquent doesn't belong in the school system as it presently exists, with both its verbal orientation and its verbal reward system. The youngster clearly feels out of it, in school and at home.

The issues of verbal intelligence and attention span may help to explain why delinquency is not a permanent condition, why it tends to die down after adolescence. Apparently, the young person finally finds a job and discovers that he can get some feeling of accomplishment from it; likewise, he forms new ties with a nondelinquent group at work. One might conclude that "curing" delinquency boils down to turning the delinquent's attention to activities that he can find rewarding.

Those young people, even from the lower classes, who intend to go to college (whether they do go or not) are involved in far fewer delinquent offenses [Pine, 1965]. In other words, the nondelinquent people are attending to and distracted by specific goals, which the delinquent doesn't have, and these goals happen to fit into society's norms. Mature social development is inadequate in delinquents, a fact reflected in their consistently low scores on tests of moral judgment. They falter in their ability to reason out problems such as this one: Should an army officer send a sick man or a troublemaker on an almost-certain-death mission to blow up a bridge? There is no specifically right or wrong answer to this problem, but delinquents in

* Regardless of where the school is located, teachers have a middle-class orientation.

this study approach the solution in an immature and relatively confused fashion [Fodor, 1972].

Support for some of these hypotheses comes from a remarkable project for delinquent youths. A special school for delinquents was established, and its curriculum consisted primarily of programmed instruction that offered immediate reward in the form of points or credits which could be used to buy nearly anything the youngsters wanted. Rewards were granted *only* if the student studied. The two key elements here seem to be, first, that the instruction relied on programmed material, which did not require that the delinquent compete with highly verbal peers, as he had to in regular school. Second, the reward system was tangible and immediate; something happened *now* if you studied. This system of tangible rewards supplanted the vague, long-term goal of going to college—a goal which the *non*delinquent can handle because he is more secure. A few months after the reward program for delinquents began, it was reported that no discipline problems existed in the classes. Thus a reorientation of traditional school activities seems to remove both learning and behavioral problems [Cohen et al., 1966]. The important element here seems to be an inability of the delinquent in the regular school system to distract himself long enough to attain goals in the future. Only the reward-now system seems to keep him going, a situation which resembles the immaturity found in children. In order to keep children on the track of long-term goals, they must be constantly provided with interesting distractions (immediate rewards) along the way [Mischel et al., 1972].

The personal world of the delinquent becomes vivid when we look closely at one thorough study that compared delinquent personality characteristics with the personalities of nondelinquents. This study used paper-and-pencil personality tests and found several important differences: Compared to nondelinquents, delinquents have *greater* need to be cared for, loved, and guided; at the same time, they have greater need to dominate others, to be aggressive and physical, and to show off [Thompson, 1969].

Thus, the delinquent personality shows a basic conflict: The delinquent is starved for affection, yet seems to have learned no other method for getting attention than a distorted form of being pushy and thereby being noticed for playing the antisocial role.

the sociopathic personality   Most delinquents grow out of their problems, but a fair number are what might be termed permanent delinquents, or *sociopaths.** From childhood on through adulthood, sociopaths usually show disturbances of an antisocial nature, and during this whole period they are aggressive, reckless, and impulsive [Robins, 1966].

---

* From *pathology* ("disease") and *social, sociopathic* literally means being diseased in social relations, or being unable to consider other people or the rules that protect them. The term *psychopathic* has also been used to describe this group. The terms are interchangeable.

The sociopath's history resembles that of the ordinary delinquent, so one might infer that the problems he encounters either begin earlier, are more intense, or both. The evidence is not clear. In a way, the sociopath has a very unusual mental disturbance; typically, the mental patient shows guilt, remorse, or anxiety about the trouble that he has in coping with society and its rules. Not so the sociopath; he doesn't seem to care about the rules, and therefore rehabilitation is a formidable task. Society and those who represent it can usually appeal to something that most of us term "conscience," but this ploy doesn't work with the sociopath.

The life history of the sociopath seems to be such that he literally does not know how to respond emotionally to others. Outwardly, this sort of person can be the ultimate in charm, grace, and friendliness—and yet he can rob you blind while smiling at you disarmingly.

Sociopathy is baffling; its origin is unknown, but we can hazard a number of fairly good guesses. For instance, one of the best predictors of continued social deviance is having a history of delinquency *and being placed in a correctional institution* [Robins, 1966]. It may well be, considering that the sociopath typically has a father who is either sociopathic himself or an alcoholic, that putting the delinquent away is more or less the last straw in the delinquent's frustration in finding some meaningful life in the company of someone who cares about him. Usually parents have been cold, forbidding, and distant, and the atmosphere in prison is not exactly that of a warm, friendly home on Christmas day [Buss, 1966].

The sociopath has been described very aptly, by two psychologists, as a person who finds himself *inconsequential* [Ullman, 1969]. If you think about this word for a moment, the personality may come into focus: the sociopath is being disregarded, and has been constantly disregarded, and when someone does pay attention to him, it usually takes the form of punishment. The sociopath seems to constantly seek new and varied experiences, especially if they will provide some form of stimulation. He is probably trying to make up for the many years in which he received no care or love, but he is not satisfied with one roller coaster ride; he needs to be on it constantly [Quay, 1965].

ALCOHOL

The average American has had a swig of alcohol by age ten, and roughly 70 percent of high school students drink occasionally, so it seems worthwhile to cover a few facts pertaining to alcoholism and the effects of alcohol [G. L. Maddox and B. C. McCall, 1964].

There is no evidence that alcohol in moderation does any damage. In large doses, over long periods of time, it can lead to muscle disease or damage; one of the muscles affected being the heart. Liver damage is one side effect of very heavy drinking, but at the present time this is thought to result from inadequate nutrition, a common fate of the alcoholic. The heavy drinker also runs the risk of irreversible brain damage after years of drunken stupors.

Whether or not alcohol becomes a problem seems to relate directly to the attitudes and behavior patterns of the parents. The lowest rate of alcoholism is found among Italian-Americans and Jewish families, two groups that traditionally introduce alcohol in diluted amounts as early as three years of age [C. R. Snyder, 1958]. One would suspect here that the positive influence in drinking behavior comes from strong family and/or religious ties. Heaviest drinking by group seems to occur where there is an ambivalence toward alcohol—that is a mixture of guilt and approval, such as we find in the traditional Anglo-Saxon Protestant Americans [A. D. Ullman, 1958]. Problems with alcohol are least likely when the parents are moderate drinkers, no moral importance is attached to drinking, and the beverage is usually consumed with a meal [National Institute Mental Health, 1972].

There is clear indication that children of alcoholics tend to become alcoholics more frequently than the general population, but the evidence to date indicates that this is not an inherited factor, rather a matter of either imitation or psychological problems created by the parents' drinking behavior [National Institute of Mental Health, 1972].

You have a problem with alcohol if you show any of the following symptoms: frequent drinking sprees; steady increase in intake; solitary drinking; morning drinking; blackouts (physical consciousness, but with a loss of memory for that period); the need to drink in order to cope with life; going to work intoxicated [National Institute on Alcohol Abuse, 1971].

Some brief notes on alcohol:

—It takes approximately one hour per drink to sober up.

—Black coffee, cold showers, or even pure oxygen are not very helpful in speeding up the process.

—Eating food while drinking can retard alcohol absorption.

—Alcohol is responsible for 30,000 automobile fatalities a year.

—Contrary to popular beliefs, there seems to be no set "alcoholic personality," just as there is no fixed kind of mental illness.

—Alcohol does not reduce anxiety or depression in chronic drinkers. Instead, it tends to increase them and adds an element of guilt, thus setting up a vicious circle because the person drinks again to get rid of these feelings.

DRUGS

Drugs, like alcohol, are not related only to adolescence.* Nonetheless, the use or abuse of either alcohol or drugs is likely to have its origin in adoles-

---

* Alcohol is a drug, of course, just as much as heroin or marijuana. For convenience, however, in this discussion we will use the term *drugs* to refer to those mind-altering substances whose sale without a prescription is illegal in this country.

cence, and in most cases it will be carried into adulthood. To make this statement, we have to stretch adolescence a little so that early college-age men and women can be included, since alcohol and drug use sometimes begins at this age.

Alcohol and tobacco are still the favorites of both adolescents and adults, but drugs seem to present as great a problem as drinking [Smart, 1970]. For instance, in New York City, the *most frequent* cause of death for males and females between the ages of 15 and 35 is drugs [Baden, 1968]. The same is true in California's major cities; for once, the problem that makes the headlines often is really something of major concern.

Drugs serve the same general function as alcohol, in the psychological sense, by providing what is called an *escape mechanism.* In other words, both are used for the purpose of escaping, in various degrees, from the realities of life. Going to a movie is also escaping from reality, and only the strictest, most puritanical person would claim that occasionally escaping from the mess we see around us is abnormal. The important factor is the degree of escape; from the psychological point of view, complete withdrawal for extended periods of time is considered abnormal. Some degree of withdrawal is considered a normal homeostatic operation, but complete withdrawal tends to indicate that the person has overstepped the homeostatic bounds and entered an unbalanced inner world that is devoid of normal social relationships or a sense of accomplishment.

When speaking of drugs, common practice is to label the user an *addict.* This is like labeling "alcoholic" everybody who takes a drink. Addiction always involves an inability to control or stop the intake of drugs and a fairly complete dependence on them. Furthermore, a distinction must be made between what is scientifically called "addiction" and habituation. Addiction is a physiological need for a drug; in other words, the body has adjusted itself in such a way that it will react physically, sometimes violently, when the drug is withheld. Moreover, addiction implies increasing tolerance for a drug. *Tolerance* is literally the body's ability to stand (tolerate) more and more of a drug. Tolerance, however, usually encompasses another factor in drug behavior: Increased tolerance means that the body comes to *need* an increased dosage in order to get the same effect.

128   (*Courtesy of the Advertising Council*)

The desire for drugs has a strong psychological component. Some drugs that are not physically addictive may be "psychologically addictive." The term for this kind of drug dependence is habituation. *Habituation* might be best explained by moving from the topic of drugs for a moment to a living laboratory, the crap game or slot machine parlor. Gambling is obviously not physiologically addictive, but it can be habituating to the point where literally thousands of people each year do face the traditionally claimed problem of flying to Las Vegas and returning home by bus (or even hitchhiking). What began as escape into a make-believe world of attaining great fortune apparently is so gratifying to a psychological need that the person cannot pass by a dice game or a slot machine without getting very nervous and upset; he regains a form of tranquility only by rolling the dice or putting a coin in the machine. An exact parallel occurs in drug habituation: The user's physical tolerance does not increase, but taking drugs becomes a habit that satisfies a psychological need to the extent that life begins to disintegrate until he can get some.

Psychological need, curiosity, or group pressure *starts off* the process of drug taking. Whether the drug taking later involves addiction or habituation depends on its chemical nature. For example, marijuana is habituating; LSD is habituating; heroin and morphine are addictive.

Reactions to habituating drugs of any kind are individual, and the reaction seems related to the degree of basic personality stability which the person has. If the individual has deep-seated problems, we can anticipate that drugs are going to be psychologically destructive because they further distort a world that is already distorted. If the person is mildly disorganized to begin with, disorganization will probably increase; and if the person is well adjusted and takes drugs, the only assumption that can be made is that he will regulate his drug intake.

We have to assume that this last person is experimenting; if he continues to take drugs in large quantities, the logical implication is that he is fighting a problem of which he is only partially aware and that he is not as sturdy psychologically as he seemed. These statements apply only to drugs such as marijuana. Though LSD is not addictive, a person better be certain of his stability before he takes it. And if he begins taking heroin, he is in serious trouble physically and psychologically, no matter how stable he once seemed to be.

In colleges, a large number of marijuana users seem to have two notable characteristics. They are basically opposed to authority, which is considered rather petty and oppressive; for example, they resent rules such as curfew hours at dormitories. And they seem sincerely to be seeking experiences such as being free and open and experiencing life deeply [King, 1970b; Bowers, 1969]. One may legitimately question that drugs provide this "gut-level" experience, but for better or worse these students are seeking far more than the raccoon-coated flask drinkers at football games in generations past. The students may be wrong, but I find it hard not to believe that many are reacting to a supercilious attitude that we flask drinkers, now grown up, have perpetuated.

In general, drugs serve to decrease awareness of the real environment and to reduce cognitive performance [Fleishman and Bartlett, 1969]. In this sense they resemble alcohol, but in another sense they are quite different, as we will discuss shortly.

drug laws   The law is obviously not always right. When it is dead wrong, from the majority viewpoint, a law is worthless, even when it is on the books, as was the case during Prohibition. But even if it were desirable to do away with drug laws, they are not going to be repealed anytime in the near future,* for at least three reasons. First, most people don't favor repeal. Second, "rebellious" adolescents, rather than executive types, are the most noticeable offenders, and lawmakers are not going to give in to them. Third, many of the drugs in question produce a state of *introspection*† that is contrary to our national drive toward constant achievement and aggressiveness [Grinspoon, 1969]. Many drugs are potentially dangerous, a fact that can't be discounted—but penalties for drug use vary so much that one must suspect that emotional factors, not actual danger, enter into the formation and continuation of many laws. The notable disparity between laws governing alcohol and those governing marijuana is a case in point.

A recent study shows that even professionals are somewhat divided—and rather confused about the ideal legal status of marijuana. Psychiatrists (mental health workers who are doctors of medicine) were polled, and 24.4 percent favored legalizing marijuana; 61.4 percent were against it; 11 percent were undecided; 0.6 percent gave no answer, and 2.3 percent offered some other solution [Keup, 1969].

Great Britain has experimented with legalizing hard-drug use (heroin), and evidence now available seems to indicate that this policy has not been as successful in practice as it was in theory. Theoretically, the drug user would be able to obtain his drugs by registering with the government and then seeing a physician to obtain his supply. This arrangement has not reduced drug violations as much as was desired [Leech and Jordan, 1970]. In fact, many users still turn to the underworld for their drugs, either because they don't want to register as addicts or because they are having more and more difficulty obtaining the drugs from physicians, who are too busy with other people in need of medical attention.‡

One advantage of the British system, however, has been the reduc-

---

* Although some penalties are being reduced.

† "Looking into yourself"; a form of self-examination and meditation that some call "soul-searching." *Introspection* is also a psychological term referring to a self-description of one's feelings.

‡ Only a few British physicians are interested in getting involved in this program because of the drain on time.

tion or at least control of underworld influence; drugs are just not as profitable in Britain as they are in the United States, where, it has been estimated, heroin *profits* alone go as high as $700 million each year [Leech and Jordan, 1970]. Crimes perpetrated in order to get money for drugs are less frequent in a country where there are legal sources of supply.

marijuana   Sometime in life we all have to face up to disillusionment and the destruction of closely held beliefs. It is therefore with considerable reluctance that I tell you that George Washington grew marijuana in his garden ("for medicinal purposes") [Grinspoon, 1971]. This, coupled with the suspicion historians have that Christopher Columbus's crew brought syphilis to the new world, can leave one's psyche in a shambles. In any case, marijuana is a plant (or a weed, depending upon your point of view), but above all it is one of the most controversial topics around.

It would seem fair to say that a large proportion of the injury resulting from drug use stems from exaggerated claims regarding the perils of marijuana; these incredible claims lead to skepticism about the *accurate* reports of danger from other drugs. The author of a recent article on the subject points out that the government has been waging a campaign against marijuana since the 1930s, when posters were published that read, "Beware! . . . This marihuana cigarette . . . contains the Killer Drug . . .—a powerful narcotic in which lurks Murder! Insanity! Death!" [Grinspoon, 1969]. Unfortunately, the evils attributed to marijuana have not been toned down very much since that time—for marijuana is not a killer drug that causes murder, insanity, and death. Nor is anyone fooled by propaganda. The typical adolescent is obviously going to discover adults' "distortions of the truth," no matter how well intentioned they are; and then, like the townspeople who heard the boy crying, "Wolf!" he is not going to believe findings about certain drugs that *are* potentially quite dangerous.

Marijuana has apparently been used at one time or another by a fairly sizeable proportion of the population. No method has been found for determining the frequency with which it is used. A clue may be gleaned from studies of usage on college campuses. Some surveys find 25 percent of students on a given campus use marijuana, some 57 percent, and some 80 percent [King, 1970; Bonier and Hymowitz, 1972]. Probably the best educated guess in terms of an average for all college students hovers around 45 percent. How well these figures represent marijuana use in the general population is unknown. Arrest records, although they show that the number is ever-increasing, reflect not the amount of usage but only that it is increasing or that the police are getting better at arresting users. Unless an individual is a very heavy marijuana smoker, little evidence exists that the smoker has personality problems, so there is not much that would call this person to the attention of the police, mental health worker, or school counselor [Bonier and Hymowitz, 1972; Grossman, 1972]. Personality tests cannot

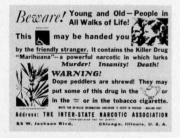

129   *(Courtesy of Lester Grinspoon)*

differentiate between the "social user"—one to four times a month—and the nonuser. Both groups are as normal as most of us hope to be. Not so, the heavy user—once a day (see below) [Cross and Davis, 1972].

effects of marijuana   The effects of marijuana last two to four hours, and unless the drug is taken again, the behavior change seems not to recur. While effective, marijuana produces lightness of limbs and euphoria—the feeling that all is wonderful with the world—and time is distorted, in the sense that it is stretched out longer than usual [Grinspoon, 1969]. The drug can also produce depression and anxiety, depending on the person who is taking it. Cognitive and motor functioning are impaired slightly, especially for new users. Although most of us would prefer to ride in a car with someone who is completely intact, if you *have to* choose an intoxicated driver, pick one high on marijuana rather than on alcohol. Marijuana can produce sleepiness, poor hearing, and a floating feeling for the driver, which makes him somewhat less than desirable, but alcohol produces accelerator, brake, signal, and speedometer errors of much greater severity than marijuana does [Hollister, 1971; Crancer et al., 1969; Weil, 1968]. The time required for effective braking by the driver is significantly affected by alcoholic intake, much less so by marijuana taken in moderation [Rafaelson et al., 1973].

Although marijuana does produce some changes in physiology—for example, pulse-rate increase, red eyes (but *not* dilated pupils), and short-term-memory impairment, there is no evidence at present of physical damage from the drug, especially the mild variety usually found in the United States [Smart, 1970; Weingartner et al., 1972]. In other words, the person first introduced to it must train himself to believe that this experience is worthwhile and meaningful; in the words of one scientist, the user of marijuana "must learn to enjoy the effects. . . . The user feels dizzy, thirsty; his scalp tingles; he misjudges time and distances. Are these things pleasurable? He isn't sure. If he is to continue marijuana use, he must decide that they are. Otherwise, getting high, while a real enough experience, will be an unpleasant one he would rather avoid" [Becker, 1963].

The major effects, then, of marijuana are psychological. Obviously certain physical changes do take place. For example, chimpanzees do not go on elaborate ritualistic marijuana binges, but their sense of time is disrupted by a normal human dosage. Given problems to solve in a certain time, they consistently overestimate the amount of time that has elapsed. Nonetheless, fake marijuana produces many of the same feelings as the real thing for humans—especially when smoked in a setting of special lighting, music, and so forth. This may explain why experienced users can get a supposed "better high" than nonexperienced; they have learned to "psyche" themselves up better [Galanter, 1972; Conrad et al., 1972]. It might be added that marijuana is almost always smoked in groups [Halikas, et al., 1972]. You might recall, in this connection, the cognitive theory of emotion discussed in Chapter 5. At that time we were talking about the fact that injecting adrenalin into a subject caused a change in him physically, but what he called this change (anger or happiness) depended on how others around him were acting. Likewise, marijuana results in certain limited but basic physical changes; the labeling of these changes as a "good high" may involve the same mechanisms.

Physical tolerance for marijuana does not increase with use [Ferraro and Grilly, 1973]. Thus, it is a habituating drug, of which continued use serves a psychological rather than a physiological need. A fair proportion of users report anxiety and panic when they take the drug, so for them it is a poor idea from the start. For others, the major danger to personality integration comes from continued heavy use which probably applies to almost anything. The continuous heavy user becomes too dependent on an artificial substance, probably to fulfill a psychological need [Cross and Davis, 1972]. The heavy marijuana smoker is not more productive because he is "freer"; instead, the reverse: He has become too preoccupied with the drug to the exclusion of other things [Glatt, 1969].

The biggest problem with taking marijuana is that the anxiety and fear a person initially feels about taking illegal drugs will be removed* [Glatt et al., 1967]. Furthermore, the marijuana user must violate the law—whether or not the law is legitimate. Once the user has overcome these problems by taking drugs, each subsequent use becomes easier; some evidence indicates that taking marijuana leads to taking other drugs that are considered dangerous and best left untouched. *Heavy* users of marijuana, for instance—those who use it daily—run a high risk of taking another drug, especially LSD [King, 1969].

In the study we're about to consider, it is important to remember that the figures may be exaggerated, first because we are dealing with adolescents who have been referred to a youth agency (but not arrested), and second because the study took place in the drug jungle, New York City. Nonetheless, the study is carefully done and suggests that it is not just an old wives' tale that one drug can in some cases lead to another. In this study, with an *N* of five hundred youngsters who were followed over a five- and a ten-year period, 50 percent who began by smoking marijuana eventually took heroin. The same group included youngsters who at the start of the study had not taken marijuana. Following this group up, of those who did not smoke marijuana at the beginning, only 15 percent got into heroin [Glaser et al., 1969].

It is extremely important to remember that in the above study we are dealing with social outcasts to begin with. Their drug usage is probably

---

* Actually, a new danger has appeared: A synthetic marijuana, called THC, can be toxic and dangerous, unlike "regular" marijuana [Keup, 1969]. One of the dangers here, as with other drugs, is that all kinds of debris, some of it poisonous, are mixed with the drug by the seller to save money.

very atypical. The study is quoted because it is the kind that produces statistics about marijuana leading to other drug use. These statistics do *not* mean that taking marijuana automatically leads to taking other drugs. For instance, in one study 57 percent of the college students took marijuana, but only 9 percent took LSD and 0.7 percent heroin [King, 1970]. Finally, most heroin users at some time took marijuana, but this equation cannot be reversed to say most marijuana users eventually take heroin.

other drugs   Although we know that marijuana is widely used by young people in our society, estimates of other drug usage are so variable and confused that we probably would do best to avoid the issue. Reports of LSD usage, for example, vary from 10 percent to 40 percent of the younger population. In general, little evidence supports the notion that use of other drugs comes anywhere near that of marijuana, a situation which, as you will notice, is quite fortunate.

To further confuse the issue of drug use, addiction and habituation in too many cases result from taking the estimated 18 billion tablets and capsules produced annually by the legitimate drug market and consumed by Americans. People may disagree about marijuana, but few would dispute the fact that LSD, amphetamines, barbiturates, heroin, and morphine are potentially dangerous drugs of the highest order [Glatt, 1969].

LSD   LSD is the chemical abbreviation for d-lysergic acid diethylamide. LSD is an overwhelmingly potent drug: 1/250,000 of an ounce produces marked alterations in behavior. The drug takes effect very rapidly, apparently reaching the lower brain centers almost as if it had a direct route [Unger, 1963]. Some research has suggested that the drug operates on the pleasure-pain areas we discussed earlier and also affects chemicals that normally transfer electrical impulses and that are found at synapses of the reticular formation, cortex, and thalamus. The composition of LSD is close enough to that of the normal chemical substances found at the synapses that it can either block or facilitate the relaying of neural messages back and forth.

The physiological effects of the drug are pronounced. What could be called "synaptic confusion" is prominent: sensations are scrambled; the user thinks he hears colors and smells music, and he can easily get burned because fire feels cool [Jones et al., 1969]. Visual changes are also notable: they include seeing bright colors and visual **hallucinations**.* Sometimes auditory hallucinations present themselves.

Permanent damage, in the physiological sense, has not been verified. Studies and stories about chromosomal damage,† for instance, have been "reported, contradicted, and then rereported." The confusion about chro-

---

* *Hallucinations*, simply put, generally involve seeing or hearing objects, persons, or events that are not present in external reality.

† *Chromosomal damage* is injury to or malformation of the chromosomes, chemical units that carry characteristics potentially inherited by one's offspring.

mosomal damage has occurred because most experiments have been performed on animals. One recent study of the rhesus monkey, which resembles man in physical structure, demonstrates that chromosomal abnormalities do occur in pregnant monkeys given LSD as part of the studies. However, the anomalies of the chromosomes tend to clear up on their own. But three of the four offspring of LSD-treated monkeys died, which should make one approach the drug with caution. Unfortunately, in most of these studies the dosage was proportionately greater than that normally taken by human beings [Kato et al., 1970].

LSD first attained scientific recognition because its effects mimic psychosis, a label attached to the most severe mental disturbances.* Hence, LSD has been called a *psychotomime*tic drug. At the time, researchers thought that if the drug produced symptoms like those of the severely disturbed, then just possibly some chemical agent in LSD might resemble one that could be found in mental patients, and thus LSD might lead to success with mental illness. So far such a substance has not been isolated.

Nonetheless, LSD does produce symptoms similar to some that are found in mental patients of a certain type—those who have unusual swings of mood from ecstasy to depression, and those who have hallucinations or feelings of *depersonalization*† [Snyder, 1969]. For some people, among the most dangerous side effects of LSD are the appearance of these overwhelming emotions, either positive or negative, and of a feeling of unreality and a fear that the self is disintegrating [Katz et al., 1968]. Another dangerous reaction is reported with some frequency: The person feels himself to be in an "intense emptiness or silence" that resembles death [Barron et al., 1964].

As far as bringing out creative potential, LSD fails, as does marijuana. Artists who have painted under the influence of LSD have later disclaimed their work; apparently, the productive side of personality is altered, even if only temporarily [Gubar, 1969; McGlothlin, 1971].

Before this begins to sound like the marijuana scare, let it be duly noted that we all know people who have taken LSD and remained relatively sane—most people who have taken LSD, in fact, do retain their sanity. When under the influence of the drug, these people can tell their own visions from reality, and for them the psychedelic experience is transitory in nature. The most serious problem of all is that *who* will react in what way to the drug is completely unpredictable. The odds are very much in favor of an adverse reaction to the drug by those who already have some personality disturbance, are relatively unstable, or have just had a crisis in their life [McWilliams and Tuttle, 1973].

---

* Psychosis will be discussed in greater detail in Chapter 22. For the moment, conceiving of it as severe mental disturbance should suffice.

† In *depersonalization* the person experiences a feeling of having lost his self-identity; he feels either that he is not himself or that he doesn't know this person he sees in the mirror.

the psychedelic
subculture

A young girl said to one experimenter, "Dropping acid and dropping out are really very similar, because, you know, in an insane world, counter-insanity is saner than plain insanity . . ." [Gioscia, 1969].

This statement, which usually requires more than one reading to understand, seems to reflect the attitude of the psychedelic drug subculture within our society. A subculture of this sort is not new to civilization as a whole, but it is a novel experience in the United States. We have had all manner of "problem" groups, but rarely have we seen large-scale, organized withdrawal from society into a never-never land.

The drug subculture presents an even more interesting ethical problem for psychology than do homosexuals. Psychology differs from some other sciences—chemistry and physics, for example—in that the latter two have more to do with objective reality. Psychology gets many of its clues about normal and abnormal behavior from the society within which the psychologist lives. What is abnormal is that which deviates from the accepted procedure of the majority of people (or of psychologists, whichever).

What about the psychedelic group whose members probably seem "abnormal" to most of us? Apparently, they are quite tolerant of others, although *we* have some difficulty being compassionate toward them. This reaction is basically the result of their behavior, of their apparent desire to remove themselves from everything—school, business, government, traditional families, and so on. If their theoretical goals were followed to a logical conclusion, society as it presently exists would freeze. Neither you nor I would have bothered, most likely, to write or read some of this material if we adhered strictly to their philosophy. Even though the world does seem insane, and withdrawing from it can be rationalized, psychology considers any person or group that withdraws, in a nonproductive way, to be abnormal. We assume that people who drop out have personality flaws that prevent them from facing life as it is, just as we would consider suicide to be an inappropriate response to the fact that wars do go on or that people are starving.

The unusual behavior of the drug subgroup is not deemed abnormal just for arbitrary reasons. If you can't accept the reasons mentioned above, consider that one popular trend in psychedelic experience has been to take a synthetic drug called STP. This drug turns you on, but no way has been found to turn you off; no treatment is available for an overdose. In fact, the drug itself is similar to the nerve gas used in chemical warfare* [Glatt et al., 1967].

amphetamines

In many respects amphetamines may be one of the most insidious drugs currently used by large numbers of people. One of the major problems is

---

* Still, determining who is sane or insane is very difficult. Supposedly rational people in the military-political establishment dumped tons of (sealed) nerve gas into the ocean in 1970.

130   Nineteen years old, this boy is dead of an overdose of heroin (*UPI*)

that this class of drugs creates a sense of elation, freedom, and energy, and it provides for many the feeling that they can accomplish a considerable amount more than is even remotely realistic [Griffith, 1968]. This is a potentially volatile situation in a society such as ours where competition is so much a way of life. Amphetamines are commonly used by persons who want to stay awake for longer periods than they should—for example, college students and truck drivers—and by persons who want to expend more energy than they should, such as athletes. Amphetamines have legitimate uses; for example, with overactive children (see chapter 24).

In all cases, however, this drug has to be carefully controlled because it is *very* susceptible to tolerance; in only a relatively short time, an individual can be taking a dosage a hundred times as great as his initial dose [Seevers, 1968].

Amphetamine is a psychotomimetic drug like LSD: It can produce severe mental disturbance and its chemical constitution resembles that of the synapses and can result in random firing of these junctions [Snyder, 1972]. Although the drug is habituating rather than addicting, in heavy dosage it produces bizarre mental images, trembling, convulsions, and a feeling that people are out to do you in. One rather curious effect of the drug, especially when it is taken by groups, is an obsession with "crazes" which resemble scavenger hunts. However, in the tradition of amphetamines, these hunts are frantic searches, day and night on end, for bizarre objects. One group was searching for "the stone of stones" until they had a tremendous stockpile of rocks they had exhaustively dug up [Fiddle, 1968].

If you must take this drug for legitimate purposes, watch the dosage carefully. When it is time to stop taking it, if intake has been too heavy, severe depression can result.

barbiturates   Barbiturates are basically tranquilizers which operate directly on the central nervous system. These drugs depress the operation of nerve and muscle cells. The most notable effect is on the brain itself, where the barbiturate interferes with oxygen consumption; in heavy dosage the result is unconsciousness and death.

Because the liver is able to remove the effective ingredient in barbiturates, larger and larger doses are required for a notable effect from the drug. A most dangerous combination is alcohol and barbiturates: while the liver can effectively remove the toxic (poisonous) elements of either one individually, when they are combined in the system the liver's functioning is reduced. Hence, the level of central-nervous-system depression is greater with this combination than with either drug by itself.

Barbiturate addiction withdrawal typically produces epileptic-type convulsions; for those accustomed to very large doses, sudden withdrawal results in death [Jones et al., 1969].

heroin and morphine   Little need be said of these two drugs. No scientist questions the danger of either one. Heroin and morphine slow down mental and physical activity by depressing the operation of the cerebral cortex, probably by acting on the hypothalamus and reticular formation. They are extremely strong depressants, and they are highly addictive. Most deaths associated with heroin or morphine use are thought to result from unsterile drugs or equipment, or from the additives put into the heroin in order to be able to sell less of it for the same price [Abelson, 1970]. Many die from an allergic reaction to the drug; others, from the worst possible thing one can do, a combination of heroin with alcohol or barbiturates [Smith and Gray, 1972].

The thoroughly addicted individual will inject himself up to a thousand times a year, and if he doesn't have a syringe available he will take a razor blade and cut open an artery to pour the drug in.

It becomes that bad.

And a final depressing note: The cure rate for this addiction is terrible. Roughly 80 to 90 percent of those treated return to drugs in a matter of weeks [Stephens and Cottrell, 1972].

SUMMARY

Juvenile delinquency is increasing dramatically each year. To some extent the problem is alarming, but part of the increase is related to better reporting techniques by police. There is also some indication that as a society becomes more repressive or up-tight, more laws and rigid enforcement procedures are enacted.

Delinquency occurs most frequently in the lower class only if official statistics are used. In reality, when people on welfare are eliminated, delinquency rates are about the same across the social classes. The major distinction between classes is that the lower-class youth tends to commit more serious crimes, involving theft of property and money, sometimes by violence.

The idea that heredity has anything to do with delinquent acts has little or no basis in fact. Most authorities suggest that the family situation is the most important factor. In the family of the typical delinquent, the parents are cold, unfriendly, and aloof, and frequently the father is missing.

The delinquent youngster seems to lack a sense of completeness; he feels that he is not the way he should be and that he is not important. The school system as it exists reinforces this feeling, contributing to his difficulties through its strong orientation toward verbal skills and abilities.

Sociopathy seems to be an exaggerated form of delinquency. One of the most important factors involved in its development is the combination of a long history of delinquency and incarceration of the individual in a correctional institution—and, we assume, a fairly severe family life.

In one respect, drugs are like alcohol, overeating, and television: they provide an escape from reality. Two types of drugs can be distinguished: those that are addictive and those that are habituating. Addiction is a physiological dependence on narcotic drugs. In habituation, the user develops a psychological dependence on the drug.

To date almost every study has shown that marijuana is not the harmful drug it has been claimed to be; for some people it can produce undesirable effects, but these are generally tied in with the personality of the user. Heavy marijuana users frequently turn to other, more potent drugs, but taking marijuana does not automatically lead to using other drugs. Synthetic marijuana is physically dangerous because of the additives.

Some people are not harmed by LSD, but the potential power of the drug entails much greater risk of experiencing bad effects than does marijuana. The odds seem to be good that LSD can produce at least psychological damage for a number of people.

Amphetamines are an extremely popular form of drug with so-called nondrug-users, the typical middle-class, middle-aged American. These drugs are very tolerance-prone and produce frantic highs when a person is on them and deep lows of depression when they are withdrawn.

Barbiturates are a central-nervous-system depressant, affecting most of all the oxygen consumption of the brain. Alcohol and barbiturates taken together are a dangerous combination because the liver has difficulty processing both of them at the same time. Withdrawal from barbiturates can result in convulsions and even death.

Heroin and morphine are without any question dangerous and to be avoided at all costs, except under medical supervision.

PART FIVE
PEOPLE

CHAPTER TWENTY
BEHAVIOR OF PEOPLE IN GROUPS

T

he passage below describes a typical evening's entertainment in a village in New Guinea in 1969:

> Father Verhaven is nestled in his favorite armchair, engrossed in a Leon Uris novel. His neighbors, who dropped by as usual after dinner, are equally absorbed.
>
> One elderly gentleman, spear scars across his chest, is concentrating on pulling hairs out of his groin with tweezers fashioned from a reed. Another guest is spreading a bit of beauty balm—pig's grease mixed with ashes—on his shoulder-length hair. A third visitor is busily tightening the vine binding on his stone axe. And a fourth neighbor is tapping his fingernails against his axe in perfect time to the static emanating from a shortwave radio. "Wa Wa WA Wa," says the older gentleman, informing the group that he is happy and contented. . . .
>
> . . . With few exceptions, [these people,] the Danis, dress as they always have. The men wear only cowrie-shell necklaces, bird-feather bracelets, penis sheaths (long gourds that extend upward to the shoulders where they are attached by a vine), and a thick coating of pig's grease and ashes smeared over the entire body. The women, hair shaved close to the scalp, wear either short grass skirts (if unmarried) or tightly bound reed around their midsection (if married). All women go barebreasted, but are scrupulously modest about covering their backs with nets. "Modesty" also characterizes the men, who are mortified if their sheaths ever slip off. . . .
>
> . . . The Dani diet consists nearly exclusively of sweet potatoes, . . . occasionally rats, insect grubs or birds unlucky enough to be hit by hunters' wobbly, featherless arrows. And of course, the Danis have sometimes eaten each other. . . .
>
> A man's status and wealth is measured by the number of pigs he owns and, to a lesser extent, the number of wives he keeps. Wives are definitely secondary. If a man has many pigs, he naturally needs some wives to take care of them and therefore trades a few piglets for a bride or two. [Kann, 1969]*

Father Verhaven seems unperturbed by his surroundings, an attitude that I feel sure few of us could share were we to join them for an evening. The strangest part of all, however, is that if the villagers reported on *our* activities, *we* would seem unusual to *them*—working all day long, as we do, for a few pieces of paper, continuously driving up one highway and down another in our metal machines, and for entertainment swinging a stick at

131 a, b   Each group has its own perspective: the Joint Chiefs of Staff, and a group of soldiers carrying their wounded toward an evacuation helicopter in Vietnam (*Wide World*)

*From P. Kann, "The Danis of Jiwika," *Wall Street Journal* 49, no. 223 (1969); reprinted by permission.

478

132 a, b Ladies and gentlemen in a drawing room of the 17th century; old women in a poorhouse, about 1870. All are members of social groups (*Bettmann Archive*)

some kind of round object. Most of all we would cause interest because we don't mind our women having their backs exposed and yet we go into a frenzy if they uncover their breasts. Such odd behavior!

We will try in this chapter to understand what goes on in groups and, to some extent, how they got that way. The behavior of people in groups is generally the domain of sociology. Psychology enters the picture because the individual person is influenced by the group, and contributes to it; psychology is concerned mainly with the reaction of the individual within the group. Psychology and sociology overlap a good deal here, as they do when we consider other social behaviors—delinquency and drug activities, for example.

SOCIAL STRUCTURE

Many people think of social order as primarily a human characteristic, but this view is incorrect. For example, in the baboon society males enjoy decided dominance over females; this arrangement is a form of social structure—a rather primitive one, but nonetheless a distinct division between one segment of a group and another.

The fact of the matter is that in the animal and insect kingdoms, social groupings are quite varied. We can return to Dr. Lorenz, the naturalist* who is renowned for his work on the imprinting of ducklings. He also made some interesting observations about social differentiation, ranging all the way from birds to monkeys. Certain birds, for instance, stand higher in rank than other birds within the same flock. This phenomenon has been called *pecking order*, referring to the fact that certain birds get to eat first, and that within a group the lower-ranking bird must move out of the way of the higher-ranking bird, even if the less prestigious bird got to the feeding tray first. Moreover, the higher bird can peck at the lower bird.

* A naturalist is a scientist who studies behavior in its *natural* state. The psychologist more often than not uses a laboratory or arranges a study to examine certain factors under his control; the naturalist watches behavior as unobtrusively as possible, not disturbing nature, and reports the outcome.

133 a, b, c Animals group together for various activities: mating; grazing; and eating their prey (*U. Boecker, Photo Researchers; Leonard Lee Rue III; Des Bartlett, Photo Researchers*)

The queen bee in a colony reigns supreme in one of the strictest of pecking orders, but she has a trick. She secretes a chemical which the other bees lick off her and regurgitate from one bee to another. This chemical is designed to eliminate her competition because once the others have absorbed it, it prevents them from rearing potential rival queens and also prevents their ovaries from developing which could produce another queen [Wilson, 1972].

Thus, although the reasons for the differentiation are not fully clear, social-class arrangements do exist among most animals, birds, and insects. Again, many people tend to think of "coming to the aid of the underdog" as a traditional human (or American) characteristic, yet this behavior is found in the bird world. When two lowly birds quarrel over who gets to eat what, one of the socially higher birds will intervene and assist the underdog in the fight [Lorenz, 1952].

These phenomena are tantalizing parallels to human behavior, and there are many more. But some psychologists, it should be pointed out, do not agree that considerable similarity exists between animal and human social orders. The disagreement is not a major dispute, though, because it is fairly obvious that humans have established more complex societies. Nonetheless, social patterns among animals are worth noticing, because it seems likely, given the universality of human grouping,* that people may start off with some instinctual, biological drive toward grouping, upon which they build a complex set of behavior patterns. The major objection of psychologists comes from labeling our own social groupings as "instinctual"; as you are aware, no end of trouble results whenever that word appears on the scene.

Almost without question, some social-grouping patterns are pre-programmed, especially in the lower animals; their behavior deviates little from generation to generation, compared to higher animals and humans. However, even in the case of birds, it is sometimes difficult to determine if refinements in the pecking order are learned or if they too are based on some innate mechanism. One can alter the pecking order by placing a radio receiver in the brain of a hen and stimulating the aggression center; this stimulation will turn a hen low in the pecking order into a wild, aggressive, demanding creature [Leonard, 1968]. Even though we have altered the animal's behavior, we haven't solved the problem of its origin—that is, whether the behavior is "instinctive" or learned.

Bees are assumed to operate on instinct because little variation in behavior patterns shows up from one generation to another. Even so, the preprogrammed changes that do take place are intriguing. For example, bees have a social structure based on the division of labor, meaning that certain

---

*Social grouping appears everywhere among humans, and thus it is doubtful we all learn it from scratch.

individuals perform certain tasks. Strangely enough, bees have more varied occupational lives than most of us, for their jobs change as they grow older. Early in life they clean cells; later they move on to become nurses to the newborn; finally, they engage in tasks such as producing wax or standing guard [Von Frisch, 1963]. Ants also have a fairly rigid division of labor based on a queen-worker and male-female dichotomy.

As we move up the evolutionary scale to more complex animals, behavior patterns become more divergent, but sex and division of labor predominate as differentiating categories, just as they do in human societies. Important exceptions can be found: We spoke of baboons recognizing a dominant male, but this is not true of some monkeys.

One most intriguing study of monkey life compared the social arrangements of urban and rural monkeys. In parts of India, some cities are inhabited by groups of monkeys that live around and in houses, although they don't socialize with the humans. Other groups of the same species of monkey live not far away in the forest. A comparison of the behavior of the two groups is startling, especially when one draws an almost unavoidable parallel with humans living in different environments. The city monkeys share food more readily, tend to have a more liberal attitude toward crowded conditions, and have a fixed living place—a home, if you will—whereas the forest monkeys camp in any convenient tree for the night [Singh, 1969]. We have, then, a case in which environmental influence alters social behavior, as it does on the human level. Among the very low animals, environment alters the behavior of an *entire* species, but in this case, with higher animals, the situation is quite different: Members of the *same* species, living not far from each other, developed different social patterns.

SOCIAL GROUPING AND TERRITORIALITY

Animals tend to live in groups and to mark off the territory they "own." This behavior is called *territoriality*. Sometimes it is an individual behavior: The family dog may mark off his territory in a distinctive manner on the trees and bushes surrounding his home. He is carrying out a plan, we assume, that would normally be in operation were he part of a group of undomesticated animals.

The buffalo really makes a production of territorial marking. He defecates, rolls in it, wipes the defecation on a tree with his shoulder, then crashes into the tree with his horn scraping a mark on it. Even worms live only one to an apple. If an apple is occupied, a worm must move on until he finds an empty one [Andrewartha, 1961]. So, territoriality is common to almost every group. It sometimes forms the basis for a "marriage": Male and female herring gulls form a semipermanent marital relationship and by squatters' rights mark off a territory roughly twenty-five yards in diameter. They usually return to this same spot with each year's migration. An intruder into the territory is greeted by lifted wings and a "threatening strut"

134   A male lion defends his territorial rights against an interloper (*Ian Cleghorn, Photo Researchers*)

[Tinbergen, 1961]. The intruder recognizes this action and retreats. Strangely enough, the threat seems to be partly *symbolic:* Throughout the animal kingdom a very small creature can defend his territory against a larger one just by making some kind of ominous gesture.*

The same behavior among human beings is most obvious in large cities, where gangs often mark off their territory, and intrusion by members of another gang is forbidden, except when a war is in progress. Suburbanites, too, are well known for their territoriality. The police are constantly plagued by major altercations involving (for instance): Part of neighbor *A*'s tree hangs over the territory of neighbor *B*, and neighbor *B* is not about to rake up the leaves. Or neighbor *C* claims one-fourth of neighbor *D*'s rosebush because it has grown over the property line. We can rescue the suburbanites from mockery by saying that possibly, rather than just being ridiculous, they are in part reverting to some natural animal state.

territoriality and smell

This subheading may make you do a double take—but some evidence indicates that odor is responsible for territorial marking, and for self-protection. Psychologically, this idea is only moderately important at the human level, probably because our brains do not devote enough space to "smell areas"—not nearly as much as many animals' brains—and because cigarette smoking and air pollution have caused large numbers of humans to lose some or all of their sense of smell [Gardner, 1968]. The animal kingdom, including man and other mammals, produces glandular secretions, *pheromones*, which have an odor. For some species—for example, the rabbit—fairly substantial evidence suggests that these pheromones, "communicate information about age, sex, reproductive stage and group membership, . . . warn of danger, and . . . define territory" [Mykytowyez, 1968]. Ants, bees, wasps, and even termites mark off their group by emitting a distinctive odor [Wilson, 1972].

Perfume, hair sprays, bath oils, soaps, and the like have just about destroyed this quality in humans, *assuming* that in our primitive state we ever were equipped to differentiate these factors. Even so, notice that you are unable to smell yourself without conscious effort—yet you can immediately smell another person. Notice, too, that you are at least vaguely conscious of a different odor when you enter someone else's territory (house).

human territoriality

The material presented so far is pretty inconclusive, but it does suggest that when humans form groups, they are operating on a basic level. In other words, we begin with a basic impulse to form groups. The variations the groups take from that point on, especially the more bizarre groups, are uniquely human. Moreover, each person† seems to form a boundary line *around himself* which resembles territorial marking. Almost all of us have

*Unless the approaching animal is a predator.
† At least in our culture.

had occasion to dislike some relative who takes the liberty of giving us a bearhug as a greeting; we recoil in horror, only approaching him again with caution or attempting to remain at a distance.

This personal boundary has been explored experimentally, and it seems to be quite real. In one study, the laboratory floor was marked off in such a way that observers could calculate through a one-way mirror how close subjects came to one another. People put under general psychological stress, but not subjected to a direct threat from another person, would not approach one another as closely as those not under stress [Dorsey, 1969]. Most of us likewise withdraw (get up and move) if we are sitting alone in a half-full movie theater and someone comes and sits right beside us. The latter case very likely involves an implied threat to our *individual* territory. We are much less likely to behave in this fashion if we attend a movie with others, probably because we are already sharing our body territory with others and the violation is not so significant.

The effect of territoriality and its relation to groups become a bit clearer if one considers two divergent cultures, the Arabs and the Americans. In Arab countries, the territory in *any* public place belongs to everyone. If you are sitting in a public bus terminal, for example, and another Arab wants your place, he will deliberately sit as close as possible to you; if he can make you uncomfortable enough to move, he has the right to take over your position. Apparently, in Arab countries, which are very crowded compared to the United States, the territory of the individual person is an internal territory. One author has interpreted the territory as internal because he notes that the Arab who wants privacy merely does not talk; in fact, he can go for days without speaking, and this privacy is respected by others. You can well imagine the confusion this sometimes causes in diplomatic circles; Americans, and many Europeans, are just the opposite, and interpret silence as a rebuff.

While we are on the subject, the same author strongly supports the possibility that humans operate on smell when they determine social grouping. He points out that among Arabs, smelling one's friend is actually desirable. Conversations are frequently held standing as close together as two people can get, and it is an insult to avoid getting another's breath directly in your face. Built into this system is social justification; it is no offense to point out to the other person that he has bad breath [Hall, 1966]. This also could cause diplomatic problems at U.N. meetings.

notes on territoriality Territoriality in humans is a fascinating area of psychology, so a few additional brief comments on studies in this area might be of interest. The below material comes from *Personal Space* [Sommer, 1969], a book devoted exclusively to this topic and a very readable and interesting addition to your library.

—Control in schools is partially enforced by the way the amount of space is divided. The teacher has fifty times more free space than the student, a fact which provides symbolic authority. Furthermore, the teacher usually can stand and move about, thus demonstrating dominance.

—In a library, the first occupant reaching a bench will usually sit at one end; the second will sit on the opposite end. This is true regardless of the sex of the individuals involved, thus indicating we are dealing with a symbol rather than a male or female person.

—In a seminar arrangement where the tables are arranged in a hollow square, students will avoid sitting next to the instructor and will take a place on the floor even if there is space available next to the teacher. On the rare occasions where a student will sit down next to the teacher he remains silent during the whole class.

—If you want to sit at a table and keep others as far away from you as possible, sit on an end chair and face away from the door (Fig. 20-1a); if you want the table all to yourself, sit in the middle and face the door (Fig. 20-1b).

PSYCHOLOGICAL FACTORS IN GROUP STRUCTURE

Directly related to territoriality is *social grouping*. Certain behaviors seem to promote and continue such grouping once it has begun. For humans, at least, a distinction should be made between group formations that are internal (formed within the group) and those that are external (imposed by one or more other groups). For instance, *internal grouping* was found in the extreme among German Nazis in World War II; they were attempting to form a supposedly "pure race" of superior people. Internal grouping was formed by the Nazis, then, against outsiders.

A rather ludicrous example of *external grouping* prevailed in the early years of the United States, when the settlers were trying to emphasize the differences between themselves and Indians. Indians were identified as a special segment of the population, to be separated from others because they were "clearly different." As a cultural group, they had evolved dangerous and specialized habits. For example, they used war paint and bows and arrows, relied on medicine men, and scalped people. What makes this distinction ludicrous is that these practices were not universal among Indians, or even unique to them; every one of the customs has been found among other peoples of the world.

Almost all groupings, external or internal, that we will discuss will seem foreign because they are arbitrary creations of the inner group, intended to bolster the "insiders" against the "outsiders," or in reference to the outer group, intended to protect themselves from, segregate, or blame the outer group. The various techniques used to segregate one group from another are group protective mechanisms; they relate to the individual in that he can gain sense of identity and a sense of belonging from his own group. He can use the group to provide standards of conduct and feelings of self-worth and to obtain companionship.

20-1 Capital letters (A, B) indicate where to sit to ward off intruders of your personal space. See text.

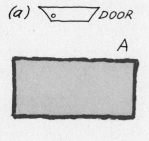

(a)   DOOR

A

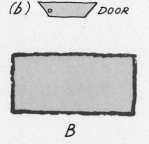

(b)   DOOR

B

This in-group, out-group business is carried to its extreme in the behavior of both the United States and the Soviet Union—behavior which is sometimes ludicrous, sometimes pathetically and tragically serious. The budgets of the CIA and that of its Soviet counterpart, the KGB, are approximately $2 billion each. Agents carry around code books, each about 250 pages long and the size of a postage stamp. Each country gets some sense of identity, some in-group, out-group identification, from this cloak-and-dagger nonsense. The KGB even has a soccer team, called the Dynamo, which is part of the largest club in the USSR, the Dynamo Sports Club. Whether the CIA has such an organization is a secret [Wise, 1967]. Even during the celebrated 1972 world championship chess match, Fischer versus Spassky, the cloak-and-dagger business surfaced. The Soviets charged the Americans with foul play, suggesting that they were influencing Spassky by use of "some electronic devices and chemical substance." The idea was not that far-fetched for them because it seems that they previously had bombarded the American embassy in Moscow with microwaves in an attempt to disrupt the intellectual process of the diplomats there [Wade, 1972].

self-reference   A quite notable characteristic of groups is what is called *self-reference*. That is, group *A* sees group *B* only from its own point of view. For example, the United States provided military aid to Laos in the form of armored vehicles. This doesn't sound too strange to us, since we live in a country that seems to treat the motor vehicle in one form or another as the solution to all problems. However, Laos has very few roads, and even those are not passable a large part of the year [O'Neill, 1971]. Closer to home, welfare programs meet with considerable opposition from the large number of Americans who embrace what is called the Protestant ethic, which stresses hard work and self-reliance. The attitude of this group is that the poor alone are responsible for their condition. Since making money is possible for *them*, reason the upholders of the Protestant ethic, it should be possible for everyone else; thus, they tend to view poverty as largely the result of laziness and lack of motivation [MacDonald and Majumder, 1972; MacDonald, 1971].

scapegoats   If things go wrong at work or at home, most of us tend to blame someone else. Even if we are fairly open-minded we are pretty likely to say, "Yes, it was partly my fault, but *he* was mostly responsible—at least, *he* started it." Psychologically, both as individuals and in groups, we maintain our balance by not taking the full blame for things that go wrong. If we were to continuously admit fault in every case, we would endanger our feelings of self-esteem. This same mechanism works with groups; others are blamed for whatever goes wrong.

A large part of our discussion will focus on negative characteristics of groups. Unfortunately, this focus reflects reality; otherwise, mankind would by now be one large human family living happily together. One

135 The "Scottsboro Seven," a group of black youths accused in Alabama in 1933 of raping two white women. Theirs was a classic case of "outsiders" being accused of trying to violate the "insider" group—the white populace (*Bettmann Archive*)

136 Stormtroopers marching in Berlin, 1933 (*Culver*)

negative factor is *scapegoating,* in which group *A* blames group *B* for the ills that befall it.* One blatant example of scapegoating is the Nazi movement, which had its seeds in the political unrest in Germany in the 1930s and used the Jewish people as the scapegoat. A man who could not even make an adequate living as a poster painter, Adolf Hitler, *did* have enough ability to say inflammatory things and incite a country to the point of mass murder. Germany had been plunged into despair; in 1933 more than 6 million Germans were unemployed and this scrawny man, Hitler, who was rejected from the military because of poor health, came up with just the right formula: "We are the results of the stress *for which others are responsible*" [Hitler, 1933; Bullock, 1953].

The integrity of the German people and their basic welfare seemed sufficiently threatened that eventually an organization of eighty thousand "technicians" (experts at murder in an efficient fashion) exterminated approximately 6 million Jews. When you read this number, it doesn't really register, does it? That is six thousand thousand individual human beings, systematically murdered. Assembly lines were set up, and each worker in a camp was assigned a specific task in the extermination: One would remove the clothing, one would form the victims into lines, some would remove gold fillings to obtain money for the cause, some would lead the people to the gas chambers; others worked on more efficient methods of producing the necessary heat to get rid of the bodies that were piling up out of control.

This description doesn't register fully, either, and it apparently didn't on the greater proportion of German people—or if it did, they repressed it or denied it just as we do when we read about conditions in a U.S. prison. Criminals are well used as scapegoats [Hughes, 1964].

The Nazis were not all madmen. However, Goering, Hitler's number-two man, was out of it: He spent a lot of time playing with his model train, which he had rigged up so that he could drop toy bombs on the cars as they passed [Davidson, 1966]. But every man shares the blame. We are all potentially able to commit such acts, sometimes under the guise of war; in 1969 the United States found itself indicted by other countries of the world for allegedly committing at least one massacre in Vietnam. But we

*The term comes from a biblical reference to a goat upon which sins were symbolically laid.

137 Bodies of prisoners at Buchenwald, 1945 (*UPI*)

were right: It was the other side's fault that the war even existed—or at least that is what was claimed. The toll of blacks lynched by frenzied whites seeking their own scapegoat is not in the millions, but that doesn't make American whites better or worse than the Germans. *Fear* is the key word; fear incites mob actions against scapegoats. The group fears the imagined or real threat from the outside. A few sadists always belong to the group, and behavior that is usually repugnant becomes temporarily "justified"; but most people who participate in such group action were rational beings before they got involved.

Probably the most bizarre scapegoating is done in the name of religion. In recent years murder, hatred, looting, and terror have marked the battle between Irish Catholics and Protestants. The cause of this behavior is not religion as such but the unification of individuals under a common umbrella. Once this unification has occurred, the basic fear and hatred within each person is allowed free reign because he has an excuse and a framework.

138 1873: Shakers dancing in their meetinghouse in New Lebanon, New York (*Culver*)

139 Catholic-Protestant demonstration in Ireland (*Peter Gould, FPG*)

Just this sort of behavior produced some rather humorous medical advice of the early 1800s; the doctrines taught at some religious revival meetings were said to be safe if you stayed at home and *read* them, but actually going to the meetings was extremely dangerous, because the large group of revivalists might be overwhelmed by contagious hysteria. One particular sect, the Millerites, was held responsible for spreading "epidemics of insanity" [Caplan, 1969].

mutual support from groups

There is the other side of the coin: Groups provide a feeling of solidarity for members. A group that is attacking another is united in a common cause: All members of "our group" are good. For instance, apparently with full knowledge of what they were doing, the United States allowed the Soviet Union to participate in the prosecution of German war criminals after World War II. The Russians had slaughtered eleven thousand Polish soldiers, an incident they blamed on the Germans—but at that particular time our allies, the Russians, were "good," and the Germans were "bad." We (the Allies) were busy being united in our horror at the behavior of an outside enemy, and we had to preserve our image, which included only "good" allies.

This discussion has been negative, for the most part, as I suggested it would be. The very nature of the group leads to undesirable behavior in so many cases that approaching the subject from the positive viewpoint is very difficult. For a specific individual, however, the group often, in fact usually, provides a considerable number of positive values. To the fraternity member, for example, the club provides a sense of belonging, of self-worth, of identification, of unity, and of protection to the *insider*. Its merit, though, rests on the idea that *outsiders* exist, and these outsiders are excluded for the benefit of insiders. For the members of any group, the most important common denominator is the mutual support that comes from belonging [Sherif, 1964].

Mutual support is sometimes the only means of survival that members have. Consider the Jewish community's solid commitment to certain beliefs in the face of constant harassment. Probably no single group has been attacked for so many reasons, over a longer period of time, than the Jews. Even Henry Ford, revered by large numbers of Americans, used the *Dearborn Independent* (a newspaper) to accuse Jews of causing the downfall of the horse and buggy, starting wars, and promoting short skirts and lipstick [Davidson, 1966].

Being attacked is unpleasant for the scapegoats, but these objects of general enmity can gain mutual support from being fired upon. Probably no other country demonstrated this principle as well as North Vietnam. Its people were taken on by two of the largest countries in the world and they continued to fight. Reporter Richard Dudman, who traveled to North Vietnam in 1972, described some of the elements that enabled the populace to remain united against such tremendous outside force:

140   A black child—an innocent "outsider"— being escorted to school; later, the school bus was overturned by white students (*UPI*)

Morale obviously is high in North Vietnam, despite the current pounding by more than 200 bomb loads a day in some of the heaviest bombing in the history of warfare. Part of the reason is that everyone is made to feel that he or she has a part in the defensive effort.

North Vietnamese leaders call their response a people's war, and its basis is getting everyone involved. Farmers are told that they are helping defend their country by growing more rice and vegetables. Children win points by writing to soldiers at the front—not identified but probably in South Vietnam, Laos or Cambodia.

Just now, since the regular bombings of the North were resumed . . . , this sense of participation is centered on shooting down American planes. . . .

. . . Shooting back, as well as the furious digging of bomb shelters throughout the country, provides a feeling of doing something about it that appears to be successful in countering the sense of helplessness that might otherwise take over. [Dudman, 1972]*

Throughout this discussion of groups, keep in the back of your mind the role religion plays in unifying groups. Notice, for example, that the Jewish religion has provided symbols, tradition, literature, rules of conduct, and behavioral patterns that have kept the Jewish people together in the face of nearly continuous terror. Blacks, on the other hand, did not have the unifying element of one common religion, and they floundered until they were united under the guidance of a religious leader, Dr. Martin Luther King. Not long after Dr. King led in the first steps toward unity, research began for the express purpose of finding symbols, tradition, and literature that relate specifically to blacks and that would provide a unifying element for black people.

The interrelationship between religion and group behavior is often

*From Richard Dudman, "Report from Hanoi," *St. Louis Post Dispatch* 94, no. 269. © 1972 St. Louis Post Dispatch. Reproduced by permission.

141   Dr. Martin Luther King, Jr., speaks in Cleveland, Ohio, to a largely black audience (*UPI*)

fascinating.* In a recent article comparing two religions, an anthropologist†
pointed out that Buddhist thought emphasizes renunciation of the political
and economic world and that Buddhist culture and society as a whole place
little value on achievement or economic growth. Judaism, on the other hand,
emphasizes the transformation of the political-economic world and is "found
in a society which places great value on social and economic revolution"
[Spiro, 1969].

Considering these interconnections, the coming years are likely to
bring a head-on collision between the Roman Catholic church and the large
segment of its "society" (that is, its own members) which approves of birth
control. A group needs members and members need a group; if things run
true to form, both sides will very likely compromise on the issue.

VERBAL COMMUNICATION IN GROUPS

The organizational structure of a group is accomplished on the human level
partly just by using words. In the military, for example, officers are called
"sir" and enlisted men are called by their last names. The barrier between
them is enhanced and perpetuated by the continued use of these different
forms of address; thus, the social structure of the group remains intact.

The most obvious kind of verbal communication for group cohesion
is the use of negative or derogatory nicknames for outsiders, especially
names that refer to country of origin or race. Often, parents who have never
shown open prejudice or used such words wonder where children pick up
these attitudes. This result can be attributed to a strange contradiction in
our society: Calling members of minorities by derogatory names is forbidden,
in the sense that teachers don't use them in front of their pupils, newspapers
don't refer to groups by such names any more than they use other taboo
words such as ———; yet the same derogatory nicknames are subtly
condoned. Jokes and whispering campaigns thus arise among children
because a specific term has a high emotional charge and using it gets a formal
negative response from many adults—thus making it more fun to use. And,
of course, many parents still think such language is cute and barely conceal
their laughter when the child comes out with one of these words. The child
finds this response rewarding enough to compensate for the parents' anger.
Of importance here is that the words in themselves attribute ominous and
evil things to the out-group and perpetuate myths that will be discussed
below, when we take up stereotypes. The myths in turn make the in-group
feel more important.

stereotypes

Stereotypes are printing plates used to reproduce printed material. When
the word *stereotype* moves over into human relations, it refers to one group's

---

* In all of these cases religion is a handy title to use. Obviously more is involved
than just prayer or organized moral codes.

† A scientist who deals with the origins, customs, and development of mankind.

ability to turn out *identical* information about *every* member of another group. For instance, all members of group *A* sleep on the floor at night, or all people of a certain race have a particular character trait—a bad one. Stereotypes can become so broad and familiar that dozens of meanings get to be summarized by just one derogatory name; when someone uses the name, all within hearing range know (or are supposed to know) all the bad characteristics of the group being stereotyped.

In the United States, stereotypes are much vaguer for Orientals than for blacks. Some theorists have suggested that whites haven't been exposed enough to Orientals to be expert at constructing stereotypes. Some clues about how stereotypes are constructed come from studies in which subjects were given verbal descriptions of certain foreigners but never actually met the people being described. Typically, the subjects tended automatically to prefer those people who were said to have characteristics similar to their own, no matter what the individual people were really like [Katz, 1958; Epstein, 1966]. In the same vein, unpleasant or unfavorable traits are attributed to college students most often by persons who have almost no contact with students. The stereotype (sight-unseen) is a beard, blue jeans, and an unkempt appearance [Hamid, 1967].

What purpose, then, do these stereotypes and name callings serve? They solidify the in-group, which can bolster its self-esteem by assuming that others are not as good as they are. And stereotypes tend to ward off the possibility that different cultural ways may encroach on the in-group. That is, the in-group wants things to stay the way they are, for safety's sake, and ridiculing the other group reduces that group's importance.

On the positive side, it should be mentioned that titles such as "doctor" not only provide some feelings of importance for the doctors, but aid the patient by reassuring him that he is in good hands (presumably, "society" would not have bestowed this title otherwise).

general role of language   The role of language, examined in terms of specific word usage, is related to group beliefs, habits, and behaviors, although the relationship here is probably quite subtle. Psychologists have known for years, for instance, that the language of a culture usually reflects the life of the people within that culture. One of the best-known studies of this kind showed that Eskimos have a tremendous vocabulary, compared to ours, for the word *snow*. They use specific words for falling snow, drifting snow, snowdrift, and so on [Boas, 1938]. This variety is intriguing, but not unexpected.

The possible effect of words on a group, however, appears to be even more subtle. It had been hypothesized for quite a while, apparently with some truth, that a great many blacks, especially those of previous generations, had adopted the white value system for skin color, light skin being more acceptable than dark [Seeman, 1946]. If Eskimos use many words for snow because snow is important to them, one could understand why blacks would develop more words for skin color than whites would. Indeed, this seems to be true; a recent study of vocabulary usage compared black children with a white control group and found the expected difference [Palmar, 1969].

Drawing broad conclusions from limited findings is a rather risky business, but speculation does no harm as long as it is labeled as such. The idea that blacks took over some white cultural values and developed a large vocabulary for skin color receives some support from a recent trend. In a phenomenon that might be called word reconditioning, which is found in many black groups, children are trained to say repeatedly, "Black is good." Blacks are attempting to reverse the trend toward accepting white values. In a study of changes in positive versus negative feelings toward various colors since 1963, evidence indicates that the movement is having an effect. Blacks now view the color black more positively than white, whereas a control group of nonblacks have shown no such change in their reactions to these colors since 1963 [Williams et al., 1971].

Group behavior, individual reactions, and social order are mainly guided by the symbol of the word. Words themselves are translated into action—or more accurately, into implied action. Certain specific behaviors and attitudes are conjured up just by identifying someone as a teenager, married, white trash, parent, and many other descriptive words. Groups react to the words themselves because certain potential actions are implied by these words [Duncan, 1968].

THE FUNCTION OF RULES IN GROUP BEHAVIOR

Rules, although sometimes unwritten, have the role of communicating structure to a group and holding it together. Rules generally evolve over a considerable period of time to meet the needs of a group, but when they don't, it is necessary for a social committee, for instance, to purchase a copy of "Robert's Rules of Order"* so that they can maintain some semblance of organization.

At the opposite extreme from the social committee is an overwhelmingly complex set of rules that fits under the heading of *law* and fills book after book on the shelves of an attorney's office. The law holds the larger society together, serving the same function as smaller sets of rules, written or unwritten. Both attempt to regulate the behavior of groups. In fact, some rules apparently are so basic to the structure of society, and to its family units, that they take effect automatically without the person's even agreeing—for example, the common-law marriage which can't be stopped if two people have lived together for a certain period of time. Such a marriage is rather like dragging in a minister and saying that the rules require you to be married, and now you are.

* A set of rules for conducting formal meetings.

Rules establish the boundaries of behavior, and they allow a sense of individual security to group members. At least in theory, a person knows where he stands. Inadvertently, rules also provide social structure within the group; it has been found that those who are most accepted within a group tend to violate the rules more than other members. Those least accepted do this, too, so in both cases the rules facilitate a form of hierarchy that differentiates "good" and "bad" members [Kiesler, 1963].

Rules are also bent and twisted in subtle ways. The old adage that you don't find rich murderers on death row is apparently true. Somewhere in the legal process the rules have been differently (or better) interpreted for these individuals.

The basic need for rules to maintain structure in any group becomes evident if we examine for a moment those groups that operate outside the law. In the early days of the Mafia, for example, if a boss became interested in the wife of a "soldier" (i.e., an underling), he could have the soldier killed. To prevent this sort of behavior, the Mafia now carries out a death sentence on anyone caught with another's wife. It is assumed that fewer members are lost this way than under the former system. The purpose of the rule is to preserve the group and to give security to the members; for the same reason, a mandatory death sentence is imposed for divulging information about the organization. A really odd Mafia rule, which may bring home the point, is that using one's *fist* against another member can result in a hearing before the "family" and lead to severe penalties [Maas, 1968]. No matter how the in-group (the Mafia) behaves toward the out-group (most of us), internal harmony and security must be preserved.

Probably one of the most peculiar rules in racketeering is that those coming up in the ranks are selected for honesty and reliability [Sutherland, 1937]. This rule makes one pause and think, but its relevance is obvious.

The rules of behavior for organized racketeering are different from those for professional armed robbers. For instance, armed robbers make up a loose confederation of individuals who get together to do a specific job. If one of them gets caught, no share of the "take" is used to aid him legally; the others have no obligation. On the other hand, with more permanent criminal activities such as organized racketeering, some profits are set aside for bail or court assistance [Einstadter, 1969].

Rules are, to some extent, flexible. Just as children sometimes need an outlet, so organizations usually have a safety-valve clause in their rules allowing for rather extreme changes in behavior. Many social and religious groups make drastic alterations in their rules. The trick in this maneuver is to make sure the original rules provide some framework for change, so that the security of the individual and his reliance on the permanency of the mystical, inflexible rules are not shaken. We can take the obvious example of war, which seems to alter rules rather dramatically. What looks

142   Rules are changing in religious orders, too—but these Trappist monks still observe the venerable traditions and wear the traditional garb of their order (*Acme*)

to be a rather straightforward statement—such as the commandment "Thou Shalt Not Kill"—has an amazing number of subparagraphs, qualifications, and elaborations, so that the rule can be changed and yet remain intact. One important authority on international law, for example, worked diligently on a number of rules for humane conduct of war, but before he was finished he had included the idea that anything that was done to "barbarians" (!?) was lawful [Wormser, 1962].

Again, the Nazis were involved in a flagrant and bizarre incident of rule changing and twisting of the law to justify a group's ends. In 1943 the law was changed to place Jews outside the law; the Nazis then had a law that said the Jews were not within the law; in other words, legal and orderly procedure was followed to enact a negative law which then allowed the Nazis to murder the Jews legally within their own system [Davidson, 1966].

SUMMARY

The group is founded on social structure—that is, differences between individuals within a given group. This differentiation can be noted in many animal groups other than man. One example is the pecking order found among birds. Throughout the animal kingdom, it would seem, social order is preprogrammed or wired into the species. Although man elaborates considerably on basic grouping patterns, some evidence, most of it indirect, suggests that he starts out with the basic principle of social ordering found in all animals and refines it. Territoriality is of interest because groups of individual animals or humans seem to mark off their living space and thereby define it as belonging to them and not to outsiders.

There are two basic principles of grouping, internal grouping and external grouping. Internal grouping stresses the difference and importance of one's own group and reinforces this by emphasizing external grouping— that is, by emphasizing that outsiders are different.

An offshoot of external grouping is not just viewing others as different, but actually blaming them for the ills that befall one's own group. This practice is known as scapegoating. Scapegoating is used to justify the actions of the in-group and to excuse inexcusable acts—for example, lynchings.

External grouping provides positive values for those who belong to the in-group: security and a feeling of belonging.

The organizational structure of a group is based on symbols and verbal communication. A stereotype symbolizes supposed characteristics, often unpleasant, of the out-groups and is passed on mainly by verbal communication.

A group is held together by rules, written and unwritten. The existence of rules is universal among groups, even such deviant ones as criminal organizations. The rules must remain flexible enough to allow some leeway for members so that the group can maintain the necessary number of members; and the rules must be rigid enough that the individual feels the protection they provide. Groups can get away with some bizarre behavior as long as they are able to construct a rule to fit it or twist an existing rule to allow for a particular act.

CHAPTER TWENTY-ONE
SYMBOLS, RITUALS AND AGGRESSION

Communicating group ideals and influencing group members sometimes involves no overt verbal behavior, especially when symbols are used. A group may communicate subtle meanings or purposes to its members; these meanings are usually found in the group's symbols. Most important, however, is the *feeling* of psychological unity, which can't be expressed in words or measured directly. Symbols are critical to this unity.

SYMBOLISM IN GROUP BEHAVIOR

Nothing is more common in human groups than symbolism. With few exceptions, group organization without symbols is rather like a séance without strange voices from on high. *Symbols* provide a unified way for the group to express itself, although the behavior may not be related to what the symbol is supposed to mean. The American flag has been used, in the not-too-distant past, as a rallying point for violence against those opposed to American war policy.

The Nazis again provide us with some striking examples; they are easy to use for illustrative purposes in these chapters because of their extremely bizarre behavior. The intelligentsia of Nazism were hard at work, for example, trying to prove that Jesus Christ was not a Jew [Davidson, 1966]. This symbolism was apparently such a threat to their cause, and to a group structure based on a "pure," non-Jewish race, that they had to change the symbol to fit their own purposes. Also, they were preoccupied with the type of blood one had, which is interesting because blood is frequently used as a *group symbol*. For example, you probably have heard the expressions "blue-blood family" or "bad blood." In the case of the Nazis, Nordic blood* was the German ideal, and some genuinely preposterous "scientific" studies were undertaken—for example, one in which a professor "found" that streetcar conductors had less Nordic blood than motormen.

The capitalist motive, ever present, entered the symbol market, bringing with it such items as soap stamped with swastikas, *Heil Hitler* stickers for cigarette packages, and even two things almost beyond imagination: a Christmas tree in the shape of a hooked cross, and swastikas for tree ornaments [Davidson, 1966].

A basic explanation for the profusion of symbols within groups is

---

* There is no such thing.

498

that they are the result of secondary reinforcement, just as gold stars are. Whatever the group means to us—security, power, affection, what have you—is translated into the symbol. In other words, the symbol is shorthand for what the group represents in our lives.

This sort of symbolism becomes clear when you examine the excerpt below, which comes from one of the wildest, most colorful trials in the history of law—the United States versus David Dellinger, Rennard C. Davis, Thomas E. Hayden, Abbott H. Hoffman, Jerry C. Rubin, Lee Weiner, John R. Froines, and Bobby G. Seale, commonly known as the "Chicago Eight." The defendants were tried on charges of crossing state lines with the intent to conspire to riot. The excerpt illustrates the struggle that ensues when the court wants to uphold its right to symbolism and when the attorney for the defense tries to get a man into the courtroom who is wearing headgear which, in the eyes of the defense, represents the man's own individual rights and beliefs:

(December 17, 1969—direct examination of Defense Witness Richard H. Perez, a CBS-TV News cameraman, by Defense Attorney [William] Kunstler.)

Mr. Kunstler: Your Honor, before the film is shown I would just like to ask your Honor's assistance. We have a young man outside, Robert Loeb, who has been denied admission to the Court because he is wearing a yarmulke* which he traditionally wears.

The Court: Oh, that is a subject not to be discussed in the presence of the jury, Mr. Kunstler. I came out here in connection with this exhibit.

Mr. Kunstler: It is a simple matter to let him—there was room and this is about the eighth time it has occurred and we would like to move the Court to have him admitted with his yarmulke.

The Court: The matter of who is admitted to the Court is a matter for the marshals and the rule of Court is that gentlemen take their hats off. This is not a church.

Mr. Kunstler: I know, but a man wears his yarmulke regularly and I think he should be admitted.

* A skullcap worn by Orthodox Jewish men as part of their religious obligations.

143-144 The Jewish star and the Nazi swastika in Germany during the 1930s; both became symbols of group unity to those who wore them (*UPI; Culver*)

145 1970: Symbols of the hippie subculture (*Ralph Garcia, Camera 5*)

The Court: We conduct trials here under the laws of the United States and not under ecclesiastical law. . . . Mr. Kunstler, I have had a prince of the Catholic Church in this courtroom who didn't wear a head-covering.

Mr. Kunstler: That may not have been his religious obligation, your Honor.

The Court: And we do not permit in this Court a man to come in with his head covered. Now I will let you or any lawyer who represents him make a record on it.

Mr. Kunstler: I am only interested in our public trial, your Honor, and we thought that this interfered with a public trial.

The Court: This is a public trial. If you don't know it, why read the newspapers, Mr. Kunstler. [Levine et al., 1970]*

In a way, when it comes to classification and storage in the brain, symbols are quite direct and simple, yet they can encompass emotion as well as fact. Just one symbol can represent a whole way of life—for example, the Roman collar worn by some members of the ministry, or the nurse's white uniform, which is only grudgingly giving way to green. This resistance to color change is interesting; supposedly, in early days, white fabric made it easier to detect dirt, so the white uniform became prominent. In the mid-twentieth century, however, many nurses violently opposed any suggestion of a color change, even though there was no reason to consider one color cleaner than another—except *symbolically*.† If you don't think you are affected by symbols, how would you react in a hospital where all the nurses and surgeons wore black? It would be a little disconcerting.

Group symbols sometimes help members to survive under almost intolerable circumstances. For instance, in a study of the possessions of poor families in Mexico City,‡ in the two poorest families of the group, religious objects had more monetary value than any other set of items, including furniture, clothing, and household equipment. In fact, 33 percent of the value of *all* objects in all the poor households studied was connected with religious items [Lewis, 1969]. At the very least, these religious objects symbolized future relief from the very difficult present problems.

**RITUAL
IN GROUP BEHAVIOR**

An outgrowth of symbolism is *ritual*. Prescribed ritual gives meaning to group activity. Having the same ritual for more than one group is worse than appearing at a party in the same dress some other woman is wearing; except by accident, each group will have a distinctive set of rituals.

---

*From *The Tales of Hoffman*, edited from the official transcript by Mark L. Levine, George C. McNamee, and Daniel Greenberg (New York: Bantam Books, 1970); reprinted by permission.

†In one large university hospital the operating-room nurses presently wear pink slacks. This is startling because we all are infected with traditional symbolism.

‡Average total value of each family's entire possessions was $338.

146-147 In different contexts, uniforms and group activities may play an important role in affirming group solidarity (*Rapho Gullimette; Culver*)

One can only speculate why rituals are so important. Perhaps very early man lived a fearful existence in which he completely misunderstood nearly everything, thinking that things in nature were animate—the wind, the sun, rain, what have you. Probably by coincidence some group activity— for instance, a dance—occurred at the same time as, say, the passing of a storm, so the ritual of the dance was later repeated to *prevent* storms.

A possible extension of this idea is that ritualistic behavior many times failed to elicit the desired result. Maybe at this point groups began to look for "outside help," so to speak, and sought the aid of some kind of demon or god [Malinowski, 1925].

In any case it is noteworthy that the advanced cerebral cortex of human beings is needed to evolve an understanding of symbolic rituals regardless of exactly how they originated.

A group's ritualistic, mystical behaviors set it and its members apart from others. Take the case of marijuana smoking: The cigarette has to be held a certain way, inhaled in a specified fashion, and the routine is rarely complete without some weird lights and music.

Even a well-established group like the Mafia can't do without ritual. It has an initiation ceremony in which a piece of paper is held in cupped hands and then lighted. While it is burning, something is said to the effect that you will burn just like the paper if you betray the secrets of the group [Maas, 1968]. Finally, it might be noted that the Boy Scouts have candle- burning ceremonies, pledges, songs, and certain signs with the fingers that are ritualistic.

A specific kind of ritual is the initiation, in which a person is required to perform certain acts in order to become a member of the group. In one intriguing study of group behavior, the experimenters set up an organization for girls in which new members were given differing degrees of severe initiation to determine the effect it would have on the person's view of the group. The subjects who received the most severe initiation were required to read an embarrassing passage before the group; those who got the least severe initiation were not required to perform any task in order

148-149 The group social function often involves ritual imbibing of special substances—marijuana, or the cocktail-party martini (*Peter Lacey, Camera 5; Mimi Forsyth, Monkmeyer*)

to get into the group. In between was a group that received a mild initiation task. Comparison of subjects showed that those who went through the most severe initiation thought the group was really something, whereas those who had no initiation or a mild one did not feel very committed [Aronson, 1959]. This study may provide a clue to the tenacity of minority groups in the face of constant difficulties; it may well be that their members are going through a kind of continuous and severe initiation and that commitment continues to increase as a result of outside harassment.

MAGIC IN GROUP BEHAVIOR

Somewhere along the line symbolism leaves off, reality disappears, and magic enters. Deciding where to draw the line between these stages is an impossible task. A man who wins for four straight hours by holding a rabbit's foot in one hand and throwing the dice with the other makes us wonder; the same man using the same technique but losing for four hours convinces us that the lucky charm is nonsense. Many groups, nonetheless, reach a level of supersymbolism—or magic, however you want to interpret it. For instance, to the Egyptians nothing was more important than that their kings be immortal. Their bodies were preserved and housed in "proper residences"—giving the world the magnificent heritage of the pyramids [McNeill, 1963].

Probably nowhere do symbolism, group behavior, magic, and the physiological aspects of psychology dovetail so well as when we consider voodoo—so it might be worth spending a little time on this topic.

Voodoo is practiced mainly on the island of Haiti. Many people think of voodoo as a primitive religion, but it contains a strange mixture of Christianity, which was introduced by early missionary work. Instead of adopting Christianity, the voodooists apparently just incorporated Christian beliefs into the existing system.*

Voodooism centers around a faith in *loa*, the spirits of God and people, which can be either good or evil. A spell of *loa*, which will cause death, can be cast by the witch doctor. This spell cannot be removed except by calling on a "greater" witch doctor or having the original one remove it.

This sounded like a lot of hocus-pocus, so some very reputable scientists decided to examine the situation [Cannon, 1942]. Among the substantiated findings were: Persons with a death-hex on them do indeed die, even though they are in good health; those on the verge of death from the hex can be brought back, so to speak, by paying off some of the witch doctors,† who then remove the spell. It was obvious to the scientists that

150　Egyptian mummy, exhumed centuries later from its "proper residence"; for the ancient Egyptians, this would be an act of wanton sacrilege (*Bettmann Archive*)

---

*Much to the dismay of the missionaries. Read Bach [1961] for an interesting and thorough account of voodooism.
†There are corrupt individuals in all societies.

151 A witch doctor performs a rite in New Caledonia, 1941 (*Bettmann Archive*)

152 A Nigerian medical practitioner treats a sick person; like Western physicians, he will be paid his fee no matter whether the patient gets well or dies (*Bettmann Archive*)

even though a person was wasting away rapidly after having a hex put on him, removal of the hex reversed the process. In other words, group belief in the power of the witch doctor apparently was strong enough so that the hexed person, who had adopted the belief, just gave up and actually began to die.

This report was picked up by a laboratory experimenter who had become aware of sudden, unexplained deaths among many zoo animals and among some of his own rats. He found that many rats, if they were restrained, had their whiskers clipped, and were doused with water, "gave up" and suddenly died. The rats seemed to have no will to live. The experimenter hypothesized that one factor causing the sudden death was overactivation of a major nerve controlling the heart, which caused the heart to stop beating. Another possibility is that the adrenal system, the hypothalamus, or cerebral cortex became overloaded [Richter, 1957, 1958].

Moving back to voodoo, we might reasonably hypothesize that human beings who have been hexed either give up, overactivating the neural network to the heart, or panic and overload the adrenal system. Thus, voodoo gives us a more than graphic example of just how much power group beliefs can hold over an individual; in extreme cases, the group controls the life and death of the individual.

The sudden-death phenomenon is not, of course, restricted to voodooland. The United States sees a number of these cases every year. The body shows no sign of injury, disease, or maladaptation before the fatal "illness" sets in; some major psychological disaster usually has occurred—for example, the death of a loved one—and presumably this event sets into motion a physiological reaction to overwhelming fear, loss, or despair. A study of unexplained sudden deaths of 26 factory workers over a period of time at a certain company has yielded some interesting clues about what might cause this. The authors found that these men had been severely depressed as the result of some misfortune. Depression reduces the level of bodily functioning, so the men were going along for a period of time with their bodies operating in low gear. The trigger for the death seems to have come from some abrupt change in their routine such as a period of anger or anxiety. The change in state elevated the level of their hormonal and nervous systems way beyond what it had been. The sudden change back and forth in the physiological mechanisms is thought to be the cause of an overloaded system. In one of the cases, a man who had been depressed got so excited over a pool shot in the recreation room that he fell over dead [Greene et al., 1972].

VIOLENCE IN GROUPS

Wars and violence seem to be as old as man. Fossil remains going back as far as our probable ancestor, the Neanderthal man of a hundred thousand years ago, show wooden weapons and spear tips that have remained em-

153   A modern witch baptizes his daughter in a black-magic ritual (*Curt Gunther, Camera 5*)

bedded in human bone [Stewart, 1969]. Some argue that man is merely an advanced animal and that aggression is a mode of life among animals of any kind [Lorenz, 1963]. Part of their logic is that animals cannot survive without aggression; although very few animals other than man kill or injure just for the fun of it, aggressive behavior seems to be part of the balance of nature. Further, a thought-provoking issue has been brought up regarding our concern about violence: We assume, presumptuously, that man is the finest and most nearly perfect species; this being so, it is inconceivable that he continue in his ways of aggression. If we stop for a moment and ponder the idea that we are not the highest *possible* form of life, human aggression takes on a different aspect; at least it doesn't seem as bizarre [Rothenberg, 1969].

In support of this assumption, societies* do exist in which a person lives his life in such a way that each day's activities are arranged to provide opportunities to cheat, gouge, and be as cutthroat as possible toward his fellows [Benedict, 1934]. But pause and consider that other societies† exist in which violence is absent and people live in harmony without destroying one another [Malinowski, 1929]. The second case makes one suspicious: How could such a society exist if man were nothing more than a creature with basically aggressive tendencies? Or is there something very strange about these peaceful groups, something that makes them abnormal?

The time we have spent so far on group behavior brings into focus the most critical issue in aggressive behavior: It is frequently based on the symbolism and unity of in-group and out-group activities. This problem is man-made, and it seems to be the common denominator for a lot of violent activity (if we ignore the rare and strange ax murder that is the quirk of an individual personality, or the man who shoots his wife because she burns the dinner). The violence of war and riot, for example, seems to be a group endeavor based on the in-group/out-group pattern. A specific country is afraid that another will somehow infiltrate and take it over and that its people are susceptible to propaganda, which threatens the country's security. We can readily see this in the behavior of our government toward Communists. In theory our Constitution allows its citizens to advocate or support *any* form of government, but sometimes the felt threat of the out-group is too much and the government oversteps the boundary of the Constitution in preventing the out-group from functioning.

The foundation for group violence undoubtedly is individual fear that is stirred up by individual fears of others—but still the basic factor seems to be social grouping. A study of the 1967 riots in Detroit and Newark compared black rioters with a black control group which came from the same areas but did not participate in the riots. The study dispels a number

---

*E.g., a group called the Dobu.
†E.g., a group called the Trobriand Islanders.

of myths. It was not the hard-core unemployed, the down-and-outers, who participated in the rioting; in fact, the rioter was better educated than the nonrioter, did not show any notable mental disturbance, and, like the delinquent, did not show any unusual desire for material possessions. Instead, investigators found, one major factor that differentiated rioters from nonrioters was the feeling of black unity—that is, the feeling that blacks are a specific and special subculture. The nonrioting blacks, on the other hand, seemed more content with whites and less specifically race-oriented [Caplan, 1968]. Not that they were happy with whites, or that they lacked racial pride—but they did seem to lack a strict in-group orientation based on frustration and the desire to form a separate subculture of blacks, in opposition to whites.

One very puzzling element in many of the riots was that blacks destroyed "their own" property and rioted in their own neighborhoods. The most plausible explanation is that the rioters were attacking the *symbols* of their ghetto existence [DeLany, 1968]. Most of us have seen this behavior on a minor scale at home when someone in the family, in a fit of complete and utter frustration, attacks an object that represents the frustrations: A housewife smashes some dishes, a child breaks toys, or a man trying to fix something becomes so exasperated that he smashes it beyond repair.

Violence, then, is directed toward others or symbols of others and is generally based on an external threat from some out-group. Sometimes the threat is real, as in the case of job discrimination against minority groups. In other cases the threat is symbolic, for the *actual* danger is unknown, as in the suspicion between the United States and China.

This national symbolism is well illustrated in the continuing complaint of Japanese officials that American television is still showing old war movies that depict stereotyped, evil-looking Orientals torturing Americans and just being bad all the way to the core. These ridiculous movies were made for propaganda purposes during World War II; we now view the

154 Damage after riots in Washington, D.C., 1968 (*Wide World*)

Japanese differently, and they view us differently: We like one another. Such a change could not have taken place if the bases for earlier disagreements were not mostly symbolic.

Japan, moreover, has developed one of the fastest-growing economic complexes in the world, and this accomplishment appeals to Americans, giving us a capitalistic common denominator for working together in areas such as exporting and importing of goods. Studies with small groups support the hypothesis that working together promotes unity; one of the most effective means of uniting two dissident groups is to force them into a situation in which they must perform a task that requires mutual assistance. In most cases, this common need provides a common purpose and a closeness that did not previously exist [Sherif, 1961].

origin of individual violence

Violent behavior can be classified into three types. None of the three has a specific name, although one author has suggested names for two of them: constructive aggression and destructive aggression. The third label I would add is pathological* destructive aggression [Rothenberg, 1969]. The names are not as important as the idea behind them, anyway.

Pathological destructive aggression is behavior that involves an emotional problem and, usually, originates in individual motivations. A man who has been belittled all his life for having a scrawny physique, for example, and who has had serious problems with his mother and with women in general may one day suddenly attack a woman in an unusually brutal fashion. The pathology or sickness involved is deep-seated, and the violence is the man's method of coping with his extreme emotional problems.

Constructive aggression should be noted carefully, for we *teach* our children to be aggressive in subtle ways—by competing in the classroom or having a "fair" boxing match with gloves on. A child also sees his parent using his automobile as a weapon in the fight for a parking place. He is encouraged to attack inanimate objects like punching bags. All these behaviors seem relatively harmless, but where do we draw the line? Obviously we are an aggressive people. Each of these responses is a method of fighting off frustration, either by trying to make ourselves better or by avoiding being thwarted in our desires. Children learn these responses by observing and participating in them.

Destructive aggression is the kind of behavior we see in mob action. It is not *necessarily* pathological, for it is the constructive aggression found in many individuals combined with the safety-in-numbers idea that gets out of control very easily. The destructive aggression of groups seems to be an offshoot of the constructive aggression of individuals. It is important to remember that society condones constructive aggression (and destructive aggression in war).†

155   American ping-pong players on their way to communist China in 1971—an unusual example of cooperation across the "bamboo curtain" (*UPI*)

* Abnormal.
† Is not police action or capital punishment a form of constructive aggression?

One set of studies on aggression involved showing part of a movie, *The Champion*, starring Kirk Douglas. In the part of the movie shown, Mr. Douglas receives a grotesque beating. After they had seen the movie, subjects were told that they were to judge the merit of a drawing made by a person who was positioned behind a screen. If they didn't like his work, they were to administer shocks to him.*

In one variation of the experiment, the "artist"† was introduced as "Kirk" to some subjects and by another name to other subjects. The intensity of shock administered to "Kirk" was considerably greater than when the stooge had another name. This suggests an important principle: We *can* identify with violent behavior, and we ourselves carry on the work just seen on the screen [Berkowitz and Geen, 1967].

In a second experiment using the same basic arrangement, some subjects were told before viewing the movie that a bad guy was receiving the beating. Another group of Ss was told that a good guy was the recipient of the blows. In other words, for the first Ss the beating was justified; for the second, it was unjustified. The experimenters found that justified violence bred greater violence (shocks) against the stooges than unjustified violence. Two principles seem important here: first, violence can breed violence; second, justified violence is more likely to breed more violence. This study and others strongly suggest that violence in the name of right, honor, and good, as portrayed in the movies and on television, actually leads to violence. One might guess that the subjects felt that society condones violent behavior if it is "right" [Berkowitz, 1964]. The problem this attitude presents is notable; who among us doesn't feel that he would be justified in doing someone in?

Children imitate all kinds of behavior, including aggressive behavior. Specific problems come up when we consider children and their viewing of television or movies. There has been a considerable amount of commotion recently about the effects of TV violence on children. First of all, in the laboratory it has been demonstrated that if children see a movie that features violence they tend to become violent themselves [Bandura et al., 1963]. Even in the Surgeon General's report on violence and television, which was quite watered down in many places and where selection of the experimenters was influenced by the political power of the networks, experiments still indicated that viewing violence leads to violence [Liebert and Neale, 1972]. Out of the laboratory, children who had had at least a moderate exposure to television violence for 10 years were about 60 percent more aggressive than a control group of children who had had little exposure [Liebert and Neale, 1972]. The latter study would suggest that the long-term effect of television violence is not good. Other studies point out that there are two

---

* The shocks were not real, although the Ss thought they were.
† Unknown to Ss, all drawings used were identical.

effects from TV violence, one short-term and one lingering. The short-term effect is a very high level of *physiological* arousal and a tendency to be very aggressive. The importance of being stirred up physiologically is demonstrated by the fact that people who are annoyed after seeing *either* a violent or an erotic film become very aggressive immediately afterward [Zillman, 1971]. After about twenty minutes, however, the physiological mechanism has lowered itself and we are left with a toned-down, but lingering level of aggression [Doob and Climie, 1972].

For the moment, we are stuck with what to do about it. Elimination of TV violence is not a complete solution because television reflects the society just as in other eras folk stories, myths, and plays told of those cultures. Current television is quite realistic in many respects: broad surveys of the content of hundreds of programs indicate that they even subtly reflect the "pecking order" of our society; white males and cartoon animals of no particular race were rarely victims compared to females, nonwhites in general, and nonwhite cartoon characters [Gerber, 1972].

To broach the question from a slightly different point of view, another study found that the hostility level of spectators after a football game was very high whether their team had won or lost, much higher than that found after a gymnastic meet [Goldstein and Arms, 1971]. Football is certainly considered an all-American sport (in its literal sense) for better or worse. Should we eliminate football?

One major change is taking place: Morality—always a difficult topic to examine—is becoming more confused as the result of a rash of realistic movies and television programs in which the distinction between good guy and bad guy is blurred and identification with "right" and "wrong" becomes difficult. Definite changes are taking place: in the past, characters were either supergood or superevil. Children, of course, always learn later that no real person fits either of these categories, but presumably most children at least wanted to emulate the supergood guys and later came to realize that human nature makes moral perfection impossible—so they compromised on something in between. Nowadays such identification with "good" is weak or obscured from the beginning, and it is difficult to guess what effect this will have on later development—if any.

Be all this as it may, from the scientific-objective point of view, one study has alarming implications—at least to me. Again using *The Champion*, experimenters have found that the level of arousal when viewing the film is significantly less ($p = <.05$) for those who have viewed considerable television than for those who have not [Cline et al., 1972]. Translated, what this study is saying is that experienced TV watchers have gotten so used to violence that it loses its impact on them. This is called ***desensitization*** (loss of sensitivity) and is the same type of adjustment people like highway patrolmen have to use to keep their sanity when dealing day-in and day-out with mangled bodies. The major area of concern, however, is that the TV viewer is becoming desensitized to the infliction of violence.

Considerable agreement seems to exist, however, that the worst kind of violence to portray is *justified violence*. The old idea that a child or an adult will learn his lesson by seeing someone punished on screen is out now; all such "examples" do is make people more perverse.

Studies in the area of violence do not lead to universal principles. The amount of aggression, for instance, can be greatly increased if the stooge insults the subject, or if someone encourages the aggression; thus, not all Ss respond in the same way. How a subject reacts depends to some extent on his motivation and personality and on external circumstances [Dahlstrom, 1970]. The long-term reaction of the child to seeing violence, however, seems to depend on whether or not the parents provide a model that offsets the television. If the children are left all to themselves, this is a bad situation [Stein, 1972].

Most studies have been conducted in a laboratory; a few have involved elaborate interviews with people actually convicted of violent behavior. The main theme repeats itself, however: Many cases involving confrontation between police and individuals clearly show that there was "justification" on both sides for the ensuing violence. Further, these same studies show that a large proportion of violent acts, even those performed by individuals, are group-related; the offended individual feels that his self-image before his peers has been violated. For example, someone in authority calls a person a name or treats him with no respect, mocking his worth in front of his peers. These persons frequently have reputations for being tough within their group; confrontation with authority suddenly challenges their position in the group, and consequently they strike out [Toch, 1969].

At least three facts about violence seem to have been demonstrated so far:

1.   Man has a potential for violence.
2.   Violence is usually group-related.
3.   Violence can be learned, or at least enhanced, by seeing violent behavior.

notes on aggression   —Contrary to popular belief, aggression is actually inhibited by hot weather and increases during periods of more moderate temperatures. One exception to this is that an individual's potential for violent outbursts is much greater if he has moved from cool, comfortable conditions into a hot atmosphere. But we cannot find evidence that riots which occur in the summer are the result of heat per se [Baron, 1972]. It may simply be that the heat of the summer is better for civil strife than the biting cold of winter. This is not too farfetched, for criminal activities follow a pattern related to the weather in the same sort of way. Crimes such as burglary, robbery, and assault decrease dramatically in the rain, snow, or generally inclement weather. Apparently villains too have a desire to stay inside when it's bad out [Pittman, 1964].

—If a person is threatened with retaliation, he is less likely to carry through with his aggression. This rule seems to hold true in many cases as long as the person who suggests retaliation comes from a different social class or different occupation [Baron, 1971]. Thus, it is probably the suggestion of the unknown about other people that makes them more frightening and makes you less likely to get them if they say they are going to get you back.

—Current theory suggests that aggression, when it occurs, is the result of neural self-activation of the rage centers (chapter 5) of the brain, resulting from stress in the environment. Thus, both learning and basic physiology are involved in aggressive behavior. Somewhat like the control of alpha waves, presumably we could learn to control our aggressive impulses [Moyer, 1973].

TECHNIQUES OF PERSUASION

Nothing is more intriguing than a spy movie in which someone has been brainwashed by a foreign power and is acting as a double agent. Some people who watch these movies are concerned about the supposed power of psychology to control the human mind. Some more optimistic men, though, view this power as an opportunity and reply to magazine ads for "mind power" books that promise to enable them to surround themselves with scantily clad girls over whom they will have complete control.

Unfortunately, real life is a disappointment in comparison to the superpowers we see illustrated in the ads or on the screen.

group pressure   One major problem in the studies we will cover is the difficulty the experimenter has in determining the extent of *earlier* group influence on an individual at the time of the experiment. For example, one might find in previous wars a few cases of Americans who have gone over to the Communist side. Were they actually brainwashed or, as some have suggested, were the original groups to which they belonged partly anticapitalist to begin with, so that little persuasion was needed? In any experiment on the effectiveness of persuasion, then, account must be taken of the person's previous *reference group*,* something that is extremely difficult to do. A partial reflection of

---

*A group with which a person identifies and which he uses to set his standards of behavior. A person can have more than one reference group—for example, family, church, work.

reference-group influence can be seen in the fact that people seem to perceive either what they want to see or what they have come to expect. For instance, a stereoscopic device was used in one experiment in which the person looking into the viewer actually had in front of him two *different* pictures, one for each eye. One picture was of a baseball player and the other of a bullfighter. Mexican subjects usually saw only the bullfighter, while American Ss usually saw only the baseball player [Bagby, 1968]. In another study, similar but broader in scope, experimenters showed subjects blatantly satirical cartoons making fun of prejudice. The most prejudiced Ss saw the cartoons as *supporting* bigotry [Cooper and Tahoda, 1964]. The producers of the famous TV series, "All in the Family," had hoped that Archie Bunker would be a useful deterrent to prejudice. Unfortunately, experimental studies have shown that the prejudiced individuals who watch the show *do not* see the satire, but merely tend to agree with Archie [Vidmar and Rokeach, 1973].

It has been found that under laboratory conditions group pressure can alter opinions of a fair proportion of individuals, but these changes do not appear to be permanent for most subjects. In a classic experiment, Ss were asked to judge the length of various lines. One member of each judging group was a genuine subject; all the others were stooges who deliberately exaggerated the length of the lines when reporting their judgments, within hearing of the one true subject. Some of the real subjects gave in to social pressure and went along with what they really thought was a preposterous evaluation of the length of the line.* When these subjects were interviewed later, most admitted that they didn't really believe the line to be that length. This experiment provides a good example of going along with the crowd, at least for a short time.†

A similar experiment was performed, but in this variation one of the stooges came over to the subject's side and agreed with him that the line was shorter than the stooges said it was. With just one stooge on his side, what had been unanimous group pressure disappeared and the subject's expressed errors in judgment decreased dramatically, even though the other stooges saw the line as very long [Asch, 1952, 1956]. The same type of resistance to group pressure can result if Ss are offered a coin for each correct guess [Sistrunk et al., 1972]. Since the amount of money involved is not large (5¢), the reward itself must be a symbol of the experimenter (who gives the money) being on the side of the subject against group pressure, and as you already know, symbols are extremely powerful.

These studies probably show us the primitive makings of a reference group [Kelly, 1968]. Since individuals use reference groups to verify what

---

*Roughly 25 percent of the Ss tended to consistently yield, and about the same proportion stood fast in their own judgment.

†Like people who go along with lynching mobs.

they see around them, noticing whether other members agree or disagree with their opinion, these studies illustrate a very small but effective reference group. If just one agreeable stooge can carry so much weight with the subject, imagine how powerful a whole reference group in real life must be!

Therefore, good evidence indicates that group pressure can operate strongly on some individuals. This force is a form of persuasion—but most people join and stay in a group because it *already* conforms to their beliefs. Thus, a group's effect on the individual has its seeds in the person's past, in the factors that led him to join the group.

An out-group's effect on the beliefs of an in-group appears to be negligible and tends primarily to reinforce the beliefs the in-group already holds. The effectiveness of various persuasive techniques seems to be based either on playing up to the sympathies of the listener, so that at least he thinks you are saying what he wants to hear, or else on putting the individual into a position in which a whole new environment is producing a new group with its own rules. The latter kind of behavior changes often occur when an adolescent moves from the norms of his family to those of his peers.

verbal persuasion   The techniques of verbal persuasion are all around us. They run the gamut from a radio and television announcer to an attorney fighting for his client's life. Persuasion itself is neither good nor bad; we all spend our lives trying to convince others of our point of view.

A little material for analyzing some psychological factors involved in persuasion is provided below, in a courtroom speech by Clarence Darrow, one of the greatest attorneys the world has ever known. Mr. Darrow is arguing before a judge for the lives of his clients, two young men convicted of having kidnapped and murdered a child. The horror of the crime led to a public outcry for the death penalty. Mr. Darrow was successful in obtaining life sentences for his clients under the most adverse circumstances. Like all attorneys, he was under an obligation to use every technique at his disposal, and he was a master at it.

1   If Your Honor, in violation of all [the progress law has made] should stand
2   here in Chicago alone to hang a boy on a plea of Guilty, then we are turning
3   our faces backward toward the barbarism which once possessed the world.
4   If Your Honor can hang a boy of eighteen, some other judge can hang him
5   at seventeen, or sixteen, or fourteen. Someday, if there is any such thing as
6   progress in the world, if there is any spirit of humanity that is working in
7   the hearts of men, someday men would look back upon this as a barbarous
8   age which deliberately set itself in the way of progress, humanity and sympathy,
9   and committed an unforgivable act.
10   . . . Now, Your Honor, I have spoken about the war. I believed in
11   it. I don't know whether I was crazy or not. Sometimes I think perhaps I was.
12   I approved of it; I joined in the general cry of madness and despair. I urged
13   men to fight. I was safe because I was too old to go. I was like the rest. . . .

156–157 Clarence Darrow defending John T. Scopes, who was tried for teaching evolutionary theory in the public schools of Tennessee; above, Darrow with the lawyer for the prosecution, William Jennings Bryan, who also possessed formidable talents of persuasion (*Culver*)

14   [Killing] was taught in every school, aye in the Sunday schools. The
15 little children played at war. The toddling children on the street. . . .
16   . . . We read of killing one hundred thousand men in a day. We read
17 about it and rejoiced in it—if it was the other fellows who were killed. We
18 were fed on flesh and drank blood. . . .
19   . . . These boys were brought up in it. The tales of death were in
20 their homes, their playgrounds, their schools; they were in the newspapers that
21 they read; it was a part of the common frenzy. What was a life? It was the
22 least sacred thing in existence and these boys were trained to this cruelty. . . .
23   . . . I know it has followed every war; and I know it has influenced
24 these boys so that life was not the same to them as it would have been if
25 the world had not been made red with blood. . . . All of us have our share
26 of it. I have mine. I cannot tell and I shall never know how many words of
27 mine might have given birth to cruelty in place of love and kindness and
28 charity. . . .
29   . . . Has Your Honor a right to consider the families of these two
30 defendants? I have been sorry, and I am sorry for the bereavement of Mr. and
31 Mrs. Franks [parents of the dead child], for those broken ties that cannot be
32 healed. All I can hope and wish is that some good may come from it all. But
33 as compared with the families of Leopold and Loeb [the accused], the Franks
34 are to be envied—and everyone knows it. . . .
35   Have they [the family of the accused] any rights? Is there any reason,
36 Your Honor, why their proud names and all the future generations that bear
37 them shall have this bar sinister* written across them? How many boys and
38 girls, how many unborn children, will feel it? It is bad enough however it is.
39 But it's not yet death on the scaffold. It's not that. And I ask Your Honor, in
40 addition to all that I have said, to save two honorable families from a disgrace
41 that never ends, and which could be of no avail to help any human being that
42 lives. [Weinberg, 1957]†

* A stripe found in a family coat-of-arms indicating an illegitimate child.
    † Quoted in Arthur Weinberg, *Attorney for the Damned* (New York: Simon & Schuster, 1957); reprinted by permission.

Darrow's rhetoric provides endless possibilities for studying the broad aspects of group psychology, individual psychology, persuasion, and use of the emotional appeals. Here, I want simply to call your attention to a few psychologically sound techniques of persuasion. Basically, the persuader must arrange logic to fit his hypothesis; then he must introduce negative feelings toward causes other than his own and positive feelings toward the cause he represents.

Lines 1–5: An effective technique in persuasion is *hyperbole* (exaggeration). His argument has some logic, but the implied result of the hyperbole is that if the defendants are executed, death penalties will be imposed on younger and younger people, possibly all the way down to children.

Lines 5–9: Here we see emotional response based on *pride*. What will future generations think of us? And we feel *guilt;* by implication, we are a barbarous age.

Lines 10–13: Here Darrow uses the *smoke screen* technique. The relationship between the war and the issue at hand seems to be present, but does a *genuine* connection exist? The purpose seems to be to distract the listener from the issue and lead him toward his own emotionally charged guilt about war.

Lines 12–13: Here Darrow uses what many people, lacking a better term, call *reverse psychology*. He criticizes himself. This technique almost always catches people off guard because it is unexpected. We find ourselves on his side, saying, "No, that is not true; if you were too old to go, that wasn't your fault, and anyway, we all approved of the war. If you're wrong, then so am I."

Lines 14–25: Here we find Darrow *scapegoating* by projecting the blame onto society. He was probably correct, to some extent, but he paints a picture so ghoulish that the defendants almost had to give in to the gore surrounding them.

Lines 25–28: Reverse psychology again. Darrow is sharing the blame and being humble, ploys that win favor with the listener.

Lines 29–34: Resorting to *personal appeal,* Darrow suggests that only the listener can possibly rectify the tragic situation. Here, the considerable smoke screen is very heavy!

Line 29: Responding to the question of the judge's "right," the judge's immediate human tendency would be to say to himself, "Of course I have the right [to do what you want]."

Lines 33–34: A call to the obvious, even though it may not be so obvious. He is saying "We *obviously* know this!"

Lines 35–42: In this passage Darrow relies heavily on highly emotional *symbolic appeal.* Note the use of the phrases *proud names, bar sinister, unborn children,* and *honorable families.*

You can find many other examples of persuasive devices in this short passage. Before leaving the issue, however, consider two small but strikingly persuasive techniques that are brought off in just a few words. In speaking of war Darrow refers to blood and killing in rather vivid terms, but in lines 31–32 when speaking of the defendants' crime, the *wording has changed* to "broken ties." And in line 39, we get the ***head-nodding technique.*** The speaker says something so obvious that the listener cannot help but agree. Consciously or unconsciously we tend to nod our heads at a statement such as "It's not yet death on the scaffold." The more a speaker can use such statements without letting them become noticeable, the more the listener will tend to agree on important issues.

brainwashing   During the Korean War, considerable interest was focused on American defectors and on "confessions" made by American prisoners of war. Rumors spread wildly that the other side had invented techniques of persuasion which could not be fought off by American troops. Naturally, our country would have liked 100 percent resistance by our own troops, but such unanimity is never possible. Furthermore, we do not feel it abnormal if some from the other side defect to us; such is just human nature, I suppose. The number of confessions and defections was relatively small considering the number of prisoners, but it was large enough, compared to World War II, to cause considerable alarm.

As we discussed earlier, a common enemy usually unites a group behind its own ideals and goals. In World War II, torture and attacks were common in prison camps, thus uniting the prisoners, but in Korea and China the prisoners were dealing with a brand-new situation: captors who did little in the way of torture; in fact, frequently they were disarmingly friendly.* This behavior is not only disconcerting but presents problems of resistance. It is much more difficult to resist a friendly enemy than a vicious one. In general, then, in Korea a considerable amount of social pressure, and frequently no deliberate physical pain, was involved in prisoner treatment [Litton, 1961].

The prisoners were subjected to many lectures, somewhat similar to those in college. Most of them could resist this pressure with little difficulty, just as college students can resist whatever they are learning. In any case, verbal messages, no matter how often repeated, have an impact only if the listener feels that the source is credible. Otherwise, attitude change is minimal even in the face of a continuous barrage [Johnson, 1971].

---

*Not always—but compared to World War II, the difference in treatment of prisoners was notable.

More difficult to fight, however, was a reward system in which the prisoners were given, say, a candy bar for providing completely inconsequential information about activities. This technique was clever, as you will see in a moment, for once a person has given in a little, each similar behavior becomes a bit easier. Along the same line, another technique was to elicit a very minor confession, again for a reward [Schein, 1961]. This behavior likewise would lead to larger confessions. Probably the most destructive aspect of the situation was that it undermined the group structure of the prisoners. Every man walking around with a candy bar was immediately suspected by the other prisoners, and it became difficult to determine who was giving significant information to the enemy and to what extent. Frequently, this same technique is used by police; they bring in two suspects and question each separately. Neither knows what the other said, but the police make certain that one thinks the game is up because they treat the other in a very friendly fashion as if he has confessed [Nizer, 1966].

So-called brainwashing, then, is based on the principle of compliance with a small request, followed by a reward, followed by a larger request. This same technique is sometimes used by advertisers who will enter your name in a contest if you simply write down the name of their product or get a boxtop and send it in. Having done this, they assume, you will probably engage in the larger behavior of buying or continuing to buy the product.

Studies in this area have been fairly consistent in showing that this is a good method for getting people to comply with one's wishes. In one study of such foot-in-the-door techniques* a group of housewives was called on the phone and asked to answer a few questions about some household product like soap. A few days later, the same group was called and asked if the experimenter could bring *five men* and take a two-hour inventory of the products in the home. Having given in to the small request, 52 percent of the housewives agreed to the larger request. A control group was given only the larger request. Naturally, compliance here was low, only 22 percent (difference between experimental and control groups, $p < .02$) [Freedman and Fraser, 1966].

The reader should be reminded, however, that there is a difference between giving in on soap and giving in on a major issue, but the principle stands as fairly effective.

Only in very rare cases, though, does a person permanently change his opinion as the result of brainwashing; it is not that effective [Brown, 1963]. In most instances, the brainwashing attempts to offset decades of training in a short time, and, if effective at all, it is usually temporary.

* A term probably dating back to a very common practice of door-to-door salesmen. Supposedly they would put their foot in the door, at least symbolically; if you agreed to this small intrusion, the salesman was on his way to a sale.

Prisoner-of-war incidents also led to increased psychological interest in a phenomenon called *sensory deprivation*, a severe type of punishment which involves no physically painful torture as such but deprives a person of the use of his senses. Such deprivation can be accomplished quite easily by using gloves, earmuffs, and a blindfold and by suspending a person in water set at body temperature. Our bodies require stimulation to such an extent that this procedure is intolerable to the average individual.* Many a cocky college student has been taken down a peg or two by this procedure: Students were asked to volunteer for a sensory-deprivation experiment in which they had to do absolutely nothing but wear the equipment and either lie on a bed or remain suspended in water. They were paid $20 or more a day. However, only the stoutest students lasted a full three days, and then even they quit. Aside from inducing a fear rather like that of being lost in a vast wasteland without a sound or sight around, such deprivation brings about temporary physiological changes; the brain begins to make up its own material, and visual hallucinations are common. Phosphene designs, mentioned earlier, are common visual experiences† [Heinemann, 1970]. Other symptoms frequently found are dreams, thought confusion, worry, disorientation to time, and regret about participating in the experiment [Zubek et al., 1971]. Even after removal from the deprivation situation, the person undergoes perceptual distortion for some time. Most of all, he feels an insatiable desire for some kind—any kind—of stimulation [Heron, 1957; Zuckerman, 1962; Bexton et al., 1954].

Sensory deprivation was used in some prisoner-of-war camps to induce compliance with the political system favored by the administration and to change a person's philosophy. Again, this technique was workable up to a point, but it rarely altered a person's beliefs permanently; many prisoners were likely to say anything just to get some stimulation again.

Laboratory studies have verified that people deprived of sensory stimulation become susceptible to any stimulus—that is, they become less resistant to suggestion. One study, for instance, used subjects who had previously been resistant to hypnotic suggestion. After sensory deprivation their suggestibility increased noticeably [Sanders, 1969]. Another study illustrated the great desire for anything in the way of stimulation that a subject develops. The deprived Ss were allowed to use a hand switch to operate the brightness on a television screen so they could see meaningless material, if they so desired. They actually increased the brightness so they could watch a series of slides that were shown upside down and backwards and had illegible subtitles. A control group, not sensory-deprived, was not

---

*Remember the monkey studies and their need to touch something soft and the effect of inadequate stimulation on children left in orphanages.

†Phosphenes are odd-shaped designs and effects produced by the eye and brain in the absence of external stimulation.

interested in this material (difference between the two groups, $p < .01$) [Roski, 1969].

defenses against persuasion

Some systems designed to fight off persuasion came out of the Korean War incidents, but most were ineffectual. For example, the soldier was given a card on which was written the beliefs he was supposed to hold. And when it was found that large numbers of Americans understood neither democracy nor communism, some attempt was made to educate them.* Education is probably more to the point, although its effectiveness is perhaps minor, because strong resistance usually comes only from those with a deeply entrenched set of beliefs.

Psychologists have studied techniques of immunization in the laboratory. The question arose: Could a subject be immunized against propaganda just as he is against measles? Results to date have not been very consistent. A few points do seem to stand out, however. As a number of authors have suggested, a two-sided argument, in which opposing viewpoints are stated and compared, seems to be a more effective immunizer than just a lecture or a one-sided argument. For example, democracy would be a favored side, but some Communist viewpoints presented [McGuire, 1964; Munn, 1969].

Similarly, a courtroom lawyer seems to gain an advantage if he presents some of his opponent's views, either in watered-down form or in a way that makes them seem insignificant; just mentioning them is important. Probably both judges and juries are impressed by this technique, which makes the lawyer seem less biased on behalf of his client and reduces the effectiveness of the opposing attorney's argument because the judge or jury has "already heard that argument" [Lawson, 1970].

Merely reading arguments does not seem to be as effective as trying to work out one's own case against something. Reading is passive, whereas building up a case is active, and most studies indicate that action is more effective. The active arguments, after a period of time, seem to be consolidated in the person's mind, and he becomes more certain of their validity— almost as if, over time, the subject forgets he was encouraged to develop the arguments and comes to think they have been part of him all along. If the person is threatened by a counterargument before this settling-in period has occurred, he seems to consolidate the arguments poorly and is not as convinced of them [Rogers, 1969].

Immunization, then, apparently is workable to a moderate degree.

---

*Amazing surveys have been conducted recently in some municipalities: When people were shown a paraphrase of the Bill of Rights (the first ten amendments to the Constitution) and asked whether they agreed with its principles (they didn't know where the material came from), many responded that they would not have anything to do with Communist or anarchical platforms.

Complete resistance is probably a fiction; a man who cannot be reached by physical torture likely can be reached by psychological methods at least temporarily. The maximally effective immunization is a way of life or a set of deeply held beliefs that run counter to the pressure being exerted on the person.

aids to persuasion and confession   The urge to confess one's misdeeds seems to be an integral part of human behavior. It is an active and symbolic method for relieving guilt and for indicating to others that the person will change in the future. The confession counteracts previous behavior and implies that it will not recur. Members of Alcoholics Anonymous, for instance, make public confessions, stating their previous transgressions, and this behavior not only serves as a form of retribution but also suggests future change.

Confession can be prompted by external devices—for example, the lie detector—but most evidence suggests that a person must have a basic desire or need to confess before such instruments will work. One author has pointed out that external devices such as the lie detector are actually quite old. For instance, in the distant past rice was often used in getting a confession. When a person is anxious or fearful, his mouth dries up and he has trouble swallowing. Capitalizing on this fact, interrogators lined up the suspects and told them to swallow a handful of dry rice. It was suggested strongly that the guilty one would have difficulty swallowing the rice. The psychological suggestion and physiological drying-up combined to locate the guilty party (sometimes) [Eysenck, 1964].

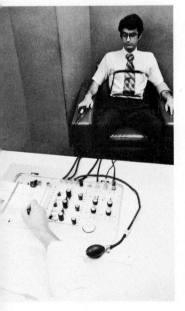

158   Application of a lie-detector test (*Los Angeles Police Department*)

Confessions to crimes have been elicited in many unusual ways. For instance, though the facts are open to question, some people's saliva does seem to contain chemicals that will indicate their blood type. Confessions have been obtained from suspects by taking saliva traces from a cigarette butt found at the scene of the crime and matching the blood type with that of one of the suspects. The scientific validity of the system wasn't as important as the fact that it trapped some suspects [Thornwald, 1967].

The lie detector works in a similar fashion. Basically, this instrument measures changes in heart rate, breathing, and perspiration. The principle upon which it rests is simple. A guilty person will show an alarm reaction when asked critical questions about his part in a crime, and this reaction will in turn alter respiration, heart rate, and degree of sweating, all of which are recorded by the machine.

The actual validity of the lie detector is argued back and forth for two reasons. First, it measures *physiological* changes that could conceivably occur whether or not the person has committed the crime. For instance, subjects can be trained to block or inhibit the amount of sweating they do, which obviously can alter results [Dean et al., 1968]. In one study Ss were able to confuse the lie detector and reduce its accuracy from 75 percent to 10 percent just by tensing their toe muscles [Smith, 1967]. In another study, the accuracy of the raters was quite variable: Some picked out only 14 of 76 lies while others spotted as many as 63 out of 76 [Moroney and Zenhausern, 1972].

In light of these facts, the second point becomes even more critical; the polygraph* operator must be *highly* skilled in interpreting the readings, and this skill varies greatly from one examiner to another.

The lie detector seems to be most accurate if well-known details about a crime are mixed with details known only to police and the guilty person. Obviously the innocent person cannot react to such information if he wasn't at the scene of the crime. But some reaction is to be expected from those who *were* present [Lykken, 1960]. In some laboratory studies in which the experimenter provided a reward for those able to deceive him, the polygraph operator achieved an accuracy as high as 92 percent in locating the "guilty" party [Davidson, 1968]. This record is impressive, but lie detector tests obviously cannot be used as evidence of guilt until the figure reaches 100 percent.† Nevertheless, it seems justifiable to say that the polygraph is effective in eliciting confessions, no matter what the graphs actually show.

The press and movies have given considerable publicity to so-called truth serums—for example, sodium pentothal. These drugs are anesthetics, the kind used to put someone "out" for an operation. Such a drug does relax a person, but it can produce a confession *only* if the person wants to confess anyway. All the drug does is lower his resistance. A person can lie under the influence of "truth serum" if he wants to, so there really is no such thing as a truth drug; there are only relaxant drugs [Brown, 1963].‡

If you remember the discussion on territoriality in the last chapter, you may already have thought of this little technique used for interrogation: Police manuals suggest that while questioning a suspect, nothing, not even a desk, should be between the policeman and the subject. This prevents the suspect from having any personal space barrier. As the interrogation proceeds, the officer should keep moving his chair closer until he eventually is sitting only a matter of inches in front of the subject. You can well imagine how unnerving this can be [Sommer, 1969].

Finally, all these methods of obtaining confessions can be negated by one strange bit of human behavior: A person can confess to crimes that

---

* Another word for lie detector—makes a record (*graph*) of many (*poly*) measurements.

† In this laboratory study, no prison sentence was involved—which might make a significant difference. In real life the lie detector may do much worse.

‡ If you are going into the medical field, remember that the brain is still registering when the person is under anesthetics, so it is best to keep quiet about any bad news regarding the patient during the operation.

are pure fantasy on his part. All policemen know this sort of behavior, for they must face a rash of confessions after any well-publicized crime. The confessors are guilty of something for which they are trying to atone, as all of us are, but they are not guilty of the crime in question. The flaws in the use of "truth serum" were made apparent by the case of the "Boston strangler," who killed thirteen women during the early 1960s. In the frantic search for a guilty party, one man who was innocent of the crime was put under a "truth" drug and made a very elaborate confession—which later was discovered to be entirely false [Frank, 1966].

It would seem, then, that psychological forces again rear their heads as the major contributor to so-called physical methods of eliciting the "truth."

SUMMARY

One of the most important elements in group cohesion is symbolism. Such symbolism can take the form of a uniform, a vestment, an armband, or what have you; the critical factor is that symbols set the group apart from out-group individuals, who are generally not wearing them or associated with them.

One form of physical symbolism is ritual. Groups are held together by a bond of ritualistic acts—that is, some form of specific action which is special for that particular group. Ritual can become so important it can influence the life of the individual, as in the case of the ritualistic behavior of the witch doctor.

Violence is not restricted to group behavior, but it is most notable in groups. Psychologists are interested in the violent individual, but frequently the basic fear that instigates violence does not appear until the person is with a group. Violence in recent years has taken a strange twist: it is aimed primarily at symbols rather than at people. Usually these symbols represent the frustrations people feel, so there are frequent attacks on police cars or burnings of buildings in ghetto areas.

Individuals are suggestible, and they tend to imitate violent behavior. Most studies indicate that the worst kind of violence to portray in mass media is justified violence—"an eye for an eye."

Clearly, people are open to persuasion, but movies and television often exaggerate the ease with which another person can be convinced. Group pressure is a basic factor in persuasion; although some resist going along with the group, it is difficult to do so, especially in the case of a reference group which is very important to the person.

Brainwashing is a potent threat, but generally the results of this technique are short-lived, lasting at most only until the person can return to his own environment. The foot-in-the-door technique is effective; one begins with a small request and moves on to bigger ones. Sensory deprivation is a form of torture which no man can stand, so at least temporarily a person will give in and agree to just about anything.

People can be "immunized" against persuasion, especially of the verbal type. This immunization is based on presenting both sides of a case to the person, with a slant toward the viewpoint you favor.

Finally, lie detectors and "truth serums" can persuade a person to give up or give in, but the actual validity of the techniques, used on their own, has been called into serious question.

PART SIX
TROUBLED PEOPLE

CHAPTER TWENTY-TWO
NORMAL AND ABNORMAL BEHAVIOR

Abnormal behavior is almost impossible to define, for its meaning varies from one society to another. It would be abnormal, for instance, for an American man to walk about in public attired only in a sheath around his penis, whereas you already know that this garb is quite dignified for men of the Dani tribe of New Guinea. Where you draw the line between normal and not normal, then, is by nature arbitrary.

WHAT EXACTLY IS MENTAL ILLNESS?

Many terms have been used to describe abnormal mental processes or behavior, but all of them mean essentially the same thing: *mental disease, psychopathology, deviant behavior, maladjustment,* or the one currently in favor, *mental illness.*

Whatever the term, to the average person "mental illness" seems to conjure up images of behavior that is far more bizarre than actually exists in real life. As you would suspect, a moderate number of mental patients are very disturbed—they talk to themselves or think they are famous people—but most books grossly misrepresent what a typical mental patient is like. If you were to go to a hospital and pick out a mental patient at random, the odds are overwhelming that in most respects this person would resemble you (or, if you prefer, your neighbor). Although complete agreement on the issue is not possible, mental illness seems to be primarily a matter of degree; that is, most mental illness is a distortion or exaggeration of behavior patterns shared by most human beings [Ullman, 1969].

159-160-161 Three creative people whose behavior was a little peculiar: the painter Vincent van Gogh; Marcel Proust, author of *Remembrance of Things Past,* who spent most of his life in a hermetically sealed, velvet-lined room; Emily Dickinson, an American poet who isolated herself almost completely from human contact (*Culver*)

Exact definitions of mental illness are hard to come by. A scene not uncommon at a murder trial is one in which three psychologists or psychiatrists* testify that the defendant is insane and three more testify that he is sane [Ullman, 1969]. Part of this confusion rests on the definition of mental illness and the sobering problem of how one determines the degree of disturbance.

One author has suggested that the difficulty in defining mental illness lies in a problem peculiar to psychology, as opposed to other sciences: our discipline mixes science and *morality*. Even though the psychologist is a scientist, he is not dealing with the behavior of an atom when he tries to evaluate a person. As a human being, he is subject, as most of us are, to equating "abnormal" with "bad." "Bad" is a moral judgment from society; "abnormal," strictly speaking, should be a purely objective evaluation [London, 1964]. I would guess that you have been subjected to this confusion if you have tried to judge for yourself whether the behavior of a homosexual is normal or abnormal; judgment on this touchy subject is usually clouded by the moral issues that are involved (or seem to be).

What we call mental illness is the United States' major health problem; it requires more hospital bed space than any other form of illness. About one out of ten people will at some time be hospitalized for mental illness. A supposedly conservative estimate of abnormal behavior is that well over 40 million disturbed people are wandering around, not counting alcoholics, drug addicts, and the mentally retarded [Coleman, 1964].

A figure such as this one, which appeared in a very popular textbook, certainly deserves some comment. It raises a number of possibilities:

1. More people are becoming mentally ill more often.
2. Mental illness is reported more often than it used to be.
3. Almost everyone who has any kind of problem is included in the list.

Any one of the three may be true. Number 2 seems to be true. Number 1 seems doubtful, although Americans seem to have more leisure time in which to become preoccupied with their problems. With the attention given to mental health, number 3 seems a distinct possibility. So far in its history, part of the human condition is to have difficulties, and such a large figure as 40 million may well indicate that the term *mental illness* has replaced the word *difficulty*.

The basic issue here can be detected by brief reflection on a current study comparing the mental illness rates among Japanese people living in four different cultures. The report from a Los Angeles agency finds high

---

* The difference between psychologists and psychiatrists will be covered in a later chapter. Until then it will suffice to substitute the words "mental health worker" in your own mind.

levels of mental illness among Japanese in the U.S. as compared with those in other countries. The author of this study forces himself into the position of arguing that the "true" rate of mental illness is higher among Japanese everywhere but that it is hidden by the fact that many Japanese do not accept mental illness. He comments, "The stereotyped Japanese gardener is an example of an occupation . . . where 'crazy' behavior can be widely tolerated" [Kitano, 1970]. The author may be right or wrong; the important question is: Does it make any difference if you are a "crazy" gardener but get your work done and live the way you want at least to some extent? The problem revolves around the issue, if you function fairly well in life can you still be considered "disturbed"?

In any case, we must settle on some definition of mental illness, and our definition must allow for the normal person and his normal problems. Usually the normal person is one who is able to function at a satisfactory level, though not necessarily a perfect level [Schoben, 1957]. Thus, a man who suffers from short periods of moderate depression, who has a temper tantrum about once a month, and who has occasional fantasies about being a superman or running away with the blonde next door is probably as close to normal as most of us get. He is normal if he is able to hold a job, has a relatively pleasant marital relationship, likes his children sometimes, and can cope with an occasional visit from mother-in-law or attend a school PTA meeting without cracking up.

The concept "normal person" is pretty vague, and it is important to notice that there is something abnormal in all "normals." In fact, experimenters have demonstrated that there is something abnormal in all of us which can be increased very simply. For instance, remembering that the abnormal is usually the deviant or highly unusual, investigators have been able to increase the number of bizarre or deviant responses to inkblots by normal Ss just by drawing attention to the deviant responses and by nodding the head favorably when they are heard. The point is that all of us may be just a step away from "abnormal" thinking [Levitz, 1969]. Haven't you ever done anything "abnormal" that you don't want others to know about?

One very workable definition of the mentally ill person (though by no means the last word) relies on three criteria, any one of which probably signals mental illness, although frequently in a mild form. First, the mentally ill person probably suffers *discomfort* more or less continuously; such discomfort is typically found in people who are always anxious, worried, or depressed. Second, the mentally ill person behaves in a *bizarre* fashion; he may see things that are not there (hallucinations), or he may constantly misinterpret what is actually going on (have delusions*), or be markedly

---

* A typical delusion of this type is a sense of inferiority. When a person who feels inferior suffers even a slight setback, which most of us would shrug off, he or she considers it a major disaster and distorts its significance to indicate—once more—his or her worthlessness. There are also more unusual delusions—for example, interpreting the world as being one's kingdom (with you as king), called *delusions of grandeur*.

different from most people, like the person who can't go to work because he is afraid to ride the elevator up to his office. Third, the mentally ill person is *inefficient*, unable to perform a life role adequately; for example, a family man may take all his savings and invest them in a stock that is highly questionable, or a housewife may be unable to face the dishes or cook the meals—ever [Buss, 1966].

For most purposes, this threefold definition—discomfort, bizarre behavior, inefficiency—works quite well. Having proposed it, I will now discuss some objections to the concept of mental illness itself. The intention here is not to cloud the definition given above, but merely to explore alternative explanations for so-called mental illness. These last three chapters as a whole are written on the assumption that mental illness, as we have defined it, does indeed exist. But first, some criticism of the concept itself. . . .

ISSUES IN MENTAL HEALTH

Society highly values its normal man. It educates children to lose themselves and to become absurd, and thus to be normal.

Normal men have killed perhaps 100,000,000 of their fellow normal men in the last fifty years. [Laing, 1967]

The psychiatrist who wrote these sentences goes on to point out that we destroy each generation of children, molding the potential of the child until it conforms to a world that has "gone mad." At first his remarks remind one of the comments of the LSD-using girl who found the effects of the drug to be an insanity saner than the insanity of the world. However, even though you may reject the girl's reasoning, the comments quoted above are not those of a voice crying in the wilderness but typify a growing wave of criticism and discontent within the mental health field. Throughout the last decade and into the present one, psychologists and psychiatrists have been attacking their own field of mental health with increasing vigor.

If I had written this book only a few years ago, it would have been simple to define mental illness and talk about how the mentally ill should be cured. No longer. The past was marked by naiveté, if you will, about mental health and the mentally disturbed. The issue was basically simple: If a person showed certain symptoms, such as claustrophobia or intense anxiety, then he was sick, and a label was attached to his sickness, just as a label is attached to having a disease like cancer. At that point, treatment began.

Very few people questioned this system; after all, it had been adapted from one of our most revered systems, the medical diagnosis of physical disease. A large part of this reverence can be traced back to Freud, who was a physician and who aided in the formulation of what was to become a very elaborate classification system. Freud basically felt that disturbances of a mental nature were determined in a physical way, just as cancer is. He specified his talking cure, which was administered much as a medicine would be: Given problem *A*, treatment *A* involves releasing the hidden (unconscious) material connected with the problem. Given problem *B*, treatment *B* will release the energy unconsciously held, and so forth. Medical doctors who had training in Freudian methodology continued and elaborated on his system, fitting it into a quasi-medical scheme of classification and treatment.*

It may be worthwhile to take a specific example and explore it. Suppose a person is subject to severe attacks of anxiety. In other words, he experiences periods of extreme fright and vague concerns about impending death or injury, accompanied by overactivity in his physiological system—rapid heartbeat, sweating, nervousness, and the like. When the person enters the hospital or doctor's office, he relates his problems to the doctor, who takes them down as *symptoms*. These symptoms fit a pattern classified as an anxiety neurosis,† so we now have a *diagnosis*. The next step is to prescribe a *cure*, just as the physician specifies treatment for tuberculosis, pneumonia, and the like.

To take an example, it is possible under the Freudian system to infer that this anxiety neurosis is caused by the person's childhood fear that his father might injure him because he felt physical desires toward his mother (this arises from the Oedipus complex discussed previously). The child was not able to resolve this fear of his father; the physical energy connected with the problem remained, and it takes the form of intense but unconscious fear, which is manifested in anxiety attacks. The prescribed cure for this anxiety is spending many hours talking with the doctor, during which time the patient will slowly come to see that the fears he is experiencing go back to childhood and are no longer appropriate. When the patient discovers this, these buried fears—which are basically at a childish level—can be brought to the surface and examined by the mature mind for what they are.

The above process makes up the typical treatment pattern: symptoms, diagnosis, cure. In psychiatric circles this pattern became so much a way of life that few thought to really question the system, except possibly to modify it a bit within its own framework. Freud's theories were changed in various ways through the years, but for the most part psychoanalysts kept the same core structure for explaining mental illness as a disease that in turn caused symptoms.

In the last ten years, it has become fashionable to attack the disease concept, and the Freudian structure has begun to give way, in many circles, to other explanations for behavior. New methods of treatment have evolved that are far removed from Freud's system. As a result, the apparently

* Although Freud provides a focal point, some who came before him were major contributors to the diagnosis system. They will be discussed shortly.
† Neurosis is covered in detail later; it refers to a mental disturbance that is moderately severe.

indestructible Freudian framework has had holes punched in it from all sides [Hersch, 1968].

In many ways, the mental health area has been reflecting the changes and challenges which now pervade our whole social structure. One major target of attack has been the definition of mental illness as *sickness*. The use of the label *mental illness*, it is claimed, is merely a means of producing conformity and ridding society of people who offend us [Sarbin, 1967]. Many societies, for instance, and some American communities have their Uncle Harrys and Aunt Marthas who spend most of each day in the attic chatting with imaginary friends. These people are tolerated by those around them because, while they are eccentric or even bizarre, they are basically harmless. The issue under attack is, simply, what right do we have to put the label *disease* to having imaginary friends, or insist that such a person undergo treatment if he does not want it?

These criticisms are rather farfetched if carried to their ultimate conclusion. Is no one disturbed? Is everybody sane? Obviously the answer is no, but the attack is still worth considering. At what point should the line be drawn? Many people follow schedules for cleaning the house or doing their work at the office that are timed almost to the second. In a psychological sense, such behavior is usually thought to result from the person's fear that if he does not keep his life exactly the same, it will somehow come apart at the seams. Now, as long as this person is performing his job in life to the satisfaction of himself and others, should we "cure" him? On the other hand there are the men called exhibitionists who expose their genitals to women whenever they have an opportunity—on the bus or in the street. These people are usually really quite harmless, except that they are a nuisance and offend society's sense of propriety [Starr, 1964]. Should they be treated? Suppose they do not want to be treated?

162   In the Middle Ages, odd behavior was often thought to be caused by demons that possessed a person's soul. Here, Catherine of Siena (right) casts the devil out of a woman (*Bettmann Archive*)

Or what about somebody like the "Boston strangler"? Should an attempt be made to cure him, even if he indicated he didn't want treatment?

Most of the criticism, then, though absurd if carried too far, *does* merit consideration. Basically, the mental health movement has gotten sidetracked in trying to correct all problems for all people; many of these dissenting writers are saying that some problems are just basic to human existence. They are also criticizing the disease concept because it too easily leads to automatic incarceration and treatment.

An alternative to the idea of mental illness as disease is now popular. In many respects, these new ideas are revolutionary. Many of them appear in *The Myth of Mental Illness*, written by a psychiatrist, Dr. Thomas Szasz. Despite its sensational title, the book is straightforward and interesting. As we cover some of Szasz's ideas, we should keep in mind that in many respects they represent an extreme view, but they have a core of truth that cannot be ignored.

First, in the traditional view of mental illness as a disease, a person could have, for example, a ***conversion neurosis***. A traditional case of conversion neurosis is paralysis of the hand or arm that has no known physical cause. On occasion, patients who feel extremely guilty about masturbating have developed such a paralysis. The symbolism is obvious: Guilt has been translated into a physical symptom that prevents the person from continuing the act. Another conversion reaction, common in wartime, is paralysis of the legs, which frequently strikes men who are up on the firing line. These soldiers are not "faking." Apparently the fear they feel is translated into a genuine physical symptom. If a skeptic comes up behind one of these soldiers and sticks a pin in his leg, he will not feel it.

Now we get to a fine-haired distinction that is important; it is tricky and requires careful reading. Most psychologists and psychiatrists interpret the inability to use a hand or a leg as a genuinely *physical* reaction which the brain has translated from a symbolic reaction. Symbolically, the fear of going into battle is too great, or the guilt about masturbation is overwhelming; the brain "realizes" that the person cannot cope with his guilt, so it develops an actual physical symptom to prevent the guilt- or fear-producing behavior. Thus, we have a disease that *automatically* deserves treatment just like any other physical disease if traditional interpretations are used.

Szasz does not give any indication that he feels the patient with a paralyzed hand or leg should *not* be treated. However, he does see the overall situation differently from the traditional view. He says that the paralysis is not a physical symptom of a disease; instead, it is body language. In effect, the person is saying, "I am afraid," or "I am guilty." The person is *not* necessarily saying, "I am sick and need treatment."

The importance of this point can be seen if we pick a less extreme example. We all learn to play certain games or roles in life. Szasz points out that the mental patient is playing a game he has learned. Suppose that, as a child, you got love and affection only when you were sick and helpless. You learned quickly that when you played the sick game your mother would show an interest in you. Later in life, if you want attention, you may use the sick-game device, even though it has become inappropriate. Nonetheless, if you are becoming sick in order to get attention, you are using body language that says, "I need love"—not, according to Szasz, "I need psychiatric help." The person who plays the sick game is not necessarily mentally disturbed; instead, he has *learned* that psychiatrists, psychologists, and friends may reward him for giving up, just as he was rewarded in childhood for the same behavior.

Hopefully, without belaboring the point, I'll present a final example, one recently discussed. The delinquent fails at the game of good verbal skills, so he joins the antisocial game that gives him some of the attention he wants. He is not sick; he is using the antisocial role to satisfy his normal need for love [Szasz, 1960, 1961].

You may seriously wonder whether there is a significant difference between the disease theory and the game-playing interpretation. The difference is significant in at least one sense: The mental patient who is seen as playing certain games in order to achieve certain ends becomes a human being who is *communicating*, rather than a malfunctioning organism that needs repair. The ideal, then, would be considering those with problems as normal people using a special form of communication. This can be important because there is such a stigma attached to the label "mental illness," a stigma which is just about impossible to get rid of once a person is marked by it. The importance of avoiding the label becomes clearer when we realize that errors can be made and that it is not necessarily true that mental health people can always detect so-called mental illness. In one study, eight normal individuals were admitted to twelve different mental hospitals over a period of time, supposedly suffering from a serious disturbance. These "patients" acted as they always had—on the outside—and none of the professional personnel at the various hospitals ever knew that "normals" were there among them. The only people who detected the phonies were some of the other patients [Rosenhan, 1973].

the normal abnormal   Probably some of the most intriguing studies to arrive on the scene in many years involved an elaborate investigation of the motives and behavior patterns of mental patients. These studies showed that a considerable amount of the mental patient's behavior fits into a specific role appropriate to the hospital setting. For example, one study showed that some patients found life in the mental hospital a workable and even satisfying mode of existence and that they did not want to be discharged. Personality tests were given to two groups of these patients (all of whom wanted to stay in the hospital), but the patients were given different reasons for being required to take the tests. One group was led to believe that the tests would be used to determine whether they were well enough to leave. The other group was led to suppose that the tests were only routine and were unrelated to discharge. The results are interesting: The patients, *no matter how sick they were supposed to be,* were able to control the outcome of the tests to fit their own desires, not those of the hospital or staff.* Those who thought it was a discharge test made themselves look "sicker." This is just part of an elaborate study; however, the partial results reported above have broad implications. The so-called mental patient is playing a role within the hospital; contrary to our assumption that he lacks any control over his environment, he does indeed know what he wants and how to get it, at least within the hospital setting.

This study is important because it shows the mental patient in some respects to be just like all the rest of us: He controls his environment with reason and purpose to obtain what he needs and desires within the institution. Such studies support Szasz and tend to refute the "hopeless disease" concept [Braginsky et al., 1969].

Other authors have zeroed in on the mental hospital itself. They point out that the patients and staff more or less feed on one another in a mutually satisfying but somewhat distorted fashion. Long-term mental patients are noted for extreme, almost childlike, dependency; staff members take the role of father (or mother) figure and dominate the patient by authoritarian behavior, frequently under the guise of scientific and medical treatment for the underdog. In fact, in some cases patients who try to end this mutual role-playing by asserting themselves wind up being committed to wards for the acutely disturbed [Rosenberg, 1970].

The mental health movement has made great strides in the past decade: none of these experimenters wants to slow the movement down or to set it back; they merely want psychology and psychiatry to be more aware of themselves and to view the mental patient from a different perspective. This trend is healthy because it means that mental health programs have become sophisticated enough that workers in the field can engage in self-criticism.

MENTAL HEALTH THROUGH THE YEARS

Considering people's fear of anything that is different or odd, it isn't surprising that treatment of mentally ill people has not been especially pleasant. Some irony does reside in the fact that only when mental illness came to

*Obviously the study included only patients who were aware of what was going on around them. Some were not, and it would be impossible to test that particular group in this manner. The latter group were in the minority, however. The ability of a patient to control his fate has been illustrated in another study; in this one a patient said, "I'm going to leave the hospital when I decide to and no damn test is going to run me out" [Shiloh, 1968, p. 31].

be considered a disease did some humanitarian reforms take place in mental hospitals; only now, when reform has taken place, is the disease concept being called into question.

Before 1700, mental illness was thought to be caused by the person being possessed by the devil, witches, or demons. Mental patients were hanged, tortured, chained, and beaten; grotesque methods were used to "bring them to their senses" [Deutsch, 1946].

People have always attributed strange events to mysterious forces, so it could have been anticipated that odd behavior would be characterized as the work of an unknown and unseen creature. The present generation is not immune. One author points out that even the least superstitious and best educated laymen attribute sicknesses to something none of them has ever actually seen—bacterial and viral microorganisms. Admittedly, practitioners of the biological sciences have had a look at these creatures, but most of us haven't—yet we have no doubt about them, showing complete faith in their existence and their ability to "cause" us to be ill [Linton, 1945]. Witchcraft and the supernatural should be viewed within context, even if not accepted by most of us.

witchcraft   Hearing voices or speaking unintelligibly commonly used to be taken as indication that a person was possessed by the devil or influenced by witchcraft. Nowadays, we are still mystical about this: We say such behavior is the result of mental illness. This explanation isn't much better than saying

163   Granny Greene, a "witch" of Salem, Mass., being arrested (*Bettmann Archive*)

THE ARREST.

164 Robert Boyle (*Bettmann Archive*)

165 George Berkeley, philosopher and theorist on visual perception, believed that most human ills could be cured by drinking a solution of tar-water. He had an unreasoning fear of being buried alive, and specified that his dead body be allowed to lie unburied until it began to stink, to make sure he was really dead (*Bettmann Archive*)

it is the product of a devil, but at least we usually treat mental patients better.

Salem, Massachusetts, has the best-known history in America of witchcraft, mainly because in 1692 the town tried and executed some of its witches. Full-scale court proceedings were held, and the accused enjoyed some rights in the trials. The "courts" were not hysterical or superstitious; instead, the "truth" came out for the judges in distorted form. For example, as in the case of voodoo mentioned earlier, the fear *itself* of witchcraft produced within the accused symptoms and behavior in the courtroom that could easily be interpreted as possession by the devil. Defendants had convulsive fits rather often, or began speaking incoherently right in front of the court. Evidence came primarily from behavior that reflected a fear of being possessed, rather than possession itself, and the judges in many cases didn't know how to interpret such behavior except as possession by the devil* [Hansen, 1969; Starkey, 1963].

Belief in magic and devils was common among some great scientists of the time. Take the example of Robert Boyle, an Irish physicist and chemist of the 1600s who laid the foundation for modern chemistry by defining the concept of chemical elements and by formulating a law for the behavior of gases. He suggested a medicine that consisted of stewed earthworms, old stockings, and human urine; he also recommended interviewing miners about any demons they met underground.

Physicians in general were very ready to diagnose witchcraft when no visible or known physiological disease was available to explain unusual behavior. And nowadays, if a patient's physiological problem seems to have no *known* cause, his difficulty is often labeled "of psychological origin" [Hansen, 1969].

The mechanisms of group behavior mentioned a few chapters back

---

*For generations it has been assumed that these trials were the work of fanatics. A very carefully documented book [Hansen, 1969] demonstrates that the Salem courts were usually quite scrupulous in gathering evidence.

166 Witches being tortured by a mob (*Culver*)

should not be forgotten either. Again fear seemed to rear its head in many cases because notable outbreaks of witchhunting occurred after natural disasters such as the black death plague in the 1300s. Lacking a plausible explanation for "God's disfavor," the persecution of scapegoat witches was rampant. When one reviews the treatment of witches in some areas, it is hard to avoid the conclusion that the same ingredients exist here as in a lynch mob. How else can we explain the following: "Extremities were jerked from the [witches'] sockets, feet were torn from limbs, thumbs were squashed and skin was torn with red-hot pincers" [Anderson, 1970, p. 1730].

With the advent of the age of science, the search began for some cause of disturbed behavior other than possession by devils. A major breakthrough occurred in the late 1700s, but it was primarily symbolic. A physician, Dr. Philippe Pinel, was put in charge of a hospital for the insane. With great fanfare he entered the hospital, which was more like a dungeon, and removed the "patients" from confinement: most had been kept chained to the wall. Given their new freedom, they did not go on a rampage and pillage the town, but instead began to show signs of improvement [Zillborg, 1941]. Thus, humanitarian treatment for mental patients began to make headway.

167 Benjamin Rush (*Bettmann Archive*)

Pinel worked with another physician, Dr. Benjamin Rush, who was an important political figure, signer of the Declaration of Independence, and the first surgeon-general in the revolutionary army. Rush gained considerable recognition for medical discoveries about arthritis. From the viewpoint of mental health, he was equally important. In the late 1700s, long before Freud entered the scene, Rush was interviewing patients and exploring their histories and problems on the verbal level.*

More important, Rush was preoccupied with the *physiological* basis for mental disease. He attributed mental disease to inadequate, inefficient, and incorrectly functioning blood vessels in the brain. He reached this conclusion because a number of autopsies of "madmen" disclosed defective

* That is, through face-to-face discussion between patient and doctor.

537

168   George III, king of England (*Culver*)

brains [Rush, 1961]. He must have singled out these cases to support his hypothesis, for except for a few of the aged and a small number of young mental patients, nothing organic seems to be wrong with most disturbed individuals. Even though Rush was on the wrong track, in a sense he was ahead of Hippocrates and the melting-brain business, because medical science was on its way to localizing abnormal physiology, which previously had been a hit-and-miss proposition at best. The mere existence of *some* documented cases of physiological difficulty correlating with mental disease lent credence to the idea that the person was ill rather than under the influence of devils—and this was the major step forward. At least as far as treatment of patients was concerned.

Another spur to more humane treatment for the mentally ill was the publicity that accompanied the alleged "insanity" of George III, king of England during the 1700s. Parliament actively investigated his illness, looking into some rough treatment he received from attendants. As one author has pointed out, this prying led to active public interest in mental illness, the entrance onto the scene of prominent physicians, and considerable concern for the king [Caplan, 1969].

classification of mental illness

Another event of interest in the 1700s was the work of a psychologist–medical student, Emil Kraeplin. He too was preoccupied with abnormal brains, but his really important work was developing a classification system for mental illness that was based on symptoms. In other words, if you had symptoms A, B, C, and D, you had mental disease X. This system has never been very successful because symptoms overlap considerably more in mental illness than they do in medicine. Nonetheless, the method was extremely important, because eventually it came to include classifications of mental illness not based just on physiology but elaborated to include behaviors resulting from psychological factors. Soon thereafter it became common practice to classify all mental patients as having one type of mental illness or another, a giant step forward from saying that they were possessed by the devil.

169   Emil Kraeplin (*Culver*)

Psychology and psychiatry have had to learn a lesson from the classification system, advanced though it was. The system has an inherent difficulty; it places patients in a social order in which some classifications are "better," while some are more hopeless than others. If the system is not highly accurate—which it isn't—a "bad" label can unjustifiably give some people a "less than human" status [Sharma, 1970].

Furthermore, it is extremely difficult to fit people into categories because thousands (millions ?) of factors go together to form a personality. Kraeplin's method had generated high hopes, because a similar technique used in zoology and botany had evolved into an elaborate and eminently workable system of animal and plant classifications and subclassifications (for example, phylum, species, etc.). These sciences made great strides using the classification system because *order* was brought to chaos. A fervent hope was that psychology, imitating the practices of zoology and botany, would have equal success. The classification system has produced a *semblance* of order in psychology and psychiatry, but because accuracy in classification is so difficult, little progress has been made in this realm, compared to the other sciences.*

After Kraeplin, Freud entered the scene and strengthened the system by giving details to the classification network, thus providing a theoretical framework that explained how the various illnesses developed—for example, anxiety reaction growing out of the Oedipal situation.

Despite all the objections to classification in mental illness, most mental hospitals of our day operate in a traditional fashion: interview, diagnosis (or classification†), and treatment.

the mental hospital   In general, the mental institutions of today are significantly better than those of Pinel's day. Some are well staffed, modern, and relatively pleasant to stay in—if you have money. But many mental institutions resemble jails more than anything else. Put another way, they become dumping grounds for people who are irritating to the majority [Goffman, 1961]. Things are not as bad as they were in 1851 when some state laws still allowed a husband to commit his wife without having to present any evidence of insanity; however, people who are disruptive, irritating, aggressive, or a nuisance are much more likely to wind up labeled sick than those who just quietly withdraw into themselves [Deutsch, 1946; Rabkin, 1972]. One of the worst aspects of current mental illness "treatment" is the flagrant abuse of the laws which allow persons to be committed involuntarily. Most of these people wind up institutionalized for an indeterminate period far worse than a fixed prison sentence [Szasz, 1972; Ennis, 1972]. To pick some extreme examples, the staff of one state hospital included only one psychologist and two psychiatrists to care for 5000 patients; some patients in this hospital are seen as infrequently as once every 19 months by a doctor, and then only for about ten minutes; the legal rights of most patients are nonexistent in practice although there are a few on the books [Ennis, 1972].‡

Other countries have been highly successful in changing their mental hospitals to retreats where the disturbed can go to recover in a countrylike atmosphere with sunshine, fresh air, and some sense of freedom [Braginsky et al., 1969]. This is going to have to be the new direction in mental health facilities for those requiring long treatment.

*Five classifications have been discussed so far in this book: sociopath, depression, anxiety neurosis, conversion neurosis, and paranoid.

†Diagnosis and classification are essentially interchangeable concepts.

‡If you are ever hospitalized against your will, remember that no matter what anyone tells you, you are always entitled to consult with an attorney. The Legal Aid Society and The Civil Liberties Union have units in almost every major city if you do not have money for your own attorney.

special problems   Strangely enough, a major crisis for mental institutions is that many patients don't want to leave. The mental hospital has become a home away from home; it cares for physical needs, provides a place to sleep, supplies companionship if it is desired, and so on. Studies show that up to 40 percent of the patients in some institutions are content where they are [Shiloh, 1968]. At first this may seem implausible, but basically what has happened is that the control exercised by the hospital has such a strong hold on the patient that he has little desire to cope with the outside world when he can have everything done for him. This trend has necessitated some major changes in mental health care. One relatively new idea is the *day-treatment center*, which has recently developed in many communities specifically to avoid the problem of overdependence on institutionalized life resulting in the patient's not wanting to leave. Day-treatment centers are what the name implies: places in which the patient spends the day receiving treatment, returning home at night. This approach has many advantages: Apparently the patients recover more quickly because they are not being labeled "inmates"; costs are cut considerably, and patients have an opportunity to live a partially normal home life [Meltzolf, 1966].

In a related study, hospitalized patients suffering from major mental disturbances were bussed each morning to a day-treatment center. Compared to a control group of patients showing essentially the same degree of disturbance who remained in the hospital day and night, the treatment-center group had more hospital discharges and fewer readmissions (p in both cases $< .05$) [Williams, 1969]. The day-treatment center seems not to foster the same degree of hopelessness which both patients and staff members feel in a traditional institution. Hospitalization for twenty-four hours a day seems by its very nature to suggest that the patient is very seriously disturbed. The day-treatment center is a quite promising development.

Another innovation in mental health treatment has been the use of nonprofessional people to assist in handling the ever-increasing number of patients. So far, research indicates that the nonprofessional who has received just a few hours of training can make significant progress with patients. In a few studies, these paraprofessionals have outperformed the professionals by a slight margin [Guerney, 1969; Hartlage, 1970].

Some rather unique things are occurring in the use of laymen. In one intriguing study arrested delinquents were provided the opportunity to visit with and "help" mental patients. These delinquents showed increased feelings of personal worth as compared with a control group of delinquents. This study holds promise for a "two-way street" of improvement [Russo, 1971].

In many respects, the outlook for mental health is promising. Outmoded issues and attitudes are gradually being replaced by innovative patient-care designs and by new hypotheses regarding the nature of mental illness.

Other significant problems remain—for example, public acceptance of the mentally ill. Although few people would blame devils or witches or advocate inhumane treatment, the phenomenon of mental illness is apparently almost as baffling nowadays as it was twenty or thirty years ago. Professionals must be included in this category of the bewildered, to some extent, because we know very little, comparatively speaking, about the causes of mental illness. Nonetheless, the public at large provides the financial and moral support for new projects. And people in general are highly suspicious of mental illness, which they find mysterious and frightening in many ways. A few studies have shown that while the public is showing more *intellectual* understanding of mental illness, few people show an increase in *emotional* understanding of the problem. Most studies indicate that little progress is being made in convincing the public that mental illness is just a form of what might, in layman's terminology, be called "sickness" [Halpert, 1969; Dohrenwend, 1967; Joint Commission, 1961].

SUMMARY

Abnormal behavior is defined within the framework of the particular society with which one is dealing. The issue is especially difficult because issues of morality and of mental illness become interwoven. Our definition states that mental illness involves at least one of three factors: discomfort, bizarre behavior, and gross inefficiency.

Typically, mental illness is handled as if it were a disease in the medical sense—that is, it automatically requires treatment. Some take issue with this approach, suggesting that the symptoms of the supposed illness are a form of communication, rather than a disease.

Some support for this assumption can be found in a number of studies which have illustrated that the mental patient is far more aware of what is going on around him than is usually assumed, and that the patient can control his environment to some extent, at least in the hospital.

Although fairly humane treatment is presently the rule, we are still far from solving many problems of earlier years. For one, the classification system has never been very successful and seems more appropriate for medical cases than psychological ones.

Major shifts are evolving in the handling of mental patients. One of the most promising is the day-treatment center, and close behind this is the use of nonprofessional personnel to help handle the problems of mental patients.

CHAPTER TWENTY-THREE
WHAT CAUSES MENTAL ILLNESS?

In this chapter we will consider some of the major theories that try to explain why a person becomes disturbed. None of these theories is definitive or the last word; each has its own followers, and some mental health workers combine two or more of them, borrowing from each what they consider useful.

These theories are mostly appeals to one's logic; they are not supported by notable evidence that one is more correct than another. No theory really has an edge over the others. Experiments that have been performed break down into two categories for each theory: those that support a given theory and those that refute it.

You may wonder how such contradiction can be tolerated. The main reason for this unusual situation is that most theories rely heavily on past experiences, usually going back into childhood, and it is very difficult, if not impossible, to locate evidence from that long ago to support a hypothesis about why the patient is the way he is today. Nonetheless, theories serve a useful function, for they provide a framework for understanding human behavior.

FREUDIAN THEORY

Freud's ideas have been mentioned so often that little elaboration is necessary. Instead, a few comments to reorient you should suffice. Basically, Freud proposed that the person developed a strong ego (self) so that he could fight off the impulses of the id (basic drives like sex) and could tone down an overstrict superego (conscience). Simply put, in Freudian theory the mentally ill person suffers from a defective ego; the defective ego control comes from inadequate satisfaction of childhood desires. The person with a sturdy ego is one who felt adequately loved and had his physical needs satisfied during his early years; for example, his desire for oral gratification was satisfied through feeding activities. If oral satisfaction is lacking, the child becomes preoccupied with oral needs. The deficiency in oral satisfaction can later create a whole mode of life: The adult is overdependent and unable to have satisfactory *mature* relationships with others, for he is still preoccupied with a stage of development that belongs in infancy. The person uses his psychic energy* trying to satisfy his oral needs, depleting the reserve, so to speak, that could be used for more productive behavior.

---

*It is important to remember that Freud thought of psychological processes as involving *actual* energy forces.

544

SULLIVAN'S THEORY

Again, at most you require only a refresher. Sullivan's system was a productive refinement of Freud's because he stressed that satisfactions in life come from *people* and from having good relationships with them. Freud had been stressing specific behaviors—for example, breast-feeding or anal activity—and their physiological aspects; only by inference did he relate these functions to behavior involving two or more people. Under Sullivan's system, the person forms a concept of himself; his self-concept is a good-me, for instance, if the mother behaves in a consistently loving fashion during almost *any* activity—breast-feeding, toilet training, or even diaper changing. The mental patient has a bad-me self-concept; it is well below par, riddled with feelings that he is essentially unloved and worthless. From these feelings come depression, feelings of inadequacy, and an inability to get along with others, to name but a few possibilities.

ROGERS, MASLOW, AND EXISTENTIALISM

You may recall that Rogers stressed that an individual is potentially able to become a well-rounded person because he, like everyone, has within himself a seed of self-actualization. The term *self-actualization* was also used in connection with Maslow's theory of motivation. The union of the two men's theories is not just chance. Some writers place them in the same category because of their somewhat existential approach.

Existentialism is a rugged word to define. Basically, it is the philosophy that a person is capable of seeing his own life ahead of him and making significant decisions that will lead him to become "that which he should become." The mentally ill, however, have not been given the opportunity to develop enough independence to bring forth this potential. The mentally ill person is thus rejecting self-actualization and falling into Szasz's negative social role of the mental patient.

The existential position is admittedly vague, from a scientific viewpoint; it sounds a lot more like faith than fact, but before discounting it, if you are so inclined, consider that *many* patients have been helped by the assumption that they are human beings who are potentially capable of controlling their own destiny.*

The existential viewpoint is gaining in popularity because it is positive, whereas most other theories are rather negative. Another factor in its popularity is the current trend among young people, including some young psychologists and psychiatrists, to let each person "do his own thing," remaining unentangled in the "establishment." This life style fits right in with self-actualization.

Finally, if you really get down to it, we cannot actually comprehend the ego, the good-me, or any of these concepts any better than we can understand self-actualization. At least self-actualization is fairly open about its basic structure being founded on faith.

* More will be said on this topic when we reach Rogers's method of treating mental patients.

LEARNING THEORY   As would be expected, the learning theory of mental illness stresses habits, conditioning, and the learning of inappropriate behaviors. The same rules apply to mental illness as apply to other kinds of learned behavior; the mentally ill person either is learning the wrong thing or has not learned the appropriate behavior for a particular situation.

A very strange case has been reported that provides an example of faulty learning occurring in mental patients. Two brothers, both quite disturbed, demonstrated a notable lack of comprehension of certain words, behavior that is fairly typical in serious mental illnesses. For example, they believed that *disagreement* meant "constipation." Viewed superficially, this bizarre reasoning could fall under the vague heading, "disordered thought patterns." In this case, however, the experimenters explored the situation a little deeper and discovered that when the boys were children and disagreed with their mother, she accused them of being constipated and gave them enemas. One might, of course, question the mother's sanity, but this issue is not the real one. Notice, first of all, that the brothers are dealing with a complex idea or symbol—that is, the word *disagreement*—and interpreting it incorrectly. Thus, when talking to them one might easily conclude that their thinking is completely out of order. Actually, it is not simply disordered, according to the learning theorists; the boys' thought-process development has followed the same *principles* as ours do, only in this particular case they learned *incorrect* associations [Lidz et al., 1958].

This example, the association of two words, has broad implications: How much of this type of faulty learning exists? How would it be possible, under such circumstances, to know what the word really means? Very few of us know all that goes on behind the closed doors of many a family, and we forget that children learn by imitation; they rely on what parents say, and they are sometimes rewarded for learning strange behavior.

I remember a case many years ago in which the patient's mother, during his whole childhood, had made him promise every day that he would not leave her; she reinforced these promises by giving him extra "love" and affection, creating a very distorted little world for the two of them. The mother finally hanged herself from the chandelier in the dining room, and the boy, now a man, kept her hanging there even during meals, faithful to his promise that they would stay together, until about a week after her death the neighbors reported to the police the gruesome odor emanating from the apartment. This case is one of *learned* abnormal behavior.

We have touched on hand-washing behavior before because it is so striking. Dirty hands require washing. The patient, having committed an act that is "dirty" in a different sense (i.e., guilt-producing), becomes more and more anxious about his bad behavior. Then he washes his hands one day,* and this act reduces his guilt feeling temporarily. The hand washing seems to do *something* about the problem, even though it is not

---

* Just as in the expression, "I wash my hands of the whole affair."

170 (*Photo Researchers, Inc.*)

very appropriate. Reduction of the guilt is rewarding, so he repeats his behavior. Learning by repetition and reward, soon he is washing his hands all the time.*

Other learning-theory people give us a slightly different interpretation that is also worth noting. A child is frequently criticized for having dirty hands; washing them relieves the fear and anxiety he builds up over being scolded. An association is solidly established between hand washing itself and reducing anxiety; then, when *any* type of anxiety threatens, the person washes his hands [Dollard and Miller, 1950].

Remember, too, that disturbed behavior such as delusions, compulsions, feelings of inadequacy, overdependence, and the like can be rewarding because they get attention for the patient—attention which the patient, like the delinquent, has never been able to obtain by appropriate behavior.†

Conditioning, a form of learning, can also help to explain some mental disorders, such as phobias (abnormal and unreasonable fears—of closed places, open places, fire, animals, heights, and so forth). Usually some traumatic event has occurred in connection with one of these objects or situations, and an extreme fear is conditioned to it, even though in adult life it is no longer appropriate. People who as children were lost from their parents, for instance, or once had trouble finding their way home, can sometimes grow up to fear crowds or open places.

Generalization can occur with phobias, too. In Watson's experiment, a child was afraid of a white rabbit, and his fear was extended to furry objects and white objects. Similarly, children may learn from parents about the dangers of germs and filth connected with bowel movements, for example, and this learned fear can spread, or generalize, to include fear of germs in restrooms or other rooms, to doorknobs, and so forth until the person is in a constant state of panic about germs; that is, he has a phobia. We all learn some of these fears; repetition and intensity of training seem to make the difference between normal and abnormal fears.

Learning theory alone may thus be used to explain personality, but it presents problems: some of the intricate complexities of human behavior are workable in learning-theory terms only with tremendous effort. On the other hand, nonlearning theories seem to belabor and elaborate apparently simple behaviors that can be covered adequately just by using learning terms. Therefore, more complete explanations are probably best obtained by using learning theory in combination with another favorite theory.

PROBLEMS CREATING MENTAL ILLNESS

Common denominators among the various theories can be found. Most theorists will agree, at least in general, that inner conflict and anxiety are common to most mental illnesses and that overuse of defense mechanisms

---

* A form of operant conditioning.
† Although this does not explain why the behavior occurs to begin with, it can explain why it persists: because it is rewarding.

and development of faulty interpersonal relationships are nearly always involved.

conflict   *Conflict* is thought to be the source of most mental illness. Each of us, from childhood onward, has certain goals and desires toward which we strive. These basic needs are not easily realized; they usually run head-on into the goals and desires of others.

Matching these needs with each type of theory, we might pair Freudian theory with the sex drive; Sullivan's ideas with the need for love; Rogerian theory with the drive for self-actualization; and learning theory with most physical needs—sex, hunger, thirst, and so forth. Frustration of these needs can be charted in similar fashion: Freud—superego interference; Sullivan—rejection; Rogers—failure to reach self-actualization; learning theories—punishment.

Although each theory emphasizes a different aspect of needs, you can see that they share a common theme expressed in different terms.

anxiety   Conflict leads to *anxiety*, or psychological stress, because the person is frustrated and sees no way out of his dilemma. All of us experience anxiety when we cannot resolve a conflict, but the mental patient's history reflects a chronic or continued anxiety, an endless frustration because he cannot cope with the world. Two major techniques can be used to combat this frustration: fighting or withdrawal. Both are appropriate in some circumstances, but continued use of these behavioral mechanisms results in inadequate coping with the environment and destruction of what ability the person still has to find a satisfactory life.

The psychological and physiological effects of anxiety attacks and of chronic anxiety are so numerous that it is difficult to see how the person would have time for much else. Those who undergo attacks of anxiety may suffer from heart palpitation, fatigue, breathlessness, chest pains, dizziness, fainting, apprehension, and headaches, to name but a few problems. To make matters worse, the body becomes so keyed up that the person overreacts to noise, light, and even heat [Pitts, 1969].

The stress of a conflict situation is clear in two types of human dilemma: the approach-avoidance situation and the avoidance-avoidance situation, especially the second. A very simple example of *approach-avoidance conflict* is the child who wants to steal some candy (approach) but is afraid of being punished (avoidance). At a more complex and serious level is the youngster who wants to engage in sexual activity but feels very guilty about doing so or is afraid of venereal disease.

The *avoidance-avoidance* arrangement is the more frustrating because the person loses either way. For example, the child is supposed to go to the dentist; if he goes it will be painful (avoidance), and if he refuses to go it will be painful because his mother will punish him (avoidance).

Again, both situations are normal: We all face them at one time or another, and they produce moderate anxiety in the average person. In mental illness, the key elements are the time period involved and the lack of compensation: a continued life pattern of such painful conflicts, especially when the person receives little love to support him, leads to chronic anxiety and weakening of the person's psychological strength. After that, *any* crisis makes the person react inappropriately, either by having an anxiety attack or by developing physical symptoms, both responses that are typical in mental illness [Wolpe, 1958].

THE SYSTEM OF DEFENSE MECHANISMS

We all use a number of behavioral responses—*defense mechanisms*—to defend ourselves against psychological attack, basically against anxiety. Each person seems to seek a balance, a psychological homeostasis, and to maintain it by warding off threats to his well-being or integrity. In other words, we all try to protect ourselves from being defeated. Some typical devices for self-protection are discussed here.

repression

At best we are only partially aware of the defense mechanisms we use. We must deceive ourselves to some extent, or by their very nature the mechanisms would not work. For instance, you are well acquainted from earlier discussions with the defense mechanism called **repression** in which we push out of our minds certain things that we do not want to face. Obviously, if we were fully aware that this repression was going on, we would not have done a thorough job of pushing back the unwanted thoughts or desires, because to be aware of repressing is to be aware of *what* we are repressing [McCall, 1963].

Repression can be unhealthy. For instance, a person may push out of awareness the feeling that his parents did not love him. Theoretically, even though the feeling has been repressed, the unconscious mind is still aware of it, and as a result the person may be unable to give or receive love in a normal fashion. A healthier response than repressing the feeling is examining it—discovering whether or not it has any basis in fact—and understanding where it comes from. A few people may be able to conduct this type of examination on their own, but usually the help of a mental health worker is needed.

Repression, or at least partial repression,* can be healthy. The death of a loved one, for instance, is not the kind of event that a healthy person needs to remember in every detail and live with every moment of his day. To remove some of the pain by repressing it is probably the only way to cope with this loss.† Some feel that fully realizing the death of a loved one

---

* Called suppression.
† From the learning theorist's viewpoint, what we are calling repression is a nonexotic form of forgetting. *Repression* is primarily a Freudian term, although it is frequently used by adherents of other theories.

is healthy, but can someone fully realize this event? I doubt it. Usually the loved one "fades away."

rationalization   *Rationalization* is describing what we do in such a way that we avoid responsibility for any consequences. A man who spends all of his money at the racetrack, for instance, might rationalize his behavior by saying that just like billionaire Howard Hughes, he is entitled to *some* enjoyment in life. In theory, he is covering up for a different and more accurate reason that would correctly explain his irrational behavior; for example, he has a constricting and confining home life, or possibly he is very insecure and indulges in a well-known pipedream: "Just one more race and I'll have a winning streak, and a winning streak will bring enough wealth so that I will no longer need to feel insecure." *

Most of us used a fairly normal rationalization when, early in adolescence, our one and only true love abandoned us for someone else. Most young men protect themselves by rationalizing the situation in this fashion: "She had bad breath and wasn't worth it anyway."

The point is that the *degree* and *extent* to which rationalization is used—how much and how often—determine whether the person's defensive reaction is abnormal. This is probably true of all defensive reactions; how often and how much make the difference between normal and abnormal behavior.

projection   *Projection* means throwing the blame for our own actions or thoughts onto another person or persons. The paranoid person who thinks that others are persecuting him and plotting against him is projecting; he is projecting onto others some problem that is really his own. For instance, perhaps the paranoid feels extremely guilty about a particular behavior and unconsciously believes that others regard him unfavorably because of this behavior. Others are probably not paying any attention to him one way or the other, and certainly they are not aware of his problems, but he projects from himself to them certain feelings which he believes they *should* have toward him, if they knew what he was up to. When the paranoid person is through translating the situation to fit his own needs, others *do* have feelings toward him, and he interprets these feelings to fit his own distorted perceptions, which seem "factual" to him.

A common example of normal projection, which could be interpreted in light of the facts (if one could find them), is the man who has been fired from a job. He maintains that his firing resulted from office politics rather than from his own poor job performance. Thus, he is projecting the responsibility onto others, rather than accepting it himself.

regression   *Regression* is a mode of behavior in which we try to defend ourselves by moving backward in time and behaving like children. This reaction is a

---

* Just to set the record straight, these examples are typical, possible explanations for such behavior, not *the* reason or the only reason that such behaviors occur.

171   Patients in a mental institution. The woman lying on the floor has taken the fetal position (*Jerry Cooke*)

defense against extreme frustration in which we cannot find any *adult* method for retaliation, so we regress to a behavior that we found effective when we were children.

Extreme regression is sometimes seen in a person going "berserk," whose behavior resembles the childhood temper tantrum, which received considerable attention from the mother or father. Crying is to some extent a regression, but whether it is normal or abnormal depends upon the degree of external motivation. Crying at the death of a loved one is certainly normal, although it is still regression because it is *primarily* a childlike behavior. Some disturbed persons have actually been known to suck their thumbs and roll up into the fetal position* when threatened. Such a person is seeking the protection he had as a child, although now he is an adult and his behavior is inappropriate.

withdrawal and suicide

A behavior commonly seen in mental illness is *withdrawal,* a very ineffective kind of reaction to stress. In withdrawal the person throws in the towel when faced with any problem or failure. Rather than fight on or try to solve the difficulty, he behaves like a child who locks himself in his room and ignores the problems he is having.

The most severe form of withdrawal is complete and irrevocable—*suicide.* Except for a person faced by the severe pain of an incurable illness, suicide is sometimes labeled as the behavior of one who is mentally disturbed, in the sense that the person has found a very poor solution to his problems. Suicide is a puzzle to most investigators, although in recent years close examination of suicide notes has turned up a few clues. A moderate number of suicides are motivated by the confusion and disturbed thought processes of severely disturbed people, and their suicide notes do not make much sense. Most suicides seem to be carried out by people who need to be pampered and cared for, in a psychological sense, most of their lives. They apparently obtained most attention when they had been hurt, and they are carrying this to the extreme, saying, "Now, you'll really be sorry and care for me because you have killed me." For such a person, suicide contains an element not only of getting attention but of enjoying a strange sort of revenge. Other people are manipulated to gratify the suicide's own need for "someone to care," although he will not be around to enjoy the rewards. Another kind of suicide, not uncommon, is based on the prospect of joining a loved one in the afterlife. Along the same line, some suicides want to start anew in the afterworld.

notes on suicide

—Married persons have the lowest suicide rate.
—More men kill themselves than women, but more women attempt suicide than men.
—Depression, confusion, and anxiety disappear a few days before a suicide;

* The position the unborn child assumes in the womb, rolled up in a ball like a cat.

likewise, a severely depressed person is most suicide-prone when coming out of a depression.

—There is no clear evidence suggesting that a tendency toward suicide is inherited.

—Incorrect: once suicidal, always suicidal.

—Suicide is as likely among the rich as the poor.

—Suicides do not happen only to the supposed mentally ill, although the rate is higher for those who have been in a mental hospital (37 per 100,000 versus 9.6 per 100,000 among never-hospitalized) [Lester and Lester, 1971; Lester, 1972].

—Suicide is increasingly a leading cause of death among adolescents, although accidents are the major cause during this period. Among those with psychological problems, adolescents are more likely to attempt suicide than adult patients [Stevenson et al., 1972].

Incidentally, a dangerous myth is still around: the false notion that people who threaten suicide do not go through with it. They do indeed. Among "successful" suicides at least three-quarters warned others about it or had otherwise threatened to take their lives [Schneidman, 1957; Darbonne, 1969].

denial   *Denial* is similar to withdrawal and repression. The person using denial as a defense just refuses to admit that anything bad has happened. Faced with major business problems, for example, the person denies that they exist; faced with the loss of a loved one, he fails to admit that the person is dead; and so on. Many authors try to make a distinction between denial and repression, maintaining that denial is partially conscious whereas repression is completely unconscious removal of the material. The distinction seems somewhat fine and probably is not especially important for our purpose.

Denial is rather like withdrawal in that the person is refusing to admit responsibility and pretending that problems don't exist. In any case, I'm sure you can detect the similarity between withdrawal, denial, and repression. Wherever they belong in the psychological scheme, each of them is an inadequate method for coping with problems; they resemble one another in that the person puts considerable distance between himself and the issues at hand so that he does not have to face his problems.

defending against anxiety   The list of defense mechanisms can be expanded endlessly, depending upon which theory one is studying or how compulsive the author is. Making lists is not as important as understanding the basic mechanism involved in defense: the person is threatened, and he responds to the threat with a counterbehavior that essentially removes him from the problem; the problem is then "gone," reduced, or blamed on someone else.

Using too many of these mechanisms often tends to create an unreal world. In theory, at least, none of us is comfortable indefinitely with an unreal world, just as the dope addict or the alcoholic can remain out of things for only limited periods without bringing some misery to himself or others. The world is still there, and apparently we have to cope with it or lose the battle [Davis, 1966]. As at least one psychologist has pointed out, one of the troubles with defense mechanisms is that they work so well. Because they do decrease anxiety, they are self-reinforcing and are used again. In fact, a person can become an interlocking mass of defenses [Peters, 1970].

FAULTY INTERPERSONAL RELATIONSHIPS

Another idea with which most personality theorists agree is that the mental patient has developed faulty interpersonal relationships (relationships among people). His relationships with others have been distorted from the beginning. One of the major problems in the life of a mental patient is confusion about how to interact with others and how to perceive others when they interact with him. Survey studies of mental patients as compared with normals seem to support the notion that one of the major difficulties the patient has is in getting along well with others. The patients emphasized interpersonal difficulties as a notable factor in their "illness"; normals tended to emphasize heredity or some physiological problem as causing mental illness [Weinstein, 1971].

One kind of faulty relationship that is a good example is again the paranoid person, who feels that others are out to get him. Basically, this person is insecure and feels overwhelmed by the frustrations of the world. No matter how he got this way, being human, he must somehow explain to his own satisfaction why everything seems to be going wrong, why computers keep sending him incorrect bills, why he is being cut off in traffic, why he has so few friends, and so on—all the frustrations of a typical day, only compounded and magnified. The paranoid has to make some sense out of this, just as you would if one day you were sitting in the library and somebody walked up to you—somebody you had never met—and slapped you in the face. Why? You'd need a reason. The paranoid reconstructs the world to fit a form of logic; this part of his behavior is normal, for the human brain seeks logic and order. What is abnormal is that he constructs a faulty system of interpersonal relationships and describes his ills as coming from the plotting of others against him. The general principle of faulty analysis of the world around them will be found to some extent among all mental patients, not just paranoids.

Distortion of interpersonal relationships can also be clearly detected in a fairly common symptom we have discussed before, fetishism. Fetishism is not a specific classification of mental disturbance, but is found in people who, usually, have a sexual problem. Fetishism means that an article of clothing, a lock of hair, or a part of the body itself becomes the object of sexual gratification. The fetishist loves or caresses the object in order to attain sexual release. The true fetishist—for example, a person who has a stocking fetish—does not need to connect a real person to the stocking, but instead can get his gratification just from the stocking alone (or shoe or lock of hair). Some theorists have pointed out that the object itself has replaced people; the person avoids the difficult interplay with other people by devoting his attention to an object. This devotion to objects is not in itself abnormal; most of us have a favorite object—a special pen, a cigarette lighter, an automobile, or some such. These objects provide security and help us to become part of the world. For instance, there are many fairly normal people who caress, love, and talk to their automobiles. The problem arises when the disturbed person is unable to relate to people and *must* substitute an object [Becker, 1969]. The important point again, is not fetishism per se, but the fact that many individuals with problems have to take refuge in objects rather than people.

No matter what theory of mental illness a professional subscribes to, the odds are greatly in favor of agreement that the typical mental patient has a history of conflict, anxiety, overuse of defense mechanisms, and faulty interpersonal relationships.

KINDS OF MENTAL ILLNESS

In any book on psychology, most readers find the parts on sex and abnormal behavior the most interesting. Although few of us know exactly why we all are so preoccupied with sex,* what interests us about mental illness usually is the startling aspects having to do with the minority of patients who provide wild and unusual behaviors—screaming, fighting, talking to themselves, and so forth. Why this myth of mental illness persists is anyone's guess—probably because it is interesting and colorful. In any case, the typical mental patient is nothing like this stereotype. In fact, as one author has pointed out, "Across the entire population of patients, . . . antisocial aggressive acts are *less frequent* than in the normal population" [Ullman, 1969, p. 355].

Nonetheless, the traditional outlines of mental illness symptomatology do provide a convenient structure for examining the topic. Supposedly, one cannot understand variations in a structure until he understands the structure itself, so most of my discussion will center on traditional kinds of mental illness. Remember, however, that these are "textbook" definitions; the overlapping of symptoms and behaviors from one patient to another is amazing [Buss, 1966].

neurosis   Strictly interpreted, the term *neurosis* comes from *neuron* ("nerve") and *-osis* ("disease"). This unusual definition—"disease of the nerves"—seems to have been the result of the unwarranted assumption made decades ago, that something had gone wrong with the person's nervous system and was

*I don't think we do know, even though we should considering the amount of time and money devoted to it.

causing his sickness. A term frequently used to replace it (although the two are interchangeable) is *psychoneurosis*. The added syllables don't help much because now the label means "disease of the mind *and* nerves." The word nerves doesn't actually belong in the term; no evidence supports the notion that the neurotic has a nerve problem in the literal sense, nor a physical defect of the brain.

In any case, whether you call his problem neurosis or psychoneurosis, the mental patient so labeled has a moderate disorder that is causing discomfort to him or others, or is interfering with his life functioning, or both. The true neurotic finds it extremely difficult to continue his everyday life without some sort of external help, whether it be in the form of tranquilizers, the assistance of a mental health worker, or actually being admitted to a hospital. Neurotic disorders can sometimes involve pronounced symptoms—for example, the often-cited cases of paralysis of one limb—but the neurotic usually has not lost contact with what we call reality. This distinction will become clearer as we differentiate neurosis from the second major classification of mental illness, the psychosis.

psychosis   The more severe form of mental illness is called *psychosis*. There are many types of psychosis, some of which we will cover shortly, but the symptoms overlap considerably from one classification to another. The mental health worker usually can tell a psychotic from a neurotic rather easily because the psychotic generally has what are called *thought disorders*. Thought disorders are difficulties in thinking the way the rest of us do. In some cases thoughts become confused; in others the person is constantly preoccupied with something others do not understand—for example, some plan or scheme that dominates the patient's whole world. Just as in the case of *disagreement* meaning "constipation," mentioned earlier, most investigators seem to feel that the thoughts probably make a distorted sense, but we are unable to understand them. In other words, the patient is speaking from a frame of reference that is entirely foreign to most of us.

We have just touched on a major distinction usually made between the psychotic and the neurotic. The psychotic seems to create his own world of reality when need be, to the apparent exclusion of the reality of others around him. The common symptoms of delusion and hallucination readily demonstrate this rejection of the real world. Things are just not the same for the psychotic as they are for us: He may claim that disembodied voices are speaking to him, or he may grossly misrepresent the external world, as the paranoid does.

Another characteristic that distinguishes the psychotic from the neurotic is *peculiarities of affect.** Most of us maintain a fairly normal, steady level of response to those around us; the psychotic can show either flat affect,

---

*Affect = emotion; hence, peculiar emotional response.

which means that he exhibits almost no response no matter what is happening, or heightened affect, which constitutes a highly agitated state typically involving jumping, giggling, shouting, and the like. In general, the psychotic does not seem able to control his emotional behavior, and this lack of control is immediately evident when one tries to communicate with him.

To make the distinction clearer, once more consider the neurotic. The neurotic may show unusual symptoms or even strange behavior, but he usually has organized thought processes, is able to communicate effectively in most spheres, and is generally well aware of what is going on around him. And although the neurotic may experience strong swings of mood, rarely does he show the excesses of flat or heightened affect typical of the psychotic.

character disorders   When hospital staff members or mental health workers are unable to fit a person into a specific category of neurosis or psychosis, the chances are good that the person's problem will be labeled *character disorder*. *Character disorder* is a misleading term when applied to mental illness, because usually the person does not show the typical signs we discussed earlier—discomfort, bizarreness, and/or inefficiency. Character disorders are not new to us, but they have been differently labeled; for example, the antisocial behavior of the delinquent, if it becomes a lifelong pattern, is labeled a character disorder. Any person who thinks first and foremost of himself, gets what he wants by stealing, cheating, or the like, and shows no guilt or "social conscience" is said to have a character disorder.

You may recall that we have called such a person a sociopath*; even though he doesn't fit the traditional pattern of mental illness, he is labeled a mentally ill person and treated as such. Although there is little question that the person who has a character disorder presents problems for society, and by inference something must be wrong with him, it is intriguing that even without overt symptoms he is still classified as mentally ill. This arrangement tends to demonstrate what we were discussing earlier—the mentally ill are first and foremost different from the rest of us, and treatment or care is designed to try to get them back into line.

KINDS OF NEUROTIC REACTIONS   Some formal classifications are used to describe types of neurosis. Remember, however, that this classification system is pretty mixed up, and any or all of the many behaviors attributed to various types can appear in the same person. Because this is so, movements have sprung up in the last decade to get rid of the classification system, but only limited progress is being made because the idea bucks tradition. Classifications are apparently here to stay for a while. They are covered in the following sections, which

---

* Essentially, the terms *character disorder*, *sociopath*, and *psychopath* are interchangeable.

provide only brief definitions and some elaboration; you are by now well acquainted with all of them, though you haven't been formally introduced.

anxiety neurosis   In *anxiety neurosis* the predominant symptom is severe anxiety. The patient may have chronic anxiety, meaning that he is always anxious, or he may have occasional severe attacks of anxiety.

phobic neurosis   The major complaint of the patient with *phobic neurosis* is acute, irrational fear of a specific kind of object, person, or situation. Phobias may include almost anything, but usually only one per patient: fear of fire, water, dogs, snakes, bugs, closed places, open places, and so forth. The patient who is faced with the object of his phobia is likely to "go berserk" and struggle, run, or even fight to get away from the traumatic object. Forcing a person to "face up to the situation" is disastrous; it can even lead to passing out or to a heart attack. Some success has been made with exposing the person gradually to the feared situation, but just flinging the person into it is always risky.

dissociative neurosis   *Dissociative neurosis* relies on the mechanism of the mind by which it cuts off (dis-associates) part of the person's life and separates it from other parts. Multiple personality is dissociative neurosis; so is amnesia (Chapter 8). In some cases this behavior is far more bizarre than many of the psychoses, but it is still called neurotic because no thought disorder occurs; even if two distinct personalities exist, each is fairly coherent.

obsessive-compulsive reaction   An *obsession* is a preoccupation with something—usually something extreme—to the exclusion of almost everything else—for example, thoughts of stripping in public, thoughts of dying, thoughts of hurting someone, thoughts of jumping off a building, and so forth. Almost never are these carried out—just constantly mulled over.

A *compulsion* is an irresistible need to perform some action, whether it be counting the cracks in the sidewalk,* washing hands, or adding the numbers on license plates. The person usually tries not to perform the act, but becomes so anxious if he doesn't that eventually the only way he can find relief is to go ahead and behave in the compulsive fashion. The anxiety built up is thus temporarily relieved, but the person is back at it within a short time, as soon as the anxiety starts again.

A person is labeled an *obsessive-compulsive neurotic* if he exhibits either of these problems. The reason goes back to theory: The obsessive thoughts and the compulsive acts are assumed to serve the same function, distracting the person and keeping him so busy that he doesn't have time to dwell on more deep-seated problems. Another reason for including them

---

*If you occasionally count cracks in the sidewalk, you are not an obsessive-compulsive, who performs continued, persistent, never-ending counting. Same thing if you occasionally wash.

in the same category is that a patient frequently shows both symptoms at the same time; for example, he may be obsessed by thoughts of cleanliness and feel a compulsion to wash his hands all the time.

Obsessions and compulsions are found in all of us. For instance, a tune that you can't get out of your mind is a mild obsession, and the act of humming it is a mild compulsion.*

The true obsessive-compulsive is usually very noticeable. I remember a secretary who gradually became more and more obsessed by the idea of typing each letter perfectly. Rather than erase, creating an imperfection, she would start over. Slowly the compulsion to type the letter grew and grew, until finally when her boss would hand her a letter, she would type it forty or fifty times, never getting it quite perfect. This process reduced her efficiency noticeably.

conversion reaction   In *conversion reaction* the patient usually has symptoms related to bodily parts—for example, paralysis or insensitivity of the limbs or other parts of the body, or temporary blindness. Such reactions are rare. They do increase somewhat among soldiers in wartime, for reasons we have already discussed, and, of course, also in cases of civil disorder such as riots, or any type of action characterized by unusual and abnormal stress. Even then, however, conversion reaction is not a common mental illness.

The term *conversion* deserves some special attention. It arises from the idea that a mental problem is converted or changed into a physical symptom and that the symptom in turn represents the mental problem. The conversion reaction does not involve an actual physical injury to the body, but the unit in question does become physically inoperative or impaired.

psychosomatic disorders   The term *psychosomatic* comes from *psyche* ("mind") and *soma* ("body"). Whereas the conversion reaction involves a bizarre symptom, usually external, the psychosomatic disorder deals with overall health and the functioning of internal organs as they are influenced by psychological problems. In the *psychosomatic disorder*, psychological factors eventually lead to *actual* physical damage to the body.

An obvious case of psychosomatic disorder is the person who feels overwhelmed by an unpleasant job and discouraged by a poor marriage and can be characterized as feeling "hopeless." Frequently this hopelessness is reflected in a bodily response of listlessness and excessive fatigue. Getting up in the morning, for example, is a monumental task. The body seems to reflect the person's psychological state; it is just too much to get out of

* Most likely you will see yourself somewhere in most of these classifications; this does not in any way even hint that you may be disturbed. Medical students are known for "catching" every disease they run across; psychology students are likewise typically developing mental illness. If you had no reason to suspect yourself before, there is no reason to do so now.

bed and face another day [Guilford, 1959]. This bodily response can lead to actual physical damage to the heart, stomach, muscles, and so forth.*

A number of clear-cut cases demonstrate the interaction between body and psyche or mind. Many experiments have tried to relate stomach ulcers to psychological stress. An ulcer is a perforation of the stomach's lining that results in an open wound. Some types of ulcer are thought to result from excessive digestive juices, with an accompanying increase in stomach acids, as a result of stress or tension. But it is possible to damage one's stomach without having psychological problems. One good way is to mix alcohol with aspirin, a combination that breaks down the protective devices of the stomach wall and induces bleeding. If you have a headache, better to decide which you need more—either alcohol or aspirin, not both [Davenport, 1972]. However, during anxiety or aggression, the walls of the stomach do engorge with blood, placing the organ under considerable stress. When we cannot relieve anger or tension, we can feel it in the stomach; the internal muscles tighten up. This feeling can sometimes be relieved by hitting a punching bag or running around the block, but unrelieved psychological tension is difficult to dissipate. In one study, subjects were angered and frustrated; one group was allowed to retaliate against (but not injure) the experimenter who had frustrated them; another group was not allowed to retaliate. In the group of Ss who could discharge their anger, what had been elevated blood pressure and accelerated heart rate decreased rapidly; this was not the case for the Ss that had to bottle up their feelings [Hokanson and Burgess, 1962]. Thus it is possible to assume that continued frustration, anger, resentment, or tension will keep the body sufficiently energized so that part of it will eventually "break down." The situation is analogous to running a machine continuously at maximum speed.

Business executives supposedly are known for getting ulcers, although this reputation is more myth than reality. Nonetheless, a large number of businessmen in middle and top management, as well as other kinds of people, do get ulcers. An unusual finding from one study of monkeys (called "executive monkeys") was that ulcers could be induced by putting the monkeys under stress. However, the ulcers seemed to develop during rest periods rather than during the stress itself. In this particular study, the monkeys were shocked at intervals, but they were given an opportunity to press a lever to relieve the shock. During this stress and lever-pressing period, stomach acidity rose only slightly; during the rest periods without shock, the acidity rose considerably [Brady, 1958]. One might speculate that fighting back by means of pushing the lever kept

---

*I haven't watched all the afternoon soap operas yet, but so far all the ones I've seen have an actor-physician saying, "Oh, she just has a psychosomatic illness," and shrugging the issue off. However, no "just" is involved—psychosomatic illnesses involve *actual* physical damage.

frustration down because the monkeys were doing something. When they were doing nothing, tension probably was building up even though the shock was not being applied at that time. A control group of monkeys was shocked but had no lever to press. They did not develop ulcers. One could speculate that anticipation of the responsibility and the tension of having to do something at the right time leads to ulcers.

It is difficult to unify the study of frustration and aggression and that of executive monkeys. In the one case, the mechanism seems to be running too fast and too long; in the other, the mechanism seems to falter if it is allowed to slow down. The two studies probably should be kept separate for the present, since they seem to illustrate two different points. First, the mechanism will eventually break down, but it will take longer if the person is actively involved in fighting back.* Second, if you can't fight back at a situation or have no responsibility, so to speak, you are unlikely to get ulcers. But, no matter how you interpret the findings, stress is a common denominator in the development of some ulcers.

In other respects also, the interrelationship between body and mind (or psyche) is intriguing.† Parts of the body—the heart, blood vessels, stomach—are controlled by the autonomic nervous system and have been assumed to operate all by themselves, without conscious or unconscious control by the person. The last ten years have seen an increase in experiments that contradict this assumption. The internal organs of the body, while controlled by the autonomic nervous system, are apparently just as susceptible to conditioning as the rest of the person is. In animals, for example, the rate of heartbeat can be altered by conditioning the animal with rewarding electrical stimulation to the brain, or by conditioning it to avoid electric shock by changing its internal responses. In other words, to obtain what it wants, the animal can change the pattern of behavior of its internal organs [DiCara, 1970]. Furthermore, by a process of conditioning, the human being can control the operation of his intestines and digestive juices and the expansion or contraction of his blood vessels [Razran, 1961].

An example of the importance of these studies is found in studies of migraine headaches, a plague to millions of people. The migraine headache is now interpreted as resulting in most cases from dilation (expansion) of a set of major arteries that run up toward the brain on either side of the head. This dilation apparently causes pressure and pain [Wolf, 1964]. Sometime in the past, the person may have been conditioned to expand these blood vessels when under stress. For instance, at one time or another

---

*Obviously we are assuming that monkeys are the same as humans; this idea is not farfetched, but it may be incorrect in *this* case. Anyway, professional ethics prohibit an experimenter from deliberately causing ulcers in humans.

† The word *mind* here is used arbitrarily, in the everyday sense of nonphysical. Some feel there is no such thing as the nonphysical; for them, we can define mind as what *seems* to be nonphysical.

a headache may have proved useful in getting out of doing something unpleasant, so the body repeats the process the next time the person faces a problem and this pattern continues.

You may have noticed that many of these studies seem to be trying to separate the physical from the psychological, and you may also remember that this issue came up when psychology first started on the path toward becoming a science. The question is, are we making any progress? In many respects we are, but one startling fact is that psychology is almost back to Descartes, who in the 1600s assumed (incorrectly) that mind and body interact with one another at a little unit in the base of the brain called the pineal gland.

How can we be making progress if we are back where we started? Actually, the answer is simple: During these intervening years we have learned so much about how the body operates that some of the pieces can now be fitted together into a coherent framework without relying on mysterious units like the pineal gland. The facts seem to indicate that body influences mind and mind influences body. In more complicated terms, an ingenious hypothesis to explain the connection between body and mind has been proposed. The cortex experiences no emotion or sensation; it merely handles concepts. A typical concept it can understand and use is "fear." The cortex, however, is connected to the hypothalamus, which exercises direct or indirect control over the body's various glands and the muscular-visceral system.* The concept "fear" is interpreted by the cortex, which then signals the hypothalamus, which signals the glandular and muscular-visceral system to respond. All of these organs together produce an emotional response. The behavior of the various glands and muscles is fed back to the cortex, which again interprets the condition and decides whether another go-round of emotion is needed. If the answer is yes, the hypothalamus is again stimulated; if no, it is not. In the life of the neurotic, the chain of events connected with fear, for example, occurs so frequently that the slightest problem activates the cortex and starts the chain of events operating. Furthermore, once this has begun, the cortex, continually interpreting severe danger, does not stop the process, and around the chain of events goes again [Kraines, 1969]. This interpretation is one way of explaining the relationship between body and mind in psychosomatic illness.

hypochondriasis   Known to most of us are people labeled *hypochondriacs*. A hypochondriac is excessively preoccupied with bodily function and tends to find ailments that are nonexistent or minor and to inflate them. This sort of person is constantly worried about his health, although he has no physical problem (unlike the person beset by psychosomatic illness). Psychological theory suggests that the hypochondriac is overdependent; in the past he received

---

* Muscles and internal organs.

love and affection primarily during periods of illness, and he is regressing in order to attain this affection again. Another possibility is that in his present adult life the hypochondriac can get the desired amount of attention (from a physician or family) only by developing physical symptoms. Psychologists and psychiatrists seem to feel most comfortable if the hypochondriac is relegated to a separate classification, thought of as a vague sort of conversion reaction, since no physical abnormality can be detected as a general rule.

When the stressful situation is removed from the life of a conversion-reaction type, the physical symptom disappears. On the other hand, the complaints of the hypochondriac are *very* resistant to treatment. This resistance has been explained as resulting from a lifelong, ingrained pattern of complaints. Although the hypochrondriac puts considerable stress on his body, he rarely develops a detectable symptom. No one knows whether or not something is physically wrong with him, although the odds seem to be against it. However, medical science and psychological science are still quite primitive, and the warning of an aforementioned author is again appropriate: Beware of labeling what is not obvious as either witchcraft or hypochondriasis. In the absence of notable psychological stress or problems, it is too easy an out just to say that the person is a hypochondriac and thereby avoid extensive physiological examination.

KINDS OF PSYCHOTIC REACTIONS

Over the years an argument has raged back and forth with little success on either side: Is the psychotic reaction simply an exaggerated form of neurotic behavior, or is it an entirely separate entity? Those who opt for a separate entity argue that many psychotic behaviors are inherited rather than just the result of psychological problems. No real solution to this question is available at present. For the time being we will assume that the psychotic is a more disturbed version of the neurotic, and later when we discuss some of the physiological factors in psychosis we will assume that it differs somewhat from the neurosis. The two approaches are not mutually exclusive. Some forms of psychosis may be caused by inherited tendencies toward this form of mental illness, by physiological alterations, or by organic damage. Other forms may be caused by primarily psychological factors. Some may involve both physiology and psychology.

When psychosis is assumed to be an exaggerated form of neurosis, the same underlying factors of faulty psychological development as mentioned by Freud, Sullivan, and others are thought to bring about the disorder. Typically, the psychotic (1) has had very cold and rejecting parents; and/or (2) has throughout his life history learned incorrect or even bizarre behavior patterns; and/or (3) has withdrawn from life because of severe trauma. The psychotic's defensive structure (defense mechanisms) is severely weakened and, under stress, gives way to the development of at least two typical patterns: (1) converting his problems into bizarre rituals and strange behaviors; and/or (2) regressing by a major withdrawal from life and reality.

The thought disorders of the psychotic can be attributed to faulty learning or to a faulty reconstruction of the world designed to fit the individual's needs. The search for obvious brain defects in the greater proportion of psychotics has proved a failure.

Some have claimed that psychosis is an artificial division of mental illness and blame the hospitalization itself for continuing and fostering the illness. Considerable evidence shows that in a few isolated societies where the psychotic's bizarre behavior is tolerated, these people lead slightly different but fairly normal lives, compared to the "normal" people around them. Hence, it *is* possible for some psychotics in our society to maintain a moderate level of adjustment, in that they carry on their life's work even while they are suffering from, say, delusions or hallucinations. Few and far between are the mental health workers who would agree that treatment is *not* indicated in these cases. An interesting parallel presents itself here; a society like ours, which makes every effort to get rid of old people by putting them in homes for the aged, also wants to get rid of those who act bizarrely, even though these people aren't doing too bad a job of living life. In any case, psychotic reactions *do* exist, and our job is to explore them.

schizophrenia   This mental illness is the best known of the psychoses and encompasses the largest number of patients. Schizophrenia includes a number of subdivisions, but the classifications overlap so much that I am going to lump them together. You can still get a picture, possibly even a clearer one, of the schizophrenic's more or less typical behavior.

The term *schizophrenia* itself comes from the Greek meaning "splitting of the mind" (*phren*). The word was coined by a mental health worker in the early 1900s because he felt the word represented the scattered (or split-apart) mental processes of this type of person. In other words, he was trying to find a term which indicated that thought associations did not fit into a coherent pattern [Bleuler, 1950]. The actual term he used was the plural German, *Schizophrenien,* and he used this form because he was referring to what he thought schizophrenia to be: the loss of harmonious balance between groups of mental functions [Cancro and Pruyser, 1970]. Someone somewhere along the way mistranslated the term to mean "split personality," and this translation in turn was misconstrued by many people to mean multiple personality.* The schizophrenic does not have a multiple personality; he has just one, but it is poorly organized or organized in a bizarre fashion.

---

* This same thing has occurred with the term *psychopath*. Somehow, possibly through movies, the word has come to mean almost any mental illness and has ironically been distorted to mean schizophrenia, which in turn many think to mean multiple personality.

172–173 Dr. Jekyll and Mr. Hyde, with Fredric March and Miriam Hopkins—a famous case of multiple personality but not schizophrenia (*Culver*)

symptoms of schizophrenia

Schizophrenia encompasses a wide range of behaviors, any or all of which may be found in a particular person. One of the most frequently seen behavior patterns of the schizophrenic is withdrawal from reality (our reality). Along with this withdrawal goes loss of interest in objects and people around him. Lack of cleanliness, for instance, is sometimes a sign of the impending development of full-blown schizophrenic behavior; this behavior is significant because the person no longer cares whether he offends people. Cleanliness per se is not significant here; what matters is that a person who will not clean up for his family or friends and is beginning to deteriorate in his interpersonal relationships.*

Communication is usually cut off between the schizophrenic and his family or friends, and to all appearances he is only minimally aware that others are around; even if he notices them, he doesn't seem to care (he lacks affect, or emotional tone).

It would be misleading, however, to assume that the schizophrenic has lost complete awareness. Typically, for example, he is quite negative about following instructions given him in psychological tests: He tends to do the opposite, and this behavior requires awareness of the instructions. Knowing exactly *how much* aware the schizophrenic is, nevertheless, very difficult. In tests that include drawing pictures, the schizophrenic usually does not expand his drawings to full size. A possible symbolic interpretation of this behavior is that he is restricting his own world to a very small space and thereby avoiding as much as possible contact with the outside world. This tendency could be unconscious. A simpler—but not necessarily more accurate—interpretation is that the patient is just refusing again to follow instructions (which requires awareness) [Taylor, 1963].

An offshoot of withdrawing from reality is the tendency of the

* Obviously we can't include in this group the roving bands of teenagers and young adults who don't bathe because being a bit dirty is part of the group ritual. The schizophrenic is detectable because he is violating *his* own group ritual. In years past, mental health workers had relied on lack of bathing as an indicator of schizophrenia. Possibly they will have to give this up.

patient to live in his own world, a world we don't understand. For example, one patient responded to all questions with "16–21 telephone pole"* [Himwich, 1969]. This and other strange utterances have some meaning in the patient's own world, but they are rather difficult for us to decipher. Frequently, however, bizarre and confusing utterances by schizophrenics appear when someone is trying to find out something personal about them or is trying to get close to them socially. So, one important aspect of their strange speech is that it reflects a fear of others and effectively prevents those around them from getting close [Shimkunas, 1972].

The paranoid schizophrenic, another example of a person living in a private world, has been mentioned before. He too lives an existence filled with feelings and thoughts about others around him that are inaccurate.

Delusions and hallucinations are frequent in schizophrenic reactions. One of the most common is the auditory hallucination, which consists of voices from the "outside" that influence the patient's behavior. These voices typically berate the patient for his supposed immoral acts, so presumably they result from guilt feelings.

To: The football department and its members present and future
     The University of New Mexico, Albuquerque, N.M.

I depend on correct, honest supplementation of this card by tele-pathy as a thing which will make clear the meaning of this card. There exists a Playing of The Great Things, the correct, the con-structive, world or universe politics, out-in-the open telepathy, etc. According to the Great Things this playing is the most feasible thing of all; but it is held from newspaper advertising and correct, honest public world recognition, its next step, by telepathic forces (it seems), physical dangers, and lack of money. Over 10,000 cards and letters on this subject have been sent to prominent groups and persons all over the world. Correct, honest contact with the honest, out-in-the-open world. This line of thought, talk, etc. rule. The plain and frank. Strangers. The Great Things and opposites idea. References: In the telepathic world the correct playings. Please save this card for a history record since it is rare and important for history.†

23–1 Postcard from a schizophrenic adolescent boy

One fact about the schizophrenic is clear: He is hyperactive (over-active), at least internally [Mirsky, 1969]. His inner bodily mechanisms are too responsive; they overreact. This could help to explain the voices: All of us hear internal talking, if you will, or we talk to ourselves; these voices probably come from the same mechanism, only in the schizophrenic they are overactivated and more real and intense than the inner voices of normal people.

Schizophrenics can sometimes be detected by their unusual motor

*This formula was apparently connected to a childhood experience in some way. The patient was believed to have lived near a telephone pole with this number on it.

†From James C. Coleman, *Abnormal Psychology and Modern Life.* Copyright © 1964 by Scott Foresman and Co.; reprinted with permission.

behavior. Such behavior includes strange postures like standing with arms in the air, strange movements like walking in exaggerated strides, giggling and silliness and strange facial expressions. Why such motor behavior occurs is unknown, but in any case it happens only infrequently, compared to most of the other symptoms.

**biological
and hereditary factors
in schizophrenia**

If you struggled through the section on inheritance of intelligence in Chapter 14, then this part will seem familiar. Almost identical problems face the experimenter who is trying to determine whether schizophrenia is inherited. Again, twins are used for a comparison. If the twins are identical, they have exactly the same inheritance; if they are not identical but fraternal twins, then their inheritance is not the same. But again we are faced with the problem that for the most part identical twins are subject to identical environments: They are usually dressed the same, they are difficult to distinguish from one another, and they are treated the same by their parents. Thus, trying to separate the environment (a predominantly psychological factor) from the inheritance (a predominantly biological factor) is the same problem which intelligence studies must face.

Literally hundreds of studies have been conducted on twins living at home, separated from one another, living with foster parents, and so forth. Experimenters have concentrated on situations in which one twin is schizophrenic. The question arises at this point: Does the illness appear in the other twin? The results of these studies are not consistent; some studies show that where one identical twin has schizophrenia the other one also does in 69 percent of the cases, while only 11 percent of fraternal twins share the illness; some find 25 percent versus 17 percent. In an attempt to unify a large number of these studies, one author obtained a combined figure, expressed as a ratio of 5 to 1 [Gottesman and Shields, 1966]. In other words, the chances are five times greater that you will become schizophrenic if you are an identical twin and your twin has schizophrenia than if you are a fraternal twin and your twin develops this problem.

Coming from a family in which there are schizophrenics among one's close relatives increases a person's chances of becoming schizophrenic and reduces the odds of an effective "cure" [Robins, 1970]. These data do not help with the issue of inheritance, however, because if a person lives with schizophrenic parents, the environment is going to be rather unusual and could be responsible for his getting the illness.

Other studies have examined foster homes with schizophrenic parents but where foster children were normal, or cases in which children of schizophrenic parents were living away from their parents. In a moderate number of these studies, biological factors seemed to operate; that is, normal foster children who lived with parents who had schizophrenic children of their own seemed to remain normal, and some children of schizophrenic parents, though reared in foster homes with normal parents, developed schizophrenia [Karlsson, 1967].

These data about twins, foster parents, and so on seem to support the hypothesis that schizophrenia is inherited; they would be fairly conclusive except that *not all sets of twins* develop schizophrenia. Furthermore, close examination of these studies reveals that in many cases parents and children were not separated until the children had lived in a home with schizophrenics for a number of years; thus, we cannot rule out the possibility of environmental influences working on them before they left [Jackson, 1960].

As in the case of intelligence studies, we cannot omit or ignore findings which tend to suggest that some predisposition toward schizophrenia can be inherited. Thus, again, we must take the position that the illness is a combination of both inheritance and environmental influences. Children who have schizophrenic *tendencies* are likely to develop full pathology if they must cope with an extremely stressful environment. A potentially weak system will give way under the pressure.

One thing is certain: Few topics have generated as much research into the physiology of the disturbed individual as that of schizophrenia. Schizophrenics have been put in plastic bags so their sweat can be captured and analyzed. Their blood has been examined until little of it is left; studies have concentrated on the chemical constitution of their urine; and on and on. However, in the words of one author who has prepared more than a hundred articles on the topic, "There are a number of promising leads, [but] there is still insufficient evidence to demonstrate unequivocally any single biochemical factor in schizophrenia" [Mirksy, 1969].

The basic supposition, yet to be proved conclusively, is that the schizophrenic has inherited a tendency to produce some toxic* substance within the body that interferes with proper cortical functioning and/or emotional normality. We mentioned earlier that some researchers think the schizophrenic produces substances resembling LSD. No chemical that is a "schizophrenic substance" has been isolated, although a number of experimenters have thought they had the answer, only to lose out in cross-validation† because the substance couldn't be found in another group. In any case, this is one line of search; attempts are still being made to isolate a chemical that interferes with brain functioning [Mirsky, 1969]. Other experimenters have offered more elaborate hypotheses, suggesting that the toxic state is connected with the emotional network and that the emotional circuit overwhelms the cortex, so to speak, without giving it time to digest the various feelings being sent to it [Kraines, 1968].

Current theories of schizophrenia focus on both physiology and psychology. To provide an example that is greatly oversimplified, the child

---

*Poisonous. A normal substance can be poisonous if there is too much of it, so overproduction is also a possibility.

    †Cross-validation is essentially the same as replication; repeating a study with different subjects.

may grow up in an environment in which the mother both hates and loves him. The child does not know how to cope with this behavior and becomes anxious and physiologically overaroused (that is, the body is keyed up beyond normal limits, which could result from an inherited tendency or just the situation itself). The child is so high-strung that any stimulus is too much for him, just as anything can set us off after a day when everything goes wrong. Only with the schizophrenic this state of affairs is continuous [Epstein, 1970]. One relatively consistent theme found in the background of the schizophrenic is that a parent either subtly or openly forces the child to expose his inner feelings and thoughts, which are then typically rejected by the parent—or the child is made to feel guilty about what he has disclosed [Heilbrun, 1972]. This background would help explain why schizophrenics fear getting close to other people.

The schizophrenic child's (and later the adult's) physiological and psychological constitutions are too sensitive. Emotions are extremely difficult to handle. They either send the person haywire or he blocks them out completely. Hence the very strange overreaction to and confusion regarding the world [Epstein and Coleman, 1970].

I have said that the schizophrenic overreacts. Another study shows that the response of the psychotic person's adrenal system is extremely pronounced during psychotic episodes; in fact, it is greater than that found in the parents of dying children or even of soldiers under attack in battle [Sacher, 1970].

manic-depressive reactions

Another classification of psychotic behavior is the *manic-depressive reaction*. This classification seems to be on the way out. In years past the basic distinction made between this kind of mental illness and schizophrenia was the marked alterations in mood shown by the manic-depressive. The word *manic* refers to extremely active, giggly, flighty behavior. The patient is so excited that he may stand on his bed in the ward and lecture and giggle for hours on end. The opposite pole is the depressive reaction, in which the patient remains in a stupor, frequently cannot even manage to walk, and spends his time sitting in a corner or staring into space. The two states are linked into one category because a few patients show mood swings from one extreme to the other; more typically, despite the hyphenated name, the patient is depressed and remains depressed.

These patients show many of the same problems schizophrenics exhibit—clouded consciousness, lack of inhibition, delusions, and the like. Hence, today most of them are labeled schizophrenic, whereas in the past they would have been diagnosed manic-depressive.

The most common depression is one called neurotic depression.* Such a depression results from a major setback in life, either real or imagined. It differs from psychotic depression in duration and severity. Psy-

---

*And obviously is a neurosis, but mentioned here to contrast the two.

chotic depression is a long-term affair, in that it is tied to deep psychological problems; the neurotic depression is usually triggered by a specific failure or disappointment, but the person has enough resiliency not to disappear completely into a psychotic world. Even though more severe, the psychotic depression is short-lived compared with the other psychoses and frequently will "cure itself" in time.

organic psychoses   What appears to be an "ordinary" psychosis—that is, marked by clouded consciousness, disordered speech, bizarre behavior, and the like—can sometimes be traced to an actual physical disorder. Common causes of *organic psychoses* are brain injury, tumor, major diseases affecting the central nervous system, alcoholism, and the deterioration of old age.

One cause of organic psychosis is syphilis. A form of psychosis called *paresis* is the direct result of syphilis. While not everyone who contacts syphilis gets paresis, the disease is sufficiently horrible to be avoided at all costs. Again, the patient can show almost any of the psychotic symptoms, only in this case the brain actually is being slowly eaten away by attacks of the syphilitic organisms and there is no way to restore it.

The rising incidence of syphilis represents a major problem of mental and physical health. Fortunately, it can be cured by massive doses of penicillin, if found in time. Syphilis first appears as a very hard pimple or open sore at the point of infection. Then, four to six weeks later, the symptoms *disappear,* deluding the person into thinking he never had the disease or is cured. But the syphilis has gone inside the body to multiply and destroy. Later, symptoms appear again as a copper-colored rash sometimes accompanied by fever, headaches, or "flulike" symptoms. Again they disappear, but by now the disease is well on its way. This stage is fairly close to the last chance to catch it before major and irreversible damage has been done. This situation is a genuine tragedy, considering that the public health service in any city will examine any person and treat the disease.

Many other diseases cause organic psychoses, but for our purposes they are not of pressing importance.

One serious problem exists regarding the conclusion that some malfunction of part of the cerebral network may cause psychotic symptoms. Many patients are diagnosed as suffering mild to moderate brain damage or malfunction, but these diagnoses are based on inference alone; the only way to know for certain is to actually enter the brain and explore—usually a rather drastic step.

The neurologist (physician expert in nerve and brain function) infers damage from problems of coordination, reflexes, lack of sensitivity to pain, and so forth, any of which could suggest damage to a specific portion of the brain. The psychologist infers brain damage from inaccurate perception, inability to memorize, inability to accurately reproduce figures (diamonds, complex circles and squares, triangles), and so forth. Psychologists and neurologists agree that brain damage does exist in a number of patients, but their opinions are educated guesses [Bachrach, 1970]. No method has been developed to determine whether minor brain damage really exists or whether the psychological problem "causes" the motor problems.

psychoses of aging   One classification of mental illness is *involutional psychosis*. The exact origin of this term is difficult to locate, but the word *involution* itself means curling or turning inward. This meaning seems accurate enough; until the age of about forty (females) and fifty-five (males) most people's life patterns seem to be going fairly well. Sometime beyond this age, however, the outside world—which has been taken up with children for most women and with occupation for most men—begins to crumble for many people, and they turn inward toward themselves; they begin to realize that the world is no longer theirs and that they are being left behind. To those of us who haven't faced this crisis yet, it seems quite remote, but when it does happen, it is a rude, startling, unpleasant awakening. The reaction of a fair number of people is understandable: They become deeply depressed and somewhat paranoid. In other words, the world is threatening and the future holds little hope [Cameron, 1963]. Although most middle-aged people do not develop involutional psychosis, it does appear even in people who have reached a fairly reasonable adjustment in the past, although most psychologists feel that these people tended toward some psychological problems to begin with. This assumption probably has some validity, but it doesn't fully take into account the type of stresses that bear on one person as opposed to another. Some pressures may be overwhelming.

Hospitalization for these patients can be lengthy, in some cases up to a few years, but for the most part the psychosis is relatively short-lived and the patient can be helped by being redirected into new and worthwhile activities, so that life again takes on the meaning it formerly had.

Even in "normal" aging a number of physiological changes take place, and their effect is to some degree correlated with psychological processes. For instance, the brain decreases in size and the number of neurons declines. The intellectual skill of the aging person decreases, although probably not as rapidly as some intelligence tests indicate.

The intelligence test presents a particular problem for the aged. First, it requires better eyesight than some old people have, and it requires coordination, which many lose. Some investigators have noted that many older people just don't care about intelligence tests—not that they should particularly, but the results do become distorted because of this lack of interest. Finally, many older persons approach problems in a relatively fixed way; after all, they have usually been handling them in the same fashion for decades, and this set pattern decreases their flexibility. Thus, while we can safely say that advancing age is accompanied by a decline in intelligence *as measured by the tests*, and possibly in "real" intelligence to some degree,

174   Elderly women in an institution; they have little to do, and their lifestyle is extremely regimented and depersonalized (*B. D. Vidibor*)

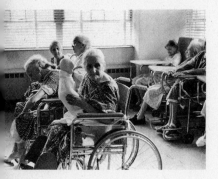

175 Tom Ingram, 101 years old, and his 96-year-old wife. Though they live in a nursing home, they are together, maintaining their family ties and interests (*UPI*)

many people are still around (some you probably know yourself) who are not far removed from the century mark and are still outwitting us [Bromley, 1966; Birren, 1959]. Although researchers have frequently reported that old people show marked deficits in learning and memory, with Ss in good physical health, employed, and active in the community these supposed deficits fail to show up [Keevil-Rogers and Schnore, 1969].

The most serious problem with the aging process is that our society does not recognize the elderly lady or man as a person deserving of respect and does not provide a place within its framework for them. Over one-half of the aged who live alone today subsist on under $1000 a year [Beva, 1972]. Thus, the psychological difficulties involved in aging are probably far more prominent than is usually realized. The major problem is *dependency* on others; the person who was once independent is no longer able to function as skillfully as the young do. Survival in old age is clearly related to independence, which in turn is based on some financial independence, good health, and, with luck, a marriage partner. All of these reduce dependence on others [Pfeiffer, 1970]. Most critical of all is good health. Studies demonstrate that poor health tends to lead to social isolation, loss of abilities, and "give-up-itis" [Ellison, 1969].

Activities such as camping, interestingly enough, are very effective in helping old people to feel more a part of things, especially if some work is involved which makes them feel useful [Hickey, 1969]. A mistake that is sometimes made is assuming that asking the elderly to help is unfair or taxing. They would far rather be taxed than be excess baggage.* Managers of some successful retirement homes, for example, have assigned jobs to the patients commensurate with their capabilities rather than hiring outside help [Kleemeier, 1960].

Institutionalization itself is not the critical factor. Loss of usefulness, drastic changes in living patterns, and physical illness that brings about some institutionalization seem to be more important in creating the negative effects that may result from being placed in an institution. The most critical phase is the *meaning* of and *anticipation* of institutionalization. These cause the most difficulty. In other words, institutionalization may present few difficulties to the elderly if there is continued enjoyment of life with grandchildren or if some meaningful activity is available [Lieberman, 1969].

Involutional psychosis occurs in late middle age; another classification of mental illness resulting from aging is called **senile psychosis**. In senile psychosis, typically psychotic behavior patterns prevail; however, the symptoms are related specifically to the onset of old age and typically involve confusion of thought processes and memory lapses. For years the assumption was made that senility is directly related to deterioration of the brain, but

---

* The late Dr. Robert Kleemeier, a genuine expert on the problems of aging, always used to tell us in class never to shy away from asking grandmothers to baby-sit (within reason).

it has been extremely difficult to find a notable correlation between this physical condition and psychological behavior. In other words, one would expect that the amount of brain damage or physical disability would have a high positive correlation with mental illness. It does not; the correlation is only moderate. In fact, some investigators have found that brain damage occurs frequently in normal people, whereas minimal brain damage is occasionally found in abnormal persons [Raskin, 1956]. This finding agrees with the fact that many people with brain tumors live out their lives with no obvious difficulty; others seem to react strongly to the tumors. Within reason—omitting massive tumors, massive brain damage, and the like—senile psychosis seems to be primarily the result of such psychological factors as major trauma, despair, or hopelessness.

SUMMARY

The various theories that try to explain the sources of mental illness are just theories, though each seems to have something to contribute to a fuller explanation of what causes mental health problems.

Freud emphasized the various stages of development and the satisfaction of needs during these particular stages. Sullivan extended the Freudian system and emphasized the specific relationships between people as more important than the stages. Rogers concentrated on an existential approach which stressed the person's need to fulfill himself or achieve self-actualization. According to any of these systems, if things go awry, mental illness could develop.

The learning theorists specifically emphasized various habits, conditionings, and learned events that occur in the development of a deviant personality. Learning inappropriate methods for handling oneself is one kind of faulty learning. Or the person might be subjected to a bizarre environment where strange associations are made, or he might learn to generalize from one set of events to many—for example, fear of mother generalizes to fear of women.

Most theorists agree that certain common elements are involved in the formation of mental illness. First is conflict, which leads to anxiety. Second is overuse of defense mechanisms, which tends to distort the real world. Third is faulty interpersonal relationships, which lead to loneliness and insecurity.

The two major categories of mental illness are neurosis and psychosis. Neurosis is a moderately severe disorder that interferes to some extent with life functioning. Psychosis is usually a major maladjustment involving unusual or disordered thought processes.

Character disorders are considered a form of mental illness, but the patient rarely shows the feelings of guilt or anxiety typically found in neurosis or the confusion typical of psychosis. Character disorder is something of a catchall category.

The major psychotic reaction is schizophrenia, which involves withdrawing from reality, living in a private world, having delusions and hallucinations, and exhibiting unusual motor behavior. Although no conclusive evidence shows that schizophrenia is inherited, data do indicate clearly that the problem runs in families. Studies of twins suggest that individuals frequently inherit a tendency toward schizophrenic behavior, which is supplemented by a poor environment, and the illness then develops.

Organic psychosis involves an actual deterioration of the brain which in turn results in many behaviors characteristic of schizophrenia.

Involutional psychosis, an illness of middle age, is characterized by depression and centers on loss of loved ones and feeling unimportant in the world. Senile psychosis can involve brain deterioration, but not always. It is a psychosis of old age which resembles involutional psychosis but is characterized by more "mental confusion."

CHAPTER TWENTY-FOUR
TREATING MENTAL ILLNESS

Throughout the preceding two chapters I have been using the terms *psychologist* and *psychiatrist* without making a distinction between them and without pointing up the differences among various kinds of psychologists. This is the place to make these differences clear.

Psychologists can be divided into an almost endless list of job categories; some counsel students in schools, some teach, some work in industry, some work in mental hospitals, and on and on. Forcing the issue, however, we can divide psychologists into two major groups, those who do research and those who work with people on a face-to-face basis. Even then, innumerable combinations exist—those who teach, do research, *and* work in industry; those who do research *and* treat mental patients; those who work in industry *and* teach; and so on.

Psychologists whose primary responsibility is research are usually subdivided into types according to their area of specialization. For instance, there are physiological psychologists, social psychologists, experimental psychologists, and experimental clinical psychologists (those who do research on mental patients; *clinical* is taken from the word *clinic*).

Psychologists who work directly with people, seeking mainly to assist them with their problems, are called either *counseling* or *clinical psychologists*. Counseling psychologists deal primarily with people who are not mental patients, and they work in a setting that emphasizes vocational assistance, resolution of troublesome problems, or ability testing. Clinical psychologists deal with patients in a mental hospital, clinic, or private practice. This distinction can become blurred, of course; the school counselor, for instance, may deal with a student's mental illness. In general, however, the terms *counseling* and *clinical psychologist* reflect a difference in emphasis, with the counselors handling normal people with problems and the clinicians abnormal people.

The typical *psychologist*, no matter what type he is, usually has a Ph.D. (doctor of philosophy degree) in psychology. After graduating from college, the psychologist continues school for about four years and obtains his degree in that specialty. The clinical psychologist puts in an additional year of internship in a hospital or mental health facility, where he receives supervised training in dealing with the problems of others. The Ph.D. clinical psychologist, then, typically receives about five years of training in psychology after earning his bachelor's degree. Psychologists in other specialties receive four years of training because they do not complete an internship.

A *psychiatrist* is a medical doctor who spends four years in medical school, earns the M.D. degree, and puts in a year as a regular medical intern dealing with physical problems. At that point he begins to specialize in the mental health field. Additional training in mental health and treatment can include one to three years of hospital residency, training which resembles an apprenticeship. The number of residency years depends on the physician and the hospital's program.

Historically, the medical doctor was first on the scene in handling mental health problems. In those early years, mental health workers were mostly physicians. The physician, like the minister, had been a traditional source of problem solving for individuals, so the transition from being a physician to being a formal physician-psychiatrist was not a difficult one to make. Freud was a physician, although he emphasized that it was not necessary to have a medical degree to treat mental patients. You may have heard at one time or another the term *psychoanalyst.* Such a practitioner is usually a psychiatrist who specializes in the Freudian technique of treating mental illness. A psychiatrist who uses *any* technique other than Freud's is called a *psychotherapist.* Either a clinical psychologist or a psychiatrist can be a psychotherapist; the term means simply one who treats others for mental problems. For that matter, *anyone* conceivably could be a psycho-therapist, although such a state of affairs probably is undesirable.

All is not well between psychiatrists and clinical psychologists, although their relationship seems to become a little more harmonious each year. The source of conflict between the two disciplines lies in the question of which group, if either, is better qualified to handle mental patients. Psychiatrists believe that they are better equipped to handle the whole person—both their physical *and* mental problems—because they hold a medical degree. Psychologists, on the other hand, feel that *they* are better equipped to handle the psychological aspects of people because they have had lengthier formal training in psychology as such.

About the only major difference that I can detect between the two groups is that the psychiatrist can prescribe drugs for the patients. As a number of authors have pointed out, however, the psychiatrist does not handle the patient's physical ailments if he suspects a major physical diffi-culty; instead, the psychiatrist calls in another physician, usually one who specializes in something other than psychiatry [Allbee, 1969]. The battle, if that is what it should be called, does not center around whether the patients need medical supervision or examination (they do); the issue is who is better qualified to administer psychological treatment.

The solution seems fairly obvious when we examine the problem historically and scrutinize research done on the effectiveness of various treatments used on mental patients. First, the psychologist entered the mental health field because during World War II a demand developed to deal with the large number of cases of mental illness. There were just not enough psychiatrists to go around, so psychologists began administering treatment to patients [Rotter, 1964]. The same situation exists today: Both disciplines are badly needed, and it is highly improbable that one is better or worse than the other. In fact, research we will cover a little later tends to indicate that treatment by psychologist or psychiatrist is equally effective (or ineffective, as the case may be).

RELIEVING MENTAL ILLNESS

A major function of the psychiatrist or clinical psychologist is to provide methods for the patient to deal more effectively with the problems he faces. *Cure* is the term used frequently, but the word is too strong; *relief* or *relearning* is more appropriate, for mental illness is a style of life that can be altered but not entirely removed. In other words, an aspirin can cure a headache, but dealing with mental illness involves providing maximum relief from problems, not removing all problems, and a process of training the patient in techniques for better handling of his problems.*

importance of the healer image

The doctor, whether a psychologist or a psychiatrist, does not help the patient to solve problems just by using the special techniques of his profession. Many researchers have pointed out that the symbolism of being a doctor is itself a major help to the patient. Just as the voodoo witch doctors were able to cause sickness or death because people believed in their powers, considerable evidence shows that the mental health worker helps the patient to some extent just because he holds a position of authority and society has labeled him a healer. The image of the healer in our society dates back to the time of Christ and the early church. Following in the tradition of Christ as a healer, the first major hospitals were built like churches; each had an altar in the center with wards for patients leading out in various directions from the altar. In keeping with this, priests were actually the first physicians, for disease was considered to be the result of sin [Cartwright, 1972]. Thus, the importance of the powers of the symbolic healer has filtered down to the present day.

To reinterpret this idea slightly, the symbolism of being a doctor provides the patient with the *belief* that help is at hand. Belief, of itself, is considered by many professionals to be the most effective ingredient in psychotherapy.† Among the many studies performed in this area is an intriguing one that dealt with warts. The wart was colored with a bright dye, and the patient was led to believe that the wart would disappear when

---

* In the following pages *cure* refers to either of these—providing relief and/or learning to handle problems.
† From *psyche* ("mind") and *therapy* ("treatment").

the dye wore off. This technique worked as effectively as other methods, including surgery [Bloch, 1961]. Even tissue damage by an ulcer can be healed by injecting distilled water if the physician assures the patient that his new medicine will cure the ailments* [Volgyesi, 1961].

These dramatic examples were deliberately picked to illustrate that the role of doctor (psychologist or psychiatrist) is of utmost importance in producing effective treatment. Obviously I don't wish to imply that these men are doing nothing more than going around being "doctorish" and evoking cures.

Nonetheless, this background is interesting, for we are going to find that the rate of cure with mental illness is essentially the same no matter what treatment is used. The power which the mental healer is assumed to have, plus some therapeutic techniques, seems to produce whatever improvement occurs.

Dozens of times within any year the newspapers report that a drug cure has been found for a certain mental illness. Strangely enough, this sort of cure often holds up for only a short time. Upon closer examination, researchers generally have discovered that patients were told they were receiving a new drug that was quite effective; the cure seemed once again to be based on hope, which wore off after the treatment no longer involved a "miracle" drug and the excitement about it died down. Hope, faith, and belief must not be discounted as therapeutic agents.

STYLES OF PSYCHOTHERAPY

Mental health professionals engage in many kinds of therapy, all of them designed to relieve the patient's problems. The best known of the therapies is psychotherapy. *Psychotherapy* is basically a technique designed to help the patient resolve his conflicts and problems, among which the most pressing issue is usually, "Who am I and what do I want in life?" [Orlinsky, 1970]. The process involves two people sitting down to discuss the problems of one of them; hence, it is probably the oldest known form of therapy and conceivably could even include two women talking over one's problems while washing clothes. The therapies with which we will deal, however, involve a relationship between doctor (psychologist, psychiatrist, or psychoanalyst) and patient.

Freudian psychoanalysis

The first organized, step-by-step therapeutic process is the one devised by Freud, *psychoanalysis.*† So many cartoons have shown a patient on the couch, or a doctor on the couch, or some such variation, that by now what goes on in psychoanalysis should be familiar to everyone. In most psychoanalysts'

---

* At least it often works. Standard medical treatment is preferable in this type of case, especially because suggestion can cover up the symptoms of actual physical illness until the illness has gotten worse.

† Analysis or examination of the psyche.

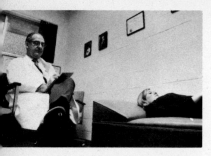

176   Classical Freudian therapy, in which the patient lies on a couch and the analyst, sitting behind her, takes notes (*Van Bucher*)

offices today, the couch has been replaced by a lounge chair, probably in reaction to the cartoons. However, the majority of psychoanalysts, beginning with Freud, have at one time or another used a couch, and for good reasons. The psychoanalyst is not a "real person" in the therapy situation; his role is to become whomever the patient wants him to become. For example, suppose the patient is trying to resolve conflicts he had with his father; in order for him to do so, the Freudians maintain, he must begin to perceive the analyst as his father.* This *transference*† does not occur literally, of course—but if the patient gets angry, the Freudians suggest, he is getting angry at his father, who is represented by the analyst. Only in this way can the patient relive his emotional feelings toward his father and examine them for what they are. The couch, then, facilitates the process of transference because the analyst is inconspicuous. A second function of the couch is to provide an atmosphere in which the patient feels free to express his inner thoughts, desires, and conflicts. He will supposedly be more free to bring these out if he is not looking the analyst directly in the eye.

Having settled himself on the couch, the patient, by reliving his past experiences with the aid of the analyst, can begin to see that his reactions at the *adult* level are the same reactions he had as a child, but they are no longer fitting or appropriate. The process of reliving the past is like a stream of consciousness, in which the patient is free to say anything he wants, anything that happens to come to his mind; this sort of thinking is called *free association*. Freud thought that free association was effective because the energy bottled up in the person would drive him—given this opportunity to be free and open—to speak about the areas of conflict that center on his problem.

Contrary to popular belief, the analyst does not sit silently, never saying a word, for so many dollars an hour. He does allow the patient to do most of the talking—because the patient himself is the only one who can work out the problem, with the doctor's guidance. However, the analyst speaks when he feels it necessary to interpret what the patient is saying or to encourage him to continue discussing certain areas which the analyst feels are important to the patient's problem.

A brief and somewhat exaggerated example of the psychoanalytic process might go:

Patient: I don't feel too well today. I had a headache and I was going to stay in bed.

Analyst (*interpreting*):   You really didn't want to come in.

Patient: Well, yes, you might say that.

*This example is one of many possibilities.
†The transfer of feelings felt for one person (in this case, the father) to another (the analyst).

> Analyst (*interpreting*): Possibly we covered some material last time that you didn't want to continue discussing?
>
> Patient: (*Silence*)
>
> Analyst: Tell me what comes to your mind.
>
> Patient (*beginning to free associate*): (*Continues association and begins to get angry*)
>
> Analyst: Possibly you are angry because I remind you of someone. (*Leading the patient toward a discussion of the cause of the anger; in our theoretical guess at his problem earlier, we now assume he will eventually begin to discuss his father and the anger associated with him, which the analyst will then interpret. Once the patient sees this anger for what it is, some of the bottled-up energy will be liberated*)

Never would an actual analyst engage in such blatant, rapid interpretation and obvious leading, but these few exchanges do illustrate a process that continues over a long period of time.

Speaking of time, psychoanalysis is the longest of the therapies; it can go on for years with two or three or even five meetings a week. Except for some Freudian psychoanalysts, most therapists today feel that such extended treatment is unnecessary.

client-centered therapy An extremely popular form of psychotherapy is *client-centered therapy,* developed by Dr. Carl Rogers. If you recall the discussion in Chapter 23 about the existential approach used by Rogers, the term *client-centered* will become significant. In classical psychoanalysis, the analyst is king and controls what the patient has to say by interpreting it; in other words, the psychoanalyst's interpretation and orientation direct the patient down a path of free association that focuses on Freudian-type material. Rogers's style of therapy takes the authority from the therapist and gives it to the client. Notice that the term *client* is far more favorable than *patient*, which has a slightly negative and inferior connotation.

Rogers assumes, in the existential tradition, that the client has the potential within himself to aim toward self-actualization; the therapist's only function is to act as a sounding board [Rogers, 1951]. The key to this system is for the therapist to be a warm, accepting person who tries to understand the client's viewpoint completely and to reflect this acceptance in tone of voice and comment. The therapist is not a robot, but rarely will he interject his own personal comments—the client is in control. The therapist does *not* interpret, but merely concentrates on what the person is saying, providing an accepting human mirror for the client so he can hear and "see" himself and take corrective action on his own. The therapist, as best as he is able, tries to put himself in the role of the client, so that when the client says something, the therapist can help clarify it, but not grossly alter the content of what the client is trying to say. The atmosphere of the counseling session is one of acceptance and permissiveness, a situation that is thought to be most conducive to the full blooming of self-actualization.

Taking the same brief interview and changing the framework to fit the Rogerian system, we come up with:

> **Patient:** I don't feel too well today. I had a headache and I was going to stay in bed.
>
> **Therapist:** You just don't feel well today.
>
> **Patient:** Yes, you might say that. In fact I should have stayed home. I didn't want to come in.
>
> **Therapist:** It's difficult to do things when you don't feel well.
>
> **Patient:** Yes, it's strange, but I think I probably wouldn't have wanted to come in even if I had felt well physically.
>
> **Therapist:** You're saying that it is unpleasant to come in? Therapy is a very taxing and difficult process.
>
> **Patient:** Yes, that's it. In a way. You see, it's so difficult to face your own problems head on, if you know what I mean.
>
> **Therapist:** Yes, it's very difficult.

Here, the client is in control of the therapy situation. The client says what he wants and the therapist accepts him for what he is feeling.

The position of the therapist as authority figure does not disappear in this situation; instead, the therapist lends his power to developing the patient's *own* hypothesis about himself, by himself. Thus, the patient can accept himself and correct what problems he has. As one author has pointed out, this method of therapy is popular because nothing fits our democratic outlook better than the assumption that even the mental patient can become a new, self-made man [Harper, 1959].

rational therapy A third kind of psychotherapy is interesting because it contrasts with the fairly "soft" approach of the Rogerian and Freudian systems. *Rational therapy* is based on the assumption that the person is intellectually able to control his problems and his emotions; hence, the patient is rational.*

Problems have arisen in a person's life because he has formed incorrect assumptions about his private world. These assumptions are stored in the person's intellect and trigger emotional responses; they are stored in the form of what are called internalized sentences [Rimm, 1969]. A person who feels inadequate as the result of past psychological difficulties, for instance, says over and over to himself a sentence something like, "I am no good." As long as the intellect is allowed to keep saying this, triggering an emotional response to the sentence, the person will remain disturbed.

*The major figure in this area is Dr. Albert Ellis, discussed briefly in Chapter 18.

Rational therapy seeks to force these sentences out into the open and then quite directly confront the patient with how absurd they are. Once this has been done, the intellect theoretically can reconstruct a better sentence—for example, "I am worthwhile."

Taking the same example:

> **Patient:**   I don't feel too well today. I had a headache and I was going to stay in bed.
> **Therapist:**   You were trying to avoid coming in.
> **Patient:**   No, I don't think so. I . . .
> **Therapist:**   Of course you were. Think about it. Weren't you saying to yourself that you really can't be helped?
> **Patient:**   Well . . .
> **Therapist:**   Saying that you were beyond help? That you don't want to face the issue?
> **Patient:**   Well, yes, I guess I was. I thought that I not only couldn't be helped but wasn't even worth helping.
> **Therapist:**   That's ridiculous, isn't it?

The first thing that probably strikes you is that this therapy is pretty rugged, or if it isn't that, at least it could make some patients hopping mad. Interestingly enough, if the client does get mad and swears at the therapist, he will probably swear back at the client [Ellis, 1962]. This therapy has a rough-and-tumble style that can be quite effective with some people. It is fairly popular, although not as popular as the Rogerian approach.

The important point about all these therapies is that certain ones seem to fit some people's temperament better than others. And each of them has effected cures for some people and not for others. No universally successful therapy exists. Studies have identified at least two clearly distinct types of patients, and one could infer that other types exist that are not as well delineated. One typical patient group wants intervention by the therapist, looks for an intimate, friendly relationship with him, and desires his approval or disapproval. A second major group wants a detached and objective therapist to aid them. Psychotherapy usually suits the first group well. Another kind of therapy called behavioral modification fits the second type of patients [Begley and Lieberman, 1970]. We will discuss this method shortly.

Many other types of therapy also involve face-to-face discussion, but the three discussed here cover the field fairly well; most therapists combine parts of these and other theories and add a dash of their own personalized techniques.

There is no right or wrong therapy, either. As you will see in a moment, other approaches utilize entirely different therapeutic devices, and

177   The contemporary slogan "Black is beautiful" that promotes healthy internalized sentences toward the self (*Ken Beckles*)

yet they seem to be neither better nor worse than face-to-face therapy. If someone could figure out how to fit the patient to the therapist, and vice versa, most of the difficulty would be solved. Some authors contend that it doesn't make too much difference which therapy you follow as long as the patient is convinced, the therapist is convinced, and the two work well together [Fingarette, 1963]. Comparisons of relationships between therapist and patient indicate that when therapists have considerable experience, their techniques tend to be similar even though formally they may claim to be one type of therapist rather than another [Howard et al., 1970].

Psychotherapy refers to *any* treatment of the psyche, so strictly speaking the behavior-modification therapies fall into that classification. However, these therapies do not involve lengthy discussions between therapist and patient—although encouragement from the therapist is still critical, as is the patient's expectation of help [Wilkins, 1972]. The therapies to be discussed, which center around specific learning-theory techniques, are separated from psychotherapy and are collectively called *behavior-modification therapy* or behavioral therapy. Under this broad heading, three fairly distinctive methods have been developed for treating patients.

behavior-modification therapies

Learning-theory therapy.   The first is a simple therapy based on learning-theory principles, especially reinforcement, extinction, and operant conditioning. While reinforcement obviously occurs in all therapies, this particular one preplans, or sets forth from the outset, certain goals (operant behaviors or acts) that are to be achieved by using learning principles. One child in a nursery school, for instance, spent 80 percent of his time alone. The experimenters decided that the teacher, who had been trying to help the child by consoling him, was actually rewarding and increasing his solitary behavior. A formal program of change was instituted. When the child stayed alone, the teacher ignored him; the moment he joined the other children, (an operant behavior), she entered the group and gave her full attention to all of them. Thus, the teacher was extinguishing the behavior of being alone and reinforcing the behavior of being with others. The child eventually was spending 60 percent of his time with the group [Bandura, 1967].

Simple learning by conditioning is not something exclusively developed by our culture. To train a male child in western Nigeria to stop bedwetting, a toad is tied by a string to the child's penis. When the child wets, the toad croaks, waking the child, until he eventually learns to control his bladder [Torrey, 1972]. Less elaborate devices for the same purposes have been used in the United States such as a buzzer sounding when the child wets the bed.

Desensitization therapy.   Currently one very popular form of behavior-modification therapy is desensitization therapy. Based on the theory of Dr. Joseph Wolpe, desensitization rests firmly on principles of learning; the goal of therapy is to recondition the patient to associate pleasantness rather than anxiety with certain feared objects or events. The patient is desensitized to his anxiety. You may recall a discussion of proactive and retroactive inhibition in Chapter 9. Ignoring the *pro-* or *retro-* for the present, the basic ingredient in the situation is that one type of material inhibits another type of material. Using this idea, Wolpe suggests that two opposite reactions to a situation cannot exist at the same time, so he attempts to replace anxiety by its opposite, relaxation. For instance, a person may live in sheer terror of being in an elevator; if this terror can be replaced by a relaxed feeling, then the problem should disappear.

Wolpe starts off at a very basic level: The patient is instructed to think of something that makes him mildly anxious. When he gets a mental image of this mildly anxiety-producing situation, he is trained to relax, thus associating the feeling of relaxation with the mildly anxious situation. Next the patient thinks of something that produces more anxiety, and again he learns to relax. These sessions continue, building up and up until the patient, at least in theory, is able to imagine one of his most feared situations and yet associate it with relaxation. By this technique, relaxation inhibits anxiety; the two cannot live together, and the symptoms are removed.

Relaxation can be induced just by talking to the patient and having him rest in a lounge chair or on a sofa. Sometimes hypnosis is effective for inducing this relaxed state. In other cases, breathing carbon dioxide* is very relaxing and sleep-inducing. Any of these methods can be used to produce the state of relaxation [Wolpe, 1966, 1958].

One major objection to this kind of therapy—that it is too superficial—is based partly on truth and partly on psychological bias. Most psychologists tend to think that problems originate in deep-seated conflicts and to regard the patient's inadequate behavior as merely a *symptom* of the conflict, not as the conflict itself. In other words, curing a compulsive hand washer of his hand washing by using inhibition techniques (via reconditioning) doesn't get at the *heart* of the problem actually causing the hand washing. If this is true, the symptom will supposedly be replaced by another one (maybe worse). The issue is whether the therapist is actually getting rid of the *problem*, or just treating its symptom. But, as one author has pointed out, some may benefit just from getting rid of the symptom. If you can be cured of claustrophobia and learn to get into an elevator without falling apart, for example, you may get enough relief to function well in life, even if you haven't resolved the problem that caused this behavior [Eysenck, 1960]. In fact, a number of studies show that a new symptom does not appear to replace the old one, but many psychologists remain unconvinced. In any case, we are again faced with the very simple but frustrating reality that desensitization works for some people but not for others.

---

* Not to be confused with carbon monoxide, which cures the patient by killing him.

There has been some discussion about whether relaxation really inhibits anxiety. Some argue that the expectation of cure itself is enough; they have supported this idea by taking one group of subjects and not going through the elaborate procedure of desensitization, but merely attaching various mechanical devices to the Ss and suggesting that this treatment would work. It did work—as well, in fact, as treatment of another group that was given full desensitization [Marcia et al., 1969]. This study reminds you, in a way, of some of the results of hypnosis studies. One major problem with the relaxation method is that it requires the patient to actually *relax*. Some cannot relax long enough for the therapy to be effective [Glick, 1970]. The mechanical device or other therapy is necessary in these cases.

Aversive conditioning.   Learning theory would naturally include punishment in its repertoire of therapies. It comes under the heading *aversive conditioning*—conditioning a person to avoid a certain response. Such conditioning is far from new. The Romans used to make their alcoholics drink wine from a jug inhabited by a live eel. The disgusting, nauseating potion caused vomiting [Coleman, 1964]. The Romans were attempting to associate the unpleasantness of sickness with drinking alcohol.

Similar conditioning is used today, only without the eels. Medications that cause severe nausea and vomiting are put in alcoholic beverages, with the hope that the two will be associated. In other cases, alcoholics are given tablets that will induce vomiting if they decide to take a drink.

The consensus is that moderate success can be attributed to such techniques, depending on the motivation and personality of the patient. Some benefit maximally from the social pressure of Alcoholics Anonymous; others respond best to conditioning. The record of AA is so impressive that it seems to be *the* method for most people; AA claims 75 percent success in removing alcoholic behavior patterns, but this figure does not take into account the thousands who won't go to AA meetings or become involved in their activities. Once an alcoholic gets involved in AA, the chances of his getting off alcohol are good. For those not suited to AA, aversive conditioning should not be passed off lightly. Among a very rugged group, "lifetime alcoholics" of skid row who don't want to be treated, aversive conditioning produced a 46 percent remission of drinking [Bourne et al., 1969].

The success of aversive-conditioning methods in affecting a continuing change in life style has not been adequately studied, but then neither have the lasting effects of other methods [Buss, 1966]. At least we know that aversive conditioning works some of the time for some people, that the rate of improvement is somewhere around 50 percent in most studies, and that this improvement lasts at least six months in most studies reported. Most important, this therapy takes little time compared to other types [Ullman, 1969].

Modifying homosexual behavior.   Behavioral modification has also progressed along the same lines in treating homosexuals. Homosexuals have been made sick to their stomachs while viewing pictures of nude men, and then injected with a sex hormone while they were viewing nude women [K. Freund, 1960]. The experimenter in this case reports that approximately 40 percent of his voluntary* patients stayed away from homosexuality for extended periods of time. The study sounds impressive, and in fact it is—but one should not be misled by the injection of sex hormones into the patients. This treatment may have had only a psychological effect; in fact, the use of sex hormones with homosexuals is at best a questionable method for inducing physical change. Probably the aversive stimuli, coupled with the reward of the experimenter's interest in the patient, is sufficient to explain the results. Furthermore, taking into consideration what we know about homosexuality, we must assume that these particular people were in some respects amenable to the idea of not being homosexuals. Some of this experimenter's subjects were not voluntary—but I do not know of a study confined to homosexuals who do *not* want to become heterosexual. Taking the above study, for instance, when the voluntary and involuntary subjects were lumped together and followed up at least three years later, the "cure rate" was down to 25 percent.

group therapy   We have touched on group therapy before without so labeling it. You may recall the behavior of the Hutterites when one of their members began to show signs of strangeness: The group came to the rescue of the individual. Essentially the same procedure operates in group therapy, except that the group is formed deliberately to handle behavioral problems; it is not a subculture.

   Group therapy is usually overseen by a psychologist, who organizes and leads the individuals until they are functioning together. At that time he still keeps part of his leadership role, but he tends to recede into the background and let the group handle itself.

   In group-therapy sessions, members share their problems with one another. This sharing process has a tremendous advantage in that the patient finds other people who have similar difficulties; he learns that he is not alone and that he can obtain support from other group members in his attempts to cope with everyday life. The group provides a more realistic world for the patient than does individual psychotherapy. If a patient attains a satisfactory level of adjustment, he is going to have to face the outside world again, and from the beginning the group provides a more realistic approximation of the outside world than does sharing problems with the therapist alone.

   Some groups operate on a deeply interpretive level; that is, leader and members deal with each other's unconscious behavior. This approach

---

*Those not brought in by the police.

can be both effective and dangerous. If the leader knows what he is doing, all is well; if not, some members of the group can become very upset from having their inner thoughts exposed.

The disadvantage of group therapy is obvious: Some people cannot bring themselves to let others know about their problems. But surprisingly few such people are around. The first sessions of group therapy may be rather deadly; it may seem that no one is going to talk, and certainly no one is going to give himself away. However, after a few weeks the group begins to move along, and sharing common anxieties and working out problems together become the norms.

You are probably acquainted with the many types of "new" group therapies that have sprung up in the past few years. In *marathon group therapy*, people have been "voluntarily forced" to stay together in intimate discussion for a day or more. Short-term personality changes do occur: The Ss generally do become more socially positive, but how long this lasts is unknown [Young, 1970]. In *nude marathon therapy*, theoretically, if everyone behaves himself, the individual is stripped bare to his soul and learns that the world is full of people who are just like him when they are nude and they free their spirits. And almost every executive has been subjected to what is called *sensitivity training*, in which Ss supposedly learn to bare their psyches and share with others.

The goals are exemplary: People learn to live together and share, and it works for large numbers of people. My negative feelings come from the fact that these therapies are much like LSD; they are disastrous for some people who cannot cope with overexposure of their psyches, who need to be left alone. Or, in the words of two authors, some of these techniques constitute interpersonal overkill, meaning that, when administered en masse,

178–179 Group therapy may consist mainly of talking about the participants' problems, or it may resort to more unusual and active forms of interaction (*Van Bucher, Photo Researchers; Ken Regan, Camera 5*)

180   (*Paul Fusco*)

they slaughter too many of the innocent [Stein, 1970; Kuehn and Crinella, 1969]. Another author has brought up a rather important question regarding these therapies: Is it absolutely necessary that the healthiest relationships involve laying bare innermost thoughts and feelings? [Smith, 1970]. Nonetheless, many benefits can be derived from these encounters. If you are a shy and sensitive person it is still possible to gain from the experience, but you run a high risk of psychological damage if you wind up in a group where the leader is very aggressive, challenging, and confronts each subject with the problems he is having, aggressively forcing him to admit them [Yalom and Lieberman, 1971]. If your leader is like this, it is probably best to quit the group and find another one.

chemotherapy   *Chemotherapy* refers to the use of drugs to relieve the symptoms of mental illness; obviously, this kind of therapy must be handled by a psychiatrist who has a medical degree, not a psychologist. The main drugs used are tranquilizers and energizers, but the distinction between them is neither precise nor simple and requires the physician to exercise a great deal of knowledge and skill in determining which drug to use. Apparently these drugs interact chemically with enzymes, altering the operation of the neural networks. The exact reaction of a particular patient to a particular drug is unpredictable; so-called tranquilizers can act as energizers *or* tranquilizers, depending upon the person's constitution and the dosage prescribed.

A case in point is the so-called hyperactive child who cannot sit still at meals, talks too much, wears out toys from constant activity, and continuously fidgets. Remarkable changes in behavior have resulted from the administration of amphetamines, an *energizing* agent. Since one of the effects of amphetamines is to stimulate the release of chemicals controlling nerve impulses in the hypothalamus and reticular formation, it is hypothesized that the child is hyperactive because there is a chemical imbalance in these areas and that the drug restores normal balance, making the child calm down [Stewart, 1970].

As a generalization, however, tranquilizers are given to anxious patients and energizers to depressed patients. In any case, patients who formerly could not be controlled are now manageable without brain surgery, which is always a drastic step to take. Drugs are *the* treatment for acute cases of schizophrenia. In some cases, psychotics have responded remarkably well to drugs alone; no major personality changes seem to have occurred, but the person was able to control himself again and became far more useful. Drugs in combination with behavior-modification therapy have been successful, but with very disturbed people psychotherapy has been of minimal value [May, 1968].

With less severely disturbed people, drugs are considered only a stepping-stone; they make the patient manageable so that psychotherapy or another therapy can be performed.

181 *(Paul Fusco)*

The major disadvantage to drugs is that they tend to fog the patient's mind, especially the psychotic, who is given heavy doses. Thought processes become even more obscure than they were before, but for the present this slight confusion is still preferable to chaining the patient to the wall or keeping him in a straitjacket, as was done in the past [Krakowski, 1969; Snyder, 1961].

One should not overlook the ***placebo effect*** of using medication. A placebo, in Latin, meaning "I shall please," is a medicine that has no physical effect but does work psychologically. Some people call placebos "sugar pills," but the placebo effect is not limited to fake pills. When the psychiatrist administers a real drug, he is still saying, "I care about you," or "This will help you." Thus, actual physical reactions are interlaced with psychological responses. The placebo effect is operative in the remarkable initial "cure" by use of wonder drugs in mental illness, and it is likely to be prevalent in any sort of therapy, even those therapies without drugs. The *act* of performing therapy gives hope and belief in cure, which conceivably can mask the effects, if any, of a specific technique used by the practitioner.

Thus, one can find a number of studies of psychotherapy or chemotherapy that may indicate success *not* because the treatment is effective but because the patient believes that it works.

electroconvulsive therapy

In *electroconvulsive therapy* (ECT), a shock is deliberately introduced into the brain of the patient in order to produce convulsions. The procedure is *relatively* safe and is not painful, but certainly can be a very frightening event. ECT is considered most effective with severely depressed patients, and in these cases it meets with frequent success, although no one knows why or how it works. It may even improve the patient because it carries a placebo effect or it may be such an unpleasant experience that it jolts the patient from his depression. The actual physical changes that occur are best summed up as confusion and temporary loss of memory, which disappear after a few hours. With continued shock treatments, however, the memory loss persists for longer and longer periods of time.

Attempts have been made to reduce the loss of abilities or memories from ECT by shocking only one hemisphere rather than the older treatment of shocking both of them. The rationale for this is that if you shock the nondominant hemisphere, then you are less likely to disrupt thought process, speech, or memory. The difference in technique has been of questionable value, something you probably could have already guessed from the discussion of the brain in the early chapters. If you recall, the various activities controlled by the brain are scattered throughout both the hemispheres, and it is difficult to avoid creating some havoc no matter which hemisphere you choose to shock [Dornbush, 1972].

In general, *psychologists* object strongly to the use of ECT. Their main objections are that no one knows what it does, why it works, or how beneficial it is. Furthermore, it completely fails to come to grips with whatever is causing the problem for the patient [Ullman and Krasner, 1969].

Psychologists would be most likely to give in on the use of ECT with *severely* depressed patients. Their major objection is that this treatment is frequently used indiscriminately—it might be used with any patient having almost any kind of problem, and its effectiveness outside of deep depression is very questionable.

It is primarily for these reasons that George McGovern's initial running mate in the 1972 elections, Tom Eagleton, was a real victim of lack of public knowledge about the workings of ECT. Receiving electroconvulsive shock tells us nothing whatsoever about the condition of the patient. Some hospitals and some physicians routinely give ECT to their patients. What justification there is for this is hard to come by, but it nonetheless happens quite frequently. Therefore, Senator Eagleton could have been suffering from something not much more severe than the occasional depressions and letdowns which all of us have in the course of our survival of the process of day-to-day living.

THE EFFECTIVENESS OF PSYCHOTHERAPY

Some similarities do exist among the various types of treatment, even though they seem entirely different on the surface. For one thing, all of them provide the placebo effect. For another, two apparently dissimilar systems, such as Freud's and Rogers's, still have in common the fact that they reward and reinforce the patient's behavior; that is, Rogers stresses that the patient can cure himself; the Freudians do the same thing by allowing the patient to bring up his own dreams, to free-associate, and to react positively or negatively to the interpretations. In other words, when you get right down to it, the therapies have a common denominator of faith in the patient, even though it is sometimes subtle. Except for the behavioral therapies, all of them stress insight, or looking into the nature of one's problems—that is, closely examining our motives in order to understand ourselves.

The major divergent therapy is behavioral therapy, which involves little discussion and is more mechanical (for lack of a better term) in its approach. Even here, though, one still has the patient's problem, recognition of its difficulty, an interested party, some technique of therapy, and the placebo effect [London, 1964].

I find it very disconcerting to end this book by pointing out a really important weakness in psychotherapy: No one knows if it works.

We do know that roughly 60 percent of patients are discharged from hospitals as improved, no matter what type of therapy they received [Schaefer, 1956]. Some studies have shown that roughly 60 percent of mentally disturbed patients improve without any therapy at all [Eysenck, 1961]. Other, more definitive studies show about 60 percent of neurotics and 40 percent of psychotics improve without outside help. Obviously the last two studies have met with violent criticism but no concrete evidence has been offered to refute them. Some rather ridiculous arguments against these studies have appeared, though. One suggested that although we don't know if therapy does any good, we don't have any evidence that it hurts anybody [Rosensweig, 1964]. This type of squabbling gets everyone nowhere fast.

In recent years, "self-cures" have come under close scrutiny. Improvement without professional help seems to be closely related to three factors: amount of education, marital status, and employment. Higher level of education reduces financial and environmental problems, allowing the person to work through some of his problems more thoroughly; being married in many instances provides a source of support from the partner; stable employment provides opportunities to feel useful and to get some companionship at work. Apparently time in and of itself does not necessarily help in the cure [Subotnik, 1972; Jansen and Nickles, 1973]. Thus, what looks like a "magical," self-induced cure often seems to have some basic and important factors working as "therapists" behind the scene [Saenger, 1970]. But since higher levels of so-called cure rates without treatment do not exist, there is always the strong possibility that psychotherapy can be of some benefit [Subotnik, 1972].

You might wonder whether any studies *support* the usefulness of therapy. Indeed, hundreds, if not thousands, do. The difficulty is that each particular therapist claims a very high rate of cure for his own therapy, which makes one wonder sometimes. Nonetheless, the patients seem to benefit from the contact, or at least they claim they do, and why question them if they feel they have been helped?

But what about the studies that show hospital patients can be "cured" without doing anything to them? This finding is dramatic, but probably somewhat distorted. Just being hospitalized is sometimes curative; hospitalization brings attention from nurses, physicians, and psychologists, and usually considerable support and love from families. If psychotherapy is a fraud—although this is not likely, even if it may be overrated—then it should be discarded. On the other hand, we have no evidence that therapy is a fake. Thousands of patients and therapists stoutly maintain that it is beneficial.

We started with a question mark, and we are ending with one. That is the frustration and the challenge of the hybrid science.

SUMMARY

Although psychologists have many different tasks, in the area of mental health they are often confused with psychiatrists, and vice versa. A psychiatrist has a medical degree and can dispense medicine as well as perform psychotherapy. The psychologist engages in psychotherapy, but cannot provide any medication. The psychologist has more years of training in the broad field of psychology, but probably about the same amount of time in actual *therapy* training. The major bone of contention is whether courses in perception, learning, intelligence, and so on make the psychologist better qualified than the physician, who has spent approximately the same amount of time in medical training. There is no answer to the dispute, and never will be. Both provide a service, and good and bad therapists work in both fields.

In any case, both the psychologist and psychiatrist benefit from the healer image and the patient's belief that help is at hand.

Freudian psychotherapy, called psychoanalysis, is based primarily on transference and free association, with the therapist seeking out conflicts rooted in childhood experiences.

Rogers's client-centered therapy differs from the Freudian approach in the great confidence that is placed in the patient and his ability to resolve conflicts and self-actualize himself.

Ellis's rational therapy, based on the restructuring of faulty internalized sentences, is quite direct and is based on a frontal attack on the patient's misconceptions, hopefully appealing to the intellect of the individual.

Behavior-modification therapy is based on learning principles. The least complex of these is simple reinforcement of desired acts—for example, the schoolchild who was rewarded by the teacher's presence when he joined the other children. More complex is desensitization therapy, which attempts to remove (that is, desensitize the patient to) anxiety-producing situations and create relaxation in the place of anxiety. Behavior modification also involves the technique of aversive conditioning, in which the patient is conditioned to avoid certain behaviors—for example, homosexuality or alcoholism.

Group therapy utilizes group pressure to help alter behavior and employs group comfort to support individuals through difficult times or to help them work out deep-seated problems.

Chemotherapy is simply the use of drugs to alter the physical constitution in such a way that the patient is more manageable or more relaxed. Although it has the disadvantage of producing sluggishness, it is quite effective with deeply psychotic people.

The most convincing proof that psychotherapy is beneficial is a fairly weak one, namely, that most patients seem to feel it helps. A number of studies demonstrate its effectiveness, but a large number call these results into question.

About 60 percent of neurotic patients and 40 percent of psychotic patients improve without formal therapy. Education, marital status, and employment are important factors in improvement, as can be the interest provided by hospital personnel, psychiatrists, and psychologists.

REFERENCES

AARONSON, B. S. 1972. Color perception and effect. *Amer. J. Clin. Hyp. 14:* 38–43.

ABELSON, P. H. 1970. Death from heroin. *Science 168:* 1289.

ADAMS, A. B. 1969. *Eternal quest: The story of the great naturalists.* New York: Putnam.

ADOLPH, E. F. 1941. The internal environment and behavior: Water content. *Amer. J. Psychiat. 97:* 1365–72.

ADRIAN, E. D. 1947. *The physical background of perception.* Oxford: Clarendon Press.

AGRANOFF, B. W. 1967. Memory and protein synthesis. *Sci. Amer. 216,* no. 6.

AINSWORTH, M. 1962. The effects of maternal deprivation: a review of findings and controversy in the context of research strategy. In *Deprivation of maternal care: a reassessment of its effects.* Geneva: World Health Organization.

AKERT, K.; KOELLA, W.; and HESS, R., JR. 1952. Sleep produced by electrical stimulation of the thalamus. *Amer. J. Physiol. 168:* 260–67.

ALBEE, G. W. 1969. Emerging concepts of mental illness and models of treatment: The psychological point of view. *Amer. J. Psychiat. 125:* 870–76.

ALDOUS, J., and KAMIKO, T. 1972. A cross-national study of the effects of father-absence: Japan and the United States. In M. Sussman and B. Corswell, eds., *Cross-National Family Research.* Leiden: E. J. Brill.

ALDRICH, H. 1972. Reported in *Behavior Today 3,* no. 40.

ALEXANDER, M., and LESTER, D. 1972. Fear of death in parachute jumpers. *Percept. Mot. Skills 34:* 388.

ALEXSEYEVA, T. T. 1967. Correlations of nervous and humoral factors in the development of sleep in non-disjointed twins. Quoted in R. F. Thompson, *Foundations of physiological psychology.* New York: Harper & Row.

ALLAND, A., JR. 1971. Intelligence in black and white. In C. L. Brace, G. R. Gamble, and J. T. Bond, eds., Race and intelligence. *Anthro. Studies,* no. 8. Washington, D.C.: American Anthropological Association.

ALLEN, M. M. 1944. The relation between Kuhlmann-Anderson tests and achievement in grade IV. *J. Educ. Psychol. 35:* 229–39.

ALPERN, H. P., and CRABBE, J. C. 1972. Facilitation of the long-term store of memory with strychnine. *Science 177:* 722–24.

ALPERN, M. 1971. The mystery pigment in color vision. *Psychol. Today 4,* no. 9.

ALPERT, D., and BITZER, D. L. 1970. Advances in computer-based education. *Science 167:* 1582–90.

AMADEO, M., and SHAGASS, C. 1963. Eye movements, attention, and hypnosis. *J. Nerv. Ment. Dis. 136:* 139.

ANAND, B. K.; CHHINA, G.; and SINGH, B. 1961. Some aspects of electroencephalographic studies in yogis. *Electroencephal. Clin. Neurophysiol. 13:* 452–56.

ANASTASI, A. 1968. *Psychological testing.* 3rd ed. New York: Macmillan.

———. 1971. Note on the concepts of creativity and intelligence. *J. Creative Behav. 5:* 113–16.

ANASTASI, A., and LEVEE, R. 1959. Intellectual defect and musical talent: a case report. *Amer. J. Ment. Defic. 64:* 695–702.

ANDERSON, J. E., ed. 1956. *Psychological aspects of aging.* Washington, D.C.: American Psychological Association.

ANDERSON, R. D. 1970. The history of witchcraft: a review with some psychiatric comments. *Amer. J. Psychiat. 126:* 1727–35.

ANDREWARTHA, H. G. 1961. *Introduction to the study of animal populations.* Chicago: University of Chicago.

ANNETT, J. 1967. Programmed learning. In B. M. Foss, ed., *New horizons in psychology.* Baltimore: Penguin.

AQUINAS, T. Of the cause of pleasure. *Summa theologica.*

ARONFREED, J. 1965. Internalized behavioral suppression and the timing of social punishment. *J. Personal. Soc. Psychol. 1:* 3–16.

ARONSON, E., and MILLS, J. 1959. Effect of severity of initiation on liking for a group. *J. Abnorm. Soc. Psychol. 59:* 177–81.

ASCH, S. E. 1952. *Social psychology.* Englewood Cliffs, N.J.: Prentice-Hall.

———. 1956. Studies of independence and submission to group pressure: I. a minority of one against a unanimous majority. *Psychol. Monogr. 70,* no. 416.

ASIMOV, I. 1965. *The new intelligent man's guide to science.* New York: Basic Books.

ATKINSON, R. C. 1968. The computer as a tutor. *Psychol. Today 1,* no. 8.

ATKINSON, R. C., and SHIFFRIN, R. M. 1971. The control of short-term memory. *Sci. Amer. 225,* no. 2.

ATTNEAVE, F. 1971. Multistability in perception. *Sci. Amer. 225,* no. 6.

AX, A. F. 1953. The physiological differentiation between fear and anger in humans. *Psychosom. Med. 15:* 433–42.

BACH, M. 1961. *Strange sects and curious cults.* New York: Dodd, Mead.

BACH, R. C.; LOWRY, D.; and MOYLAN, J. 1972. Training state hospital patients to be appropriately assertive. *Proceed. 80th Annual Conv. Amer. Psychol. Assn.,* vol. 7.

BACHRACH, H. 1970. Cerebral dysfunction in psychiatric patients. *Bull. Menninger Clin. 34:* 23–30.

BADEN, M. J. 1968. Drug abuse: its current status. *New York Med. 24:* 464–68.

BAGBY, J. W. 1968. Quoted in J. D. Frank, The face of the enemy. *Psychol. Today 2:* 24–29.

BAILEY, F. L. 1971. *The defense never rests.* New York: Stein & Day.

BAILEY, P. 1962. Cortex and mind. Quoted in J. M. Scher, ed., *Theories of the mind.* New York: Free Press.

BAKER, J. W., II, and SPIELBERG, M. J. 1970. A descriptive personality study of delinquency-prone adolescents. *J. Res. Crime Delinq. 7:* 11–23.

BALL, R. A. 1969. Why punishment fails. *Amer. J. Correct. 31:* 19–21.

BANDLER, R. J., JR.; CHI, C. C.; and FLYNN, J. P. 1972. Biting attack elicited by stimulation of the ventral midbrain tegmentum of cats. *Science 177:* 364–66.

BANDURA, A. 1954. The Rorschach white space response and "oppositional" behavior. *J. Consult. Psychol. 18:* 17–21.

———. 1967. Behavioral psychotherapy. *Sci. Amer. 216,* no. 3.

BANDURA, A., and PERLOFF, B. 1967. Relative efficacy of self-monitored and externally imposed reinforcement systems. *J. Personal. Soc. Psychol. 7:* 111–16.

BANDURA, A.; ROSS, D.; and ROSS, S. 1963. Imitation of film-mediated aggressive models. *J. Abnorm. Soc. Psychol. 66:* 3–11.

BANDURA, A., and WALTERS, R. 1959. *Adolescent aggression.* New York: Ronald Press.

BARBER, T. X. 1959. The "eidetic image" and "hallucinatory" behavior: a suggestion for further research. *Psychol. Bull. 56:* 236–39.

———. 1961. Anti-social and criminal acts induced by hypnosis: a review of experimental and clinical findings. *Arch. Gen. Psychiat. 5:* 301.

———. 1963. The effects of "hypnosis" on pain. *Psychosom. Med. 25:* 303.

———. 1965a. Experimental analysis of "hypnotic" behavior: a review of recent empirical findings. *J. Abnorm. Psychol. 70:* 132–34.

———. 1965b. Physiologic effects of "hypnotic suggestions": a critical review of recent research 1960–1964. *Psychol. Bull. 63:* 201–22.

———. 1969. An empirically-based foundation of hypnotism. *Amer. J. Clin. Hypn. 12:* 100–130.

———. 1969. Multidimensional analysis of "hypnotic behavior." *J. Abnorm. Psychol. 74:* 209–20.

———. 1970. Suggested "hypnotic" behavior: The trance paradigm versus an alternative paradigm. Harding, Mass.: Medfield Foundation.

BARBER, T. X., and CALVERLEY, D. S. 1965. Empirical evidence for a theory of hypnotic behavior: effects of suggestibility of five variables typically induced in hypnotic induction procedures. *J. Abnorm. Psychol. 29:* 98–107.

BARBER, T. X., and GLASS, L. B. 1962. Significant factors in hypnotic behavior. *J. Abnorm. Soc. Psychol. 64:* 222.

BARBER, T. X., and SILVER, M. J. 1968. Pitfalls in data analyses and interpretation: a reply to Rosenthal. *Psychol. Bull. 56:* 236–39.

BARDWICK, J. M. 1971. *Psychology of women: a study of bio-cultural conflicts.* New York: Harper & Row.

BARLOW, H. B.; NARASIMHAN, R.; and ROSENFELD, A. 1972. Visual pattern analysis in machines and animals. *Science 177:* 567–75.

BARON, R. A. 1971a. Exposure to an aggressive model and apparent probability of retaliation from the victim as determinants of adult aggressive behavior. *J. Exp. Soc. Psychol. 7:* 343–55.

———. 1971b. Magnitude of victim's pain cues and level of prior anger arousal as determinants of adult aggressive behavior. *J. Personal. Soc. Psychol. 17:* 236–43.

———. 1972. Aggression as a function of ambient temperature and prior anger arousal. *J. Personal. Soc. Psychol. 21:* 183–89.

BARRON, F. 1963. *Creativity and psychological health.* Princeton, N.J.: Van Nostrand Reinhold.

———. 1965. The psychology of creativity. In *New Directions in psychology.* New York: Holt, Rinehart & Winston.

BARRON, F.; JARVIK, M.; and BUNNELL, S., Jr. 1964. The hallucinogenic drugs. In *Psychology: the biological bases of behavior.* San Francisco: W. H. Freeman.

BARZUN, J. 1941. *Darwin, Marx, Wagner.* Boston: Little, Brown.

BASH, K. W. 1939. Contribution to a theory of the hunger drive. *J. Comp. Psychol. 28:* 137–60.

BEACH, F. A. 1948. *Hormones and behavior.* New York: Hoeber Press.

———. 1956. Characteristics of masculine "sex drive." In M. Jones, ed., *Nebraska symposium on motivation*. Lincoln: University of Nebraska.

———. 1967. Cerebral and hormonal control of reflexive mechanisms involved in copulatory behavior. *Psychophysiol. Rev. 47:* 269–316.

BECK, S. J. 1951. The Rorschach test: a multi-dimensional test of personality. In H. H. Anderson and G. L. Anderson, eds., *An introduction to projective techniques*. Englewood Cliffs, N. J.: Prentice-Hall.

BECKER, E. 1969. *Angel in armor: a post-Freudian perspective on the nature of man*. New York: Braziller.

BECKER, H. S. 1963. *Outsiders: studies in the sociology of deviance*. New York: Free Press.

BEECHER, H. K. 1959. *The measurement of subjective responses*. New York: Oxford University Press.

———. 1961. Surgery as placebo. *J. Amer. Med. Assn. 176:* 1102–7.

———. 1966. Pain: one mystery solved. *Science 151:* 840–41.

BEGLEY, C. E., and LIEBERMAN, L. R. 1970. Patients' expectations of therapists' techniques. *J. Clin. Psychol. 26:* 112–16.

BEILIN, H.; KAGAN, J.; and RABINOWITZ, R. 1966. Effects of verbal and perceptual training on water level representation. *Child Develop. 37:* 317–29.

BELL, R. R., and CHASKES, J. B. 1970. Premarital sexual experience among co-eds, 1958 and 1968. *J. Marriage Fam. 32:* 81–84.

BELLOWS, R. T. 1939. Time factors in water drinking in dogs. *Amer. J. Physiol. 125:* 87–97.

BENEDICT, R. 1934. *Patterns of culture*. Boston: Houghton Mifflin.

BENNETT, E. L.; DIAMOND, M. C.; KRECH, D.; and ROSENZWEIG, M. R. 1964. Chemical and anatomical plasticity of the brain. *Science 146:* 610–19.

BERGER, A. 1966. Selected review of studies on the effectiveness of various methods of measuring reading efficiency. *J. Read. Specialist 6:* 74–87.

BERGER, D. F. 1969. Alternative interpretations of the frustration effect. *J. Exp. Psychol. 81:* 475–83.

BERGER, R. J.; OLLEY, P.; and OSWALD, I. 1962. The EEG, eye movements and dreams of the blind. *Quart. J. Exp. Psychol. 14:* 183–86.

BERGER, S. M., and ELLSBURY, S. W. 1969. The effect of expressive verbal reinforcements on incidental learning by models and observers. *Amer. J. Psychol. 82:* 333–41.

BERITASHVILI, I. S. 1969. Concerning psychoneural activity of animals. In M. Cole and I. Maltzman, eds., *A handbook of contemporary Soviet psychology*. New York: Basic Books.

BERKOWITZ, L. 1964. The effects of observing violence. *Sci. Amer. 210*, no. 2.

BERKOWITZ, L., and GEEN, R. G. 1967. Stimulus qualities of the target of aggression: a further study. *J. Personal. Soc. Psychol. 5:* 364–68.

BERLYNE, D. E. 1969. The reward value of indifferent stimulation. In J. T. Tapp, ed., *Reinforcement and behavior*. New York: Academic Press.

BERLYNE, D. E.; KOENIG, I. D.; and HIROTA, T. 1966. Novelty, arousal, and the reinforcement of diversive exploration in the rat. *J. Comp. Physiol. Psychol. 62:* 222–26.

BERNARD, L. 1970. Quoted in *Psychology today: an introduction*. Del Mar, Calif.: CRM Books.

BERTRAND, S., and MASLING, J. 1969. Oral imagery and alcoholism. *J. Abnorm. Psychol. 74*, no. 1.

BETTELHEIM, B. 1969. *The children of the dream.* New York: Macmillan.

BEVAN, W. 1972. On growing old in America. *Science 177*, no. 4052.

BEVAN, W., and PRITCHARD, J. F. 1964. The influence of hypnotically induced expectancies upon anchor-effectiveness. *J. Gen. Psychol. 71:* 79–85.

BEXTON, W. H.; HERON, W.; and SCOTT, T. 1954. Effects of decreased variation in the environment. *Can. J. Psychol. 8:* 70–76.

BIEDERMAN, I. 1972. Perceiving real world scenes. *Science 177:* 77–80.

BILLER, H. B. 1970. Father absence and the personality development of the male child. *Develop. Psychol. 2:* 181–201.

BILLER, H. B., and WEISS, S. D. 1970. The father-daughter relationship and the personality development of the female. *J. Genet. Psychol. 116:* 79–93.

BIRNBAUM, M. P. 1972a. Morality and judgments: tests of an averaging model. *J. Exp. Psychol. 93:* 35–42.

———. 1972b. Morality judgments: tests of an averaging model with differential weights. *Symposium, Western Psychological Assoc.* April, 1972.

———. 1972c. Personal communication.

BIRNBAUM, M. P. 1972. Anxiety and moral judgment in early adolescence. *J. Genet. Psychol. 120:* 12–26.

BIRREN, J. E., ed. 1959. *Handbook of aging and the individual: psychological and biological aspects.* Chicago: University of Chicago Press.

BISHOP, P. M. 1953. Sex hormones and human behavior. *Brit. J. Animal Behav. 1:* 20–22.

BLEULER, E. 1950. *Dementia praecox: the group of schizophrenias.* New York: International Universities Press.

BLICK, K. A., and WAITE, C. J. 1971. A survey of mnemonic techniques used by college students in free-recall learning. *Psychol. Rep. 29:* 76–78.

BLIXT, S., and LEY, R. 1969. Force contingent reinforcement in instrumental conditioning and extinction in children. *J. Comp. Physiol. Psychol. 69:* 267–72.

BLOCH, B. 1961. Uber die Heilung der Warzen durch Suggestion. Quoted in J. D. Frank, *Persuasion and healing: a comparative study of psychotherapy.* Baltimore: Johns Hopkins.

BLOCK, J. M. 1973. Conceptions of sex role. *Amer. Psychol. 28:* 512–26.

BOAS, F., ed. 1938. *General anthropology.* Lexington, Mass.: Heath

BOBROW, S. A., and BOWER, G. H. 1969. Comprehension and recall of sentences. *J. Exp. Psychol. 80:* 455–61.

BODMER, W. F., and CAVALLI-SFORZA, L. L. 1970. Intelligence and race. *Sci. Amer. 223*, no. 4.

BOLLES, R. D. 1969. The role of eye movements in the Muller-Lyer illusion. *Percept. Psychophys. 6:* 175–76.

BOLTWOOD, C. E., and BLICK, K. A. 1970. The delineation and application of three mnemonic techniques. *Psychon. Sci. 20:* 339–41.

BOND, E. A. 1960. Tenth grade abilities and achievements. Quoted in L. J. Cronbach, *Essentials of psychological testing.* 2nd ed. New York: Harper & Row.

BONIER, R. J., and HYMOWITZ, P. 1972. Marijuana and college students: set, setting and personality. *Proceed. 80th Annual Conv. Amer. Psychol. Assn.*

BOTTRILL, J. H. 1969. Personality change in LSD users. *J. Gen. Psychol. 80:* 157–61.

BOUCHARD, T. J., JR., and HARE, M. 1970. Size, performance, and potential in brainstorming groups. *J. Appl. Psychol. 54:* 51–55.

BOURNE, P. G.; ALFORD, J. A.; and BOWCOCK, J. Z. 1969. Treatment of skid row alcoholics with disulfiran. Quoted in L. P. Ullman and L. Krasner, *A psychological approach to abnormal behavior.* Englewood Cliffs, N.J.: Prentice-Hall.

BOUSFIELD, W. A. 1953. The occurrence of clustering in the recall of randomly arranged associates. *J. Gen. Psychol. 49:* 229-40.

BOUSFIELD, W. A., and WICKLUND, D. A. 1969. Rhyme as a determinant of clustering. *Psychon. Sci. 16:* 183-84.

BOWER, G. H., and BOLTON, L. S. 1969. Why are rhymes easy to learn. Copy undated, received from author 1969.

BOWER, G. H., and CLARK, M. C. 1969. Narrative stories as mediators for serial learning. *Psychon. Sci. 14:* 181-82.

BOWER, G. H., and WINZENZ, D. 1969. Group structure, coding and memory for digit series. *J. Exp. Psychol. Monogr. 80,* no. 2, pt. 2.

BOWER, T. G. R. 1966. The visual world of infants. *Sci. Amer. 215,* no. 6.

———. 1967. The development of object-permanence: some studies of existence constancy. *Percept. Psychophys. 2:* 411-18.

———. 1971. The object in the world of the infant. *Sci. Amer. 225,* no. 4.

BOWERS, M., JR. 1969. Student psychedelic drug use: an evaluation by student drug users. *Int. J. Addict. 4:* 89-99.

BRACE, C. L. 1971. Introduction to Jensenism. In C. L. Brace, G. R. Gamble, and J. T. Bond, eds., Race and Intelligence. *Anthro. Studies,* no. 8. Washington, D. C.: American Anthropological Association.

BRACE, C. L., and LIVINGSTONE, F. B. 1971. On creeping Jensenism. In C. L. Brace, G. R. Gamble, and J. T. Bond, eds., Race and Intelligence. *Anthro. Studies,* no. 8. Washington, D.C.: American Anthropological Association.

BRADY, J. V. 1958a. Ulcers in "executive monkeys." *Sci. Amer. 199,* no. 4.

———. 1958b. The paleocortex and behavioral motivation. In H. F. Harlow and C. N. Woolsey, eds., *Biological and biochemical bases of behavior.* Madison, Wis.: University of Wisconsin Press.

BRAGINSKY, B. M.; BRAGINSKY, D. D.; and RING, K. 1969. *Methods of madness: the mental hospital as a last resort.* New York: Holt, Rinehart & Winston.

BRANAN, J. M. 1972. Negative human interaction. *J. Counsel. Psychol. 19:* 81-82.

BRASCH, R. 1967. *How did it begin?* New York: McKay.

BRECHER, R., and BRECHER, E. 1966. *An analysis of human sexual response.* New York: Signet Books.

BREGER, L.; HUNTER, I.; and LANE, R. W. 1971. *The effect of stress and dreams.* New York: International University Press.

BRINKMAN, J., and KUYPERS, H. G. 1972. Splitbrain monkeys: cerebral control of ipsilateral and contralateral arm, head, and finger movements. *Science 176:* 536-38.

BRITTAIN, C. V. 1967. An exploration of the bases of peer-compliance and parent-compliance in adolescence. *Adolescence 2:* 445-58.

BROME, V. 1967. *Freud and his early circle.* New York: Morrow.

BROMLEY, D. B. 1966. *The psychology of human aging.* Baltimore: Penguin.

BROWN, D. G. 1966. Female orgasm and sexual adequacy. In R. Brecher and E. Brecher, *An analysis of human sexual response.* New York: Signet Books.

BROWN, J. A. C. 1963. *Techniques of persuasion.* Baltimore: Penguin.

BROWNING, H. L. 1969. Timing of our lives. *Transaction 6*, no. 11.

BROWNING, R. C. 1968. Validity of reference ratings from previous employers. *Pers. Psychol. 21*, no. 3.

BRUCH, H. 1969. Hunger and Instinct. *J. Nerv. Ment. Dis. 149:* 91–114.

BRUNER, J. S. 1968. Foreword in A. R. Luria, *The mind of a mnemonist.* New York: Basic Books.

BRUNER, J. S., and GOODMAN, C. C. 1947. Value and need as organizing factors in perception. *J. Abnorm. Soc. Psychol. 42:* 33–44.

BRUNER, J. S.; OLIVER, R. R.; GREENFIELD, P. M.; et al. 1966. *Studies in cognitive growth.* New York: John Wiley.

BRYAN, J. H., and TEST, M. A. 1969. Models and helping: naturalistic studies in aiding behavior. Quoted in P. H. Mussen and M. R. Rosensweig, eds., *Annual review of psychology.* Palo Alto, Calif.: Annual Reviews.

BULLOCK, A. 1953. *Hitler: a study in tyranny.* New York: Harper & Row.

BURT, C. 1958. The inheritance of mental ability. *Amer. Psychol. 13:* 5–10.

BUSS, A. H. 1966. *Psychopathology.* New York: John Wiley.

BUTTERFIELD, E. C., and ZIGLER, E. 1970. Preinstitutional social deprivation and IQ changes among institutionalized retarded children. *J. Abnorm. Psychol. 75:* 83–89.

BYRNE, D., and LAMBERT, J. 1970. The effect of erotic stimuli on sexual arousal, evaluative responses, and subsequent behavior. In *The report of the commission on obscenity and pornography.* Washington, D.C.: U.S. Government Printing Office.

CALDWELL, B. M.; WRIGHT, C. M.; HONIG, A. S.; and TANNENBAUM, J. 1970. Infant day care and attachment. *Amer. J. Orthopsychiat. 40:* 397–412.

CALLOWAY, N. O. 1972. IQ: methodological and other issues. *Science 178:* 230–32.

CAMERON, N. 1963. *Personality development and psychopathology.* Boston: Houghton Mifflin.

CANCRO, R., and PRUYSER, P. W. 1970. A historical review of the development of the concept of schizophrenia. *Bull. Menninger Clin. 34:* 61–70.

CANNON, W. B. 1939. *The wisdom of the body.* New York: Norton.

————. 1942. Voodoo death. *Amer. Anthropol. 44:* 169.

CANNON, W. B., and WASHBURN, L. 1912. An explanation of hunger. *Amer. J. Physiol. 29:* 441–54.

CANON, L. K., and MATHEWS, K. E. 1972. Concern over personal health and smoking-relevant beliefs and behavior. *Proceed. 80th Annual Conv. Amer. Psychol. Assn.*

CAPLAN, N. S., and PAIGE, T. M. 1968. A study of ghetto rioters. *Sci. Amer. 219,* no. 2.

CAPLAN, R. B. 1969. *Psychiatry and the community in nineteenth century America.* New York: Basic Books.

CARPENTER, B.; WIENER, M.; and CARPENTER, J. T. 1956. Predictability of perceptual defense behavior. *J. Abnorm. Soc. Psychol. 52:* 380–83.

CARRINGTON, P. 1972. Dreams and schizophrenia. *Arch. Gen. Psychiat. 26:* 343–50.

CARROLL, J. B. 1964. *Language and thought.* Englewood Cliffs, N.J.: Prentice-Hall.

CARTWRIGHT, F. F. 1972. *Disease and history.* New York: Thomas Y. Crowell.

CARTWRIGHT, W., and BURTIS, T. 1968. Race and intelligence: changing opinions in social science. *Soc. Sci. Quart. 49:* 603–18.

CARVER, R. P. 1971. *Sense and nonsense in speed reading.* Silver Springs, Md.: Revrac Publications.

———. 1972. Speed readers don't read: they skim. *Psychol. Today 6,* no. 3.

CARVER, R. P., and DARBY, C. A., JR. 1971. Development and evaluation of a test of information storage during reading. *J. Educ. Meas. 8:* 33–44.

CATANIA, A. C. 1969. Concurrent performance: inhibition of one response by reinforcement of another. *J. Exp. Anal. Behav. 12:* 731–44.

CATTELL, J. McK. 1890. Mental tests and measurements. *Mind 15:* 373–80.

CAUTELA, J. 1958. Misconceptions: intelligence and the IQ. *Education 78:* 300–303.

CERASO, J. 1967. The interference theory of forgetting. *Sci. Amer. 217,* no. 4.

CHAMBERS, J., and DUSSEAULT, B. 1972. Characteristics of college-age gifted. *Proceed. 80th Annual Conv. Amer. Psychol. Assn.*

CHAPLIN, J. P., and KRAWIEC, T. S. 1968. *Systems and theories of psychology.* 2nd ed. New York: Holt, Rinehart & Winston.

CHARMAN, W. N. 1972. Eye marks in vertebrates as aids to vision. *Science 177:* 367.

CHAVES, J. F. 1968. Hypnosis reconceptualized: an overview of Barber's theoretical and empirical work. *Psychol. Rep. 22:* 587–608.

CHEVALIER-SKOLNIKOFF, S. 1971. Homo- and heterosexual behavior in stumptail monkeys (*Macaca Speciosa*). Paper. AAAS meeting, December, 1971.

———. 1972. Sexual behavior of the male and female stumptail monkeys (*Macaca Speciosa*), and its implications for understanding the sexual behavior of other primates. Portland, Ore.: *Symposium, 4th Int. Cong. Primatol.,* August, 1972.

CHILD, I. L. 1946. Children's preference for goals easy or difficult to obtain. *Psychol. Monogr. 60,* no. 4.

CHILD, I. L.; FRANK, K. F.; and STORM, T. 1956. Self-ratings and TAT: Their relation to each other and to childhood background. *J. Personal. 25:* 96–114.

CHRISTIANSEN, T., and LIVERMORE, G. 1970. A comparison of Anglo-American and Spanish-American children on the WISC. *J. Soc. Psychol. 81:* 9–14.

CLAIRBORN, W. L. 1969. Expectancy effects in the classroom: a failure to replicate. *J. Educ. Psychol. 60:* 377–83.

CLARK, G. R.; TELFER, M. A.; BAKER, D.; and ROSEN, M. 1970. Sex chromosomes, crime, and psychosis. *Amer. J. Psychiat. 126:* 1659–63.

CLINE, V. B.; CROFT, R. G.; and COURRIER, S. 1972. Desensitization of children to television violence. *Proceed. 80th Annual Conv. Amer. Psychol. Assn.*

COATES, B.; ANDERSON, E.; and HARTUP, W. 1972. Interrelations in the attachment behavior of human infants. *Develop. Psychol. 6:* 218–30.

COHEN, H. L.; FILIPCZAK, J. A.; BIS, J. S.; and COHEN, J. E. 1966. *Contingencies applicable to special education of delinquents.* Silver Springs, Md.: Institute for Behavioral Research.

COLE, M., and BRUNER, J. S. 1972. Preliminaries to a theory of cultural differences. *Yrbk. Nat. Soc. Study Educ.,* pt. 2, no. 8, 161–80.

COLEMAN, J. C. 1961. *The adolescent society.* New York: Free Press.

———. 1964. *Abnormal psychology and modern life.* Glenview, Ill.: Scott, Foresman.

CONANT, J. B. 1951. *On understanding science.* New York: New American Library of World Literature.

CONRAD, D. G.; ELSMORE, T. F.; and SODETZ, F. J. 1972. Δ^9-tetrahydrocannabinol: dose-related effects on timing behavior in chimpanzee. *Science 175:* 547–50.

COOPER, E., and TAHODA, M. 1964. Quoted in W. W. Lambert and W. E. Lambert, *Social psychology.* Englewood Cliffs, N.J.: Prentice-Hall.

COPPERSMITH, S. 1968. Studies in self esteem. *Sci. Amer. 218,* no. 2.

CORBALLIS, M. C., and BEALE, I. L. 1971. On telling left from right. *Sci. Amer. 224,* no. 3.

CORY, D. W. 1965. Quoted in A. Ellis, *Homosexuality: its causes and cures,* 25. New York: Lyle Stuart.

COTTLE, T. J.; HOWARD, P.; and PLECK, J. 1969. Adolescent perceptions of time: the effect of age, sex and social class. *J. Personal. 37:* 636–50.

CRANCER, A., JR.; DILLE, J. M.; DELAY, J. C.; WALLACE, J. E.; and HAYKIN, M. D. 1969. Comparison of the effects of marijuana and alcohol on simulated driving performance. *Science 164:* 851–54.

CRIST, J. 1971. Are American men afraid of women? *Sex. Behav.,* May, 1971.

CRONBACH, L. J. 1960. *Essentials of psychological testing.* 2nd ed. New York: Harper & Row.

CROPLEY, A. J. 1972. A five-year longitudinal study of the validity of creativity tests. *Develop. Psychol. 6:* 119–24.

CROSS, H. J., and DAVIS, G. L. 1972. College students' adjustment and frequency of marijuana use. *J. Counsel. Psychol. 19:* 65–67.

DAHLSTROM, W. G. 1970. Personality. In P. H. Mussen and M. R. Rosenzweig, eds., *Annual review of psychology.* Palo Alto, Calif.: Annual Reviews.

DALAL, A. S., and BARBER, T. S. 1969. Yoga, "yogi feats," and hypnosis in the light of experimental research. *Amer. J. Clin. Hypn. 11:* 155–66.

DANA, R. H. 1970. A hierarchical model for analyzing personality data. *J. Gen. Psychol. 82:* 199–206.

DANA, R. H., and HANDZLIK, A. L. 1970. Clinical judgment as fantasied identification. *Psychol. Rep. 26:* 437–38.

DARBONNE, A. R. 1969. Study of psychological content in the communications of suicidal individuals. *J. Consult. Clin. Psychol. 33:* 590–96.

DARDEN, E. 1972. Masculinity-femininity body rankings by males and females. *J. Psychol. 80:* 205–12.

DAVENPORT, H. W. 1972. Why the stomach does not digest itself. *Sci. Amer. 226,* no. 1.

DAVIDSON, E. 1966. *The trial of the Germans.* New York: Macmillan.

DAVIDSON, P. O. 1968. Validity of the guilty knowledge technique. *J. Appl. Psychol. 52:* 62–65.

DAVIDSON, R., and KRIPPNER, S. 1972. Biofeedback research: their data and their implications. In *Biofeedback and self control 1971.* Chicago: Aldine Atherton.

DAVIS, C. M. 1928. Self-selection of diet by newly weaned infants. *Amer. J. Dis. Child. 36:* 651–79.

DAVIS, D., and BROCK, T. C. 1972. Paradoxical instigation of self-criticism by inordinate praise. *Proceed. 80th Annual Conv. Amer. Psychol. Assn.*

Davis, D. R. 1966. *Introduction to psychopathology*. 2nd ed. New York: Oxford University Press.

Davis, F. B. 1962. Measurement of improvement in reading skill courses. *11th Yrbk. Nat. Read. Conf.:* 30–40.

Davis, G. A. 1969. Training creativity in adolescence: a discussion of strategy. *J. Creative Behav. 3:* 95–104.

Davis, H. V., Sears, R. R.; Miller, H. C.; and Brodbeck, A. J. 1948. Effects of cup, bottle and breast feeding on oral activities of newborn infants. *Pediatrics 2:* 549–58.

Dawes, R. M. 1972. IQ: Methodological and other issues. *Science 178:* 229–30.

Dayton, D. H. 1969. Early malnutrition and human development. *Children 16:* 210–17.

Dean, S. J.; Martin, R. B.; and Streiner, D. 1968. Mediational control of the GSR. *J. Exp. Res. Personal. 3:* 71–76.

Deitz, G. E. 1969. A comparison of delinquents with nondelinquents on self-concept, self-acceptance, and parental identification. *J. Genet. Psychol. 115:* 285–95.

de Kruif, P. 1926. *Microbe hunters*. New York: Harcourt Brace Jovanovich.

Delany, L. T. 1968. The other bodies in the river. *Psychol. Today 2,* no. 1.

Delgado, J. M. R. 1969. *Physical control of the mind*. New York: Harper & Row.

Dellas, M., and Gaier, E. L. 1970. Identification of creativity: the individual. *Psychol. Bull. 73:* 55–73.

Dement, W., and Kleitman, N. 1957. Cyclic variations in EEG during sleep and their relations to eye movements, bodily motility and dreaming. *Electroencephalog. Clin. Neurophysiol. 9:* 673–90.

Dennis, W. 1943. On the possibility of advancing and retarding the motor development of infants. *Psychol. Rev. 50:* 203–18.

———. 1948. *Readings in the history of psychology*. New York: Appleton-Century-Crofts.

Deregowski, J. B. 1972. Pictorial perception and culture. *Sci. Amer. 227,* no. 5.

Deutsch, A. 1946. *The mentally ill in America*. New York: Columbia University Press.

Deutsch, J. A. 1968. Neural basis of memory. *Psychol. Today 1,* no. 12.

———. 1972. Brain reward: esp and ecstasy. *Psychol. Today 6,* no. 2.

Deutsch, J. A., and Deutsch, D. 1966. *Physiological psychology*. Homewood, Ill.: Dorsey.

DeVoto, B. 1943. *The year of decision, 1846*. Boston: Houghton Mifflin.

DiCara, L. V. 1970. Learning in the autonomic nervous system. *Sci. Amer. 222,* no. 1.

Didato, S. V. 1969. Some recent trends in juvenile delinquency. *Ment. Hyg. 53:* 545–49.

Dimond, S. J., and Beaumont, J. G. 1972. Hemispheric control of hand function in the human brain. *Acta Psychol. 36:* 32–36.

Dohrenwend, B. P., and Chin-Shong, E. 1967. Social status and attitudes toward psychological disorder: the problem of tolerance of deviance. *Amer. Socio. Rev. 32:* 417–33.

Dollard, J., and Miller, N. E. 1950. *Personality and psychotherapy: an analysis in terms of learning, thinking, and culture*. New York: McGraw-Hill.

DOOB, A. N., and CLIMIE, J. R. 1972. Delay of measurement and the effects of film violence. *J. Exp. Soc. Psychol. 8:* 136–42.

DORNBUSH, R. L. 1972. Memory and inducted ECT convulsions. *Seminars Psychiat. 4:* 47–54.

DORSEY, J. A., and MEISELS, M. 1969. Personal space and self-protection. *J. Personal. Soc. Psychol. 11:* 93–97.

DOTY, R. W. 1969. Electrical stimulation of the brain on behavioral context. In P. H. Mussen and M. R. Rosenzweig, eds., *Annual review of psychology.* Palo Alto, Calif.: Annual Reviews.

DOUGLAS, J. W. B.; ROSS, J. M.; and SIMPSON, H. R. 1969. New society. Quoted in *Transaction 6,* no. 3.

DUANE, T. D., and BEHRENDT, T. 1969. Extrasensory electroencephalographic induction between identical twins. Quoted in D. Krech, R. Crutchfield, and N. Livson, *Elements of psychology.* New York: Knopf.

DUBIGNON, J., and CAMPBELL, D. 1969. Discrimination between nutriments by the human neonate. *Psychon. Sci. 16:* 186.

DUBOS, R., and PINES, M. 1965. *Health and disease.* New York: Time, Inc.

DUKES, W. F., and BEVAN, W. 1967. Stimulus variation and repetition in the acquisition of naming responses. *J. Exp. Psychol. 74:* 178–81.

DUNCAN, H. D. 1968. *Symbols in society.* New York: Oxford University Press.

DUNLOP, R. 1965. *Doctors of the American frontier.* Garden City, N.Y.: Doubleday.

DURANT, W. 1933. *The story of philosophy.* New York: Simon & Schuster.

EAGLY, A. H. 1969. Sex differences in the relationship between self esteem and susceptibility to social influence. *J. Personal. 37:* 581–91.

EAKIN, R. M. 1970. The third eye. *Amer. Sci. 58:* 73–79.

EATON, J. W., and WEIL, R. J. 1955. *Culture and mental disorders.* New York: Free Press.

EICHLER, R. M. 1951. A comparison of the Rorschach and Behn-Rorschach inkblot tests. *J. Consult. Psychol. 15:* 185–89.

EINSTADTER, W. J. 1969. The social organization of armed robbery. *Soc. Probl. 17:* 64–83.

EISENBERGER, R. 1972. Explanation of rewards that do not reduce tissue needs. *Psychol. Bull. 77:* 319–39.

ELLIS, A. 1962. *Reason and emotion in psychotherapy.* New York: Lyle Stuart.

———. 1965. *Homosexuality: its causes and cures.* New York: Lyle Stuart.

ELLISON, D. L. 1969. Alienation and the will to live. *J. Gerontol. 24:* 361–67.

ENNIS, B. J. 1972. *Prisoners of Psychiatry: mental patients, psychiatrists and the law.* New York: Harcourt Brace Jovanovich.

EPSTEIN, H. T. 1972. A new agenda for school reform. *Change 4,* no. 9.

EPSTEIN, R., and KOMORITA, S. 1966. Childhood prejudice as a function of parental ethnocentrism, punitiveness, and outgroup characteristics. *J. Personal. Soc. Psychol. 3:* 259–64.

EPSTEIN, S. 1970. Anxiety, reality, and schizophrenia. *Schizophrenia 2:* 11–35.

EPSTEIN, S., and COLEMAN, M. 1970. Drive theories of schizophrenia. *Psychosom. Med. 32:* 113–40.

Erikson, K. T. 1964. Notes on the sociology of deviance. In H. S. Becker, ed., *The other side: perspectives on deviance.* New York: Free press.

Estes, K. W. 1944. An experimental study of punishment. *Psychol. Monogr. 57*, no. 263.

Evans, F. J.; Gustafson, L. A.; O'Connell, D. N.; Orne, M. T.; and Shor, R. E. 1969. Sleep induced behavioral response. *J. Nerv. Ment. Dis. 148*, no. 5.

Eysenck, H. J., ed. 1960. *Behavior therapy and the neuroses.* London: Pergamon Press.

———. 1961. The effects of psychotherapy. In H. Eysenck, ed., *Handbook of abnormal psychology.* New York: Basic Books.

———. 1964. *Sense and nonsense in psychology.* Baltimore: Penguin.

Ferraro, D. P., and Grilly, D. M. 1973. Lack of tolerance to Δ^9-tetrahydrocannabinol in chimpanzees. *Science 179:* 490–92.

Festinger, L. 1961. The psychological effects of insufficient rewards. *Amer. Psychol. 16:* 1–11.

Fiddle, S. 1968. Circles beyond the circumference: some hunches about amphetamine abuse. In J. Russo, ed., *Amphetamine abuse.* Springfield, Ill.: Charles C Thomas.

Fingarette, H. 1963. *The self in transformation.* New York: Basic Books.

Fisher, C.; Kahn, E.; Edwards, A.; and Davis, D. M. 1973. A psychophysical study of nightmares and night terrors. *Arch. Gen. Psychiatr. 28:* 252–59.

Fisher, D. F. 1971. The effects of delay interval on word recall and clustering. *J. Psychol. 77:* 67–77.

Fiske, D. W., and Maddi, S. R. 1961. *Functions of varied experience.* Homewood, Ill.: Dorsey.

Fitzgerald, H., and Porges, S. 1971. A decade of infant conditioning and learning research. *Merrill-Palmer Quart. Behav. Develop. 17*, no. 2.

Fleishman, E. A., and Bartlett, C. J. 1969. Human abilities. In P. H. Mussen and M. R. Rosenzweig, eds., *Annual review of psychology.* Palo Alto, Calif.: Annual Reviews.

Flexner, L. B., and Flexner, J. B. 1968. Intracerebral saline effect on memory of trained mice treated with puronycin. *Science 159:* 330–31.

Fodor, E. M. 1972. Delinquency and susceptibility to social influence among adolescents as a function of level of moral development. *J. Soc. Psychol. 86:* 257–60.

Ford, D. H., and Urban, H. B. 1963. *Systems of psychotherapy.* New York: John Wiley.

Foulkes, D. 1967. Dreams of the male child: Four case studies. *J. Child Psychol. Psychiat. 8:* 81–98.

Foulkes, D.; Pivik, T.; Steadman, H.; Spear, P.; and Symonds, J. 1967. Dreams of the male child: An EEG study. *J. Abnorm. Psychol. 72:* 457–67.

Fox, M. W., ed. 1968. *Abnormal behavior in animals.* Philadelphia: Saunders.

Frank, G. 1966. *The Boston Strangler.* New York: New American Library.

Freedman, D. A., and Brown, S. L. 1968. On the role of somesthetic stimulation in the development of psychic structure. *Psychoanal. Quart. 37:* 418–38.

FREEDMAN, D. G. 1968. Longitudinal studies in the social behavior of twins: birth through five years. Paper, APA convention, 1966. Quoted in A. T. Jersild, *Child psychology*. 6th ed. Englewood Cliffs, N.J.: Prentice-Hall.

FREEDMAN, J. L., and FRASER, S. C. 1966. Compliance without pressure. *J. Personal. Soc. Psychol. 4:* 195–202.

FREUD, S. 1933. *New introductory lectures on psychoanalysis.* New York: Norton.

———. 1936. *Inhibitions, symptoms and anxiety.* London: Hogarth.

———. 1938. The history of the psychoanalytic movement. In A. A. Brill, ed., *The basic writings of Sigmund Freud.* New York: Random House.

FREUND, J. E. 1960. *Modern elementary statistics.* 2nd ed. Englewood Cliffs, N.J.: Prentice-Hall.

FREUND, K. 1960. Some problems in the treatment of homosexuality. In H. J. Eysenck, ed., *Behavior therapy and the neuroses.* London: Pergamon.

———. 1970. The structure of erotic preference in the nondeviant male. *Behav. Res. Ther. 8:* 15–20.

FRIJDA, N. H. 1972. Simulation of human long-term memory. *Psychol. Bull. 77:* 1–31.

FRISCH, C. VON. 1963. *Man and the living world.* New York: Harcourt Brace Jovanovich.

FRUMKIN, R. M. 1961. Beauty. In A. Ellis and A. Abarbanel, eds., *The encyclopedia of sexual behavior.* New York: Hawthorne.

FULLER, J. L. 1967. Experimental deprivation and later behavior. *Science 158:* 1645–52.

FULLER, R. 1972. A new theory of intelligence which allows reading with comprehension in low IQ subjects. Presented at 80th annual meeting, Amer. Psychol. Assn., Sept. 6, 1972.

FUNKENSTEIN, D. H. 1955. The physiology of fear and anger. *Sci. Amer. 192,* no. 5.

GALAMBOS, R.; NORTON, T.; and FROMMER, G. 1967. Optic tract lesions sparing pattern vision in cats. *Exp. Neurol. 18:* 8–25.

GALANTER, M.; WYATT, R. J.; LEMBERGER, L.; WEINGARTNER, H.; VAUGHN, T. B.; and ROTH, W. T. 1972. Effects on humans of Δ^9-tetrahydrocannabinol administered by smoking. *Science 176:* 934–36.

GALBRAITH, J. K. 1961. *The great crash: 1929.* Boston: Houghton Mifflin.

GARCIA, J. 1972. IQ: the conspiracy. *Psychol. Today 6,* no. 4.

GARDINER, H. M.; METCALF, R. C.; and BEBBE-CENTER, J. G. 1937. *Feeling and emotion: a history of theories.* New York: American Book.

GARDNER, E. 1968. *Fundamentals of neurology.* Philadelphia: Saunders.

GARRETT, H. E. 1951. *Great experiments in psychology.* New York: Appleton-Century-Crofts.

———. 1958. *Statistics in psychology and education.* 5th ed. London: Longmans, Green.

GARY, ROMAIN. 1970. *White Dog.* New York: New American Library.

GATES, A. I. 1958. Recitation as a factor in memorizing. Quoted in J. Deese, *The psychology of learning.* 2nd ed. New York: McGraw-Hill.

GAY, P. 1966. *The enlightenment: an interpretation.* New York: Knopf.

GAZZANIGA, M. S.; BOGEN, J. E.; and SPERRY, R. W. 1965. Observations on visual perception after disconnection of the cerebral hemisphere in man. *Brain 88:* 221–36.

GEBHARD, P. H.; GAGNON, J. H.; POMEROY, W. B.; and CHRISTENSON, C. U. 1965. *Sex offenders: an analysis of types.* New York: Harper & Row.

———. 1969. Quoted in L. P. Ullmann and L. Krasner, *A psychological approach to abnormal behavior.* Englewood Cliffs, N.J.: Prentice-Hall.

GERARD, R. 1972. Quoted in B. S. Aaronson, Color perception and effect. *Amer. J. Clin. Hyp. 14:* 38–43.

GERBER, G. 1972. Communication and social environment. *Sci. Amer. 227,* no. 3.

GESCHWIND, N. 1972. Language and the brain. *Sci. Amer. 226,* no. 4.

GESELL, A. 1929. Maturation and infant behavior patterns. *Psychol. Rev. 36:* 307–19.

GESELL, A., and THOMPSON, H. 1929. Learning and growth in identical infant twins: an experimental study by the method of co-twin control. *Genet. Psychol. Monogr. 5:* 1–124.

GETZELS, J. W., and JACKSON, P. W. 1962. *Creativity and intelligence.* New York: John Wiley.

GIBBENS, T. C. N., and AHRENFELDT, R. H., eds. 1966. *Cultural factors in delinquency.* Philadelphia: Lippincott.

GIBSON, E. J., and WALK, R. D. 1960. The visual cliff. *Sci. Amer. 202,* no. 4.

———. 1970. The development of perception as an adaptive process. *Amer. Sci. 58:* 98–107.

GIFFORD, R., and SOMMER, R. 1968. The desk or the bed? Quoted in R. Sommer, *Personal space: The behavioral basis of design.* Englewood Cliffs, N.J.: Prentice-Hall.

GINSBERG, G. L. 1972. Quoted in *Human Behavior 1,* no. 3.

GIOSCIA, V. 1969. LSD subcultures: acidoxy versus orthodoxy. *Amer. J. Orthopsychiat. 39:* 428–36.

GLASER, D.; INCIARDI, J. T.; and BABST, D. V. 1969. Later heroin use by marijuana-using, heroin-using, and non-drug-using adolescent offenders in New York City. *Int. J. Addict. 4:* 145–55.

GLATT, M. M. 1969. Is it all right to smoke pot? *Brit. J. Addict. 64:* 109–14.

GLATT, M. M.; PITTMAN, D. J.; GILLESPIE, D. G.; and HILLS, D. R. 1967. *The drug scene in Great Britain: "journey into loneliness."* London: Edward Arnold.

GLICK, B. S. 1970. Conditioning therapy with phobic patients: success and failure. *Amer. J. Psychother. 24:* 92–101.

GLUECK, S., and GLUECK, E. T. 1950. *Unraveling juvenile delinquency.* Cambridge, Mass.: Commonwealth Fund.

———. 1959. *Predicting delinquency and crime.* Cambridge, Mass.: Harvard University Press.

———. 1970. White delinquents in the core city: as boys and men. *Soc. Sci. 45:* 67–81.

GOFFMAN, E. 1961. *Asylums.* New York: Doubleday.

GOLDSTEIN, J. H., and ARMS, R. L. 1971. Effects of observing athletic contests on hostility. *Sociometry 34:* 83–90.

GOMBRICH, E. H. 1972. The visual image. *Sci. Amer. 227,* no. 3.

GORDON, R. A. 1967. Issues in the ecological study of delinquency. *Amer. Socio. Rev. 32:* 927–44.

GORDON, W. J. 1969. *Synectics.* Quoted in G. A. Davis, Training creativity in adolescence: a discussion of strategy. *J. Creative Behav. 3:* 95–104.

GOTTESMAN, I. I., and SHIELDS, J. 1966. Schizophrenia in twins: 16 years' consecutive admissions to a psychiatric clinic. *Brit. J. Psychiat. 112:* 808–18.

GOUGH, H. G. 1952. *The adjective checklist.* Berkeley: University of California Press.

GRAF, R. G., and RIDDELL, J. C. 1972. Helping behavior as a function of interpersonal perception. *J. Soc. Psychol. 86:* 227–31.

GREEN, E. 1973. Quoted in *APA Monitor 4,* no. 4.

GREENE, W. A.; GOLDSTEIN, S.; and MOSS, A. J. 1972. Psychosocial aspects of sudden death. *Arch. Intern. Med. 129:* 725–31.

GREGORY, R. L. 1966. *Eye and brain: the psychology of seeing.* New York: McGraw-Hill.

———. 1968. Visual illusions. *Sci. Amer. 219,* no. 5.

GRESHAM, W. L. 1959. *Houdini: the man who walked through walls.* New York: Holt, Rinehart & Winston.

GRIFFITH, J. 1968. Psychiatric implications of amphetamine abuse. In J. Russo, ed., *Amphetamine abuse.* Springfield, Ill.: Charles C Thomas.

GRIM, P.; KOHLBERG, L.; and WHITE, S. H. 1968. Some relationships between conscience and attentional processes. *J. Personal. Soc. Psychol. 8:* 239–52.

GRINSPOON, L. 1969. Marihuana. *Sci. Amer. 221,* no. 6.

———. 1971. *Marihuana reconsidered.* Boston: Harvard University Press.

GROSSMAN, D. S. 1972. Variables associated with marijuana use in college students. *Proceed. 80th Annual Conv. Amer. Psychol. Assn.*

GROTJOHN, M. 1971. Are American men afraid of women? *Sex. Behav.,* May, 1971.

GUBAR, G. 1969. Drug addiction: myth and misconceptions. *Pa. Psychiat. Quart. 8:* 24–32.

GUERNEY, B. G., JR., ed. 1969. *Psychotherapeutic agents: new roles for nonprofessionals, parents and teachers.* New York: Holt, Rinehart & Winston.

GUETZKOW, H., and BOWMAN, P. H. 1946. *Men and hunger.* Elgin, Ill.: Brethren Publishing House.

GUILFORD, J. P. 1959. *Personality.* New York: McGraw-Hill.

———. 1967. *The nature of human intelligence.* New York: McGraw-Hill.

GUTHRIE, E. R. 1952. *The psychology of learning.* Rev. ed. New York: Harper & Row.

GYR, J. W. 1972. Is a theory of direct visual perception adequate? *Psychol. Bull. 77:* 246–61.

HABER, R. N. 1958. Discrepancy from adaptation level as a source of affect. *J. Exp. Psychol. 56:* 370–75.

———. 1969. Eidetic images. *Sci. Amer. 220,* no. 4.

———. 1970. How we remember what we see. *Sci. Amer. 222,* no. 5.

HALIKAS, J. A.; GOODWIN, D. W.; and GUZE, S. B. 1972. Pattern of marihuana use: a survey of one hundred regular users. *Comp. Psychiat. 13:* 161–63.

HALL, C. S. 1951. What people dream about. *Sci. Amer. Offprint Series No. 434.*

———. 1953. *The meaning of dreams.* New York: Harper & Row.

HALL, E. T. 1966. *The hidden dimension.* New York: Doubleday.

HALL, K. R., and STRIDE, E. 1954. The varying responses to pain in psychiatric disorders: a study in abnormal psychology. *Brit. J. Med. Psychol. 27:* 48–60.

HALPERT, H. P. 1969. Public acceptance of the mentally ill. *Public Health Rep. 84:* 59–64.

HAMID, P. N. 1967. Social distance and stereotypes characterizing university students. *New Zealand J. Educ. Stud. 2:* 148–54.

———. 1968. Style of dress as a perceptual cue in impression formation. *Percept. Skills 26:* 904–6.

———. 1969. Changes in person perception as a function of dress. *Percept. Mot. Skills 29:* 191–94.

———. 1972. Some effects of dress cues on observational accuracy, a perceptual estimate, and impression formation. *J. Soc. Psychol. 86:* 279–89.

HAMILTON, A.; MADISON, J.; and JAY, J. 1952. The federalist. In R. M. Hutchins, ed., *The great books of the western world, no. 79.* Chicago: Encyclopaedia Britannica.

HAMILTON, E. 1942. *The Greek way.* New York: Norton.

HANSEL, C. E. M. 1966. *ESP: a scientific evaluation.* New York: Scribner's.

HANSEN, C. 1969. *Witchcraft at Salem.* New York: Braziller.

HARDEMAN, M. 1972. Children's moral reasoning. *J. Genet. Psychol. 120:* 49–59.

HARLOW, H. F. 1959. Love in infant monkeys. *Sci. Amer. 22,* no. 6.

———. 1969. Quoted in F. Beach, It's all in your mind. *Psychol. Today 3,* no. 2.

HARLOW, H. F.; BLAZEK, N.; and McCLEARN, G. 1956. Manipulatory motivation in the infant rhesus monkey. *J. Comp. Physiol. Psychol. 49:* 444–48.

HARLOW, H. F.; GLUCK, J. P.; and SUOMI, S. J. 1972. Generalization of behavioral data between nonhuman and human animals. *Amer. Psychol. 27:* 709–16.

HARLOW, H. F., and SUOMI, S. J. 1970. Nature of love–simplified. *Amer. Psychol. 25:* 161–69.

HARPER, R. A. 1959. *Psychoanalysis and psychotherapy.* Englewood Cliffs, N.J.: Prentice-Hall.

HARRIS, D. H. 1960. Questionnaire and interview in neuropsychiatric screening. Quoted in L. J. Cronbach, *Essentials of psychological testing.* New York: Harper & Row.

HARRIS, J. A.; JACKSON, C. M.; PATERSON, D. G.; and SCAMMON, R. E. 1930. *The measurement of man.* Minneapolis: University of Minnesota.

HARRISON, S. I. 1970. Reared in the wrong sex. *J. Amer. Acad. Child Psychiat. 9:* 44–100.

HARTLAGE, L. C. 1970. Subprofessional therapists' use of reinforcement versus traditional psychotherapeutic techniques with schizophrenics. *J. Consult. Clin. Psychol. 34:* 181–84.

HARTMANN, E. 1968a. The 90-minute sleep-dream cycle. *Arch. Gen. Psychiat. 18:* 280–86.

———. 1968b. On the pharmacology of dreaming sleep (the D state). *J. Nerv. Ment. Dis. 146:* 165–73.

———. 1969. Pharmacological studies of sleep and dreaming: Chemical and clinical relationships. *Biol. Psychiat. 1:* 243–58.

HARTMANN, E.; BAEKELAND, F.; ZWILLING, G.; and HOY, P. 1971. Sleep need: How much sleep and what kind? *Amer. J. Psychiat. 127:* 1001–8.

HARTSHORNE, H., and MAY, N. A. 1928–1930. *Studies in the nature of character. vol. 1, studies in deceit; vol. 2, studies in self control; vol. 3, studies in the organization of character.* New York: Macmillan.

HARVEY, W. 1952. On the generation of animals. In R. M. Hutchins, ed., *The great books of the western world, no. 28.* Chicago: Encyclopaedia Britannica.

611 *References*

HAWES, G. R. 1972. The decline of the SATs. *Change 4,* no. 9.

HAWGOOD, J. A. 1967. *America's western frontiers.* New York: Knopf.

HEBB, D. O. 1951. The role of neurological ideas in psychology. *J. Personal. 20,* no. 45.

———. 1969. *The organization of behavior.* Quoted in J. R. Phillips, Jr., *The origins of intellect: Piaget's theory.* San Francisco: W. H. Freeman.

HEBB, D. O., and FOORD, E. N. 1945. Errors of visual recognition and the nature of the trace. *J. Exp. Psychol. 35:* 335–47.

HEILBRONER, R. L. 1961. *The worldly philosophers.* New York: Simon & Schuster.

HEILBRUN, A. B. 1972. Distinctiveness of maternal control: a further link in a theory of schizophrenic development. *J. Nerv. Ment. Dis. 154:* 49–59.

HEINEMANN, L. G. 1970. Visual phenomena in a long sensory deprivation. *Percept. Mot. Skills 30:* 563–70.

HEINSTEIN, M. I. 1968. Behavioral correlates of breast-bottle regimes under varying parent-infant relationships. *Monogr. Soc. Res. Child Develop. 28,* no. 4. whole #88, quoted in A. T. Jersild, *Child Psychology,* 6th ed. Englewood Cliffs, N.J.: Prentice-Hall.

HENAHAN, J. F. 1966. *Men and molecules.* New York: Crown.

HENDRICKS, S. B. 1968. How light interacts with matter. *Sci. Amer. 219,* no. 3.

HENRY, J. 1963. *Culture against man.* New York: Random House.

HERNANDEZ-PEON, R.; SCHERRER, H.; and JOUVET, M. 1956. Modification of electrical activity in cochlear nucleus during "attention" in unanesthetized cats. *Science 123:* 331–32.

HERON, W. 1957. The pathology of boredom. *Sci. Amer. 199,* no. 1.

HERSCH, C. 1968. The discontent explosion in mental health. *Amer. Psychol. 23:* 497–506.

HERSEN, M. 1972. Nightmare behavior: a review. *Psychol. Bull. 78:* 37–48.

HESS, E. H. 1972. "Imprinting" in a natural laboratory. *Sci. Amer. 227,* no. 2.

HESS, E. H. 1959. Imprinting: an effect of early experience. *Science 130:* 133–41.

HETHERINGTON, E. M. 1965. A developmental study of the effects of sex of the dominant parent on sex-role preference, identification and imitation in children. *J. Personal. Soc. Psychol. 2:* 188–94.

———. 1973. Girls without fathers. *Psychol. Today 6,* no. 9.

HICKEY, T. 1969. Psychologic rehabilitation for the "normal" elderly. *Ment. Hyg. 53:* 369–74.

HICKS, J. D. 1954. *The federal union.* Cambridge, Mass.: Riverside Press.

HIMWICH, H. E., 1969. Psycholpharmacologic drugs. Quoted in N. L. Munn, L. Fernald, Jr., and P. Fernald, *Introduction to psychology.* 2nd ed. Boston: Houghton Mifflin.

HIPPOCRATES. 1952. On the sacred disease. In R. M. Hutchins, ed., *The great books of the western world,* no. 10. Chicago: Encyclopaedia Britannica.

HIRNING, L. C. 1961. Clothing and nudism. In A. Ellis and A. Abarbanel, eds., *The encyclopaedia of sexual behavior.* New York; Hawthorne.

HIRSCHI, T. 1969. *Causes of delinquency.* Los Angeles: University of California Press.

HITLER, A. 1942. Speech of February 24, 1933. In N. H. Baynes, ed., *The speeches of Adolf Hilter, vol. 1,* 252. Oxford: Oxford University Press.

HOFFMAN, E. 1971. The idiot savant: a case report and a review of explanations. *Ment. Retard. 9:* 18–21.

HOFFMAN, M. 1968. *The gay world: male homosexuality and the social creation of evil.* New York: Basic Books.

HOFFMAN, M. L., and SALTZSTEIN, H. D. 1967. Parent discipline and the child's moral development. *J. Personal. Soc. Psychol. 5:* 45–57.

HOKANSON, J., and BURGESS, M. 1962. The effects of three types of aggression on vascular process. *J. Abnorm. Soc. Psychol. 64:* 446–49.

HOLLAND, J. G., and SKINNER, B. F. 1961. *The analyses of behavior: a program for self instruction.* New York: McGraw-Hill.

HOLLISTER, L. E. 1971. Marihuana in man: three years later. *Science 172:* 21–28.

HOLMES, C. S., and SCHALLOW, J. R. 1969. Reduced recall after ego threat: Repression or response competition? *J. Personal. Soc. Psychol. 13:* 145–52.

HOLT, R. R. 1970. Yet another look at clinical and statistical prediction; or is clinical psychology worthwhile? *Amer. Psychol. 25:* 337–49.

HOMER. 1952. The odyssey. In R. M. Hutchins, ed., *The great books of the western world, No. 4.* Chicago: Encyclopaedia Britannica.

HOMME, L. E.; DEBACA, P. C.; DEVINE, J. V.; STEINHORST, R.; and RICKERT, E. J. 1963. Use of the Premack principle in controlling the behavior of nursery school children. *J. Exp. Anal. Behav. 6:* 544.

HONIGMANN, J. 1959. *The world of man.* New York: Harper & Row.

HONORTON, C., and KRIPPNER, S. 1969. Hypnosis and esp performance: a review of the experimental literature. *J. Amer. Soc. Psychical Res. 63:* 214–52.

HONZIK, M. P.; MCFARLANE, J. W.; and ALLEN, L. 1948. The stability of mental test performance between two and eighteen years. *J. Exp. Educ. 17:* 309–24.

HOOD, A. B. 1963. A study of the relationship between physique and personality variables measured by the MMPI. *J. Personal. 31:* 97–107.

HOOK, E. B. 1973. Behavioral implications of the human XYZ genotype. *Science 179:* 151–57.

HOOKER, E. 1957. The adjustment of the male overt homosexual. *J. Proj. Tech. 21:* 18–31.

———. 1962. The homosexual community. In *Proceed. 14th Int. Cong. Appl. Psychol.,* vol. 2. *Personality research.* Copenhagen, Denmark: Munksgaard.

HORNEY, K. 1950. *Neurosis and human growth.* New York: Norton.

HORTON, M. 1972. Personal communication.

HOWARD, K. I.; ORLINSKY, D. E.; and TRATTER, J. H. 1970. Therapist orientation and patient experience in psychotherapy. *J. Counsel. Psychol. 17:* 263–70.

HUBBARD, R., and KNOPF, A. 1967. Molecular isomers in vision. *Sci. Amer. 216,* no. 6.

HUBEL, D. 1963. The visual cortex of the brain. *Sci. Amer. 209,* no. 5.

HUBEL, D., and WIESEL, T. N. 1962. Receptive fields, binocular interaction and functional architecture in the cat's visual cortex. *J. Physiol. 160:* 106–54.

HUGHES, E. C. 1964. Good people and dirty work. In H. S. Becker, ed., *The other side: perspectives on deviance.* New York: Free Press.

HUMPHREYS, L. 1970. *Tearoom trade: impersonal sex in public places.* Chicago: Aldine.

HUNT, J. M. 1969. Black genes—white environment. *Transaction 6:* 12–22.

Hurvich, L. M., and Jameson, D. 1969. Human color perception: an essay review. *Amer. Sci. 57:* 143–66.

Husni-Palacios, M., and Scheur, P. 1972. The high school student: a personality profile. *Proceed. 80th Annual Conv. Amer. Psychol. Assn.*

Hutchins, R. M., ed. 1952. The major works of Sigmund Freud. In *The great books of the western world.* Chicago: Encyclopaedia Britannica.

Inhelder, B., and Sinclair, H. 1969. Learning cognitive structures. In P. Mussen, J. Langer, and M. Covington, eds., *Trends and issues in development psychology.* New York: Holt, Rinehart & Winston.

Irvine, S. H. 1970. Affect and construct: a cross-cultural check on theories of intelligence. *J. Soc. Psychol. 80:* 23–30.

Irvine, W. 1955. *Apes, angels and victorians.* New York: McGraw-Hill.

Jacks, I. 1972. Religious affiliation and educational, political and religious values of college freshmen and sophomores. *Adolescence 7,* no. 25.

Jackson, D. D., ed. 1960. *The etiology of schizophrenia.* New York: Basic Books.

Jackson, R. H., and Dick, A. O. 1969. Visual summation and its relation to processing and memory. *Percept. Psychophys. 6:* 13–15.

Jacobson, L. I.; Berger, S. E.; and Millham, J. 1970. Individual differences in cheating during a temptation period when confronting failure. *J. Personal Soc. Psychol. 15:* 48–56.

Jacobson, L. I.; Millham, J., and Berger, S. E. 1969. Individual differences in information processing during concept learning. *Psychon. Sci. 14:* 287–89.

———. 1970. Effects of intelligence on the speed and frequency of problem solution in concept learning. *Psychon. Sci. 19:* 337.

Jacobson, M., and Hunt, R. K. 1973. The origins of nerve cell specificity. *Sci. Amer. 228,* no. 2.

James, W. 1890. *Principles of psychology.* New York: Holt, Rinehart & Winston.

Jansen, D. G., and Nickles, L. A. 1973. Variables that differentiate between single and multiple admission psychiatric patients at a state hospital over a five year period. *J. Clin. Psychol. 1:* 83–85.

Jastrow, R. 1967. *Red giants and white dwarfs.* New York: Harper & Row.

Jensen, A. R. 1969. How much can we boost IQ and scholarly achievement? *Harvard Educ. Rev. 39,* no. 1.

Jersild, A. T. 1968. *Child psychology.* 6th ed. Englewood Cliffs, N.J.: Prentice-Hall.

Jersild, A. T., and Holmes, F. B. 1935. Children's fears. *Child Develop. Monogr. 20.* New York: Teachers College, Columbia University.

Johdai, K. 1955. Extinction as due to the changed direction of a psychological force. *J. Exp. Psychol. 49:* 193–99.

John, E. K. 1967. *Mechanisms of memory.* New York: Academic.

John, E. R. 1972. Switchboard versus statistical theories of learning and memory. *Science 177:* 850–64.

Johnsgard, P. A. 1967. *Animal behavior.* Dubuque, Iowa: Wm. C. Brown Co.

JOHNSON, H. H., and WATKINS, T. A. 1971. The effects of message repetitions on immediate and delayed attitude change. *Psychon. Sci. 22:* 101–3.

JOINT COMMISSION ON MENTAL ILLNESS AND HEALTH. 1969. *Action for mental health.* New York: Basic Books.

JONES, H. E. 1949. *Motor performance and growth.* Berkeley: University of California Press.

JONES, K. J., and JONES, P. P. 1970. Contribution of the Rorschach to description of personality structure defined by several objective tests. *Psychol. Rep. 26:* 35–45.

JONES, K. L.; SHAINBERG, L. W.; and BYER, C. O. 1969. *Drugs and alcohol.* New York: Harper & Row.

JONES, R. M. 1970. *The new psychology of dreaming.* New York: Grune & Stratton.

JONES, V. 1970. Attitudes of college students and their changes: a 37-year study. *Genet. Psychol. Monogr. 81:* 3–80.

JOSEPHY, A. M., JR., ed. 1962. *American heritage history of flight.* New York: American Heritage.

———. 1968. *The Indian heritage of America.* New York: Knopf.

JOVANOVIC, U. J. 1971. *Normal sleep in man.* Stuttgart: Hoppokrates.

JUNG, C. G. 1925. *Psychology of the unconscious.* New York: Dodd, Mead.

———. 1933. *Modern man in search of a soul.* New York: Harcourt Brace Jovanovich.

———. 1938. *Psychology and religion.* New Haven, Conn.: Yale University Press.

———. 1958. Transformation symbolism in the mass. In V. S. de Laszlo, ed., *Psyche and symbol: a selection of writings of C. G Jung.* New York: Doubleday.

KAGAN, J. 1972. Do infants think? *Sci. Amer. 226,* no. 3.

———. 1973. Quoted in *APA Monitor 4,* no. 2.

KAGAN, J., and MOSS, H. A. 1962. *Birth to maturity.* New York: John Wiley.

KAHN, E.; FISHER, C.; EDWARDS, A.; and DAVIS, D. 1972. Psychophysiology of night terrors and nightmares. *Proceed. 80th Annual Conv. Amer. Psychol. Assn.*

KALLMAN, F. J. 1952. Comparative twin study on the genetic aspects of male homosexuality. *J. Nerv. Ment. Dis. 115:* 283–87.

KAMIYA, J. 1968. Conscious control of brain waves. *Psychol. Today 1,* no. 11.

———. 1969. Operant control of the eeg *alpha* rhythm and some of its reported effects on consciousness. In C. Tart, ed., *Altered states of consciousness.* New York: John Wiley.

KANDEL, D., and LESSER, G. S. 1969. Parent-adolescent relationships and adolescent independence in the United States and Denmark. *J. Marriage Fam. 31:* 348–58.

KANDEL, E. R. 1970. Nerve cells and behavior. *Sci. Amer. 223,* no. 1.

KANN, P. H. 1969. The Danis of Jiwika. *Wall St. J. 49,* no. 223.

KAPATOS, G., and GOLD, R. M. 1972. Tongue cooling during drinking: a regulator of water intake in rats. *Science 176:* 685–86.

KARLSSON, J. L. 1967. Evidence of hereditary transmission of schizophrenia. *J. Schizophrenia 1:* 239–54.

KASTENBAUM, R. 1959. Time and death in adolescence. In H. Feifel, ed., *The meaning of death.* New York: McGraw-Hill.

KATO, T.; JARVIK, L. F.; ROIZIN, L.; and MORALISHVILI, E. 1970. Chromosomal studies in pregnant rhesus macaque given LSD-25. *Dis. Nerv. Syst. 31:* 245–50.

KATONA, G. 1940. *Organizing and memorizing.* New York: Columbia University Press.

KATZ, D., and BRALY, K. 1958. Verbal stereotypes and racial prejudice. In E. Maccoby, T. Newcomb, and E. Hautley, eds., *Readings in social psychology.* New York: Holt, Rinehart & Winston.

KATZ, I. 1964. Review of evidence relating to effects of desegregation on the intellectual performance of Negroes. *Amer. Psychol. 19:* 381–99.

KATZ, M.; WASKOW, I. E.; and OLSSON, J. 1968. Characterizing the psychological state produced by LSD. *J. Abnorm. Psychol. 73:* 1–14.

KEEVIL-ROGERS, P., and SCHNORE, M. M. 1969. Short-term memory as a function of age in persons above average intelligence. *J. Gerontol. 24:* 184–88.

KEITH, A. N. 1947. *Three came home.* Boston: Little, Brown.

KELLOGG, W. N., and KELLOGG, L. A. 1933. *The ape and the child.* New York: McGraw-Hill.

KELLY, H. H. 1968. Two functions of reference groups. Quoted in D. Cartwright and A. Zander, eds., *Group dynamics: research and theory.* New York: Harper & Row.

KERCHOFF, A. C., and BACK, K. W. 1968. *The june bug.* New York: Appleton-Century-Crofts.

KESNER, R. P., and CONNER, H. S. 1972. Independence of short- and long-term memory: a neural system analysis. *Science 176:* 432–34.

KETCHUM, R. M., ed. 1959. *The American heritage book of the pioneer spirit.* New York: American Heritage.

KEUP, W. 1969. The legal status of marihuana. *Dis. Nerv. Syst. 30:* 517–23.

KEYS, A.; BROZEK, J.; HENSCHEL, A.; MICKELSON, O.; and TAYLOR, H. L. 1950. *The biology of human starvation.* Minneapolis: University of Minnesota Press.

KIESLER, C. A. 1963. Attraction to the group and conformity to group norms. *J. Personal. 31:* 559–69.

KING, F. W. 1969. Marijuana and LSD usage among male college students: prevalence rate, frequency, and self estimates of future use. *Psychiatry 32:* 265–76.

——. 1970a. Personal communication.

——. 1970b. Users and nonusers of marijuana: some attitudinal and behavioral correlates. *J. Amer. Coll. Health Assn. 18:* 213–17.

KINSBOURNE, M. 1972. Eye and head turning indicates cerebral lateralization. *Science 176:* 539–41.

KINSEY, A. C.; POMEROY, W. B.; and MARTIN, C. E. 1948. *Sexual behavior in the human male.* Philadelphia: Saunders.

KINSEY, A. C.; POMEROY, W. B.; MARTIN, C. E.; and GEBHARD, P. H. 1953. *Sexual behavior in the human female.* Philadelphia: Saunders.

KITANO, H. H. L. 1970. Mental illness in four cultures. *J. Soc. Psychol. 80:* 121–34.

KLEEMEIER, R. W. 1960. Personal communication.

KLEITMAN, N. 1949. Biological rhythm and cycles. *Psychol. Rev. 29:* 1–30.

——. 1963. *Sleep and wakefulness.* Chicago: University of Chicago Press.

KLEITMAN, N., and KLEITMAN, H. 1953. The sleep-wakefulness pattern in the Arctic. *Sci. Monthly 76:* 349–56.

KLINE, K. E. 1971. Quoted in G. G. Luce, *Body time*. New York: Random House.

KLINE, M. V. 1972. The production of antisocial behavior through hypnosis: new clinical data. *Int. J. Clin. Exp. Hyp. 2:* 80–94.

KLUCKHOHN, C. 1949. *Mirror for man*. New York: McGraw-Hill.

KOFSKY, E. 1966. A scalogram study of classificatory development. *Child Develop. 37:* 191–204.

KOHLBERG, L. 1963. Moral development and identification. In H. W. Stevenson, ed., *Yearbook of the national society for the study of education: pt. 1, child psychology*. Chicago: University of Chicago Press.

KOLERS, P. A. 1972. Experiments in reading. *Sci. Amer. 227*, no. 1.

KOMAROVSKY, M. 1950. Functional analysis of sex roles. *Amer. Socio. Rev. 15:* 508–16.

KORNER, A. F. 1969. Neonatal startles, smiles, erections, and reflex sucks as related to state, sex and individuality. *Child Develop. 40:* 1039–53.

———. 1973. Sex differences in newborns with special reference to differences in the organization of oral behavior. *J. Child Psychol. Psychiat. 14:* 19–29.

KOULACK, D. 1969. Effects of somatosensory stimulation on dream content. *Arch. Gen. Psychiat. 20:* 718–25.

———. 1972. Rapid eye movements and visual imagery during sleep. *Psychol. Bull. 78:* 155–57.

KRAINES, S. H. 1968. Schizophrenic physiopathology. *Psychosomatics 9:* 19–29.

———. 1969. The neurophysiological basis of neurosis. *Psychosomatics 10:* 285–88.

KRAKOWSKI, A. J. 1969. General principles of chemotherapy of mental illness. *Psychosomatics 10:* 82–87.

KRECH, D. 1962. Cortical localization of function. In W. Postman, ed., *Psychology in the making*. New York: Knopf.

KREMER, M. S., and RIFKIN, A. H. 1969. The early development of homosexuality: a study of adolescent lesbians. *Amer. J. Psychiat. 126:* 129–34.

KRIGER, S. F., and KROES, W. H. 1972. Child-rearing attitudes of Chinese, Jewish and protestant mothers. *J. Soc. Psychol. 86:* 205–10.

KRIPPNER, S. 1970. The use of hypnosis and the improvement of academic achievement. *J. Spec. Educ. 4:* 451–60.

———. 1972. Experimentally-induced effects in dreams and other altered conscious states. *20th Int. Cong. Psychol.* Tokyo, August, 1972.

KRIPPNER, S., and DAVIDSON, R. 1971. The use of convergent operations in bio-information research. Lecture, Academy of Pedagogical Sciences. Moscow, June, 1971.

———. 1972. Parapsychology in the U.S.S.R. *Saturday Rev.*, March 18, 1972.

KUBIE, L. S., and MARGOLIN, S. 1944. An apparatus for the use of breath sounds as a hypnagogic stimulus. *Amer. J. Psychiat. 100:* 610.

KUEHN, J. L., and CRINELLA, F. M. 1969. Sensitivity training: interpersonal "overkill" and other problems. *Amer. J. Psychiat. 126:* 840–45.

KURTZ, R. M. 1969. Sex differences and variations in body attitudes. *J. Consult. Clin. Psychol. 33:* 625–29.

KURTZ, R. M., and HIRT, M. 1970. Body attitude and physical health. *J. Clin. Psychol. 26:* 149–51.

LAING, R. D. 1967. *The politics of experience*. Middlesex, England: Penguin.

LANDAVER, T. K. 1969. Reinforcement: a consolidation. *Psychol. Rev. 76:* 82–96.

LANDSBAUM, J. B., and WILLIS, R. H. 1971. Conformity in early and late adolescence. *Develop. Psychol. 4:* 334–37.

LANGER, J. 1969. *Theories of development.* New York: Holt, Rinehart & Winston.

LAWSON, R. G. 1970. Relative effectiveness of one-sided and two-sided communications in courtroom persuasion. *J. Gen. Psychol. 82:* 3–16.

LEARY, T. 1973. The principles and practice of hedonic psychology. *Psychol. Today 6,* no. 8.

LEBOVITZ, P. S. 1972. Feminine behavior in boys: aspects of its outcome. *Amer. J. Psychiat. 128:* 1283–89.

LEE, E. S. 1951. Negro intelligence and selective migration: a Philadelphia test of the Klineberg hypothesis. *Amer. Rev. 16:* 227–32.

LEECH, K., and JORDAN, B. 1970. *Drugs for young people: their use and misuse.* Oxford: Pergamon Press.

LEEF, R. 1969. Effects of punishment intensity and consistency on the internalization of behavioral suppression in children. *Develop. Psychol. 1:* 345–56.

LEIBOWITZ, H. W. 1965. *Visual perception.* New York: Macmillan.

LEONARD, G. B. 1968. *Education and ecstasy.* New York: Delacorte Press.

LESTER, D. 1972. *Why people kill themselves.* Springfield, Ill.: Charles C Thomas.

LESTER, G., and LESTER, D. 1971. *Suicide: the gamble with death!* Englewood Cliffs, N.J.: Prentice-Hall.

LETTVIN, J. Y.; MANTURA, H. R.; McCOLLOCH, W. S.; and PITTS, W. H. 1959. What the frog's eye tells the frog's brain. *Proceed. Inst. Radio Engr. 47:* 1940–51.

LEVENTHAL, H. 1967. Fear for your health. *Psychol. Today 1,* no. 5.

LEVINE, M. L.; McNAMEE, G. C.; and GREENBERG, D., eds., *The tales of Hoffman.* New York: Bantam.

LEVITZ, L. S., and ULLMAN, L. P. 1969. Manipulation of indications of disturbed thinking in normal subjects. *J. Consult. Clin. Psychol. 33:* 633–41.

LEVY, M. R. 1970. Issues in the personality assessment of lower-class patients. *J. Proj. Tech. Personal. Assess. 34:* 6–9.

LEVY, M. R., and KAHN, M. W. 1970. Interpreter bias on the Rorschach test as a function of patient's socioeconomic status. *J. Proj. Tech. Personal. Assess. 34:* 106–12.

LEWIS, A., and *The New York Times.* 1964. *Portrait of a decade: the second American revolution.* New York: Random House.

LEWIS, O. 1969. The possessions of the poor. *Sci. Amer. 221,* no. 4.

LIDDELL, H. S. 1954. Conditioning and emotions. *Sci. Amer. 190,* no. 1.

LIDZ, T.; CORNELISON, A.; TERRY, D.; and HECK, S. 1958. Intrafamilial environment of the schizophrenic patient: The transmission of irrationality. *A.M.A. Arch. Neurol. Psychiat. 79:* 305–16.

LIEBERMAN, M. A. 1969. Institutionalization of the aged: effects on behavior. *J. Gerontol. 24:* 330–40.

LIEBERT, R. M., and NEALE, J. M. 1972. TV violence and child aggression: snow on the screen. *Psychol. Today 5,* no. 11.

LIFTON, R. 1961. *Thought reform and the psychology of totalism.* New York: Norton.

LINDSLEY, D. B. 1960. Attention, consciousness, sleep and wakefulness. In J. Field, ed., *Handbook of physiology, vol. 3.* Washington, D.C.: American Physiological Society.

LINDZEY, G., and HEUMAN, P. S. 1955. Thematic apperception test: a note on reliability and situational validity. *J. Proj. Tech. 19:* 36–42.

LINDZEY, G.; LOEHLIN, T.; MANOSEVITZ, M.; and THISSEN, D. 1971. Behavioral genetics. In P. Mussen and M. R. Rosenzweig, eds., *Annual review of psychology.* Palo Alto, Calif.: Annual Reviews.

LINTON, R. 1945. *The cultural background of personality.* New York: Appleton-Century-Crofts.

LIPMAN-BLUMEN, J. 1972. How ideology shapes women's lives. *Sci. Amer. 226,* no. 1.

LONDON, P. 1964. *The modes and morals of psychotherapy.* New York: Holt, Rinehart & Winston.

LORENZ, K. 1952. *King Solomon's ring.* New York: Thomas Y. Crowell.

———. 1963. *On aggression.* New York: Harcourt Brace Jovanovich.

LUCE, G. G. 1971. *Body time.* New York: Random House.

LUCHINS, A. S. 1942. Mechanization in problem solving: the effect of *einstellung. Psychol. Monogr. 54,* no. 248.

LUDWIG, A. M.; BRANDSMA, J. M.; WILBUR, C.; BENDFELDT, F.; and JAMESON, D. 1972. The objective study of a multiple personality. *Arch. Gen. Psychiat. 26:* 298–310.

LURIA, A. R. 1968. *The mind of a mnemonist.* New York: Basic Books.

———. 1970. The functional organization of the brain. *Sci. Amer. 222,* no. 3.

LYKKEN, D. T. 1960. The validity of the guilty knowledge technique: the effects of faking. *J. Appl. Psychol. 44:* 258–62.

MAAS, P. 1968. *The Valachi papers.* New York: Putnam's.

MACCOBY, E. E., ed. 1966. *The development of sex differences.* Stanford, Calif.: Stanford University Press.

———. 1972. The meaning of being female. *J. Contemp. Psychol. 17:* 369–72.

MACDONALD, A. P., JR. 1971. Correlates of the ethics of personal conscience and the ethics of social responsibility. *J. Consult. Clin. Psychol. 37:* 443.

MACDONALD, A. P., JR. and MAJUMDER, R. K. 1972. Do the poor know how we see them? Preliminary study. *Percept. Mot. Skills 34:* 47–49.

MACKINNON, D. W. 1962. The nature and nurture of creative talent. *Amer. Psychol. 17:* 484–95.

MACKWORTH, N. H. 1965. Visual noise causes tunnel vision. *Psychon. Sci. 3:* 67–68.

MADDOX, G. L., and McCALL, B. D. 1964. *Drinking among teenagers.* New Brunswick, N.J.; Rutgers Center of Alcohol Studies.

MAIER, H. W. 1965. *Three theories of child development.* New York: Harper & Row.

MAIER, N. R., and JANZEN, J. C. 1969. Are good problem solvers also creative? *Psychol. Rep. 24:* 139–46.

MALINOWSKI, B. 1925. Magic, science and religion. In J. Needham, ed., *Science, religion and reality.* New York: Macmillan.

———. 1929. *The sexual life of savages in northwestern Melanesia.* New York: Harcourt Brace Jovanovich.

MALPASS, R. S. 1969. Effects of attitude on learning and memory: the influence of instruction induced sets. *J. Exp. Soc. Psychol. 5:* 441–53.

Mancuso, J. C., and Dreisinger, M. 1969. A view of the historical and current development of the concept of intelligence. *Psychol. Sci. 6:* 137–51.

Mann, L. 1970. Perceptual training: misdirections and redirections. *Amer. J. Orthopsychiat. 40:* 30–38.

Manning, A. 1967. *An introduction to animal behavior.* Reading, Mass.: Addison-Wesley.

Manuel, F. E. 1964. *The new world of Henri Saint-Simon.* Quoted in F. W. Matson, *The broken image.* New York: Braziller.

Marcia, J. E.; Rubin, B. M.; and Efran, J. S. 1969. Systematic desensitization: expectancy, change or counter conditioning? *J. Abnorm. Psychol.* 74: 382–87.

Margules, D. L., and Olds, J. 1962. Identical "feeding" and "rewarding" systems in the lateral hypothalamus of rats. *Science 135:* 374–75.

Marshall, J. 1969. The evidence. *Psychol. Today 2,* no. 9.

Martin, J. M. 1961. *Juvenile vandalism: a study of its nature and prevention.* Springfield, Ill.: Charles C Thomas.

Maslow, A. H. 1954. *Motivation and personality.* New York: Harper & Row.

———. 1962. *Toward a psychology of being.* New York: Van Nostrand Reinhold.

Mason, A. S. 1961. *Health and hormones.* Baltimore: Penguin.

Mason, R. F. 1961. *Internal perception and bodily functioning.* New York: International Universities Press.

Massaro, D. W. 1970a. Forgetting: interference or decay? *J. Exp. Psychol. 83:* 238–43.

———. 1970b. Perceptual processes and forgetting in memory tasks. *Psychol. Rev.* Received in mimeographed form.

Masters, W. H., and Johnson, V. E. 1962. The sexual response cycle of the human female 3. The clitoris: Anatomic and clinical considerations. *West. J. Surg. Obst. Gynec. 70:* 248–57.

———. 1966. *Human sexual response.* Boston: Little, Brown.

Matefy, R. E. 1972. Operant conditioning procedure to modify schizophrenic behavior: a case report. *Psychother. Theor. Res. Pract. 9:* 226–30.

Matson, F. W. 1964. *The broken image.* New York: Braziller.

Maxwell, J. 1969a. Assessing skimming and scanning improvement. *18th Yrbk. Nat. Read. Conf.:* 229–33.

———. 1969b. *Skimming and scanning improvement.* New York: McGraw-Hill.

May, P. R. 1968. *Treatment of schizophrenia: a comparative study of five treatment methods.* New York: Science House.

May, R. 1967. *Psychology and the human dilemma.* New York: Van Nostrand Reinhold.

Mayer, J. 1968. *Overweight: causes, cost and control.* Englewood Cliffs, N.J.: Prentice-Hall.

McCall, R. B.; Hogarty, P. S.; and Hurlburt, N. 1972. Transitions in infant sensorimotor development and the prediction of childhood IQ. *Amer. Psychol. 27:* 728–48.

McCall, R. L. 1963. The defense mechanisms reexamined: a logical and phenomenal analysis. *Catholic Psychol. Rec. 1:* 45–64.

McCann, J. J. 1972. Rod-cone interactions: different color sensations from identical stimuli. *Science 176:* 1255–57.

McClearn, G. E. 1962. The inheritance of behavior. In L. Postman, ed., *Psychology in the making.* New York: Knopf.

McClelland, D. C. 1973. Testing for competence rather than for "intelligence." *Amer. Psychol. 28:* 1–14.

McClelland, D. C.; Atkinson, J. W.; Clark, R. A.; and Lowell, E. L. 1953. *The achievement motive.* New York: Appleton-Century-Crofts.

McConnell, J. D. 1968. Effects of pricing on perception of product quality. *J. Appl. Psychol. 52,* no. 4.

McCormack, P. D. 1972. Recognition memory: how complex a retrieval system? *Can. J. Psychol./Rev. Can. Psychol. 26:* 19–41.

McDaniel, C. O., Jr. 1969. Dating roles and reasons for dating. *J. Marriage Fam. 31:* 97–107.

McGaugh, J. L., and Hostetter, R. C. 1967. Retention as a function of the temporal position of sleep and activity following waking. Unpublished manuscript quoted in E. R. Hilgard and R. C. Atkinson, *Introduction to psychology,* 4th ed. New York: Harcourt Brace Jovanovich.

McGlothlin, W. H., and Arnold, D. O. 1971. LSD revisited: a ten year follow-up of medical LSD use. *Arch. Gen. Psychiat. 24:* 35–49.

McGraw, M. B. 1939. Swimming behavior of the human infant. *J. Pediat. 15:* 485–90.

McGuire, W. J. 1964. Inducing resistance to persuasion: Some contemporary approaches. In L. Berkowitz, ed., *Advances in experimental social psychology.* New York: Academic.

McKee, J. P., and Leader, F. 1955. The relationship of socioeconomic status and aggression to the competitive behavior of preschool children. *Child Develop. 26:* 135–42.

McKendry, J. M.; Snyder, M. B.; and Gates, S. 1963. Factors affecting perceptual integration of illustrated material. *J. Appl. Psychol. 47:* 293–99.

McKenzie, R. 1973. Quoted in *APA Monitor 4,* no. 4.

McMahon, F. B. 1969. Psychological testing: a smoke screen against logic. *Psychol. Today 2,* no. 8.

McNeill, W. H. 1963. *The rise of the west.* Chicago: University of Chicago Press.

McWilliams, S. A., and Tuttle, R. J. 1973. Long-term psychological effects of LSD. *Psychol. Bull. 79:* 341–51.

Mead, G. H. 1934. *Mind, self and society.* Chicago: University of Chicago Press.

Mead, M. 1928. *Coming of age in Samoa.* New York: William Morrow.

——. 1935. *Sex and temperament in three primitive societies.* New York: William Morrow.

——. 1949. *Male and female: a study of the sexes in a changing world.* New York: William Morrow.

Medinnus, G. R. 1962. Objective responsibility in children: A comparison with Piaget's data. *J. Genet. Psychol. 101:* 122–33.

Melton, A. W. 1963. Implications of short-term memory for a general theory of memory. *J. Verb. Learn. Behav. 2:* 1–21.

Meltzoff, J., and Blumenthal, R. 1966. *The day treatment center: principles, application and evaluation.* Springfield, Ill.: Charles C Thomas.

Melzack, R. 1961. The perception of pain. *Sci. Amer. 204,* no. 2.

Melzack, R., and Casey, K. L. 1970. The affective dimension of pain. In M. B. Arnold, ed., *Feelings and emotions: the Loyola symposium.* New York: Academic Press.

Melzack, R., and Scott, T. H. 1957. The effect of early experience on response to pain. *J. Comp. Physio. Psychol. 50:* 155–61.

Melzack, R., and Wall, P. D. 1965. Pain mechanisms: a new theory. *Science 150:* 971–79.

Menaker, M. 1972. Nonvisual light reception. *Sci. Amer. 226,* no. 3.

Mencken, H. L. 1950. *In defense of women.* New York: Knopf.

Mercer, J. R. 1972. IQ: the lethal label. *Psychol. Today 6,* no. 4.

Merrill, M. A. 1938. The significance of IQs on the revised Stanford-Binet scale. *J. Educ. Psychol. 26:* 641–50.

Merz, W. R., and Rutherford, B. M. 1972. Differential teacher regard for creative students and achieving students. *Calif. J. Educ. Res. 23:* 83–90.

Michael, C. R. 1969. Retinal processing of visual images. *Sci. Amer. 220,* no. 5.

Milgram, S. 1965. Some conditions of obedience and disobedience to authority. *Hum. Relat. 18:* 57–76.

Miller, G. A. 1962. *Psychology: the science of mental life.* New York: Harper & Row.

Miller, N. E. 1948. Studies of fear as an acquired drive, i. fear as motivation and fear-reduction as reinforcement in the learning of new responses. *J. Exp. Psychol. 38:* 89–101.

———. 1971. Learning of visceral and glandular responses, in *Biofeedback and self control.* Chicago: Aldine-Atherton.

Miller, N. E., and Murray, E. J. 1952. Displacement and conflict: learnable drive as a basis for the steeper gradient of avoidance than of approach. *J. Exp. Psychol. 43:* 227–31.

Mirsky, A. F. 1969. Neuropsychological bases of schizophrenia. In P. H. Mussen and M. R. Rosenzweig, eds., *Annual review of psychology.* Palo Alto, Calif.: Annual Reviews.

Mischel, W. 1969. Continuity and change in personality. *Amer. Psychol. 24:* 1012–18.

Mischel, W.; Ebbesen, E. B.; and Zeiss, A. 1972. Cognitive and attentional mechanisms in delay of gratification. *J. Personal. Soc. Psychol. 21:* 204–18.

Modell, W., and Lansing, A. 1967. *Drugs.* New York: Time, Inc.

Money, J. 1961a. Components of eroticism in man: i. the hormones in relation to sexual morphology and sexual desire. *J. Nerv. Ment. Dis. 132:* 239–48.

———. 1961b. Hermaphroditism. In A. Ellis and A. Abarbanel, eds., *Encyclopaedia of sexual behavior.* New York: Hawthorne.

Montagu, A. 1962. *Man: his first million years.* New York: New American Library.

———. 1964. *Man's most dangerous myth: the fallacy of race.* 4th ed. New York: World Publishing.

Morgan, C. D., and Murray, H. A. 1935. A method for investigating fantasies: the thematic apperception test. *Arch. Neurol. Psychiat. 34:* 289–305.

Morgan, C. T. 1965. *Physiological psychology.* 3rd ed. New York: McGraw-Hill.

Moroney, W. F., and Zenhausern, R. J. 1972. Detection of deception as function of galvanic skin response recording methodology. *J. Psychol. 80:* 255–62.

Mosher, D. W., and Greenberg, I. 1969. Females' affective responses to reading erotic literature. *J. Consult. Clin. Psychol. 33:* 472–77.

Moss, C. S. 1965. *Hypnosis in perspective.* New York: Macmillan.

Moss, T., and Generelli, J. A. 1967. Telepathy and emotional stimuli: a controlled experiment. *J. Abnorm. Psychol. 72:* 341–48.

Moyer, K. E. 1973. The physiology of violence. *Psychol. Today 7,* no. 2.

Mrosovsky, N. 1968. The adjustable brain of hibernators. *Sci. Amer. 218,* no. 3.

Munn, N. L.; Fernald, L. D.; and Fernald, P. 1969. *Introduction to psychology.* 2nd ed. Boston: Houghton Mifflin.

Munroe, R. L. 1945. Prediction of the adjustment and academic performance of college students by a modification of the Rorschach method. *Appl. Psychol. Monogr. 7.*

Munsinger, H., and Kessen, W. 1964. Uncertainty, structure and preference. *Psychol. Monogr. 78:* whole 586.

Murdock, G. P. 1949. *Social structure.* New York: Macmillan.

Murphy, G. 1961. *Challenge of physical research.* New York: Harper & Row.

Murray, E. J. 1964. *Motivation and emotion.* Englewood Cliffs, N.J.: Prentice-Hall.

Murray, J. B. 1969. The puzzle of pain. *Percept. Mot. Skills 28:* 887–99.

Mussen, P. H. 1963. *The psychological development of the child.* Englewood Cliffs, N.J.: Prentice-Hall.

Mykytowyez, R. 1968. Territorial marking by rabbits. *Sci. Amer. 218,* no. 5.

Nash, J. 1970. *Developmental psychology: a psychobiological approach.* Englewood Cliffs, N.J.: Prentice-Hall.

Nathan, P. E.; Andberg, M. M.; Behan, P. O.; and Patch, V. D. 1969. Thirty-two observers and one patient: a study of diagnostic reliability. *J. Clin. Psychol. 25,* no. 1.

National Institute of Mental Health. 1972. *Alcohol and alcoholism.* Washington, D.C.: U.S. Government Printing Office.

Neisser, U. 1968. The processes of vision. *Sci. Amer. 219,* no. 3.

Neubauer, P. B., ed. 1965. *Children in collectives.* Springfield, Ill.: Charles C Thomas.

Neverovich, Y. Z. 1969. Mastery of movements of objects at pre-preschool and preschool ages. In M. Cole and I. Maltzman, eds., *Contemporary Soviet psychology.* New York: Basic Books.

Newton, I. 1952. Optics, book 3. In R. M. Hutchins, ed., *Great books of the western world no. 34.* Chicago: Encyclopaedia Britannica.

Newton, N. 1968. Breast feeding. *Psychol. Today 2,* no. 1.

Nicholls, J. G. 1972. Creativity in the person who will never produce anything original and useful: The concept of creativity as a normally distributed trait. *Amer. Psychol. 27:* 717–27.

Nizer, L. 1966. *The jury returns.* New York: Doubleday.

Noton, D., and Stark, L. 1971. Scanpaths in eye movements during pattern perception. *Science 171:* 308–11.

Nourse, A. E. 1964. *The body.* New York: Time, Inc.

Offer, D.; Marcus, D.; and Offer, J. L. 1970. A longitudinal study of normal adolescent boys. *Amer. J. Psychiat. 126:* 917–24.

Offer, D., and Offer, J. L. 1969. Growing up: a follow-up study of normal adolescents. *Semin. Psychiat. 1:* 46–57.

Olds, J. 1956. Pleasure centers in the brain. *Sci. Amer. 195,* no. 4.

——— . 1969. The central nervous system and the reinforcement of behavior. *Amer. Psychol. 24:* 114–32.

O'LEARY, K. D.; POULOS, R. W.; and DEVINE, V. T. 1972. Tangible reinforcers: bonuses or bribes? *J. Consult. Clin. Psychol. 38:* 1–8.

O'NEILL, W. L. 1971. Coming apart: an informal history of *America in the 1960s.* Chicago: Quadrangle Books.

ORBACH, J.; EHRLICH, D.; and HEATH, H. A. 1963. Reversibility of the necker cube: 1. An examination of the concept of satiation of orientation. *Percept. Mot. Skills 17:* 439–58.

ORLINSKY, D. E.; HOWARD, K. I.; and HILL, J. A. 1970. The patient's concerns in psychotherapy. *J. Clin. Psychol. 26:* 104–11.

ORNE, M. T. 1962. Antisocial behavior and hypnosis. In G. H. Estabrooks, ed., *Hypnosis: current problems.* New York: Harper & Row.

OSBORN, A. F. 1963. *Applied imagination.* New York: Scribner's.

OSTER, G. 1970. Phosphenes. *Sci. Amer. 222,* no. 2.

OSWALD, I. 1966. *Sleep.* Baltimore: Penguin.

OWEN, D. R. 1972. The 47,XXY male: a review. *Psychol. Bull. 78:* 209–33.

PALMER, R. I., and MASLING, J. 1969. Vocabulary for skin color in negro and white children. *Develop. Psychol. 1:* 396–401.

PARDUCCI, A. 1968. The relativism of absolute judgments. *Sci. Amer. 219,* no. 6.

PASKEWITZ, D.; LYNCH, J.; ORNE, M.; and CASTELLO, J. 1970. The feedback control of *alpha* activity: conditioning or disinhibition. *Psychophysiol. 6:* 637–40.

PENFIELD, W. 1959. The interpretive cortex. *Science 129:* 1719–25.

PENGELLEY, E. T., and ASMUNDSON, S. J. 1971. Annual biological clocks. *Sci. Amer. 224,* no. 4.

PETERS, J. 1970. Personal communication.

PETERS, R. S. 1965. Freud's theory in psychology. In B. B. Wolman and E. Nagel, eds., *Scientific psychology: principles and approaches.* New York: Basic Books.

PETERSON, L. R. 1966. Short-term memory. In *Psychology: the biological bases of behavior.* San Francisco: W. H. Freeman.

PFEIFFER, E. 1970. Survival in old age: Physical, psychological and social correlates of longevity. *J. Amer. Geriat. Soc. 18:* 273–85.

PHILLIPS, J. L., Jr. 1969. *The origins of intellect: Piaget's theory.* San Francisco: W. H. Freeman.

PIAGET, J. 1929. *The child's conception of the world.* New York: Harcourt Brace Jovanovich.

———. 1948. *The moral judgment of the child.* M. Gabin, tr. New York: Free Press.

———. 1952. *The origins of intelligence in children.* New York: International Universities Press.

PIERCE, C. S. 1962. The doctrine of necessity. In W. Barrett and H. Aiken, eds., *Philosophy in the twentieth century,* vol. 1. New York: Random House.

PINE, G. J. 1965. Social class, social mobility and delinquent behavior. *Pers. Guid. J. 43:* 770–74.

PITTMAN, D. J. 1964. Personal communication.

PITTS, F. N., Jr. 1969. The biochemistry of anxiety. *Sci. Amer. 220,* no. 2.

PLATO. 1952. Phaedo. In R. M. Hutchins, ed., *Great books of the western world, no. 7.* Chicago: Encyclopaedia Britannica.

Pomeroy, W. B. 1972. *Dr. Kinsey and the institute for sex research.* New York: Harper & Row.

Postman, L.; Adams, P. A.; and Phillips, L. W. 1955. Studies in incidental learning: ii. The effects of association value and the method of testing. *J. Exp. Psychol. 59:* 439–49.

Premack, A. J., and Premack, D. 1972. Teaching language to an ape. *Sci. Amer. 227,* no. 4.

Pribram, K. H. 1969. Neurophysiology of remembering. *Sci. Amer. 220,* no. 1.

Quay, H. C. 1965. Psychopathic personality as pathological stimulation-seeking. *Amer. J. Psychiat. 122:* 180–83.

Rabin, A. I. 1958. Kibbutz children: research findings to date. *Children 5:* 179–85.

Rabkin, J. G. 1972. Opinions about mental illness: a review of the literature. *Psychol. Bull. 77:* 153–71.

Racinskas, J., and Vogel-Sprott, M. 1969. Rigidity induced through reward and punishment. *J. Exp. Res. Personal. 3:* 221–27.

Rafaelsen, O. J.; Bech, P.; Christiansen, J.; Christrup, H.; Nyboe, J.; and Rafaelsen, L. 1973. Cannabis and alcohol: effects on simulated car driving. *Science 179:* 920–23.

Ralston, N. C., and Thomas, P. 1972. America's artificial adolescents. *Adolescence 7,* no. 25.

Rank, O. 1929. *The trauma of birth.* New York: Harcourt Brace Jovanovich.

Raskin, N., and Ehrenberg, R. 1956. Senescence, senility and Alzheimer's disease. *Amer. J. Psychiat. 113:* 133–36.

Ratliff, F. 1972. Contour and contrast. *Sci. Amer. 226,* no. 6.

Ratner, S. 1968. Personal communication as reported by R. Rosenthal and L. Jacobson. *Pygmalion in the classroom: teacher expectation and pupils' intellectual development.* New York: Holt, Rinehart & Winston.

Raymond, B. 1969. Short-term storage and long-term storage in free recall. *J. Verb. Learn. Behav. 8:* 567–74.

Razran, G. 1961. The observable unconscious and the inferable conscious in current Soviet psychophysiology: Interoceptive conditioning, and the orienting reflex. *Psychol. Rev. 68:* 81–147.

Reichenbach, H. 1931. *Phantom fame.* New York: Simon & Schuster.

Reiff, R., and Scheerer, M. 1960. *Memory and hypnotic age regression.* New York: International Universities Press.

Reisman, J. M. 1966. *The development of clinical psychology.* New York: Appleton-Century-Crofts.

Reiss, A. J., Jr., and Rhodes, A. L. 1963. Status deprivation and delinquent behavior. *Social Sci. Quart. 5:* 135–49.

Report of the commission on obscenity and pornography. 1970. Washington, D.C.: U.S. Government Printing Office.

Reyher, J. 1962. Posthypnotic stimulation of hypnotically-induced conflict in relation to anti-social behavior. *J. Soc. Ther. 7:* 92.

RICHTER, C. P. 1957. On the phenomenon of sudden death in animals and man. *Psychosom. Med. 19:* 191–98.

———. 1958. The phenomenon of unexplained sudden death in animals and man. In W. H. Gantt, ed., *Physiological bases of psychiatry.* Springfield, Ill.: Charles C Thomas.

RICHTER, C. P.; HOLT, L. E.; and BARELARE, B. 1937. Vitamin B$_1$ craving in rats. *Science 86:* 354.

RIEFF, P. 1959. *Freud: the mind of the moralist.* New York: Viking.

RIESIN, A. H. 1965. Effects of early deprivation of photic stimulation. In S. Osler and R. Cooke, eds., *The biosocial basis of mental retardation.* Baltimore: Johns Hopkins.

RIMM, D. C., and LITVAK, S. B. 1969. Self verbalization and emotional arousal. *J. Abnorm. Psychol. 74:* 181–87.

ROBINS, E., and GUZE, S. B. 1970. Establishment of diagnostic validity in psychiatric illness: its application to schizophrenia. *Amer. J. Psychiat. 126:* 107–11.

ROBINS, L. N. 1966. *Deviant children grown up: a sociological and psychiatric study of sociopathic personality.* Baltimore: Williams & Wilkins.

ROBINSON, I.; KING, K.; and BALSWICK, J. 1972. The premarital sexual revolution among college females. *Fam. Coord. 21:* 189–94.

ROFFWARG, H. P.; MUZIO, J. N.; and DEMENT, C. 1966. Ontogenetic development of the human sleep-dream cycle. *Science 152:* 604–19.

ROGERS, C. R. 1942. *Counseling and psychotherapy.* Boston: Houghton Mifflin.

———. 1951. *Client-centered therapy: its current practice, implications and theory.* Boston: Houghton Mifflin.

ROGERS, R. W., and THISTLETHWAITE, D. L. 1969. An analysis of active and passive defenses inducing resistance to persuasion. *J. Personal. Soc. Psychol. 11:* 301–8.

ROHLES, F. H., JR. 1967. Environmental psychology: a bucket of worms. *Psychol. Today 1,* no. 2.

ROSENBERG, S. D. 1970. Hospital culture as collective defense. *Psychiatry 33:* 21–35.

ROSENHAN, D. 1967. Aloneness and togetherness as drive conditions in children. *J. Exp. Res. Personal. 2:* 32–40.

ROSENHAN, D. L. 1973. On being sane in insane places. *Science 179:* 250–58.

ROSENSWEIG, S. 1964. Quoted by A. W. Astin in P. London, *The modes and morals of psychotherapy.* New York: Holt, Rinehart & Winston.

ROSENTHAL, R., and JACOBSON, L. 1968. *Pygmalion in the classroom: teacher expectation and pupils' intellectual development.* New York: Holt, Rinehart & Winston.

ROSENZWEIG, M. R. 1962. The mechanisms of hunger and thirst. In L. Postman, ed., *Psychology in the making.* New York: Knopf.

ROSENZWEIG, M. R.; BENNETT, E. L.; and DIAMOND, M. C. 1972. Brain changes in response to experience. *Sci. Amer. 226,* no. 2.

ROSENZWEIG, M. R., and LEIMAN, A. L. 1968. Brain functions. In P. R. Farnsworth, ed., *Annual review of psychology.* Palo Alto, Calif.: Annual Reviews.

ROSS, N. P., ed. 1961. *The epic of man.* New York: Time, Inc.

ROSS, W. S. 1968. *The last hero: Charles A. Lindbergh.* New York: Harper & Row.

ROSSI, A. M.; NATHAN, P. E.; HARRISON, R. H.; and SOLOMON, P. 1969. Operant responding for visual stimuli during sensory deprivation: effect of meaningfulness. *J. Abnorm. Psychol. 74:* 188–92.

ROTHENBERG, M. B. 1969. Violence and children. *Ment. Hyg. 53:* 539–44.

ROTHMAN, M. A. 1970. Response to McConnell. *Amer. Psychol. 25:* 280–81.

ROTTER, J. B. 1964. *Clinical psychology.* Englewood Cliffs, N.J.: Prentice-Hall.

RUCH, B. 1961. Medical inquiries and observations upon the diseases of the mind. In T. Shipley, ed., *Classics in psychology.* New York: Philosophical Library.

RUCH, F. L. 1967. *Psychology and life* 7th ed. Glenview, Ill.: Soctt, Foresman.

RUSSO, J. R. 1971. *A study of the effect upon the self-concept of delinquents when interaction takes place with mental patients.* Washington, D.C.: U.S. Department of Health, Education and Welfare, Proj. 9–E-098.

RUST, S. M., and BLICK, K. A. 1972. The application of two mnemonic techniques following rote memorization of a free recall task. *J. Psychol. 80:* 247–53.

RUTNER, I. T. 1970. A double barrel approach to modification of homosexual behavior. *Psychol. Rep. 26:* 355–58.

SACHAR, E. J.; KANTER, S. S.; BUIE, D.; ENGLE, R.; and MEHLMAN, R. 1970. Psychoendocrinology of ego disintegration. *Amer. J. Psychiat. 126:* 1067–78.

SACKETT, G. 1968. Abnormal behavior in laboratory-reared rhesus monkeys. In M. W. Fox, ed., *Abnormal behavior in animals.* Philadelphia: Saunders.

SAENGER, G. 1970a. Factors in recovery of untreated psychiatric patients. *Psychiat. Quart. 44:* 13–25.

———. 1970b. Patterns of change among "treated" and "untreated" patients seen in psychiatric community mental health clinics. *J. Nerv. Ment. Dis. 150:* 37–50.

SAFILIOS-ROTHSCHILD, C. 1972. The options of Greek men and women. *Sociol. Focus 5,* no. 2.

SAGHIR, M. T., and ROBINS, E. 1969. Homosexuality 1. Sexual behavior of the female homosexual. *Arch. Gen. Psychiat. 20:* 192–201.

SAGHIR, M. T.; ROBINS, E.; and WALBRAN, B. 1969. Homosexuality 2. Sexual behavior of the male homosexual. *Arch. Gen. Psychiat. 21:* 219–28.

SAINT-EXUPERY, A. DE. 1940. *Wind, sand and stars.* New York: Harcourt Brace Jovanovich.

———. 1942. *Night flight.* New York: Harcourt Brace Jovanovich.

SALK, L. 1973. The role of the heartbeat in the relations between mother and infant. *Sci. Amer. 228,* no. 5.

SANDERS, P. S., JR., and REYHER, J. 1969. Sensory deprivation and the enhancement of hypnotic susceptibility. *J. Abnorm. Psychol. 74:* 375–81.

SANTILLANA, G. DE. 1955. *The crime of Galileo.* Chicago: University of Chicago Press.

SANUA, V. D. 1969. Religion, mental health, and personality: a review of empirical studies. *Amer. J. Psychiat. 125:* 97–107.

SARASON, S. B.; MANDLER, G.; and CRAIGHILL, P. G. 1952. The effect of differential instructions on anxiety and learning. *J. Abnorm. Soc. Psychol. 47:* 561.

SARBIN, T. R. 1950. Contributions to role-taking theory: i. hypnotic behavior. *Psychol. Rev. 57:* 255.

———. 1967. The concept of hallucination. *J. Personal. 35:* 359–80.

SCHACHTER, S., and SINGER, J. 1962. Cognitive, social and psychological determinants of emotional state. *Psychol. Rev. 69:* 379–99.

SCHAEFER, C. E. 1969. The self concept of creative adolescents. *J. Psychol. 72:* 233–42.

SCHAEFER, L. F., and SCHOBEN, E. J., JR. 1956. *The psychology of adjustment.* Boston: Houghton Mifflin.

SCHAWLOW, A. L. 1968. Laser light. *Sci. Amer. 219,* no. 3.

SCHEIN, E. H.; SCHNEIDER, I.; and BARKER, C. H. 1961. *Coercive persuasion.* New York: Norton.

SCHICKEL, R. 1968. *The Disney version.* New York: Simon & Schuster.

SCHILL, T., and CHAPIN, J. 1972. Sex guilt and male's preference for reading erotic magazines. *J. Consult. Clin. Psychol. 39:* 516–17.

SCHMELL, J. A. 1972. The Fuller reading system: a scientific method for teaching those who are ready or not. Presented at 80th annual meeting, Amer. Psychol. Assn., Sept. 6, 1972.

SCHMIDT, G., and SIGUSCH, V. 1970. Psychosexual stimulation by film and slides: a further report on sex differences. In *The report of the commission on obscenity and pornography.* Washington, D.C.: U.S. Government Printing Office.

SCHMIDT-NIELSEN, K. 1971. How birds breathe. *Sci. Amer. 225,* no. 6.

SCHNEIDMAN, E. S., and FAREBEROW, N. L. 1957. Comparisons between genuine and simulated suicide notes in terms of Mowrer's DRQ. *J. Gen. Psychol. 56:* 251–56.

———, eds. 1957. *Clues to suicide.* New York: McGraw-Hill.

SCHRAMM, W. 1964. The research on programmed instruction: an annotated bibliography. Washington, D.C.: U.S. Office of Education.

SCHULMAN, R. E., and LONDON, P. 1963. Hypnosis and verbal learning. *J. Abnorm. Soc. Psychol. 67:* 363.

SCHULTZ, D. P. 1969. *A history of modern psychology.* New York: Academic.

SCHWARTZ, F. 1969. Some problems and notes about short-term memory. *Psychol. Rep. 24:* 71–80.

SCHWARTZ, G. E. 1971. Cardiac responses to self-induced thoughts. *Psychophysiol. 8:* 462–67.

———. 1972. Voluntary control of human cardio-vascular integration and differentiation through feedback and reward. *Science 175:* 90–93.

SCOTT, J. P. 1962. Critical periods in behavior development. *Science 138:* 949–57.

SCOTT, J. P., and MARSTON, M. U. 1950. Critical periods affecting the development of normal and maladjustive social behavior in puppies. *J. Genet. Psychol. 77:* 25–60.

SCULLY, D., and BART, P. 1972. Quoted in *Psychol. Today 6,* no. 7.

SEARS, R. R.; MACCOBY, E. E.; and LEVIN, H. 1957. *Patterns of child rearing.* Evanston, Ill.: Row Peterson.

———. 1965. Dependency. Unpublished manuscript quoted in H. W. Maier, *Three theories of child development.* New York: Harper & Row.

———. 1966. Development of the gender role. In F. A. Beach, ed., *Sex and behavior.* New York: John Wiley.

SEEMAN, M. 1946. Skin color values in three all-negro school classes. *Amer. Socio. Rev. 11:* 315–21.

SEEVERS, M. 1968. Use, misuse, and abuse of amphetamine-type drugs from the medical viewpoint. In J. Russo, ed., *Amphetamine Abuse.* Springfield, Ill.: Charles C Thomas.

Selcer, R. U., and Hilton, I. R. 1972. Cultural differences in the acquisition of sex roles. *Proceed. 80th Annual Conv. Amer. Psychol. Assn.*

Seligman, M.; Maier, S. F.; and Geer, J. H. 1968. Alleviation of learned helplessness in the dog. *J. Exp. Psychol. 73:* 256–62.

Sellin, J. T. 1959. *The death penalty.* Philadelphia: American Law Institute.

Shapiro, D., and Schwartz, G. 1970. *Psychophysiological contributions to social psychology.* Palo Alto, Calif.: Annual Reviews.

Sharma, S. L. 1970. A Historical background of the development of nosology in psychiatry and psychology. *Amer. Psychol. 25:* 248–53.

Shaw, C. R. 1929. *Delinquency areas.* Chicago: University of Chicago Press.

Sheldon, W. H. 1936. *The varieties of temperament: a psychology of constitutional differences.* New York: Harper & Row.

Shepard, R. N. 1967. Recognition memory for words, sentences, and pictures. *J. Verb. Learn. Behav. 6:* 156–63.

Sheridan, C. L., and King, R. G., Jr. 1972. Obedience to authority with an authentic victim. *Proceed. 80th Annual Conv. Amer. Psychol. Assn.*

Sherif, M.; Harvey, L. J.; White, B. J.; Hood, W. R.; and Sherif, C. 1961. *Intergroup conflict and cooperation.* Norman: University of Oklahoma Book Exchange.

Sherif, M., and Sherif, C. 1964. *Reference groups: exploration into conformity and deviation of adolescents.* New York: Harper & Row.

Sherman, M. 1927. Differentiation of emotional responses in infants. *J. Comp. Psychol. 7:* 265–84.

Sherwin, R. V. 1961. Laws on sex crimes. In A. Ellis and A. Abarbanel, eds., *The encyclopaedia of sexual behavior.* New York: Hawthorne.

Shevrin, H.; Smith, W. H.; and Fritzler, D. E. 1969. Repressiveness as a factor in the subliminal activation of brain and verbal responses. *J. Nerv. Ment. Dis. 149:* 261–69.

Shiffrin, R. M., and Atkinson, R. C. 1969. Storage and retrieval processes in long-term memory. *Psychol. Rev. 76:* 179–93.

Shiloh, A. 1968. Sanctuary or prison—responses to life in a mental hospital. *Transaction 6:* 28–36.

Shim Kunas, A. M. 1972. Demand for intimate self-disclosure and pathological verbalizations in schizophrenia. *J. Abnorm. Psychol. 80:* Oct., 1972.

Shirley, M. M. 1933. The first two years: a study of twenty-five babies ii. intellectual development. *Inst. Child. Welfare Monogr. Ser.*

Shlaer, R. 1972. An eagle's eye: Quality of the retinal image. *Science 176:* 920–22.

Shoben, E. J., Jr. 1957. Toward a concept of the normal personality. *Amer. Psychol. 12:* 183–89.

Shopland, C., and Gregory, R. L. 1964. The effects of touch on a visually ambiguous three-dimensional figure. *Quart. J. Exp. Psychol. 16:* 66–70.

Shuman, J. B. 1972. *Results from teaching the Fuller reading system to those with low comprehension expectation, pt. 2.* Presented at 80th annual meeting, Amer. Psychol. Assn., Sept. 6, 1972.

Siegel, P. 1960. Does bath water enter the vagina? *Obstet. Gynecol. 15:* 660–61.

Siegman, A. W. 1966. Father absence during early childhood and anti-social behavior. *J. Abnorm. Psychol. 71:* 71–94.

SIGAL, C. 1960. *Weekend in Dinlock.* Boston: Houghton Mifflin.

SIMMONS, K. 1944. The Brush foundation study of child growth and development, ii. Physical growth and development. *Monogr. Soc. Res. Child Develop. 9,* no. 1.

SIMON, W. 1969. Sex. *Psychol. Today 3,* no. 2.

SIMON, W., and GAGNON, J. 1969. Psychosexual development. *Transaction 6:* 9–17.

SIMSARIAN, F. P. 1948. Self demand feeding of infants and young children in family settings. *Ment. Hyg. 32:* 217–25.

SINGH, S. D. 1969. Urban monkeys. *Sci. Amer. 221,* no. 1.

SINNOTT, E. W. 1955. *The biology of the spirit.* New York: Viking.

SISTRUNK, F.; CLEMENT, D. E.; and ULMAN, J. D. 1972. Effect of reinforcement magnitude on nonconformity. *J. Soc. Psychol. 86:* 11–22.

SKEELS, H. M. 1966. Adult status of children with contrasting early life experiences. *Monogr. Soc. Res. Child Develop. 31:* 1–65.

SKINNER, B. F. 1938. *The behavior of organisms: an experimental analysis.* New York: Appleton-Century-Crofts.

———. 1954. The science of learning and the art of teaching. *Harvard Educ. Rev. 24:* 86–97.

———. 1957. *Verbal behavior.* New York: Appleton-Century-Crofts.

———. 1967. Autobiography in E. G. Boring and G. Lindzey, eds., *A history of psychology in autobiography.* New York: Appleton-Century-Crofts.

———. 1971. *Beyond freedom and dignity.* New York: Knopf.

SLACK, C. W. 1973. Tim the unsinkable, a short, excellent biography of Timothy Leary. *Psychol. Today 6,* no. 8.

SMART, R. G. 1970. Some current studies of psychoactive and hallucinogenic drug use. *Can. J. Behav. Sci. 2:* 232–45.

SMITH, B. M. 1967. The polygraph. *Sci. Amer. 216,* no. 1.

SMITH, D. E., and GAY, G. R. 1972. *It's so good, don't even try it once.* Englewood Cliffs, N.J.: Prentice-Hall.

SMITH, R. H. 1972. *OSS: the secret history of America's first central intelligence agency.* Berkeley: University of California Press.

SMITH, R. J. 1970. A closer look at encounter therapies. *Int. J. Group Psychother. 20:* 192–209.

SNODGRASS, R. E. 1966. Some mysteries of life and existence. In W. P. True, ed., *Smithsonian treasure of 20th century science.* New York: Simon & Schuster.

SNOW, C. P. 1966. *Variety of men.* New York: Scribner's.

SNYDER, C. R. 1958. *Alcohol and the Jews.* New Brunswick, N.J.: Rutgers Center of Alcohol Studies.

SNYDER, F. 1969. Sleep of the body. *Biol. Psychiat. 1:* 271–81.

SNYDER, S. 1961. Perceptual closure in acute paranoid schizophrenics. *Arch. Gen. Psychol. 5:* 406–10.

SNYDER, S., and LAMPARELLA, V. 1969. Psychedelic experiences in hysterical psychosis and schizophrenia. *Commun. Behav. Biol. 3:* 85–91.

SNYDER, S. H. 1972. Amphetamine—a sketch. *Psychol. Today 5,* no. 8.

SOCIETY FOR THE PSYCHOLOGICAL STUDY OF SOCIAL ISSUES. 1969. Council statement on race and intelligence. *J. Soc. Issues 25:* 1-3.

SOLOMON, R. L., and WYNNE, L. C. 1964. Cited in S. A. Mednick, *Learning.* Englewood Cliffs, N.J.: Prentice-Hall.

SOLZHENITSYN, A. 1963. *One day in the life of Ivan Denisovich.* New York: Dutton.

SOMMER, R. 1969. *Personal space: the behavioral basis of design.* Englewood Cliffs, N.J.: Prentice-Hall.

SONTAG, L. W.; BAKER, C. T.; and NELSON, V. L. 1958. Mental growth and development: a longitudinal study. *Monogr. Soc. Res. Child Develop. 23,* no. 68.

SPERRY, R. W. 1964. The great cerebral commissure. *Sci. Amer. 210,* no. 1.

———. 1968. Hemisphere deconnection and unity in conscious awareness. *Amer. Psychol. 23:* 723–33.

SPINKS, G. S. 1967. *Psychology and religion: an introduction to contemporary views.* Boston: Beacon Press.

SPIRO, M. E. 1969. Religious symbolism and social behavior. *Proc. Amer. Phil. Soc. 113:* 341–49.

SPREY, J. 1972. On the origin of sex roles. *Sociol. Focus 5,* no. 2.

STAFFIERI, J. R. 1972. Body build and behavioral expectancies in young females. *Develop. Psychol. 6:* 125–27.

STANFORD WOMAN, THE. 1972. Reported in *Behav. Today 3,* no. 50.

STANLEY, E. J.; GLASER, H. H.; LEVIN, D. G.; ADAMS, P. A.; and COLEY, I. L. 1970. Overcoming obesity in adolescents. *Clin. Pediat. 9:* 29–36.

STARKEY, M. L. 1963. *The devil in Massachusetts.* New York: Time, Inc.

STEIN, A. 1970. The nature and significance of interaction in group psychotherapy. *Int. J. Group Psychother. 20:* 153–62.

STEIN, A. H. 1972. Mass media and young children's development. In *Early childhood education, 1972.* Chicago: National Society for Study of Education, 71st Yearbook.

STEINBECK, J. 1969. *Journal of a novel: the east of Eden letters.* New York: Viking.

STENT, G. S. 1972. Cellular communication. *Sci. Amer. 227,* no. 3.

STEPHENS, R., and COTTRELL, E. 1972. A follow-up study of 200 narcotic addicts committed for treatment under the narcotic addict rehabilitation act (NARA). *Brit. J. Addict. 67:* 45–53.

STERNBERG, S. 1966. High speed scanning in human memory. *Science 153:* 652–54.

STEVENSON, E. K.; HUDGENS, R. W.; HELD, C. P.; MEREDITH, C. H.; HENDRIX, M. E.; and CARR, D. L. 1972. Suicidal communication by adolescents. *Dis. Nerv. Syst. 33:* 112–22.

STEVENSON, H. W. 1967. Developmental psychology. In P. R. Farnsworth, ed., *Annual review of psychology.* Palo Alto, Calif.: Annual Reviews.

STEWART, M. A. 1970. Hyperactive children. *Sci. Amer. 222,* no. 4.

STEWART, T. D. 1969. Fossil evidence of human violence. *Transaction 6:* 48–53.

STOLLER, R. J. 1970. Pornography and perversion. *Arch. Gen. Psychiat. 22:* 490–99.

STONE, L. A., and COLES, G. J. 1971. Dimensions of color vision revisited. *J. Psychol. 77:* 79–87.

STORR, A. 1964. *Sexual deviation.* Baltimore: Penguin.

STOTT, D. H. 1966. *Studies of troublesome children.* London: Tavistock.

STRAYER, L. C. 1930. Language and growth: the relative efficacy of early and deferred vocabulary training studied by the method of co-twin control. *Genet. Psychol. Monogr. 8:* 209–319.

Subotnik, L. 1922. Spontaneous remission: fact or artifact? *Psychol. Bull. 77:* 32–49.

Sullivan, H. S. 1953. *The interpersonal theory of psychiatry.* New York: Norton.

———. 1954. *The psychiatric interview.* New York: Norton.

Summers, S. A., and Fleming, J. S. 1971. Construction and reconstruction in memory. *Amer. J. Psychol. 84:* 513–20.

Suppes, P. 1966. The uses of computers in education. *Sci. Amer. 215:* 206–23.

Sutherland, E. H., ed. 1937. *The professional thief.* Chicago: University of Chicago Press.

Sutton-Smith, B., and Rosenberg, B. 1965. Age changes on the effects of ordinal position of the sex-role identification. *J. Genet. Psychol. 107:* 61–73.

Swanson, D. W., and Dinello, F. A. 1970. Severe obesity as a habituation syndrome: evidence during a starvation study. *Arch. Gen. Psychiat. 22:* 120–27.

Szasz, T. S. 1960. The myth of mental illness. *Amer. Psychol. 15:* 113–18.

———. 1961. *The myth of mental illness: foundations of a theory of personal conduct.* New York: Harper & Row.

———. 1972. Introduction. In B. Ennis, *Prisoners of psychiatry.* New York: Harcourt Brace Jovanovich.

Tanner, J. M. 1968. Earlier maturation in man. *Sci. Amer. 218:* 21–27.

Taub, J. M. 1970. Dream recall and content following various durations of sleep. *Psychon. Sci. 18:* 82.

Taub, J. M., and Burger, R. J. 1969. Extended sleep and performance: the Rip Van Winkle effect. *Psychon. Sci. 16:* 204–5.

Taylor, I. A.; Rosenthal, D.; and Snyder, S. 1963. Variability in schizophrenia. *Arch. Gen. Psychiat. 8:* 163–68.

Taylor, S. E. 1965. Eye movements in reading: Facts and fallacies. *Amer. Educ. Res. J. 2:* 187–202.

Teft, L.; Wapner, S.; Werner, H.; and McFarland, J. H. 1964. Relation between perceptual and conceptual operations: numerical distance and visual extent. *Brit. J. Psychol. 55:* 421–27.

Terman, L. M., and Oden, H. H. 1959. *The gifted group at mid-life: thirty-five years' follow-up of the superior child.* Stanford, Calif.: Stanford University Press.

Thigpen, C. H., and Cleckley, H. M. 1957. *Three faces of Eve.* New York: McGraw-Hill.

Thomas, E. L. 1968. Movements of the eye. *Sci. Amer. 219,* no. 2.

Thompson, G. 1961. *The inspiration of science.* New York: Oxford University Press.

Thompson, G. G., and Gardner, E. F. 1969. Adolescents' perceptions of happy-successful living. *J. Genet. Psychol. 115:* 107–20.

Thompson, R. F. 1967. *Foundations of physiological psychology.* New York: Harper & Row.

Thorndike, E. L. 1911. *Animal intelligence.* New York: Macmillan.

———. 1924. Mental discipline in high school studies. *J. Educ. Psychol. 15:* 83–98.

Thorwald, J. 1967. *Crime and science: the new frontier in criminology.* New York: Harcourt Brace Jovanovich.

Tillich, P. 1962. Courage and individualization. In W. Barrett and H. D. Aiken, eds., *Philosophy in the twentieth century.* New York: Random House.

TINBERGEN, N. 1961. *Herring gull's world.* New York: Basic Books.

TOBIAS, J. J. 1970. The affluent suburban male delinquent. *Crime Delin. 16:* 273–79.

TOCH, A. H. 1969. *Violent men.* Chicago: Aldine-Atherton.

TOLMAN, E. C., and HONZIK, C. H. 1930. Introduction and removal of reward and maze performance in rats. *Univ. of Calif. Publ. Psychol. 4:* 257–75.

TOLMAN, E. C.; RITCHIE, B. F.; and KALISH, D. 1946. Studies in spatial learning versus response learning. *J. Exp. Psychol. 36:* 221–29.

TORDA, C. 1969. Biochemical and bioelectrical processes related to sleep, paradoxical sleep, and arousal. *Psychol. Rep. Monogr. Supp. 24:* 807–24.

TORRANCE, E. P. 1960. Educational achievement of the highly intelligent and highly creative: eight partial replications of the Getzels-Jackson study. *Res. Memo., BFR-60-18.* Minneapolis: Bureau of Educational Research, University of Minnesota.

———. 1962. *Guiding creative talent.* Englewood Cliffs, N.J.: Prentice-Hall.

TORREY, E. F. 1972. What western psychotherapists can learn from witchdoctors. *Amer. J. Orthopsychiat. 42:* 69–76.

TRABASSO, T., and BOWER, G. 1968. *Attention in learning.* New York: John Wiley.

TRENT, S. E. 1972. Pain inhibition. *Science 177:* 294.

TRIANDIS, H. C., and TRIANDIS, P. 1969. The building of nations. *Psychol. Today 2,* no. 10.

TROELSTRA, A.; ZUBER, B. L.; MILLER, D.; and STARK, L. 1964. Accommodative tracking: a trial and error function. *Vis. Res. 4:* 585–94.

TRUZZI, M., and EASTO, P. 1972. Carnivals, road shows and freaks. *Society 9:* 26–34.

TSANG, Y. C. 1938. Hunger motivation in gastrectomized rats. *J. Comp. Psychol. 26:* 1–17.

TURIEL, E. 1969. Developmental processes in the child's moral thinking. In P. Mussen, J. Langer, and M. Covington, eds., *Trends and issues in developmental psychology.* New York: Holt, Rinehart & Winston.

TYLER, L. E. 1963. *Tests and measurements.* Englewood Cliffs, N.J.: Prentice-Hall.

———. *The psychology of human differences.* 3rd ed. New York: Appleton-Century-Crofts.

ULLMAN, A. D. 1958. In *Mental health aspects of adult education.* Washington, D.C.: U.S. Public Health Service.

ULLMANN, L., and KRASNER, L. 1969. *A psychological approach to abnormal behavior.* Englewood Cliffs, N.J.: Prentice-Hall.

ULLMANN, M., and KRIPPNER, S. 1970. An experimental approach to dreams and telepathy, ii. *Amer. J. Psychiat. 126:* 1282–89.

UNGER, S. N. 1963. Mescaline, LSD, psilocybin and personality change: a review. *Psychiat. 19:* 111–25.

VALENSTEIN, E.; COX, V.; and KAKOLEWSKI, J. 1968. Modification of motivated behavior elicited by electrical stimulation of the hypothalamus. *Science 159:* 1119–21.

VAN DER KLOOT, W. G. 1968. *Behavior*. New York: Holt, Rinehart & Winston.

VAN DER POST, L. 1967. *A portrait of all the Russians*. New York: Morrow.

VAN DOREN, C. 1948. *The great rehearsal*. New York: Viking.

VARON, E. J. 1935. The development of Alfred Binet's psychology. *Psychol. Monogr.* *46:* 1–129.

VIDMAR, N., and ROKEACH, M. 1973. Archie Bunker's bigotry: perceptions in the eye of the beholder. Paper: *East. Psychol. Assc.* May, 1973.

VOGEL-SPROTT, M., and RACINKAS, J. 1969. Suppression and recovery of a response in humans as a function of reward and punishment. *Behav. Res. Ther.* 7: 223–31.

VOLGYESI, F. A. 1961. Quoted in J. D. Frank, *Persuasion and healing: a comparative study of psychotherapy*. Baltimore: Johns Hopkins.

VON FRISCH, K. 1963. *Man and the living world*. New York: Harcourt Brace Jovanovich.

WADE, N. 1972. Fischer-Spassky charges: what did the Russians have in mind? *Science 177:* 778.

WAGNER, A. R. 1966. Frustration and punishment. In R. N. Haber, ed., *Research on motivation*. New York: Holt, Rinehart & Winston.

WAHLER, R. G. 1967. Infant social attachments: a reinforcement theory interpretation and investigation. *Child Develop. 38:* 1079–88.

WALLACE, R. K., and BENSON, H. 1972. The physiology of meditation. *Sci. Amer. 226,* no. 2.

WALSH, R. P. 1969. Generalization of self-control in children. *J. Educ. Res. 62:* 464–67.

WANTLAND, J. A. 1970. Unpublished essay.

WARD, W. D. 1969. Process of sex-role development. *Develop. Psychol. 1:* 163–68.

WATERS, E., and SAMUELS, C. 1951. *His eye is on the sparrow*. New York: Doubleday.

WATSON, G. 1957. Some personality differences in children related to strict or permissive parental discipline. *J. Psychol. 44:* 227–49.

WATSON, J. B. 1928. *Psychological care of infant and child*. New York: Norton.

WATSON, P. 1972. IQ: the racial gap. *Psychol. Today 6,* no. 4.

WATSON, R. I. 1968. *The great psychologists*. 2nd ed. Philadelphia: Lippincott.

WATSON, R. S. 1972. Twins: early mental developments. *Science 175:* 914–17.

WATTS, A. 1961. *Psychotherapy, east and west*. New York: Pantheon.

WEBB, B. B., and AGNEW, H. W., JR. 1971. Stage 4 sleep: influence of time course variables. *Science 174:* 1354–56.

WECHSLER, D. 1958. *The measurement and appraisal of adult intelligence*. 4th ed. Baltimore: Williams & Wilkins.

WEIL, A. T.; ZINBERG, N.; and NELSEN, J. 1968. Clinical and psychological effects of marihuana. *Science 162:* 1234–42.

WEINBERG, A., ed. 1957. *Attorney for the damned*. New York: Simon & Schuster.

WEINGARTNER, H.; GALANTER, M.; LEMBERGER, L.; ROTH, W.; STILLMAN, R.; VAUGHN, T.; and WYATT, R. 1972. Effect of marijuana and synthetic Δ^9THC on information processing. *Proceed. 80th Annual Conv. Amer. Psychol. Assn.*

WEINSTEIN, R. M., and BRILL, N. Q. 1971. Conceptions of mental illness by patients and normals. *Ment. Hyg. 45:* 101–8.

WEINSTOCK, A., and LERNER, R. M. 1972. Attitudes of late adolescents and their parents toward contemporary issues. *Psychol. Rep. 30:* 239–44.

WEISBERG, P., and WALDROP, P. B. 1972. Fixed-interval work habits of congress. *J. Appl. Behav. Anal. 5:* 93–97.

WEISSTEIN, N. 1969a. What the frog's eye tells the human brain: Single cell analyzers in the human visual system. *Psychol. Rev. 72:* 157–76.

———. 1969b. Woman as nigger. *Psychol. Today 3,* no. 5.

WEITZMAN, E. D.; KRIPKE, D. F.; GOLDMACHER, D.; McGREGOR, P.; and NOGEIRE, C. 1970. Acute reversal of the sleep-walking cycle in man. *Arch. Neurol. 22:* 483–89.

WERBLIN, F. S. 1973. The control of sensitivity in the retina. *Sci. Amer. 228,* no. 1.

WESSLER, R. L. 1968. Experimenter expectancy effects in psychomotor performance. *Percept. Mot. Skills 26:* 911–17.

———. 1969. Experimenter expectancy effects in three dissimilar tasks. *J. Psychol. 71:* 63–67.

———. 1970. Estimating IQ: expertise or examiner effect. *Percept. Mot. Skills 30:* 268.

WEYER, E., JR. 1961. *Primitive peoples today,* New York: Dolphin Books.

WHEATLEY, R. E.; MENKIN, M. F.; BARDES, E. D.; and ROCK, J. 1965. Tampons in menstrual hygiene. *J. Amer. Med. Assoc. 192:* 697–700.

WHITING, J. W.; KLUCKHOHN, R.; and ANTHONY, A. 1958. The function of male initiation ceremonies at puberty. In E. E. Maccoby, T. M. Newcomb, and E. L. Hartley, eds., *Readings in social psychology.* 3rd ed. New York: Holt, Rinehart & Winston.

WHO'S WHO OF AMERICAN HIGH SCHOOL STUDENTS. 1972. Survey. Quoted in *Behav. Today 3,* no. 44.

WILKINS, W. 1972. Desensitization: getting it together with Davidson and Wilson. *Psychol. Bull. 78:* 32–37.

WILLIAMS, J. D.; DUDLEY, H. K., JR.; and GUINN, T. J. 1969. Use of day treatment center concepts with state hospital inpatients. *Amer. J. Orthopsychiat. 39:* 748–52.

WILLIAMS, J. E., and TUCKER, R. D. 1971. Changes in the connotations of color names among negroes and caucasians: 1963–1969. *J. Personal. Soc. Psychol. 2:* 222–28.

WILLOWS, A. O. D. 1971. Giant brain cells in mollusks. *Sci. Amer. 224,* no. 2.

WILSON, E. O. 1972. Animal communication. *Sci. Amer. 227,* no. 3.

WILSON, J. R. 1964. *The mind.* New York: Time, Inc.

WISE, D., and ROSS, T. B. 1967. *The espionage establishment.* New York: Random House.

WISHY, B. 1968. *The child and the republic.* Philadelphia: University of Pennsylvania.

WISSLER, C. 1901. The correlation of mental and physical tests. *Psychol. Rev. Monogr. Supp. 3,* no. 6.

WITTENBORN, J. R. 1957. Inferring the strength of drive. In M. R. Jones, ed., *Nebraska symposium on motivation.* Lincoln: University of Nebraska.

WOLF, A. 1959. *A history of science, technology, and philosophy in the 16th and 17th centuries.* New York: Macmillan.

WOLFF, H. G. 1964. Quoted in J. C. Coleman, *Abnormal psychology and modern life.* 3rd ed. Glenview, Ill.: Scott, Foresman.

WOLFF, P. H. 1970. Biology and behavior. *Semin. Psychiat. 2:* 106–11.

WOLINS, M. 1970. Young children in institutions: some additional evidence. *Develop. Psychol. 2:* 99–109.

WOLPE, J., and LAZARUS, A. A. 1966. *Behavior therapy techniques: a guide to the treatment of neurosis.* Elmsford, N.Y.: Pergamon.

WOLPE, T. 1958. *Psychotherapy by reciprocal inhibition.* Stanford, Calif.: Stanford University Press.

WOOLDRIDGE, D. E. 1963. *The machinery of the brain.* New York: McGraw-Hill.

WORMSER, R. A. 1962. *The story of the law.* New York: Simon & Schuster.

YALOM, I. D., and LIEBERMAN, M. A. 1971. A study of encounter group casualties. *Arch. Gen. Psychiat. 25:* 16–30.

YATES, A. J. 1961. Hypnotic age regression. *Psychol. Bull. 58:* 429.

YOUNG, E. R., and JACOBSON, L. I. 1970. Effects of time extended marathon group experiences on personality characteristics. *J. Counsel. Psychol. 17:* 247–51.

YOUNG, P. T. 1967. Affective arousal: some implications. *Amer. Psychol. 22:* 32–39.

YOUNG, R. W. 1970. Visual cells. *Sci. Amer. 223,* no. 4.

YOUNG, V. R., and SCRIMSHAW, N. S. 1971. The physiology of starvation. *Sci. Amer. 225,* no. 4.

YOUTZ, R. P. 1968. Can fingers "see" color? *Psychol. Today 1,* no. 9.

ZEILER, M. D. 1963. The ratio theory of intermediate size discrimination. *Psychol. Rev. 70:* 516–33.

ZELAZO, P. R.; ZELAZO, N. A.; and KOLB, S. 1972. "Walking" in the newborn. *Science 176:* 314–15.

ZERN, D. 1969. Some trends in the development of concrete reasoning in children: a note to Jan Smedslund's "Concrete reasoning: a study in intellectual development." *J. Genet. Psychol. 115:* 3–5.

ZILBOORG, G., and HENRY, G. W. 1941. *A history of medical psychology.* New York: Norton.

ZILLMAN, D. 1971. Excitation transfer in communication-mediated aggressive behavior. *J. Exp. Soc. Psychol. 7:* 419–34.

ZIPF, S. 1960. Resistance and conformity under reward and punishment. *J. Abnorm. Soc. Psychol. 61:* 102–9.

ZUBEK, J. P.; HUGHES, G. R.; and SHEPHARD, J. M. 1971. A comparison of the effects of prolonged sensory deprivation and perceptual deprivation. *Can. J. Behav. Sci./Rev. Can. Sci. Comp. 3:* 282–90.

ZUCKERMAN, M.; ALBRIGHT, R.; MARKS, C.; and MILLER, G. L. 1962. Stress and hallucinatory effects of perceptual isolation and confinement. *Psychol. Monogr. 76,* no. 549.

ZUNG, W. W. K., and WILSON, W. P. 1971. Time estimation during sleep. *Biol. Psychiat. 3:* 159–64.

Professor Ivan N. McCollom of San Diego State College has compiled a list of books in the area of psychology which contains titles that have been consistent favorites among students over the years. With Dr. McCollom's permission the list is reproduced below in the hope that you might find some of them of interest. Listed alphabetically by author.

ADCOCK, C. J. 1964. *Fundamentals of psychology*. Baltimore: Penguin. (Paperback, Pelican edition)

ALLPORT, G. W. 1950. *The individual and his religion*. New York: Macmillan. (Paperback, Macmillan edition, 1960.)

AXLINE, V. 1964. *Dibs: In search of self*. Boston: Houghton Mifflin. (Paperback, Ballantine edition.)

BLATZ, W. E. 1966. *Human security: Some reflections*. Toronto: University of Toronto Press.

CANTRIL, H., and Bumstead, C. H. 1960. *Reflections on the human venture*. New York: New York University Press.

DETHIER, V. F. 1962. *To know a fly*. San Francisco: Holden-Day.

GREEN, H. 1964. *I never promised you a rose garden*. New York: Holt, Rinehart & Winston. (Paperback, New American Library, Signet.)

GRIER, W. H., and Cobbs, P. M. 1968. *Black rage*. New York: Basic Books. (Paperback, Bantam, 1969.)

HALL, C. H. 1954. *A primer of Freudian psychology*. Cleveland: World. (Paperback, New American Library, 1955.)

HESSE, H. 1951. *Siddhartha*. New York: New Directions.

LORENZ, K. 1952. *King Solomon's ring*. New York: Thomas Y. Crowell. (Paperback, Apollo edition.)

NEILL, A. S. 1960. *Summerhill*. New York: Hart.

SKINNER, B. F. 1948. *Walden two*. New York: Macmillan.

VOEKS, V. 1964. *On becoming an educated person*. 2nd ed. Philadelphia: Saunders.

WILSON, J. R., ed. 1964. *The mind*. New York: Time.

Here is an additional list of titles recommended by the author of this book.

CRICHTON, M. 1972. *The terminal man*. New York: Knopf. (Paperback, Bantam Books, 1973.)

EYSENCK, H. J. 1964. *Sense and nonsense in psychology*. Baltimore: Penguin. (Paperback, Pelican edition.)

HARRIS, THOMAS A. 1969. *I'm OK—You're OK*. New York: Harper & Row. (Paperback, 1969.)

KESEY, K. 1962. *One flew over the cuckoo's nest*. New York: Viking Press. (Paperback; also Signet, New American Library.)

LAING, R. D. 1967. *The politics of experience*. New York: Pantheon Books. (Paperback, 1967.)

MORRELL, D. 1972. *First blood*. New York: M. Evans. (Paperback, Fawcett Crest Book, 1973.)

TRYON, T. 1971. *The other*. New York: Knopf. (Paperback, Fawcett Crest Book, 1972.)

GLOSSARY

Accommodation: Changes in the shape of the lens of the eye to fit the distance of the object. A perceptual cue.

Achievement test: A test which measures learning of specific subject matter up to a specific point in time, e.g., a history achievement test.

Addiction: Physical dependence on a drug.

Adrenalin: A hormone secreted during an emotional reaction of fear or anger. Seems to play a predominant role in fear reactions.

Afferent sensory neurons: Incoming sensory fibers, e.g., to the spinal cord.

Age regression: Use of hypnosis to return an individual to a previous era of his life to examine the problems found there.

Alpha wave: Relatively slow brain wave indicating the individual is entering a stage of greater alertness.

Amino Acids: Basic chemicals which bond together in a complex fashion to form the protein molecule which presumably contains memory information.

Anal stage: Freudian developmental stage in which the individual is preoccupied with elimination and the anus.

Androgen: Male sex hormone.

Anxiety neurosis: Patient suffers from continuous anxiety.

Approach avoidance conflict: Desires conflict with reality, e.g., wants candy, but willing to face punishment for stealing it.

Aptitude test: Tests which measure a specific ability, e.g., mechanical aptitude.

Archetype: Carl Jung's concept that there exist certain universals which are inherited from one generation to the next. The archetype is the original from which each generation borrows. Example: Mother archetype.

Association areas: Portions of the brain which contain highly complex connections between neurons. These areas are assumed to produce our more complex thought patterns, actions, and feelings.

Attention: A critical factor in learning. Means orienting toward or focusing on in order to learn.

Attention span: The length of time a subject can focus his attention on an object or material to be learned.

Aversive conditioning: Association of unpleasantness (e.g., nausea) with undesirable behavior (e.g., excessive drinking) in an attempt to remove that behavior.

Avoidance-avoidance conflict: Stress created by a "double bind." He hates his job, but has no prospects for another if he quits.

Axon: An elongated tentacle that takes messages from the cell body. Connects to muscles, glands, sensory receptors, etc.

Behavioral Modification Therapy: Changes in behavior are brought about in one of three ways. Learning Theory Therapy—Retraining based on principles of reward, reinforcement, and extinction; Desensitization Therapy—Reconditioning by association of pleasantness in lieu of previous unpleasant feeling toward a behavior, and the reduction of anxiety toward an object or behavior.

Binet: *See* Stanford-Binet.

Biofeedback: Technique for allowing a subject to monitor his internal bodily reactions with the aid of machines. He then attempts to control internal behavior to correspond to certain readings on the machine, e.g., blood pressure.

Blind spot: Portion of the retina at which we cannot see because it is the point where the optic nerve exits.

Blood-sugar level: The level of concentration of sugar in the blood. A signal which alerts the organism to eat more or to cease eating.

Brainstorming: A group gives free-flight to imagination and attempts to solve problems in a new and "creative" or unexpected fashion.

Buddy stage: Period of adolescence, according to Sullivan, when the individual forms very close personal attachments to individuals of his own sex.

Cannon-Bard Theory of Emotion: Both the body and the emotional response act in unison through the action of the hypothalamus.

Categorizing: *See* clustering.

Central nervous system: The spinal cord and the brain as a unit.

Cerebellum: Portion of the brain responsible for coordinated physical activities.

Cerebral cortex: Literally, the outer layer of the brain. However, as commonly used, refers to the convoluted mass of brain cells composing the highest brain center. Usually called the cortex.

Character disorders: *See* sociopath.

Chemotherapy: The use of drugs to alter behavior and/or mood. Most frequently involves energizers or tranquillizers.

Circadian rhythm: The cycle of the body which follows a rhythmic pattern, basically 24 hours in length, resembling that of the light-dark cycle in our country.

Clairvoyance: ESP, in which predictions are made without the benefit of a sender.

Classical conditioning: Basic traditional conditioning discovered by Pavlov. Unnatural stimuli are associated with natural stimuli to elicit responses identical to those of the natural stimuli.

Client-centered therapy: Therapy which emphasizes the solving of problems by the client with the therapist available only to assist.

Closure: The tendency of the eye to close partially-open figures until they are

Clustering: The tendency of the mind (or brain) to group items together for the sake of order and/or clarity.

Coding: A physiological mechanism of the brain for categorizing or clustering. The exact mechanism is not fully understood.

Cognitive dissonance: An imbalance between beliefs and behavior or between thought and feeling. According to the theory, one or the other must change so that the two are no longer dissonant.

Cognitive map: The ability we have to reorder or reconstruct pieces in order to provide for ourselves a whole picture of the given situation, e.g., a route from place *A* to place *B*.

Cognitive Theory of Emotion: Emotion involves a physiological response, but we know what emotion we are feeling only because we attach a label to it.

Concrete operations stage: Second stage of cognitive development in which the child is learning to actively manipulate the objects of the real world, which are, by then, permanent to him. (*See* object permanency.) During this stage objects are replaced by symbols eventually and much exploration of the environment is symbolic rather than physical.

Conditioned response: The response of an organism to a stimulus to which certain behaviors have become associated.

Conditioned stimulus: A previously neutral stimulus, e.g., a bell, which comes to elicit a response as the result of association.

Conditioning: The process of learning by association. (*See also* Classical conditioning.)

Cones: Receptors within the retina which are more responsive to the red end of the color spectrum. Cones are responsible for color vision and are most responsive in daylight.

Conservation: The concept that altering the shape of a body does not change its mass. Concept is learned during the concrete operations stage.

Consolidation theory: The memory theory which assumes that material is solidified (consolidated) in the brain after learning. This occurs during rest.

Constitutional psychology: A theory of personality which emphasizes that our personalities are a reflection of our body size and shape.

Construct validity: Validity based on a hypothesis or construct on the part of the test designer. Intelligence is a construct since we do not know what intelligence *really* is, and the IQ test is designed to measure what the constructor thinks intelligence is.

Contact comfort: The basic physical and psychological need of the animal and human to be touched and comforted, or to touch.

Content validity: Validity based on the assumption that the items are measuring what they claim just because the items are specific in their content. For example, a math test with math items has content validity.

Contrast detectors: Sensors in the visual network which respond to variations in contrast to the object being viewed.

Control: The experimental process of arranging an experiment in such a way that unwanted factors cannot contaminate the results.

Convergence: The movement of the eyes onto a given point. The position of the eyes provides information to the brain regarding distance.

Conversion reaction: Transformation of a psychological problem into a physical symptom. In its extreme, paralysis of the leg during combat.

Cornea: Clear outer covering of the eyes filled with a clear liquid.

Corpus Callosum: A unit in the middle of the brain between the two hemispheres which acts as a transfer agent for information from one hemisphere to the other.

Correlation: A statistical measure which indicates the degree to which two variables are related, e.g., height of parents and height of children.

Creativity: A construct defined by psychologists as the ability to break set.

Critical period: A certain event in an animal's life must occur during a specified period of time to be effective.

Cross-validation: *See* Replication.

Dark adaption: The process by which the daylight cone vision is taken over by night-time rod vision. Eyes are considerably more sensitive after dark adaption.

Data: Information obtained from a scientific study.

Decay theory: The theory that assumes that one forgets because the traces of memory decay over time. (*See* trace theory.)

Delusion: Misrepresentation of the "real" world, e.g., delusion of grandeur, in which one believes he is king.

Dendrites: Tentacles that bring stimuli to the cell body of the nerve cell.

Denial: A defense mechanism in which we merely deny that a problem exists.

Dependent variable: The variable in an experiment which reflects the changes introduced by the experimenter via his independent variable.

Depersonalization: The feeling an individual has that he has lost his self-identity. He feels either that he is not himself or that he doesn't know who he is.

Depth perception: Perceptual cue which gives us the feeling of both the distance and solidity of objects.

Deviant: One who violates the rules, mores, or dictates of society.

Discrimination learning: The process by which we differentiate one object or event from another because of detected differences.

Dissociative neurosis: One part of the "mind" is disassociated from another in symbolic terms. Multiple personality; amnesia.

Drive: Basic (assumed) cause for much of human behavior. Man is driven by hunger, thirst, sex, etc.

Ductless glands: Glands which dump their chemical material into the bloodstream directly for the purpose of widespread bodily activity, e.g., the adrenal glands.

Ectomorph: A thin person.

Efferent motor neurons: Outgoing fibers responsible for bodily acts.

Ego: In Freudian terminology, the control panel of the person that checks on the outside world and determines the amount of regulation needed for the superego or id. A balancing unit.

Eidetic imagery: What the layman calls "photographic memory." It is the ability to retain an image for a sufficiently long period of time so that certain perceptual actions can be performed, e.g., counting the stripes on an "image" of a zebra.

Electrode: Electrically activated, very thin wire, primarily used in brain experiments as described in this text.

Emergency reaction: A physiological response in which the body is prepared to fight or flee. Breathing rate is accelerated, liver secretes more sugar, heart rate increases.

Empirically keyed test: Test in which the items do not necessarily reflect what they seem to be asking. Norms are established by tabulating responses from a given group of subjects regardless of how they answered the question. The answer is most important, not the question.

Endomorph: A fat person.

Environmental cue: An object which triggers a secondary drive, e.g., water fountain.

Epicurianism: The seeking of pleasure for the long term, greater good. May involve periodic pain.

Estrogen: Female sex hormone.

Experimental group: The group of subjects upon whom the experimenter performs whatever task is required by the independent variable.

External grouping: Use of characteristics of other groups in a negative sense in order to develop strength for one's own group.

Extinction: The process by which one forces forgetting. Extinction can occur just from the absence of reward or it can occur by punishment.

Fixed internal reinforcement: A reward is provided for the organism at a fixed rate; for example, every five minutes a rat is given a food pellet.

Forced choice technique: Objective test in which subject must select from two or more equally undesirable or desirable items.

Formal discipline: The belief that certain scholastic activities such as Latin, mathematics, and logic provide "exercise" for the mind. Incorrect.

Formal operations stage: From adolescence on, the young person is developing the ability to engage in highly complex symbolic manipulations, e.g., those of mathematics or logic.

Fovea: Located in the center of the retina, this area predominates in cones and provides sharpest vision.

Free nerve endings: Mechanoreceptors. Disturbance creates chemical electrical impulse of pain.

Frontal lobe: Portion of the brain with considerable space devoted to association areas. Plays an important part in personality, but is not the entire seat of personality.

Ganglion cells: In the eye, translate photosensitive information from the rods and cones into suitable electrical messages for the optic nerve fibers.

Generalization: The spreading of a response from one object or set of circumstances to another, e.g., the fear of a rat is spread to the fear of other furry animals.

Genital stage: Freudian developmental stage in which the individual is preoccupied with heterosexual interests.

Gestalt: The whole; complete. That group of psychologists emphasizing that we come into the world programmed to perceive objects as whole units, not in parts, e.g., a house is a house, not brick, shingle, etc.

Glands: Units of the body which trigger chemical changes in order to prepare the body for certain tasks. For example, salivary glands secrete saliva for the digestion of food.

Glial cell: Small chemical unit in the brain used as a "screen." Thought to feed or nourish the brain cells.

Gonads: Sex glands—testes in male, ovaries in female.

Group test: A paper and pencil test which is administered to groups of individuals.

Group therapy: Many kinds, but all based on the principle of exercising group pressure and reassurance to modify the patient's unacceptable behavior.

Habituation: Psychological dependence on a drug.

Hallucination: Seeing or hearing (occasionally smelling) objects or events which do not exist in the real world.

Hedonism: One of the oldest theories of motivation. We seek that which is pleasurable and avoid that which is painful.

Hemisphere: The cortex is divided into two units, each of which is a hemisphere. The right hemisphere is responsible for control of the left part of the body and the left hemisphere is responsible for control in the right portion of the body.

Hermaphrodite: An individual who is more than one sex, generally having a combination of sex organs for both the male and the female.

Hierarchy of needs: A theory of motivation developed by Abraham Maslow in which more basic needs must first be met before higher order needs come into play—physiological, safety, belongingness, self-esteem, self-actualization.

Homeostasis: A mechanism by which the various bodily functions or units remain in balance, e.g., regulated temperature. Homeostasis is assumed to operate in the area of emotion, motivation, and psychological defense.

Hormones: Chemical units which instigate alterations in physical or psychological behavior.

Hypochondriasis: Patients suffer from illnesses which cannot be located by present medical techniques. Illnesses are presumed to be imaginary. Excessive preoccupation with the body and its minor problems.

Hypothalamus: Portion of the brain which regulates many of our needs. Involved in hunger, thirst, and emotion. Also functions in the complex interplay of hormonal activity during adolescence.

Hypothesis: The stated results the experimenter anticipates finding in his experiment.

Id: In Freudian terminology, the unit which contains the basic desires of the individual.

Identical twins: Twins who come from the same egg. Hence, they share identical heredity.

Identification: The process of incorporating into oneself the goals and purposes of others, e.g., a child identifies with his mother.

Idiot savant: A person who can perform amazing feats of memory but usually has a very low IQ.

Imprinting: The process by which an animal's brain is programmed to receive an object at a particular time, e.g., mother imprinting.

Independent variable: The specific variables of an experiment which are manipulated by the experimenter in order to produce a change in the dependent variable.

Individual test: A psychological test which is administered on a face-to-face basis with the psychologist.

Infant intelligence test: A primarily motor development test designed to predict later intelligence. Generally inferior in this task.

Instinct: A presumably automatic behavior "pre-wired" into the organism and resulting in a certain fixed behavior pattern. Is generally not considered valid for humans.

Intelligence quotient: MA/CA $\times$ 100.

Interference theory: Forgetting occurs because previously learned material interferes with present learning or recalling previous material is interfered with by present learning.

Intermittent reinforcement: A reward is provided at unexpected intervals. For example, a pigeon is given some food after pecking at a disk for 5, 7, 3, and 6 times.

Internal grouping: Heavy concentration on characteristics of one's own group to differentiate it from other groups.

Internalization: The incorporation into oneself of the values, goals, or purposes of others with whom one identifies.

Iris: Circular muscle of the eye that opens onto the lens and changes the lens from larger to smaller.

James-Lange theory of emotion: We feel an emotion *after* the body has reacted, e.g., we run and then we are afraid.

Latent learning: Behavior which is learned, but does not become evident until the organism is provided with a reward or incentive for engaging in that behavior.

Libido: In Freudian terminology, the sexual energy responsible for most of our behaviors. From the Latin for lust.

Light: A form of energy movement based on a transmission principle of waves. Waves, in turn, vary as a function of frequency and wave length.

Limbic system: The area of the older brain containing a primitive cortex. Is apparently responsible for pleasure responses, rage, and emotional reactions.

Long-term memory: The presumed storage of memories in a permanent memory storage bank, after having passed through the short-term memory.

Manic depressive psychosis: Psychosis characterized by swings in mood from grand elation to deep depression. Category is gradually losing favor. Most patients in this category are primarily depressed.

Manipulation motive: The unexplained "need" of higher animals to seek an opportunity to manipulate objects.

Masochism: The deliberate seeking of pain for "pleasurable" or sexual experience.

Maturation: The process by which the organism develops in an orderly sequence and at a fixed individual rate.

Mean: The average in layman's terminology. Sum of the entries is divided by the number of entries.

Median: The number used to represent the halfway mark or midpoint in a list of numbers.

Medulla: Portion of the brain responsible for most automatic functions, e.g., breathing and heart pumping.

Mental age: *See* Stanford-Binet.

Mesomorph: An athletic person.

Mnemonic device: Unusual tricks or combinations that assist us in remembering.

Mode: The most frequently appearing number in a set of numbers.

Moral realism: First stage of moral development in which the child blindly follows rules without reason. This is followed by the *reward stage* in which the child is actively seeking praise or gratification for following rules. In turn, this is followed by a developmental sequence of concern about disapproval from others and then from incorporation of this disapproval, the stage which is called *disapproval of self*. The final stage is the *sharing stage* which involves active and concerned interpersonal relationships.

Motor area: Portion of the brain which creates a motor response, i.e., a response of the arms, legs, trunk, etc.

Moving edge detectors: Sensors in the visual network which respond to moving edges, i.e., the edges of moving objects.

Muller-Lyer illusion: Two lines which are the same size. One has arrowheads, the other "feathers." The lines are perceived as one being longer than the other.

Necker cube: Two overlapping squares which provide the perception of a changing square, first one direction then another.

Negative transfer: The general phrase encompassing any learning which is interfered with by some previous learning.

Neo-Freudians: Individuals who basically follow many of Freud's core ideas, but emphasize the ego rather than the id. Further emphasize social interaction rather than biological determinism.

Nerve: A group of neurons which together transmit information.

Neuron: The individual nerve cell with its attachments.

Neurosis: Somewhat debilitating mental illness characterized by a reduced level of functioning in life. Individuals in this category generally have minor distortions of reality, but basically are quite aware of the "real world."

Nonsense syllables: Three consonants which are designed to have minimal or no previous associations for the subject. Hence, in memory experiments, each subject starts from "scratch."

Norm: The base line or typical expected score on a test to which others are compared.

Normal curve: A visual representation of the distribution of individuals on certain basic characteristics such as height, weight, and intelligence test results. The majority of individuals fall in the middle of the curve.

NREM sleep: The sleep during which there is minimal eye movement and no dreaming.

Object permanency: A portion of the sensorimotor stage in which the child gradually learns that certain objects are a permanent part of the environment.

Objective test: A test consisting of fixed or structured questions. Term usually is used as a comparison with the projective test, which is loosely structured.

Obsessive compulsive neurosis: Obsession is preoccupation to the extreme with certain thoughts. Compulsion is the continuous performance of certain ritualistic acts, e.g., counting cracks in the sidewalk.

Occipital lobe: Portion of the brain primarily functional in visual activity.

Oedipal conflict: The male seeks to do away with his father and take his place with the mother.

Older brain: As used in this text, refers to the animal portion of the entire brain, the part responsible for most of our non-voluntary activities. Developed first from an evolutionary point of view.

Operant conditioning: Conditioning or learning which occurs from the actual behavior of the organism (its operations). Certain acts lead to certain desirable consequences and hence are repeated.

Oral stage: Freudian developmental stage in which the individual is preoccupied with use of his mouth.

Organic psychosis: Symptoms of major mental illness appear as the result of brain damage either from disease or injury.

Orienting reflex: A portion of the body is oriented in a certain direction in order to assimilate something seen or heard.

Overlearning: The process of learning material well beyond the level of being able to recite it one time through perfectly.

Paranoid: Psychotic who thinks others are out to do him in. Typically has delusions; frequently has hallucinations.

Parapsychology: The scientific study of anything in the realm of extrasensory perception.

Pecking order: Direct reference to birds; indirect to people. One bird has higher "social rank" than another, gets to eat first, and can, if he so desires, peck at the lower birds.

Peers: Members of one's own age group—school, neighborhood, etc.

Perception: The ability of an organism to comprehend or understand by use of the senses. Visual perception is most important for humans.

Perceptual cues: Information which provides us with data by which we organize and interpret the world around us.

Perceptual defense: The ability we have to ignore or not "see" that which is undesirable.

Performance test item: An intelligence test item which minimizes verbal skills, but tries to continue to emphasize symbolic reasoning.

Peripheral nervous system: The units of the nervous system contained outside the spinal cord and the brain.

Peripheral vision areas: Portions of the retina on either side of the fovea which are extremely sensitive to movement and trigger an orientation response of the foveal area. Reds predominate.

Persona: Mask. The mask of personality each of us wears (Carl Jung).

Phallic stage: Freudian developmental stage in which the individual is preoccupied with sex as a sensual experience of self-gratification.

Pheromenes: Glandular secretions of a specific odor used for identification of territory or for communication purposes.

Phi phenomenon: The perception of inevitable movement. A Gestalt principle illustrated by the movement of the donkey's tail in the text, or the lights on a movie house which provide the sensation of movement.

Phobic neurosis: Acute fear of object, person, or situation. Typical fears include those of fire, water, dogs, snakes, closed places, etc.

Phosphenes: Patterns, designs, images created by the visual network without external light stimulation. Can sometimes be aided by pressing lightly on the edge of the eyeball.

Photopic vision: *See* cones.

Photosensitive: The ability to react to the stimulation of light, usually in a chemical fashion.

Phrenology: The belief that the various bumps or knots on the skull represent specific abilities or personality factors. Theory was most important in turning science toward localized function within the brain.

Pituitary: Gland responsible for growth activities and for the activity of hormones during the adolescent period.

Pleasure principle: An organism seeks pleasure and avoids pain. Found in the Freudian theory and the learning theory of personality devised by Dollard and Miller.

Ponzo illusion: An illusion in which one rectangle looks longer than another. Two logs on a roadbed were used in the text to illustrate this illusion.

Predictive validity: See definition for validity. Asks question, "How valid is test as a predictor of furture behavior?"

Primal scene: Sexual intercourse between parents witnessed by a child.

Principle learning: Very effective device for remembering. Items are brought together under a single unifying principle.

Proactive inhibition: A previous learning interfering with a present learning.

Probability: As used in psychological experiments, the probability level (.05, .01, .001) indicates the probability that a certain event could occur by chance alone. Corresponds to the layman's concept of odds.

Programmed learning: The presentation of school material in an orderly sequence with learning carefully structured into units. Is a self-instructional device.

Projection: Blaming our own problems or difficulties on others. Attributing to others feelings which we ourselves have.

Projective test: Unstructured stimulus designed to elicit deeper layers of personality. The subject projects his own thoughts and impulses onto the stimulus, since it is very vague.

Protein molecule: In memory, highly complex building blocks which contain chains of amino acids which are assumed to represent memory items.

Psychiatrist: Therapist with a medical degree. Additional training in mental illness quite variable; typically two or three years.

Psychoanalysis: Therapy for mental patients following the Freudian framework and theory.

Psychologist: Scientist or therapist with a doctor of philosophy degree. Usual minimum training beyond bachelor's degree, four years.

Psychopath: *See* sociopath.

Psychopathology: Abnormal behavior. Literally, sickness of the psyche.

Psychosis: Major mental disturbance characterized by the individual withdrawing from our reality into his own. Frequently characterized by hallucinations, and/or delusions, and thought disorders.

Psychosomatic disorder: Actual physical damage resulting from psychological stress.

Psychotherapy: Any form of treatment, actually, of the "psyche," but usually restricted to face-to-face contact between a psychiatrist or psychologist and his patient. Usually involves verbal interaction between the two individuals.

Pupil: Merely an opening in the eye.

Purkinje phenomenon: At twilight, objects that are red darken more quickly than objects at the blue-violet end of the spectrum. (*See also* rods and cones.)

Rationalization: Explaining away, for ourselves and/or others, our behavior in such a way that we avoid any responsibility for our actions.

Rational therapy: Quite direct and forceful therapy in which the patient is told to restructure his faulty "internalized sentences."

Recall: The ability to bring back learned material by detailed recitation.

Recitation theory: The theory of learning which emphasizes that memory will be greatest if material is rehearsed.

Recidivism: The tendency of an individual to return to his criminal ways.

Recognition: The ability to bring back learned material by stating that one has seen it before. Specific details are not required.

Reference group: A group (or groups) with which we identify and use as our standard of behavior.

Reflex arc: An automatic behavior of the body involving only reflex, e.g., withdrawing hand from a fire. Typically, involves the spinal cord.

Regression: Movement backward in time in behavior patterns. Individual acts in a more child-like manner.

Reinforcement: The tendency of an act to be repeated. Presumably this occurs because the animal has been rewarded.

Reliability: A measure of a psychological test which asks the question: "Does the test consistently measure from one administration to the next?"

REM sleep: Rapid eye movement. Sleep in which the individual is having major movements of his eyes. Corresponds to periods of dreaming.

Replication: The process of repeating a study one or more times to ensure that the results of the study found the first time were not due just to chance. Also called cross-validation.

Repression: The pushing down, or removing from consciousness, of unwanted desires or feelings.

Reticular formation: The alertness control center of the brain which regulates the activity level of the body.

Retina: The back portion of the eyeball which contains rods, cones, and portions of the visual network.

Retroactive inhibition: Previous learning being interfered with by a present learning.

Reward: Something which is satisfying to the organism. Will tend to reinforce whatever behavior led to the reward.

Rods: Receptors within the retina which are more responsive to the blue-violet end of the spectrum and function best in semi-darkness.

Role conflict: Each of us plays different roles in life, one at home, one at work, etc. When these do not fit with one another, role conflict develops.

Rorschach test: Ink blots used to evaluate an individual's unconscious impulses and thought integration.

Scan path: A pattern of eye movements used to examine an object. The scan path varies from one object to another.

Schizophrenia: Major mental disorder (a psychosis) characterized by a withdrawal from reality in one's own world. Most psychoses are labeled schizophrenia.

Scotopic vision: *See* rods.

Secondary drives: Needs or desires which are attached to the basic needs of sex, hunger, thirst, etc. Secondary drives are usually intimately involved in symbols and words.

Self-actualization: The highest level of development of the individual. Used in this text to represent also the highest level of striving for the individual under the system of Carl Rogers. Rogers called this level "fully-functioning," Maslow coined the term "self-actualization."

Self-report test: A questionnaire or test in which the individual evaluates himself, as opposed to being evaluated by an outside observer, e.g., a psychologist.

Sensorimotor stage: First stage of cognitive growth characterized by learning experiences that combine sensation and movement.

Sensory deprivation: Removal of all stimulation from the environment. Produces disorientation and hallucinations.

Set: The tendency we all have to do things in the present in the way they always have been done.

Sex role: Learned social behavior which conforms to society's expectations for acts appropriate to a given sex.

Sexual behavior: A rather interesting bit of activity engaged in by many species.

Short-term memory: The initial "receptor" of environmental information. If memories are lost in this area they do not make it to the long-term storage areas of the brain.

Size constancy: The ability of the perceptual apparatus to maintain a fixed size for an object even though the actual image on the retina changes.

Sociopath: One who continuously violates the norms of society and shows little remorse. Same as psychopath.

Spinal cord: Functions as an automatic brain. Is a relay station for impulses to and from the higher brain and acts independently to instigate reflex actions.

Standardization: The process of making test administration uniform from one administration to another. Instructions given and behavior of administrator are rigidly fixed.

Stanford-Binet intelligence test: A highly verbal intelligence test with greatest accuracy for children. The test was originally designed to locate mentally defective children. Test compares mental age with chronological age.

Statistics: A numerical process which is used to group, assemble, organize, or analyze information received by the experimenter.

Subjects: Individuals who participate in an experiment.

Superego: In Freudian terminology, the unit which acts as the conscience.

Synapse: The junction of two neurons. Actually is a "space" over which the nerve impulse jumps when it connects pathways.

Tachistoscope: A mechanical device which provides exposure of words or objects for very short spans of time. Is sometimes used in perception of "dirty word" experiments.

Telepathy: ESP, in which there is a sender and a receiver.

Territoriality: The marking off of a certain space (or landmark) as belonging to oneself or one's family.

Thalamus: Portion of the brain which functions primarily as a central relay station for incoming and outgoing messages.

Thematic apperception test: Projective test consisting of vague pictures to which the subject tells a story. Presumably the subject is talking about himself.

Tolerance: The body's ability to adapt and withstand increased amounts of a drug. In common psychological usage, also refers to the fact that an individual tends to increase his dosage.

Trace theory: The theory of learning which assumes that memory leaves a ''trace'' on the neural networks of the brain.

Transfer: The process by which a previous learning, because of its similar aspects, provides assistance in a present learning.

Trial and error learning: Behavior in which the organism learns by attempting various solutions until one proves rewarding.

Unconditional positive regard: The concept coined by Rogers which refers to an acceptance of the client as a person even if one does not approve of his actions.

Unconditioned response: The response of an organism to a stimulus which automatically elicits a certain reaction, e.g., salivation to meat on the tongue.

Unconditioned stimulus: A stimulus which automatically elicits an unconditioned response, e.g., meat.

Unconscious: The portion of the psyche which contains impulses and desires of which we are unaware.

Validity: A measure of a psychological test which asks the question: ''Does the test measure what it is supposed to measure?'' (*Also see* construct and content.)

Verbal cue: A word which triggers a secondary drive, e.g., the word eat.

Visual cliff: Especially designed table which contains a glass protector giving the impression to the baby that he will fall off. Is used to illustrate innate depth perception.

Wechsler adult intelligence scale: Intelligence test which gives performance, verbal, and overall intelligence scores. More effective than the Binet for adults.

White light: Light derived from the sun. Contains all available colors.

A Aborigines, 50
Accomodation, 155
Achievement, need, 114
Acupuncture, 109
Adaptation, 221
Adolescence:
  "buddy stage," 288
  conformity, 429
  coordination, 433
  and death, 434
  in Denmark, 435
  drugs, 436
  grouping, 429, 431–32
  growth hormones, 430–32
  growth spurt, 429, 431, 434
  homosexuality, 443ff.
  hormones, 390, 430–31
  initiation rites, 432
  kibbutz, 431
  marriage, 438
  masturbation, 269
  mother relationships, 436
  nutrition, 438
  obesity, 433
  parents, 435–36
  persuasion, 512
  physiological changes, 429
  pituitary, 430
  puberty, 437
  reference groups, 512
  religion, 436
  sense of time, 434
  sex, 439
  sex behavior, 436ff.
  sex hormones, 430–31
  sharing stage, 422
  Sullivan, H. S., 288
  values, 434–36
  weight changes, 429, 433
Adrenalin, 112, 118, 431, 433, 468, 503, 568
  injection, 118, 120
Afferent neurons, 74

Aggression (*see also* Violence):
  brain center, 480, 510
  dreams, 251
  female, 387
  Freud, 272
  group, 504
  notes on, 509–10
  social role, 276
  societal, 301
Aging, 570–71
Aircraft:
  fatigue, 23
  set, 20ff.
Aircrib, 199
Albert, B., 91
Alcohol:
  Alcoholics Anonymous, 519, 586
  automobile driving, 467
  aversive conditioning, 586
  body rhythm, 23
  and brain, 63
  and delinquency, 456
  effects, 60
  effects of price, 96
  ethnic groups, 462
  Freudian theory, 266
  in high school, 461
  homeostasis, 116
  and marijuana, 23
  nutrition, 461
  sex roles, 388
  social pressure, 97
  stereotypes, 97
  tolerance, 377
Alcoholics:
  Alcoholics Anonymous, 519, 586
  aversive conditioning, 586
  oral, 266
  Rorschach, 310
  sex role, 387
Alcoholics Anonymous (*see* Alcohol)
Alger, Horatio, 176
All in the Family, 511

Alpha rhythm, 246, 248
Amnesia, 193, 557
Amphetamines, 471
Androgen, 106
Anger:
   stomach 97–98
Animal intelligence, 68
Animal psychology, 45ff., 82
Animal speech, 48
Anxiety, 394, 530, 559
   and fear, 121, 380–81
   and hypnosis, 243
   learning theory, 291
   and morality, 422
   Neofreudian view, 287ff.
   symptoms, 548, 552
   test, 23
Aptitude tests, 360–61
Aquinas, Saint Thomas, 8
Aristotle, 8, 17
Association areas, of brain, 64,
   190–91
Astrology, 5
Astronaut, diet, 99
Attention, learning, 213
Attitudes, learning, 206
Autonomic nervous system, 247
Average (*see* Mean)
Avoidance behavior, 292
Axon, 66

B Barber, Theodore, 244
Barbiturates, 472
Beagle, H.M.S., 45
Beasties, 18
Beauty, conditioning, 83
Beer, pricing, 96
Bees, ultraviolet light, 140
Behavioral modification, 584–87
   alcoholics, 586
   aversive conditioning, 586
   delinquents, 460
   desensitization, 584–86
   homosexuals, 587
   learning theory, 584
   phobias, 557
Behaviorism:
   Skinner, B. F., 199ff.
   Watson, John, 91
Bell-shaped curve (*see* Normal
   curve)
Beyond Freedom and Dignity, 203

Binet, Alfred, 330ff., 346, 349
Biofeedback, 247ff., 560
   alpha rhythm, 246, 248
   blood pressure, 248
   meditation, 248
   yoga, 248
Biological clocks, 22–23
Birds:
   bones, 20, 47
   migration, 142
   pecking order, 479
   wings, 20
Black Bart, 212
Blind persons, 253, 382, 403
Blood clotting, 112
Blood distribution, 67
Blood flow, 17
Bloodletting, 66
Blood pressure, 248
Blood sugar, 98
Boyle, Robert, 18, 536
Brain, 59ff.
   aggression center, 480, 510
   and alcohol, 60, 63
   association areas, 64, 190–91
   blood, 244
   cerebellum, 77
   cerebral cortex, 61ff.
   convoluting, 61–62
   corpus callosum, 70–71
   damage, 462, 569
   development, 58
   discovery, 63ff.
   discrimination of objects, 169–70
   division, 62ff.
   electrical stimulation, 6
   electricity, 68ff., 168
   elephant, 347
   enlargement in animals, 355
   evolution, 76–77
   exercise, 355
   fissure, 69
   Dr. Fludd's version, 67
   frontal association areas, 62
   frontal lobes, 72
   glial cells, 61
   Greek philosophy, 7
   hearing, 63
   hemispheres, 70
   hypothalamus, 77
   injury, 70
   and intelligence, 62
   localization of function, 66ff.

Brain (cont.)
  location, 17
  medulla, 77
  memory, 228
  mind vs., 61
  motor area, 69
  neurons, 64ff.
  older, 73, 76–77
  operation of, 64
  oxygen, 244
  pain, 72
  parts of, 69
  phrenology, 67
  reticular formation, 60–61
  size, 347, 355, 570
  and spinal cord, 67
  surgery, 48, 68, 72
  and symbols, 500
  thalamus, 77
Brainwashing (*see* Persuasion)
Brainwaves, 168, 180, 181, 246,
     248, 303 (*see also* Biofeedback)
Breast-feeding, 382–83
Breuer, Joseph, 265
Bruner, Jerome, 400ff.
Bull:
  color vision, 138
  fear center, 110–11

C Cancer, 107
Cannibalism, 96
Cannon, W. B., 119
Cannon-Bard theory, 119
Capote, Truman, 442
Carnival, 272
Carson, Kit, 96
Cat:
  dreams, 250
  night vision, 138
  vision, 147
Cave paintings, 50
Central nervous system, 74–75, 126,
     256
Cerebellum, 77
Cerebral cortex (*see* Cortex)
Chance, 171ff.
Character (*see* Morality)
Character disorders, 556 (*see also*
     Delinquency; Mental illness;
     Neurosis)
Charcot, Jean, 245, 264–65
Chemotherapy, 589

Chicago Eight, 499
Child (*see also* Morality):
  aggression, 411
  birth, hysterical, 265
  cognitive growth, 400ff.
  concrete operations stage, 407
  conservation, 408
  dependency, 412
  effects of culture, 385
  evolution, 58
  father influence, 268–69
  formal operations stage, 409
  intelligence tests, 400
  intelligence training, 376
  internal conversation, 409
  love withdrawal, 414
  malnutrition, 378
  moral development, 409, 421
  mother relationships, 381
  Neofreudian view, 287–88
  object permanency, 406
  punishment, physical, 412
  rearing, effects, 382
  rearing, monkeys, 54
  reward, 460
  self-concept, 415
  sensorimotor stage, 405
  sex-role development, 114–15
  size constancy, 402–3
  social development, 378
  speech, 407
  stages of development, 405
  swimming behavior, 58
  vision, 401–4
  walking, 57, 376
Children:
  amphetamines and, 472
  anxiety, 380
  avoidance behavior, 292
  birth trauma, 379
  blind, 222, 382
  brain injury, 70–71
  breast feeding, 382–83
  vs. chimpanzees, 375
  contact comfort, 381
  creativity, 386
  culture and, 384
  day-care centers, 386–87
  depth perception, 154
  developmental sequence, 375–76
  deviant, 385
  diet, 95, 99–100
  divorce, 392

Children (cont.)
  dreams, 253
  early development, 266
  early social behavior, 55–56
  eidetic imagery, 197
  emotions, 91–92
  extinction with, 231
  fears, 90–92, 380–81, 404
  Greek, 385
  growth cycles, 378
  health, 377
  Hutterite, 385
  hyperactive, 589
  identification, 389
  imitation in, 384
  infant behavior, 114
  kibbutz, 386–87
  language, 55, 405
  learning, 206
  maturation, 58, 375ff.
  milk, fingers in, 231
  and mother absence, 382
  obedience, 409–10
  orphans, 54, 386
  physical skills, 377–78
  prejudice, 440
  preprogramming, 56
  punishment, 232
  reading, 355
  reared in isolation, 56
  rearing techniques, 91–92
  rejecting fathers, 457–58
  reversing letters, 71
  reward, 232
  schizophrenia, 568
  sexuality, 268–69
  smiling, 381–82
  social development, 381, 411
  strangers, 404
  talking, 376
  television, 507–9
  thumb sucking, 382
  toilet training, 384
  violence, 507–9
  visual cliff, 154
  vitamin deficiencies, 99
  weaning, 384
  welfare families, 457–58
  without cortex, 78
  work laws, 374
Chimpanzees:
  brain of, 71
  development of, 375

Chimpanzees (cont.)
  and marijuana, 467
  speech, 48
CIA, 441, 485
Cigarettes and homeostasis,
    115–16
Circadian rhythm, 249
  sleep, 253
Clairvoyance, 176
Classical conditioning, 84ff., 90,
    93, 198
  and Soviet Union, 93
Closure, 156, 204
Coal, color of, 140
Cognitive dissonance, 297
Cognitive theory, 120
Color(s):
  dreams, 258
  extrasensory perception, 180
  lights, 139
  major, 135
  psychological aspects, 170–71
  and race, 492
  response of eye, 135
  sex role, 275–76
  spectrum, 135
Color vision (*see also* Eye;
    Vision):
  defects, 139
  mystery pigment, 139
  phosphenes, 140
  psychological aspects, 139
  rods in, 138
  theories of, 138ff.
Communes, 386–87 (*see also*
    Children; Delinquents)
Competition, social, 33
Concentration camps (*see* Prisons)
Concrete operations, 407
Conditioning (*see also* Biofeedback;
    Learning; Sensory deprivation):
  association, 82ff.
  aversive, 586
  beauty, 83
  behavioral modification, 583,
    584–87
  classical, 86–87, 198
  emotion, 90ff.
  etiquette, 83
  food, 87, 99
  and internal organs, 93
  kinds of, 198
  neurosis, 89

Conditioning (cont.)
   operant, 198ff.
   pain, 198
   reinforcement and reward, 200
   religion, 83–84
   salivation, 85
   sexual, 87, 106
   shock, 88
Cones, 136ff., 146
Congress, operant conditioning of, 203–4
Consciousness, Watson's view, 90
Conservation, 408
Constitutional psychology, 281ff.
Control:
   experimental method, 19ff.
   groups, 22ff.
Convergence, 155
Coordination, 63
Copernicus, Nicolas, 10
Copilia, 144–45
Cornea, 142
Corpus Callosum, 70–71
Correlation, 26ff., 32
   causation, 32
   interpretation of, 29ff.
Cortex, 61ff., 473, 503
   electrical firing, 403
   internal conversation, 409
   removal, 71, 250
   and sex, 442
Crandon, Mina, 177
Creativity, 363ff.
   achievement tests, 366
   characteristics of, 368
   construct, 364–65
   Greeks, 385–86
   and IQ, 366–68
   kibbutz, 386
   mental illness, 364, 368–69
   personality, 366–69
   prediction of, 367
   rote memory, 219
   set, 364–65
   students, 365–66
   training for, 369–70
Criminals:
   punishment, 233
   recidivism, 233
Critical periods:
   children, 54
   dogs, 55

Critical periods (cont.)
   ducks, 52
   imprinting, 55
   monkeys, 55
"Crowbar" case, 71
Cycles (*see also* Biological clocks):
   light-dark, 22–23, 142, 378

D Dance fly, 49
Dancing mania, 5
Dark adaptation, 138
Dark Ages, 8, 9
Darrow, Clarence, 512ff.
Darwin, Charles, 8, 45ff., 118, 160, 271, 285, 328
Death:
   sudden death phenomenon, 503
   voodoo, 502–3
Decapitation, 73
Defense mechanisms (*see also* Drugs; Mental illness):
   denial, 552
   projection, 485, 550
   of psychotic, 562
   rationalization, 550
   regression, 266–67, 550–51
   repression, 266, 273–74, 315, 549–50
   withdrawal, 551
Delinquency:
   birth order, 417
   family patterns, 457
   gangs, 458
   goals, 458
   and Greek children, 385
   juvenile, 454ff.
   moral judgments, 459
   parental attitudes, 458
   personality, 458ff.
   physical defects, 417
   rates, 454–56
   and religion, 459
   reporting, 454–56
   school, 459
   social class, 454–55
Delinquents:
   body type, 284
   as therapists, 540
Dendrites, 65–66
Dentists, pain, 109
Dependent variable, 19ff.
Depth perception, 153ff.

Descartes, René, 64, 132, 141, 561
Deviance, 301 (*see also* Mental
    illness)
Diet, food selection, 99–100
Digestive glands, 85
Digit symbol task, 24
Discipline (*see* Child; Morality)
Discrimination, 220
Disney, Walt, 300
Dissection, 18
Dissonance (*see* Cognitive
    dissonance)
Distribution curve:
    normal curve, 36
    other curves, 38
Divorce, 392
DNA, 192
Dogs:
    avoidance behavior, 292
    critical period, 55
    extrasensory perception in,
        178–79
    imprinting, 55
    sensory deprivation, 108
    shocking of, 410
    sleep patterns, 250
    smell, 403
    social behavior, 55
    territoriality, 481
    thirst, 100
Dollard, John, 290
Dolphin, sleep, 249
Donner Party, 96
Dormouse, 117
Dowry, human and animal, 49
Dreams, 250ff.
    alpha, 255
    body rhythm, 249
    eye movements, 253–54
    Freud, 255, 269
    Greek, 8
    internal, 255
    length of, 253
    mental illness, 257
    need for, 254
    nightmares, 258–59
Drives:
    basic, 93, 124
    Maslow, 124
    sex motivation, 105
Drugs:
    addiction, 463
    alcohol, 461

Drugs (cont.)
    amphetamines, 471, 589
    barbiturates, 472
    with children, 472
    death rates, 463
    escape mechanism, 463
    food, 433
    Great Britain, 465
    in Greek culture, 385–86
    habituation, 464
    heroin, 465, 472–73
    laws, 465
    LSD, 464
    marijuana, 465, 466–69
    with mental patients, 472, 589–90
    morphine, 472–73
    placebo effect, 579
    STP, 471
    tolerance, 463
    user personality, 464
    vision, 140
Ducks:
    conversation, 53
    imprinting, 51

E Earth: views of, 4, 9ff.
Efferent neurons, 74
Eidetic imagery, 196
Einstein, Albert, 26
Eisenhower, Dwight, 300
Electrical brain stimulation, 6,
        68–69, 72, 98, 100, 107, 111, 201
Electroencephalogram (*see*
    Brainwaves)
Electroencephalograph (*see*
    Brainwaves)
Ellis, Albert, 448, 582
Emergency reaction, 112
    and homeostasis, 116
    in schizophrenics, 568
Emotions, 104 ff.
    in accidents, 67
    adrenalin, 112, 120
    artificial, 118
    Cannon-Bard, 119
    changes from lobotomy, 72
    in children, 90–91
    cognitive theory, 120
    conditioning, 90–91
    effects on stomach, 97
    emergency reaction, 112
    fear, 90–91

Emotions (cont.)
 fear in monkey, 54
 Greek philosophy, 7
 homeostasis, 115
 hypothalamus, 110, 119
 James-Lange theory, 118
 and limbic system, 119
 location in brain, 72
 mechanistic viewpoint, 90–91
 orienting reflex, 119
 physiology of, 109
 rage, 110
 Soviet theory, 119
 stomach, 97–98
 symbols and, 247
Encounter (*see* Psychotherapy)
Enlightenment, 8
Epicurianism, 122
Epilepsy, 7
ESP (*see* Extrasensory perception)
Estrogen, 106
Eugenics, 343
Evans, Oliver, 7
Evolution, 45ff.
 and Freud, 45
 and geology, 45
 psychological, 46
Existentialism, 123, 545
Experimental method:
 control(s), 19ff., 22ff., 283
 dependent variable, 19ff.
 experimental groups, 22ff.
 hypothesis, 19, 24
 independent variable, 20ff.
 rating forms, 315
 replication, 367
 reporting results, 23ff.
 subjects, 21
 trials, 24–25
Extinction, 231–32
Extrasensory perception, 171ff.
 for color, 180
 dreams, 181–82
 Grateful Dead, 182
 sleep, 182
 twins, 181
Eye:
 accommodation, 155
 camera, 141, 144
 color response, 135
 complex cortical cells, 148ff.
 convergence, 155
 copilia, 144–45

Eye (cont.)
 dark adaptation, 138
 development of, 142
 early theories, 141
 fixation, 145, 151, 169
 frequencies of light, 135
 image, 144
 movement in sleep, 253ff.
 movements, 145, 151
 ox, 141
 parts of, 142ff.
 peripheral vision, 147
 photosensitivity, 142
 pigments, 138ff.
 processing, 147ff.
 receptors, 136ff.
 retinal ganglion cells, 147ff.
 scan path, 145
 sensitivity, 137ff.
 simple cortical cells, 148ff.
 and television, 145
 third, 141
 visual acuity, 138
Eysenck, Hans, 178

F Fathers, influence of, 268
Fear, 112
 and anxiety, 121, 380–81
 centers, 122
Feeding, monkeys, 54
Festinger, Leon, 296
Fish, memory, 194
Fissure, brain, 70
Fixation, eye, 145
Flourens, Pierre, 68
Fludd, Robert, 67
Fly, dancing fly and evolution, 49
Food:
 eating habits, 87
 pin-ups, 95
 prisoners, 94–95
 selection, 99
 social aspects, 96
 tastes, 96
 vitamin deficiencies, 99
Ford, Henry, 488
Foreign language, 55, 217
Forgetting:
 curve, 214
 decay, 229
 extinction, 231
 frustration, 231–32

Forgetting (cont.)
  hypnosis, 245
  inhibition, 230
  interference, 229–30
  punishment, 232–33
  repression, 273
  retrieval, 228
  synapse, 189
  transfer, 230
Formal discipline, 218
Fovea, 143, 146
Frankenstein, Dr., 64
Franklin, Benjamin, 60, 140
Freud, Sigmund:
  aggression, 272
  biological theory, 285
  child rearing, 266
  classification of mental illness,
    539
  dreams, 121, 255, 269–70, 273
  flying, 105
  free association, 580
  homosexuality, 444
  hypnosis, 264–65
  id, ego, superego, 270–71, 309
  identification, 388–89
  libido, 269–70
  mental illness, 544
  Neofreudians, 272
  Oedipus complex, 267
  pleasure principle, 291
  psychoanalysis, 577–80
  regression, 266–67
  repression, 266, 273
  sex emphasis, 266, 269, 444
  sex role, 388
  sexual stages, 266
  slips of tongue, 273
  talking cure, 265, 529–30
  unconscious, 6, 273, 309
Fritsch, Gustav, 68
Frog:
  bug catcher, 148
  decapitated, 73
  nerves, 65
  vision of, 147–48
Frontal lobes, 72
Fuller, René, 355

G Gage, Phineas, 71
Galilei, Galileo, 10–11, 178
Galileo (*see* Galilei)
Gall, Franz, 67ff.

Galton, Francis, 26ff.
  eugenics, 342ff.
  personality test, 309
Galvani, Luigi, 65
Gandhi, Mahatma, 122
Ganglion cells, 148
Generalization, 219
Genes (*see* Inheritance)
"Genius" (*See* Intelligence)
Geology, and Darwin, 45
George III, 538
Gesell, Arnold, 376
Gestalt, 160–61, 204
Glands, 105ff.
  adrenals, 112
  digestive, 84ff.
Glandular system, 112ff.
Glial cells, 61
Glueck, S., and E. T., 284
Goats, conditioning, 90
Gonads (*see* Sex)
Grand Canyon, 152
Graphs, 23ff.
Gravity, 16
Greeks:
  Aristotle, 8, 17
  armchair speculation, 6ff., 10,
    16, 17
  Hippocrates, 7
  mental illness, 7
  philosophy, 6ff.
  Plato, 7, 8
  and sex, 395, 447
  Socrates, 7
Gregory, Dick, 97
Gregory, Richard L., 155
Group behavior:
  dancing mania, 5
  similar characteristics, 169
Grouping:
  into categories, 36
  normal curve, 36
Groups (*see also* Social grouping):
  animal, 479–81
  bees, 480–81
  brainwashing, 516
  Catholics, 490
  fear, 487–88
  identity, 458, 484–85, 488
  initiation, 432
  Jews, 488
  kibbutz, 386–87
  Mafia, 493
  Nazis, 486, 494, 498

Groups (cont.)
  personal boundary, 481–84
  prejudice, 490
  pressure, 203, 510ff.
  pressure and child development,
    411
  prisoners, 515ff.
  protective mechanisms, 484ff.
  purpose, 506
  reference, 510
  religion, 489–90
  riots, 96
  rituals, 500ff.
  rules, 492–94
  scapegoating, 485–86
  Scottsboro Seven, 486
  social class, 34, 479
  social grouping, 484ff.
  starving, 96
  stereotypes, 491
  suggestion, 240
  symbols, 490ff., 498ff.
  territoriality, 481–84
  Vietnam, 489
  violence, 503 ff., 506
Group therapy, 587
Guillotine, 73

H Hallucinations, 528, 565
  drugs, 469
Handedness, and brain function, 70
Harlow, Harry, 125
Harvey, William, 17, 67
Hawk, fovea, 146
Headache, cures for, 64
Hearing, 63, 403
  frequencies, 134
Heart, 17, 67
Hedonism, 121, 207
Helping behavior, 167–68
Hemispheres:
  of brain, 69ff.
  disconnection, 71
  dominance, 70
  learning, 71
Hereditary Genius, 342
Heredity (*see* Inheritance)
Hermaphrodites, 446
Heroin:
  college students, 470
  physical effects, 472–73
Hibernation, 117
Hierarchy of needs, 123ff.

Hipprocrates, 7, 66, 538
Histogram, 334
Hitler, Adolph, 486
Hitzig, 68
Hoarding behavior, 95
Hoffman, Martin, 447
Homeostasis, 115ff., 270, 297,
    377, 413, 463, 549
Homosexuality, 443ff.
  acceptance, 443
  adolescence, 443–44
  in animals, 447
  bisexuality, 445
  conditioning, 445
  environments, 446
  family relations, 444–45
  female, 445
  Freud and, 444
  hormones, 106, 446
  incidence, 443
  inheritance, 445–46
  "marriages," 444
  myths, 446–47
  normality, 447–48
  "primal scene," 444
  psychological explanations, 443
  Sullivan, 289, 443
  therapy, 587
  twins, 445
Hormones, 105–6, 389, 446
Horney, Karen, 380
Horse:
  evolution of, 46
  telepathic, 177
Houdini, Harry, 176–78
Hunger, 93ff.
  blood sugar, 98–99
  cues, 293
  hoarding behavior, 95
  hypothalamus, 77, 98
  overeating, 286
  pangs, 98
  secondary drives, 293
  social theories, 286
  stomach contractions, 98
Hunger drives, monkeys, 54
Hunting, and evolution, 49–50
Hutterites, 385
Hypnosis, 240ff., 517
  age regression, 242
  and anxiety, 243
  blindness, 246
  childbirth, 245
  Freud, 264

Hypnosis (cont.)
  highway, 241
  and immorality, 243
  and learning, 243
  and pain, 245
  reticular formation, 252
  self, 245
  and sleep, 241, 247
  stage, 242
  surgery, 245
  and unconscious, 264–65
  and yoga, 244
Hypothalamus, 473, 503, 589
  emotion, 110, 119
  in hunger and thirst, 77, 98, 100
  in pleasure and pain, 107
  and temperature, 117

Idiot savant, 195–96
Illusions (*see* Visual illusions)
Imprinting, 50ff.
  and critical period, 52
  ducks, 50ff., 377
  heartbeat, 53
In Defense of Women, 82
Independent variable, 20ff.
Indians, 484
  Hopi, 57
  intelligence, 345
  perception, 152
  slaughter, 96
Individual differences, 33–37
Infant intelligence, 400
Inheritance:
  alcohol, 462
  chromosomes, 186
  criminal behavior, 457
  and delinquency, 457
  details of, 186–87
  developmental patterns, 375ff.
  disease, 346
  and environment, 377
  fears, 380
  homosexuality, 445–46
  intelligence, 342ff., 346ff.,
    376ff.
  and LSD, 469–71
  personality, 298
  proteins, 192
  and psychosis, 562
  racial differences, 346
  twins, 377
  visual apparatus, 401

Initiations, 501–2
Ink blots (*see* Rorschach)
Instinct, 58–59, 91, 154
Institutions, effects of on aged,
  571
Intelligence, 328ff., 340ff.
  and adjustment, 283–84
  and aging, 570
  average, 333
  Binet, 330ff.
  blacks, 354
  and body type, 283–84
  brain, 62, 68
  and brain convolutions, 61–62
  brain size, 347, 355
  changes, 351ff.
  children, 400
  conditions affecting, 335
  and creativity, 366–68
  decreases, 352
  definitions, 341
  distribution, 334
  education, 329
  environment, 343
  errors, 336
  eugenics, 343
  evaluation of, 355
  expectation, 352ff.
  female, 393
  group tests, 339
  and hypnosis, 243
  individual tests, 339
  inheritance, 342ff., 346ff., 376ff.
  and institutions, 352
  IQ, 332–33
  Jensenism, 348ff.
  malnutrition, 378
  memory, unusual, 195–96
  mental age, 332
  mind and body, 330
  normal curve, 333–34
  performance, 338
  phrenology, 328
  and physical skills, 329–30
  quotient, 332–33
  and race, 345ff., 349
  reading speed, 152
  reliability, 336
  school influence, 361–62
  school performance, 335
  standardization, 336
  symbols, 329
  synapses, 355
  testing, 329ff.

Intelligence (cont.)
  testing-motivation, 351ff.
  testing-purpose, 360
  theories of, 328–29
  "training," 376
  twins, 343–45, 377
  validity, 335–36, 340
  verbal, 337
  walking, 378
  Wechsler, 337ff.
  women, 354
Inverting glasses, 146
Invisible college, 17
Iris, 142

J James, William, 118
  James-Lange theory, 118
  Japanese Americans, 169
  Jensen, Arthur, 348ff., 355
  Jung, Carl, 297ff.
  Juvenile delinquency (*see*
    Delinquency)

K Kepler, Johannes, 10
  Kibbutz, 386–87 (*see also*
    Communes):
    adolescence in, 431
  King, Martin Luther, 489
  Kinsey, Alfred, 437
  Kohlberg, Lawrence, 421–22
  Kool-Aid (*see* Conservation)
  Kraeplin, Emil, 538

L Laing, R. D., 529
  Language, 405, 407, 491–92 (*see also*
    Social grouping; Symbols):
    foreign, 55, 217
  Latent learning, 205–6
  Learning (*see also* Memory):
    ability and age, 571
    anxiety, 291
    association, 82ff.
    attention, 206, 213
    attitude, 206
    avoidance, 292
    behavioral modification, 584–87
    categorizing, 221–22
    classical conditioning, 84ff.
    clustering, 221–22
    coding, 222
    cognitive map, 197

Learning (cont.)
  consolidation, 225
  curves, 213ff.
  discrimination, 220
  and emotion, 113, 114
  environmental cues, 293
  by exposure, 205
  and forgetting, 214
  formal discipline, 218
  generalization, 219, 291
  and hypnosis, 243
  and intelligence, 329
  languages, 217–19, 222
  latent, 205
  meaningfulness, 222
  and mental illness, 546
  mnemonic devices, 223
  and motivation, 113, 206, 213
  motor skills, 216
  nonsense syllables, 193
  overlearning, 214
  pain, 108
  personality theory, 289ff.
  primary drives, 293
  principle, 223–24
  programmed, 233–35
  punishment in children, 232
  recall, 226–27
  recitation, 226
  recognition, 226–27
  reinforcement and reward, 200
  reward and, 233
  secondary drives, 293
  secondary reinforcement, 415
  and sex role, 115
  sexual behavior, 442
  and sleep, 256
  social, 82ff., 299, 301, 383
  social behavior, 383
  study habits, 218
  synapses, 188ff.
  teaching machines, 233–35
  transfer, 217
  trial and error, 200
  verbal cues, 293
Leary, Timothy, 207
Leeuwenhoek, A., 18ff.
Lefthandedness, 70
Lie detector, 519–20
Light averaging, 140
Light-darkness cycle, 22–23
Light waves, 133–35
Limbic system, 111, 120
Lindbergh, Charles, 156

Lizard, third eye, 141
Lobotomy, 72
Long-term memory, 193ff., 225–26
Lorenz, Konrad, 51, 377, 479
LSD:
　chromosome damage, 469–71
　creativity and, 470
　dancing mania, 5
　dosage, 469
　effects, 469–71
　hedonism, 207
　and marijuana taking, 469
　synaptic confusion, 66, 469
　use, 469
Luther, Martin, 9

M McClelland, David, 114
Mafia, 501
Magic, 502
Maladjustment (*see* Mental illness)
Mammoth, 50
Marathon group therapy, 587–89
Marijuana (*see also* Drugs):
　and alcohol, 23
　and automobile driving, 467
　creativity and, 468
　effects, 467–69
　and heroin, 468–69
　laws, 466, 468
　LSD taking, 468
　personality and, 464, 466, 468
　tolerance, 468
　use, 466
　Washington, George, 466
Marx, Karl, 33
Masculinity:
　self-image, 284
　society's definition, 284
Maslow, Abraham, 123, 294
Masochism, 122
Masters, William (and Johnson, Virginia), 440
Maturation, 58, 95, 376, 378ff., 408
May, Rollo, 186
Mazes, and set, 21
Mead, Margaret, 431, 438
Mean, 38ff.
Mechanoreceptors, 107
Median, 38ff.
Medicine, prescientific, 16
Meditation, 93, 248
Medulla, 77

Memory;
　and age, 571
　amino acids, 191
　amnesia, 193
　association areas, 190–91
　chemical, 188–91
　coding, 222, 227
　cognitive map, 197
　consolidation, 225
　decay, 229
　eidetic, 196
　extinction, 233
　facilitating, 189
　grouping, 228
　increasing, 226
　inhibition, 189, 192, 194
　intelligence, 329
　location of, 72–73, 190
　long term, 193ff.
　meaningfulness, 195
　mnemonic devices, 223
　and motivation, 194
　and pain, 106
　and persuasion, 518
　photographic, 196–97
　phrenology's version, 67
　physiology of, 188ff.
　protein, 191ff., 194, 225
　recall, 226–27
　recitation, 226
　recognition, 226–27
　reconstruction, 190
　short term, 193ff.
　split brain, 190
　storage, 189ff., 226–27
　storage in brain, 191ff.
　storage of symbols, 329
　synapse, 188ff.
　trace theory, 229
　unusual, 195–96
　visual, 194
　waveform, 189
　witnesses, 167
Mencken, H. L., 82
Menstruation, 394
Mental hospital, as cause of illness, 534
Mental illness (*see also* Defense mechanisms; Neurosis; Psychosis):
　age regression, 243
　aggression in, 554
　animal, 89

Mental illness (cont.)
  anxiety, 530, 548
  behavior during, 533–34
  brain defects, 537–38
  brain surgery, 72
  and breast-feeding, 382
  character disorders, 556
  in children, 385
  classification, 538–39
  conditioning and, 89
  conflict, 548
  as conformity, 531
  and creativity, 364, 368–69
  criticism of concept, 529–33
  cultural differences, 527
  cycle, 250
  day treatment centers, 540
  definition problems, 527
  definitions of, 527–28
  in delinquents, 533
  delusions, 528, 547
  depersonalization, 470
  depression, 312, 385, 394, 503
  depression and amphetamines,
    471
  diagnosis, 312–13
  as disease, 530–31
  dreams, 257
  exhibitionists, 531
  fetishes, 553
  Greek philosophy, 7
  hallucinations, 528
  history of, 534ff.
  homosexuality, 527
  hospitals, 539
  Hutterites, 385
  hypnosis, 265
  inheritance, 562
  and intelligence, 283–84
  interpersonal relationships,
    553–54
  in kibbutz, 386–87
  labeling, 301
  and LSD, 469
  and medicine, 529–30
  and morality, 527
  multiple personality, 303, 557
  nonprofessionals in, 540
  normal behavior, 527–28, 533
  number of cases, 527
  operant conditioning, 202
  origin of:
    anxiety, 547–49

Mental illness (cont.)
    conflict, 547–48
  paranoia, 312, 550, 553
  phobias, 547
  psychosomatic illness, 84
  punishment and, 418
  reactions toward, 541
  in religious communities, 385
  Rogers, Carl, 297
  and school PTA meetings, 528
  similarities in treatment, 591
  sleep, 254
  sociopath, 460–61
  suicide, 313
  surgery, 110
  symptom replacement, 585
  symptoms, 530
  tests, 309ff.
  theories of:
    Freud, 529–30, 544
    learning, 546–47
    Rogers, 545
    Sullivan, H. S., 288, 545
    Szasz, 532
  thought disorders, 555
Mental patients:
  assertiveness, 39
  general behavior, 555
  nightmares, 258
Mesmer, Anton, 240
Micro-organisms, 18–19
Middle Ages, 8
Miller, Neal, 290
Mind, views of, 5, 44
Miss America, 83
Mnemonic devices, 223
Mode, 38ff.
Monkeys (*see also* Chimpanzees):
  contact comfort, 53–54, 381
  emotion, 54
  evolution, 47
  "executive" ulcers, 559
  imprinting, 50ff.
  and puzzles, 125
  sensory deprivation, 53
  sexual activity, 390
  social patterns, 481
Morality:
  birth order, 416
  bribery, 415
  cheating, 421
  delinquents, 459
  disapproval by others, 421

Morality (cont.)
 discipline, 409
 group pressure, 410ff.
 guilt, 413
 helping behavior, 423
 honesty, 420–21
 internalization, 412
 knowledge of, 419–21
 love withdrawal, 414
 moral realism, 421
 normal curve, 421
 obedience training, 409
 and perception, 169–70
 and physical defects, 417ff.
 physical punishment, 412–14
 religion and, 420
 reward and, 414ff.
 reward stage, 421
 secondary reinforcement, 414
 self-criticism, 415
 self-esteem and, 416
 self-regulated, 415
 sharing stage, 421–22
 and social class, 423
 social pressure, 423
 training, 218, 423
Morgan, C. D., 311
Morphine, 472–73
Motivation, 104ff.
 achievement, 114
 attention, 206
 curiosity, 125
 emotion, 113
 gestalt, 204
 glands, 105–6
 hedonism, 121
 hierarchy of needs, 123ff.
 homeostasis, 115
 hormones, 105–6
 hypnosis, 244–45
 instinct, 59
 and IQ, 352ff.
 latent learning, 205
 learning, 113, 206
 manipulation, 125
 Maslow, 123
 and memory, 194
 non-tissue needs, 125
 obscure, 200, 204
 operant conditioning, 199
 pain, 106ff.
 pleasure, 106ff.

Motivation (cont.)
 sexual, 105ff.
Motor systems:
 area of brain, 69
 neurons, 69
 spinal cord, 73
Multiple personality, 303
Murphy, Gardner, 181
Murray, Henry, 311

N Naturalist, 51, 377, 479
Nazis, 410
Neanderthal man, 50
Needs, hierarchy, 123ff.
Neo-Freudians, 272, 286ff.
Nerves:
 afferent, 74
 axon, 65
 in brain, 64
 cells, 45
 central nervous system, 74
 dendrites, 65
 discovery, 63ff.
 efferent, 74
 electrical operation, 65
 free nerve endings, 107
 hypnosis, 246
 impulse pathways, 109
 maturation of, 404
 motor, 73–74
 pain receptors, 109
 peripheral nervous system, 74
 sensory, 73–74
 synapse, 65
Neuron (*see* Nerves)
Neurosis (*see also* Defense
  mechanisms; Mental illness):
 animal, 89
 anxiety, 557
 classification, 556ff.
 conditioning, 89
 conversion, 532, 558
 cortex and hypothalamus, 561
 defined, 554–55
 depression, 312, 385, 394, 503
 dissociative, 557
 fetishes, 553
 goats, 90
 hypochondriasis, 561
 multiple personality, 303, 557
 obsessive-compulsive, 557–58

Neurosis (cont.)
  phobias, 557
  psychosomatic disorders, 536,
    558–59
  sheep, 90
Newton, Isaac, 16, 141
Nightmares, 258–59
Night vision, 136–37
Nonsense syllable, 193
Normal curve (frequency
    distribution), 33ff., 173ff.
Norming (*see* Normal curve)
Nudity, 271
Nutrition, 461

O Obedience training, 409–10
Obesity:
  adolescence, 433
  factors in, 286
  neo-Freudian view, 286
Object permanency, 406
Occipital lobe, 136, 139, 143, 148
Odds (*see* Probability)
Older brain, 107, 111, 190, 255
Operant conditioning, 198ff.
  anticipation, 201
  behavioral modification, 584–85
  biofeedback, 248
  brain, 201
  vs. classical, 200
  Congress, 203–4
  factory workers, 203
  homosexuality, 445
  human, 200
  mental patients, 202, 547
  pain, 201
  Skinner, B. F., 199
  Skinner box, 199–200
  teaching machines, 234
  trial and error, 200
Opsins, 138
Orientation reflexes, 119, 146–47
Origin of the Species, 45, 55
Orphans, 386
  death rate, 54
Overlearning, 214

P Pain:
  anticipation, 109
  areas, 111

Pain (cont.)
  avoidance, 122
  boxes, 107
  brain cells, 72
  centers, 107
  conditioning, 198
  emotions, 106ff.
  free nerve endings, 107
  hedonism, 121
  hypnosis, 245
  learned, 108
  masochism, 122
  mechanoreceptors, 107
  memory, 106
  pathways, 109
  philosophical ideas, 8
  receptors, 107
  reticular formation, 109
  suggestion, 108
  tolerance, 108, 242
Parapsychology (*see* Extrasensory
  perception)
Patton, George S. III, 281
Pavlov, Ivan, 84, 198
Penitentes, 122
Percentages, 30
Perception, 132ff.
  abstract, 167–68
  anticipation, 167ff.
  categorizing, 222–27
  in children, 401ff.
  cities of gold, 166
  coins, 168
  color, 170
  in context, 169
  cues, 152ff., 402–3
  defense, 168–69
  depth, 153–54
  dirty words, 168–69
  distance, 152ff., 401ff.
  dolphin, 132
  extrasensory, 171ff.
  factors in, 132
  group affiliation, 511
  helping behavior, 167–68
  individual, 139
  inherited, 160
  morality, 169–70
  numbers, 167
  prejudice, 511
  psychological, 166ff.
  sensory deprivation, 517

Perception (cont.)
  similarities, 169
  size constancy, 152–53
  tachistoscope, 168
  touch, 180
  unconscious, 168
  vision in man, 132ff.
  wearing apparel, 167–68
  witnesses, 166–67
  words, 131–33
Peripheral nervous system, 74–75
Peripheral vision, 147
Personality:
  archetype, 299
  and body image, 281ff.
  changes with hunger, 95
  cognitive dissonance, 297
  and communal living, 386–87,
    431
  constitutional psychology, 281ff.
  delinquents, 458ff.
  diagnosis, 308ff.
  Dollard-Miller system, 290
  drug users, 464
  fluids in the body, 7
  frontal lobe, 72
  Greek philosophy, 7
  inheritance, 298
  Jung, Carl, 297ff.
  learning theory, 289ff.
    avoidance, 292
    vs. Freud, 290
    generalization, 291
    pleasure principle, 291
    secondary drives, 293
  multiple, 303
  persona, 297–99
  phrenology, 67ff.
  and physique, 281–85
  ratings, 315
  Rogers, Carl, 295
  secondary drives, 293
  self-actualization, 123
  and sex role, 387ff.
  and sleep, 256
  social learning, 82ff., 299, 301,
    383
  social roles, 302
  social theories, 301
  somatotype, 282
  testing, 308ff.
  tests, 283, 318, 320
  theories and conflict, 280–81

Persuasion:
  and beliefs, 510, 516–17
  brainwashing:
    advertising, 516
    compliance, 516–17
    confession, 515–16
    defenses, 518–20
    Korean War, 515–17
    resistance, 511
    rewards, 511, 516
    sensory deprivation, 517–19
    verbal messages, 515
  Clarence Darrow, 512ff.
  confession, 519–21
  courtroom, 518
  drugs, 520
  education, 518
  group pressure, 510–11
  lie detector, 519–20
  reference group, 511–12
  territoriality, 520
Phi phenomenon, 161
Phosphenes, 140
Photographic memory, 196–97
Photopic vision, 138
Phrenology, 67ff., 328
Piaget, Jean, 400ff.
Pig, smell, 403
Pigeons, shaping, 201–2
Pinel, Philippe, 537
Plato, 7, 8
Pleasure:
  brain centers, 107, 111, 201
  dreams, 121
  hedonism, 121
  limbic system, 107, 111
  and pain, 122
  philosophical ideas, 8
  receptors, 109
Pornography, 440–41
Prejudice (*see also* Groups):
  All in the Family, 511
  attention, 220–21
  discrimination, 220
  and perception, 511
  transfer, 220
Principles of Psychology, 118
Prisons, 302, 515ff.
  concentration camps, 515–17
Probability, 171, 176
  coin tossing, 171ff.
  dice, 171
Problem solving, 23–24

Programmed learning, 233–35
Programming in children, 56ff.
Projection, visual, 95
Projective tests (*see* Testing)
Protein inhibitor, 192
Protein molecule, 191ff., 194
Psychiatrists, 576
Psychoanalysis, 577 (*see also*
  Psychotherapy)
Psychologists, 577
Psychoneurosis (*see* Neurosis)
Psychopathology (*see* Mental illness)
Psychosis (*see also* Defense
    mechanisms; Mental illness):
  affect (emotion), 555–56
  aging, 570
  causes, 562
  defined, 555
  delusions, 528
  depressive, 568–69
  hallucinations, 528
  hospitalization, 563
  involutional, 570
  manic depressive, 568–69
  organic, 569–70
  paranoid, 565
  schizophrenia:
    causes, 563–68
    defined, 563
    delusions, 565
    drugs, 589
    hallucinations, 565
    inheritance, 562, 566–67
    motor behavior, 565–66
    origin of term, 563
    physiology, 567–68
    reality orientation, 564–65
    symptoms, 564–65
  senility, 571
  thought disorders, 555, 563
Psychosomatic disorders (*see*
    Stress; Neurosis)
Psychotherapy:
  age regression, 243
  and anxiety, 584–87
  behavioral modification, 583,
    584–87
  chemotherapy, 589–90
  client-centered therapy, 581–82
  defined, 578, 584
  effectiveness, 578, 583, 591–92
  electroconvulsive therapy,
    590–91

Psychotherapy (cont.)
  free association, 580
  group, 587–89
  length of, 581
  nonprofessionals in, 540
  placebo effect, 579, 589–90
  psychoanalysis, 579–80
  psychotherapists, 577
  rational therapy, 582–83
  self-cures, 591–92
  similarity in types, 591
  styles, 579ff.
  suggestion, 578–79
Punishment, 232–33, 268, 412ff.
Pupil, 142
Purkinje phenomenon, 136

R Race:
  brain size, 345–49
  differences, 345–46
  heat tolerance, 346
  and intelligence, 345ff.
  verbal skills, 345
Rage, 107, 111
Rank, Otto, 379
Rats, hoarding behavior, 95
Reading:
  college students, 151
  errors in, 133
  Fuller system, 355
  and intelligence, 152
  letter processing, 133
  skimming, 151–52
  speed of, 151
Recall, 226ff.
Reflexes, 73ff.
  arc, 75
  in lower animals, 67
  pain, 110
Reinforcement, 200
Reliability, 314
  IQ tests, 336
  personality tests, 314ff.
Religion:
  adolescent, 436
  conditioning, 83–84
  pain, 123
Renaissance, 10
Replication (cross validation),
  367
Representative numbers:
  mean, 38–39

Representative numbers (cont.)
median, 39
mode, 39
Response:
conditioned, 86–87
unconditioned, 86–87
Reticular formation, 60–61, 109, 126,
249, 251, 252, 259, 473, 589
Retina, 144ff., 197, 402–3
retinal disparity, 155
Reward, 200
Rhine, Joseph, 177
Rhodopsin, 138, 143, 197
Rhythms, bodily (*see* Biological
clocks; Cycles)
Riots, 96, 505
Rituals (*see also* Symbols):
Boy Scouts, 501
cerebral cortex, 501
early man, 501
God, 501
Hopi culture, 57
hunting, 49–50
initiations, 501–2
Jung, Carl, 297ff.
Mafia, 501
marijuana, 501
mating, 49
painting, 50
voodoo, 502–3
RNA, 192
Rods, 136ff.
Rogers, Carl, 294ff., 581–82
Roles (*see also* Sex role):
conflicts, 302–3
hypnosis, 243
Rorschach, Herman, 309–10
food items, 266
with normals, 528
repression, 274
test, 309ff.
Rush, Benjamin, 537

S Saint-Exupéry, Antoine, 104, 123
Scan path, 145
Scapegoats, 485–86
Schachter, Stanley, 120
Schizophrenia (*see* Psychosis)
Scientific method, 11
Scotopic vision, 138
Sears, Robert, 383–84

Selective attention, 206
Self-actualization, 123, 248,
294ff., 545
Sensitivity training, 587–89
Sensory deprivation, 517–18
children, 56, 108
dogs, 108
dreams, 256
and memory, 195
monkeys, 53
and sleep, 254
September Morn, 272
Set, 20ff., 219, 355, 364–65
Sex:
adolescence, 390, 431, 436ff.
and aggression, 411
behavior, female, 394–95
behavior and sex role, 394,
437
bisexuality, 390–91
and breast feeding, 382–83
as conflict, 436ff.
cortex, 442
and courts, 395
and culture, 432, 436
differences, 114–15, 389–90
drive, 105–6
fantasies, 439
father absence, 392
fears, 251–52
fetish, 106
Freudian, 266, 269
glands, 105–6, 431
gonads, 105–6
Greece, 395
hermaphrodites, 390–91
homosexuality, 443ff.
hormones, 105–6, 389–90, 430–31,
442
identification, 392
Kinsey, 437
learning, 269
lesbians, 275
and masochism, 122
masturbation, 269, 442
maturity and diet, 478
monkeys, 390
motivation, 105ff.
and nose, 389
nudity, 271
offenders, 441
organ development, 440

Sex (cont.)
  physiology, 441
  pornography, 439–41
  premarital, 394
  psychological factors, 389–90
  rituals, 271–72
  and sex role, 275
  and society, 106, 276
Sex role, 387ff.
  adolescence, 436ff.
  alcohol and, 388
  animals, 390
  biological aspects, 389
  and color, 275
  conflicts, 302–3
  and crime, 388
  culture, 388ff.
  dating, 434
  dependency, 411
  development, 391
  dominance, 274–75
  family, 268
  father, 268
  female, 267–69
  and female occupations, 395
  Freud, 388
  hermaphrodites, 390–91
  in homosexuality, 448–49
  hormones, 430–31
  identification, 388, 392
  IQ decline, 393
  learning, 275, 442
  male, 268–269
  menstrual cycles, 394
  Old Testament, 394
  prostitutes, 302
  punishment, 392
  sex differences, 389–90
  and sexuality, 411
  and siblings, 392
  and society, 411
  submissiveness, 390
  training, 391
  universality, 274–75
Sexuality, Greek philosophy, 7
Shaping, 201
Sheep, 90
Sheldon, William, 281ff.
Shock, conditioning, 88–89
Short-term memory, 193ff.
Significance, levels of, 175
Size constancy, 152

Skimming, reading, 151–52
Skinner, B. F., 199ff., 234
Skydiving, homeostasis, 117
Sleep, 249ff.
  amount of, 252
  brain waves, 247
  circadian rhythm, 249
  dreams, 253
  effects of, 252
  ESP, 182
  hypnosis, 241, 247
  laboratory, 246
  learning, 256
  length of, 256
  and memory, 225
  need, 254
  NREM, 253ff.
  physiology, 252–53
  REM, 253ff.
  reticular formation, 249
  Rip Van Winkle effect, 252
  sensory deprivation and, 254
  sleeping pills, 254
  synapses, 251
Smell, 403
Smiling, 381–82
Smoking, homeostasis, 116
Snake, infrared receptors, 140
Social:
  acceptability, 166–68
  behavior, 167–68
  class, 33
  drinking, 97
  food selection, 100
  learning, 82ff., 269
  pressure, 203, 411, 510
  psychological theories, 285ff.
  roles, 299, 302
Social grouping:
  external grouping, 484ff.
  individual benefit, 488
  internal grouping, 484ff.
  and languages, 490ff.
  mutual support, 488–90
  and religion, 489–90
  and rules, 492–94
  scapegoats, 485–86
  and social class, 34, 455
  and stereotypes, 491
  territoriality, 481
Socrates, 7
Soul, 6, 44

Soviet Union, 33–34, 93, 304, 485–86
    emotional theory, 119
Speech, animal, 48, 53
Speed reading, 151ff.
Spider:
    reflex actions, 76
    and unicorn, 17
Spinal cord, 67, 73ff.
Spock, Benjamin, 92
Sponge, 44
Standardization, normal curve, 336–37
Starvation, 93–94
Statistics, 37
Steinbeck, John, 312
Stereoscopic vision, 155ff.
Stereotypes, 301, 491
Stimulus, generalization, 91
    conditioned, 86–87
    unconditioned, 86–87
Stomach:
    acid, 559
    aggression, 559
    contractions, 98
    digestion studies, 97–98
    emotion, 97
    removal, 98
Stone Age man, 49–50
Stress:
    confession, 515–16
    conflict, 548–49
    mental illness, 548–49
    personal boundary, 483
    and physical problems:
        conversion reaction, 532, 558
        cortex and hypothalamus, 561
        headaches, 560
        hypochondriasis, 561–62
        psychosomatic disorders, 84, 558
        ulcers, 559–60
Sudden death, 503
Suggestion, 586
    cognitive theory, 120
    dancing mania, 5
    death, 502–3
    emotional responses, 121
    and hypnosis, 240
    pain, 108–9
Suicide, 313, 471, 551–52
    kamikazi, 58
Sullivan, Harry S., 286ff., 379
    adolescence, 443

Sullivan, Harry S. (cont.)
    "bad me," 287, 545
    "good me," 287, 545
Sumerians, 4
Surrogate mother:
    ducks, 53
    monkeys, 53ff.
Swimming behavior, child, 58
Symbols (*see also* Rituals; Jung, Carl):
    and aggression, 498–99, 506
    in birds, 482
    blood, 498
    brain storage, 329, 500
    in children, 403
    clothing, 499–500
    criminal activity, 501
    doctor, 578
    early man, 50
    food, 88
    and group communication, 490ff., 498ff.
    hunting, 50
    and intelligence, 329
    Jung, Carl, 298–99
    language, 491–92
    learning, 500
    in mental illness, 546
    and morality, 415
    nurses, 500
    paintings, 49–50
    pecking order, 479
    prejudice, 490
    in psychotherapy, 579
    and religion, 490
    religious, 500
    secondary reinforcement, 293, 499
    sexual, 106
    sexuality, 437
    speech, 407
    and stereotypes, 491
    symbolization, 294–96
    territoriality, 481–84
    thought disorders, 555, 563
    words as, 133, 492
Synapses, 65–66, 109, 188ff., 251, 355, 405, 469, 472
Syphilis, paresis, 569
Szasz, Thomas, 532–33

T Tachistoscope, 168
Teaching machines, 233–35

Telepathy, 176–78
Television:
  satiation, 126
  violence 507–9
Temperature:
  adaptation, 125
  body regulation, 115, 117
  tongue receptors, 100
Terman, L. M., 283
Territoriality, 481–84, 520
Testing, 308ff. (*see also*
    Intelligence):
  anxiety and, 23–24
  conditions, 308ff.
  group, 339
  normal curve, 173, 333–34
  norms, 308, 320
  objective, 318
    empirical, 321–22
    faking, 320–21
    forced choice, 321
    norms, 319
    problems, 323–24
  personality, 307
  projective, 95, 309, 316
  reliability, 314, 322–23
  Rorschach, 309ff.
  of schizophrenics, 564–65
  self-report, 455
  standardization, 336
  TAT, 311–12
  validity, 313–14, 320, 322–23
  word association, 309
Tests:
  achievement, 361–62, 366
  adjective check list, 368
  aptitude, 360–61
  BITCH, 350, 355
  creativity, 363
  empirical, 321–22
  forced choice, 321
  infant, 400
  interpretation, 317
  personality, 307ff.
  profile, 361
  speeded, 361
  uses for things, 365
  and working class, 317
Thalamus, 77
Therapy (*see* Psychotherapy)
Thinking:
  mechanistic viewpoint, 91–92
  physical movements, 92
  Watson's view, 91–92

Thirst, 93ff.
  body cells, 100
  hypothalamus, 77, 100
  physical mechanisms, 97
  salt, 101
  social, 96
Thought control, 112
Tolman, E. C., 197
Transfer:
  areas of brain, 70–71
  formal discipline, 218
  and generalization, 220
  languages, 218–19
  negative, 219
  positive, 217
  prejudice, 220
Tribes:
  Boloki, 83
  Hottentot, 83
  Kafir, 83
Truth serum, 520
Twin studies:
  ESP, 181
  fears, 380
  homosexual, 445
  inheritance, 377
  intelligence, 343
  maturation, 377
  schizophrenia, 566
  Siamese, 249
  walking, 56–57

U Ulcers, human, 559
Unconscious, 6, 264ff., 290, 309
Unconscious perception, 168
Unicorn, 17–18

V Validity, 313–14
  construct, 340
  content, 319
  IQ tests, 335–36, 340
  personality tests, 313–19
  phrenology, 68
  prediction, 323
  of ratings, 323–24
Vietnam, 232
Violence:
  aggression:
    constructive, 506
    destructive, 506
    pathological, 506
  city riots, 504–5

Violence (cont.)
  desensitization, 508
  fear, 504
  justified, 507
  sports, 508
  symbols, 504–5
  and television, 507–9
Vision, 132ff. (*see also* Color
    vision)
  brain, 403
  child, 401–3
  color, 138ff.
  color defects, 139
  constancy, 140
  detectors, 147–48
  dominance, 157
  and drugs, 140
  electrical aspects, 140
  peripheral, 147
  phosphenes, 140
  photopic, 138
  "psychological," 139
  Purkinje phenomenon, 136
  scotopic, 138
  sharpness, 138
  three worlds of, 140
Visual acuity, 138
Visual cliff, 153–54
Visual illusions, 156ff.
  colored weights, 158
  movement, 160
  Müller-Lyer, 159
  Necker cube, 158
  Phi phenomenon, 161
  Ponzo illusion, 159
  size constancy, 159
  tilted room, 157
Visual processing, 147ff.

Visual texture, 155
Vitamin deficiencies, 99
Volta, Allessandro, 65
von Braun, Werner, 26
Voodoo, 502–3, 578

W Walking, 51, 56–57, 376, 378, 400
Warts 578–79
Washington, George, 466
Watergate, 410
Waters, Ethel, 289
Watson, John B., 90ff., 199, 290,
    547
Wavelength, 135
  brightness, 139–40
Wechsler, David, 337
  test, 337ff., 362
White light, 134–35
Witchcraft, 9, 535–37
Witnesses, perception, 166–67
Wolpe, Joseph, 584–85
Women:
  "beauty," 82
  curves of, 82
  dating, 433–34
  intelligence, 393
  interests, 393–95
  sex behavior, 393ff.
Woodworth, R. S., 318
Wooldridge, Dean, 186
Wright, Orville, 21

Y Yoga, 93, 248

Z Zombie, Blue, 192, 195